The Creative Connection

Expressive Arts as Healing

The Creative Connection

Expressive Arts as Healing

Natalie Rogers

Science & Behavior Books, Inc.
Palo Alto, California

Printed in the United States of America.

Library of Congress Card Number 93-083958

ISBN 0-8314-0080-3

Cover and interior design by Paula Goldstein
Cover art by Natalie Rogers
Interior art on pages ii, xxiv, 182, and 219 by Natalie Rogers. Art on pages 220 and 229 by Connie Smith Siegel. "Tomales Bay" acrylic on canvas, 52" × 66". 1981.
Editing by Rain Blockley
Black-and-white photography by Bernie Lustgarten, except for photos on pages 130 and 156, by Rebecca Gerendasy
Typesetting by Bookman Productions
Printing by Haddon Craftsmen

I would like to thank the following colleagues for permitting me to use photographs of them in action throughout this book:

Svend Anderson, Nancy Bloom, Spencer Conway, Shellee Davis, Gretchen Delaney, Elizabeth Eisenman, Maria Gonzalez-Blue, Liana Nan Graves, Sadja Greenwood, Mukti Khanna, Bodil Lahelle, Gail Laird, Fran Macy, Joseph McIntyre, Ruth Miller, Alexander Orlov, Sandy Scotchler, Masako Shimamura, Nina Utigaard-Simon, Peter Wrycza.

In memory of
my mother and father,
Helen Elliott Rogers and Carl R. Rogers

Dedicated to
my creative daughters,
Janet, Frances, and Naomi, and
my delightfully evolving grandchildren,
Satya, Simon, Jazmin, and Megan

Another book by this author:

Emerging Woman: A Decade of Midlife Transitions
(Personal Press, P.O. Box 6518, Santa Rosa, CA 95406)

For information regarding the Person-Centered Expressive Therapy Institute, write or call:

The Person-Centered Expressive Therapy Institute
P.O. Box 6518
Santa Rosa, CA 95406
U.S.A.
(707) 526-4006
(800) 477-2384

Contents

3 Beginning Explorations 27

4 The Creative Connection, Part I: Movement and Writing 43

5 The Creative Connection, Part II: Art, Music, and Meditation 69

7 Further Applications of the Expressive Arts 131

8 Accepting the Shadow, Embracing the Light 157

9 Discovering Spirituality Through the Arts 183

Expressive Arts Exercises

Preface

The expressive arts are ancient forms being rebirthed to bring much-needed integration and balance into our world. In early times people knew well that dance, song, art, and storytelling were all part of the same process: that of being fully functioning and creatively human. They also used the arts as a connection to each other and the forces of nature. Dancing and song release feelings, energize the body, and evoke community spirit. The visual arts bring forth imagery and metaphor.

I am presenting a philosophy of psychotherapy and creativity and a statement about the connectedness of one art form to another—the *Creative Connection process.* I offer this process for your personal enjoyment and self-discovery as well as for deep psychological healing. My purpose is to inspire you to rediscover your innate creative ability and to learn ways to explore that creativity with a freedom of self-expression that is healing and transformative. I hope that, having experienced healing through self-expression, you will be motivated to use these methods professionally. This book is intended to serve as a guide to psychotherapists, educators, parents, and others whose mission it is to offer a safe, nurturing environment for self-exploration, insight, and communication.

People often ask how my interest in the expressive arts evolved. My mother, Helen Elliott Rogers, was a talented artist and gave my brother and me the stimulus and encouragement to draw, paint, and sculpt. My father, Carl Rogers, was a psychologist who developed an outstanding theory and practice which he named *client-centered* therapy. As his theories developed, they were also applied in education, administration, and mediation work and became known as the *person-centered approach.*

So it is natural that my interest in both the arts and psychology came about. I also loved to use movement for self-expression. As a young girl I can remember putting on music to inspire me to dance in the livingroom. In college I majored in psychology but also took art courses. Later, after marriage and childrearing, I reentered college to get a Master's degree in psychology at Brandeis University (where Abe Maslow was my mentor) and trained further as a psychotherapist. My first work was with children as a play therapist. The arts were a natural mode for their expression.

When employed in mental health clinics and psychiatric settings, I experimented with using the arts as a method for helping clients express feelings and gain insight. Also, during my many years in private practice, I evolved my psychotherapeutic approach, expanding my father's person-centered philosophy to include the expressive arts.

After twenty years of marriage and a divorce, I moved to California and eventually wove all of my interests into an intensive person-centered expressive arts training program. Over the past ten years, as I have seen the participants of this program evolve and have witnessed with awe and wonder their art, movement, song, and writing, I have been stimulated and enriched. Since participants return several times over a period of two years, I have observed them bursting forth with enlivened creativity and self-empowerment.

I have tried to bring this material to you in a way that will help you feel it in your heart and your bones. The beginning chapters describe ways to use expressive art playfully by yourself, or with family and friends. Learning to enjoy the process without worrying about the product is the secret to rediscovering the childhood pleasure in creating. However, not all environments are conducive to creativity. Chapter 2 puts forth my expanded view of the person-centered principles for developing an environment that *does* foster creativity. Chapters 4 and 5 describe the Creative Connection process—how it evolved and how the interweaving of movement, writing, art, music sound, and meditation are used to journey into the inner realms of the psyche and to reach out to be connected to others. Trying to put the expressive arts process into words is like trying to tell a woman from Mars what an orange tastes like. Really, you must taste it to understand it.

Chapters 6 and 7 describe the theory and practice of the Creative Connection process with psychotherapy clients and other populations. I emphasize acceptance of a universal consciousness, which is sometimes ignored in psychotherapeutic theories. Chapters 8 through 11 attempt to address the major philosophical/political/spiritual crises of our times: our need to accept our shadow, embrace our light, discover our spirituality, find our universality across cultural boundaries, and develop a humanitarian, egalitarian, and creative consciousness for the future. The expressive arts are potent processes for understanding and communicating our feelings and thoughts on these issues.

Like most human beings, I have my own blocks to creativity. As I was writing this book, a fortuitous event allowed me to use the Creative Connection process to work through those blocks. My computer was in the room next to the kitchen, which was being remodeled. As the carpenters hammered and played loud rock music, I said to myself, "This will not do!" So I moved the computer to my art studio. What a blessing! When I needed a break, I turned on music as inspiration to dance and sing. My gratitude goes out to the new age artists Paul Winter, Susan Osborn, Steven Halpern, Gabrielle Roth's The Mirrors, and Olantunji and other drummers. As I got the beat, got the rhythm, shook loose, expressed my frustrations and victories, let out sound, stretched, yelled, softened, curled up, and melted, I moved from using my left brain to my right brain, bringing richness and balance into my writing. I needed to practice what I was writing! I have had to delve further and further to integrate my logical and linear mode with my intuitive processes and metaphoric mind. As is true with the creative process, the object—in this case, the book—started to have a voice of its own. I finally surrendered to that voice.

Storytelling is part of rebirthing the ancient forms, and I now turn to tell you another true story, "The Sun Dance," that serves as a metaphor for this book. It happened May 22, 1987, in Switzerland. I awoke to drizzling rain, soggy clouds, and chilly winds. My balcony window looked out over rolling verdant green hills sloping down to Lake Konstanz. Cowbells chimed melodiously in the distance, waking me each morning. Some days I laughed at the unusual alarm clock and felt glad to breathe in the Swiss mountain air, tinged slightly with cow dung. It was Spring and the blue forget-me-nots and golden dandelions filled the fields with color.

"Rain brings flowers and green grass, that's for sure, but today I cannot greet this gloomy drizzle with my usual inner sunshine," I said to myself. Poking my head out the French doors, I yelled at the splashing rain drops,"I'm tired of you! I want to have fun today!" I wanted to roam with my newfound friend, Dr. Paolo Knill, and explore the remarkable Swiss landscape. Driving on winding roads in the rain and trying to see the mountains when they were overcast with fog did not seem like a pleasant journey. But traveling together to Paolo's home town in the Alps could be a delicious possibility after these past ten days of intense, emotional work together. "Come on, sun, let's see you shine!"

Paolo is a Swiss psychologist, a perfoming artist and professor at Lesley College, Cambridge, Massachusetts. He had invited me to cofacilitate, or teach, ten days of "Creativity and Expressive Arts Therapy" to professionals, both Swiss and German. Here in the Swiss countryside, he and I had created an environment for the students to tap into their innate creativity. They had been flourishing, finding new ways to express themselves through movement, art, music, theater, journal writing, and personal discussions. The week had been full of rich experiences as students and faculty alike had traveled on inner journeys and learned new skills to help others be more creative.

But today was different. We were to have the afternoon and evening free; a rest from our intensity, and a chance to assimilate our learnings in a relaxed way. Paolo met me at breakfast. "Well, what do we teach this morning?" he asked with his usual Swiss/German accent.

I said, half jesting, "This morning we shall dance to bring out the sunshine." After saying it in such a serious tone, I realized we might actually try it.

The group met—twelve of us, which seemed the right sort of number. I opened the session by saying, "I think we need—at least, I know *I need*—sunshine for our free afternoon and evening. I suggest we create a ritual to bring out the sun. Native Americans do it, other cultures do it; let's create our own way."

As we began, some of us started to dance and drum, slowly. Others used art materials to create their own projects. I took felt-tip pens and drew a large picture of the sun, placing it in the center of the room. At first I was annoyed that not everyone was in the mood to enter the pulse and beat of the ritual dance. (But I also knew that allowing people the freedom of choice not to participate was also important.) Paolo kept a steady beat, first on the drum, then on the piano. There was an insistent and relentless rhythm that others picked up with bells and wood blocks and other percussion instruments. My mood changed. I realized that it didn't matter how many joined in; it was the spirit of those who were really involved that mattered. I put my full intent, my heart and body, into evoking the sun. So did the others.

Inwardly, I was chuckling at myself for such an outrageous thought: that we might actually influence the weather. On the other hand, I really had the belief, the faith, that such things were possible. The realist in me said, "This is really silly." The believer in me said, "This is exactly the right thing to do, and it will happen."

The sounds and pulse became one, in harmony. Many feet kept the beat as we chanted, sang, and cried out. Did one hour or two go by? I'm not sure. Then it came. The sun came beaming into our huge windows, placing three feet of bright, warm light on the grey carpet.

Our songs burst into celebration. Our feet stomped. The drums got louder and we cheered. I sat in the rectangular pattern of light, laughing and singing. Others clapped. Our crescendo built and then eased off. Someone threw wide the windows, which opened on to lush, dripping wet trees. The birds came close on nearby branches. Their songs joined ours.

Eventually we quieted down and sat in a circle. There was chit chat, giggles, and laughter. The conversation was scattered. Then I remembered, "We must spend time being grateful that our call was answered. Whether we evoked the sun or whether it 'just happened' is not the issue. We had our wish answered."

As we meditated in silence, the song of the birds became louder. The sun did seem like magic. The morning had been completely overcast, yet here was brilliant light coming through the grey clouds. Those clouds disappeared. The afternoon and evening were filled with freshly washed landscape illuminated with dazzling sun.

We called that day "The Day of the Sun Dance." One might believe that our music, our art, our focused dancing and prayers brought out the great SOL. Or one might say that it was time meteorologically for the sun to appear, after ten rainy days. It doesn't really matter to me. What does matter was our sense of self-empowerment. And yes, the sense of magic. A faith in the possible.

As one participant said, "The Day of the Sun Dance is a metaphor, for me, of personal growth. If we have faith, and if we work on our issues or problems with intention and focus, if we believe in the possible and if we find ways to express our feelings by channeling them through the arts, we can create our own magic. Our internal miracles do happen."

I would add to that statement: if we have such faith and intention as a collective, as a group, and if we collaborate in an egoless way, we have great impact on each other and the planet. When we can be fully receptive and active at the same time (listening to each other's music and beat while dancing our own dance), we can call in many universal forces: the sun, good will, and love. It is one path to a collective consciousness for the future.

This book is about that process, a process of creativity and consciousness. It is not as simple as the two-hour sun dance. Many factors, many forces are involved. Some of the questions that I raise are: How do we help people unblock their creative abilities? How does movement or dance affect our art? How does creating art affect our writing? How do we create an environment, both physical and psychological, that allows people to use their innate creativity? How do we deal with the negative or dark forces within each of us? How do we change personal and global consciousness? And how might all of this help our world?

Acknowledgments

It is the participants, faculty, and board of directors of the Person-Centered Expressive Therapy Institute that have brought life and meaning to the body of this work. They have enriched my learnings as we have journeyed together by sharing their personal art, writing, and growth processes. By permitting me to to show and quote their work, they are providing the rich color and texture to the fabric of the concepts presented. The same is true of my former clients and my students at John F. Kennedy University, the University of San Francisco and the Institute of Transpersonal Psychology.

In particular, I want to thank my daughter, Frances Fuchs, for her initial support as cocreator of the Person-Centered Expressive Therapy Institute and Shellee Davis for taking on the responsibility of being codirector and a key faculty person. I am grateful to Gail Laird for her emotional support, generosity, and willingness to share her personal story in these pages. I also owe special gratitude to Carol Griffin, Liana Nan Graves, Connie Smith Siegel, Mary McClary, and Bobbi Chaney —who have allowed me to use their art and writing. Liz Campbell and Char Horning have been exceptional friends and staunch supporters of the Institute from its conception. My heart was warmed and the lens from which I viewed the world expanded as Fran Macy, Claire

Fitzgerald, and I worked together in the former Soviet Union. Paolo Knill and Ben Hedges have been delightful, collaborative colleagues who have renewed my faith that men can enjoy dancing, painting, and being playful as well as being brilliant conceptualizers. I appreciate the ever-growing leadership and involvement in this work of Maria Gonzalez-Blue, Nina Utigaard-Simon, and Sadja Greenwood. I would like to thank my colleagues for permitting me to use photographs of them in action throughout this book: Svend Anderson, Nancy Bloom, Spencer Conway, Shellee Davis, Gretchen Delaney, Elizabeth Eisenman, Maria Gonzalez-Blue, Liana Nan Graves, Sadja Greenwood, Mukti Khanna, Bodil Lahelle, Gail Laird, Fran Macy, Joseph McIntyre, Ruth Miller, Alexander Orlov, Sandy Scotchler, Masako Shimamura, Nina Utigaard-Simon, and Peter Wrycza. I also thank Sharon Springer for offering to index this book. My hat goes off to Joseph McIntyre for taking on the responsibilities of being our executive director, which has given me the time to write.

I always appreciate the friendship, love, and support from my three daughters, who inspire me profoundly.

To Rain Blockley, my incredible editor, I say, "Thanks for understanding the message of this book and gently teaching me how to order my thoughts and words." I am also grateful to Bob and Becky Spitzer, owners of Science & Behavior Books, for their trust in my ability to manifest the manuscript. Thanks to Hal Lockwood and Paula Goldstein at Bookman Productions for bringing the book into aesthetic form.

I especially want to express my appreciation to Mel Suhd. Mel's perceptive understanding of the contribution and depth of person-centered expressive therapy, along with his strong encouragement and gentle guidance, have been my beacon.

With heartfelt thanks,
Natalie Rogers
Santa Rosa, California
Valentine's Day: February 14, 1993

The Creative Connection

Expressive Arts as Healing

I

A Path to Wholeness: Person-Centered Expressive Arts Therapy

When art and psychotherapy are joined, the scope and depth of each can be expanded, and when working together, they are tied to the continuities of humanity's history of healing.

—Shaun McNiff,
The Arts and Psychotherapy

Part of the psychotherapeutic process is to awaken the creative life-force energy. Thus, creativity and therapy overlap. What is creative is frequently therapeutic. What is therapeutic is frequently a creative process. Having integrated the creative arts into my therapeutic practice, I use the term *person-centered expressive arts therapy.* The terms *expressive therapy* or *expressive arts therapy* generally denote dance therapy, art therapy, and music therapy. These terms also include therapy through journal writing, poetry, imagery, meditation, and improvisational drama. Using the expressive arts to foster emotional healing, resolve inner conflict, and awaken individual creativity is an expanding field. In the chapters that follow, I hope to encourage you to add expressive arts to your personal and professional lives in ways that enhance your ability to know yourself, to cultivate deeper relationships, and to enrich your methods as an artist, therapist, and group facilitator.

What Is Expressive Arts Therapy?

Expressive arts therapy uses various arts—movement, drawing, painting, sculpting, music, writing, sound, and improvisation—in a supportive setting to facilitate growth and healing. It is a process of discovering ourselves through any art form that comes from an emotional depth. It is *not* creating a "pretty" picture. It is *not* a dance ready for the stage. It is *not* a poem written and rewritten to perfection.

We express inner feelings by creating outer forms. *Expressive* art refers to using the emotional, intuitive aspects of ourselves in various media. To use the arts expressively means going into our inner realms to discover feelings and to express them through visual art, movement, sound, writing, or drama. Talking about our feelings is also an important way to express and discover ourselves meaningfully. In the therapeutic world based on humanistic principles, the term *expressive therapy* has been reserved for nonverbal and/or metaphoric expression. Humanistic expressive arts therapy differs from the analytic or medical model of art therapy, in which art is used to diagnose, analyze, and "treat" people.

Most of us have already discovered some aspect of expressive art as being helpful in our daily lives. You may doodle as you speak on the telephone and find it soothing. You may write a personal journal and find that as you write, your feelings and ideas change. Perhaps you write down your dreams and look for patterns and symbols. You may paint or sculpt as a hobby and realize the intensity of the experience transports you out of your everyday problems. Or perhaps you sing while you drive or go for long walks. These exemplify self-expression through movement, sound, writing, and art to alter your state of being. They are ways to release your feelings, clear your mind, raise your spirits, and bring yourself into higher states of consciousness. The process is therapeutic.

When using the arts for self-healing or therapeutic purposes, we are not concerned about the beauty of the visual art, the grammar and style of the writing, or the harmonic flow of the song. We use the arts to let go, to express, and to release. Also, we can gain insight by studying the symbolic and metaphoric messages. Our art speaks back to us if we take the time to let in those messages.

Although interesting and sometimes dramatic products emerge, we leave the aesthetics and the craftsmanship to those who wish to pursue the arts professionally. Of course, some of us get so involved in the arts as self-expression that we later choose to pursue the skills of a particular art form. Many artist-therapists shift from focusing on their therapist lives to their lives as artists. Many artists understand the healing aspects of the creative process and become artist-therapists.

Using the creative process for deep inner healing entails further steps when we work with clients. Expressive arts therapists are aware that involving the mind, the body, and the emotions brings forth the client's intuitive, imaginative abilities as well as logical, linear thought. Since emotional states are seldom logical, the use of imagery and nonverbal modes allows the client an alternate path for self-exploration and communication. This process is a powerful integrative force.

Traditionally, psychotherapy is a verbal form of therapy, and the verbal process will always be important. However, I find I can rapidly understand the world of the client when she expresses herself through images. Color, form, and symbols are languages that speak from the unconscious and have particular meanings for each individual. As I listen to a client's explanation of her imagery, I poignantly see the world as she views it. Or she may use movement and gesture to show how she feels. As I witness her movement, I can understand her world by empathizing kinesthetically.

The client's self-knowledge expands as her movement, art, writing, and sound provide clues for further exploration. Using expressive arts becomes a healing *process* as well as a new language that speaks to both client and therapist. These arts are potent media in which to discover, experience, and accept unknown aspects of self. Verbal therapy focuses on emotional disturbances and inappropriate behavior. The expressive arts move the client into the world of emotions and add a further dimension. Incorporating the arts into psychotherapy offers the client a way to use the free-spirited parts of herself. Therapy may include joyful, lively learning on many levels: the sensory, kinesthetic, conceptual, emotional, and mythic. Clients report that the expressive arts have helped them go beyond their problems to envisioning themselves taking action in the world constructively.

What Is *Person-Centered*?

The person-centered aspect of expressive arts therapy describes the basic philosophy underlying my work. The *client-centered* or *person-centered approach* developed by my father, Carl Rogers, emphasizes the therapist's role as being empathic, open, honest, congruent, and caring as she listens in depth and facilitates the growth of an individual or a group. This philosophy incorporates the belief that each individual has worth, dignity, and the capacity for self-direction. Carl Rogers' philosophy is based on a trust in an inherent impulse toward growth in every individual. I base my approach to expressive arts therapy on this very deep faith in the innate capacity of each person to reach toward her full potential.

Carl's research into the psychotherapeutic process revealed that when a client felt accepted and understood, healing occurred. It is a rare experience to feel accepted and understood when you are feeling fear, rage, grief, or jealousy. Yet it is this very acceptance and understanding that heals. As friends and therapists, we frequently think we must have an answer or give advice. However, this overlooks a very basic truth. By genuinely hearing the depth of the emotional pain and respecting the individual's ability to find her own answer, we are giving her the greatest gift.

Empathy and acceptance give the individual an opportunity to empower herself and discover her unique potential. This atmosphere of understanding and acceptance also allows you, your friends, or your clients to feel safe enough to try expressive arts as a path to becoming whole.

The Creative Connection

I am intrigued with what I call the *creative connection*: the enhancing interplay among movement, art, writing, and sound. Moving with awareness, for example, opens us to profound feelings which can then be expressed in color, line, or form. When we write immediately after the movement and art, a free flow emerges in the process, sometimes resulting in poetry. The Creative Connection® process that I have developed stimulates such self-exploration. It is like the unfolding petals of a lotus blossom on a summer day. In the warm, accepting environment, the petals open to reveal the flower's inner essence. As our feelings are tapped, they become a resource for further self-understanding and creativity. We gently allow ourselves to awaken to new possibilities. With each opening we may deepen our experience. When we reach our inner core, we find our connection to all beings. We create to connect to our inner source and to reach out to the world and the universe.

Some writers, artists, and musicians are already aware of the creative connection. If you are one of those, you may say, "Of course, I always put on music and dance before I paint." Or, as a writer, you may go for a long walk before you sit at your desk. However, you are not alone if you are one of the many in our society who say, "I'm not creative." I hope this book entices you to try new experiences. You will surprise yourself.

I believe we are all capable of being profoundly, beautifully creative, whether we use that creativity to relate to family or to paint a picture. The seeds of much of our creativity come from the unconscious, our feelings, and our intuition. The unconscious is our deep well. Many of us have put a lid over that well. Feelings can be constructively channeled into creative ventures: into dance, music, art, or writing. When our feelings are joyful, the art form uplifts. When our feelings are violent or wrathful, we can transform them into powerful art rather than venting them on the world. Such art helps us accept that aspect of ourselves. Self-acceptance is paramount to compassion for others.

The Healing Power of Person-Centered Expressive Arts

I discovered personal healing for myself as I brought together my interests in psychotherapy, art, dance, writing, and music. Person-centered expressive therapy was born out of my personal integration of the arts and the philosophy I had inherited. Through experimentation I gained insight from my art journal. I doodled, let off steam, or played with colors without concern for the outcome.

Unsure at first about introducing these methods to clients, I suggested they try things and then asked them for feedback. They said it was helpful. Their self-understanding increased rapidly and the communication between us improved immensely.

The same was true as I introduced movement, sound, and free writing for self-expression. Clients and group participants reported a sense of "new beginnings" and freedom to be. One group member wrote: "I learned to play again, how to let go of what I 'know'—my successes, achievements, and knowledge. I discovered the importance of being able to begin again." Another said: "It is much easier for me to deal with some heavy emotions through expressive play than through thinking and talking about it."

It became apparent that the Creative Connection process fosters integration. This is clearly stated by one client who said, "I discovered in exploring my feelings that I could break through inner barriers/structures that I set for myself by moving and dancing the emotions. To draw that feeling after the movement continued the process of unfolding."

It is difficult to convey in words the depth and power of the expressive arts process. I would like to share a personal episode in which using expressive arts helped me through a difficult period. I hope that, in reading it, you will vicariously experience my process of growth through movement, art, and journal writing in an accepting environment.

The months after my father's death were an emotional roller coaster for me. The loss felt huge, yet there was also a sense that I had been released. My inner feeling was that his passing had opened a psychic door for me as well as having brought great sorrow.

Expressive arts served me well during that time of mourning. Two artist-therapist friends invited me to spend time working with them. Connie Smith Siegel invited me to spend a week at a cottage on Bolinas Bay. I painted one black picture after another. Every time I became bored with such dark images, I would start another painting. It, too, became moody and bleak. Although Connie is primarily an artist, her therapeutic training and ability to accept my emotional state gave me permission to be authentic.

Also, I went to a weekend workshop taught by Coeleen Kiebert and spent more time sculpting and painting. This time the theme was tidal waves—and again, black pictures. One clay piece portrays a head peeking out of the underside of a huge wave. My sense of being overwhelmed by the details of emptying my parents' home, making decisions about my father's belongings, and responding to the hundreds of people who loved him was taking its toll. Once again, my art work gave free reign to my feelings and so yielded a sense of relief. Coeleen's encouragement to use the art experience to release and understand my inner process was another big step. I thought I *should* be over my grief in a month, but these two women gave me permission to continue expressing my river of sadness. That year my expressive art shows my continued sense of loss as well as an opening to new horizons.

As is often true when someone feels deep suffering, there is also an opening to spiritual realms. Three months after my father's death, I flew to Switzerland to cofacilitate a training group with artist-therapist Paolo Knill. It was a time when I had a heightened sense of connectedness to people, nature, and my dreams. Amazing events took place in my inner being. I experienced synchronicities, special messages, and remarkable images. One night I found myself awakened by what seemed to be the beating of many large wings in my room. The next morning I drew the experience as best I could.

One afternoon I led our group in a movement activity called "Melting and Growing." The group divided into pairs, and each partner took turns observing the other dancing, melting, and then growing. Paolo and I participated in this activity together. He was witnessing me as I slowly melted from being very tall to collapsing completely on the floor. Later I wrote in my journal:

> I loved the opportunity to melt, to let go completely. When I melted into the floor I felt myself totally relax. I surrendered! Instantaneously

> I experienced being *struck* by incredible light. Although my eyes were closed, all was radiant. Astonished, I lay quietly for a moment, then slowly started to "grow," bringing myself to full height.

I instructed the group participants to put their movement experiences into art. All-encompassing light is difficult to paint, but I tried to capture that stunning experience in color.

Reflecting on these experiences, it seems that my heart had cracked open. This left me both vulnerable and with great inner strength and light. A few days later another wave picture emerged. This time bright blue/green water was illumined with pink/gold sky.

These vignettes are part of my inner journey. I share them for two reasons. First, I wish to illustrate the transformative power of the expressive arts. Second, I want to point out that person-centered expressive therapy is based on very specific humanistic principles. For instance, it was extremely important that I was with people who allowed me to be in my grief and tears rather than patting me on the shoulder and telling me everything would be all right. I knew that if I had something to say, I would be heard and understood. The transformative power of being deeply understood is often underestimated. When I told Paolo that I had the sensation of being struck with light, he could have said, "That was just your imagination." However, he not only understood, he told me he had witnessed the dramatic effect on my face.

Humanistic Principles

Since not all psychologists agree with the principles embodied in this book, it seems important to state them clearly as the foundation for all that follows:

- *All people have an innate ability to be creative.*
- *The creative process is healing.* The expressive product supplies important messages to the individual. However, it is the process of creation that is profoundly transformative.
- *Personal growth and higher states of consciousness are achieved through self-awareness, self-understanding, and insight.*
- *Self-awareness, understanding, and insight are achieved by delving into our emotions.* The feelings of grief, anger, pain, fear, joy, and ecstasy are the tunnel through which we must pass to get to the other side: to self-awareness, understanding, and wholeness.

- *Our feelings and emotions are an energy source.* That energy can be channeled into the expressive arts to be released and transformed.
- *The expressive arts—including movement, art, writing, sound, music, meditation, and imagery—lead us into the unconscious.* This often allows us to express previously unknown facets of ourselves, thus bringing to light new information and awareness.
- *Art modes interrelate in what I call the creative connection.* When we move, it affects how we write or paint. When we write or paint, it affects how we feel and think. During the Creative Connection process, one art form stimulates and nurtures the other, bringing us to an inner core or essence which is our life energy.
- *A connection exists between our life-force—our inner core, or soul—and the essence of all beings.*
- *Therefore, as we journey inward to discover our essence or wholeness, we discover our relatedness to the outer world.* The inner and outer become one.

My approach to therapy is also based on a psychodynamic theory of individual and group process:

- Personal growth takes place in a safe, supportive environment.
- A safe, supportive environment is created by facilitators (teachers, therapists, group leaders, parents, colleagues) who are genuine, warm, empathic, open, honest, congruent, and caring.
- These qualities can be learned best by first being experienced.
- A client–therapist, teacher–student, parent–child, wife–husband, or intimate-partners relationship can be the context for experiencing these qualities.
- Personal integration of the intellectual, emotional, physical, and spiritual dimensions occurs by taking time to reflect on and evaluate these experiences.

The diagram on the following page illustrates how discovering the essence of the self through the expressive arts connects us to the universal energy source helping us relate to our community and the world.

Come with me, if you will, on a journey of inner exploration to awaken your creativity. Perhaps you are a writer who shys away from visual art, or an artist who says,"I can't dance," or a therapist who would like to discover methods for enhancing the counselor–client relationship. I invite you into your own secret garden.

Black Wave: "In my grief I felt overwhelmed. Painting the black tidal waves over and over expressed my sense of helplessness."—Natalie Rogers

White Wings: "I was awakened by what seemed to be the beating of many large wings in my room."—N. R.

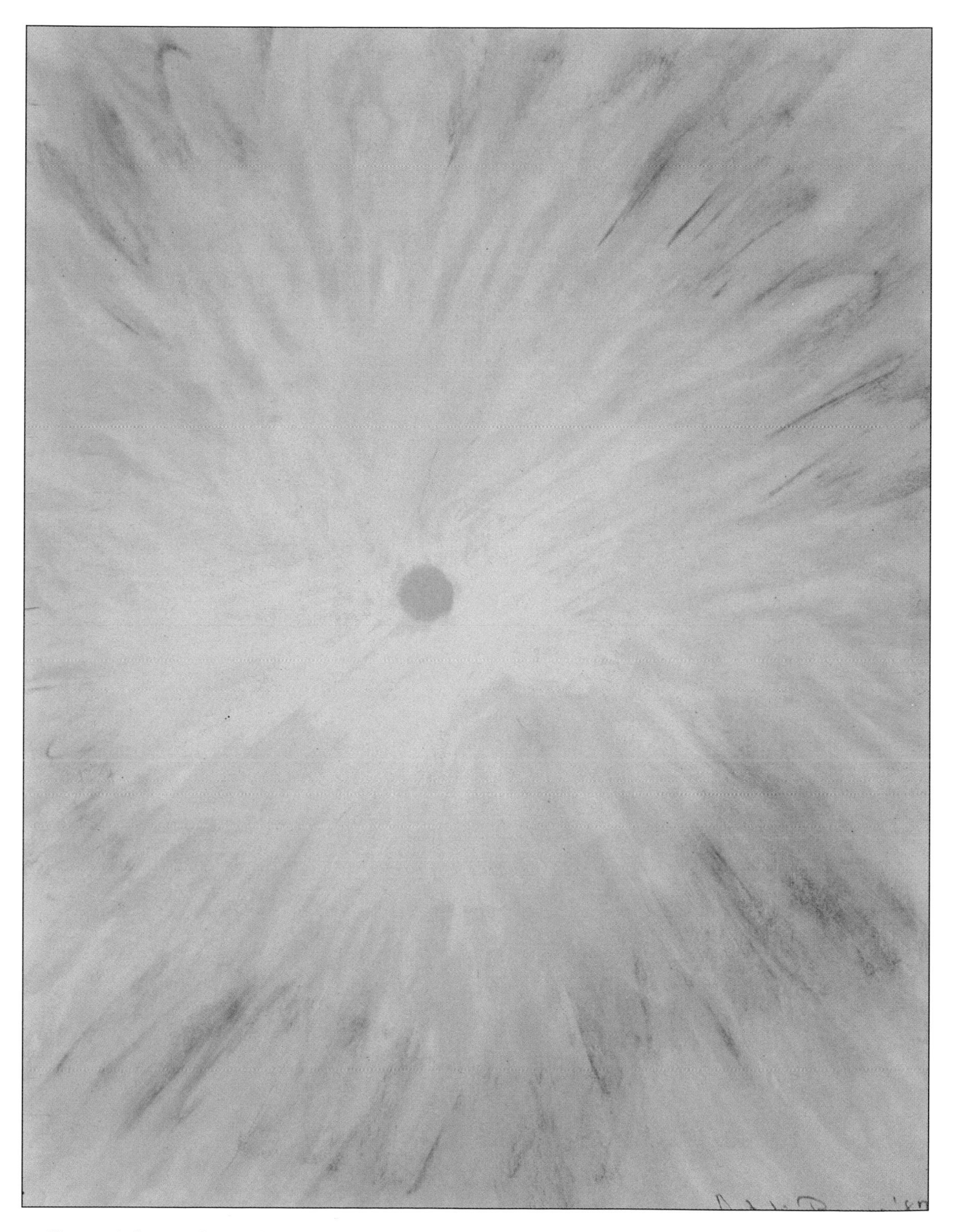

Yellow Light: "I danced 'Melting and Growing.' As I melted into the floor, I felt myself surrender. Instantaneously I experienced being struck by incredible light. All was radiant." —N. R.

Blue/green Wave: "A few days later, another wave image emerged. This time bright blue/green water was illumined with pink/gold sky."—N. R.

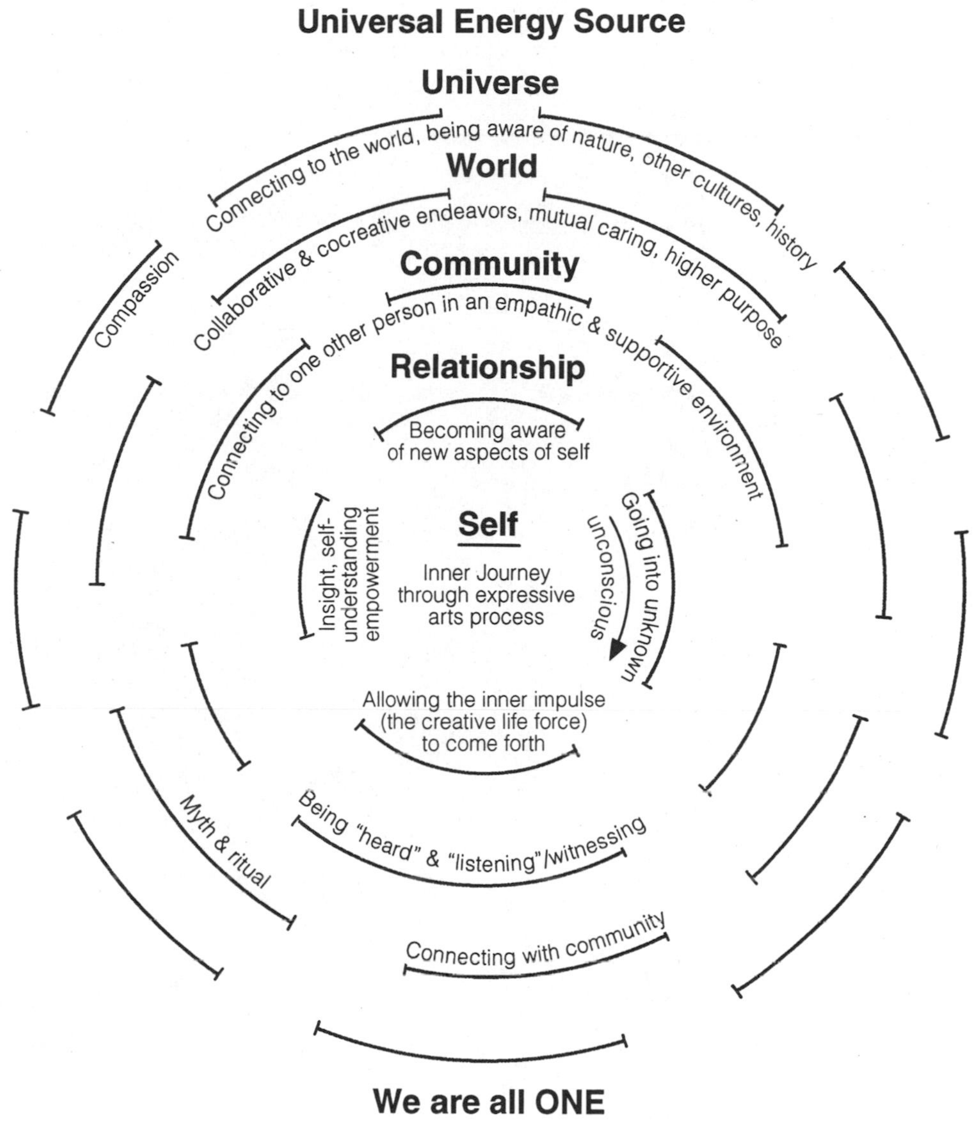

Universal Energy Source
Universe
Connecting to the world, being aware of nature, other cultures, history
World
Collaborative & cocreative endeavors, mutual caring, higher purpose
Community
Connecting to one other person in an empathic & supportive environment
Relationship
Becoming aware of new aspects of self
Self
Inner Journey through expressive arts process
Going into unknown unconscious
Insight, self-understanding empowerment
Allowing the inner impulse (the creative life force) to come forth
Being "heard" & "listening"/witnessing
Connecting with community
Compassion
Myth & ritual
We are all ONE

The Creative Connection Process: The above diagram shows how, as we first journey inward through the expressive arts, we tap into the unconcious and become aware of new aspects of self, thus gaining insight and empowerment. Then, by connecting to at least one other person in an empathic and supportive environment, we learn ways to relate to the community. As we learn how to be authentic and empowered in a small community, we are then inspired to move to the larger circle. We become cocreative and collaborative, being able to access our higher purpose and powers. This connects us to the world—other cultures and nature—with compassion.

2

Facilitating Creativity

From the very nature of the inner conditions of creativity it is clear that they cannot be forced, but must be permitted to emerge.

—Carl Rogers,
On Becoming a Person

Within each of us is a secret garden: a place where our true self exists. It may be a garden of roses with many thorns, or a garden of exuberant wildflowers. It probably includes moldy and rotten tree stumps and some poisonous mushrooms. Whatever grows in the garden, it is all part of being human. It is all material that can be used in the creative process.

Feelings are a source for creative expression. We can channel them into visual art, movement, sound, or writing—thus releasing and transforming them. So the moldy tree stumps as well as the bright wildflowers can become meaningful art.

Some people are reluctant to go into their own secret garden, their inner life. Others roam within their secret walls but are unwilling to invite friends or colleagues into that space. Many folks also feel a reluctance and fear about using art media, whether for self-exploration or for the pleasure of creating. Fear keeps us from taking a look at our own garden, at the full variety of plants and animals growing there. We need some way of feeling safe to enter that space.

We are thus looking at two issues: personal apprehension about using dance, painting, sounds, or writing; and the fear of going into our own secret garden, taking a look at all aspects of ourselves. Two pertinent questions are, "What holds us back from using expressive art media?" and "What will make it safe for us to use those media to enter our secret garden?"

Each secret garden must have fertile soil that allows the individual to become his or her unique, magnificent self. Fostering the creative process is like preparing that soil. We loosen the hard-packed earth to allow for oxygen. We feed it with nutrients so that the seeds will be nourished, will germinate, and will sprout. We pay attention to the details that nurture growth and watch each plant develop at its own pace. As gardeners we have a belief, even a strong faith, that each seed can grow to its full beauty and usefulness.

Likewise, the job as facilitator is relatively simple yet takes considerable knowledge, experience, and constant attention. A nourishing and nurturing environment—a fertile soil—is needed for people to use feelings for self-expression. The gardener/facilitator/therapist creates an environment or container in which the people can actualize their full potential.

Seeds can grow and blossom fully on their own in a natural field. Sometimes plants grow in reaction to a very hostile environment, such as the twisted cypress growing out of the granite rocks on the windy Monterey coast of California. Similarly, some creative people just grow themselves without any apparent gardener. Others develop strong creative impulses in reaction to, and as a way to survive, a hostile environment. Most of us, however, find our creative juices flowing when we are in an aesthetically pleasing physical environment and we sense that it is safe to be authentic and to express our true feelings.

It is the facilitator (teacher, counselor, parent, personnel manager, etc.) who creates the psychologically safe environment, the fertile field. The facilitator's values, attitudes, and way of being establish a safe space for the participant (student, client, child, etc.) to take emotional risks: to venture into the land of authenticity. If the facilitator has the intention of fostering creativity and her behavior models respect for the wide variety of possible expression, she will have tilled the soil for each plant to grow.

As facilitators, it is helpful to understand that creativity comes from our *whole being* and that each of us has an inherent drive and need to express ourselves: to use our imagination and inner resources. Some authors describe the process of creativity as though it comes only from the mind. Dancers and artists know from their own experiences that creativity comes from the senses as well. The creative process originates in our whole body/mind/emotions/spirit system.

Knowing or believing or experiencing this helps you understand that using movement, art, sound, creative writing, and guided imagery can be stimuli as well as channels for that creative energy.

It is important to have experienced personally that which you wish to adopt professionally. When you have discovered this process to be healing for yourself, you are ready to take the next step: using the arts to aid others in expressing themselves. Knowing that you are offering your client an opportunity, rather than insisting on a method, helps you feel comfortable as a facilitator. Giving the client the option to accept or reject expressive arts as a mode of expression enhances her sense of safety and aids in establishing a facilitative relationship.

Conditions that Foster Creativity

My approach draws in part on the work of my father and his colleagues, who did vast amounts of research to discover the conditions that enhance the client's ability to feel safe and trusting. The same conditions they found basic to fostering a facilitative client–counselor relationship also help support an environment for creativity.

In his book *On Becoming a Person,* Carl Rogers discusses the desperate social need for creative individuals and puts forth a theory of creativity:

> the mainspring of creativity appears to be the same tendency which we discover so deeply as the curative force in psychotherapy—*man's tendency to actualize himself, to become his potentialities.* By this I mean the directional trend which is evident in all organic human life—the urge to expand, extend, develop, mature—the tendency to express and activate all the capacities of the organism, or the self.[1]

This deep faith in the individual's innate drive to become fully herself is basic to my work in the expressive arts. I appreciate the words "curative force" since it is my experience that individuals have a tremendous capacity for self-healing if given the proper environment. Think, if you will, of those times when you have felt appreciated, trusted, and given support to use your individuality to develop a plan, create a project, write a paper, or to be your authentic self. Most likely the challenge was exciting, stimulating, and gave you a sense of personal expansion.

This tendency to actualize and become our full potential is undervalued, discounted, and frequently squashed in our society. I urge us to tune into this aspect of self! As you acknowledge and appreciate the actualizing drive in yourself, you will more fully appreciate this precious force in all people.

In fostering creativity, we need to recognize that there are both internal and external conditions needing attention. Carl Rogers defines the internal conditions as *openness to experience* and *internal locus of evaluation.* He defines the external conditions as *psychological safety* and *psychological freedom.*

Openness to experience is a lack of defensiveness, and an ability to perceive the existential moment as it is without prejudgment. This includes a lack of rigidity, an openness to new concepts and beliefs, and a tolerance for ambiguity. For the artist, being open to experience may mean seeing the forested mountain as lavender; for a spouse, it may mean acknowledging the tenderness behind a stern facade, or seeing manipulation behind the sweet-talk. For a politician, it may mean seeing the worthwhile aspects of opposing views. Being fully open to any experience—seeing its many facets—is not easy. Most of us screen out what we don't want to see or experience. To expand our ability to be creative, we need to practice being open to experience as it is rather than viewing it through filtered lenses.

When an individual is able to listen to the response of others but not be overly concerned with their reactions, she has developed her *internal locus of evaluation.* Since most people have a strong need for approval, gaining a sense that self-evaluation is more important than that of peers is difficult. Also, most of us are more critical of ourselves than of others. As you develop an internal locus of evaluation, you are able to give yourself credit and appreciation when it is due. Having a keen sense of your talents and abilities goes along with developing a sense of self-esteem. As you become able to evaluate yourself honestly, you dispense with the need to have continual praise from others.

Certain external conditions also foster and nurture the foregoing internal conditions for creativity. Carl Rogers outlines two conditions; I have added the third.

1. Psychological safety
   a. Accepting the individual as of unconditional worth
   b. Providing a climate in which external evaluation is absent
   c. Understanding empathically
2. Psychological freedom
3. Offering stimulating and challenging experiences

These concepts are expanded in the following pages.

Psychological Safety

An environment of psychological safety—one in which you feel free to explore a variety of feelings, responses, and projects—is paramount to your ability to be creative. Such an environment depends on acceptance, empathy, and nonjudgmental facilitation.

What does it mean to accept the individual as of *unconditional worth?* It is when the facilitator conveys her belief that each individual is precious regardless of any present words or behavior. Here are two examples: a friend says she feels ashamed and guilty for having lied to her sister. It would be facilitative to let her know you understand her feelings—they are real. At the same time, you can convey your belief in her as a worthy person. A response such as: "Yes, I understand how terrible you must feel for having told that lie. I value our friendship, regardless," acknowledges the validity of the guilt while valuing the worth of the friend.

Here is another example. When a child shouts and screams as he smears the finger paint, or stamps his feet in a dancing rage, the facilitator accepts those feelings, although she may need to set physical limits on the behavior. A statement such as: "I know you are really angry and that's okay! You need to keep the finger paint on the paper, however," conveys acceptance of the feeling while putting socially acceptable limits on the behavior.

Also, to accept a person's feeling—such as embarrassment about dancing, or shyness or fear about using colors—rather than trying to talk her out of that feeling, gives the individual a sense that she is safe to be herself.

Providing *a climate in which external evaluation is absent* is also important in developing a safe environment. We work and play in a society in which competition, grades, and evaluation are constantly with us. It is truly amazing and refreshing to be in an environment where judgment and evaluation of any kind are at a minimum or nonexistent. It is freeing and invigorating. It is like letting a bird out of a cage.

It is particularly important the facilitator be nonjudgmental when an individual is experimenting and exploring with expressive arts media. If judged or evaluated, most people halt their budding creative endeavors. Also, if the individual experiences an atmosphere of nonjudgment, she is able to develop her own internal standards of evaluation. Rather than counting on an authority figure for her standards, she values her own judgment.

You might ask, "If I am not going to judge or evaluate my client's work [or student's work, etc.] how *do* I respond?" The answer is to express reactions without using them to rate the work. Judging a product differs, although subtly, from reacting to it. If we *own* our reactions to the art, poem, or dance, etc., we are giving a reaction response, not a judgment.

By owning our reactions to the product, I mean that we make such first-person statements as, "*In my opinion* this writing is . . . [boring or exciting]" or "*I experience* that painting as . . . [sensual or depressing]" or "When I look at that sculpture *I feel* . . ." These types of statements are quite different from saying, "Your poem is no good," or "Your painting is excellent," or "Your sculpture is ugly." These latter statements are categorical judgments. However, when we own our reactions, we allow the creator of the product to discriminate between our reaction and her own internal evaluation.

Creating a safe environment also includes genuinely, empathically understanding the individual. The word *empathy* is often misunderstood to mean sympathy. The dictionary defines empathy as an "understanding so intimate that the feelings, thoughts, and motives of one are readily comprehended by another." *Sympathy,* on the other hand, is described as "a relationship between persons in which whatever affects one correspondingly affects the other." Words such as *pity* and *commiseration* are included in the definition of sympathy. To have empathy is to fully comprehend the feelings of the other without taking on those feelings, whereas sympathy includes taking on those feelings or feeling sorry for the other. There is a vast difference between the two.

It is one thing to understand empathically and to accept a person in your heart and mind, it is another to convey this understanding accurately to that individual. The facilitator needs to respond verbally in a way that lets the individual feel understood. *Paraphrasing, reflecting, mirroring,* and *active listening* are all terms that describe verbal responses that demonstrate the facilitator's ability to understand. Often, these words have been misunderstood and misapplied in ways that encourage facilitators to be parrotlike. The key to empathy and understanding is to have a *genuine intention* of accurately understanding both the feelings and the intellectual content of the client. I particularly like this metaphor: to respond to the music as well as the words. It implies an intuitive and imaginative response that gets at the individual's deeper meaning or feelings. The client or the person who is trying to communicate is our best teacher. If she says, "No, that is not exactly what I meant," she can then rephrase what she has said.

Psychological Freedom

In discussing psychological freedom as an external condition for creativity, Carl Rogers says:

> When a teacher, parent, therapist or other facilitating person permits the individual a complete freedom of symbolic expression, creativity is fostered. This permissiveness gives the individual complete freedom to think, to feel, to be, whatever is most inward within himself. It fosters the openness and the playful and spontaneous juggling of percepts, concepts and meanings, which is a part of creativity.
>
> Note that it is complete freedom of *symbolic* expression that is described. To express in behavior all feelings, impulses, and formings may not in all instances be freeing. Behavior may in some instances be limited by society, and this is as it should be. But symbolic expression need not be limited.[2]

The emphasis on the word *symbolic* interests me. The expressive arts are an ideal means for expressing through symbols and metaphors. Symbolically expressing feelings toward any hated person, for instance, releases pent-up feelings without damaging that person. Using drawing, painting, and sculpting to express feelings about that person gives a tremendous relief and a new perspective. Also, symbols carry messages that go beyond the meanings of words.

The foregoing principles are valid for creating a safe environment wherever we work and play. For example, they are sound principles for parents creating a safe environment to foster communication with children. They are also profoundly effective in the teacher–student relationship, the couple relationship, and even in the business world.

Offering Stimulating and Challenging Experiences

For my work, the third category of external conditions that foster creativity is offering stimulating and challenging experiences. Psychological safety and psychological freedom are the soil and nutrients for creativity, but seeds must be planted. What I found lacking as I worked with my father were stimulating experiences that would motivate and allow people time and space to engage in the creative process. We can sit and talk about being creative but never involve ourselves in the process. Since our culture is particularly geared to verbalizing, it is necessary to stimulate the client or student by offering experiences that challenge her. Carefully planned experiments or experiences designed to involve the individual in the expressive arts (if she chooses to take the opportunity) help her focus on the process of creating.

Most of us have tried to be creative in an unsafe environment. We have been offered art materials in a classroom or studio where the teacher said there was a right or a wrong way to do it. Or we have danced or sung and then been corrected, evaluated, or graded. It is an entirely different experience, for most people, to be offered an opportunity to explore and experiment with a wide variety of materials in a supportive, nonjudgmental space. Such a setting gives permission to be authentic, to delve deep, to be childlike.

It is possible, of course, just to put out the materials and say, "Go to it." We have found it helpful, however, to suggest projects or experiences that have no right or wrong outcome but that stimulate the creative juices. The next chapter gets you started on such experiments, and many other suggestions for exercises appear throughout this book.

What Holds Us Back?

The creative process includes exploring, experimenting, messing around with materials, being playful, entering into the unknown. Such words may arouse apprehension. "Who, me, creative? I can't draw a straight line!" "I will never get up nerve to dance or use movement to express my feelings!" These are reactions many people have about themselves in relation to their own ability to use expressive media.

Time and again I have listened to touching stories from clients, friends, and group participants who can pinpoint the exact moment they stopped using art, music, or dance as a form of pleasure and self-expression. A teacher gave them a poor grade, others ridiculed them as they danced, or someone told them to mouth the words while others sang. They felt misunderstood and judged negatively. The self-image that remained was, "I can't draw," "I'm not musical," "It's no fun anymore." Music and drawing then become confined to singing in the shower or doodling on the note pad.

What a pity. This society has squeezed the tasty juice of the creative process right out of most of its citizens. We need to find ways to recapture our spontaneous freedom of expression, without looking to others for approval. We cheat ourselves out of a fulfilling and joyous source of creativity if we cling to the idea that we need to be "artists": specialists who have fully developed the craftsmanship of expression. Instead, the rest of us can use the arts to focus on self–expression and personal growth rather than developing a skill or mastering a medium.

Carl Jung said, "The dynamic principle of fantasy is play, which belongs to the child, and as such it appears to be inconsistent with work. But without this playing with fantasy no creative work has ever yet come to birth." It seems that the creative bud in each of us is very delicate. Although the urge to express ourselves is powerful, it seems to be easily squashed in childhood. Many people then feel afraid and reluctant to try again.

Most of us think of the artist as someone else, "those *other* talented, creative people." But as children we were comfortable with this language. We were unself-conscious. We would take a paint brush, dip it in the jar of color, smear it on the large paper, and be pleased! "Look, Mom, a TREE!" We didn't worry about others liking it or whether Mom also saw it as a tree. We were happy expressing ourselves. It felt good. It was both playful and serious. We felt free to experiment with color, splashes, dots, and scribbling lines. It was an investigation, a learning process.

Then, at some point, it all changes. It becomes important that people not only see it as we see it, but that they like it. The tales I have heard are incredible yet universal. One woman said, "I was in second grade and came home from school with a picture of a rabbit. I was really proud of my picture. My mother looked at it and said, 'What a nice dog you drew.' I insisted it was a rabbit. My mother put it on the refrigerator door and kept talking about it as a dog. I decided not to draw pictures any more."

Another woman who is a talented artist-therapist, said:

> When I was five years old and lived in a little village in Bavaria [Germany] I enjoyed making pretend bread loaves out of mud. One of my sisters and I also mixed colored brickstone powder into water and made red lemonade and filled little bottles with it. We created many of these images and played country grocery store. I loved all that.
>
> Whenever I was able to draw freely, which I loved, I got recognition for it. But later I realized that my teacher was only interested in realistic drawings. In the third grade we had to draw a bicycle from memory and it was judged to be good when it had all the details of a real bike. That was frustrating for me and I was disappointed that my teacher didn't care about the beauty and soul I put into my drawing. Very soon I felt inhibited about drawing.[3]

I also think of Antoine St. Exupery and his story of the Little Prince. In the opening chapter, the boy draws a snake that has swallowed an elephant. To him it is obvious that it is an elephant inside of a snake. To the adults it is a hat or some other form. The Little Prince is mightily discouraged with the lack of *real* understanding on the part of the adults.

Here is another example. I was asked to present my work to twenty highly intellectual, professional people. They were at a retreat center in the Redwoods of California, discussing psychology and philosophy for a week. I laid out art materials and a few percussion instruments and talked about the art of play: of using our bodies in movement to free our ability to use color and form.

I could see their bodies stiffen as the fear set in. I guessed what they were experiencing and said, "For some of you, when you see the art materials, you can hardly wait to get to them. For others, you are probably saying to yourself, '*Not me,* I can't draw or paint or dance.'"

Many heads were nodding in agreement. I had understood their panic. Saying it out loud for them eased the tension.

I laughed. "I promise you you'll have a good time and learn if you *wish* to take a risk and try. And if you would rather sit on the sidelines and watch, that is perfectly okay, too."

Muscles relaxed. I could hear people breathing with greater ease. By the time the afternoon was over, a sense of joy and self-worth prevailed as people shared their sculptures and pictures. *Having me understand their apprehension and knowing they did not have to participate allowed them to enjoy themselves.*

Blocks to Creativity

Many reasons or excuses exist for stopping ourselves from being creative. By becoming aware of when and how we block ourselves, we can make a conscious effort to change our habitual behavior. We can let go of those excuses and give ourselves the opportunity to enjoy our wondrous creative energy.

The inner critic seems to be sitting on the shoulder of each of us. It is difficult to think of a time when I have created a picture or written an article or danced that I did not, at some point, judge myself: "Am I doing this well, or is it terrible?" Most people seem to go through this same thought process, constantly. Yet as young children (before entering school) we were able to be creative without any concern about something's "rightness," "beauty," or "good" or "bad" qualities. We were simply involved in exploring and experimenting.

We have incorporated this critic for many reasons: to help us discriminate aesthetically, to aid us in improving the way we approach a project, or to be useful people in society. But the inner critic is not useful when it puts shame, embarrassment, and terror into our lives. This prevents us from being creative.

We can get acquainted with our inner critic so that it does not dominate our feelings and behavior. One way to let go of that harsh judge is merely to notice it and tell it to pass by: "Oh, I'm feeling judgmental about myself. I can continue to be hard on myself or get back into the process of doing this project." Using this kind of meditation allows the inner critic to be a part of life but keeps it from blocking our ability to act. Or we can tell ourselves, "Mr. Critic, you may be useful later in this project, but not now."

We also have a *need for approval* that may block creativity. "Will anyone like my sculpture?" "What will people think of me if I try to dance and I'm clumsy?" "If I am off tune and someone hears me sing, they will wish I would shut up."

We are asking the basic question: "Will anyone love me if I'm all of me?" One woman wrote:

> Now that I have learned some of the behavior patterns of adult children of dysfunctional parents and co-dependency, I know that my need for approval was not met in my childhood and so I have tried to get this approval from substitute parents. I realize how uncertain and weary I feel, always depending on the approval of others so that I can feel that my life has value. I know that a way to heal these childhood wounds is to feel that anger and rage and despair at not having my basic needs met and finally to forgive and learn to be my authentic self to gain my own approval. I realize too that the deeper I go, the more I see, and that I am always in a process of becoming more true to myself.[4]

We all need love and approval. Yet the key to unleashing our creative energy is finding the deepest sense of approval within ourselves. If we place the locus of our worth in the hands of others, we doom ourselves to a life of trying to please. Women particularly know how self-destructive this can be. My generation of women was brought up to serve their husbands and children. In the process, many of us lost a sense of self. On the other hand, Mother Teresa, who serves in the highest sense, is not trying to *please* anyone.

Our culture also overemphasizes the logical, linear, hi-tech, and masculine qualities so that many men are trained to disapprove of their aesthetic, imaginative, receptive, and playful selves. Expressing feelings through dance or color seems foolish to them. To open to their full creative abilities, these men first need to overcome a stern inner critic and learn self-approval. One man in the person-centered expressive arts training program wrote about it this way:

> As a male I have gotten my self-esteem largely through achievement, performance, competition, maintaining control, being dominant, rational, obedient, and most importantly by suppressing all feelings. What happened to me at the expressive arts program was an opportunity to find self-esteem by accessing my expressive emotional, spiritual, compassionate aspect: that part which I regard as my "feminine" side and therefore not acceptable into my masculine identity. . . . It was the atmosphere of trust—knowing that I wasn't competing with others, that my expressions of art, movement, writing, and play weren't being judged—that was integral to my ability to go within and get in touch with feelings. I could be vulnerable and intimate without risking ridicule. . . . By taking the risk of expressing myself, I broke through old conditioning that a man should not engage in behavior that might seem foolish, childlike or feminine.[5]

The creative process as experienced through the expressive arts is one path to self-discovery, self-esteem, and self-empowerment. The man quoted here had discovered self-empowerment by appreciating his tender side.

Becoming our own best source of approval may take some time. You can practice paying attention to the part of you that needs approval. Accept it gracefully but don't let it dominate your behavior. A helpful affirmation might be: "I am aware that I would like someone to tell me I am doing well. I can give myself that pat on the back for now."

Our need for love and approval is legitimate. But that need is a tricky, elusive little elf. The more we long for love and approval, the less we seem to get. It has never seemed fair to me, but life experience tells me that when I am the neediest for love and approval, I don't get them. When I am in love or loving, more comes my way. Being authentic or true to our highest self is a straighter path to receiving genuine love and appreciation.

Fear of failure is another hurdle to allowing ourselves our full creativity. What is failure, anyway? The school system grades us every step along the way and can play havoc with our sense of self and our sense of failure. I was fortunate to have grown up in a progressive school system and was never graded until I went to college. Instead, the teachers gave us suggestions for improvement. These reports

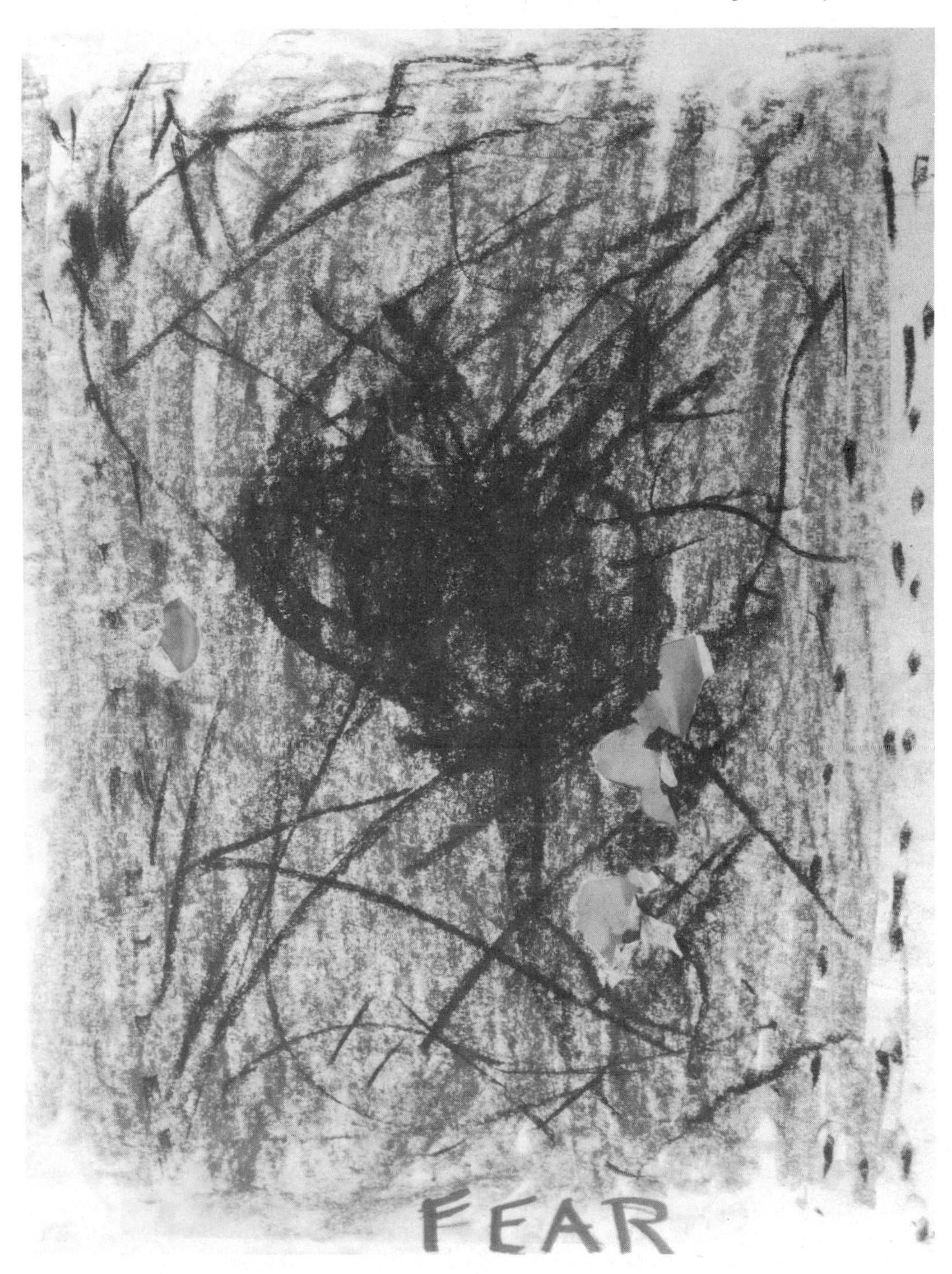

Fear: Fear of criticism, fear of failure, fear of being misunderstood, fear of the unknown—these may hold us back from using our innate creativity.—N. R.

never gave me a sense of failure. On the contrary, they always included something good, which was much more motivating than the negative remarks.

What is failure? "I did it wrong," "I'm no good," "I made a big mistake!" In the creative process (as in life), none of these statements is useful. More helpful attitudes include: "What can I learn from this situation?" "What would make this process or product more to my liking?" As a therapist or group facilitator, I see people struggling with their art or feeling embarrassed by their dance, and I say, "There is no right or wrong to what you are doing." I can see them release the tension in their bodies.

Another block to using our creative potential is the *fear of the unknown*: that we will discover monsters and demons within. Often the question arises, "What happens if I tap the source of my deepest pain?" As I discuss in chapter 8, "Accepting the Shadow, Embracing the Light," the basic principle is this: to lock up these demons takes a great deal of energy; and the longer they are imprisoned, the larger they grow. It is best to look at the angry, pained, violent aspects of ourselves rather than keeping them buried. Bringing them to consciousness diffuses their energy. Accepting that such feelings are part of being human actually makes allies of them. The monster of fear can be transformed to compassion. The angry, violent creature inside each of us can become our energy for creativity and positive action.

For instance, harboring long-term resentments toward a spouse or business partner saps your energy. Keeping this anger secret and holding it in takes a toll on your body, mind, and spirit. If you express those feelings through color or dance and write about them in your journal, you release the volcanic aspect of that energy and come to some new insights about yourself in relationship to your partner. This paves the way for appropriate communication.

Using the expressive arts in an accepting, supportive environment helps greatly in overcoming these blocks to creativity. Some of the participants in the person-centered expressive arts program find this worth comment: "I feel like the lid has been taken off and a wealth of creativity and feeling is emerging—creativity is a part of me and gives me such energy" and "I found the importance of a playful attitude to rediscover my serious sides and experience a fresh perspective."

Creating a safe environment is not magic. It is a learnable skill. People who participate in this environment end up thinking, "We created this community of safety ourselves." Indeed, they did do much of it themselves. It also takes a skilled facilitator to set the stage for that kind of caring community to evolve. That skill is based on the principles of psychological safety and freedom described earlier in this chapter.

It is possible to create an environment for yourself, alone, to reawaken your creativity. The following chapter is on expressive arts explorations and affirmations that can help you give yourself a safe, permissive environment.

NOTES

1 Carl Rogers, *On Becoming a Person* (Boston: Houghton Mifflin, 1961), p. 351.

2 Ibid.

3 Hermine Glaser, "My Path to Creative Therapy" (Santa Rosa, CA: Person-Centered Expressive Therapy Institute, intern paper, 1989).

4 Ibid.

5 Alex Rush, "Masculinity and PCETI" (Santa Rosa, CA: Person-Centered Expressive Therapy Institute, intern paper, 1987).

3

Beginning Explorations

Play is the taproot from which original art springs.

—Stephen Nachmanovitch, *Free Play*

If you are one of those persons who has stopped painting, dancing, singing, and writing, it is time to awaken the juicy flow of creativity. Where to begin, you ask? We begin playfully to recapture that sense of freedom and abandon we had as a child: the curiosity, inquisitiveness, and urge to explore that was once ours. As you play and create, your self-consciousness about being the creator dissolves.

Involving yourself in the creative process actually releases the blocks that have kept you from being creative. That is, as you explore and experiment with various forms of expression in a nonjudgmental environment, the inner critic, the need for approval, the fear of failure, and fears of the unknown can disappear. Classes and workshops only aggravate these blocks if they demand perfection, emphasize grades, or encourage comparisons. That is why I continually emphasize the safe, person-centered environment.

Plunging into creating takes you into a different state of consciousness. Cares and worries of the day and self-evaluation are temporarily shed while you focus on the evolving product. Entering the creative process with a spirit of play reduces the possibility of being overly concerned with that product. We don't need to be serious as we create. In fact, being childlike or free-spirited is an asset.

Affirmations

Fostering a creative environment for yourself includes being aware of your blocks to creativity as they arise and using affirmations to release them. Before you start your creative play, review the following affirmations and then try these explorations. Later, you can offer them to a friend or to family members.

- There is no right or wrong to what I am doing. I am here to experiment and to explore and enjoy the process.
- Oh. I'm being judgmental about myself. I can *choose* to let go of the inner critic for now.
- I am aware that I would like someone else's approval of my picture or movement or writing, but I can give myself that approval, for now.
- I can *choose* to explore new aspects of myself through these expressive modes. The more I can know and accept about myself, the stronger and more compassionate I become.

Explorations

What follow are some playful beginnings. The first step is to relax and enjoy the art materials. Any experimentation you do is fine. Here are two projects for a rainy afternoon by yourself, with kids, or with a friend or partner.

THE BIG DOODLE

Materials

Newsprint pad 18″ × 24″ (or newspaper)
Felt-tip pens, broad tip
Masking tape

The Process

Place the newsprint pad on your kitchen table or on the floor. Tape down the two free corners so the paper won't slip around as you work on it. Or you may prefer using newspapers which truly gives you the feeling that it doesn't matter how much paper you use. Tape it down some way.

Create a Big Doodle: Relax, sing a song, experiment.

Start by taking a colored marker in each hand. Close your eyes. Sing a song and wave your hands in the air. You are first doodling in the air, letting your hands dance to your humming.

Open your eyes for a second to find your paper. Using both hands, start doodling on the paper. Experiment with your eyes closed, then with your eyes open. Continue singing your song. Let anything happen. Don't worry about what the doodle looks like. Go on to do another big doodle.

Each picture takes only two or three minutes. Do another one. And another one. Enjoy yourself.

When you've done enough doodles to satisfy your playful urge (it may be three, it may be twenty), go back and select one or two that appeal to you for any reason. (You may wish to choose the most bizarre one, or one whose lines intrigue you.) Take any of the felt-tip pens and fill in parts, cross-hatch, make dots, or add more scribbles. You can add anything new that you wish. You can create a design or you may find figures, flowers, animals. It doesn't matter what you find. Delight in the process.

Now look at the doodle. Be open and receptive to it. Practice being nonjudgmental.

Write five words that come to mind as you look at your doodle. Any words are okay. There is no right or wrong.

Put a few of your doodles on the wall or the refrigerator for a few days. Let them speak to you. You may say, "Those are foolish." Accept the foolishness. Or you may see rhythm or lines or forms that you want to expand on. Do it.

DOODLE-DANCE TO MUSIC

Before you begin, put on some music—any type that suits your present mood. (If you are using this experiment with a client or friend, have a wide variety of music available and let that person choose something that suits her mood.) Close your eyes and let your body sway and move to the music. Then go to your art pad and spend a few minutes letting your arms dance with the markers on the page. If you find a table where you can stand up and work, you can involve your whole body rather than just your hands and arms. Swing and sway while you draw.

Try several doodles this way. Pick one and expand on it in any way you wish. Write five words or five sentences to go with it. Tape it up on the wall.

Dance the picture. Stand facing it. Receive it. What movement does it suggest? Is there a feeling or mood to your doodle? Can you let you body get into the posture of that mood? Close your eyes as you move so that you experience your inner movement. Let yourself experiment with using the line, rhythm, and color of your picture as a starting point for your movement. Let the dance evolve. If you worry about what you look like, acknowledge the thought and let it pass. Trust expressing yourself.

Let out sound while you move. Let out a hum, a groan, a sigh, or a song. Most of us inhibit ourselves from letting out sound. Give yourself permission. (When you do this with others, give each other permission. Try it together.)

Other Materials

You may want to vary the coloring materials. You can use oil pastels or chalk pastels (see equipment list in appendix).

The Purpose

What have you done? In doing the preceding exercise, you experience some aspects of the Creative Connection process. By waving your hands in the air before drawing, you experience elements of movement that free you to draw. By drawing with your eyes closed, you start the process of going inward to express yourself. If you write words after the art, you may experience the connection between free art expression and writing. When you work with both hands, either simultaneously or separately, you begin to experience the use of your right- and left-brain hemispheres. If you hum or sing, you bring in the sounding aspect of the creative connection. With the variation of the Big Doodle, you learn to experience through movement. And if you dance your picture, you may begin to see how the creative connection spirals you into a variety of self-explorations. If you practice nonjudgment of yourself, you are understanding the importance of creating a safe environment in which to explore and be creative.

COLLAGE

Collage is an easy-going way to get involved in the creative process. As children we were fascinated with cutting and pasting. This activity lets us again drop into that dreamlike frame of mind, puttering with scissors and glue, meandering through magazines to pick out images that have meaning to us. It is a relaxing, fun way to "speak out." With collage (more easily than with drawing) we can suspend our self-criticism. We are so busy with the looking and clipping that we don't worry much about the product. The images in front of us capture our imagination as we lay them out in a design that has personal appeal. Collage is particularly well suited to those of us who are fearful of drawing or are very analytic and intellectual.

Materials

Magazines
Scissors
White glue or glue sticks
A piece of stiff paper or cardboard
Optional: colored paper, fabric, found objects from nature (feathers, leaves, small twigs), stapler, transparent tape

The Process

The process for creating a collage can vary according to your feelings, needs, or purposes. Relaxing into a spirit of play is a good beginning.

Free form. Cut out any pictures or words that appeal to you. Arrange and glue them on the cardboard or paper. Fine! Hang up your collage where you can see it often.

You can end the project here, or you might like to:

- Give it a title.
- Write a short story as you look at it.
- Let out a sound or create a dance that it suggests.

"This is Me." Pick images, colors, and words that represent various aspects, moods, or feelings that you recognize in yourself. Arrange and glue them to the cardboard. Spend some time letting the images speak back to you. You can end the project here, or continue.

If you wish, take a piece of paper and spontaneously write five sentences that begin with "I have" or "I feel" or "I am."

An Issue. You can consciously choose an issue to depict in your collage, such as: "My relationship to my boss (or partner, child, or parent)" or "An important decision I am making" or "A dilemma I have."

First, sit quietly and meditate on the issue. Let feelings emerge. Allow your inner dialogue to be active. Then go to the collage materials and choose images and words from the magazines without censoring yourself. Don't worry about whether the images actually have anything to do with your issue. Let the images pick themselves.

After arranging and gluing them, take time to let the pictures speak to you. You can add to your understanding of the collage if you:

- Write a "Once upon a time" story to go with it. Start by writing the words "Once upon a time" and let any story evolve.
- Do some free writing while the collage is in your consciousness. Just keep your pen moving for ten minutes without stopping or censoring what you write.
- Get input from others you trust.

If you have tried some of these explorations, congratulate yourself. Any of them can be done on a purely playful level, or you can choose to search out the meanings these art products symbolize for you.

Dialogue with the Inner Critic. By now you have had some fun but probably have experienced your inner critic sitting on your shoulder, nagging you with judgments. It helps to have a dialogue or imaginary conversation with that critic. It might go something like this.

ME: Here you are again, haunting me, telling me that what I do and say is not good enough! Why do you torture me this way?

CRITIC: I get pleasure out of blocking you, seeing you feel inadequate.

ME: I don't deserve this! I want my creativity to flow spontaneously, without you haunting me. I want to banish you!

CRITIC: You'll never banish me. I have a function in your life, you know.

ME: Tell, me, what value are you?

CRITIC: I insist that you have high standards for yourself.

ME: But you are getting in my way all the time!

CRITIC: I don't really want to get in your way. If you just acknowledge my presence and appreciate me for what I am, I'll not haunt you so often.

ME: Is that all I have to do? Just say, "Hi, you're here again?" and "I don't need you now," and you'll go away?

CRITIC: Yep! That's about all it takes.

The story may continue. What you will learn about yourself can be rewarding. By taking time to write about your inner critic and learning how to quell its negative aspects, you may save yourself many difficult moments during your creative process.

THE ART JOURNAL

Keeping your own art journal is another way to experience the power and depth of self-expression. An art journal is similar to a written diary, except that it is in visual form.

Materials

A blank sketch book 6″ × 8″ or larger

Felt-tip pens, colored pencils, or oil pastels

Use oil pastels if you wish to be able to blend colors on the page, smearing them with your fingers. You can also lay one color over another for a vibrant, intense effect. Felt-tip pens are good, too. Chalk pastels are quick and soft in hue but get pretty messy in a notebook.

The Process

Taking ten to twenty minutes a day, record your feelings through quick artistic expression. Capture your outlook on the world for that moment. The quick expressions of moods and images in color can be abstract or pictorial. In creating several consecutive pages of art, you may find you have several moods in rapid order or that your frame of mind changes as you do these.

I recommend keeping an art journal for six months. To combine your art and writing journals choose an unlined book. You can use any sequence: write about your art or create pictures to express your feelings after writing. Try to set aside any worry about the product.

Do a ten-minute doodle or scribble or feeling picture. Choose times of frustration, sadness, or anger to let the feelings pour out through your arm and fingers onto the paper. See if you can express any feelings with color, line, or images.

Try using your nondominant hand at times. Alternate your right and left hands. Your nondominant hand is less controlled, allowing you to draw more spontaneously.

Try drawing with your eyes closed. Be aware of your present mood. Feel the connection your crayon has with the paper. Let the crayon lead the way, exploring in any direction. Let it go at any pace. This process can break up the habitual movement patterns of the hand, opening up new possibilities. When you are through, open your eyes and allow yourself to accept whatever is there. You may wish to add more to this free form, or just leave it as it is.

Try art expression when you feel stuck or bored. Your art can become a way to open doors, recharge your bored batteries, or help you find your way back to your feelings.

Make mood pictures when you are joyous or ecstatic. Again, alternate drawing with your nondominant hand and with your eyes closed.

Draw your dreams, or your feelings about your dreams of the night before.

You don't need to show your art journal to anyone unless you choose to. So allow yourself full freedom to express your feelings. Don't censor yourself. This process is for you: to release your feelings, to let the colors and images speak for themselves. Later you can review them to gain further insight and self-knowledge.

Although I had always been encouraged to paint and draw, both at home and at school, and had taken a few art classes at college, I was only introduced to the process of self-exploration in an art therapy workshop in 1973. The workshop facilitator, Janie Rhyne, was one of the pioneers in humanistic art therapy. I still have the little art pad she handed out with the instructions that we were to use felt-tip pens to doodle two or three times a day. I doodled and wrote. This is what it says on the first page:

> I want to become less self-conscious of my unconscious. I want to be able to work more directly from my unconscious to paper or art media. I want to integrate my life force, which is surging, with the one–ness with the universe that I feel. I want to explore the left side of me. I want to explore the me transcending; the flow of energy *thru* me to others and back. Is it real? I want to know what, if anything, is in the white (empty) space in the self-portrait I just did.

Having just pulled this art journal out of storage, I realize that what I wrote then is just as valid for me today. These questions seem to be part of my life search.

During that workshop I stopped worrying about the product and just enjoyed the process. *Enjoyed* is perhaps the wrong word. I used the process to unload some of my feelings about my divorce, and of my frustration, loss of identity, and loss of love. I didn't look back at those doodles for many years. When I did, I found a wave-like progression of feelings coming to a peak, crashing, churning, stirring around, and then coming to a peak again. Some of the doodles are stark and angry, others are full of passion and ecstasy. The pads of paper grew from five by seven inches to much larger tablets. The smaller sizes could no longer hold my process.

My daughter Frances Fuchs, an expressive art therapist herself, puts it this way:

> Much of my own psychological pain has occurred when I felt my possibilities narrow, when the world seemed small and closing. It has been at those times that I have used my art journal most, that color and shape have pried open doors that were unknown to my conscious self.[1]

THE WRITING JOURNAL

Many people keep a diary or writing journal to allow for personal and spiritual development. Through writing, we become aware of our feelings and our patterns of behavior. Out of this come self-understanding and empowerment.

The Process

Here are some guidelines and suggestions that may expand your notion of the writing aspect of your journal.

Write every day, if possible. It is more important to write short, frequent entries than long but erratic ones.

Write for yourself. Try not to censor what you write. This is a personal letter to yourself. Include your feelings, fantasies, dreams, and thoughts. If your censor persists, write about whatever feelings and thoughts block your self-expression.

Write about your ups and downs, good times and bad, joys and disappointments.

Allow the chaos and confusion to happen. Don't try to organize your writing. Let it out in whatever fashion it takes.

Try free writing. Just keep your pen moving for ten minutes, without worrying about grammar or punctuation. If you get stuck, write about the stuckness until something else comes.

MOVEMENT EXPLORATIONS

Earlier sections in this chapter encourage you to move to music before you draw. Now, let me suggest you start by moving for self-expression. Our bodies are vehicles for expression, yet most of us freeze if someone asks us to express what we feel through movement. If you feel safe and supported in the environment you create for yourself, try some movement explorations at this point. It can be a wonderful adventure for self-expression and getting reacquainted with your body. Doing so also helps you understand others who may be reluctant to move.

Shadow dancing is one way you can engage in free movement. All you need is a darkened room, a bright light on the floor, and a blank wall on which to project your shadow. Put on some music, if you wish, and let the shadow dance. (Kids usually love this, too. Children can often inspire us to play with movement.)

While trying the movement, remember to affirm yourself. Tell yourself, "There is no right or wrong. I don't need to judge myself negatively. The important thing is to enjoy using my body. I can listen to the messages of my body."

Moving from the inside, out. Tune in to what you are feeling at the moment: playful? silly? anxious? rushed? Whatever you are feeling, let your body express it. Let the feelings from within come out through your arms, legs, torso, and head.

To add authenticity and intensity to the experience, try *moving with your eyes closed* (or slightly open, to see where you are going; this is called *soft focus)*. Notice how you can have a heightened sense of your body as you shut out the outer world. Let the impulse begin in your body. It will move you.

Having a witness or empathic observer as you move with your eyes closed allows you to focus inward, becoming more fully aware of your feelings as you move. If you have a friend you trust as being empathic and nonjudgmental, try having that person be a witness to your movement. It is important that the witness have the intention of being present in a supportive role and be willing to experience you, the mover, without analyzing or interpreting.

When you discuss the movement later, be sure that the mover speaks first, saying what the experience was like for her. When the witness speaks, she needs to talk about the mover's experience in the "I" language, for example: "When you curled into a little ball, *I felt* safe." This is very different from saying, "When you curled up into a little ball *you were* safe." The mover may have curled up in a tight ball because she was experiencing fear. This form of speaking allows the mover to distinguish her experience from the impact she had on her witness. It also lets the witness respect the world as the mover experiences it, which supports the safe, trusting environment.

Try free-form moving to music. (This experiment is fun to do with family and friends.) To better understand the influence of music on your psyche, select a variety of music—a bit of bluegrass, classical, new age, and rock, for instance—and try ten minutes of each as you move to it with eyes closed or in soft focus. Pay attention to how you feel as the tempo and mood of the music changes. Then draw to the music.

While you are moving and drawing, let out some sound. Different aspects of yourself may emerge as you respond to each type of music through movement, color, and sound. (Or, if you don't enjoy moving, put on the various background selections and use color to do quick, abstract drawings while you listen.) To deepen the process, do some free writing after each drawing.

Shadow Dancing: The shadows can play, argue, fight, or join.

As you responded to each type of music through movement, color, and sound, which parts of your body were active? As you danced to a drum beat? To classical music? To rock? What were your moods and feelings during each?

EXPERIMENTS WITH SOUND

Some easy experiments with sound can give you a sense of the importance of vocal/vibrational release. If you are shy about letting others hear you, wait until you are driving on the freeway, or are in an isolated room, or are walking in the woods.

Try finding your own note. Close your eyes, open your mouth, and play around with your sound, up and down, until you find a vibration that pleases you. See if you can let that sound come from down deep in your belly. Feel how it jiggles your insides and warms your gullet. Be silly with your sound. Let it jump around, howl, groan. Breathe deeply between sounds. Open your mouth and

Let your shadow tell you what to express.

throat and let go. Even if you are trying soft sounds, let them come from your belly.

Sounding with a friend can heighten the experience. Facing one another, first with eyes closed, each of you can play with sound until you find your own note. Be aware of your breathing and the vibrations. Then open your eyes, look at each other, and keep sounding your own note. If you keep this up for three or four minutes, the vibrations begin to alter your state of consciousness. You can literally become more in tune with your inner and outer worlds.

Next you might *try having a conversation with sound*. You can each "talk" or sing your conversation together. Be aware of the mood that you are conveying with your "conversation" sounds.

Then take time to *be quiet for a few minutes*. After sounding, be receptive to whatever may happen. In my experience, sounding for two or three minutes (or more) creates an empty space within. If I allow time for quiet, this process brings forth higher states of awareness.

Your Secret Garden

Why do these experiments? What is your answer to yourself? Do you feel release? Are you finding any new power and strength in yourself? Are you tuning in to anything different? The experiments suggested here serve to get you playfully involved in the creative process. Reawakening the pleasure of creating is the first step. As we become tuned into our bodies and our senses, we uncover a path to self-discovery and personal growth.

Trying some of the explorations in this chapter opens the gate to your secret garden. These reconnect you to your innate creativity. As you use various media, what do you find? Are you willing to explore your secret garden—your inner self? Can you make the process exciting? Can you toss off the inner judge and critic for awhile? Do you find forget-me-nots and gardenias? An oak tree? Wolves?

What happens when you find a monster in your garden? Within each of us is the potential for fear and pain and anger. If we wish to realize our full potential, it is necessary to acknowledge each aspect of ourselves. Using expressive art is a safe way to begin to see and experience the wolves or rotten tree stumps in our garden. Can you look at those images, accept them, and let them speak to you?

What do you find? Is it fear? Anxiety? Rage? Depression? Or just a lurking presence without name or form? Through the drawings, clay, collage, writing, or sound, you may begin to accept even unknown aspects of yourself. Acknowledge the existence of a darker side within every person, including yourself.

As you look around at your garden, can you accept and enjoy its beauty? Can you genuinely appreciate your creativity? Do you see the flowers, the bright sun, and the budding leaves? Many people have more difficulty accepting their own worth and beauty than accepting their pain or anger. Take time to appreciate yourself.

Perhaps you have shared some of your experiments with family, friends, or colleagues and have found companionship as you engage in the creative process. More than one person participating in the process frequently stimulates creativity. Something is magical about working together, side by side. Also, new depths of communication often evolve as people share their experiences.

If you have found new energy by channeling some of your emotions into expressive art, give yourself credit. If you are experiencing the creative connection—experiencing how one art form can nurture and unblock another—you are acquiring knowledge that will be useful throughout your life. If in some of your experiments you feel any "negative" force transforming into constructive energy, you are discovering a potent method of self-healing. The next two chapters expand on the theory and concepts of the Creative Connection process you have been experiencing.

NOTES

1 Frances Fuchs, "Women's Creative Process" (Rohnert Park, CA: Sonoma State University, master's thesis, 1982), p. 18.

4

The Creative Connection
Part I: Movement and Writing

Each art must nourish the other, each one can add to the other. And I would take into writing what I learned from dancing, what I learned from music, what I learned from design. . . .

—Anais Nin,
A Woman Speaks

One sunny day I was driving down the freeway, mulling over my marketing list, when three words came flashing into my head: *the creative connection*. "What is that?" I asked myself. I dismissed the experience momentarily, but the words kept haunting me. Later I realized they described the work I had been evolving over many years. Now, I find my students saying, "Let's do the creative connection."

The Creative Connection Concept

The creative connection describes the process of allowing one art form to influence another directly. Using various expressive arts in sequence heightens and intensifies our journey inward. When we start by expressing ourselves through movement and sound—moving in response to our feelings—and then go immediately to color or clay, our art work changes. Frequently what we then create comes from the unconscious. We may be surprised by what appears. And if we follow the visual art with journal writing, the writing also comes from a deep place within. By moving from art form to art form, we release the layers of inhibition that have covered our originality, discovering

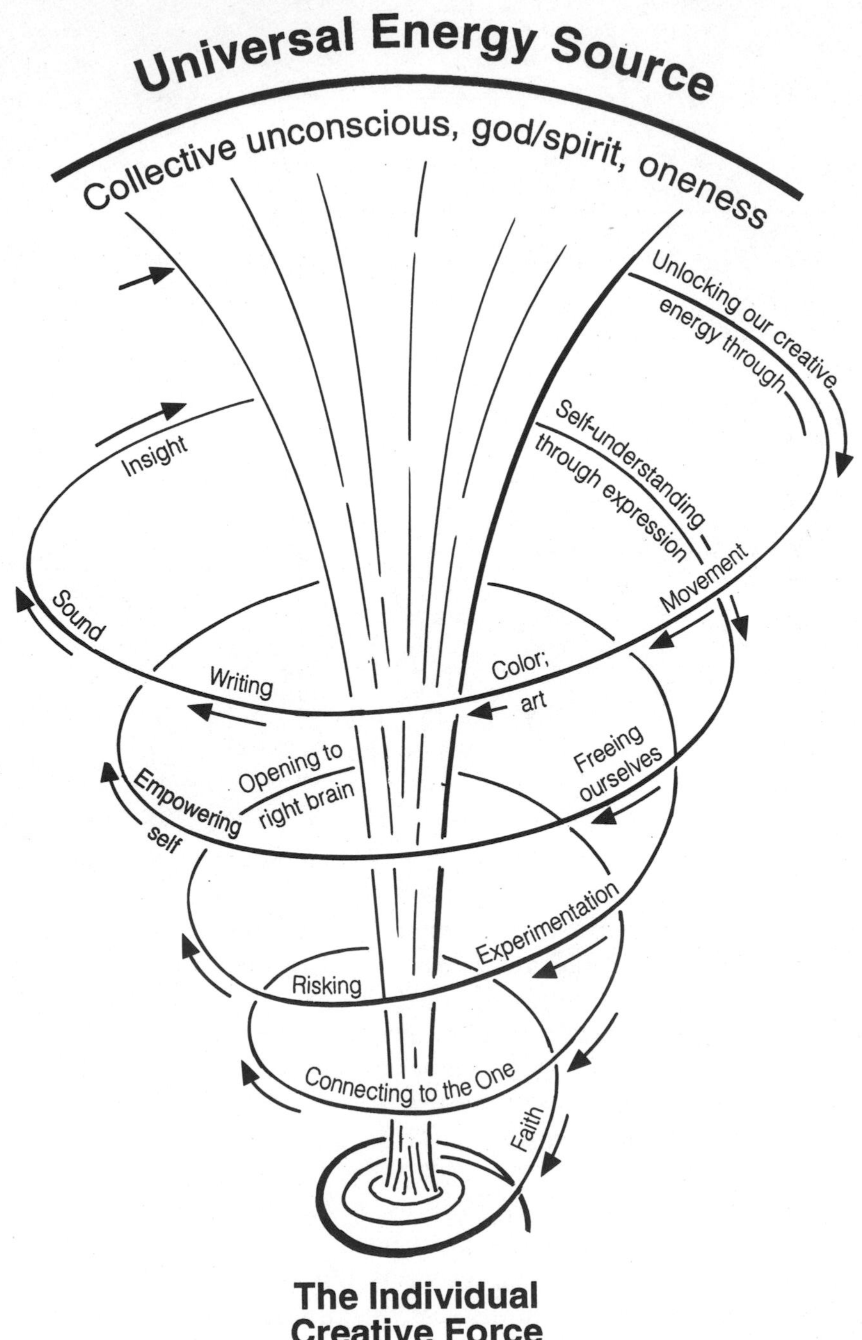

The Creative Connection Process: By moving from art form to art form, we release layers of inhibitions, bringing us to our center—our individual creative force. This center opens us to the universal energy source, bringing us vitality and a sense of oneness.

our uniqueness and special beauty. Like a spiral, the process plumbs the depths of our body, mind, emotions, and spirit to bring us to our center. This center or core is our essence, our wellspring of creative vitality (see accompanying diagram).

Movement, art, sounding, music, writing, and meditation help us enter our inner core or essence. Most people can identify this as a physical experience: they usually locate the center of their energy in the abdomen or solar plexus. As we touch into that core, we discover energy that flows up and out, connecting to a universal energy source. When that channel opens, the universal energy can also flow into us.

Many artists and therapists have discovered the potency of integrating the arts and therapy. College courses and a few books now exist using the term *intermodal therapy.* (I particularly recommend Shaun McNiff's book, *The Arts and Psychotherapy.*) This has similarities with what I call the creative connection. Since there were no courses or books on expressive arts during my training as a psychologist, I stumbled on the concept through my own experience. I discovered how movement affects art and writing when I took my art journal to Anna Halprin's dance training program. At lunch time I created quick, expressive drawings with oil pastels. (Later, when I reviewed them, I was astonished. Those small, impressionistic drawings held an unusual intensity of color, freedom, and power.) Or when I wrote, at lunch, poetry came out. I was amazed because I shy away from writing poetry. It was apparent that the intensive work in movement was allowing my visual art and my words to burst forth in more authentic ways.

By studying my own process, I became intrigued with the power of the creative connection. Since then I have been reading whatever I can find on expressive arts and intermodal therapy. McNiff's books emphasize the interconnection of the arts. Jean Houston's *The Possible Human* particularly supports the theory and practice of attaining higher states of consciousness through mind–body and right–left brain integration.

To get a different perspective on the creative connection, I invited my friend and noted anthropologist Angeles Arrien to my home in Santa Rosa, California for an informal discussion. Here are some excerpts:

NATALIE: Angie, when we were talking the other day, I noticed that you had a lot to say about the process that I call the creative connection. To me, these words give a label to the expressive arts process in which we use movement, art, sound, writing, and guided imagery to tap into the deep wellspring of creativity that is within each of us. I know you are enthusiastic about this process, but I also noticed that you have a different vocabulary to describe it. Tell me, from your personal and anthropological point of view, what this process is.

ANGIE: It is a therapeutic model that incorporates all of the four intelligences: the mental, the emotional, the physical, and what I would consider the energetic or the intuitive intelligence. It is also a model that teaches people how to integrate different aspects of the creative spirit.

NR: What do those words "creative spirit" mean to you?

AA: I would say the creative spirit within an individual is that impulse which is deeply connected to a spiritual essence that is *relentless* about being expressed. It is an impulse that, in its relentlessness, is always seeking how it can be expressed in multiple forms. One form that it seeks is visual. At another time, it may be expressed through movement. Another form can be through sonics, sound, or music. Sometimes the creative or healing arts, or the therapeutic arts segment, try to develop portions of, the creative spirit rather than address the creative spirit as a whole.

What I think is so wonderful about what you are doing in the expressive arts is that you have developed a container that is able to hold all the forms. Archetypically, it is what I would consider a cauldron, or a well, or a chalice. For me, it's really interesting that instead of art therapy—because that is just the visual arts—you also include dance, music and sonics, and writing and imagery. I like your term *multimodal,* but I also think that what it is, is a container that honors the full expression of the creative spirit rather than parts of the creative spirit.

This model honors the four intelligences. It is a model that, regardless of what profession or what ideology, belief system, or culture you come from, here is a container that holds the four universal healing salves: singing, dancing, storytelling, and silence. And what holds those healing salves together are the visual arts. You have a training that ultimately produces healing, transformation, and is a training in reclamation of the soul—or soul retrieval work, or curing what indigenous cultures would call *soul loss.* In modern day terms, we would call it depression, or dispiritedness, or disheartenment.

A linguist, Theodore Misner, did a cross-cultural study on languages, and in a footnote he said, "I think it is very interesting that all cultures use three words synonymously: creativity, intuition, and spirituality." I thought to myself, isn't it interesting that those three words are really doorways for the spirit.

For instance, someone says, "Oh, I'm not spiritual, but I'm going to explore my creativity." They don't realize that through the creative doorway, they are ultimately going to reclaim their spirit.

NR: The spiritual aspect of this work came as a surprise to me. I know that our methods awaken the creative energy in people, but it took me awhile to realize the creative connection process was helping people find their spirituality. As you say, creativity is a door to spirituality.

AA: It's "soul work."

NR: That seems like a good name for it, but I would not have used those words spontaneously, myself. I feel very cautious about using words like *soul* and *shamanic* and *spiritual.*

AA: Well, this work totally reaches into the spiritual. Just like intuitive work. Someone says, "I'm not spiritual and I'm not creative but I am going to go study with Helen Palmer about my intuition." That's another doorway to spirituality and another way to creativity. They are all connected.

NR: That's why these words, *the creative connection*, fascinate me. They came to me out of the blue and I didn't understand what they were until I realized it was a name for my work.

AA: Interesting . . . because, you see, what creativity does is to take people into a transcendent place, always. There is loss of time—timelessness; space and time change. There is a loss of self-consciousness, and a total focus, and every art piece is somehow an expression of the soul.

NR: What do you think there is about creativity that is destructive? I realize that I always think of creativity as healing, and then I realize that the creative process can be used for negative or evil purposes. Someone could be creative in thinking up the worst torture chamber. And it must have been a highly creative process to develop the nuclear bomb. So I worry when I always talk about creativity as a transformative and healing process. I say to myself, "Wait a minute, it may not always be a healing process. There can be a dark side to this process, too."

AA: What I think is interesting is that the creative spirit is relentless about finding a form. The creative spirit always moves like sonar to vision, or sonar to intention. So if my intention is a good one and my vision is for purposes of healing and transformation, then the creative spirit has a wonderful container. But if my intention is for shadow purposes, one can be equally creative in that. I love what Carl Jung and Marie von Franz said: that the greatest destruction takes place when there is no outlet for the creative spirit.

The thing that came to mind when I read the description of your work was the part I mentioned, about the four healing salves.

NR: Where do you get these words, "the healing salves"? Is that your own language?

AA: Yes, it is. In indigenous cultures where there is singing, dancing, storytelling, and silence, they ask the questions, "Where in your life did you stop singing? Where in your life did you stop dancing? Where in your life did you stop being enchanted with stories? And where in your life did you become uncomfortable with the sweet territory of silence?" Because their belief is, where I stopped singing, where I stopped dancing, where I stopped being enchanted with stories, or became uncomfortable with silence, is where I began to experience soul loss.

NR: That's fascinating.

AA: So that if I return to singing, dancing, storytelling, and silence, then it is like soul retrieval work.

NR: When you say people of indigenous cultures, who do you mean, exactly?

AA: They would be any native or tribal peoples that are indigenous to a particular culture. In Africa, the tribal people would see it that way. The native peoples of the Americas and the Oceanic peoples—which would include the Aborigines, the Maoris, and Polynesian societies or Island peoples—would see it that way. In all their ritual ceremonies and healing work, they picture health and well-being as someone who is still singing, dancing, enchanted by stories, and loves the sweet territory of silence. It is interesting to me that the majority of art work is done in silence. It is like a double connection.

NR: Yes, it always seems to be a profound silence.

AA: It is a transcendent time.

NR: When we have a group of thirty-five people who are all doing their own expressive art at one time, the silence is exquisite and profound. I call it the sacred space. Sometimes I stop my own art work for a few minutes just to "listen" to the silence created by such intense, creative focus of so many people. It is awesome. So, wherever people stop singing and dancing . . .

AA: Is where they experience soul loss.

NR: I'm trying to think about that for my own life. I was wondering when I stopped dancing. It was when I got married—about age twenty-one. I was supposed to be a responsible wife and mother.

AA: Also, the other thing I was struck with about your work is that it is focused on people getting in touch with their own psychomythology instead of being fixated on their psychopathology.

NR: That's true. We emphasize finding the joy and playfulness in life as well as delving into the problems.

AA: And that psyche is the union of *eros* and *logos*, which are the love and wisdom natures. And mythology is *mythos*, the life dream. So it is like you are really teaching people to reconnect back to their *eros* or love nature, or their wisdom nature, in connection with their life dream. That work is inspirational and empowering work because it is not so fixated on what isn't working.

NR: Long ago I felt the need to go beyond healing the wounds or fixing the problem. I've always been involved in creating environments where people can discover their full potential—and that is a lot more than solving their relationship problems or job problems. It is helping people rediscover their joy and ecstasy.

As Angeles Arrien points out, the creative connection revives some ancient knowledge to help us become whole, integrated human beings. It is my belief and my experience that these expressive arts processes help us become aware of:

- Our past: our childhood and early years
- Our present mood: "What am I feeling, now?"
- Our inner reality, or unconscious
- Our spirit, or higher consciousness

This awareness gives us the option to improve and transform our self-concept, self-esteem, and our states of consciousness. Connecting our childhood experiences with our inner reality and our present state of consciousness is a necessary integration, if we wish to realize our full potential. As discussed in the humanistic principles in chapter 1, self-discovery and self-insight foster an openness to the richness in life. This also affords us the opportunity to envision the highest good for ourselves and the planet.

It continues to intrigue me to ask, "What happens in my body, mind, psyche, and spirit when I am totally involved in the creative process? Why does this intense involvement change who I am and how I perceive?" We may have to conclude that—as with conception, birth, and death—we can describe the physical and psychological events but the transformative quality of the creative process remains a mystery.

Although I talk about the interrelation of one art form to another, the pages that follow look at them separately as movement, writing, visual art, improvisational music, sound, and meditation. The major art forms that I use (because they are most familiar to me) are movement, art, and writing. Although I am continually experimenting with improvisational music and sound, I am less familiar with these modes of expression. I know that creating music and using our voices for expressive sounds are powerful creative avenues. I discuss improvisational music as distinct from *sounding* (as I use these words, here) in that music is made with instruments, sound is made with our vocal chords.

Meditation, although not classified as an art form, is also an essential aspect of the creative process. The other expressive art forms I discuss are active. Meditation, or being receptive, is often overlooked as an essential element in the creative process.

The Healing Aspects of Movement

Movement is life, life is movement. If you don't believe it, just try holding completely still for a minute. Impossible. Movement is a human need. Breath is movement. Our bodies express our internal state all the time. We know intuitively if someone is sad or angry. How? We are picking up the person's body language and movement.

Our bodies are our temples. They were given to us to inhabit while we exist on this earth. We may love our bodies, we may hate them. They are what we have to move around in while we live this temporal life. We might as well enjoy them. Strange, how our high-tech culture and so many religions have disconnected us from our bodies and movement.

Movement therapist Barbara Mettler writes about movement as underlying all other arts:

> Movement is our primary medium of expression, upon which all other means depend. Speaking, writing, singing, drawing, painting, using any tool or instrument, building, all begin with a movement impulse which is then transformed into word, tone, line, color or some other material. In every other medium our inner experience is externalized in some material apart from ourselves. In movement expression, the movement of our own body is the material. Material and instrument and idea are one in the expressively moving body.[1]

Our bodies and movement reflect our physical health and well-being. Do we have a sense of balance and of being grounded? Or are our heads in the clouds? Are we flexible or stiff, fast or slow, angular or flowing? As we begin to be aware of our way of moving in life, we also become conscious of how our emotional and physical well-being are connected. Movement can affect how we feel, and how we feel can affect our way of moving. A reciprocal relationship exists between movement and emotions.

Since many of you are probably hesitant to use movement for your own self-healing, let me tell you how I was catapulted into this arena. For years I cut myself off from my love of moving to music—not dance steps, but improvisational movement—and in the process became psychologically less mobile. I thought I was either too big to dance or too old or too sedate as a wife and mother, and I moved accordingly. Then, as I mentioned earlier, I moved to California in midlife (age forty-two). After a divorce and an uprooting from my Boston suburban home, I took the big plunge into the pool of self-expression through movement by joining Anna Halprin's dancer's workshop training in San Francisco. Walking into this dance studio contrasted outrageously with my former life. I was used to my grassy neighborhood, my efficient homemaking, my carefully ordered day, and a generally buttoned-up existence. Here is how I experienced the first day.

> Getting off the bus at Divisadero Street, I find myself at dusk in a multicultural neighborhood complete with barred liquor store windows, trash on the sidewalks, and high-energy people talking, laughing, and shouting.
>
> Up the old, narrow wooden stairs, worn with years of use, I find studios that speak of a free spirit. Political posters, friendly photographs, and creative art work are tacked up here and there. "This is what they call *funky*," I say to myself. The casual disarray of furniture, clothes, and food, with their accompanying strange smells, prompt me to admonish myself, saying, "Don't be uptight, Natalie."
>
> Since I am a late joiner of this weekly evening class, there is no warm-up session for me. This first evening plunges me into immediate, intense use of my body for self-expression, human contact, and inner knowledge. As the group sits in a circle discussing the proposed events for the evening, I am astonished at the colorful leotards and sashes, dangling earrings, and the lithe, muscular black leader. "Tonight we will do some shadow dancing," she says. "Each person can take a turn using the spotlight to create his or her shadow on the wall. Play with your image, create your dance with yourself."

> "My god," I think, "do I have to do that?" I freeze. Then, watching as others engage with their shadows I become fascinated. There are tall bodies, short bodies, fat and slim bodies. More importantly, the relationship these people are finding with their shadows is mesmerizing.
>
> The lively interplay (was the shadow doing its own dance?) pulls me into the spirit. As my turn approaches I look for the nearest exit. Then, with cold hands and feet I find myself standing in front of the spotlight looking at the giant I had created on the wall. "Is this really me?" I ask myself as I begin to move. Can I somehow disappear or leave, now? The giant shadow begins to sway and melt, its arms stretched out and around. The dark image stretches tall, tall, and taller until its hands move from wall to ceiling. Then it shrinks to a humped-over heap, only to have its fingers find a way out to play a game of hide and seek. The fingers lead the way to a flowing, undulating arm, then the body follows the arms and the feet follow the body.
>
> Suddenly I am aware that people are at my back, watching me dance—something I had always avoided like the plague. Sweat trickles from my armpits. I become self-conscious. "I must look like a klutz," I murmur to myself. Then I realize I have a choice: a choice to let their presence inhibit me or to shut them and their possibly negative opinions out of my awareness. In a flash I choose the latter. I tell myself, "If I just focus on my shadow, I'll be okay." I engage with the dark image on the wall once again, putting the viewers out of mind.
>
> I become a clown being foolish, a tree swaying, a snake in the grass. My shadow is teaching me to play. I am enraptured, full of new energy, hooked into the process of using my body, once again—after 20 years—to express myself.
>
> I bring the movement to an end as I collapse into a curled up position. After a few moments of silence in which all I can hear is my own loud heartbeat, I return to the sitting circle. At first I can't look these strangers in the face. But as I do, I see genuine, gentle approval in their eyes. I feel accepted. I have joined the clan.

Perhaps my story of taking the risk to move and dance will give you courage to take some risks for yourself. You don't need to jump in at the deep end, as I did. You may begin one step at a time, reawakening your appreciation for expression through movement.

To dance my feelings is still helpful. When I get lethargic or blue, I try to remind myself to move: to put on some drumbeat music to get grounded and be connected to the earth; or to put on a classical piece and let the message move through my body; or to close my eyes and let my body make the first move. Moving "from the inside, out," I experience my lethargy or droopiness and accept that aspect of myself. It brings me to a new awareness. Unknown feelings get unclogged and move out through the muscles, nerves, veins, and pores in my body. Feelings of helplessness first become intensified and then fall away. New energy and determination begin to emerge. Going to the source of my feeling—even if it is unknown—transforms the feeling.

In movement we get in touch with our sensuality, and sexuality, and we are able to integrate them with our spirit. Certain movements allow us to release—to release anger, frustration, blockage—with explosive, angular, stamping, fist-fighting energy and motion. It is a healthy, creative, instructive way to be aware of ourselves and to release those energies constructively. Holding in all those feelings builds up a head of steam, making our bodies into pressure cookers.

We could sit and talk about being frustrated, blocked, or angry for hours and hours and the energy might not shift. If we use our bodies to express our emotions through movement (in a safe and accepting environment), we can deeply experience, accept, release, and transform them. We let the monster out of the cage, look at it, and ultimately accept it as part of ourselves. The raging beast eventually becomes our ally for strength, determination, and the will to move on.

People's biggest fear, of course, is that their raging beast will strike out and do damage: that their rage will turn into real violence. Indeed, the rage *will* turn into real violence if we bottle it up continually. On the other hand, a safe environment offers an opportunity to put our anger into dance—to express it freely without hurting others or ourselves. This, in turn, transforms the anger into strength and self-empowerment, thus shifting this potentially destructive energy into constructive form. Healing occurs.

Certain other delicate, soft, leisurely movements flow quietly from a clear inner pond of love and hope. Forceful, tall, forward movements may bring awareness of mission and destiny. In movements of stillness and inner quiet, the focus is peaceful, meditative. Finding the movements to express such feelings brings the inner and outer realities into alignment. When we *feel* hope and *dance* our expression of it, that kinesthetic experience brings us into a state of total congruence. When we feel fear and express it through movement, the inner and outer match. Through such congruence, we can come to accept and appreciate all aspects of ourselves as being necessary to our vitality.

Movement as Self-Discovery

When you move, you can start from any of four places:

1. A feeling you are experiencing: joy, grief, anger, etc.
2. An image: "I am a silly child," or "I am a tree in the wind"
3. A concept: "I will try experiencing being powerful"
4. A body impulse: "I will let my body move me"

This section describes these starting points merely to help you be aware of your movement process. Where we start may not be of great importance. The distinguishing and healing aspect of movement is that it comes from genuine expression.

In the following example, I begin with a feeling: I dance my feeling of agitation and as the dance continues my mood changes and changes again.

> I wake up feeling agitated. I don't know why. Perhaps it was the dream I had. Perhaps it is the frustration I felt during the meeting last night. I put on my sweatsuit and decide to dance. Closing my eyes, I am aware of the agitation inside my body. I don't conceptualize it or *think*, "How do I express this agitation?" Instead I tell my body, "Express yourself."
>
> After a long pause, my feet begin to stamp a bit. It shakes my spine. My shoulders begin to follow the beat of my feet. I notice that my hands are clenched. They begin to keep the beat, too. The motions take over, I stop thinking. The feelings are leading the way. My head is bowed as my feet stamp harder and harder. My elbows and shoulders are getting into the mood. My jaw is clenched. I let it open. These movements continue for awhile. My heart is beating with strength, rapidly.
>
> Then my eyes look upward. My head follows. My hands reach up, my feet still stamping. A new mood is entering my body. My feet prance a bit, carrying me around the room. My knees lift up as I prance. A pony image fleetingly enters my mind. A lightness in spirit is coming into my being.
>
> I am tired. I melt to the carpet. My body curls in, slowly. I'm a small child on the beach. I allow rest to overtake me. Quiet. Peace. A few minutes later, my arms reach up over my head to a full stretch. I elongate myself. How big can I be? Consciously, I allow the floor to support me. I sink into it, relaxing, giving way. I open my eyes. I see

the jade green leaves on the Japanese maple outside my window. I check out how my body feels, what my emotions are now.

My brief example starts with a feeling and with allowing my body to dictate the movement of that feeling. Then that feeling transforms itself: from agitation to the spirit of a pony, which in turn transforms into a peaceful little child curled up on the beach. In summary, I experience it like this:

- I feel (agitation).
- My body moves (stamping and shaking).
- A new feeling emerges (spirited).
- My body moves the new feeling.
- Another feeling arrives (childlike).
- My body moves accordingly (into a child's pose).
- Another feeling comes (warmth and comfort).
- My body accepts it (the warmth and comfort).
- My body eventually stretches, my eyes open, and I am keenly aware of all senses.

By starting with the awareness of a feeling and allowing that feeling to create a dance, the feeling shifts, transforms, and gives me information I did not have before. The original cause of the agitation does not disappear. But my body can now relax, and my mind has new information that helps me take an action.

Most of us are familiar with taking a long walk when we are troubled. This is the same process. The kinesthetic experience realigns the body, emotions, and thoughts, helping to bring clarity to the problem. We can bring this method into our psychotherapeutic practice.

It is also possible to start moving with a concept, an idea, or an image. One example is, "I think I will dance as if I were feeling competent." You can then act out your concept through movement. When you work with concepts such as this, your body actually feels increasingly empowered as you move, and your self-image can begin to change.

Awareness can also occur when we start with an image. Try this experiment as you read this section. Stretch your arms up, just for the sake of stretching. Do this now. Then try the same movement with a different *intention*. Close your eyes and imagine feeling warm sunlight and an ocean breeze. You are lifting your arms to receive those elements. Breathe in the ocean air and warm sun. Do you feel a difference between the first stretch and the second? Where do you feel it? In your chest? Your heart? Your psyche?

The witness is an empathic observer who creates the container for the mover to go inward.

Having an image of warm sun and fresh air changes your movement and your experience. The same is true if I get out of my chair and walk to get a glass of water. It differs if I imagine myself stalking a lion as I walk down the hall. My movement takes on the expression of excitement and fear.

These two examples tell us we can change how we feel by the way we move. If we move as though we felt helpless, we may accentuate that helplessness and be seen as incompetent. If we have the intention to move as though we were self-confident, we may actually feel more self-confident. Also, others will experience us as confident.

What happens when we allow our bodies to tell us how to move? Starting to move according to a body impulse is something you may not have experienced. The first step is to close your eyes and go inward. Wait for an impulse in your body that moves you. You may think this is impossible: that it is your thoughts that move you. If you wait long enough and let go of your thought process, however, your body will have an impulse to move. It may be a tiny gesture or a sweeping movement, but it will happen. Dance therapist Mary Whitehouse explains the process as one of being moved and moving at the same time. Movement therapist Janet Adler calls it authentic movement. Or, as one man in my workshop put it:

> I have to say, I didn't dance. **IT danced me!** I'm just a businessman. I've never seen a ghost or a spirit, but it danced. I did something important for me. It gave me tremendous pleasure.

At such times, people are no longer thinking about their bodies. They *are* their bodies. It is an astonishing event.

Certain movements allow release of frustration or blockage.

Regardless of how the movement begins—from a feeling, an idea, an image, or an impulse—it is important to understand the different parts of the healing process. Looking at our inner process is essential, rather than focusing on the product (the dance or movement itself). The mover goes through several phases of awareness as she explores her inner being. These phases seem to be: becoming aware of a feeling, fully experiencing it, experiencing its transformation, integrating it, understanding it, and assimilating it.

We become aware of feelings by paying close attention to the messages of the body. Sometimes we experience an element of surprise: "Oh, that is who I am, at this moment." We fully experience a feeling in the body through movement. This can include exploring the unknown: the feelings we usually deny.

The third phase involves a transformation of the feeling as it flows into movement. This includes being aware of the shifts of energy such as experiencing helplessness shifting into a sense of empowerment.

Healing ultimately occurs as the body accepts and experiences aspects of the self that have been denied awareness. Many of us experience integration as a melding or joining of opposites, and a new balancing or centering of ourselves as a result. For example, we might dance some inner polarities, such as anger/pain or fear/trust, and then create a third movement to explore whether meaningful kinesthetic and personal integration follow.

Cognitive understanding of the process comes through reflecting, writing, or creating art (or any combination of these) immediately after the movement. Taking time to think about the process that just happened and to write about it clarify the emotional and physical experience and bring intellectual understanding. Expressing the experience through different media can deepen the meaning of the event.

To some extent, we integrate, understand, and assimilate our healing simultaneously. We also continue these processes over time. We reminisce about our experiences. Assimilation is a receptive mode, in which we take take in all of the knowledge on a physical and metaphoric level. It can also be the beginning of leaving the experience behind in order to move on to something new.[2]

You may want to record your own experiences as you explore the possibilities of movement for self-expression and healing. This process is evident in the following examples.

"Panic and Joy"

Frank, a man in his forties, describes the tumult he went through as he involved himself in the exercise called "Melting and Growing." This class had spent time establishing trust and experiencing the philosophy of respect for each person's way of being. In "Melting and Growing," I gave these instructions:

> Choose a partner with whom you will spend the next half hour. That partner will be your movement witness and you, hers. I will put on some gentle music, and one partner—the mover—closes her eyes, and spends ten minutes "melting and growing" to the music. To do this, just let the sounds in. Imagine yourself melting and growing, knowing that there is no right or wrong to the movements. Observe your own feelings as you allow yourself to melt and grow. You may feel like staying on the floor or you may never want to melt. There is no success or failure to this. It is a process to learn more about yourself.
>
> The witness is an empathic observer, creating the space or container for the mover to go inward. She will not judge or evaluate you. She is present to hold the safe space—emotionally and physically—for you to go inward and move.
>
> After about ten minutes of doing this, I will tell you to bring it to a close. At that time, the witness and the mover will each briefly discuss their experience. The mover speaks first. The witness puts her impressions in the first person. For instance she might say, "When you curled up in a ball, *I felt like* a child." She does not say, "You *were* a child." After the discussion you will switch roles. The witness moves and the former mover now witnesses. (This experience is followed by visual art—clay or color—and then free writing.)

Frank wrote the following account and titled it, "Panic and Joy."

I tend to see myself as moving in linear ways. My lines are too straight, too disciplined. I feel that my early athletic training incessantly indoctrinated the notion of repetition into my movements.

Each move was supposed to be the same as before, no room for spontaneity. I respect the fact that early in my life, athletics were my main outlet for self-expression. However, now, I would like to make the rigid, old ways more graceful and introduce more curves and blurs to my movements.

When you briefly described what the exercise entailed, there was an immediate freeze throughout my body. Could I allow myself the opportunity to move freely? Could I perform in front of someone else? My partner did not ease the tension when she declared that because of her anxiety, I would have to go first. So, in the next moment, which seemed like an eternity, I decided, "You wanted this opportunity, dummy! Now that you have gotten your wish, do something with it. Be as graceful as your center yearns. Dance with the angels. Be in touch with your core and do not be afraid of the Frank that emerges. On the contrary, welcome him as a lost friend. . . ."

In this moment of bravado, I closed my eyes, breathed deeply, and summoned the remainder of my courage. Now was the time, be set free. The music was supportive, soothing like soft rain on an early spring day. It encouraged growth. Initially, I found myself doing familiar things, yogic moves which helped loosen my lower back muscles and vertebrae. This was my melting phase, or more appropriately, my birth. I found myself not wanting to stay on the floor for very long, once my body temperature increased and muscles loosened. I wanted to get on with growth.

A dilemma occurred when I tried to make a fluid transition from ground to upright. My attempts were awkward, unsteady. My mental reaction was, "You've blown it." My physical reaction was to stop, balance myself in a squatting position, focus on my breathing and relax. Once I calmed the critical voice, I envisioned myself moving slowly, gracefully, to a vertical posture. With that mental picture I fluidly proceeded. I was elated. Sweat and a smile covered my face. I was past the difficult part and was moving toward enjoyment. Once standing, the movements were instinctive, as free and unrehearsed as anything I had ever done. The motions were similar to Tai Chi, but with a Latin flavor. I had more rhythmicity. I had more syncopation with the music, which by now had saturated every pore.

Slowly, I could feel the end of the dance approaching. No sorrow, just an appropriate ending. I felt personally satisfied, accomplished. I felt an unusual mixture of exhaustion and replenishment. A pride engulfed my body that I had explored the core and was joyous for it.[3]

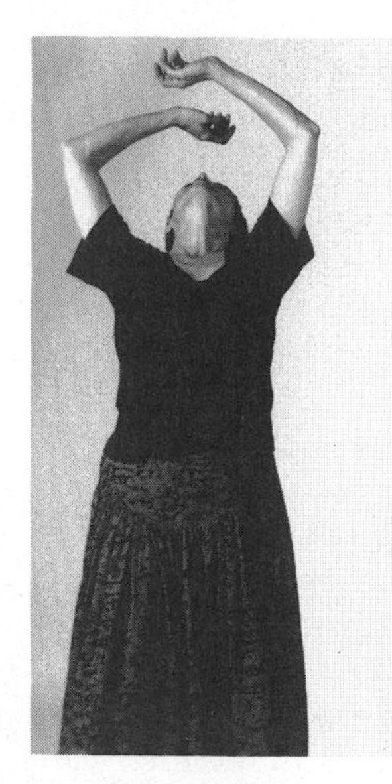

Some movements bring forth an experience of fluidity and inner peace.

Although Frank moved through panic to joy in this experience, he describes his difficulty in fully accepting it:

> Surprisingly, the feedback from [his witness] was much harder to accept than doing the movements. I found myself in total disbelief of her observation. I listened suspiciously as she told me of her wanting to cry. Could the movements have affected her that much? Was she really sincere, or over-reaching for expression? While I wanted to believe her, doubt lingered. Or, better put, my critical mind was coming back to power. Yet, even with the distrust of her data, I knew that I had danced with spirit and the fear would not be as great the next time.

If we review Frank's experience, we can see the steps or stages as perceived by him.

1. *Frank became aware of a feeling* by letting his body take the lead, despite his strong inner critic. His body knew things his mind did not know: that he needed internal balance, and that gracefulness and flowing movement were the balance to his angular, linear mode. His body yearned to be graceful.
2. *He fully experienced that feeling* of flowing and grace within himself.
3. As he did so, *his emotions shifted* from fear to pride, accomplishment, and joy.
4. He began to *experience the integration* of the opposites within.

First, the mover tells of her experience. Then the witness gives her impressions, stating them in the first person.

5. Finally, by writing and reflecting—*through cognition*—he understands what is happening to him intrapsychically. He makes the connection between gracefulness and internal balance.
6. He *assimilates* his process as he writes and as time gives him perspective on his experience.

One more example gives the reader a sense of how individuals experience the same exercise differently.

"Overcoming Resistance"

Dean was also terrified by the movement instructions, yet took the opportunity to explore. Her poignant writing tells the tale of how any feeling—in this case, resistance—can be put into movement and, in moving, becomes transformed. She had spent the first ten minutes being a witness to her partner but also anticipating her own upcoming dance. Later, she wrote:

> Some of those minutes were absolutely excruciating—almost as bad as sitting in the dentist's chair, eyes tightly closed, waiting for the high-speed drill to attack a poor unsuspecting molar tucked way back. . . . I knew my turn was coming and I feared I would have nothing, would be able to think of nothing to do with my body, and like the molar, my internal pain would be uncovered. . . . Those moments were simply excruciating. . . .

And finally, it was almost my turn. . . . I reluctantly stood up, moved away a little—to give some space and my partner some perspective—and slowly closed my eyes.

And I stood there, not moving, for what seemed like an eternity. And then I started to shiver-shudder in a sort of defiance and resistance to the exercise. And something in my body said yes to the feeling of resistance. To go ahead and really experience resisting. To really experience resistance to melting, to letting go. Because that was the way it really had been for me. Strong, strong resistance.

Resistance to the concept of maybe even needing help.

Resistance to asking for help.

Resistance to sharing my cares, uncertainties, and fears.

Resistance to letting go of the armor of self-sufficiency.

Resistance to acknowledging that I was not perfect.

And then the little shiver of excitement of finally giving in just a little, of melting, just a tad, and of feeling a sort of warmth in letting go. Of being momentarily supported by someone or something other than my own sheer will. And the renewed resistance, coming on strong, protective, but from a slightly different place, a slightly different perspective. The yielding again. This time for a little longer. Then two, three, four more cycles, each time sensing a bit more that the world of me did not disintegrate when I allowed myself to experience the state of "not in control." And ultimately, the total absence of resistance and simply the experience and the knowledge of what it is to yield completely and still be conscious.

I found it to be a very special place. But something in the totality of letting go—of total melt—was, after all, terrifying. Not terrifying in the sense of screaming out or fleeing from pursuit or anything dramatic. Rather it was a fear, I think, of melting still further into a sort of nothingness. As if resistance (and control) were life, and letting go would mean to not be. And then a dawning realization that the resistance is really just a special form of the life forces of growth. A way of keeping the self alive when emotional and spiritual growth is not possible.

As I lay there on the floor experiencing a physical oneness with it, and as the fears of nothingness mounted, my body, my torso, began to feel the forces of life, of movement, of growth. Its need to pulse, to contract and expand, defied the weighty aspect of my limbs and head and they were called into response. Into taking energy from my torso, transmitting it into the floor and into pushing up off into a triumphant

> victory over gravity. And with victory, a marvelous sense of well-being that again went from the core, the torso, to the extremities, causing great, large, waving motions that gradually subsided, quietly, gently into a state of yielding, relaxation—melting in a little way. And then again the beginning, pushing this time not resonating off the floor but more as sound waves, intense at the source and moving without resistance in all directions, growing, dissipating. Losing the strength of interaction. Feeling lost . . .
>
> Natalie's voice coming over the music into the center of my being, asking that we bring our experience to a close. The sense of frustration and helplessness. Of wanting to give up. And then the sensory memory of having yielded totally and of having found strength in the resonating, the grounding, literally, of my being.
>
> I can't begin to share with you the joy of my discovery of the floor. Really feeling it was like the feeling of being, of being grounded and being centered. I crouched down. Feet to floor, hands to floor, and I rebounded. And again. With glee. Stretching out. Stretching out the experience. Growing beautifully as one can grow on a warm spring day with the breezes softly blowing.
>
> The art and sculpture I did that day expressed much of what I felt finally, and it seemed to communicate that message to other people, for their feedback was most incredibly wonderful: "evolving gracefully," "a whale's tail? or a horn of plenty?," "at sea," "rejoice."
>
> And the statement of truth that evolved out of the work? Well, in seeing the role of resistance in the movement sequence and how essential it was to all the experiences that came after [her art work and writing], I realized that this is the way it has been in my life. And instead of putting myself down for feeling the stirrings of resistance, I need to work with it. Let it be a part of the growth process. . . .[4]

Here we have two dramatic examples: Frank, who has yearned to move gracefully; and Dean, who experiences her strong resistance. Each goes through a similar process. When Dean became aware of her resistance, she allowed herself to experience it fully, kinesthetically. As is so often true, when we allow ourselves to experience fully the most feared aspect of the self, that aspect takes on a new face and can even become a friend or a positive energy source.

Dean took a big risk to allow her body to "give in just a tad" to yielding or melting. How beautifully she describes the physical and emotional transformation as being cycles of resisting and yielding to the letting-go process: the fear of nothingness. When her body was convinced she would not disappear, she began trusting the new experience. The transformation occurred as she felt the forces of life, movement, and growth enter her body. "Feet to floor, hands to floor, and I rebounded . . . with glee . . . stretching out." Acknowledging her resistance rather than fighting it meant she could use it as her ally—as an energy source and part of her growth process. Cognition came as she did her art work and journal writing.

This is an excellent example of how the person-centered philosophy can extend into the movement realm. When we can experience and accept all aspects of ourselves, we discover a great impulse to become our fullest selves. In this instance, Dean's experience was kinesthetic and emotional, which adds a dimension to the more traditional psychotherapy of verbal and emotional experiencing. Her experience is the creative connection exemplified.

Writing for Self-Expression

Although movement may be a foreign medium for many of you, writing is something familiar to us all. Having had to write school papers, personal letters, or business documents, most of us have had some degree of experience. This book uses writing to tap into the unconscious and help us gain self-insight. Those of you who keep personal journals of your unspoken thoughts and feelings know how this process promotes self-understanding.

Writing for self-expression may not be easy at first. A simple exercise that gets us out of our intellects and into feelings and images is called *free writing*. I learned about this from Patsy Cummings and a group of her colleagues from the Humanities Department at MIT. Patsy describes the free writing they use in their classes:

> Free writing is a basic and very simple exercise; one of those like touching your toes with alternate hands or diaphragmatic breathing that everyone ought to do every day because it is easy (it only takes ten minutes), and its moral, spiritual, and physical benefits are incalculable. It helps you to know yourself; it can free you from the mundane or show you that you are hopelessly enmeshed in it. It is better than aspirin for tension and has no counter-indications. It helps when you are depressed and sometimes you find out what you were concerned about. These are the instructions we give classes, friends, ourselves:
>
> Write for ten minutes. Do not stop writing. Do not worry about spelling, punctuation, complete sentences, grammar. If you can't think of anything to say, write, "I can't think of anything to say" over and over again until you do think of something. Do not read over what you have written (at least for awhile).

> Free writing is not only a way of finding out what one is thinking but also how, in what rhythms, words, phrases; it is a way for people who are locked into textbook language or other people's thoughts to find their own.
>
> It is important, especially at first, that people should have an accepting audience for their free writing.[5]

I agree with Patsy. We definitely need empathic and encouraging listeners for our newly born word-poems. I preface my instructions to people with, "Don't censor what you write. You will not have to share this with anyone unless you wish to. Be honest with yourself, now, as you write. You can decide later if you wish to read it to anyone." When people do decide to share by reading, I remind the listeners to be empathic and supportive and to give feedback in the first person: "In my opinion, this sentence . . . ," or "When I hear your words I feel . . ."

Try Patsy's ten-minute exercise for yourself. Free writing can be a wonderful experience alone or with others, independently or in workshops. If you do it with family or friends, be sure to follow the person-centered principles. Respect the author's right not to read. And, as you listen, put yourself in the reader's frame of reference: ask yourself what it is like to be that other person (rather than judging her writing).

The Creative Connection process helps tap our inner source for writing and expands authentic expression. To add juice to your free writing, use any of the movement and art experiences that you find appealing.

Most people say that free writing is quite different from any other writing they have done. Here are three examples.

"I Feel Like a Diamond Today"

This first example of free writing is from a man who is a professor at Northeastern Illinois University.

> I feel like a diamond today—many-faceted and chiseled and shining. I haven't always felt that way and after last night, I don't even have good reasons to feel that bright, shiny, or faceted. This morning with my son wasn't much better—but hell, basically I have the stone. It's me. I've been carving away on that rock—me—for 51 years.
>
> It's a long way from that Iowa farm and the drudgery, misery that were part of my life there. But after umpteen shifts, directions and degrees, I know who I am and it's time to cash in on some of the facets, begin to use them and then also enjoy what's been created.

> I'm me—imperfect—yet the diamond symbolizes that struggle for perfection . . . Don't even want to look back over the long road . . . (have to keep this pen moving) . . . Leave some time for me to be lazy —to see Lake Michigan out the windows. Better yet, to feel the water on my feet—to run along its shores and get high on the beauty of the sunrise and sunset over it. Let me handle loneliness and not have to have a significant other to share it. Share more of me with me and find meaning there.[6]

The second example is elegant in its simplicity. The author was in a leadership conference group I led in Chicago.

"The Highs and Lows"

> The highs and lows—Notes
>
> The near and far—Reach
>
> The earth and sky—Touch
>
> The black and white—Mix
>
> The same and different—All men are created equal
>
> The weak and strong—Space
>
> Life and death—Man

The next piece is by one of the probation officers with whom I have worked. These people's jobs were demanding and not equally rewarding, so I had hoped that the material in the two-day program would be useful with their clients. "No," they said, in essence, "we cannot adapt your material to our work with our clients since we only have fifteen to twenty minutes with each person and need to get information from them. But we desperately need the sense of renewal and creativity we are getting for ourselves."

"A Rose, When Cut, Rises"

> Her beauty is like a rose which, cut down, rises slowly from the soil, sending shoots of stems slowly stirring toward the sun, and soon the tiny twisted streamers stretched out a bud. This tiny baby begins and sends a cry to all its neighbors, "Here I am" and they come running. First the ant comes scampering out, foraging for supplies, runs on by, comes back and leaves again, then stops, antlers twitching in the morning glare, runs hurriedly back and forth the self-same route. Others join one by one, and then the cavalcade, all coming to and fro anxious to greet the new arrival. . . .[7]

Although the foregoing examples describe things that make sense to us as readers, frequently the contents of free writing are so loosely associative as to have no immediately apparent meaning. Finding ways to tap the unconscious as we write brings forth potent imagery and shakes up stilted, overused forms. Words sometimes voice unseen aspects of the self, adding depth to our awareness.

So many excellent books have been written to help people express themselves through creative writing that I refer you to my bibliography, particularly to the books by Natalie Goldberg, Carolyn Heilbrun, Gabriele Rico, Brenda Ueland, and Ira Progoff.

Soul Retrieval

Where and when did you stop dancing or writing? Would you like to find the lost parts of your soul? Beyond reading about my theory of the creative connection, you can begin your journey by using movement and writing as healing processes. The many examples in this chapter may help you vicariously experience these two expressive arts: moving from within and writing as a free-association process. You may have tried some of these methods and experienced the pleasure of reawakening your creative juices. The next chapter explores the visual arts, music, sound, and meditation as further aspects of the creative connection. Are you curious as to how using color and sound can take you to your unknown territories? The opportunity awaits to continue your journey into your secret garden.

NOTES

1 Barbara Mettler, "The Art of Body Movement" (unpublished manuscript).

2 These process steps are similar to those discussed by Coeleen Kiebert in *All of a Sudden: The Creative Process* (Aptos, CA: self-published, 1980). She describes the process of creativity in general and with visual arts in particular. I have adapted her steps to discuss movement as a creative process.

3 Frank Hernandez, untitled student paper (Orinda, CA: JFK University, 1987).

4 Dean Lockhart, untitled student paper (Orinda, CA: JFK University, 1987).

5 J. Brown et al., *Free Writing: A Group Approach* (Rochelle Park, NJ: Hayden Books, 1977), p. 6.

6 Anonymous participant, Chicago workshop, 1988.

7 Joseph Doherty, Probation Office workshop participant, 1979.

5

The Creative Connection
Part II: Art, Music, and Meditation

Art is a way of emptying the mind and centering the self.

—Alan Watts, *A Way of Zen*

For over thirty-five years, I have spent time creating environments for either children or adults, disturbed or healthy, where they feel free to explore both their inner and outer worlds through the various arts. As a facilitator of creativity and as an expressive arts therapist, I provide an atmosphere in which we can reexperience the direct communication with color and form that we knew as children. There is no way to be that child again. We know too much. But we can recapture the healing aspects of spontaneous self-expression through art.

Healing Aspects of Visual Art

Color, line, and form speak to us. Art is a direct visceral experience. It does not need to go through the word mill. Color, line, and form can reveal our energy levels, our feeling states, and our self-concepts. Color can be soft or intense, brilliant or dull, delicate or powerful, and as such can "speak" for us. Line can be jagged or smooth, flowing or disconnected, simple or complicated. All bear kinesthetic messages.

Images come from the unconscious to help us understand our inner world. Another language of the body, art comes from our sensations and perceptions. We can use art media as bridges between our inner and outer realities by allowing the art process and the images we create to bring us messages. Artist Connie Smith Siegel says, "Art is very close to meditation and therapy in that it is a sensory and perceptual language: a language of feeling."[1]

When we talk about person-centered expressive visual arts, we are not talking about learning how to see (as in Betty Edwards' books) in order to draw with greater skill. We are discussing the process of experiencing a feeling, either conscious or unconscious, and expressing it through art without concern for the product.

Expressive arts emphasize the process of self-expression. It is the process rather than the product that heals, informs, and creates avenues for insight and development. Visual arts offer the opportunity to express ourselves dramatically, poignantly, and colorfully, thereby gaining insights as to who we are. We can release our feelings, expressing them nonverbally, and gain insight into our deeper selves by viewing the art.

Through our intense focusing during the creative act, we actually transform the repressed feelings into constructive energy. We also heal ourselves by integrating our inner polarities or opposites, coming into fuller balance and alignment. We can use the visual arts to explore these conflicting elements and discover ways to become whole. The examples and discussion in this chapter illustrate and expand these concepts.

An intellectual understanding of any emerging symbolic images also provides for psychological growth. Recognizing the healing qualities of the creative process and the symbolic image opens the door to acknowledging the mystical and transcendent qualities of expressive art.

Self-Discovery Through Visual Art

Since the images we create are lasting, the visual arts are particularly useful on the inner journey. Over and over again, we can look at our work, reflect on it, and let it speak to us. Frances Fuchs, a counselor skilled in the use of art and hypnotherapy, says, "Art has the capability of being both the midwife and child of our inner selves."[2] Being keenly aware of the inner self helps us connect our inner reality to the outer world, bringing us closer to nature and other humans. It can also foster a global perspective.

As with any self-exploratory medium, expressing ourselves through art may put us in touch with our anger, greed, envy, jealousy, or any emotion we might rather keep out of sight. It is important that we acknowledge this dark side and then find constructive ways to use or transform that energy. Using art media is a dynamic way to journey safely through the tunnel to become whole, integrated, constructive individuals.

Following are three examples of self-discovery through expressive art, taken from written work of participants in the Person-Centered Expressive Therapy Institute training program. They illustrate the power and effectiveness of self-expression through imagery and color. A potent image or a strong feeling (even if the feeling lies just below the surface of consciousness) are two of the doorways through which people enter the expressive arts process. Images and feelings are motivating fuel for personal growth.

Art that Comes from an Image: "Spirit Bear"

In the first anecdote, Carol Griffin's experience shows how an image springs forth from the unconscious and, when put into visual form, releases negative energy. This process transfers the energy into vital, positive motivation.

> Ben Hedges, co-facilitator of this group and Director of Expressive Art Therapy at JFK University, led us in a guided meditation. He asked us to connect with the earth, to feel roots sinking downward. I felt the golden hills again, and experienced fine root tendrils growing out of me. I felt connected with the elements. He suggested that we find a need to come to us as a spirit. My need . . . was to unblock the flow of my art.
>
> As I lay deepening in meditation, a presence came over me, a big, powerful spirit. As if out of a deep cave, came my spirit bear, awakening from long slumber within me. As he awoke, his strength grew, his fur glowed with a blue magnetism, his eyes became very intense. As the group began to move and embody their spirits, I slowly arose, a low guttural growl emerged from my throat, and I lumbered about. I kept myself focused on the inner need, supported by the earth. This bear was a powerful, surprising ally in my need to manifest art. My determination and power grew. I interacted with the other spirits. Many were birdlike and airborne; quite a contrast to my earthiness. The bear spirit rose up on his hind legs and with a mighty earth roar held out clawed paws, energy streaking from them. This was the power of art flowing from my hands, from my bear spirit, from the earth.

> We proceeded to the art materials and I prepared to use acrylic paint. . . . *The Bear with Blue Hair*. It was exhilarating and intense to create my spirit bear and express all of his magnetism and power in the art.[3]

Carol was discovering an important inner strength and strong need to create art. Her bear was giving her both the message and the courage to follow the message. Later, she shared her painting with a small group. She explained that she had been "too nice" too long in her life and that the slumbering bear inside her was now awakening:

> full of power, anger power, that I had always been afraid of. That power could now be my ally. Just like a bear, I could be my own authority. My bear claws of art energy gave me my purpose, my focus. My inner male, the animus, that had learned to inhibit me as I had allowed outer men to do, now was healing. His strength could be with me, for me, supporting me.

The next day she went to the art materials, cut a large sheet of paper, and wrote out words of what anger is. Using red and black ink, she wrote and, in the process,

> felt deeply the pain and hurt, the energy of anger. It felt again exhilarating to make art, this time as a release of emotion. *I put my whole body into it*. The movement in the art took on the form of a heart—the heart is the seat of anger, as well as its victim and healer. [Emphasis added.]

Carol started this particular process with a feeling rather than an image. Her bear image had brought forth both the fear of and the strength in her anger. So she pursued the journey into the "forbidden" anger, knowing she was in a safe environment in which to explore it.

> Later, during a free afternoon, I decided to lead myself in a guided meditation. This process seemed to be a way to access my creativity. I had watched the swans on the pond and was struck by their beauty and wanted to paint them. I again let the fine tendrils of roots grow out of me down into the earth. The bear was not about to let those swans in. Suddenly I was again the bear, powerful and necessary, with yellow piercing eyes and big clawed hands of streaking energy. I painted the bear with mighty paws, the intense message to manifest art and anger.
>
> [The next day:] the bear comes in wanting admiration—this great energetic part of me is finally on the move. I feel him in my belly and am content and willing to hold that energy.[4]

Carol's experience shows that important personal imagery sometimes comes out of deep meditation, which puts us in touch with the uncon-

Bear with Blue Hair: "A powerful ally in my need to manifest art."—Carol Griffin

Bear with Mighty Paws: "This great energetic part of me is finally on the move."—Carol Griffin

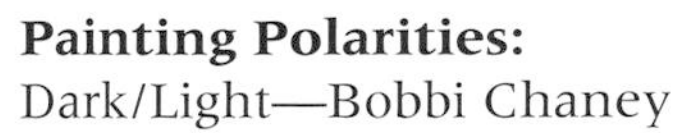

Painting Polarities:
Dark/Light—Bobbi Chaney

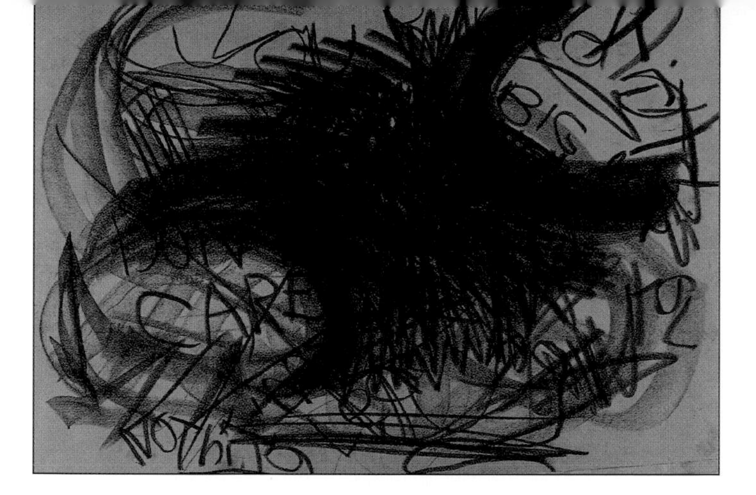

#1 "My dark side—a big mess; despondence, self-dissatisfaction."

#2 "My light side—fluid, warm, sensual, caring."

#3 "My synthesis—includes the gold color with strength, power, and mobility."

“My spirit guide, the egret, lifts off, leaving the crocodile part of me behind.” —N. R.

Free writing after creating the picture:

The crocodile poked his warted head out of the muddy water, blinking, his eyes full of tears. “Please don’t eat me!” he said beseechingly to the huge white egret who had already set sail. Her large form was full of graceful power-energy. Her destination was unknown. She barely had time to look back, but as she did, her compassion for the ugly reptile tore at her heart.

”Why not leave you?” she said to herself (though the dark, slimy monster had been her life-long companion).

“Why not leave me?” he thought.

His longing for her touched her. What would she be without him, she wondered. “Spirit without a body,” she said to herself. “Is that what I want? Hmmmm . . . I don’t think so.” But why associate with this stuck-in-the-mud creature? she asked herself. Why, indeed? He keeps sliding back down into the muck. But then, she thought, “Spirit with no *body? Nobody?”*

scious. Creating movement and sound gave her the kinesthetic experience of her image. Through movement, her bear spirit became more than an image: it was a sensory experience as well. Using color brought this image into form—a form that continued telling her things about herself and her need to create art. Power and anger, two emotions she would usually suppress, came welling up to be painted, danced, written about, and painted again.

Many women hide their power and anger, which puts their energy into a straightjacket. After releasing her feelings through dark lines, Carol realized anger is an energy that can be channeled for creativity. Out of this experience she drew added self-understanding, self-esteem, and personal empowerment.

Carol's experience illustrates the expressive arts process; during this one sequence of paintings, she discovered repressed feelings of anger, her *inner mood,* and her *unconscious feelings* and desires. Simultaneously, she uncovered an important *symbol,* which will continue to have meaning as her life unfolds. She was also aware of a *higher state of consciousness* as she entered into the all-enveloping process of creativity. And if she chooses to research the symbolic meanings of the bear (e.g., what it symbolizes for Native Americans or Europeans), she may find it a rich resource.

Art that Comes from a Feeling

Carol started with an image. It is also possible to explore a feeling without using specific images, letting the color and line flow freely to see what may appear. Such a process plumbs the unconscious quickly. Bobbi Chaney describes drawing conflicting elements of her personality:

Painting Polarities: "Dark/Light"

> I began with my "dark side." On that day my dark side was a very negative thing that I described as a "big mess." The feeling was of despondence and criticalness . . . depression and self-dissatisfaction.
>
> The second drawing was of my "light side." This was done in orange–gold (a power color for me) with a light touch and wavy lines. It felt fluid, warm, caring and bright.

Bobbi was then invited to try a third picture. A synthesis emerged.

> I began with the black line in the center. I realized how strong a statement this black made, and how powerful an emotion it was. With the inclusion of the gold, I found that [the gold] could move easily around the black. The black was the strength and even the

> center of the piece, but the gold could move happily and easily around it. In this drawing, I actually liked the strength and power of the black very much. The synthesis gave the piece mobility and character. I realized that I could deal with my "black" moods in a similar way, as a source of power rather than a debilitator.[5]

Again we see that when we look at and accept the part of us that is an angry, ugly "mess" and proceed to express it through the arts, we find important energy that has been cooped up in that dark side. To function fully requires learning how to use that energy constructively. Bobbi's unplanned, abstract, feeling pictures gave her a new analogy for her own life. This example also illustrates how the unconscious comes forth as color and line flowing freely from feelings. The metaphoric mind sees the importance, in life as well as on paper, of using black to bring forth the brilliance of the gold.

Expressing Pain: "The Black Box"

Knowing she had an inner conflict, Bobbi decided to put that dialogue on paper. Her approach was deliberate; what emerged was spontaneous. But what about when even stronger emotions well up? What do we do when our feelings seem overwhelming? Should we swallow them? Scream? Cry? The following example shows how journal writing helped one participant become aware of her emotional pain. Here is the essence of what she wrote to me:

> Before I came to the workshop I had been working on a very difficult personnel problem involving myself and two other people. . . . One day during the workshop . . . I wrote in my personal journal: "I got rid of her! I won, goddamn it! . . . I want people to come to me—these are things that sound terrible about myself. I'm not a terrible kind of person. I try to make things happen. I want life to be fair and kind—I'm 44 years old and I still don't have my act cleaned up—I organize the shit out of things—I want recognition—I won!"

This highly competent woman, a college administrator, was owning up to a lot of anger and need to be in control.

> Sometime during my rambling thoughts I began to cry and pictured myself as having all of my emotions and feelings locked up inside of me in a heavy metal black box. As I sat on my bed I could actually feel an uncomfortable, painful sensation in my chest where the black box was located. Then I envisioned a drawing that I wanted to produce and I sketched it on a corner of the note pad. . . . It was late evening before I was able to do the drawing. [The next] morning I did two more drawings . . . something of a series. [Each] showed a figure

> rising from darkness into brighter light and the black box within the figure opened up and completely disappeared. I also began going around touching and feeling objects, people, plants, much more than I had ever done before. I remember walking back to the dorm and stopping along the way to caress a rose in my hand.
>
> . . . since I returned to work I find that I'm more spontaneous in my reactions to others and that others are responding to me in a much different way. My relationship with my administration has taken on a much more successful bearing.[6]

When this person paid full attention to her emotional pain, she found it was located in a very specific part of her body. It conjured up a dramatic image. As she pursued the image through a series of drawings, her perceptions and physical sensitivities transformed.

Her strong need to be in control suddenly emerged as a physical sensation in her chest and the image of a black box. Drawing the box again and again allowed the imagery to shift spontaneously, actually changing how she felt as well. It seems like a miracle! Expressive art is a wondrous process. It works. Creating these drawings actually opened up all of her senses so that she could "smell the roses" and be more understanding and compassionate.

Art that Begins with a Concept

We have seen how self-discovery through art can begin with an image or a feeling. A third way is to start with an idea. Recently, for instance, my clay sculptures seem to be about my relationship to my lover. They depict male and female interactions in various versions (abstract as well as realistic). Since that theme is what is coming forth, I looked at the series and made an intellectual decision: "I will take the clay, slice it in half with a wire, and form the two pieces so that they fit together, closely." In this instance, I let the sculptures emerge out of an intellectual concept.

Since starting from the intellect in this way sometimes leads to dead art, it is important to involve the emotions during the process of creation. With my own sculptures, it didn't take long before I began to relate emotionally and kinesthetically to the two pieces I was fitting together. I also came to realize that, metaphorically, I was sculpting the masculine and feminine aspects of myself as they integrate within me at this stage of life. The yin and the yang feel like three-dimensional puzzle pieces joining to making a strong unit.

As mentioned, looking at the symbols that emerge in our art can add to our intellectual understanding of our identity and the dynamics of our behavior. Since many symbols appear in other cultures, both ancient and modern, we may get a sense of our connectedness across boundaries of geography and time.

Carl G. Jung contributed a great deal to our understanding the universality of symbols. Although the Jungian therapeutic approach is too intellectual for me, I appreciate what I have learned from its approach to art and symbol. For instance, I find it fascinating to learn that the "spirit guide" image that frequently comes to me, the egret, is a symbol of freedom, spirituality, and transcendence in some cultures. Such intellectual understanding fits what I feel about the image of my great white bird lifting off this earthly planet with her head reaching for the clouds, her long legs stretching out behind her. The many snake and serpent dreams, images, sculptures, and drawings that I have brought forth become even more important to me when I read that one meaning for the serpent is a link between earth and heaven. I am captivated by the long, undulating serpent paintings on the corridor wall in an Egyptian tomb, and I read that this creature is the guardian of the tomb: the connection between life and death. Such cross-cultural or universal symbols bring me closer to my ancient past and give me perspective on my inner being.

Most of my transformation and healing comes in the process of creating my serpents in various forms, however, not in the intellectual understanding of their meaning. Some of my snakes have a meditative quality, others are in an assertive pose. One dream image was of two cobras facing each other with dynamic energy surging between them. As I take in the messages of my serpents, I see they reflect my state of energy and spirit at the time.

The person-centered approach to symbols leaves room for educating ourselves as to the meanings of our symbols, but in the final analysis we are our own message-givers. Although our understanding of a particular piece of art is likely to change over time, its meaning for us still reflects our unconscious speaking to us.

Respecting the Artist and Her Product

The structured experiences in this book are based on the theory that each person has the capacity for self-understanding, insight, and an ability to find the path or direction she needs, if given an environment of empathy and support. Intellectual understanding of your expressive art—whether it is visual art, writing, sounding, or movement—may come later, even years later.

In viewing the art, the goal for the facilitator (therapist) is *to better understand the world of that individual.* Looking at another person's art affects us. What we see is *our* view of that person's inner world. It is not necessarily, and usually is not, her view of her inner world. The important questions for the facilitator are: "How does this person experience her art, her life? How can I be fully present for this individual while she examines her inner world?"

When people create art—whether it is a doodle, an expressive painting or sculpture, a personal dance, or a piece of journal writing—it always reveals an aspect of the self. It may reveal an aspect of the unconscious self. If you intend to lead an individual in an exercise to stimulate art expression and self-awareness, then you have the tasks of helping her talk about it and giving constructive feedback. Knowing that the artist takes a risk in sharing that unknown aspect of the self, you need to treat the product with great respect. Those of us who are therapists or group facilitators also carry some responsibility for sensitively helping the artist discover the meaning of the product. The following passage helps facilitate discussion of the visual arts product.

How do you show respect for the product and the artist?

- By asking the artist (participant or client) to explain what the process was like and the meaning the art has for her. One inquiry could be, "What do you feel when you look at your picture or sculpture?"
- By waiting to give your response until the artist has described the meaning for her. Then *ask* the artist if she wants your impressions or input.
- By owning your feelings and thoughts as personal reactions, rather than analyzing or interpreting the art. For example, you might say: "When I look at this picture, I feel lonely [or agitated, or sad]. Is that the mood you experience?" or, "To me, it looks like. . . ." This helps differentiate between your truth and the artist's truth of the image.

Ways of Processing the Art

The following descriptions bring together, for easy access, the various ways of exploring and expanding the meaning of visual art.

The Gestalt Art Process

Ask the artist to describe each part of the art in the first person: for example, "I am a blue curving line flowing out of the page. I am dark green blobs. I am a yellow sun radiating over many dark clouds," etc. It is difficult for people to express themselves this way, in the first person, when looking at their art, so you need to remind them gently to return to that process. As the artist tries this, she may get flashes of insight.

Enlarging or Expanding a Section

One part or section of the art may be vague, poorly defined, or troubling to the artist. Make a frame for this part by cutting out an appropriate size hole from a piece of white paper. Place the frame over the section and suggest expanding or enlarging this part of the picture on another piece of paper. Although this notion may not appeal to the artist, this process can bring light to unconscious material. That which was only vaguely perceived in consciousness becomes more defined.

Writing About the Art

People can write about their art in several ways that enhance self-discovery.

Identifying with the Picture

Here are three ways to identify with the art.

- Have the artist write five sentences to accompany her art, starting with, "I am," "I have," or "I feel."
- Give a title to the image. If the artist wanted to refer to this picture a year from now, what title would arouse her memory?
- Have the artist write five words that spontaneously come to her as she looks at her picture. Write them on the picture, or on the back of it.

Free Writing

After doing any art, write for ten minutes without stopping, without editing, without lifting your pen off the paper, and without worrying about spelling, grammar, or punctuation. If you can't think of anything, just write: "I can't think of anything to write"—and keep going. You may have your art nearby, but don't worry about whether you are writing *about* your art.

Dialoguing

Speak to your image in writing and let that image have a voice as well. You can argue, debate, agree to disagree, or try to understand each other's point of view. Let the writing take you wherever it will. (See dialogue of egret and crocodile on color plate preceding page 75.)

Storytelling

While looking at your art, start a story with: "Once upon a time . . ." and let it flow.

Moving Your Art

Alone or in combination with other ways of processing visual art, people can use movement to deepen their self-expression.

Posing
Look at your art and use your body to sculpt yourself, taking the shapes in your picture or sculpture.

Dancing Your Picture or Sculpture
Start as in the preceding exercise, "Posing." Once in a pose that expresses the shape or feeling of your picture, try moving with the rhythm and flow of the lines you see. Use the picture or sculpture as a starting point, then move in any way to further explore the meaning of your picture or sculpture. Use sounds as you move. Or let words flow out freely. As you move, you can create a dance/story.

Sounding Your Art

Allow yourself to make vocal sounds to dramatize the feelings you have when you look at your art work. If you are doing this with another person, have her join you in making sounds. This gives you support to explore the sounds you wish.

You can also use musical instruments—percussion or harmonic instruments—to create music to express the feelings in your art.

Whether you use these explorations for yourself or with another person, they can transform your outlook on life. The expressive arts take you beyond the daily doldrums or self-centeredness to an awakening of the spirit and enlivening of the soul.

Sounding for Healing

Sound can be a very sensitive subject. Using our voices in any manner other than normal conversational tones is definitely discouraged in our culture. When I was a child, my parents seldom raised their voices; and even now, I tend to retreat in the face of heated arguments. In some homes, shouting and fighting with words dominate the scene. Many survivors of such noise never want to hear loud voices again.

Our society offers very few outlets for uninhibited sounding. Children are told to be quiet in school. Lovers muffle their exuberant sounds so no one will know they are enjoying themselves. Loud

Dancing Your Art: Use your picture as a starting point, then move in any way to further explore its meaning.

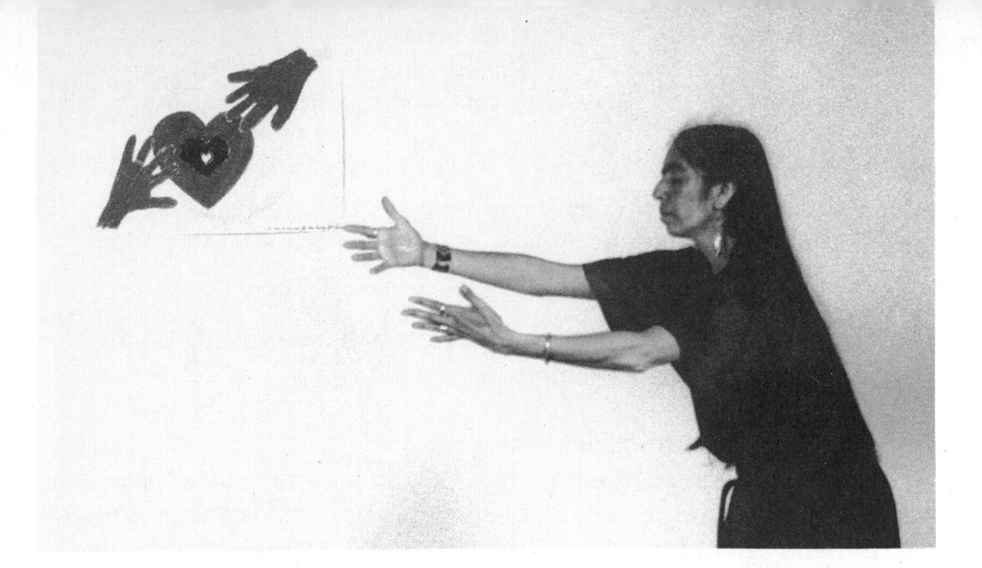

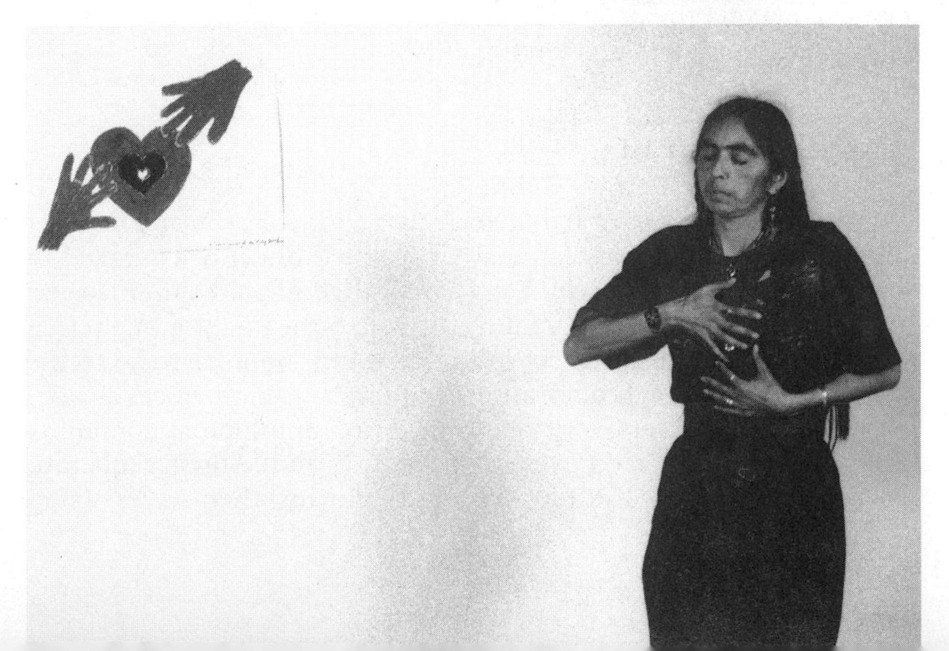

sounds can invade the privacy of others. If *you* need to have a quiet time and *I* need to be noisy, we may both have difficulty getting what we need or want. Most people end up singing in the shower or screaming in their cars, insulated by freeway noise.

Early childhood experiences of speaking and singing influence our attitudes about our own voices. You may have been one of the loud kids in school whose teachers reprimanded them to quiet down. Or you may have been told to mouth the words rather than sing the Christmas carols. Perhaps you were constantly told to speak up, or told, "I can't hear you!" Whatever our past experiences, the way we speak and sing now says a lot about who we are.

In North America we tend to keep quiet unless speaking. In other cultures, chanting, wailing, singing, moaning, and laughing are part of life. Each is a powerful mode of emotional release. Most religions use singing and chanting to bring people to altered states of awareness to evoke an opening of the heart. Singing and chanting can also be used to stir political allegiance or revolutionary force, to help mourn death, or to be used to praise the Lord. Singing is a potent voice for the emotions. It is the language of the spirit. Liberating the voice helps us make contact with deep levels of the self. It has healing powers.

Singer Bobby McFerrin said in an interview:

> our culture poses obstacles to a widespread rediscovery of the spiritual power of music. "It's something that is looked down upon in society, because we think it's all pagan, superstitious hogwash," he says. "But our ancestors were a lot closer to the Earth, a lot closer to the elements—and had a reverence for life that we're losing rapidly. They were a lot closer to the spirit realm, but because of technology and the cities where we live and the onslaught of media, we are losing touch with a really valuable part of ourselves, which is our ancestral memory—the genetic memory of the old songs, the old chants, the old rhythms, the things that our ancestors used to bring these spirit beings up. It sounds other-worldly, but what I'm talking about is actually of this world."[7]

The voice is where the body and mind meet. Our vocal chords, located between our head and body, are the channel through which we link these two aspects of self.

Sound is vibration. And the world is made up of vibration. Physicists are telling us that all matter is vibration. When we make sounds as a form of self-expression and personal discovery (rather than performance), we find ways to release the emotions and massage ourselves from the inside, out.

Usually we think of our voices as a medium for communication or for singing and performing. However, your voice can be used for

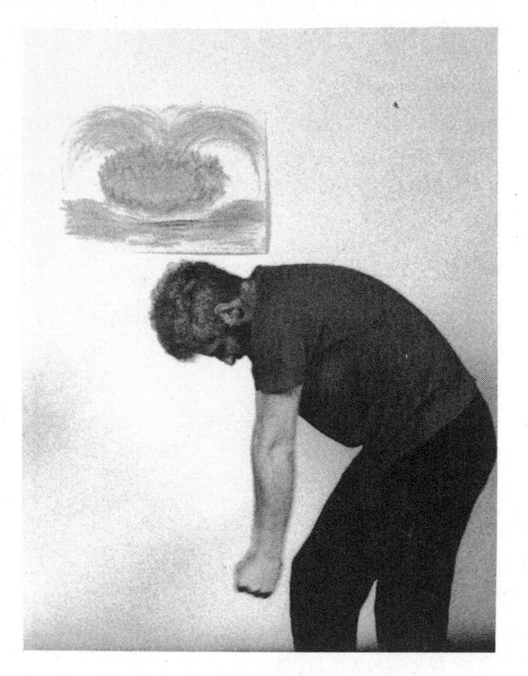

Sounding Your Art: As you move, allow yourself to make sounds.

self-healing as well. Don Campbell has spent many years researching the healing effects of using the voice as a means of integrating the mind, body, emotions, and spirit. His books and tapes describe the process of using vocal sound to create inner vibrations to bring about inner alignment as well as connecting to the vibrations of the planet and the universe.[8]

His beginning exercises suggest spending two or three minutes experimenting with each vowel sound, with a rest of one minute between sounds. You might want to try this now. As you experiment with the qualities of your sounds, close your eyes and place the palm of one hand firmly on your chest to feel the vibration. This helps you release, relax, lower your blood pressure and tension, and come into alignment and balance. Campbell also states that sounding allows us to open up our ability to *hear* the world because we have released our tension.

It is one thing to experiment with making sounds in the privacy of our own homes. However, my heart still pounds hard when I decide to make sounds in public. Knowing that I am inhibited about singing, I signed up for an "Everyone Can Sing" weekend workshop with

vocalist Susan Osborn. I was a little early but extremely nervous as I walked into the room where she was getting things ready. Should I go through with this weekend? As I considered leaving, I went to her and said, "I don't think I can do this because every time I start to sing, I cry." Her gentle reply was, "That's what it is all about." I stayed for the weekend and found more of my singing voice.

I still belt it out only when I am in my car with a tape accompanying me. However, over the years as I have empowered myself as a woman, my voice has become stronger and more resonant. I think again of Angie Arrien's comment, "Wherever you stopped singing was where you lost your soul. What we need is soul retrieval work." When my first daughter was born, I sang her to sleep every night and sang to her as she sat next to me in the car seat. She is now an accomplished musician and voice teacher. I wonder, "When did I stop singing?"

Another experience with sound came through a weekend workshop on Mongolian and Tibetan overtone chanting with Jill Purce, author of *The Mystic Spiral* (a book about the evolution of consciousness). Interested in the magical properties of the voice, she led us as we practiced during the weekend. I came home with unusual energy, my whole body vibrating, and created three large watercolors in an hour. One, a Zen-like circle in rainbow colors with a large white space in the center (used for the cover art of this book) portrays well my experience with sound that day. Every time I experiment with sound, I draw circles enclosing receptive space. The sound vibrations open my body and heart in magnificent ways.

Sounding helps to find our own voices. Making our own sounds taps into the vibrations of matter around us. We can change our states of consciousness by using our voices to vibrate and massage our bodies. Sounding with others puts us in tune with each other, physically and psychologically.

One of my weekend classes agreed to experiment with sound. Here is the report of one woman, an accomplished artist, writer, and photographer. Her detailed account gives us a feeling for the potency of the experience.

> My experience with sound. Sound is a release for me. If I do something that is not quite right, the judge in me condemns me and I let out a barely audible squeal, more like a whimper. Over the weeks and months these add up. There is so much hurt, guilt, not-able-to-pleaseness, and frustration. Friday I let out a scream that came from my gut—I know it did because right before it was released I felt such a turmoil going on down there. I didn't want to let out any feelings. I was trying so hard to sit on them, to contain them, telling myself *don't let it out,* don't let it out . . . *let it out!* . . . hold on, contain, put your feelings away. . . . LET IT OUT! Aaaaaaaaaeeeeehhhh! I collapsed into myself, exhausted, crying, spent.
>
> The next day I got to act out frustration. There is so much frustration built up in my life. . . . I pounded my feet, shook my fists in the air, tightened my jaw and let out primitive-sounding noises of "unh." It came from my chest cavity and pushed through my throat. It was an effort for the sound to come out. . . . I continued the pounding and the jutting of my arms and legs and the grunts until I became exhausted and hoarse. I felt cleansed. I felt I had released the balloon of frustration and it had floated away to disperse itself into the universe.
>
> My background and life has always been visual art. In the past few years I have delved into journal writing and have been enjoying what comes out of this process . . . now I am beginning to discover another ingredient: sound. It feels so primitive to make utterances without forming words, and yet so much more in tune to essence—that part of myself that has no body, form, language. . . .

The work with sound over the weekend tapped into my spiritual self, without a doubt. It was my strongest experience over the two-day class. I was warming up to letting out my inner sounds while stretching. The tightness in my neck and shoulders came across my vocal chords and up through my throat then out my mouth. . . . Instead of telling myself to keep it all in, don't bother anybody about it, don't speak unless spoken to, and good girls are seen but not heard, I gave myself permission to let it *all* out during these exercises.

The exercise that blew me away the most was the one where we faced a partner, looked into one another's eyes, and began to let our own personal sound out. Mine was gentle and low at first, but I felt the fires build within and knew I had to throw on more coals in order to get the heat really rising. I expanded my diaphragm and rose in pitch and level of output. With each breath it became more intense for me. As my decibel level rose, so did my spirit and body. As I was putting out my maximum amount of sound, the true essence of my spiritual being emerged. I was floating in space, in a void with sparkles of light, and there was much movement flashing by me. I was ecstatic. I felt free and the sense of no restrictions, expectations, needs or wants enveloped me. I felt very alive also.

The sound kept coming out without any effort. I had no breath left, my diaphragm was empty and yet I was still putting out sound. . . . I knew my feet were still on that dark gray-blue carpet though my head was in another realm. My body began to shake, my fingers were stretched out wide at the side of my body and I felt my face begin to turn red.

It was time to return. I stopped, took another breath and slowly descended. I went back out there one more time. It was not quite as intense as before, but I knew I had reached out of my body once again. Upon my second descent . . . I noticed being in tune with my partner. We were breathing in at the same time and our noise levels were similar. I felt very connected to her as we traveled along our sound pathways.

Behind me I heard someone telling me it was time to end the journey. My partner and I came to a slow run and then it turned into laughter. Ah! More release! We laughed and laughed, and laughed some more as we sat down. She asked where I thought the laughter might have taken us if we hadn't run out of time. Probably to crying, I said. She smiled and nodded in agreement. I feel crying would have been the final cap on the whole sound experience. . . .

So much had come out: inhibitions, bravery, fear, scaredness, the unknown, the little girl in me, hate, lots of built up anger, confusion

> and innocence lost. . . . I felt very energized at the end of the exercise and very *hot.* My shoulders were steaming, and that is where I had been holding all my tension.
>
> Integration was the word that kept coming to me at the end of the class. There are so many ways to reach the inner path . . . movement, drama, writing and sound. Each has its own strengths and virtues to help me look deeper within myself.[9]

I give this example to alert you to the depth to which sound can take us and also to caution readers about using this as a parlor game. Sound brings up very deep emotional experiences. My own sense of it is that sound is the element that can crack the cosmic egg. It is a potent force to be respected. It can tap into violent memories as well as evoking high spiritual states. In some of our group experiments with sound, people have had memories of physical trauma as well as mystical and magical experiences. Therapists and group facilitators need to prepare themselves to spend time working with the emotional states that surface through experiments with sound.

The next chapter, "Using Expressive Arts with Clients," describes a demonstration therapy session using voice and sounding. If you initiate sounding with clients, it is very important to be in a soundproof room or an isolated building where a wide range of sounds can be expressed without inhibition and without causing alarm. The therapist needs to become "shockproof" if she is to allow the journey of sounding to complete itself. That is, the therapist must be able to accept her client's loud sounds, whether those include a high note, wailing, or screaming. If such sounds trigger the therapist's fear or embarrassment, she won't be much help to the client who needs permission and support to become uninhibited.

Music as Therapy

Making music and listening to music are different aspects of using sound for healing. In stores, offices, and even elevators, we are bombarded with music because marketing specialists know that music soothes the soul or stimulates appetites. Music is part of most ritual ceremonies: marriages, funerals, graduations, parades, and so on. Rhythm and drumbeats keep us in step or stir our earthy emotions. Religious and spiritual groups use a constant beat to foster trance states. Choirs touch into our feelings of love and compassion. Much classical music stirs passions of the soul, evoking feelings that range from a sense of gloom and tragedy to the angelic or ecstatic.

Listening to a piece of music allows us to move into a deep sensory state of feeling. We can use recorded music to help us profoundly experience a feeling in order to transform that emotional energy. To acknowledge that feeling and to select music accordingly can be helpful in personal healing. We may play mournful tunes during times of grief, brass horns and drumbeats to acknowledge a sense of accom-

Music Improvisation: finding a new sense of our musical selves

plishment, sweet strings and Tibetan bells to tune into sensuality and spirituality. Often people say, "I can't cry, although I know I am sad," or "I have just accomplished something in my life, but I don't really feel good about it." Finding music that accentuates the identified feeling helps you or your client plumb that feeling source.

Occasionally individuals seem to get stuck in one emotional condition. In such instances, music that elicits an opposite emotion may be of value. To hear songs of joy when feeling depressed can be as helpful as dancing a jig in the face of death.

Music therapy—creating music as a form of self-understanding and healing—is an important field in its own right. Personally, I frequently bask in music, letting it inspire my art, dance, and spirit. However, I have not been trained in this field. In this section I am more comfortable quoting from colleagues who share my humanistic approach and have more experience and training. One music-therapist colleague, Therese Marie West, had this to say to me:

> Music bypasses the intellectual defenses and goes to the nexus that connects the body, mind, emotions, and spirit. Music is a powerful transmitter of emotional energy. It evokes emotion and is also a medium to express emotions. Music provides a structure to organize and contain feelings that could otherwise seem overwhelming. Healing takes place when we fully experience ourselves. People are afraid to experience themselves fully because of the possible pain they may discover. Music is a nonverbal form in which to explore all aspects of self on a sensory level and is a channel for releasing and communicating.
>
> I work with a Hospice program serving families caring for a member facing a life-threatening disease. I am very person-centered in my approach as I improvise and work with this multi-generational group. We will talk, of course. Also, I introduce music (and frequently art) as a mode of self-expression. We may make music together with instruments, or singing. I will play my flute in response to what they are saying and experiencing. My playing actually reflects back to them the emotions they are feeling. The nonverbal expression of *my* experience of *their* deep feelings is compelling and often helps the person to go deeper.

It touched me when Therese said a neurologist referred patients to her who couldn't speak—that her music, and the music they could make together were an important link to the world. As is true with so many therapists, she offers many art forms to her clients to facilitate their mutual communication. Movement, art, and play frequently go along with the music.

Music therapy is highly beneficial in helping people face physical or emotional pain, serious illness, losses, or grief, as well as being a medium for creativity and joyful expression. These methods can be used with children, with disabled people, and with individuals in psychiatric wards.

I enjoy music, realize its impact on our lives, and have experienced the sense of finding more of myself through musical improvisation with instruments. Several participants in our training program have educated me as they volunteered their expertise to our group. Sadja Greenwood, a medical doctor by profession, is also an avid facilitator of improvisational music. She wrote a brief paper on some of her musical experiments, which I pass along to you.[10]

> There are many routes beyond words to artistic self-expression and communicating feelings. Singing, humming, drumming or playing an instrument are forms of expression and creativity that appeal greatly to many individuals and to groups. Improvisational music can be an art form, a technique for expressing and discharging emotion, and also a means to build group cohesion, enabling the players to lose their self-consciousness and enter trance states as they create rhythmic sound together.
>
> I have been inspired by the workshops and musical philosophy of David Darling[11] and his organization Music for People, which enunciates the belief that music is a natural creative expression available to everyone. There are as many ways to improvise as there are people, and any combination of people and instruments can make music together. There are no wrong notes or wrong sounds!
>
> To improvise alone, play or sing one note, making what David Darling calls a "quality sound" coming from the easiest and most favorite place in your voice or instrument. Hold the sound, loving it, for as long as possible. Make another quality sound. Honor the silence between sounds. A melody begins to emerge. Go slowly, relishing your sounds, alternating between loud and soft. Let it happen rather than *make* it happen.
>
> Play or sing a simple tune you know, a nursery rhyme perhaps. After a time, begin to extend or change it; change the melody, perhaps, or the rhythm. Put it up or down in pitch; play it loud, soft, or with different texture. Let it keep changing.

> Play a walking song—begin by tapping your foot to the beat of your walking or actually walk around the room, slowly and steadily. Start singing or playing your instrument, one note per beat. Stay on the same note for a while until you are ready to change. Gradually let a walking song evolve.
>
> Start with movement before you begin to play or sing. In silence, begin to move or dance in any way that suits you, listening to the sounds of your feet and body. Gradually begin to let out sound when you exhale. See if the rhythm of your feet, the claps of your hands, and the sounds of your voice make a song for you. Sustain it; put words or merely syllables to it if you wish; play it on your instrument.[12]

We tried some of these improvisations with Sadja, finding a new sense of our musical selves as well as release and pleasure.

Meditation and Receptivity

The Creative Connection work discussed so far is active. Movement, art, writing, and sound are creative processes in which we are physically involved in producing something, even though the emphasis is not on the product. We are physically active in moving our bodies, creating art, writing in journals, or using our vocal chords.

Equally important, I believe, is to go inward in a quiet, receptive mode. Tuning in to ourselves and the universal energy source is a powerful method of opening to our creativity. Meditation helps evoke our inner strength and wisdom.

In his jewel-like book, *How To Meditate: A Guide to Self-Discovery,* Lawrence LeShan describes a small conference of scientists, all of whom practiced meditation on a daily basis. When asked why they meditated, they gave various answers until one man said:

> "It's like coming home." There was silence after this, and one by one all nodded their heads in agreement. There was clearly no need to prolong the inquiry further.[13]

LeShan continues by saying that we meditate to

> find, to recover, to come back to something of ourselves we once dimly and unknowingly had and have lost without knowing what it was or where or when we lost it. We may call it access to more of our human potential or being closer to ourselves and to reality, or to more of our capacity for love and zest and enthusiasm, or our knowledge that we are a part of the universe and can never be alienated or separated from it, or our ability to see and function in reality more effectively. As we work at meditation, we find that each of these

> statements of the goal has the same meaning. It is this loss, whose recovery we search for.[14]

This brings me back again to Angeles Arrien's comment about Creative Connection work as soul retrieval. Where and when did we lose our ability to be silent and to be open to all that is?

A few minutes of attunement, or going inward and getting centered, can be vital for me before each important activity—whether it is working with a client, creating a sculpture, having a board meeting, giving a lecture, or facilitating an expressive therapy group. Attunement brings me to a state of inner quiet that helps me be more effective as well as compassionate during that event. Much of the frantic busyness sheds from my mind and body like the dry skin of an onion peeling away. Petty grievances and nervous agitation disappear, and I am fully present for the occasion.

Being open and receptive has a great deal to do with the flow of creativity. And creativity is directly connected to our internal source of energy, our self-esteem, and our self-empowerment. Too long we have tried to control everything and everyone in our lives. By contrast, allowing events to evolve and emerge is part of the creative process and part of the meditative state.

A dramatic experience brought this to my attention in 1980 when I was feeling out of the professional mainstream and anxious about my ability to earn money. I decided to try meditation. I sat quietly, counting my inhalations and trying to let go of the many intruding thoughts. I felt brief moments of inner peace. Then two sentences came from out of the blue: "You are blessed" and "You don't have to be in charge." I was startled.

During the ensuing week, those two sentences kept coming to mind. Being "blessed" was not in my lexicon. But somehow it felt good. At first I felt special. Then I realized it would be a burden to be especially blessed. Finally I recognized the real message: we are all blessed if we take the time to realize it.

The second message, "You don't have to be in charge," was in direct contrast to my efforts to be in control of all of my life. It seemed like a strange message. But as I thought it over, I understood it was exactly what I needed to hear. I did not have to work so hard to push my way into the professional world. I could let the path evolve.

Having had two profound messages early in my meditation work, I expected to get more. When none came, I realized that those two messages were good for a lifetime. They were all I needed.

I suggest you try sitting quietly, with eyes closed and paying attention to your breath, before writing or making art in your journal, or before using any of the movement exericses presented here. Allow stillness to become part of your creative process.

The River of Creativity

In discussing the creative connection, we have been looking at how each art form can help us discover the mystery of the self. Using the expressive arts, we can enter realms of the unconscious to bring forth messages through our movements, our sounds, words, and images. It seems that the more we use our creative power, the more we have. Tap the source and the wellspring flows. In doing so, we open ourselves to a universal energy force.

Movement, art, writing, sound, and meditation intertwine in the flowing river of creativity. If we think of creativity as our deep well, we can see that sometimes it becomes still and stagnant. Movement can stir the waters, unblock the source, and allow the spring to come bubbling up. The visual arts allow those bubbling waters to manifest into color, shape, and form. Those shapes, forms, and colors may be dark, threatening whirlpools or languid streams or brilliant waterfalls. Free writing becomes the voice of the stream, as do sounding and music. It is possible to dance the poem, sing the art, and write the whole journey. This is the creative connection.

NOTES

1 Connie Smith Siegel, untitled intern paper (Santa Rosa, CA: Person-Centered Expressive Therapy Institute, 1985).

2 Frances Fuchs, "Exploring Women's Creative Process" (Rohnert Park, CA: Sonoma State University, master's thesis, 1982), p. 18.

3 Carol Griffin, "Tools For Self-Discovery" (Santa Rosa, CA: Person-Centered Expressive Therapy Institute, intern paper, 1987).

4 Ibid.

5 Beatrice (Lowry) Chaney, "Person-Centered Expressive Therapy: Exploring Creativity as a Path to the Heart" (Rohnert Park, CA: Sonoma State University, master's thesis, 1986), p. 90.

6 Anonymous, "My Experience at the Person-Centered Expressive Therapy Institute Held at Sonoma State University from July 21 to 28, 1985."

7 In "Medicine Music" by Phil Catalfo, in *New Age Journal* (March/April 1991), p. 33.

8 Don Campbell, *The Roar of Silence* (Wheaton, IL: The Theosophical Publishing House, 1989).

9 Anonymous (Orinda, CA: JFK University, student paper, 1986).

10 Sadja Greenwood, "Improvisation Music as Creative Expression" (Santa Rosa, CA: Person-Centered Expressive Therapy Institute, intern paper, 1991).

11 David Darling, Music for People / RD 4, Box 221A / Keene, NH 03431.

12 Greenwood, op cit., p. 2.

13 Lawrence LeShan, *How To Meditate: A Guide to Self-Discovery* (Boston: Little, Brown, 1974), p. 3.

14 Ibid, p. 4.

6

Using Expressive Arts with Clients

The art experience is one way to contact yourself through your senses. Dancing, drumming, working with clay, drawing and painting—without trying to figure out why you are doing what you are doing—can help you know yourself on the sensory level. Without trying, you make sense.

—Janie Rhyne,
The Gestalt Art Experience

The following pages focus on the necessary preparation for and use of expressive arts with clients in the therapeutic setting. Much of the same preparation is useful if you are an artist, writer, musician, teacher, or parent. I hope you will adapt the following discussion for your own purposes.

Most clients come to me either because they have read my book *Emerging Woman: A Decade of Midlife Transitions* or because they know I am a client-centered therapist. When they discover that I also use the expressive arts as a form of self-expression, self-understanding, and communication, they may feel timid about engaging in such activities. Although times are changing and eventually clients will expect to have many media as forms of therapy, at present most people seeking help expect the therapy to be verbal.

Using expressive arts to enhance and deepen verbal psychotherapy is a natural evolution. More and more we are coming to understand the need to engage in processes that integrate all aspects of self: the body, mind, emotions, and spirit. Simply put, we cannot integrate all aspects of self without involving all aspects of self. We do not become creative by thinking about it. We reawaken our creativity by engaging in the process of creativity.

In our culture, we are accustomed to expressing ourselves with words only. In psychotherapy, encounter groups, Twelve-Step programs, staff meetings, organizational planning meetings, and as teachers or lecturers, we express our thoughts and feelings verbally. We are also used to sitting at desks, in our cars, and at our computers. It is rare, indeed, that someone uses art or movement to communicate. Therefore, it is necessary that a catalyst—a therapist or guide—invite the client (or group members) to get up out of the chair to experiment with expressive media.

What I am suggesting is not new. Ancient cultures did not separate their arts from healing. It was all one and the same thing. Dance, song, and visual art were part of everyday life, and it was understood that all aspects of self must participate in life to be whole. With so many personal-growth and self-help groups now emphasizing creative visualization, sensory awareness, breath work, sounding, drumming, and movement, clients are now much more open and even eager to work in these more holistic ways: approaches that involve the whole body, mind, heart, and spirit.

The Benefits

Changing our own perspective on the creative process is one of the most helpful things we can do in preparing the environment for others to be creative. People have a right as well as a need to fulfill their creative capacities. An inherent impulse or drive within each of us longs for creative expression. Incorporating movement, sound, art, journal writing, and guided imagery enhances our therapeutic relationships in many ways. Using the expressive arts helps clients:

- Identify and be in touch with feelings
- Explore unconscious material
- Release energy
- Gain insight
- Solve problems
- Discover intuitive, mythological, and spiritual dimensions of the self

Using creative arts is a powerful and effective way to help clients identify and be in touch with their feelings. This approach is particularly useful for people who tend to be highly rational and verbal. Clients often become experts in talking *about* their problems rather than allowing authentic feelings to well up. If you agree with the humanistic psychological principles stated in chapter 1, then as a therapist you are trying to create an environment where clients can experience their feelings at their deepest level, thus gaining release, insight, and transformation.

Using expressive arts also allows clients to tap into and explore unconscious material. The Creative Connection sequence plunges people into the deep waters of the unconscious. Color, form, and symbols emerge from the unconscious into visual art. In a person-centered environment, the client can begin to put meaning to those images and symbols. In using authentic movement, or movement that comes from the inside-out, unconscious material is experienced kinesthetically. When we introduce sounding, the client opens a vibrational channel—the throat—which connects the mind and the body. Sound sometimes evokes experiences from the past. Also, chanting and sounding can bring forth the experience of connecting kinesthetically and emotionally to matter and spirit. This unconscious material is the rich loam in the secret garden of the self. Out of it grows a wide variety of plants preparing to bloom.

The expressive arts readily facilitate emotional release and insight. The first chapter recounts the healing I experienced in using expressive arts after my father's death, creating my black paintings and painting of waves. Many clients and workshop participants affirm how releasing the expressive arts can be. The client example later in this chapter shows how one man used movement to face his ultimate fear: that of being a madman. Movement plus insight released much of that haunting shadow from his life.

Color, movement, sound, free writing, and guided imagery can also be very useful in solving problems and making decisions. Many times I lead a guided imagery journey for clients who are trying to make decisions. It helps them go down the path of each potential decision and experience the consequences of that decision in their imaginations. I then ask them to draw and move each scenario. This allows them to *experience* each decision. Intuition, imagination, symbols, and kinesthetic experience are all brought to bear on the issue. Much new information comes to clients in this fashion. They can add this process to the more logical pros-and-cons lists with which they may be struggling.

The expressive arts allow clients to discover their own intuitive, mythological, and spiritual aspects. Many people now realize that life offers much more than day-to-day events and practical problems. Each of us is a spiritual being. Each of us has our own mythos in life. We are on a journey in time. There is a beginning and an end. There are peaks and valleys, challenges and victories. We are involved in the writing of our own life stories. The expressive arts are a magnificent vehicle for allowing these stories to come forth. Art and writing, movement and dance, chanting and song—all evoke the mythological from within.

The Facilitative Therapeutic Relationship

Knowing the benefits of expressive arts therapy is a starting point for using these methods. It is also important to understand the philosophy and principles for creating a facilitative relationship. The psychological principles for creating a safe, permissive environment (see chapters 1 and 2) outline the necessary conditions for such a therapeutic relationship. Much of this you already know if you are a therapist, social worker, or other mental health professional.

The person-centered expressive therapist uses the arts as a healing process and for self-exploration and understanding. We differentiate our approach from those medical models that believe the therapist has the "real knowledge" and an accurate interpretation of the client's art, and that the client's growth comes about by accepting that interpretation. We believe in the ability of individuals to find appropriate self-direction if the psychological climate is empathic, honest, and caring. Our tradition draws from many humanistic psychologists—notably, Carl Rogers, Abraham Maslow, Rollo May, Clark Moustakas, Ross Mooney, Arthur Combs, Sidney Jourard, and Prescott Lecky—who defied the authoritarian medical model and created a relationship model of personal growth in which the therapist respects the client's dignity, worth, and capacity for self-direction.

Several excellent humanistic psychotherapists have authored books that shed brilliant light on the process of psychotherapy from the client's vantage point as well as that of the therapist. I particularly recommend the work of James Bugental, Frances Vaughan, Clark Moustakas, as well as the classic *On Becoming a Person* by Carl Rogers. (See the bibliography for books by the authors mentioned above.)

The Human as a Trustworthy Organism

One basic principle that humanists uphold is that the human being, if given the proper environment, has potential for positive growth. In his book *Carl Rogers on Personal Power*, my father put it this way:

> A person-centered approach is based on the premise that the human being is basically a trustworthy organism, capable of evaluating the outer and inner situation, understanding herself in its context, making constructive choices as to the next steps in life, and acting on those choices.[1]

My experience as a therapist corroborates this premise. Sometimes it is difficult to let go of the notion that we, as therapists, must fix things for the client or give advice that solves their problems. Yet letting go of our ego needs—the need to have an answer—is one of the great healing powers. Many clients have told me, "You seem to have more faith in me than I have in myself." It is that faith—my belief in each client's inherent capacity for self-direction—which affords them the opportunity to empower themselves. In creating the climate for self-direction, I may offer reading materials or give out educational information that might aid clients in making decisions, but that merely prepares the ground for their self-empowerment. If clients are to have lasting behavior changes, those changes must come from an inner conviction, not an outer authority. I like the way Tom Hanna put it:

> It is not a matter of the therapist following the old authoritarian medical model of keeping the patient in the dark as a patriarch might treat a child. . . . It is a matter of the habituated, unhappy individual regaining self-control and self-maintenance of his own wholeness and health.[2]

In a world where old political forms are crumbling, those of us who believe in democratic principles now face a challenge: the challenge to continue developing and maintaining a therapeutic process based on self-determination and democratic principles.

> The politics of the client-centered approach is a conscious renunciation and avoidance by the therapist of all control over, or decision-making for, the client. It is the facilitation of self-ownership by the client and the strategies by which this can be achieved; placing of the locus of decision-making and the responsibility for the effects of these decisions.[3]

Empathy, Congruence, and Unconditional Positive Regard

The basic conditions for a therapeutic relationship were tested and researched by Carl Rogers and colleagues for more than thirty years. These three conditions have often been misunderstood or oversimplified in literature. Therefore I would like to quote from Carl's own concise summary statement:

There are three conditions which constitute this growth-promoting climate, whether we are speaking of the relationship between therapist and client, parent and child, leader and group, teacher and student or administrator and staff. The conditions apply, in fact, in any situation in which the development of the person is a goal. I have described these conditions at length in previous writings.[4] I present here a brief summary from the point of view of psychotherapy, but the description applies to all of the foregoing relationships.

The first element has to do with genuineness, realness, or congruence. The more the therapist is him- or herself in the relationship, putting up no professional front or personal facade, the greater is the likelihood that the client will change and grow in a constructive manner. This means that the therapist is openly being the feelings and attitudes that are flowing within at the moment. There is a close matching, or congruence, between what is being experienced at the gut level, what is present in awareness, and what is expressed to the client.

The second attitude of importance in creating a climate for change is acceptance, or caring or prizing—unconditional positive regard. It means that when the therapist is experiencing a positive, nonjudgmental, acceptant attitude toward whatever the client is at that moment, the therapeutic movement or change is more likely. It involves the therapist's willingness for the client to be whatever immediate feeling is going on—confusion, resentment, fear, anger, courage, love, or pride. It is a non-possessive caring. When the therapist prizes the client in a total rather than a conditional way, forward movement is likely.

The third facilitative aspect of the relationship is empathic understanding. This means that the therapist senses accurately the feelings and personal meanings that are being experienced by the client and communicates this acceptant understanding to the client. When functioning best, the therapist is so much inside the private world of the other that he or she can clarify not only the meanings of which the client is aware, but even those just below the level of awareness. Listening of this very special, active kind is one of the most potent forces for change that I know.

There is a body of steadily mounting research evidence which by and large supports the view that when these facilitative conditions are present, changes in personality and behavior do indeed occur. Such research has been carried on in this and other countries from 1949 to the present. Studies have been made of changes in attitude and behavior in psychotherapy, in degree of learning in school, and in the behavior of schizophrenics. In general, they are confirming. (See Rogers, 1980[5] for a summary of the research.)[6]

Empathy needs to be conveyed through words and body language.

In discussing these concepts, participants of my person-centered expressive therapy training program have added their own thoughts based on their experience. They developed these statements to define congruence: "Congruence is being in touch with and honest about your experience—honest with yourself and with your client." "Being congruent means staying connected with self, client, space, and time." "To be congruent is to share a persistent thought or feeling."

Carl emphasized this last point when he was on our expressive arts faculty (in 1985 and 1986). "The therapist cannot expect, nor would it be wise, to share all feelings at all times," he would say. "It is when a persistent feeling keeps welling up and is getting in the way of staying present with the client—that is when it is important to be congruent and share that feeling."

The concept of *unconditional positive regard* is often misunderstood. In some discussions, we agreed on the following statements: "It is acceptance without judgment." "It is acceptance at the deepest level. I may disapprove of the behavior of that person but I accept who he or she is at a much deeper level." "It is valuing wholeness of being." My father always emphasized that this kind of deep prizing or caring was something to strive for in the therapeutic relationship but is actually achieved only some of the time. I use the phrase "coming from the heart" to describe my experience of being with a client.

I define *empathy* as "seeing the world through the other person's eyes, ears, and heart." Another way to describe it is: "to walk beside, to be on the path with." It is not enough for the therapist just to feel empathic. It needs to be conveyed through words and body language. The client frequently needs a verbal response to know that the therapist is indeed on the path beside her.

The client-centered or person-centered approach with these three conditions for facilitating growth were the theme of Carl's professional life. They sound almost elementary, yet most people admit it takes a great deal of practice to live these conditions fully as a therapist.

Respecting the inner world of the artist and her interpretations extends client-centered theory into the field of expressive arts. Person-centered expressive therapy builds on the solid foundation of theory, research, and practice of client-centered psychotherapy. It expands the methods by offering stimulating and challenging avenues of the expressive arts. The Creative Connection process can stimulate the client to use her innate creative capacities to open windows to her unconscious. The therapist offers this stimulus in a way that leaves the authority and decision-making process with the client. Information gleaned by the client is respected by the therapist.

I came to my distaste for analytic art therapy through my own experience. When I began my training in art therapy and my work was being supervised, briefly, by a well-known psychoanalytic art therapist, I felt myself rebelling—rebelling very seriously. Since I enjoyed doing my own art work, it was easy to put myself in the place of the client and to wonder, "How would I feel if someone told me what my art signified?" Even if the therapist had good intentions, I knew I would resent having her tell me that my passionate, red-orange and pink sensual drawings were really "angry statements coming from my unconscious." I knew that such interpretation would seriously inhibit any future attempts at expressing myself through color.

It seems counterproductive, to me, to have diagnostic categories for symbols and colors. How could I, as a client, feel spontaneous or free to create if my works were to be judged and labeled? Such labeling would make me self-conscious about exposing unconscious feelings through art. I like to give my clients (and students) the same respect and consideration that I need.

A second experience came during a staff discussion at a family clinic where I interned. The case of an emotionally disturbed child was being presented. An art therapist steeped in the theories of Melanie Klein insisted that this child's red fire engine was a symbol for sexual aggression. My sympathies went to the kid. "Maybe he just likes fire engines," I thought. It seemed like one more way to play god, be the authority figure, and inhibit the client from creating art.

My reactions to using art for diagnosis and analysis come from my experiences with clinicians trained as Freudian art therapists. I have also been appalled at a few humanistic psychologists who use art to "read" a person's past and predict the future. Being a fortune-teller in this way contradicts the basic rights of and respect for the individual that is inherent in the humanistic principles. I view such practices as dangerous.

Each of us has her own value system as a psychotherapist. It is important to be aware of these values when using the Creative Connection process with clients. The credo I have developed over the years summarizes, in a very personal way, my adaptation of the person-centered philosophy.

My Credo

I am aware that going on one's inner journey can be a frightening, exhilarating, exhausting adventure.

I will be present for you but not intrusive.

I have faith that you know how to take care of yourself. I won't be responsible for you or take away your power.

Nor will I abandon you.

I will respect you and your decisions for yourself. I have faith in your ability.

I will support you and encourage you on your inner journey.

I may challenge you and your belief system, at times, but I will always respect you and your truth.

I will encourage you to try new things, to take risks into the unknown of your inner world, but I will never push you.

I will offer you expressive arts media to help you open to your innate creativity and discover your inner essence. You are free not to use these media.

At times I will give you my opinions and feedback but will always check it out to see if it is meaningful to you.

I will honor my own boundaries and yours to the best of my ability.

I will share my value system and beliefs with you so that you know why I am saying and doing what I say and do.

I am open to learning from you at all times.

I make mistakes, do things I'm not pleased with, and am misguided at times. In such instances I will say so. I am able to say "I'm sorry."

Preparing the Physical Space and Materials

Having an office that invites the use of expressive arts media is helpful. This does not mean you need a large space or a studio. If you have a medium-size table and room for some minimum movement, that is enough. As difficult as it is to have an office where loud sounds do not intrude on neighboring offices, most therapists know the importance of letting the client cry or let out angry sounds. Much Gestalt therapy and Reichian work requires such space. As more therapists require soundproof rooms, architects will design them.

I am also a firm believer in natural light, fresh air, and plants, and in conveying an aesthetic sense through pictures and furnishings. Emotional healing comes through all of our senses. Windowless rooms with fluorescent lighting are an abomination to me. It is incredible how many people now have to work in such conditions. The high technology of our society is fostering our disconnection from nature and our own inner nature.

You need to have appropriate materials available in your office. These materials need not be elaborate. Specific suggestions appear in the appendix; what follows is a general list of the minimum materials you need.

For visual art

Newsprint pad 18″ × 24″

A set of broad felt-tip pens

Oil pastels

Masking tape

A table to work on (or, to work on the floor, a masonite board 20″ × 26″ to which you can tape paper)

For movement

A drum

A few other small percussion instruments

For writing

A pen

Tablet of lined paper

Additional materials to add as you continue using the arts for self-expression:

Ceramic clay
Paper plates (the large, flat variety: for putting the clay on)
Collage material: construction paper, magazines, scissors, glue

Preparing Yourself

Many psychotherapists and people aspiring to be in the helping professions ask, "How do you introduce these methods? How do you determine whether you will use art or movement or guided imagery? And how do you manage to get the clients involved?" The environment for fostering creativity and using the expressive arts with clients is prepared when you have experienced the healing qualities of expressing yourself through these media (and assuming you are a trained therapist open to exploring new avenues with your client).

Having experienced the profound process of the inner journey through any of the art modes, you can introduce this material from a sense of confidence in its effectiveness. If you have plumbed your inner depths through movement, art, writing, or sound, you have the essential ingredient to introduce this to your clients: you have a trust in the process. Coming from this conviction is imperative. Creativity is not a tool. It is a mystery that you enter: an unfolding: an opening process.

Although many therapists are intrigued with the expressive arts and can imagine how these methods might enhance their work, some are shy about introducing them to clients. I certainly remember the first therapeutic sessions when I timidly advanced the notion of using drawing as an adjunct to our talk therapy. Would the client be threatened, or think me foolish, or think we were wasting our valuable and expensive time together? Since I had had no expressive arts in my therapeutic training nor had I been exposed to it in my own therapy, I had no models to go by. But I knew that my own explorations in art had given me insight, and that the classes in which I had used yoga and free movement brought new energy and light to my life.

What gave me the courage to offer expressive arts to clients was my strong foundation in client-centered counseling. I knew that the client is our best teacher. I knew that if I offered something to a client as an experiment and continued asking for feedback, we could evolve a process that would be meaningful to her. I also knew that I would not analyze or interpret the client's art. I did not need to be an expert on symbolic meanings. I would follow the client-centered philosophy that each person has the inner capacity to discover meanings for herself. *I saw myself not as an authority in expressive arts, but as a companion in the process of the client's self-discovery.*

The client chose whether to use the art methods I offered. I had to be genuinely offering this method as a choice. If the client preferred not to use art, movement, or guided imagery, I would accept the "no" answer without feeling foolish or rejected. I saw my role as one of creating a trusting environment in which the client would be heard at the deepest level, and where various means of self-exploration would be available.

Along the same lines, I prefer to tell you how I function as a therapist and let you choose what is helpful to you. There is no one right way. You need to experiment and practice to see what best fits your therapeutic philosophy.

Opening Sessions

Most clients are anxious as they come to the therapeutic hour. At the outset I say, "It is important for me to get centered and be fully present with you. It is useful to me if we can have a minute or two in silence, together, with our eyes closed, to let go of the hustle and bustle of getting here. Does that seem okay to you? Is meditation anything that is familiar or comfortable to you?"

As we are quiet together, I may suggest we close our eyes and "allow ourselves to breathe deeply, feel the support of the chair underneath us, and tell our muscles to relax." This simple beginning has proved monumentally helpful to me as a therapist as well as to clients. It allows me to become fully present and brings me (and frequently the client) to a state of consciousness that moves us directly into the core of whatever is emotionally charged within the client.

An opening meditation also sets the stage for introducing the process of guided imagery. As the client becomes familiar with this centering process, subsequent sessions may include more specific awareness methods such as: "Now be aware of your inner thoughts and feelings. Does any imagery come to you? Are these images located in any particular part of your body?" Images and body locations can be a direct route to deeper feelings, energy blocks, and insights. They also suggest possibilities for using either art or movement as a method for further exploration.

During the first or second session, I say something like: "I am an expressive arts therapist, meaning that I have training in the use of movement and art and guided imagery to help you explore—or go on

Opening Sessions: I invite the client, "Would you like to try expressing that feeling or image in color?" (Natalie demonstrates with colleague Mukti Khanna.)

your inner journey through—symbolic, nonverbal modes. At times I will suggest these methods, offer them to you. I am particularly interested in the healing process of this work, not the product, although the product can speak back to you, giving you new information about yourself. I don't use art to diagnose you or interpret you. The art and movement processes are available to you as another avenue of self-exploration and healing."

At this point, I ask for some reaction from the client. Some people are eager to use the materials; others say, "I can't draw" or "I'm not a creative person" or "I've got two left feet and can't dance." Their fear of needing to perform or create a nice product is evident. Briefly, I reassure them that it is not a test of their creativity, or drawing or dancing ability, but a method of self-discovery.

I also assure clients that whenever I do offer them the opportunity to express themselves nonverbally, they always have the option to say, "No." I might say, "I will suggest and encourage you, but the decision is up to you. I will respect it." I may hear a sigh of relief from the client. Often I find that many are eager to use the expressive arts modes. It may be the therapist who feels insecure in offering them.

When working with an individual client, I engage my intuitive abilities as well as my intellectual knowledge to enter into a relationship that fosters trust, openness, and self-exploration. I describe this, metaphorically, as creating a large, translucent eggshell around the two of us in which we have plenty of air, light, and an aura of safety.

What mode to use depends on the work at hand. When a client is delving into her inner being to discover aspects of herself that are blocking her full potential, she frequently uses body language that says, "I need to move." She may be gesturing repeatedly as she describes her feelings. Or she may remain very controlled physically and be motionless as she talks but be using imagery to describe events and feelings. These are clues for me as to what avenue of expressive arts might be useful.

When the client is already using gestures as she talks, I may invite her to co-design some specific movement activities to help her go deeper. If she is tapping her foot hard as she says, "I am in a real quandary as to what to tell my boss," I might ask her to observe her foot tapping and exaggerate it. I may invite her to get up out of the chair and let her foot do the talking. I may ask if I can join her in the movement to see what it feels like. In this way, I am a companion on the kinesthetic journey with her. As I tap my foot, I begin to feel what she *might* be feeling. To check it out with her, I may ask, "What does the foot tapping say to you?"

"I'm very impatient with my boss."

I then might suggest she exaggerate the tapping even more and put sound and words with it. Her impatience may turn to frustration or anger. Experiencing this shift may point up to the client that her current situation is associated with past experiences that are similar. Following the lead of the client supports her kinesthetic experience and helps her to delve more deeply into the issue. I do not need to know where to take her. She shows me. Any movement, small or large, can hold a key to self-discovery. Focusing attention on her movement brings forth material from the unconscious. She can then become aware of its meaning.

At times the client may use a lot of imagery, such as: "It feels like my heart is cracking open" or "I imagine myself in a black box." Such statements suggest that visual art might be useful. I invite the client this way: "Would you like to try expressing that feeling or image with color?" If the answer is yes, I remind her: "Try using your nondominant hand. Choose colors with that hand. Don't be concerned about the product."

Sometimes I offer the option of using clay. I suggest, "Start by closing your eyes to feel the texture of the clay. Play with the clay for a while and then let anything emerge." Some people prefer to keep their eyes open and construct an image they have in mind. It is involving oneself in the process that is important.

Inviting the client's involvement in the visual arts is easier for many therapists than inviting movement. Visual art yields a product that both client and therapist can look at and use for further communication. Movement is more elusive. Since most therapists seem to be more comfortable using art as a mode of their own expression, it comes more naturally to offer it to clients. A way to ease into using movement is to ask the client to look at her picture and create movement to express the picture. This could start with a pose which then begins to shift into bigger movement. I suggest moving freely to the lines, rhythm, and color of the image. As therapist, I join my client in moving and let her tell me what the movement feels like. Out of this, another picture or clay object could emerge.

Trusting the Client's Path

People who observe me in a demonstration counseling session often ask, "How did you know whether to use art or movement or sound with that client?" I don't *know,* in the sense that there is a right or wrong art form to offer. I use my intuition, clues from the client and, most importantly, I trust the client to tell me the appropriate path. That is, I always ask if that medium is something she wants to use.

It helps to imagine the client going on a journey down a path to her inner self. The path twists, turns, explores deep caverns, and crosses bridges, leading to a home at the end. We do not know this path. Therapists are merely companions helping to light the way. We may suggest dancing down the path; we may use guided imagery to move us along, or use visual art or sound. Whatever the method, we are on *her* path and she can use or refuse any of the modes we offer.

I am trying to give you some courage to try these methods, first for yourself and then with your clients. However, I do not minimize the need for getting training in the use of expressive arts therapy. Reading books about the person-centered philosophy and expressive arts is no substitute for experience. Many people think they understand the philosophy and practice of client-centered therapy after reading books by Carl Rogers. This is not enough. Being in an environment where you actually experience full acceptance and permission to be your true self brings your intellectual understanding into being a more complete awareness. In-depth experience is crucial for those methods you wish to adopt professionally.

When you have fully experienced the challenge, the risk, and the powerful healing process of using expressive arts, you are then ready to adopt the methods professionally. As therapists practice using the expressive arts modes in supervised counseling sessions, they gain confidence in suggesting movement or art, sound or writing. Practice helps them understand how to be *with* the client as she creates images or uses movement and sound for self-exploration. In our training program, as people practice these new approaches to counseling, they learn ways to help clients explore the meaning of their imagery. Trainees can also request videotapes of their sessions as an added learning opportunity to be used during group supervision.

Multilayered Awareness

Being fully present with the client and at the same time creating special modes of expression for her self-exploration are a very sophisticated art. It takes practice to feel self-confident and to learn to be creative in quickly designing an experience that might be useful for the client. I compare my inner experience as a therapist to functioning like an eight-track tape player. One track is fully present with the client, listening, responding, reflecting. Another track is being aware of my own feelings and physical sensations. This may lead to an inner dialogue such as: "Am I nervous? If so, what do I do to relieve my nervousness? Shall I offer a silent meditation to help both of us?" Or my inner dialogue might be, "I'm feeling a pain in the pit of my stomach. Is it my indigestion or am I picking up something from her that I should report to her, thus staying congruent?"

A third track is observing her physical state: "She is speaking very softly now and can't seem to look at me. This must be difficult for her." A fourth track is wondering if this is a good time to be offering an expressive arts experience. A fifth track may be designing that experience from the things she is saying. A sixth track is remembering a childhood experience this client related last week that might be relevant to her present exploration. A seventh track may be aware of the time, knowing that only a half hour remains to our session. An eighth track may be wondering about an outside event in my life, as in whether an important letter will arrive today.

We all operate on many of those tracks all of the time. Trained to be self-aware, therapists become very familiar with them. Often only three or four of these tracks are going simultaneously. As my attention shifts, I activate different tracks. For me, being on any combination of those eight tracks creates an altered state of consciousness. It means bringing my intense focus to the world as the client views it, entering her frame of reference to try to understand fully who she is and how she feels. This altered state is probably very familiar to you, as well. I bring it up to reiterate that while I encourage you to use the expressive arts in your therapeutic practice and I try to make it sound simple, the process has many levels to be learned.

Time Management

Some therapists have told me they don't have time to use art therapy in their fifty-minute sessions. This says to me that they believe words are a more effective therapeutic mode than the expressive arts. They seem to think expressive arts are an adjunct to therapy to fill in the gaps. Actually, the opposite is true. Expressive arts plunge people rapidly into their inner journey. The therapist needs to be ready to handle the strong emotions stirred by these processes.

It is also true that fifty minutes is not the perfect time allotment for expressive arts work. In my own practice, I see people for an hour and twenty minutes. This gives us time to do the art and movement and to discuss its significance. However, I have also found one hour adequate time to include the arts.

If we do not conclude the discussion within the session, I suggest the client write more at home that evening and even continue the process by doing additional drawings and writing. Much of the therapeutic process routinely happens outside any therapist's office as the client ponders and struggles during the week with the material stirred in the session. We therapists need to give clients explorative processes to use on their own. Self-expression through art is a wonderful practice for life-long learning.

I am not advocating we do away with verbal therapy. Words are as important as the expressive arts. I continually communicate my empathy and understanding to the client through words. And she gains release and insight through talking. The point is that we can combine the use of expressive arts and words into a creative connection that speeds and deepens the therapeutic process.

Guidelines for the Client

When suggesting expressive arts exercises to clients, you may want to offer them these guidelines.

- Be aware of your feelings as a source for creative expression to be channeled into art (color, clay, collage) or writing or movement. For example, if you are feeling confused, you can dance or draw or write the confusion. If you are bored, tired, or stuck, you can dance or draw those feelings, as well. If you are sad or happy, you can use colors or a poem, sound, or movement to express those feelings.
- Be aware of your own body and take care of yourself. Create movements that suit your ability.
- With these exercises, you are your own boss. You always have the option not to do them even though I (the therapist) am suggesting them.
- These experiences stir up many feelings. You may need to cry or let out loud sounds, which can be extremely helpful as you involve yourself in the Creative Connection process.
- There is no right or wrong way to create the movement or art, sound or writing. The purpose is to involve yourself in the process of creativity for self-learning.

Interweaving and using the expressive arts in sequence is the Creative Connection theme. To simplify the presentation of this material, I discuss each art mode separately. When you start with visual art, however, movement, sound, and writing can follow. Or when you start with movement, visual art adds further depth to the exploration.

Using Visual Arts

As stated, the therapist can offer the visual arts process any time the client is using imagery and color to describe herself. The flow of the therapy is thus enhanced rather than interrupted. The client experiences no break in her train of thought or feeling. She is using the visual art mode to enter more deeply into the image or issue she has been sharing.

You can also offer the client specific exercises or, as I prefer to call them, *explorations*. At times clients get stuck or become repetitive in their self-explorations. Highly verbal clients get into "telling their story," which seems to go nowhere, therapeutically. Here are several useful explorations you might offer to help them gain insight and perspective.

"This Is Me"

Ask the client if she would like to go on a short guided imagery journey that could lead to using some expressive arts. (You may have tried this in collage form, as suggested in chapter 3.) The guided imagery goes as follows:

> Close your eyes, breathe deeply, let your shoulders relax. Let go of all tension. [*Pause.*] Now imagine that your mind is a slide projector and that various scenes of this week or this month pass through. Don't dwell on any one vignette very long, but be aware of the feelings stirred by each picture. Take three or four minutes to do this.
>
> Now focus on one scene that has some emotional content you would like to understand more fully. Stay with those feelings for a while. It might be a feeling of frustration, shyness, sexuality, hope, fear, anger, or a combination of feelings—anything you wish to explore.
>
> As you look at those slides, those vignettes, what colors, lines, and images come to mind? [*Pause.*] Now open your eyes and, with your nondominant hand, use colors to create quick images or feelings that come to you. You can use one piece of paper or as many as you like. You have about ten minutes for creating the picture.

As therapist you can be a witness to the client as she draws. Or do a drawing yourself. I find that most clients appreciate having me be the silent witness as they work. Since I am not judging or interpreting their work, they feel my presence as a support and encouragement. Again, I ask clients what they prefer and soon we establish a routine that is comfortable for each of us.

A few clients feel self-conscious if I am a witness. And some therapists feel self-conscious being an observer to the client as she draws. They say they feel like voyeurs or that they are intruding on the client's private space. However you work it out with each client, it is important that each of you be honest about what you want and need and then come to some agreement. There is no right way.

After the client is finished with the art, you can suggest any of the several ways of processing and expanding on the meaning of the experience (as discussed in chapter 5). These include suggesting the client move in response to the art, or spend five minutes in free

"This Is Me" in clay. Play with the clay. Twist it, poke it, smooth it. Feel the texture. Let the shape emerge.

writing, or use the Gestalt process of owning each aspect of the picture. Or simply let the client tell you about the picture.

"This Is Me" in Clay

Rather than work in color, your client might prefer to work in clay. It helps if you suggest she take the clay and close her eyes, letting anything emerge as she keeps her vignettes in mind.

A Life Mandala

If you would like your client to get a full picture of the important events in her life, you can modify the preceding guided imagery. One example appears here.

The paper should be prepared in advance. Draw a circle on paper that is about 18 by 24 inches. You can do this by tying a string to a pencil, holding down the string's free end in the center of the paper, and letting the pencil swing around to create a circle. Or you can trace around a large round platter. Have oil pastels, felt-tip pens, or chalk pastels available.

Then lead your client in the following guided imagery:

> Rest quietly on the floor. Imagine your mind as a screen upon which your slide projector casts images of past events. Start with your *early childhood*, recalling scenes and images. As you review these experiences, be aware of sights, sounds, smells, tastes, and colors. Rather than dwelling on any one vignette, let the slide show continue. Remember to breathe deeply as you watch your own picture show.
>
> Next, recall your *adolescent years*, allowing scenes to come and go. Again, be aware of your feelings, sensations, and moods. Then recall your *young adult life*. Let the scenes come to awareness and let them pass by. Do the same with your *midlife* and *senior years*. Pause to let the feelings and thoughts and images sink in.
>
> Finally, *imagine your future*. Spend some time seeing yourself in situations that are fulfilling. Allow colors, feelings, and scenes to come from your imagination.

When you have finished the guided journey, suggest that your client go to the paper circle. These are the guidelines:

> Portray your feelings through color, line, and form. You can be representational by using stick figures and other real-life images, or you can portray your feelings by drawing abstract images. Don't worry about what it looks like. Draw something for each period of your life. Also spend time drawing your feelings about your future.
>
> You may keep within the circle, or you may wish to extend your image beyond its borders. If you feel self-conscious about your images, try using your nondominant hand. Be involved in the process of expressing your feelings through imagery.

Your client may want to talk about the images first, or you might suggest she move to the images and then share her feelings and thoughts. If she wants to move, you might say:

> Study your mandala. Put it on the wall. Let it speak to you. Dance or move to your various life stages, letting out any sounds as you do so.

Then suggest she do some free writing about the images she has created. It often helps to write in the third person. Suggest she take the mandala home and write a "Once upon a time" story as she looks at it.

Looking at one's life through this Creative Connection sequence provides information from the unconscious as well as the conscious mind. If the client puts the mandala on a wall at home where she can refer to it over a period of time, she may see important patterns in her life.

A Life-Line

A variation on the Life Mandala project is to use a long piece of butcher paper or shelf paper on which to draw a life-line, rather than putting the images in a prepared circle. I prefer the circle image, but some people may prefer the linear mode.

When the client finishes with her life images, she has new information about herself and about her attitude toward the future. Looking at the sequence of events in our lives can bring us rich information.

Although delightful memories may be part of the picture, unpleasant events may be uncovered. However, being able to recall one's history or "herstory" illuminates areas for deeper exploration. By understanding our past, we gain perspective on our present and our potential future. Envisioning the future is an important step in manifesting it.

The client may want to expand vague parts of the picture into subsequent paintings. Similarly, parts that carry a great deal of emotional content may indicate an opportunity to do other images (or movement or writing and sound) to delve more deeply into their meanings.

The visual arts are an excellent avenue of expression for any issue or feeling the client is discussing. Anger, grief, jealousy, pain, sorrow, depression, anxiety, boredom, stuckness, fear, confusion, chaos—all are feelings that can be channeled onto paper or into clay. As a therapist, I say: "You seem to have a lot of feelings around this issue. Would you like to put some of those feelings onto paper or into clay?" This very simple invitation can lead to some of the most profound work.

Not only do pictures speak back to the client and therapist, but the process of creating often transforms the feeling. When a client is in a highly emotional state, offering her the use of art media can be a real gift. Focusing attention on experiencing the emotion and letting that emotion be expressed in rhythm, color, and form is releasing. Taking the picture home and viewing it over time allows for further insights.

Opening the Session with Art

Occasionally clients prefer to come into my office/studio and, after our brief meditation together, start with art work before saying much. These clients discover what they wish to pursue in the therapy session by beginning the hour with art.

Using Movement

The therapist makes good use of the movement method by inviting the client to use movement to expand on any feeling or image she has at the time. Giving the client an opportunity to experience her feelings more fully by putting them into kinesthetic form is a potent avenue. Here is a simple invitation: "Would you be interested in exploring that feeling through movement? Find your space, close your eyes, and let that feeling express itself through your body."

> The basic premise is that movement is essential in discharging suppressed emotions and in releasing energy from psychic and somatic blocks. Such an energy release facilitates new levels of perception, which lead toward the integration of body, mind, and spirit. Dance/movement therapy fosters respect for individual differences, aids in the development of a positive body image, and encourages creativity through exploration of inner feelings.[7]

It can also be important to hold very still for a long time, if that is the kinesthetic impulse the client is experiencing. You can say, "No movement counts as moving, if that is your intention."

Susan Frieder Wallock lists the following three stages in movement therapy.[8] *"The first step is to assist the client in becoming aware of her body."* Our movements in daily life become so automatic that we are not necessarily aware of how we move or what emotional content those movements convey. We can become conscious of our bodies by focusing on our movements. For example, I may be walking with my head leading my body. Once I become aware of this posture, I can then focus on how it feels. I can exaggerate my posture to understand what it is doing to my body (and my self-concept). I can also reverse the process by tucking my chin in tightly. Then I can feel the emotions I am carrying and conveying by living life "sticking my neck out."

"The second step of the process is to help her trust her body's inner impulses and to allow movement to happen." Here the client can let go of the thought process or stop analyzing what she is doing. The uncon-

scious supplies the spark that sets the body in motion. It means letting something happen rather than doing something.

"The third stage is to [help the client] make the outer connection to what was happening intrapsychically." For example, one client started his movement on the floor, curled into a tight ball. He slowly uncurled to reach out, then went back into a tight ball. He experimented with this, making sounds of different pitch with the movement. Gradually he became aware of the connection to his life: that he felt safe in his own tight little world, and that he felt fear and excitement as he stretched out, being open and vulnerable.

He had moved through all three stages: becoming aware of his body, then trusting his inner impulse and, finally, recognizing the metaphoric movements as a lesson for his own life. In this way, he connected his spontaneous movement with his psychological reality.

This man could now create a movement or dance that depicts and exaggerates the elements of safety and fear in his life. He could explore integrating these movements to find some kinesthetic resolution. When we dance our feelings, we can change our emotional state —sometimes permanently.

Particular concepts are important to using movement as an expressive art. *Intentional focus* refers to the mover making a conscious decision to be aware of her feelings and let those feelings be expressed through her body. I call this "moving from the inside, out." When a person places intentional focus on a feeling and moves from the inside, out, genuine expression ensues. This can be riveting to observe, even if the movements are subdued or awkward. When a mover is congruently expressing a genuine feeling, she creates an energy field that is palpable.

When I focus on a feeling and allow it to flow through my body in dance, I am using movement for self-expression. However, when I don't know what it is I am feeling and I close my eyes, letting a body impulse come to me to start me moving, I am using movement for self-discovery. Self-expression can lead to self-discovery and vice-versa. The difference is in the starting point. I either start with a feeling or thought that I wish to express, or I wait to let my body tell me what I am feeling/thinking.

Moving with awareness means moving with an intentional focus on the feelings being expressed. It includes being aware of how the feelings shift as the movement develops. For example, if I am feeling sad, I let my body express sadness. If I feel anxious and I dance my anxiety, the feeling may shift to playfulness. So, in moving with awareness, I note the shift. I am conscious of the feelings changing as I move.

The therapist as witness is a term I borrow from Janet Adler and her work in authentic movement. I am an admirer of Janet and her work, having experienced it deeply for myself. My definition of the witness is somewhat different, though, in that I am defining it from my client-centered theoretical frame.

When the client is moving for self-discovery and self-expression, the therapist becomes a witness to her movements. This witnessing is an important aspect for both the mover and the therapist. As with the counselor–client team, the mover–witness dyad is in a specific relationship. The therapist is not "looking at" the client in the usual sense, in the way she might look at a dance performance. The therapist is staying in her role of being fully present: being empathic, congruent, and present with an open heart (unconditional positive regard).

The mover begins with her eyes closed and goes deeply inward to listen to her body messages. The therapist-witness is being fully present, not judging or evaluating. Experiencing the mover, the therapist also allows her own imagery and intuition to be active.

When they discuss the event later, the mover speaks first, sharing anything she wishes about her experience. The therapist-witness then tells of her experience, owning it as she does. She might make such statements as, "When you lifted your arms, I experienced relief. When

The Therapist as Moving Companion: When moving with the client, I try to understand the world as she experiences it.

you curled up in a little ball, I experienced being a little child." This kind of response from the witness allows the mover to retain full identity and to own her separate experience. I view this kind of response as being fully in accord with the client-centered philosophy of respecting the client's individuality. The therapist is careful not to project onto the client.

On the other hand, if the therapist says, "When you were all curled up you were moving like a little child," she is interpreting the client's movement. The client may not have been experiencing herself as a little child, she may have experienced something very different.

Just as the therapist owns her impression of the client's art rather than interpreting it, so too does the therapist own her experience of the movement. This gives the mover an opportunity to feel the authenticity of her experience. When I witness a client doing her art work, I am creating an environment or container for her while she draws. I likewise create this safe space as a witness to the mover. In both cases, dynamic energy flows between the therapist and client, even without words.

The Therapist as Moving Companion

An intuitive decision on my part is whether I move with the client or stay as witness. If I am in doubt as to the appropriateness of accompanying her movement, I ask, even while we are moving, "Does it feel right, for you, that I am moving too?" Most people find the accompaniment supportive. When I move with the client, I dance her dance, not in a mimicking way, but with a sense of the feelings she is expressing. A deeper sense of her experience develops, even though I am having my own experience.

Sounding with the Movement

Movement naturally elicits sound. As the client expresses feelings of the moment through movement, I suggest that she release her body's voice as well. "If you feel like letting out any sound, feel free to do so," is the way I put it. Sometimes I see a client holding in the sound. It is a natural phenomenon in our culture, to keep quiet even though we may be moving energetically.

The following exercises give umbrella-type instructions so that each mover can express her uniqueness. Suggesting either the Museum Pose, the exploration of an issue through movement, or starting from a body impulse helps clients express how they feel at the moment.

The Museum Pose

This is a short guided imagery journey resulting in movement.

> Close your eyes, breathe, relax. Now, imagine you are in a wonderful museum. You are walking down a long corridor and you see a rotunda at the end of the corridor. As you walk into that room, you see only one statue in the center of the room. When you look at it, you say to yourself, "Oh, that is exactly how I feel right now!" Take a walk around the statue and look at it carefully. With your eyes still closed, take the pose of that statue.
>
> Notice how you are feeling. What emotions and associations do you connect with this pose?

With her eyes closed, the client can tell you what she is feeling in the pose. Then, suggest the client put herself in a new pose, one that depicts: "This is how I would *like* to feel." She can move around until she finds that position. Discuss the emotions and thoughts that are evoked in that position.

Finally, invite the client to try moving between the first pose and the second, noticing the transitional movements. What does it take, literally and metaphorically, to move from the one position to the other?

Insight can come kinesthetically, metaphorically, and conceptually with such an exploration.

An Issue

Any issue can be transposed into movement. Clients can use movement to express their experiences of dependency, feeling stuck, chaos, fear, facing a decision or dilemma, being in love, and so on. Delving into the unconscious through movement releases energy and brings dramatic insight.

Moving from a Body Impulse

For a client who seems ready to use movement, you can suggest she start in any position she wishes. Invite her to begin with her eyes closed, letting the impulse in her body tell her how to move. She can add sounds or words to the movement, gaining further insight.

Here is one example of client-centered movement therapy, in which a forty-year-old male client, whom I had seen for a year, cocreated his movement process. This allowed him to experience his emotional states kinesthetically, releasing those emotions to find new aspects of himself.

This man works in the computer field. His values and high hopes are of environmental and ecological renewal, and of a world that has a sane economy: one in which resources are valued, not wasted. He tends to hold himself back from fully exploring his life options. He is fearful, sad, and longing for togetherness and community, while designing his life (unintentionally or unconsciously) for isolation.

In my office, he describes his inner dichotomy. He speaks of the "me" that should be at the office with computers, on the one hand, and the "me" that wants to "go with the flow" of life to see what happens, on the other. This polarity is one that could be explored through visual arts—color, clay, or collage—or through movement. I suggest we go into my studio room, adjacent to my office. He is familiar with this room, the art supplies, and working with me in movement. I ask him if he would prefer to start with the art materials or movement.

"Let's move," he says.

I sense his agitation and suggest, "Let's just walk for a few minutes, finding our own path and pace. Be aware of your breath, your breathing, your pace. You don't need to change anything, just be aware." We spend a few minutes this way. I am walking to open my own energy channels, to be in tune with myself and sensitive to his movement. I am not relating to him. At this point, I am finding myself as he finds himself.

"Imagine yourself on your way to work. How do you feel?" He walks rapidly with stiff arms, and stiff legs.

"Also, imagine yourself at work, what movements portray how you feel at work?" He immediately discovers the kinesthetic sense of himself at work. Since he seems to want to go deeply into this on his own, I decide to become the witness rather than continuing to move with him. I sit on the couch at the side of the room with my large Taos Indian drum and accompany his fast movements.

"Is it okay for me to drum while you move?" I inquire, checking to see that my action is supportive rather than leading him or disrupting him.

He nods a strong affirmation. He is lean, wiry, and slightly slumped. He walks in a circle, clapping his hands, around and around, stiff and robotlike. His feet keep him moving hurriedly. The tin soldier is wound up. His rote clap keeps beat to his rote feet. Finally he stops, crouching to contain his dizziness.

"No wonder I'm sick," he declares. "My life makes me dizzy. I'm going in a circle all the time, making myself dizzy. I want to vomit! It makes me sick!"

This ten minutes of moving from the inside, out has allowed him to experience in his body something he has talked about for many sessions: "The way I live my life makes me sick."

Then he moves spontaneously, pushing out of the crouch into a pose of fear. "When I stop the circling, I become fearful. I'm really afraid." This seems to be a new insight. He moves in the circle again. "When I'm moving like this, the fear goes away; but then I get dizzy." He stops moving again, experimenting with the sensations, listening to what his body is telling him. "When the dizziness stops, I realize my fear."

My sense of it is that the fear is generic, global. I wait, allowing him to experience that fear fully. I resist asking him, "What are you afraid of?" I'm picking up that he is not afraid of some *thing*. He seems generally fearful, or full of fear.

When he has finished exploring his fear, I ask if he would like to try moving to the other aspect of himself: the part he had described as "floating with the current of the river."

> "I would like to start here on the floor." He knows it is his responsibility to create or cocreate his own healing experiences, whether this means hiding under a blanket to feel the longed-for sense of womblike protection or, in this situation, capturing the experience of the current of the river.
>
> Slowly he uncurls from the floor, letting his right hand lead him. He moves gently in the room, this way and that. My drum beat is soft, following his lead. Eventually his right hand leads him to the box where I keep the music cassettes. "May I use one of these?" he inquires. I nod.
>
> He picks a tape quickly, barely looking at the choices. His hand goes to the Gregorian chants. As it plays, he closes his eyes to go inward, standing perfectly still, hands in prayer fashion near his face. He walks, slowly, methodically, still holding his hands in prayer.
>
> Softly, I keep the beat with the drum. Bending to kneel on the floor, he places his forehead on the carpet, his hands outstretched. He remains in that pose for nearly five minutes, listening to the music. I stay fully present: witnessing, feeling the depth of his involvement. As the music stops, he reaches to turn off the tape deck and then raises his head. Tears brim in his eyes, his body shakes.
>
> I move to be closer and ask if it is all right to touch his back. A nod of appreciation. Sensing the tears are stuck, I move my hand on his spine from his waist toward his neck. I sense this will help bring the tears forth. I find I am not interested in comforting him, at this point. I am urged to give him permission to let out the tears.

> Through his tears he says, "I don't know what this is about."
>
> "That's okay," I reply. "Allow yourself that deep experience. The meaning can come later."[9]

I wrote this description immediately after our session. If we had had more time, I might have suggested he do some art work and writing. Using the Creative Connection process as well as movement and words allows people to go even deeper into their polarities. Meanwhile, as it was, this session was one of those times when I felt totally in tune with or on the same wavelength as the client, although not fully understanding the meaning of it all. As such, it is an example of client-centered movement therapy at its best: it incorporates deep respect for the client, always letting him take the lead, while offering him some stimulus (such as the suggestion to move) and an environment of acceptance.

The client takes the lead by describing imagery that is coming to him. He chooses to do movement. The therapist merely suggests he go inward and reimage before he starts to move. The therapist participates in the movement event by supporting the client's movement with sound (the drum). She is fully present as a witness, being there with an open heart. She stays in the here-and-now, accepting each moment as it is.

The therapist checks with the client as to the appropriateness of touching. (If he had indicated, or if I had sensed this to be inappropriate, I would not have stroked his back.) She gives permission for the client to move into his feelings and shed his tears as a way to discover new aspects of himself. Both client and therapist are in a state of altered consciousness—a process that is healing in and of itself.

It is interesting to note that the client felt fearful and explored the fear on a surface level. In the next session, the following week, the explorations bring him to face that fear.

> We start with an attunement, or silent meditation, together. Then he speaks of an image that came forth during the meditation. "I am connected to the earth through roots and the universe, through energy flowing in and out of my head and arms. But I am standing in a void. There is nothing around me of substance, and I'm terrified by something that is behind me."
>
> We go into the studio and I ask if he would like to take the pose of his image. He stands with his face close to the blank white wall. After experiencing this void, he squats down, putting pillows over himself. He starts to growl. His sounds grow louder.
>
> Wondering what new images have occurred, I ask, "What is happening now?"

> "I feel fear that something grotesque is behind me," he says, "a crazy madman." He protects himself with pillows.
>
> I suggest he might want to move as well as sound. He takes the big pillow as protection as he turns to face the ogre. He stamps and growls and moves as he starts to talk to the fear. "I hate you, I'll kill you! You are a stinking, ugly, crazy madman! I'm stronger than you. I'll get you!" He goes on and on in a gruff, growling voice. I feel I am with him in his facing of the Shadow, and it seems he recognizes this demon as part of himself as he continues to rant.
>
> Gradually he lets the pillow down and faces the creature. With eyes closed, he squats and growls some more, then begins to raise himself to his full height and creates a ritual movement of the conqueror.[10]

In this session his imagery, body, and sounds took him to a place of facing the ultimate fear experientially. He hid from it, attacked it, faced it, danced with it, conquered it. The kinesthetic experience amplified what he had said in words before.

Facing the unknown can be terrifying, whether we face it through words, art, movement, sound, or writing. In this instance, the client chose to experience it kinesthetically, which seemed very appropriate. Once we bring the unknown to consciousness, the terror it holds begins to diminish. This man's hidden secret—hidden to himself as well as to others—was his fear of being crazy, of being a raging madman. To dance it, face it, say it out loud, and to let me witness it was, for him, like turning on the light when wakened by a nightmare. Further discussions, pictures, and movement brought the fear down to manageable size.

In looking at my part of this process, I realize I spent most of my time being the witness with this client. At many moments in other therapy sessions, I move with the client, mirroring what she is doing to understand her movements empathically.

When I first experimented with doing my version of the client's movement, I felt self-conscious. When I asked for feedback from my clients, however, they consistently said it felt very supportive. This demonstrates one of my strongest edicts as a therapist: if I am in doubt as to whether something is helpful or appropriate, I always check it out with the client. The client is the best guide and feels respected when I ask.

Besides its obvious physical benefits, movement reawakens all of the senses, allows intuitive aspects of the self to emerge, discharges suppressed emotions, opens up energy blocks, and improves our breathing. This leads to changes in self-image and perceptions of the world around us. Experiencing and listening to the messages of our bodies give us the opportunity to integrate and empower ourselves. The body is our personal temple. As we revere and honor it, and as we use it as a vehicle for self-understanding and creative self-expression, we become integrated, whole, and connected to all life forms.

I agree wholeheartedly with Shaun McNiff when he says:

> Probably no single feature of artistic and general human expression is as consistently missing in training psychotherapists as the language of the body. . . . As we begin to grow in our awareness of the expressive potential of our senses of movement and touch, we will see how they can augment the power and scope of psychotherapy, as well as our lives as a whole.[11]

Using Sound

Sound is an extremely powerful tool for therapy. I encourage you to give permission to your clients to use their vocal chords as they move, draw, or use clay. Using sound is a natural extension of moving. Using sound in a therapy office can be a problem, on a practical level, however, unless your space is isolated or soundproof.

Since loud sounds are frequently associated with violence, anger, argument, attack, trauma, and tragedy, they may evoke many feelings. This also means that sound can release those same feelings. While many sounds are joyful, the painful sounds rapidly take the client into her deepest feelings. It is important, as a therapist, to accept those sounds without judgment and to be fully present for the client in her grief, anger, fear, or pain.

During one demonstration counseling session, the volunteer "client" (a participant in the training program) triggered her impulse to use sound, which I encouraged. This community had been together more than a week, so the client and I worked within a circle of trust and support. I later suggested she write up the session for her own insight. In reading it again now, I see it illustrates how many clients can use sounding as part of the therapeutic experience.

> I'm volunteering . . . there, I've said it. Whew! No one will want to hear my issue. . . . I feel numb. I'm sitting in the chair, feeling numb. Everyone has gathered. Natalie is sitting, giving me an introduction. She suggests a beginning attunement—I like that. She suggests I pay attention to inner sensations, images, etc. That's easy. My body is developing lots of problems—my back hurts, my fingers tingle, my legs feel heavy, my breath is shallow and forced (in spite of the deep breathing), and my head is throbbing in one place. There are no images just now.

Natalie is asking me what I'd like to say—what I'm here for. That client-centered approach sure makes you work, right from the start. I hate explaining myself, and I'm glad I've learned to speak calmly without so many intonations, giggles, etc. I am describing my throat problem and my theories about the abortion and the need to express something. I'm telling her a brief history of some things I've done to work with this situation. . . . I'm telling my history of "swallowing" things forced on me—literally and figuratively. I don't feel any emotional or physical responses to telling this. I can stay calm, now, while I talk about this. Natalie is asking what sensations I felt during the meditation, and I report them. I'm more comfortable, now. She's telling me that my voice is soft and she has trouble hearing me. I'm surprised, as this isn't normally true. She is asking me if I want to be heard—oh, such grief! I'm crying and saying "yes." She's nodding and saying she'd like to hear me. . . .

She's asking about my body's desires, now, and I'm aware that my tongue wants to stick out and move around. This surprises me, I don't know why it wants to do this. As I play with my tongue, my mouth begins to want to blow. I start blowing and the force gets stronger. I want to blow hard. I want a blue river to come up out of my body through my mouth. I'm blowing harder and the air is being forced up through my gut and out my mouth. I'm feeling greatly agitated and as I blow, sound begins to come. I don't know what this sound is. I've done yelling and screaming in therapy and groups, but this is different. I've howled uncontrollably from my gut in a group, but this is different. I am so controlled by the air forcing itself through my body and the wailing sound—a part of me I'm not aware of is doing this. I'm also aware I'm able to observe all this as I'm doing it. I sound like I'm wailing and I don't know why.

No! No! No . . . I'm wailing and sobbing. I'm back in the abortion again. I thought I'd finished with this. How could there be more? I'm so deeply sad. They're taking my baby. I can't stand it. I'm crying so hard. I want to be held and rocked. I want to hold and rock my baby, but she's gone. I can't stand it. I'm so empty—so sad. I'm crying, wailing, moaning. Why do I have to go through this again?

I'm beginning to slow down. I'm almost done crying. I feel clearer. I'm blowing my nose—thank goodness. Natalie has been asking me what was happening through all of this. It's interesting that I could tell her and keep in my own process.

The session has been over a few hours, now, and I'm beginning to be tired . . . and feeling insecure. I've really opened up more pain. I just want to hide.

> I feel compelled to do this collage. It's been building for so long. I'm doing it . . . it's all fitting into place . . . an obsession to complete it. Closed-up faces and mystery on the right side, blood around the baby, water and wind flowing through it all, bringing out the words, the feelings, the expression, the life! Yes, that's better. . . . I can live now. It's done. It's all out. I feel complete.[12]

As we entered into the relationship during this demonstration, I was particularly aware of this woman's faint voice. I could have strained harder to hear, or thought, "It's because we are sitting in the middle of a circle of people and she may be self-conscious or afraid of what she may uncover as she enters into this exploration." But as I paid attention to the immediate situation and was congruent with my own feelings, I pointed out, "I cannot hear you." This is quite different than saying "You are not speaking loudly enough," which makes it the other person's problem, or blames her. I was also being true to myself when I said, "I would like to be able to hear you, do you want to be heard?" One never knows what will trigger an emotional response, but it is true that "being heard" at a deep level is a rare experience for most people. I happened to touch on her longing.

Since the client was describing troubles with her throat, we paid attention to that part of her body. I encouraged her to listen to the messages of her throat. She led herself into the sounds. But she needed empathic support to know that it was all right to blow and sob and wail. Just a few statements from me—such as, "It's okay to be as loud as you want" and "You can explore this feeling any way you wish"—were all she needed.

Her own description tells, far better than I can, the profound sense of release and insight that evolved from this forty-minute session. Sound is a powerful vehicle for transformation.

Using Writing

So many therapists understand writing as a powerful tool for self-discovery that I don't feel the need to say much here. Also, chapter 3 gives methods for approaching the writing process and suggests combining the art and writing journal as an added dimension. Many therapists ask clients to keep a journal between sessions. It is always appropriate to ask clients to write after they have explored through the other media. Many people find writing to be the greatest healer of all.

Conclusion

Using any of the expressive arts or the Creative Connection sequences gives therapists many ways to help clients experience themselves on the kinesthetic, symbolic, mythological, and spiritual level, bringing the unconscious or unknown into awareness. The unknown is not only about fear, anger, and grief. It often includes the capacity to experience joy and love, which can be buried deep.

Using expressive arts with clients is one aspect of this field. The following chapter discusses the application of the expressive arts with specific client populations and other professions or interest groups.

NOTES

1 Carl Rogers, *Carl Rogers on Personal Power* (New York: Delacorte, 1977), pp. 14–15.

2 Tom Hanna in Rogers, ibid.

3 Rogers, op. cit., p. 14.

4 Particularly in *On Becoming a Person,* and C. R. Rogers, "A Theory of Therapy, Personality and Interpersonal Relationships as Developed in the Client-Centered Framework," in S. Koch (Ed.), *Psychology: A Study of a Science, Vol II: Formulations of the Person and the Social Context* (New York: McGraw Hill, 1959).

5 Carl Rogers, "Client-Centered Psychotherapy," in H. I. Kaplan, B. J. Sadock, A. M. Freedman (Eds.), *The Comprehensive Textbook of Psychiatry III* (Baltimore, MD: Williams & Wilkins, 1980).

6 Carl Rogers, "A Client-Centered, Person-Centered Approach," unpublished paper for the Center for the Study of the Person, date unknown. Also, an expanded verison of this appears in Carl Rogers, *A Way of Being* (Boston: Houghton Mifflin, 1980), pp. 114–18.

7 Susan Frieder Wallock and Daniel G. Eckstein, "Dance/Movement Therapy: A Primer for Group Facilitators," in *The 1983 Annual for Facilitators, Trainers and Consultants* (San Diego, CA: University Associates Press), p. 195.

8 Susan Frieder Wallock, "Reflections on Mary Whitehouse," *American Journal of Dance Therapy,* 1981, pp. 51–52.

9 Author's journal regarding an anonymous client.

10 Ibid.

11 Shaun McNiff, *The Arts and Psychotherapy* (Springfield, IL: Charles Thomas, 1981), p. 131.

12 Anonymous participant.

7

Further Applications of the Expressive Arts

Art, if it is to heal, cannot be a defense against suffering . . . therapeutic art knows only one value: to show the truth as far as that is possible.

—Stephen K. Levine, *Poiesis*

This chapter focuses on using the expressive arts for special client issues, such as with people recovering from drug addiction, sexual abuse, or the loss of a loved one. It also discusses using expressive arts for professional groups, such as artists, writers, or educators. The application of the person-centered expressive arts process is limited only by the boundaries of our imagination.

Psychotherapists, social workers, mental health professionals, paraprofessionals, and self-help groups find the expressive arts effective in helping people explore their feelings and change behaviors. People involved in Twelve-Step programs find that using expressive arts adds depth to their personal growth in each step. Alcohol treatment centers have utilized the expressive arts to give residents an opportunity to go beyond recovery to reawaken their creativity and find hopeful images for their future. With women and men who have suffered sexual abuse and have denied those experiences to awareness, expressive arts can help uncover those wounds in order to heal them. Hospice workers and counselors or paraprofessionals assisting people with grief have found these nonverbal methods particularly rewarding.

If you are not a mental health worker, you may wonder how to use these methods in your own field. The expressive arts are useful for anyone who wishes to foster creativity, self-understanding, and self-empowerment. They also help promote personal integration of body, mind, emotions, and spirit. If you are considering adapting these expressive arts methods to your professional setting, you might ask yourself if it would be useful and appropriate to introduce methods that:

- create opportunities for self-healing
- awaken creativity
- foster self-understanding and insight
- allow constructive expression of all feelings
- foster self-empowerment
- offer opportunities to be playful or childlike
- enhance access to the right brain or to intuitive, spontaneous processes
- use nonverbal modes of communication
- tap into unknown or unconscious aspects of the individual
- promote personal integration of body, mind, emotions, and spirit
- offer opportunities to experience higher states of consciousness

Nurses can introduce expressive arts to hospital patients, for example, giving them the opportunity to help heal themselves through drawings before and after an operation or during a long illness. Working with the elderly can expand to using forms of movement, art, and journal writing. Artists, musicians, dancers, and writers may discover new freedom of expression through the expressive arts. Using the creative connection can release vital creative energy. Teachers use expressive arts to strengthen self-esteem and learning and to bring life to academic subjects. Individuals working in cross-cultural situations find the expressive arts an aid to communication.

Applications abound for using various modes in various settings. Ensuing sections elaborate on ways to create appropriate expressive arts experiences.

The Basic Design

When offering expressive arts experiences to individuals in any context, the most important thing to remember is that the expressive arts process has two aspects: it is a process of inner exploration, and it is also a language. The first aspect allows people to discover feelings and thoughts. The second allows them to communicate those feelings and thoughts. Both are vital to designing fruitful experiences.

Creating a basic design for expressive arts work does not mean organizing techniques in some logical order. I don't think of the expressive arts as techniques. A technique is a procedure by which a task is accomplished. Doctors and dentists have techniques for surgery. The expressive arts are not something you do *to* somebody. They are a process which you *offer* to someone for self-exploration and personal communication. I dwell on this because it relates to my next point: it does not take complicated methods or elaborate experiences to give an individual the opportunity to use the arts as a healing process. It does take an environment of trust and safety so that the individual feels free to explore and express herself.

Offering the expressive arts is appropriate when you believe your client, student, or colleague might benefit from being in touch with deeper feelings. It is appropriate to offer the expressive arts any time that you would ordinarily ask: "How do you feel about that?" or "Would you want to say more about that?" or "Would you want to explore that in more depth?"

If the person says yes, your next question might be: "Would you like to try using color or movement to explore those feelings?" If the answer is "I am not sure," you have the opportunity to suggest this as a new form of self-exploration. You might suggest taking a risk that could be beneficial. If the person declines interest, it is important to respect that choice.

If, on the other hand, the answer is yes, you offer the choice of materials and mention that it is the process, not the product, that is important. Being fully present, although usually silent, while the individual uses art or movement to explore her feelings is also crucial. Creating the safe, non-interpretive, person-centered way of exploring the meaning in those creations builds trust and encourages self-empowerment.

Although this book provides various experiments or exercises, if you never do anything other than suggest to your clients or participants, "Would you like to explore that feeling through color or clay or movement, sound, or writing?" *you will have done a lot.* This invitation is the basic design for in-depth work. I use these same words again and again with clients, groups, and friends. After working with one art medium, I ask again, "Would you like to try another medium? Would you like to dance the drawing, or write about it, or make sounds to go with it?" Or, if the client has been moving, I ask, "Would you like to put some of your movement experience into clay or color or writing?"

The design does not need to be elaborate to evoke important material. Simple ways of offering the basic Creative Connection process can be useful with individuals in addiction recovery, hospital patients, elderly people, those in mourning, prisoners, students who have experienced some trauma (such as an earthquake or the death of a classmate), individuals in a psychiatric ward, or friends who need your support and interest.

Once you have offered the process, it is important to respect the individual's personal interpretation of her work. The person-centered theme in this book spells out the requirements for a safe, understanding, nonjudgmental, non-interpretive environment who allows for self-expression, self-direction, and creativity.

Applications for Addiction

In looking at ways to prevent addiction as well as ways to assist in the addict's recovery, we need to look at the reasons people turn to mind-altering drugs or behaviors. We can only touch on this vast topic here, but the addict's search for a "high" or an altered state of consciousness relates directly to using the expressive arts to serve that same function.

My hypothesis is that our hi-tech culture and industrial civilization have separated us from our innate creativity, thus cutting us off from a vital sense of personal satisfaction. To create is a profound event. The process entails a state of focusing in which all else drops away. We can call this an altered state of consciousness or a time of highly energized, purposefully directed behavior. Whatever we call it, it is enlivening.

Without the opportunity to be creative, we lose much of life's zest and flavor. Our society does not afford many opportunities to continue the free expression of our childhood years, so we become blocked and frustrated. We then look for ways to experience stimulation and excitement. Drugs are one avenue to that altered state. Compulsive behaviors are another.

In an article titled "Addictions and Consciousness," Pat Perrin and Wim Coleman ask, "Is the addict's dilemma truly different from the spiritual strivings of the rest of us? How many of us can say that we are not addicts in one way or another?" They posit that many individuals who eventually become addicts began by seeking something worthwhile.

> The new consensus of many health professionals is that addiction does not necessarily begin as a self-indulgent search for pleasure without responsibility. To the contrary, it may be a failed attempt at a legitimate goal.[1]

In this same article, Andrew Weil, professor of Addiction Studies at the University of Arizona, says:

> the social model is that addiction is a matter of will and humans have weak wills. The public believes in weakness.
>
> Instead, we should emphasize what the addict is fundamentally *after*. All addicts are striving to experience wholeness. . . . Research approaches that do not acknowledge this desire are doomed to failure as are treatment approaches that do not teach alternative ways to satisfy it.[2]

The expressive arts obviously come into this picture as such an alternative. Substance abuse or self-abusive behaviors frequently begin when people are looking for ways to be in touch with their creativity. They act out or use drugs as the stimulus and then get hooked on the substance or process. Most of us know of people who have become addicted to alcohol or other drugs after they experienced the substance as helping to free them in their creative endeavors. We may know the writer who takes a glass of wine to help the words flow freely, the musician who snorts cocaine to enhance his drumming, the corporate type who uses drugs to make the day livelier and her thoughts more creative. As years go by, the drug becomes the master. The addicted person's mind turns fuzzy and dull. She is sidetracked away from self-expression into self-destruction.

In terms of preventing addiction, engaging in the Creative Connection process can be one path to becoming more spontaneous and uninhibited. Drumming, dancing, painting, writing, meditating, improvising, and singing become the vehicles for transporting them to their creativity. It seems imperative that we offer many ways and many opportunities for people—particularly youth—to use their creative energy constructively. We currently have stifled so much of the individual's playful, spontaneous expression that the society is functioning like a pressure cooker about to explode. If we were to emphasize and integrate creative self-expression within our homes and schools, our young people would not be so attracted to drugs. They could get their excitement and their highs through expressive dancing, trance dancing, sculpting, painting, and writing in a safe, ungraded, nonevaluative environment.

In addition to prevention, the expressive arts can also be an important aspect of addiction recovery. The first step in treatment is to get the addict off the drug, whether this is voluntary or by planned intervention methods. The second step is to help the addict control her behavior. The necessary third step is to offer ways in which the recovering addict can envision and experience her potential self, including her spirit.

To illustrate this third step, let me recount a daylong workshop for fifty recovering addicts at the Sierra Tucson treatment center. The staff were at an in-service training program that day, so the entire residential population was with me from nine in the morning until five in the afternoon for a day of Creative Connection work. To start, I established an important ground rule: "Everyone must stay in this large room, but you do not need to participate unless you want to." I also explained the guidelines for expressive arts work, emphasizing that any feeling—whether it is shame, anger, love, or loneliness—can be channeled into art. Saying that the work is designed to help them discover their feelings, I emphasized that the process is important, not the product.

Most of the residents participated. These were blue-collar workers, ministers, businessmen and -women, housewives, doctors, and drop-outs. The onlookers were a handful of people in their first week of detoxification.

We spent an intense day with the Creative Connection process, focusing on the inner journey of each individual. After closing their eyes and experiencing some movement to express "This is me," people made drawings, sculptures, or collages to explore their identities further. Some people were in tears as they worked, others were humming. A few were obviously feeling anxious or agitated. I suggested they put their agitation into the art process. Free writing followed the art work.

People then were invited to share their personal discoveries in dyads. Then we all looked at each other's art. I asked them to talk about some of their learnings with the whole group. In this feedback hour, several people said they appreciated the chance to see who they could be when they had recovered from substance abuse. They felt they were on the road to abstinence but needed this opportunity to experience themselves as persons beyond addiction. One participant said, "This gives me a sense of hope. I've been looking at all of my behavior and struggling to change, but today has been my chance to have a vision." Another person said the Creative Connection process had brought him back in touch with his spirituality, something he had long been missing. Many people had been through deep emotional states during the day and now felt released.

Program directors had brought me into this situation as an experiment. It became obvious to me and to those who participated that a person-centered expressive arts component would round out a treatment plan for residential recovery programs. If we listen to the residents of such programs, we hear that abstinence is just the beginning of recovery. Developing a new identity and recovering one's creativity are also a necessary step to stabilized growth toward full potential. The expressive arts can be a path.

Expressive Arts with Twelve-Step Programs

The expressive arts methods described in this book are particularly suitable to Twelve-Step programs such as Alcoholics Anonymous (AA) and Overeaters Anonymous. These remarkably successful self-help programs rest on people's mutual support for being honestly self-revealing and for changing their own behaviors. Week after week, participants share their individual stories of abuse and recovery. Acknowledging failures as well as successes enables them to let go of their shame and their need to be perfect. In turn, this allows personal growth and behavior change to proceed at a gradual but steady pace.

Strict rules govern the group dynamics. The official format does not allow cross-talk (responding to each other) or such personal-growth processes as the expressive arts. However, many private groups adapt AA's twelve steps and incorporate other methods to enhance self-understanding and communication. For example, Step Four in the Alcoholics Anonymous process starts: "Made a searching and fearless moral inventory of ourselves. . . . Step Four is our vigorous and painstaking effort to discover what these liabilities have been and are."[3] This refers to exploring how our social drives for emotional security, sex, money, and power are necessary for survival yet are often misdirected and run wild. Using imagery to help the recovering addict become aware of needs and drives can be useful. A picture can be worth a thousand words, particularly when the individual feels guilty, ashamed, or embarrassed.

Here is one expressive arts experience to help a person acknowledge such aspects. This could be done at home, alone, or in a group.

EXPLORING DRIVES

1. My Wild Side
Close your eyes and meditate for a moment on your social drives, particularly ones that might get out of control or run wild. This could include drives for power, money, or sex, or any other needs that are important to you. Let any feelings or images emerge. (Pause for a minute.)

Now go to the collage box (for magazines) and let pictures find you. Don't try to find pictures to match the images you had in your meditation. Choose any pictures that speak to you at the moment. Arrange and glue them on the page in a way that satisfies you.

When you are finished, study the picture and do some free writing to go with it. Or write five sentences starting with: "I am [or I have, or I feel]. . . ."

Stand up and put the picture on the wall. Try doing some movement and sound to the picture. What kind of feelings emerge? Say any words as you move such as, "I feel driven . . . I need . . . I want. . . ." What feelings arise as you do this?

Next, quickly express your feelings in color, line, rhythm, and form. Try using your nondominant hand. Or take the clay, close your eyes, and let anything emerge.

Try writing about or moving to that picture or sculpture. What are you discovering about yourself?

2. Using My Social Energy Constructively

When you feel you have finished exploring any feelings of being wild or out of control, create a collage or picture or sculpture that expresses who you are when you use that energy in constructive ways. Close your eyes and remember the energy you experienced when you were in touch with your drives for sex, food, or power. Also, remember times when you have used that energy in useful or constructive ways. It may have been something simple, such as going for a walk in the woods or fixing something; or something more complex: developing an intimate relationship, cooking for a party, leading a meeting, giving a speech, writing a poem, building something, or developing a new idea. See if you can imagine useful ways to channel your energy into creative endeavors.

Now go to the collage box and select pictures that seem to speak to you. There is no right or wrong to this exercise. When you finish with the collage, write about it. Then dance it. (Or dance it and then write about it.) See how it feels, kinesthetically, to use your power in productive ways.

Compare how you feel when you are out of control (eating too much, demanding too much, etc.) and how you feel when you channel your energy constructively. I am not suggesting you limit or put bounds on your energy. I am suggesting you find avenues in which to express it.

3. Bridging

After looking at and moving to each of your two collages, allow a third piece of art to emerge. This can portray the bridge between the two states of being: wild drives and drives that are channeled into constructive action.

Out of this picture can come another movement. Movement is particularly useful for gaining insight about the bridging process. To move as the wild drives and then to move into constructive energy gives a kinesthetic understanding of how to change from one feeling state to another. As you shift from the one mood to the other, you can detect your transitional steps. "Oh, I need to slow down and be less frantic and ground myself" might be the information you gained from your movement.

The pictures that come out of this experience are reminders of the inner work that needs to be done. Experiencing the wild side in contrast to "the me when my energies function in a way that benefits my life" can give new perspective on the possible.

It is possible to design expressive arts experiences for any situation that calls for self-exploration. I have suggested one possibility. You will think of others. The facilitator needs to ask herself, "What expressive arts process might help this individual to explore her inner experiences?" There is no one perfect design. Many paths lead to the same inner core. If we create expressive arts experiences that have no right or wrong outcome, the individual can use the opportunity to discover new aspects of herself. With any of the twelve steps, you can design arts processes that help the individual, whether she is a recovering alcoholic or an adult child of an alcoholic, or someone recovering from another addiction. The expressive arts process can help her explore her feelings and her future possibilities.

Life Inventory

Using the arts process to inventory one's life can be extremely helpful for anyone, including people who are in recovery or have suffered sexual abuse. To stimulate memories and images of the past, use the exercise "Life Mandala" or "Life-Line" detailed in chapter 6. Letting the unconscious and imagery bring up past events helps illuminate them for purposes of self-understanding and making choices about behavior in the future.

Working with Sexual Abuse Survivors

People who are dealing with the consequences of sexual abuse or are in the early stages of discovering that it existed in their lives frequently find that art imagery uncovers hidden information. One counselor

Sexual Abuse Survivors: Expressive art may help evoke suppressed memories. It can also be used as an avenue of release for unspoken feelings.—N. R.

who participated in my expressive arts class started to draw pictures that she described as grotesque and horrible. (They didn't appear so horrible to us, which again points up the importance of respecting the artist's feelings about her images.) They appeared so hideous to her that she preferred not to talk about them in class. She knew they were important.

Later she told me she took them to her therapist, who helped her explore their meaning. The woman was pleased that her therapist although not trained in art therapy, was willing to help her use the art to discover the hidden meanings regarding her sexual abuse. This student was grateful that the frightening imagery had surfaced. Although it was painful and disturbing to uncover this material, it was a necessary part of her healing.

Expressive arts exercises that let the individual be in touch with her inner child—which may range from being lighthearted and playful to being wounded or abandoned—are helpful in looking at sexual abuse issues. The "Life Mandala" is one such exercise. Another is to suggest that the individual draw herself as the wounded child or draw the feelings of being that wounded person. A third possibility is to draw or make a collage entitled "The Unspeakable." Shame, guilt, self-deprecation, and emotional trauma are so intertwined with sexual abuse that the experiences are frequently layered over with years of denial. The visual arts offer an opportunity for images to come forth when words are not yet formed.

Therapists or group facilitators using the expressive arts should be aware that movement, art, guided imagery, and sound do evoke forgotten experiences. It is important to respect the pace of the individual who begins to uncover traumatic events. Don't push. Accept the explanations of the participant at face value. She will sense the importance of the images and decide for herself whether she wishes to involve herself in their mystery.

Insisting on peeling the scab off a wound is counterproductive. The scab serves as a protection. Allowing it to soften and fall away gently is more appropriate to healing. Sometimes it takes many months of exploration to bring these experiences into consciousness and healing. Other times it happens quickly.

One student of mine once created a collage and then moved to that collage. A poem burst forth into her writing. Then she said:

> My writing process allowed me access to the deep despair which is surfacing just now in my life around the sexual abuse I received as a child. The slashing movements in my dance process released a great deal of rage that I have been having in my body due to the sexual abuse and it felt very good and satisfying to have a means to let go. . . . underneath the rage lies the despair *and* my dark side, *and* the light.
>
> As I reclaim my sexuality, my understanding of my wholeness takes on a new perspective. It became very clear to me in the process of putting my collage together that my essence or spirit was pulling the work together. . . . One of the recurrent themes in my collage is a lack of wholeness in the many different faces. Eyes are split off from noses, mouths are torn away from eyes, and in one picture, Princess Di's head is completely ripped off and her body turned upside down.

> Because of the sexual abuse of my childhood, I have been unable to accept my sexuality as truly part of me. I feel a great deal of shame and guilt associated with my sexuality.
>
> Yet it became quite apparent, as I completed the collage, that the resolution of this split-off of my sexuality was to be found in the collage.[4]

Awareness is a first step. The movement and art allowed this woman to experience unconscious messages through her body that were then expressed in the collage. By studying the collage and dancing to it, she allowed further aspects to reveal themselves. This woman ended her paper by saying she was finding healing by being more aware of Mother Earth and that she spent time appreciating nature as well as learning how to appreciate her body.

Working with Overeaters

Using the expressive arts may uncover some of the early childhood trauma underlying eating disorders. I again suggest a collage to start the process of self-exploration because the words and images we pick from magazines relate directly to the body-beautiful media images that affect our self-esteem.

THE IMPORTANCE AND MEANING OF FOOD

Take a few minutes to meditate on the importance and meaning of food in your life. Then select pictures and words from magazines or newspapers, and make a collage. When finished, write five statements beginning with "I am," "I have," or "I feel."

Next, hang your collage on the wall and study it. Do the images evoke any feelings? Create some movement and sound that express those feelings. What are you discovering about yourself?

Now try a clay sculpture titled "This Is Me." To fully experience the texture of the clay, start with your eyes closed. Let something emerge. Then do some free writing about the sculpture. Finally, put yourself into the pose of the sculpture and then allow yourself to move. What else are you discovering?

With this sequence of making a collage, using movement or sound, creating a sculpture, and then writing and dancing the sculpture, you are tuning in to the messages of your body and allowing the unconscious to become conscious. You are gaining information about yourself through your personal explorations. It is not easy to make behavior changes. Becoming aware of what motivates you is the first step.

Grief Work

Everyone eventually experiences the death of a loved one, whether it is a parent, a child, a spouse or partner, or a dear friend. Small children may experience the death of a loved animal. When someone dies for whom we care deeply, a reaction process evolves. After the first shock, we may enter a denial period. Such statements as, "This is not

Saying Goodbye: Accepting the ending can start the healing process. Imagery can speak when there are no words.—N. R.

possible! This could not be true! I don't believe it." are typical when the news of death comes as a surprise. Disbelief is frequently followed by anger: anger at the loved one for leaving or anger at the world or God for taking the person away. (Sometimes people quickly take that anger out on the family members around them.) Sorrow and grief follow. Eventually, if the individual allows the deep feelings to surface and finds ways to express them in a compassionate setting, she reaches acceptance of the loss. Inner healing proceeds.

These feelings may occur all at the same time and happen immediately, or they may stretch out over a long period. Some people stay in denial. Others never get beyond the anger. Still others stay sad or depressed for years. Frequently grief is so profound that people stuff it down inside, like pushing cotton batting into a pipe. This stifles and muffles all life experience, beginning with the crying out and screaming that are natural impulses when we are shocked by the news of sudden or unexpected death. Most cultures encourage wailing as part of the funeral ceremony. In our stoic culture, however, we exacerbate the grieving process by frowning on overt displays of emotions. For some strange reason, we tend to admire the widow who does not shed a tear.

Helping people face the loss is crucial to moving through the stages of mourning and living a full life. Most of us know people who have suppressed their feelings of loss or grief for many years before some incident allows the painful blister to burst. As therapists, we know that going beyond the terrible suffering of grief begins with accepting the loss. This acceptance may be gradual or rapid. It brings relief and creates an opening to a new life. Being able to acknowledge and accept the ending—that someone has really left this world—is the beginning of the healing process.

As therapists, we also know it is extremely important that each person be allowed to grieve at her own pace. Time is one of the healing salves. Each individual has her own sense of timing. The following exercises can be offered freely within a person-centered environment. If the mourner is not ready, she needs to feel safe to say no or to call a halt to her experience, as needed. (For an account of working in depth with a grieving individual see "Gail's Herringbone" in chapter 9.)

Opportunities abound for the expressive arts therapist to permit sound, movement, and visual art to release people's pain and help them acknowledge loss. Several examples of using visual art and sound in grief work appear throughout this book. Let me merely remind the reader that when words are caught in someone's throat, or buried deep within her heart, it is appropriate to ask if she would like to express those feelings through movement or visual art. I frequently encourage the use of sound by telling the client I will sound with her.

Saying Goodbye to a Loved One

Usually we think of many things we wished we had told the person who has now departed. Here is one expressive arts experience that helps facilitate the process of saying goodbye.

> As you sit quietly in your chair, allow yourself to remember some of the time and events you shared with the person who is now deceased. Allow yourself to experience the loving times, the frustrating times, the discordant times, the playful times. Notice all the feelings you have had toward this person. Be aware that loving someone includes times of anger and distrust as well as of warmhearted feelings.
>
> After reviewing some of those events, go to the paper and with your nondominant hand quickly make as many pictures as you need to express the many feelings you have toward the person who has died. On each picture write five words: whatever words first come to you when you look at your picture.
>
> It helps to dance each picture you have drawn. Letting your body move and flow and stomp and pound are all useful ways to release grief, anger, and sorrow.

Now write the deceased person a letter. Start it with, "Dear ———, there are some things that I did not have the chance (or the courage) to tell you. I want you to know. . . ." Try to say all the things that are in your heart and mind, whether they are loving or sad or angry. Don't censor yourself. You do not need to read this to anyone unless you choose to do so.

This may be a difficult letter to write. You may cry or feel rageful during the process, but let it flow. Like a river, the water needs to rush on. Damming the river can damage our bodies as well as our minds.

Hospice workers and paraprofessionals working with victims of disasters such as earthquakes, floods, and fires benefit by training in person-centered expressive arts. Post-Traumatic Stress Disorder can be alleviated by using the expressive arts. When trauma is too great for words, people may find that symbols, colors, movement, and sound provide acceptable paths for expression. Classroom teachers have found the arts useful when children have undergone such trauma. It is just as appropriate for adults as for children.

Grief Work with Children

Using expressive arts with children is a broad and exciting topic worthy of a separate book. Meanwhile, one of the graduates of our training is cocreating a program that merits mentioning.

Anne Black and Penny Simpson Adams decided to use the expressive arts to provide support for grieving children. They are developing a program called HEALS: Hospice Expressive Arts Loss Support. After presenting their idea to several principals, guidance counselors, and teachers in their area, it became evident they had been uncomfortable about discussing death with their grieving students. They welcomed the opportunity to learn how to use the expressive arts and ritual to create paths for healing and caring in a group setting. The guidance counselors also used the training as an opportunity to share their own losses, thus experiencing the expressive arts as healing. The pilot project involved forty children attending eight-week-long support groups (eight children per group) in the schools.

> HEALS was also asked to assist the schools following four separate death crises: a teenager with a congenital heart defect died at a school dance; a three-year-old daycare child was accidentally run over by his father's car; the suicide of a teenager who learned her cancer had returned; and the murder of a beloved music teacher who had taught in four schools. In each of these cases, we went into the schools with death crisis protocols, teddy bears, and art materials. These experiences became our teachers, and each one became part of our ongoing training.
>
> The HEALS training program that developed out of this pilot project is both experiential and conceptual. The experiential portion uses guided imagery, movement, sound, art and writing. In addition to the therapeutic process, the participants are presented with the signs and developmental stages of grief in children and given ritual ideas for commemoration and closure. The philosophic foundation for all of this work is the person-centered approach to empathic listening.[5]

Other such experimental programs probably exist for children who have lost a significant family member. This one was brought to my attention and, although it is in an early developmental stage, it is noteworthy in its use of the expressive arts in a person-centered environment as a mode of self-understanding and healing.

Working with Seniors

Using the Creative Connection process with able-bodied seniors is not very different from working with any other population. Designing arts processes that help people to be expressive necessitates thinking through the needs and personal issues of that particular population. Seniors seem to be particularly self-critical in terms of their ability to be creative. The judge or self-critic has been around for a long time with these folks. Facilitators need to accentuate that it is the process, rather than the product, that is important.

Nonetheless, many seniors are set in their ways and want a pretty product. The facilitator's challenge is to think of projects that can be satisfying in terms of their products and yet have some real qualities of self-expression. One possibility is to create a favorite persona by decorating a mask, a hat, or a shawl. Explore some of the senior person's favorite characters: people that she might like to be if she had the chance. Start with eye masks (the inexpensive Halloween variety) and offer textured items to decorate them (feathers, satin, beads, etc.). Or bring in second-hand hats or shawls to redecorate. Suggest some special character or emotion (a queen, a devil, or peace or fear). Encourage people to extend their self-expression to simple movements, which they can do sitting or standing.

Fragile seniors are sometimes more interested in reminiscing than looking toward the future. Many welcome projects that tap into this desire to harvest life's experiences. Using guided imagery, you can help individuals remember happy moments or exciting years and then suggest ways to express their feelings through storytelling ("Once upon a time . . ."), collage, clay, drawing, or writing. Their art products can become symbols that help each individual share her life story with others.

My colleague Maria Gonzalez-Blue spent many months working several hours a week with a group of "special needs" seniors in a convalescent home. Given their lack of mobility, their inability to communicate verbally, or their potential to disrupt activities, these residents did not go to other activities. Asking herself, "What do these people want or need?" Maria realized they needed a very slow pace and someone to listen and encourage them to express themselves. She says, "I learned to slow myself way down to a nonexpectant place of simply being with these individuals, offering my methods not from a place of trying to help them but from my heart, as a means of letting them know someone cared about them."

Through experimentation, she found that they responded most to things that stimulated their senses. This knowledge inspired her to bring items of color and texture, including flowers, scraps of silk and satin, and dolls. They also enjoyed it when she invited them to help her draw. As they collaborated, the art expression emerged.

Patience, simple expectations, understanding the needs of the individuals, and coming from the heart helped create a pleasant and peaceful atmosphere. This seemed to fill these people's needs.

Applications for Life Transitions

We all go through major life transitions of some sort, such as career changes, marriage, the birth of a child, children leaving home, moving from one part of the country to another, divorce, or retirement. By understanding that these transitions have various stages and by paying attention to these stages, we can move through them more gracefully. In my book *Emerging Woman: A Decade of Midlife Transitions*, I discuss the stages involved in uprooting from my twenty years in the Boston area and moving to California. I experienced those stages as: making a decision, creating a bridge, saying farewell, letting go, limbo, and rerooting. Bill Bridges, author of the helpful book *Transitions*, defines three stages: endings, the neutral zone, and beginnings.[6]

Whether we break down the process into six steps or three is less important than learning how to help ourselves and others appreciate, rather than dread, such life changes. To approach life transitions consciously helps. It also helps to tune in to the messages of our intuition, the messages of our bodies, and any imagery that may arise through the expressive arts. While we always have rational thoughts and responses to the important events in our lives, we need to balance the rational with our intuitive and emotional reactions to each stage.

Using the arts facilitates that balancing process. Here are some examples.

Making a Decision

If you or a friend or a client are considering a major life decision, this expressive arts process might shed light on your choices.

> Sit meditatively in your chair or rest quietly on the floor. See yourself on the floor and see yourself as you are in your present situation. Take a few minutes to be aware of your daily activities. Acknowledge the frustrations and the pleasures, the conflicts and the excitement. Be aware of sights, smells, sounds, tastes, and touch in your present situation. Breathe deeply. Take it all in.
>
> Using your nondominant hand, now create an abstract picture that expresses how you feel in your present situation. Then put your picture on the wall and move to it. Notice the lines and colors, and let

them speak through your body. Allow sound to accompany the movement. What are you learning about your present situation?

When you are finished moving, find a comfortable spot where you can relax again. Now imagine yourself in your forthcoming situation. You may envision yourself in your new career, or as a married person, or as a newly single person; or you may see yourself living in another part of the world.

First, call on all the information you have about being in that new environment. You may know where you will be living or working or have other information. Also, call on your intuition as you imagine yourself having made this life change. Be receptive to feelings, hunches, metaphors, and images that surface as you imagine yourself in this new life.

Now try moving or dancing to explore how it might feel to be in that new place. Dance each aspect that comes to you: the excitement, fear, productivity, loneliness, adventure, or security. Whatever comes to mind, use your body to express that feeling.

Now draw a picture or create a sculpture. Set aside any worry about the product, and don't necessarily try to be realistic. The movement left you with some conscious and unconscious feelings. Let those pour out through your arms and hands into your art.

When you are finished, let the two images—of the present and the future—be the subject for your free writing. Write in the first person, present tense. For instance, it might read: "In my present situation, I am two heads looking in opposite directions. I am also a red jagged line and a dagger. In my future situation, I am a bright sun and I am a big brown bear with teeth. I feel light and powerful." Continue writing in this vein for five minutes. Later, see what new information you have gleaned about your transition or decision.

Endings

Endings are new beginnings. Elements of sadness mix with the excitement of what is to come. The end of a job, the end of schooling, leaving a community, the end of a relationship—all bring forth the bittersweet, the pathos, and the beauty. Even if we are glad to leave an oppressive job, or excited about graduating, or relieved to be leaving an unsatisfying relationship, there are also usually aspects of that situation that have been gratifying. The ending therefore has more than one flavor.

In the last ten years, we have learned to create ceremonies and rituals to honor the passage of an ending. Women, particularly, have been reclaiming the ceremonial wisdom of ancient cultures to ease the transitional passage. The expressive arts are an integral part of those rituals as people express their journey in dance and music and painting.

Another simple but elegant way to use the arts is to put your feelings into color or clay. It may take a series of creations done over several days to tap into your multifaceted mood. Dance the pictures, or the sculpture. Is there a metaphor that comes to mind when you think of this ending? Is it like slamming a door? Or swimming upstream? Is it like getting onto an elevator? Or like being a bird flying away?

Dance the metaphor. Write about it. Journal writing is particularly effective for expanding our understanding as we leave a situation. What is it you are leaving? What smells, sounds, tastes, and touches are you leaving? What people are you leaving? How do you feel about leaving them? Be honest with yourself.

Limbo

The most uncomfortable stage of a transition, usually, is what I call *limbo*. Bill Bridges calls it the neutral stage; others call it the nowhere land. It is similar to the artist's void. The lack of any single compass point can be unnerving. "Where am I? Who am I? This is confusing and chaotic!" are typical laments from the person in this stage of transition. It is helpful to know that such stages exist and that, in time, we do move through them.

It is also helpful to portray our stages. Creating art during this chaotic period may bring forth products that are not highly aesthetic —and that is not the point. Drawing, dancing, sounding, and writing the limbo can be extremely beneficial. Identifying the chaos, looking at it, and experiencing it kinesthetically are grounding and healing. Just as a lot of energy exists within us in the "stuck place" or the artist's void, so too can we discover a lot of energy in the chaos or neutral zone.

New Beginnings

When you have made your change—when you can actually say you have left the old and are now embarking on the new—you may continue finding it useful to use the arts for self-discovery. Do you have a metaphor for this beginning? Have you come through a tunnel? Jumped into the deep end of a pool? Are you at the end of a rainbow? Are you like a newborn infant? A butterfly unfolding its wings? What image comes to mind? Try drawing it, or dancing it, or writing about it. Make sounds that express your new state of being.

Limbo: Drawing, dancing, sounding, and writing about this chaotic stage will help you acknowledge it, accept it, and move on.—N. R.

The Creative Connection process clearly elicits new and helpful information for any shift in your life. The expressive arts are not solutions; they embody a process that helps us gain insight into almost any situation. Such insight creates an inner balance and perspective in our daily lives.

Working in Hospital Settings

I am puzzled that the powers that be in hospital settings do not give more attention to using the arts as part of the healing process. Encouraging hospital patients to use simple materials for an art journal, for example, would serve several purposes. It would help take their minds off the annoying details of hospital life, stimulate the creative mind, and actually be an aid in the physical healing process.

Aware of the healing aspect of imagery, many physicians ask their patients to meditate daily on the physical area that needs to mend. Using the visual arts to enhance that kind of imagery can be both powerful and delightful. The expressive arts can help people release tension and transform anxiety and fear into more manageable emotional states.

Having an art journal for a bedridden patient seems a natural way to foster self-healing. Some felt-tip markers or crayons and a sketch pad with a few simple instructions might help bring many people home sooner. With time on their hands, patients could use the art journal to express fear, anxiety, boredom, and frustration. They might imagine the body area that needs healing and then draw that part as healed. The image can be symbolic rather than anatomically realistic.

Creating mental and artistic images of a whole, healthy body actually can speed recovery. Here is an excerpt from Teresa Benzwie, a dance therapist who used art and imagery to help herself prepare for and heal after hip replacement surgery. An author and group facilitator, she had also been a participant in our expressive arts training.

> Two weeks before surgery I began to keep an art journal, something I could easily take to the hospital and continue at home afterwards. A small colorful set of watercolors, a set of magic markers and an 8½″ by 11″ sketchbook were my materials. When beginning a drawing I would have nothing special in mind. I let myself be drawn to a color, place the brush or magic marker anywhere on the paper, and let it do whatever happened, somewhat like doodling. Most of the time I couldn't interpret the results. Sometimes the drawing pleased me, sometimes not.
>
> The most important thing was that something seemed to happen inside me during the process. It was like taking a deep breath and having all my separate pieces move into place. A feeling of peace and contentment would wash over me as if the healing process were going on.[7]

Teresa also used her extensive knowledge of movement to aid her in pre- and post-operative strengthening exercises. Along with the movement and art, she also did some free writing. The art, the writing, and her dreams helped her realize she was afraid of the upcoming surgery. Acknowledging this, writing about it, and talking with her friends helped relieve her anxiety and confusion. She put it this way:

> My ambivalence and conflicting feelings also found expression in my art work and writings.
>
> . . . can't tell the monsters from the clouds—the clouds from the islands—the islands from the sea—the sea from the sky—the sky from the mountains—the mountains from the waves—the waves from the ripples—the ripples from the beasts. Lost in it all—swirling sun drenched or is it bleeding-beautiful-confusion-moving-dancing-drifting.[8]

In the hospital, Teresa continued writing and drawing, listening to music, and using as much movement as possible before and after surgery. She felt these methods aided her in maintaining a positive attitude toward the surgery and toward her body, helping it to heal.

Working with Creative Blocks

Artists, musicians, dancers, and writers find the expressive arts a powerful process for unleashing spontaneity and creativity. During periods of feeling blocked, stuck, or empty, this can be particularly valuable. The experience is: "I'm drained dry. There is no more creativity in me" or, "I'm in a rut. My art [or writing, music, or dance] hasn't changed in years."

Even though facing the void is part of the artist's life, this can be a frightening time. Many artists seem to think they have to find their way out of this void by themselves. However, in our person-centered expressive training program, we have witnessed the emergence of exceptional creativity as artists go into the realms of their unconscious to discover new material for artistic expression. One of the most useful experiments is to dance, paint, draw, or write the stuckness, as reflected in the following excerpt from a student.

> The most powerful experience for me during the creative connection process was when I danced to three pictures I had drawn titled "Stuck," "Creative," and "Discover." When the exercise was introduced I couldn't even imagine what it would be like—maybe jumping off a diving board for the first time, you just do it and hope you hit okay! . . . I imagined that when I tried to dance "stuck" there would be nothing to do. Initially I felt a bit awkward and wondered what to do next. I wasn't moving much since I was with stuck. After a few moments I forgot all thoughts and simply felt the "stuck." I was amazed at how intense it felt to me, and how easy it was to simply flow. As I moved through the rest of the pictures I felt as if my body was telling me things that I didn't know. When I had finished I had an overwhelming feeling of surprise, it had felt good and interesting.

> And very freeing. Not at all how I had imagined. . . . I realized I had discovered a lot of energy in my "Stuck" dance and then had released it in my other dances. I had never thought about there being energy and intenseness in stuckness. I had always thought of it as lifeless and still.[9]

Artists can also take any of the other experiments described in this book and use them at home or with friends to find new avenues of spontaneity. Visual artists and singers frequently find movement to be the process that frees them. Musicians may find the visual arts stimulating. Writers find that both the movement and art affect their creativity.

Musicians, visual artists, writers, dancers, and performers know that inspiration comes from a deep inner source. To be creatively productive requires having access to that source. Being able to perceive through all of our senses—hearing, smell, touch, sight, and taste—helps us avail ourselves of that inner source. Consciously focusing attention on our bodily senses, one by one, awakens them. Music, movement, voice, and the visual arts also arouse these senses.

Using the right hemisphere of the brain is paramount to creativity. The expressive arts stimulate that part of the brain. Spontaneity, playfulness, intuition, and being able to tolerate ambiguity are all parts of the creative process that are fostered by the creative connection.

One special-education teacher was blocked while writing her Master's thesis. She was pondering important philosophical questions, such as: "What is my philosophy of education? What do I truly believe is the best way for people to learn? How does my actual teaching relate to my beliefs?" I suggested she use the expressive arts to see if it would help her writing. In her first chapter she describes her process:

> At first I attempted to organize and make sense of these questions by thinking and writing, but the words came out jumbled and provided no clues in finding the answers. I became quite frustrated that the words did not cooperate to help me write my philosophy, and so with a sense of resentment I abandoned the words and turned instead to drawing.
>
> I grabbed a piece of drawing paper and a box full of crayons and with my left (nondominant) hand I began to exert my frustration and anger onto the paper. When this first paper was filled with lines and colors, I moved on to a clean sheet and then on to another and another. Slowly, as my frustration and anger were released, there emerged from the drawings some very clear images relating directly to my questions. As I continued to work on the drawings my thoughts became more clearly defined and soon I was free-writing (writing whatever comes to mind without interpretation) about each drawing. My drawings had bridged my feelings and thoughts to written words and had provided a vehicle with which to answer my many questions.[10]

This is a vivid description of how the creative connection releases frustration and brings forth material from the unconscious. As she studied and wrote about the images she had drawn, new cognitive material emerged. Not only did her thought processes clear, but she had pictorial images that defined the problems she was contemplating.

Summary

The container in which to offer the expressive arts is a learning environment. The individual is listened to with empathy, and her ability for self-understanding and self-direction is honored. By putting yourself in the other person's shoes, you can imagine the thoughts and feelings she may have and so design an appropriate expressive arts experience. It it always helpful to ask whether any proposed exercise feels appropriate or if she thinks it might help her situation. If she says no, it is time to rethink what you are offering.

Many expressive arts projects are adaptable to various populations. You can use your own creativity in developing such projects as you explore the needs of the population with whom you are working.

NOTES

1 Pat Perrin and Wim Coleman, "Addictions and Consciousness," *New Realities*, Sept./Oct., 1987.

2 Ibid, p. 25.

3 Alcoholics Anonymous, *Twelve Steps and Twelve Traditions* (New York: Alcoholics Anonymous World Services, Inc./P.O. Box 459, Grand Central Station/New York, NY 10017; 1952), p. 42.

4 Alexandra Folts, "Modalities of Expressive Arts: The Creative Connection" (Orinda, CA: JFK University, student paper, 1988).

5 Anne Black, The Center for Creative Healing/The HEALS Program/P.O. Box 1576, Brattleboro, VT 05302 (manual available).

6 William Bridges, *Transitions* (Menlo Park, CA: Addison-Wesley, 1980).

7 Teresa Benzwie, "Elective Surgery: A Voyage to Growth and Power" (unpublished paper).

8 Ibid.

9 Colleen Sjollema, "Creative Connection and Group Process" (San Francisco, CA: University of San Francisco, student paper, 1990).

10 Jean E. LaSarre, "The Seed of a Child: Personal Growth and the Expressive Arts Process in Education" (Santa Monica, CA: Sierra University, master's thesis, 1987), p. 7.

8

Accepting the Shadow, Embracing the Light

One does not become enlightened by imagining figures of light, but by making the darkness conscious. The latter procedure, however, is disagreeable and therefore not popular.

—Carl Jung,
The Philosophical Tree

Accepting the shadow, embracing the light—this is the personal task for each of us if we wish to come into individual and world balance. We act on our feelings and beliefs. If we hold the belief that evil is "out there," we project our own dark parts onto "those others." We tend to put those unwanted parts of self on someone else or some other group, making them the carriers of our own unfinished work. If we, as individuals, could face our dark sides and learn to transform the energy fused to those shadowy parts into constructive action, it would be a monumental step toward changing the world. Instead of a "we/they" attitude of blame, each of us would take responsibility for all that happens in the world.

I will never forget the moment I became aware of a frightening shadow aspect of myself. I grew up in a loving family and was seldom exposed to anger. I am a pacifist. Therefore I was shocked on the day that I realized I had the real urge to kill. At one point in my life I felt extremely intimidated, verbally trapped and cornered. I remember my rage mounting and finally, the god-awful experience of "let me at him, I want to KILL!" Horrified that I could have such a feeling, I felt ashamed and guilty. (For years, I never told anyone.) But I vowed not to forget that I, too, had the potential for violence. An ugly shadow aspect had surged forth unexpectedly. It brought me to a deeper understanding of the potential for violence in each of us. My compassion expanded to include those who feel so oppressed that their rage brings them to the brink of striking out.

In Jungian terms, the *shadow* is that aspect of the self that is unknown or that lives in the realm of the unconscious. The shadow is composed of *all* that became unconscious as a result of early experiences and conditioning. It is the part of the self that we have rejected, denied, or repressed. As children we discovered that certain behaviors were unacceptable: little girls may hear such statements as "You don't look pretty when you are angry" or "That's not ladylike!"; little boys, "Big boys don't cry" or "Can't you hold still?" As we grow up, other such admonitions tell us that some behaviors are acceptable, others not. What happens to the girl's need to stand up for her rights, or the boy's needs to let out his emotions? As Robert Bly says, when we learn that some of our behavior is not welcome, we toss it in our "long black bag and drag it behind us." When we later look in the bag, we discover that we tossed out much good stuff, too.[1] In these examples, the girls have stuffed the black bag with their ability to assert themselves, and the boys have tossed in their ability to express feelings.

Repressed thoughts, feelings, and behaviors have a lot of power as they rumble around in our unconscious with their potential for volcanic eruption. As with a pressure cooker, the repressed aspects build force by tight containment. Keeping those rumblings in check takes a lot of personal energy. Tension in our muscles, pain in our joints, and constriction of the heart result from keeping such thoughts and feelings under cover. Most of us fear looking into the unconscious but seldom realize how much physical and emotional energy we spend keeping the lid on.

The denied or rejected aspects of self are frequently thought of as destructive or evil impulses: the urge to kill or plunder, or to dish out revenge. Often, however, we also relegate to the realm of the unconscious our creativity, strength, rebelliousness, sensuality, sexuality, and our willingness to love. So when we risk exploring the depths of the unconscious, we also find many lost treasures.

Actually, accepting our shadow may be less difficult than embracing the light. A certain mystery exists when we talk about embracing the light. We are, in effect, talking about opening to our spirituality: our ability to experience love, compassion, and all-encompassing states of consciousness. In my years as a therapist and group facilitator, I have found that people are uncomfortable acknowledging and feeling love. Readily they accept negative thoughts about themselves and others but find themselves fending off compliments, caring, and love. Being open to love is available to anyone, without cost. Yet we tend to armor ourselves against receiving it. Being able to receive love fully, whether it is from another person or from a universal energy source, may be the prerequisite for being able to offer unconditional love.

When we give love it feels good, yet we are fearful of giving it: afraid of being rejected, hurt, and vulnerable. However, it is often those who have suffered most deeply who offer their love most freely. Love is the most powerful force in the universe. Opening our heart to others brings us joy. In the act of loving we give ourselves a great gift. It seems that loving—in the highest meaning of the word—is the bliss we long for.

This chapter discusses the dynamic process of facing and transforming the shadow through the use of expressive arts. We discover the juxtaposition of dark and light and look at how we can integrate our inner polarities. Although I discuss discovery and integration as two different events, they are actually both part of the same circle, the whole, the self. As in the yin/yang symbol, there is a dark dot in the light, and a light dot within the dark. There is no way to be truly loving and compassionate without being open to one's darker side. Finally, I give examples of people who have had transcendental experiences of light and love.

Discovering the Shadow

To know, accept, express, and release the dark side in nonhurtful ways is essential to prevent these powerful forces from being acted out in violent forms. The expressive arts are natural media for journeying into the shadow to bring forth images, movement, sound, and creative writing that illuminate those unknown aspects. If we give ourselves permission, the expressive arts can plunge us into the mythical, metaphoric, and kinesthetic aspects of the unknown. As we become aware of the shadow, we may find many useful, exciting messages for our lives. Discovering our unknown parts brings those aspects to light, allowing them to become allies: long-lost subpersonalities that we need to be complete.

My insistence that we look at and accept our shadow distinguishes my philosophy and my work from that of my father. In his later years, Carl admitted that he was often not in touch with his own anger. I was acutely aware of this as I worked with him in a collaborative team effort at the Person-Centered Approach workshops held each summer from 1975 through 1980. Although the other staff members and I were able to speak honestly to each other and the group of one hundred participants when we were angry, Carl never seemed to *get* angry. Since many aggravating and frustrating situations arose during these events, his lack of response put pressure on us, I felt, to speak his anger for him. It is probably my father's inability to experience his anger that has me spotlighting this feeling as an important and potentially very constructive emotion. The word *anger* is not listed in the index of any of his books. The posthumously published *Carl Rogers' Reader* indexes four references to anger, one of the texts being a disguised description of *my* anger (my life-saving energy) as I fought for a divorce. In that book, Carl explains that "Jennifer's" marriage might have been saved if she had known how to be aware of and be able to own her anger within the relationship. (But "Jennifer" had no family model—no experience of seeing two people get angry with each other in a constructive way in order to come to a resolution.)

With clients, with groups, and in my own life, I do my best (and I am always learning) to be aware of anger and to give support to its verbal and artistic expression as a path to self-understanding and self-empowerment. I am suspicious when people proclaim they never experience anger. I do what I can, through the expressive arts, to help them acknowledge and express it when it arises.

Anger is an important motivator for constructive action. I found this out as I transformed myself from being an accommodating wife to a self-empowered person. (My art journals show some of that growth.) Although this transformation took years, the lessons I learned then have sustained me at each crossroad. As an active feminist in the 1980s I became outraged at every injustice I saw: the dearth of women in the Senate, the House, the Supreme Court, and on editorial boards, as conference keynote speakers, as corporate executives —all of the inequalities as they are acted out in our country and the world. Like most women who speak out against injustice, I was ridiculed and put down for being "an angry woman." However, being in touch with that anger and allowing it to surface gave me a great deal of energy to do something about those injustices rather than staying home feeling depressed. I learned that if I was aware of my anger, I could use it as rocket fuel to initiate projects.

Women particularly need to be able to tap their anger-energy and channel it into creative acts rather than turning it inward. For instance, when publishers turned down my personal/political book *Emerging Woman: A Decade of Midlife Transitions* because they "didn't

Anger: Becoming aware of and using anger-energy constructively can be an extremely useful motivating force.—Anonymous

want to advocate my lifestyle," I first thought I was a lousy writer and felt inadequate. When I realized they were wrong, I used my anger to motivate me to self-publish. (Twelve years later, this book is still selling and has been translated into five languages.) Also, when I was upset and angry at the ending of a relationship, I realized I could focus some of that energy on my work. Doing so led me to start the Person-Centered Expressive Therapy Institute, which has been the sustenance for my professional work and many personal friendships.

Thus, my experience is that becoming aware of and using anger-energy can be an extremely useful motivating force. These learnings get passed along as I guide others who either have put a lid on their rage and need constructive channels for it or are venting it through their art, their drama, or in political action. Acknowledging our anger is the first step to channeling it constructively. Although anger is certainly not the only emotion in the long dark bag that holds the shadow, it is a potent one.

Carl Jung captures my interest since he personally explored and expressed his shadow through painstakingly beautiful art in his Red Book. As a therapist he was willing to look at his anger and fear. Although my father could not easily access his anger, his faith in the individual was remarkable. I find myself drawn to integrating the thinking of Carl Jung as he discusses the shadow with that of Carl Rogers as he discusses the trustworthiness of the human potential. The Creative Connection process, as I teach and facilitate it, actually integrates many of my learnings from each of these men, but comes from the deep feminine principle—a holistic principle—that acknowledges the tremendous value of our intuitive and receptive qualities.

Learning to uncover our disowned parts can be called *shadow-work*.

> Doing shadow-work means peering into the dark corners of our minds in which secret shames lie hidden and violent voices are silenced. Doing shadow-work means asking ourselves to examine closely and honestly what it is about a particular individual that irritates us or repels us; what it is about a lover that charms us and leads us to idealize him or her. Doing shadow-work means making an . . . agreement with one's self to engage in an internal conversation that can, at sometime down the road, result in an authentic self-acceptance and a real compassion for others. . . . In this war between the opposites, there is only one battleground—the human heart. And somehow, in a compassionate embrace of the dark side of reality, we become bearers of the light. We open to the other—the strange, the weak, the sinful, the despised—and simply through including it, we transmute it. In so doing, we move ourselves toward wholeness.[2]

How do we peer into the dark corners of our mind? How do we consciously make the effort to illuminate our unconscious? If we agree that embracing disowned aspects of ourselves enables us to become more whole, energized, and compassionate people, we need some methods to unveil our shadow.

A safe environment is always the first requisite for becoming more deeply aware of the unconscious. Knowing that the person(s) within that space will not judge or condemn us for "shameful" thoughts or actions gives us permission to explore them through painting, mask making, ritual dances, drumming, sounding, and dramatic improvisation. It was in such an environment that one woman in a group began the process of unveiling her "Little Devil" nature:

My Little Devil: "I have a little devil . . . quietly, quietly, shhh . . . ." A Russian participant explores her stuttering.

This lithe young Russian woman was in our training group in Moscow. She was bothered by episodes of stuttering when facing her boss. At first she was very reluctant to look at her troubling behavior. However, others in the group were also investigating their shadow aspects, helping her feel that this was a safe environment. When she volunteered to be a demonstration client, I asked if she would be interested in drawing a picture of her stuttering self. Quickly and spontaneously she drew "a little devil." She was using body language as she described the meaning of her picture, so I encouraged her to move as though she were her little devil and to receive messages from him. I stood and moved with her, inviting her to explore this image kinesthetically.

She began a dialogue with her devil part and realized he was a very important aspect of self. He insisted that she have a mind of her own and not be dominated by others. Her drawing showed her that her devil was impish, not fearsome. Through movement, sound, and drawing she discovered the spirited little devil in her psyche that both helped and hindered her in tense situations. She had never before acknowledged the *positive* devilish self.

When she first contemplated investigating what triggered her stuttering, she was truly frightened. An hour later that fear had been softened to realistic proportions. It is often true that what is most feared turns out to have some helpful aspects. This insight could, in time, lessen the tension that triggers the stuttering.

Many of us honor our intellect and think of it as part of our creativity. Yet one other woman spent more than an hour painting dark pictures and then used her hands and feet to stamp out her anger at her own intellect. She discovered she was very angry at herself for not doing what she really wanted in life. Her blackish, wrinkled, stamped-on picture emerged with the words: "You dark, heavy, serious intellect, you will not extinguish my creative flame and my joy to play!"[3]

For this person, intellect was an extinguisher of creativity. Her stern, judgmental mind was not giving her artistic talents room to explore. Her left-brain functions were overpowering her intuitive, spontaneous self. Releasing this dark energy allowed her to paint with a sense of freedom and abandon.

The Creative Connection process thus helps us discover attitudes and judgments that block our capacity to be fully ourselves. According to Joseph Campbell, Jung's idea was that

> the aim of one's life, psychologically speaking, should be not to suppress or repress, but to come to know one's other side, and so both to enjoy and to control the whole range of one's capacities; i.e., in the full sense to "know oneself."[4]

For some people that "other side" might be the intellect; for some it is the spontaneous self.

Facing the blank page, the void, the emptiness is part of the shadow that is often overlooked. For beginning artists (and perhaps all artists), the blank white page can be terrifying. Emptiness in life holds that same fear. Here a man in his thirties opened the door to his unknown and found emptiness.

VOID VOID VOID VOID
VOID IF SPINDLED
VOID IF MUTILATED
A VOID AVOID
VOID
A VOID IS A SPIRAL

VOID IS VORTEX
TO VOID IS TO ELIMINATE
The Quick Brown Fox Jumped
Over The Void
AVOIDANCE
DANCING IN THE VOID
THIS VOID
IS
disappearing
down
the
vortex

Notice how, even as he wrote, the empty feeling started to "disappear down the vortex." It always seems somewhat magical to me, but extensive evidence shows that to face the fear (or emptiness) is to begin its demise.

This same man, a Vietnam War veteran, drew a picture and wrote more about his need to look at his shadow. His image released some of his scream and let him know that he was angry. Better to see it, acknowledge it, and talk about it in a caring atmosphere than to bottle it up. Writing after creating his picture, he furthered the process.

> Shadow side dark mirror of light. What lurks behind your closed doors in dusky corners? Fogs swirl, mists veil the light. Gazing through cloudy windows vague shapes emerge and disappear. Grey gates beckon and close. Dusky, dank shadows descend. Shades of our dark selves merge and turn in delicate Dervish dance, slow spinning. We long for light, but light cannot emerge without darkness. Life without death, flower without dormant deep darkness seedtime. . . .

Shadow-art, shadow-writing, and dancing the shadow can stir many emotions in the facilitator or therapist. How do I respond when the client's artist-intellect is battling herself on paper? First, I let her know by my physical presence that I am there for her. If we are in a group setting, I can stroll by several times as she works, or stand quietly and witness the conflict she is enacting. I say nothing. I don't cheer her on or tell her to stop making a mess. I am totally present, supporting her self-exploration. When she discusses her picture and her sense of accomplishment in confronting herself, I, too, get excited with her discoveries. I do my best not to evaluate. (All the same, when people are enraptured with their new beginnings, I frequently say, "That's wonderful. I'm glad you've found your direction." Or I might say, "I really support you in that.") Being supportive of growth that has come through self-understanding and insight is very different from giving advice and then patting the person on the back for accepting it. My sense of joy is obvious when I see people blossoming.

When someone is digging into her fearful shadow, I also make sure I am fully present to hold the psychological space for that exploration. I do not need to be witnessing each moment, but participants know that even as I move around, I am attentive and am inviting them to go deep. I am always drawn to the pictures or dances, the masks or writing that reveal the dark side. I ask the poet if he is willing to share his poem, *The Void*. If he reads it shyly or without feeling, I ask if I can read it to him, as well. I use my voice to emphasize the emotional affect it conveys: the loneliness or fear. As he hears his own words read with dramatic emphasis, he senses the full impact of what he has written.

What I am doing, in these instances, is to support the self-directed learnings of these individuals. I am not feeling sorry for or trying to fix their situations. I am being a companion as they journey through the wilderness of their psyches. I deeply trust the process: as we acknowledge, confront, and accept unknown parts of self, those parts become our allies.

Integrating Polarities

Accepting our shadow and embracing our light appears to integrate inner polarities. Frequently, as we journey into our inner world, we experience certain things as being diametrically opposed. As we fantasize or write about or dramatize those polarities, often an integration begins to evolve. As integration occurs, something more than acceptance of the two parts happens. Carl Jung talks about the *transcendent function* arising from the union of conscious and unconscious contents:

> The shuttling to and fro of arguments and affects represents the transcendent function of opposites. The confrontation of the two positions generates a tension charged with energy and creates a living, third thing, . . . a living birth that leads to a new level of being, a new situation. The transcendent function manifests itself as a quality of conjoined opposites. So long as these are kept apart—naturally for the purpose of avoiding conflict—they do not function and remain inert.[5]

This next example illustrates this activation and joining of opposites. Mary, a thirty-seven-year-old woman, writes about the creative connection and her transformative experience. First she describes her reluctance to go on an inner journey.

"Agony Gives Birth to Three Eggs"

> I am still floating on the surface, feeling as if a part of me sleeps. I yawn and laze, keeping mostly to myself and enjoying the freedom to indulge my solitary ways. . . . I have watched as others drew and painted. I have done one or two drawings but mostly regard myself as uncreative and unskilled with art media. I feel disturbingly like a colorless nonentity doing nothing, being no one.
>
> Then comes Hiroshima Day. Some participants have asked that we observe the anniversary of Hiroshima . . . so we are led through a process of intuitive drawing. Using my nondominant hand, I find myself drawing powerful, expressive images which flow onto the paper without thought or plan. Each image captures exactly my feelings in that moment of the horror and meaning of Hiroshima. Then out of agony and death expressed in slashing forms of red and black, the next image emerges as a pink egg traced in rounding movements, symbol of the promise of nurture and new life. My final drawing becomes a resurrection—a vivid, bursting affirmation of renewed life. In a great, expanding blossom of orange and hot pink, the YES! within me declares itself. It has been a revelation to me from myself of the beauty and vitality that live inside.
>
> Now my creativity seems released and I begin drawing more freely. The next few drawings are dark and reveal my sense of being shadowed by some inner burden. Yet over the dark colors, I fill in brighter colors, determined to create this in my life. And in this act of adding color over darkness, I know that I have made a choice—the choice to push through somehow into my inner light and promise.
>
> I watch and wait for something to precipitate my breakthrough. It begins the day I draw a stylized face showing two sides of me: one lovely side sleeps while the other hovers watchful, dark, angry, and powerful. As the group members share their drawings . . . I quietly cover mine up.
>
> My unveiling comes the next day in a process of drawing, then dancing the right and left sides of our bodies. I have drawn another face, one side a mask, the other a bright, simple oval. The mask-woman speaks: "I am powerful, hungry, sorrowful, wise, damned." The clear yellow oval chirps, "Who me? I am bright, cool, careful, smart. I am a mask."

> I hang back now, not wanting to expose the dark woman in me. Then the moment comes and I meet it. My dance is brief and dramatic, an uncovering of the powerful, denied woman hidden beneath my careful social face. The group responds with warm support. . . .
>
> My next drawings vibrate with vivid colors depicting rebirth. I do a series of three eggs bursting with released energy.

A further step in Mary's integration occurred in a demonstration counseling session with Carl Rogers (who was one of our faculty during that training program). Mary used her art to discuss her long-held fears:

> at my core I am a strong, creative woman at odds with a world which values very different qualities in a female. [As Carl accepts, listens to, and queries Mary about her images, a new image comes to her:] . . . the image of a snake with jaws opening wide enough to swallow the whole world. I am the snake choosing to accept and be nourished rather than denied by the world.
>
> Through this extraordinary experience I have moved to a new level inside. I feel all of a piece within. . . . I am feeling full, complete. . . . I am in equilibrium.[6]

Mary's description illustrates how delving into the polarities can bring forth the birth of a new image, a new identity. The Hiroshima Day exploration lit her emotional fuse, sparking her to express deep feelings. Out of the black emerges blossoming hot pinks: confirmation that we must go into the dark to find inner light. This surge of deeper expression frees her to use bright colors over the dark picture she creates next. Discovering new polarities, drawing them, dancing them, she experiences release and vitality. As she enters the verbal aspect of the therapeutic process, a transformative image appears: a snake opening its jaws to take in the whole world. This helps Mary feel a sense of inner balance and resolution. It is accompanied by drawings that express hope.

"Delicate Flower Turns Tiger"

The process of exploring inner polarities frequently evokes this third experience of integrating and transcending. One of our lively Japanese participants discovered this process. I wrote about her in my journal:

> I guided the group in movement to express "This Is Me," suggesting that they close their eyes to go inward to let the impulse of the body lead the way. I was observing Mako. Like a delicate Japanese flower,

Agony Gives Birth to Three Eggs

#3 **Resurrection:** "The YES within me declares itself." —Mary McClary

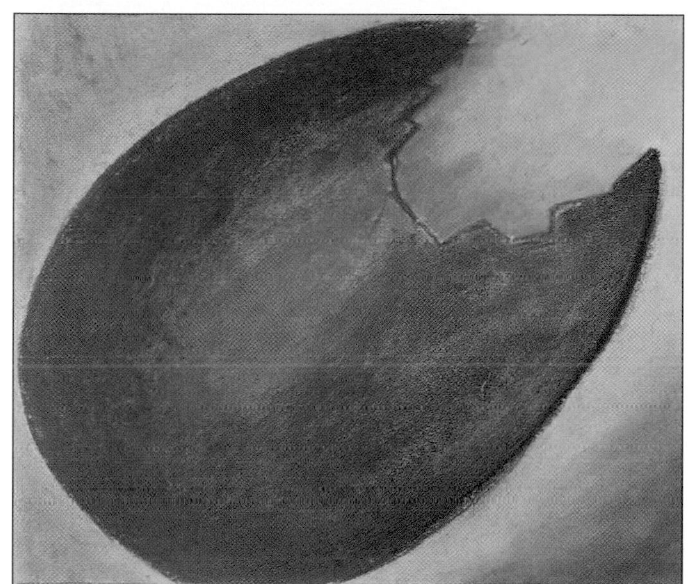

#2

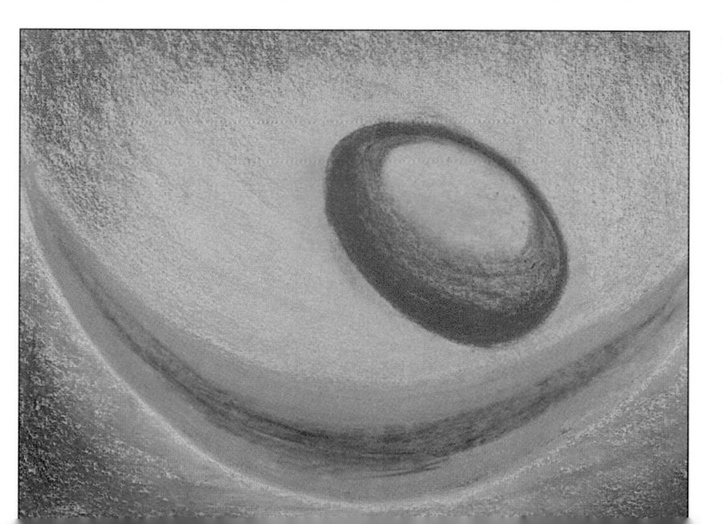

#1 The Promise of New Life

Liana‘s Journey #1: Javelina—a wild, ugly pig. (This represents discovering the terror of being unloved if one‘s dark side is shown.) Art by Liana Nan Graves.

(above) **Liana's Journey #2:** Bleeding Heart Plight: "signals of agonized distress."

(left) **Liana's Journey #3:** Soul Light: "I felt a protective light shield in the form of a divine being that is in us always."

Liana's Journey #4: Bird Flight: "I launch myself upward with all my strength, and a great cry."

> she entered the room first smiling and automatically bowing to people. As the movement exercise began, she closed her eyes. She began like a flowing river moving with fluidity and grace. Then she became a forceful wind that sends clouds through the sky. After seven minutes of this kind of dance, I gave a new instruction to the group. "Now do movements that express, 'This is *not* me! I am hardly ever like this!'"
>
> Mako becomes a raging, growling tiger. This delicate flower of a woman becomes a fierce, clawing animal. She transforms into a hunter prowling, tracking for the kill.
>
> Later she put this into art form, creating a clay "mask of fury." She tells me she has never used clay before, but her motivation is so strong that a grotesque face emerges, looming up at us.
>
> Later, in the discussion, Mako says, "I didn't know I was so angry and so strong! I loved getting so wild. I own the fact that this is part of me. I can accept the dark, stormy, angry side. I release it, making the mask and dancing the rage. It is not with me, now, at this moment. It flowed out of me into the clay and the dance." She sits tranquilly. I am looking at an open, relaxed body and face—one without tension, in peace. Peace within.

The two preceding examples describe the gradual manner of approaching one's shadow. Shy Mako, with an always-sweet smile, is stimulated by the words "This is *not* me" to try out her tiger-self. Such stimulus gives the individual permission to explore the unknown. At the other workshop, a genuine request from participants and the leader (Connie Smith Siegel) to think about the implications of the U.S. bombing of Hiroshima involved us in recalling that world event. The visceral emotions were raw. We plunged deeply into personal and political tragedy. Although it took time, allowing the despair to surface and be shared ultimately led us to a sense of new beginnings and courage to act. If outrage, despair, anger, and sound are taboo parts of our culture, then releasing these emotions physically through dance, sounding, and art is a step toward integrating the shadow.

Sometimes I invite a client to express anger by beating pillows with a tennis racquet. I encourage her to make sounds during the physical activity. This process helps people face the fear that their emotions will get out of control (which indeed happens if people bottle them up too long). Letting off some of the steam is helpful. It starts the healing process. But, as one woman stated:

> For me, the hitting and pounding didn't move the rage through to something else—it didn't transform it. But when I used paint again and again, I found the rage being transformed into something mean-

Delicate flower turns tiger.

> ingful. The pictures took on new form. I gained insight into my rage while releasing it through imagery.

Guided imagery is another avenue to explore the shadow. With one client, my suggestion was to close his eyes and to take an elevator down into his chest, where pain often gnawed at him. His written description shows his tremendous courage in looking at the dark side:

"Black Bird Opens the Heart"

> I see my heart, and see that it has big black veins around it—no, it is the claw of a huge, malevolent black bird. My heart is in its talon. If I move my heart at all, the talon will puncture it; and the bird knows that and laughs that it would be my fault. This bird clearly has the full force of shadow. I feel its power and incredibly strong will. It says, "If you think you're going to get loose, think again."

I suggested the heart and the bird talk to each other. This is what he reported:

> HEART: I need for you not to grip so hard, to let go.
>
> BIRD: You feel my talon as a prison. But I also hold you back from dangers that you cannot see. . . . I am outside of that deceit, that god stuff, so I'm the only one that can see clearly and save you because I don't *have* to believe anything.
>
> HEART: I believe and trust your friendship and care, when you say that.

In the imagery that follows, Bird then takes this man to a high plateau where scattered shards indicate that Bird's heart has been stolen by God. Worse yet, the pain and grief of this loss cannot be communicated because God owns all words. Bird's anger and pain are condemned to silence.

> It seems that what is to be done is to offer my heart to Bird. This is a kind of deep trust. And as this sense deepens in me, I all of a sudden feel on a much deeper level that I am God's messenger returning this stolen heart to Bird. It is not only a personal event, but some deep act of spiritual rearrangement that is unfolding here through me.
>
> I feel small light-beings in my chest, like fireflies, undoing all the ribbons that hold my heart in my chest. [As the heart is transferred to Bird:] I feel myself in the presence of a love so complete that all I want to do is be near the center of its streaming light where everything is given without fear. I feel myself emptying, emptying. . . . And it's done. I'm exhausted. I feel like a big black bird with a heart—and a heart with a new force and strength; a fierce heart whose feeling and love has raven's blood mixed in with it. I think of how much I've held onto my heart as my "special" center, my "best part". . . . And that Bird was saying to me, "Okay, you want to hold onto your heart? You think that's the right path? Okay, then I'll really put a hold on your heart!" The feeling that remains, now, is that the shadow side, Bird, will never appear again as a stranger—he and I are interwoven in the deepest possible way, and so he is not alien, but a friend.[7]

As this example shows, facing the fear of the shadow, discovering that it has important survival qualities, and shedding some of the intrinsic fear of that shadow lead to integrating polarities to find new personal strength. Offering his heart to the evil bird is an act of trust and surrender that results in a sensation of love and light.

I am not saying that one such event transforms a person's life forever. Just as we must grieve over and over again to release the pain and loss of a loved one, so must we persevere in accepting the dark and embracing the light. It is an ongoing challenge.

Embracing the Light

As the personal examples in this book illustrate, the expressive arts are a healing medium for transitional and transcendental experiences. The arts allow the possibility of making our darkness visible, concrete, real. Moving from dark to light, incorporating and integrating all aspects of self, finds a voice through the Creative Connection process.

Becoming enlightened, entering the light, feeling light, receiving light—all require an openness or *receptivity.* Chapter 1 recounts my experience of kinesthetically "melting into surrender," which brought about a sensation of being struck by a flash of light. I was surprised later by a student paper describing something similar. Reporting on a movement experience, she wrote:

> When I was prostrate and helpless my body felt warm, comfortable, relaxed. I loved the feeling of stretching out my fingers and digging into the carpet. I didn't want to move except to sink further into the floor and stretch out as far as I could. My body resisted getting up; I just wanted to stay there, at peace. It felt like my body was saying surrender! My emotional experience was very strong, almost overwhelming. . . .Then I saw the yellow light. . . . I knew it would leave if I stopped surrendering. . . .
>
> The yellow light was my higher power and was, I believe, sending me a message that I must surrender my self-will to my higher power in order to grow and regain my personal power. . . . The message relates directly to a major life decision which I carry with me constantly. A big part of the struggle for me is to get out of my head, where I am confused, scared, and projecting. In trying to find answers in my head, I just keep going in circles and I find myself paralyzed with fear and confusion. . . . I know that if I give in, surrender to my higher power, I can walk my path with dignity and personal power.[8]

This is yet another account of how our intellect can get in the way of our spiritual self. To surrender and let go of the analytic opens the door to receiving guidance from one's higher self.

Liana's Journey

Anthropologist and educator Liana Nan Graves describes several experiences of facing the shadow and embracing the light. When her group was asked to "Dance and draw your dark dream animal," she drew a javelina, a wild, ugly pig. After drawing the pig, she made a clay piece. Then she wrote a dialogue with the shadow figure. This kind of writing can be a highly instructive exploration. Liana describes her process:

> I made a clay piece which celebrated raw feminine power in a way some would consider ugly. I did not strive to make it aesthetically pleasing, and spent a good deal of the first part of the activity slamming the clay down on the board with great force. The only important thing was to express this kind of energy within me and witness it to the outside world. . . . I spoke to the piece in the following dialogue after dancing its energy:

LIANA: Who are you?
MEDUSA: I am Medusa, I am angry snakes, threatening to bite, hissing, growling. I am the door to the underworld. I am fear and rage, but never groveling. No groveling, only defense, or attack, pain, agony, sharp spikes, twisting, turning, fighting, struggling, moving, shifting, never the same, always exploring all the cracks, all the openings, moving into the holes and out again, biting and screaming, shrieking and strangling.
LIANA: Why are you here?
MEDUSA: Because I want to show ugliness, to allow ugliness to be seen, embraced, loved. There is room for my beautiful angry ugliness. I am tired of being in the dark, in the blackness. I deserve the light. My snakes have grown blind from never seeing the light of day. I am angry I have no place in your world!
LIANA: What do you want from me?
MEDUSA: Acceptance. I want to be embraced and seen. I want to be opened to.
LIANA: Why have you been hidden in the dark?
MEDUSA: Because no one wanted an ugly, angry child, no one wants an ugly woman. "You look ugly when you're angry." "Your art is ugly, why not draw something pleasant, something nice?" "No one will like you if you get angry." "Don't act in that ugly way!" Because you needed love and approval to survive. Because you still need love and approval from your family and friends, and you're afraid no one will give it to you if I'm around.

Whose open hand is that? Can you tell me *anyone* who will witness my ugliness, my rage, my desire to rip and tear and bite and fight and tear down and destroy? NO! They will lock me back up in the dark dungeon and shut the iron door. Or *you* will, before they get a chance.
LIANA: Who do you want to witness and give you a hand?
MEDUSA: First of all, you. Then a friend or several friends. Your partner, your family. I have tremendous power. Bring me to light. NOW NOW NOW! [9]

In this dialogue as she writes in the first person, Liana owns both aspects of self: the "me" that is looking at the image, and the "me" that is the image. This process leads to an experiential self-acceptance: giving voice to the dark self brings it into clear, clean focus.

Liana discovers the terror of being unloved if she shows her dark, angry face. The strong edicts of childhood to be nice and make pretty art encouraged her to banish her anger and ugliness. By doing so, she pushed much of her strength into the "long black bag" of the unconscious. This shadow-voice had gained amplitude during its confined years. It wanted to be acknowledged and accepted. Bringing these urges and desires into creative writing, art, dance, and sound in an empathic environment kindled Liana's fire of self-acceptance, assertiveness, and empowerment.

To dramatize the point that in expressing our feelings through art, the feelings shift, change, and transform, I particularly like presenting a series of expressive art created in one day or evening. Liana created such a series in one evening at home, which attests to the possibility of healing oneself in solitude. She writes:

> The next time I had an unpleasant experience and couldn't sleep, I rose from bed and drew my feelings. All the old hurts from the past came back, but as the brief sketches continued I found them quickly becoming healed. Afterwards I wrote about the sequence:
>
> *"Bleeding Heart Plight"*
>
> This picture is painful to look upon again, yet at the time I drew it the pain in my chest gradually disappeared until by the end it was completely gone. I was a red blob in the center of the page which gradually grew into a heart and seemed to throb from the middle outwards. I felt a sore spot in the center, purple, bruised, and dripping blood. . . . Icy blue surrounds the red drops . . . I think it is attempting to cool down the injured heart like an ice-pack on a nosebleed. A blue arrow enters the heart from above and cracks it . . . excruciating pain. Orange-yellow shock waves scream out . . . like signals of agonized distress.
>
> I don't like this picture aesthetically at all. I find it ugly and frightening in its intensity, but doing it was extremely healing. . . . I have no pain or resentment left, as though it had drained out onto the paper.

Many people have described this phenomenon, this emotional healing as energy drains out onto the paper. This body of evidence reminds us that the process of doing the art as well as the insights gained bring a sense of wholeness. The experiential process and the intellectual understanding are both important requirements for self-actualization to take place.

Liana continued her pictures and her healing that same night. She drew the next picture, then wrote about her associations:

> *"Soul Light"*
>
> I begin with a feeling of light at the center of my child self. . . . Images of myself in photos at ages four months to two years come to me. I was full of the joy of living, exploration, discovery. The soul shone through my eyes and body. I remembered the photo where, as a toddler, I ran forward, showing my parents the Easter egg I had found. "Look! Isn't it beautiful?" I seem to be saying.

> From this center all life and light radiate outwards. . . . Making this picture was a real high. I felt a protective light shield in the form of a divine being that is in me always.

One of the most exciting aspects of this work is that it allows people to go beyond their pain into new realms of joy and light. With the third picture comes a further transcendental experience:

> *"Bird Flight"*
>
> I am a bird yearning toward the Light of Heaven. I launch myself upward with all my strength, and a great cry. My chest is blue. All my energy is streamlined toward the one goal. Nothing holds me back. I am already off the ground. Only a few strokes lift me.
>
> I completed this picture with very few strokes, beginning with my nondominant hand and ending with my dominant one. I like everything about the picture. It speaks to the longing and yearning, the ability to soar, and it is just taking off.[10]

From a cracked, bleeding heart to divine light, to soaring—these feelings and concepts evolved in an evening. Time and again, self-expression through art plunges us so deeply into the cracked heart that the only place to go is toward healing. Our survival tendency and self-actualizing tendency take over.

Summary

For some people, the transformational process takes years of therapeutic process. For others, dramatic turnarounds happen in weeks or months, or even in an instant. All the examples in this book are written by competent adults. The clients and group members that I am quoting are functioning people wanting to explore their inner journey, become more fully themselves, and participate in protecting and enhancing the world. Perhaps you are surprised by the overwhelming pain, the monster/demons, and the soaring figures of functioning people. It is important to know that these are parts of each of us. These feelings are part of the human condition.

For years I have tried to explain why self-expression through the process of drawing, dancing, singing, or writing heals the spirit, the soul. All my explanations—that it releases energy, unlocks inhibitions, brings the unconscious to consciousness—do not really answer the question, *"Why the healing?"* They are merely further descriptions of the process itself. Also, there is no real answer to the question, "Why do individuals have this push toward self-actualizing, toward becoming whole individuals who use their full capacities?" The formative tendency towards growth and the healing that occurs in the act of creativity is a very mysterious process. Yet both operate fully in the person-centered approach to expressive arts therapy.

People are often reluctant to claim their inner light, feeling that it is too "special." The sensation is so dramatic that we tend to ascribe this capacity to only Christlike or Buddhalike people. We may be embarrassed or ashamed to admit we have this ecstatic sensation or powerful beauty. If as individuals we begin to acknowledge and accept this inner light, we pave the way for others to come forth with their ecstatic experiences. In a world that rumbles with heavy storm clouds, we certainly need this light to shine through.

In becoming whole people, fully actualized and empowered, our journey must include searching the unconscious to uncover those aspects of self we have pushed aside, ignored, repressed, or hidden. Awareness is always the first step. Without awareness we have no choices. Becoming aware of our fear, shame, guilt, anger, pain, light, sensuality, or creativity is the first move toward accepting each part for what it is: an important and useful aspect of self. Personal integration is part of the natural flow of events when we use symbolic and expressive media. Once we uncover the unknown, the process then includes letting these parts find their rightful places in our psyches. When we have accepted the dark and embraced the light, we are able to experience the ecstatic universal oneness, a connectedness to all life forms.

Exercises

The following two exercises are suggested ways to tap into your unconscious to accept your shadow and embrace your light.

Inner Polarities

To discover the energy that comes from the dynamic tension between polar opposites, try the exercise "Inner Polarities." It begins with brainstorming or becoming conscious of your inner polarities. I suggest you start with the visual art, following it with movement and sound (although starting with the movement would work well, too).

Writing
Brainstorm (by yourself or with a friend) the inner polarities that are familiar to you, such as: love/hate, fear/confidence, passivity/aggression, playfulness/seriousness, joy/sorrow, attraction/repulsion. What others can you think of?

Meditation
Take a few minutes to sit quietly, close your eyes, breathe deeply, and let all these words float in your consciousness. Which polarities are you drawn to explore? Choose one pair.

Visual Art
Facing a large piece of newsprint (18 by 24 inches), use your nondominant hand to choose the colors and express your feelings about each side of the polarity. Don't worry about what the picture looks like. Experiment with closing your eyes as you draw. Use one page for each aspect of the polarity, or put both on the same page.

Writing
On each picture, write five words or five sentences that begin with "I."

Movement and Sound
As you look at the first picture, let your body move to the line, the rhythm, and the colors you see. Let out sounds to express your feelings as you move. Remember, when you move you have high and low space, wide and narrow space. You can move slowly, or quickly. You can be angular or flowing. Experiment with all kinds of sounds as you move.

Writing
Take ten minutes to do free writing. Don't censor yourself, don't stop writing. Or, have a dialogue between the two poles.

Visual Art
Now, quickly create a third picture. Use both hands at the same time. Let anything happen. What words come to mind when you look at this picture?

Meditation
Reflect on what you have done. Close your eyes, breathe deeply. Let go. How are you feeling now? What are you learning about yourself and your inner conflicts?

Opening to Shadow and Light

Since exploring the shadow means going into the unknown, it can be difficult to do on your own. Discovering your shadow requires an inner journey to face those aspects of self that are denied or repressed. As previous examples illustrate, you may discover beautiful treasures in this chamber, or your worst ogre, or both. The ogre may have important messages for you and become an ally.

The optimal condition is to work with a therapist during the following exercise. If that is not possible, be with a friend who can read the guided journey for you and can accept your dark self as well as your bright side. Or you can record the guided imagery journey on tape and then listen to it, giving yourself plenty of time to use the Creative Connection process to express what you find.

This guided imagery asks you to open the door to two aspects of yourself: one that you keep hidden in the dark, one in the light. These could be archetypal images (a witch, devil, jester, magician, emperor, empress, etc.) or animal images, or they may come to you as colors or feelings. These are the persona behind the social mask. Although these qualities are usually kept in the closet under lock and key, they have power in your life.

Preparation

Unless you are having a therapist or a friend read this to you, dictate it slowly and meditatively onto an audiotape. Then arrange for forty-five minutes of quiet time. Turn off the telephone. Have drawing paper, colors, and clay available.

With any guided journey, whether you have taped the instructions for yourself or have a friend read it to you, you are always in charge. You can change the instructions to suit yourself or you can end the journey whenever you wish. Light trance states help you tap into your unconscious, but you can always come out of it at will. (If you are guiding someone else, read this paragraph to them.)

Guided Imagery

(*To be read slowly:*) Sit or lie down. Feel the support underneath you. Breathe deeply. With each exhalation, take time to relax the muscles in your feet, your calves, your thighs, and your pelvis. (*Pause.*) Continue to inhale and exhale, deeply. As you exhale, allow the muscles of your abdomen, chest, shoulders, arms, and hands to relax. (*Pause.*) Continue your deep breathing. Relax your neck, your face, your jaw, your scalp. Inhale deeply and, as you exhale, tell all the muscles of your body to relax.

Imagine yourself walking down a hillside. Notice the air you breathe. Notice what is to the left of you, to the right of you. Look toward the sky and down the hill. With each step down, breathe and relax. As you go down the hillside path, you notice it goes into a cave. Decide whether you wish to follow the path into the cave. (*Pause.*)

As you enter the cave, the dim light allows you to see the steps down. There are five steps. Count them as you descend, slowly, exhaling and relaxing with each step down. (*Pause.*)

You are now in a rotunda—a round room. There is plenty of space to move and plenty of air to breathe. You are safe. If for any reason you do not feel safe, bring what you need into the rotunda. (*Pause.*) Explore this waiting area. What do you smell? What can you touch? Notice that there are two doors in this area. On one it says, "Shadow." On the other it says, "Light." Decide which one you will open first.

Take the doorknob, turn it, and gradually open the door. You may see something immediately, or it may take some time for an image to appear. It may be a person, an animal, a color, a word, a sentence, or a feeling. Whatever appears first, accept it. Acknowledge it. (*Pause.*)

You may ask this image a few questions such as, "Who are you? (*Pause.*) What do you want from me? (*Pause.*) What are your powers?" (*Pause.*) Listen carefully. What qualities does this image have? How can this inform you? Notice your feelings. (*Pause.*) Now, say goodbye and close the door.

Now, go to the other door. Notice the sign on the door. Gradually open it. An image or color or feeling will be there for you. Accept it. Again, you may ask it a few questions: "Who are you? (*Pause.*) What do you want from me? (*Pause.*) What are your powers?"(*Pause.*) Listen to the response. How can these two images inform you? What gifts do they have? When you are through, close the door and return up the steps to the daylight and come back to the here and now.

Writing or Visual Art

Take time to either write or draw your impressions of this exploration. If you choose to write first, include the dialogue between yourself and each image. Follow the writing with visual art, using clay or color to express your feelings about your "shadow" figure and your "light" image.

Movement and Sound
As you look at your art pieces, stand and let your body move to express the lines, colors, and shapes. Let out sound as you move.

Meditation
Look at your pictures or sculptures and read your writing out loud. Reflect on your thoughts and feelings. In your guided journey, did you meet up with a frightening shadow image? If so, what were its messages? What does it want from you? What power does that entity have that could be harnessed for your benefit? Is it actually an ally?

When you opened the door marked "Light," did an entity appear? Was this easy or difficult to accept? How can you use the energy of that entity? What would you like to explore further?

Writing
To carry this one step farther, have the dark and light images talk to each other. Record their dialogue.

Remember, there are no correct images. We can learn from whatever happens, even if nothing appears behind the doors. What does the nothingness have to say to you? Going into the dark without getting trapped, overcome, or stuck—that is confronting the fear. Frequently the greatest fear is in opening the door. Once it is opened and the unknown becomes known, the shadow is less awesome. Usually these figures become allies with important strengths and good advice.

Embracing the light can be just as overpowering as the shadow. Actually experiencing light or facing a radiant figure may bring tears of compassion and ecstasy. The boundary between compassion and suffering is delicate. Embracing the loving, nurturing, radiant qualities in ourselves is often more difficult than accepting the darker impulses.

NOTES

1 Connie Zweig and Jeremiah Abrams (Eds.), *Meeting the Shadow* (Los Angeles: J. P. Tarcher, 1991), p. 6.

2 Ibid. pp. 271–73.

3 Hermine Glaser, "My Path to Creative Therapy" (Santa Rosa, CA: Person-Centered Expressive Therapy Institute, intern paper, 1989).

4 Joseph Campbell (Ed.), *The Portable Jung* (New York: Penguin, 1976), p. xxvii.

5 Ibid, p. 298.

6 Mary McClary, untitled report (unpublished).

7 Anonymous client.

8 Jeri Spencer, untitled paper (Orinda, CA: JFK University, 1988).

9 Liana Nan Graves, "Living the Dream: Connecting the Creative to My Life Path" (Santa Rosa, CA: Person-Centered Expressive Therapy Institute, intern paper, 1990), p. 45.

10 Ibid.

9

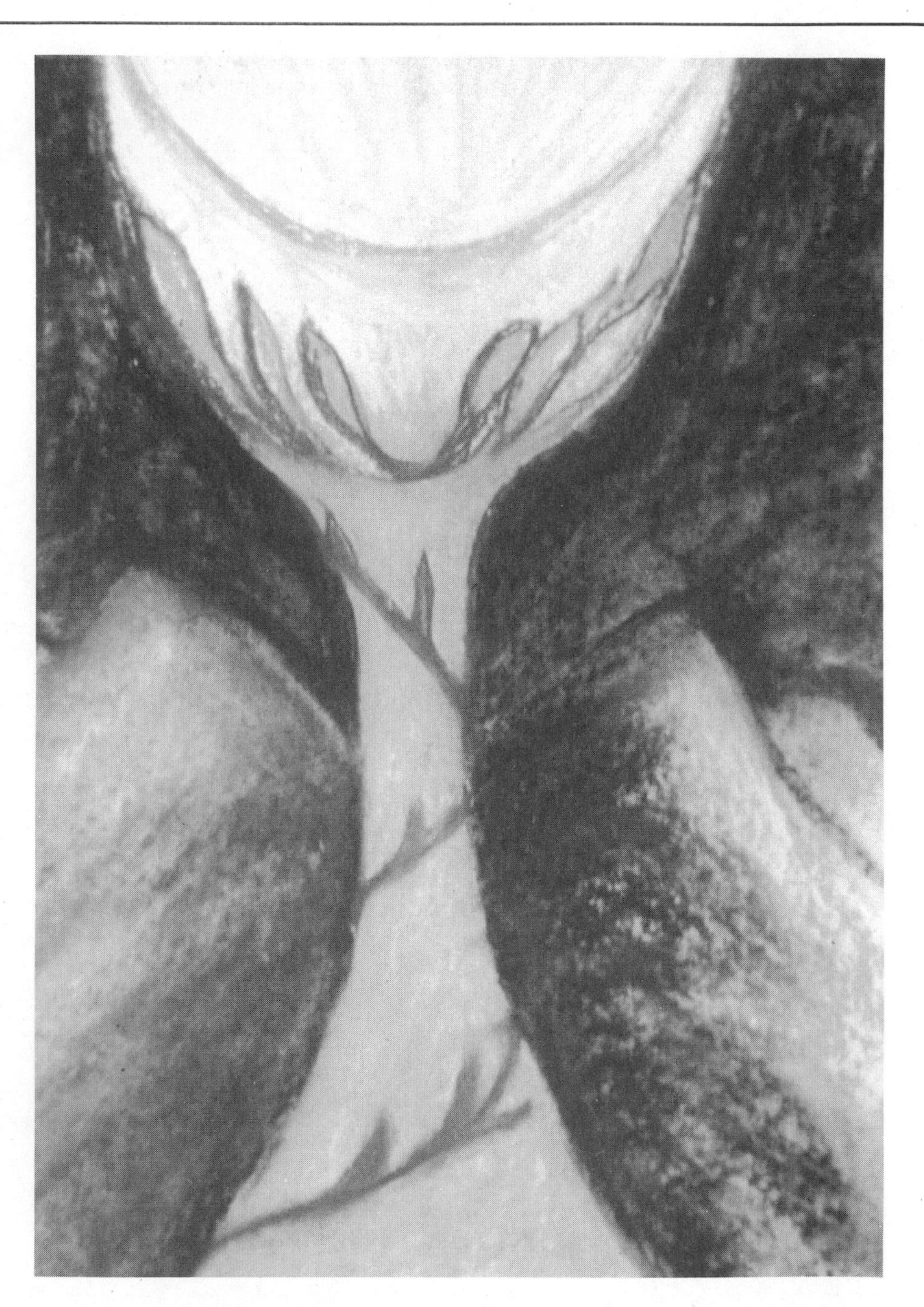

Discovering Spirituality Through the Arts

The experience of art is an experience of transcendence through the senses. That is why the artist in each person is to be nourished and valued. It is a way of experiencing connection.

—M. C. Richards, *Centering*

In developing a training program in the expressive arts, my intention has been to offer psychotherapists, mental health professionals, artists, and educators methods that would enhance their work and a place where they could activate their creativity. As the program evolved, it came as a surprise to me that many people were reporting an awakening to their higher selves or an opening to what they called the God spirit or universal energy. This was not part of my plan, although it fit with my experience of the very special ambience in the room when we were all involved in our expressive art simultaneously. I call it the *sacred space*. Others refer to it that way, as well.

During the many years of facilitating this work, my own art has become lighter, brighter, more flowing, and symbolically more open and evocative of spiritual energy. My experiences during the expressive arts program have included receiving blessings, love, and a sense of internal peace. These developments could be a product of my aging and maturity, but my growth has also been stimulated and nurtured through the expressive arts programs in which the group consciousness is so poignant. Movement and sounding particularly put me in touch with things spiritual. It is through my body and sound vibrations that I gain access to my deepest feelings. It can be a time when

I feel every cell opening to the cells of all beings. Art is the form in which those feelings become visible.

Since I have had no religious training of any sort (my father rebelled against his puritanical upbringing and his theological training), I tend to be cautious about any claims to spiritual awakening. Also, I abhor the possibility of being seen as any kind of a guru. In the past I kept most of my personal experiences of universality to myself. But as I told friends and colleagues about my experiences of receiving light, or possibly angels, or messages from beyond, I found they too had kept such experiences to themselves. It seems important to share these events to explore their meaning and significance.

Listening to clients and participants who have been touched by numinous experiences has validated my own. Rather than being skeptical, I find myself more receptive to the efficacy of these happenings. The following examples from two participants illustrate how people open to their spirituality during the Creative Connection process. The first is from a man who has experienced war and now spends much of his time as a librarian and poet.

> In the criss-cross pattern of the creative connection a moment can open wide enough to allow a glimpse of Being. The body with its seemingly infinite cellular past moves in a stew of sound, vision, color, and feeling, opening new pathways to the space of now. . . . The body, mind, spirit reality are where we glimpse the unknowable.[1]

In the following expressive arts experience, an image of empty space evoked awe and a sense of potential:

> I began to experience myself as a channel of golden light surrounded by reds, oranges, purples which I experienced as high intensity energy becoming "white hot" in the middle as the energy gained clarity and purpose—my purpose. . . . I created a hollow yellow cylinder which represented the clear channel that would be the vehicle for my directed energy. It was, to me, the empty space that could now be filled, the potential that could now become the actual, the meeting of heaven and earth . . . me. I felt like crying as I saw the tremendous potential self that could act as a channel of Divine Energy on earth.[2]

These poignant examples manage to convey the depth of the personal experience. They are also testimony to the fact that involving oneself intensely with the creative process brings an alignment of mind and body, creating an opening to receive divine energy. Discovering one's spirituality through creativity actually happens. This raises the question of what we mean by *spirituality*.

What Is Spirituality?

During an evening class held in my livingroom, we talked of our spiritual experiences and asked ourselves, "What is spirituality to us?" Here are some of our free associations:

Opening to
The universal spirit
To what is, surrender
Fusion with the oneness
Tapping into the unconscious or to a universal source
The collective unconscious
Faith
Belief
Clarity
Intuition
Inner truth
Perspective
Inner calm, peace
Sense of Oneness
Existential aloneness
Facing our shadow, dancing with it, releasing it constructively
Integration of the polarities within: male/female, yin/yang
Reconciliation of opposites
Sexual union leading to spiritual union
Creativity
Centering
Grounding
Connecting with the inner eye
Wholeness/Holiness/Healing
Knowingness
Purpose
Suffering the valleys to reach the peaks
Death/Life/Rebirth
Opening of the heart
Compassion
Love

Most of these associations could be prefaced with "Opening to. . . ." Becoming enlightened, entering the light, feeling light, receiving light —all require an openness or receptivity. The experience of melting, being struck by a flash of light, letting go completely of mental control—or physically letting go—is an act of surrender. It can be ecstatic or frightening, depending on the circumstances. In a caring, nurturing environment, letting go may open a door to the higher self.

The foregoing list highlights much of the process presented in this book: tapping into the individual and collective unconscious, facing the shadow, accepting and integrating those feared or disliked aspects, and going deeply inward through pain, anger, fear, and suffering to become whole and to reach the peaks of knowing, compassion, and love. When we search inward for what is most deeply personal, we touch the universal. This is a death-rebirth process. What I am describing is a journey on the spiritual path. Frances Vaughan describes it this way:

> The spiritual life, which affirms and includes all experience in awareness, tends to manifest joy that radiates from an inner source. It cannot be found by searching in the outer world, but when the source within is awakened it is reflected in all things. In the words of Kalu Rinpoche, a Tibetan Buddhist teacher, "When you practice the Dharma the clouds of sorrow will drift away and the sun of wisdom and great joy will be shining in the clear sky of your mind."[3]
>
> What is important for the person on the spiritual path . . . is to discover and honor the creative inspiration that is uniquely his or hers to express.[4]

The results of a doctoral research project shed light on the connection between creativity and spirituality. Psychologist Mukti Khanna researched creativity as experienced by participants who had completed or were in the third level of the person-centered expressive therapy training program. She interviewed eighteen adults, ages twenty-seven to sixty-five, asking them to describe specific times during this program when they were aware of feeling creative and to identify the feelings they had during those creative moments. After transcribing each interview, she found that seven themes emerged, universality being one of them. *Universality* referred to a particular experience of feeling creative in which people also had a sense of the numinous, of unity, and of their connectedness to all life forms. They felt more in touch with their spiritual side and/or a sense of transcendental connectedness than in everyday life. Eleven of the eighteen participants talked of such a universal or transpersonal experience. Most said this was an unexpected part of the training for them since they had signed into the program knowing it had a psychological focus.[5]

One person experienced a closeness to God:

> it's not only the creative part—I even feel like sacred spaces were open for things to happen in a very spiritual way, as you would suppose it would happen in a church—a space where God can be made more visible, closely felt, and I felt quite surprisingly, I didn't think this would happen.

Another person felt the link between ecstasy and agony:

> I'm channeling my spirit, that creative force is being let free, and that is like a spiritual awakening—it's kind of an ecstatic feeling of tears and joy, it's some fine line between pleasure and pain. I find myself thinking, "This feels wonderful, this is a safe place to be all of me," and that's what I associate with the spirit.[6]

I value Mukti's research since it is based on reports of the subjective experiences of those who have just been immersed in the process of creativity. Since no names were attached to these interviews (they were coded) and no grades given in our program, these sharings can be trusted as authentic. It is further data showing that the expressive arts not only heal psychological wounds but frequently allow people to feel ecstatic and to have a sense of oneness.

Referring back to the list of qualities that describe spirituality, it is no accident that the last and largest word is LOVE. The quest to experience light and universal love is part of all religions. Many people have such experiences but, because the experiences are not logical or based in science, they may dismiss them as irrelevant or unimportant. However, most of us appreciate and even long for these supremely peaceful moments. Such times can bring about personal change or new perspectives that last a lifetime.

Spirituality and Creativity

What is the relationship of creativity to spirituality? Two thoughts come to mind. First, creativity is a life-force energy that flows like a river through each of us. Dam it up and we become psychically ill, blocked, and physically stressed. The expressive arts offer a way to keep the river flowing. Reawakening our creativity leads us to the spiritual path. The radical Dominican priest Matthew Fox put it this way:

> I talk about my new devotion to creativity—a *vow* to creativity. I think creativity is the only hope Mother Earth has for survival. We have to recover our creativity and our divine power.
>
> Creativity is so satisfying. That's why it's so important, not because it produces something, but because the process is cosmological, spiritual, centering and satisfying.
>
> There is joy and delight in giving birth.[7]

My second thought is that denial is our biggest personal and global enemy. To deny our personal grief, suffering, despair, or evil impulses is to carry these as a heavy, unknown burden. This leads to lethargy, depression, and apathy or violence. On the other hand, to become aware leads us into the powerful emotions that need to be channeled appropriately into creative projects. Using our creativity for awareness, release, insight, and action again leads us to the path of spirituality.

Frances Vaughan summarizes this well:

> Psychologically healthy integration of the spiritual seems to require a foundation of personal integrity based on self-knowledge and a willingness to see things as they are. It implies a compassionate response to suffering and a commitment to telling the truth to oneself as well as to others. Healthy integration of the spiritual is the result of an authentic response to ultimate questions such as the meaning and purpose of birth, life and death, and the universal human confrontation with aloneness and with existential freedom. The transcendence of egocentric concerns does not imply that interpersonal relationships must suffer as a result. Attention to all aspects of life with love, compassion and open-mindedness is a more natural result of a psychologically mature spirituality.[8]

Achieving inner peace involves coming to terms with the totality of our physical, emotional, mental, and spiritual states. People do not find peace if they try to bypass the difficulties and unpleasant parts of life by using meditation or some other spiritual discipline as an escape rather than as an addition to confronting their problems. Shortcuts are always tempting. But there is no shortcut to higher states of consciousness. This is where the expressive arts are so helpful. If the clear, calm lake is the goal, and the river is the flow of creativity, then the expressive arts are one canoe in which we can travel.

Spiritual Imagery

In using the Creative Connection process, people often find themselves in nonordinary states of consciousness. What may emerge in the resulting art work are symbols that exist in many cultures. The individual may say things such as, "I don't know where this particular image came from. I've never related myself to a butterfly [or bear or cross or serpent or Easter egg] before," or "How did this symbol, which is also on a tomb in Egypt and a vase in China, appear in my art when I have never thought of it before?" Such symbols are found in ancient and modern cultures and become archetypal or universal, although their meanings may be specific to each culture. As Carl Jung and other psychologists and anthropologists have found, these images come from a collective unconscious. Participants who reflect on their expressive art may become fascinated with this universal symbology. When powerful images come out of "nowhere," even the skeptical person may wander into the halls of mysticism.

As I have said often, I do not interpret symbols for people. Even if I had the expertise, I would ask them to pursue the meaning of these symbols for themselves rather than rely on any external authority. By discovering their own internal relationship to the symbol, people find its real power. For the intellectually curious, looking into the meaning of those symbols as defined by other cultures may add interest and dimension.

Spiritual symbols abound in churches, caves, sand paintings, weavings, tombs, and temples. They range from the cross in all its varied forms to the rose window, chalice, lingam (phallus), yoni (vulva), spirit-guide animals, and sacred plants. When these and other symbols arise spontaneously in expressive art, I encourage the artist to delve further, with more movement, art, sound, and writing involving that symbol. Sometimes I also encourage looking into references that describe its meaning as others have defined it.

Gail's Herringbone

A very meaningful piece of symbolism came from an afternoon session with my good friend and colleague Gail Laird, who was at that time facing the grief of her mother's death. Personally moved by our work together, I wrote about it in my journal that evening. With her permission, I offer you my account of that day to illustrate many of the methods described in this book. By looking at the dynamics of this counseling session as well as the spiritual symbol that emerged spontaneously, I then comment on many aspects of person-centered expressive arts therapy.

Overcoming grief takes time. The process is helped if the person in mourning is able to release feelings in the presence of a compassionate and understanding person. It is possible, of course, to grieve alone; but, as many hospice workers know, the presence of a peer who can accept the kaleidoscope of feelings speeds the healing. Grieving has stages of denial, sadness, anger, catharsis, acceptance, and finally healing of the wound of loss. The searing pain of loss chokes words: they get stuck in the throat. At such times people can release their feelings through color and line; through images and metaphor in visual art, poetry, and journal writing; or kinesthetically, through movement and sound. The expressive arts are thus a particularly helpful means for releasing emotions and communicating to a trusted other.

Going into the well of grief means plunging into suffering. When experienced and accepted fully, this suffering leads to a path of enlightenment and spirituality.

> Those who will not slip beneath
> the still surface on the well of grief
> turning downward through its black water
> to the place we cannot breathe
> will never know the source
> from which we drink,
> the secret water, cold and clear,
> nor find in the darkness glimmering
> the small round coins
> thrown by those who wished for
> something else.
>
> —David Whyte, "The Well of Grief"[9]

Gail had told me, "During the past three months I made trips to the East Coast to nurse Mother as she was dying. Then, after the third trip, my husband and I arrive home to get word that *his* father had died. Then Mother dies." She continued, "And, during the previous year my very good friend—my colleague and mentor—was shot to death. And my former therapist died of AIDS. It's too much, *just too much!"*

Gail is an extremely competent, well balanced professional, usually full of bounce and humor. At this point in time she had *had* it!

Since she had used her skills to help me through a very tough month in my life, I wanted to offer her some time in my studio. She had completed our expressive therapy training, so she knew how to use this work for herself and with others. We set aside a time. On the appointed day, we began by sitting on two large cushions. Our agreement was that for the afternoon I would be her counselor, giving her the space to focus on any issue she wished. The almost verbatim account in my journal reads:

> "Would you like to meditate together for a few minutes?" I ask. She nods, yes. As we begin to settle into the quiet I say, "I think I'll guide us a bit to help us get here." She responds softly, "I'd like that. It would help me get into myself."
>
> I guide us in a meditation something like this: Breathe deeply. Let your shoulders relax. Feel the support underneath you as you sit on the cushion, which is resting on the floor. Feel the support that comes from the floor and below the floor. You might imagine roots going down deep into the earth. Let those roots spread out. If you like this image, imagine the earth's energy coming up through the roots into your whole body, giving you earth energy. Watch the energy as it rises through every cell, every organ in your body. [Pause.] Now imagine the clear blue sky above. If you like this image, imagine the sky energy coming into the top of your head and washing down through every cell, every organ in your body. Let it mix and mingle with the earth energy. [Pause.] Breathe. Relax. Now, check into your body. What feelings do you have? [Pause.] Where, in your body, are they located? [Pause.] Are there any colors or images that appear? [We are quiet awhile.] Take your time, but when you are ready, gradually open your eyes and let me know.
>
> We look into each other's eyes silently for a while. I feel compassion for the pain and exhaustion I see. She begins:
>
> "I had an image of a fish. It was hanging, vertically. It was in black and white, only. There was a head and a tail but the whole body was just a skeleton. The vertebrae and the ribs were visible but there was no flesh and no skin."
>
> I sit quietly, allowing her image into my perception. She continues, describing it in more detail. "The sun has been on its bones. They are bleached white and dry." When she seems finished, I ask her to review that image, putting the description into first-person statements. This is a Gestalt art practice that we have found to be extremely beneficial, and Gail was familiar with it.

"I am a fish, hanging vertically. My head is intact. There is a link that holds my head part to my skeleton part." She slumps as she speaks. "I see that my tail is all there. But I see that there is only a skeleton in between. I have a vertebrae and bleached white ribs, and that is all."

"Can you say any more about that middle section?" I ask. She thinks for a while. "Well, nothing is left of me. There is no liver, no intestines, no bowel, no stomach, no heart." (A long pause and a big sigh.) "I don't have any heart." Her voice is sad, silently weeping. "I don't have any heart, I am all intellect."

I am disturbed by her inaccurate perception of herself. After some inner debate, I decide to be congruent and give her my perception.

"I understand that you are feeling that you have no heart, now, and that you are seeing yourself as ruled by intellect, but I think if we asked your friends and colleagues if you have a heart, they would say you are a very heartfelt person. At least that is my perception of you. You always seem to come from the heart. *I do hear you, however*—that at this time, now, you definitely feel you have lost your heart."

Gail is upset about losing her heart. She describes the excruciating details of her mother's death: that her mother was gasping for each breath, not being able to get enough air to live, and not being able to give up, to die. The loving daughter felt helpless yet stayed present for days. Gail speaks of the horror of watching her mother leave the world in this way. She weeps as she speaks.

I move around behind her and, kneeling at her back, place my knees at the base of her spine, giving her support. I am aware of not wanting to "comfort" her in the sense of making her feel better but to give her the necessary support and touch that will allow her tears to be unrestrained. I let my intuition and hands guide me. When I start to stroke her hair, she breaks into deep sobs. "My mother always loved my hair. When I was a child she would brush it and stroke it and tell me it was beautiful. Your hands found the right place. It feels wonderful." She continues to cry. My comment is simply, "It is okay to cry. You can let it out."

After a while I ask, "Is there anything you would like to tell your mother?" Barely audible, she says, "I'll miss you, mother, I love you so much. You were really wonderful to me." In a more cheerful voice she says, "By the way, your little dog is okay. She's with me." Then to me, she says, "I really finished all of my business with my mother during all those trips to the East Coast."

I am still supporting Gail with my body, stroking her hair. When I ask, "Could you tell your mother about your heart, what's happened to it?" A large pillow is sitting in front of Gail, and she talks to it as though this is her mother. "Mom, I've lost my heart, I can't feel it any more. It's gone." A sad sigh comes forth.

"Where is it?" I inquire.

"I've left it with you, Mom. I left it with your body in the casket." Gail vividly describes the scene in the funeral parlor, saying, "When they closed the casket, it closed on my heart."

"What would your mother say to that?" I ask. Gail's voice changes, sounding rather perky and tough. "'You take your heart back right away!' she'd say."

"And what is *your* reaction to that?" I ask.

Gail replies to the pillow, wistfully, "Well, I'd say it may take some time, Mom. You were always more impatient than I. I'm afraid it will take some time before I get it back." A long silence ensues.

My own heart goes out to Gail as I empathize, reflecting back her conclusion. "Even though your mother may want you to have your heart back immediately, as far as you're concerned it will take some time." I am still at her back, letting her talk to the mother in front of her.

Gail offers, "I really feel her presence, here. She is all over this room!" We talk about it as a possibility. "I feel she has been present so often, in my dreams and actually around my house."

I admit, "I have to agree. I've been wondering about that possibility, here, myself. I've certainly been aware of some different quality in this room during this hour." It was true, I had felt the possibility of a "spirit" in the room.

Eventually I move back to sit on my own pillow. "You must be exhausted," Gail says, being protective of me.

"No, it may be exhausting for you, but to be with you through this sorrow feels very precious to me. I'm moved, not exhausted." She realizes there is more she needs to do. "I would very much like to try doing a picture of my image."

"Wonderful!" I respond, feeling the pleasure of being with someone who knows the healing aspects of the art process. She goes to the art table where a large pad of drawing paper, oil pastels, and chalks are available. I suggest she first close her eyes, putting her hands on the paper to explore it in a meditative state. Then I also remind her that one effective way to approach the art process is to use her non-dominant hand, thus eliminating the judgmental critic. "Thanks for reminding me," she says. Immediately she is completely engrossed in the process.

I can see she would like to work alone, so I take her suggestion to do my own art. I go to the clay table, not having any notion of what to do. I take a hunk of cool gray clay and with my eyes closed start rolling it gently. I realize I am in a very soft/strong mood, having been very centered and grounded during the last emotional hour yet extremely open to all that came in. Unlike Gail, I have no image in mind. I spend some time just playing with the clay, rolling and rolling, first a ball, then it becomes more of a cylinder, then my fingers begin to open it. It is smooth on the outside. I open my eyes. There are some lines that appeal to me, I emphasize them with strong finger strokes. As I begin to open the cylinder, I wonder what it will become. Part of it becomes hollow, like a fat, hollow log. Still, I just follow the shapes that appeal to me. The clay and I are mutually engaged in the "something" that is happening.

All of a sudden I see the beginnings of a woman's figure. In an abstract way, she looks like a Madonna. My fingers move to give her breasts and a lap. She already has an arm reaching out to embrace. She is cloaked with a large wrap. "Of course," I say to myself, "the title of this piece is 'Mother.'"

I have been feeling very openhearted and embracing while Gail has been delving into her grief. Although images of my own mother's death occurred while she was speaking, I stayed focused on Gail's more immediate experience. Now, my art work is speaking for me. Lovingly I am creating not my mother, or Gail's mother, but Mother, in the best sense of the word. This clay piece brings my experience to fruition.

In the meantime, Gail finishes her picture and tells me she is going to do some writing. When we are both finished, we look at her picture. Again, I am moved. The image is stark. It fills the page. A large fish with a black head and black tail is dangling. Between the head and tail is a set of skeleton-white ribs held together by carefully drawn black circles for vertebrae. "How can it be?" she queries. "I'm no artist and I used my left hand and it came out exactly as I had wanted! I love it."

There is no need to discuss the art in depth at this point. She has "owned" every aspect of it through her verbal description. Although the picture gives a bleak impression, intense focus as she created each detail with care seems to have lifted the dark mood a bit. I ask if she would like to do some free writing at this point. She likes the idea.

When we finish we go to the patio to have some iced tea. I show her my sculpture, and she reads her writing:

> Imagery—Herringbone. Fish with head and tail intact, but no mid-section. Bones and vertebrae, no guts, no intestines,

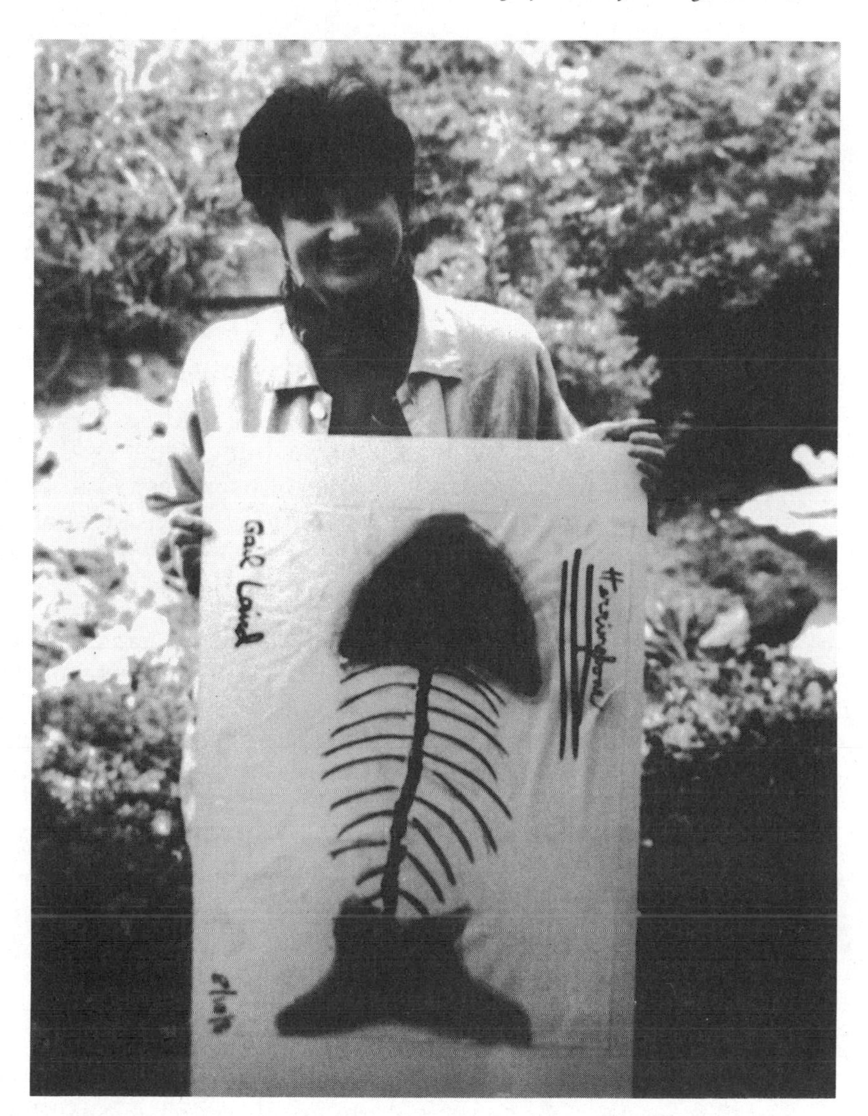

Gail's Herringbone: "There is no liver, no intestines, no bowel, no heart . . . . I've lost my heart."

stomach, bowel, heart. NO HEART. I am a fish with a head and tail and no heart. So I can decide where to go; my tail will propel me there; but if I have no heart what will it matter if I go there? My heart cares, my head doesn't.

Where is my heart? I trace it to Mother's casket in the ground at Pulteney, Lakeview Cemetery. When asked, mother wanted me to retrieve it RIGHT NOW! However, I want it to stay there til I return to New York next week.

> Sounding is vibration—the connection between heaven and earth. My singing and sounding has been good and clarifying—clearing me out—making space for thoughts, ideas, maybe making room for a larger heart when it comes back to me.
>
> Natalie works so sensitively with me, gently probing, suggesting—touching my back, my head, my hair. Was it Mother's spirit guiding Natalie's hands and fingers to my hair? Mother so appreciated my hair.
>
> Thank you Natalie for this special time—time to be and time to do and for your depth so that I could trust and go so deeply myself. I am worn out.

As we finish the afternoon, one remaining topic is the symbolic meaning of the fish. Although neither of us is steeped in symbolism, we both know that the fish is a profound religious symbol, and that in the Christian religion it is the symbol of Christ. I have since looked up some of the symbolism to share with her.

> The fish symbol has a double aspect. On the one hand it is a cold-blooded creature of the depths and thus represents unconscious instinctuality. . . . On the other hand it is a symbol for Christ. Thus it symbolizes both the redeemer and that which is to be redeemed.[10]

The Process Reviewed

The vignette about Gail stands by itself as an afternoon of self-exploration through words and imagery in a supportive environment. Yet this example also embodies certain nuances of the client-centered art process as healing.

Empathic Listening

Listening to a person's "music" as well as her words is the heart and soul of empathic listening. It is the counselor's task to hear the deepest nuances of the client's emotional statements. Feeding back those feelings to the client helps her look at them and get perspective on herself, as if looking into a mirror.

How tempting it might have been to comfort (and thus smother) Gail's grief, or to take the side of the mother who said, "You need your heart back, immediately!" Letting the individual be her own guide ("It will take *time*, Mom") is what is ultimately empowering and healing for the client.

The importance of that moment was to accept and understand Gail's felt sense that she had really lost her heart. I came close to side-tracking that meaningful moment when I started to try to convince her she "really was a heartfelt person." Quickly I realized I was saying this out of my own need, and it was useless and possibly detracting input. I went back to the poignant point she was making: "You *feel* you have lost your heart." My acceptance allowed her to feel deeply understood—a rare event for people in emotional pain. Being understood on that level gave her strength to go one step deeper: to review the excruciating details of her mother's death and funeral. Being accepted and listened to on this level, she continued into her pain: "I'll miss you, Mother. My heart is in your casket."

The therapist who finds the agony of the story more than she can tolerate will unconsciously steer the client away from that pain. Although my heart was aching for Gail's sorrow, and memories of my own mother's death fleetingly intruded on my thoughts, I found my internal strength by focusing even more diligently on the depth of the experience *for Gail*. At a crucial point like this, my mind runs on several tracks:

> "I want to be fully present for Gail."
>
> "This chokes me up as I feel her pain and remember my mother's death."
>
> "I need to refocus on her pain, not mine, and see to it she feels fully and deeply understood."
>
> "Ah, that's better, I sense she is relieved as she feels accepted and understood."
>
> "Now I feel in better control of my own emotions, having focused in appropriately on her."

Such mind-talk happens within seconds. I share it because therapists in training ask how I cope with my feelings. "How do you remain so present yet keep your boundaries?" As I reflect on this question, I realize I do not shield myself or put up a boundary. Being aware that I am feeling personally touched by the grief during the moment allows me to shift back intentionally to verbal and emotional acceptance of the client's experience, thus helping me contain my emotions. I feel so rewarded, knowing that the troubled person confiding in me finds strength by my presence, that I seem not to take on her pain.

Many colleagues and students have told me that absorbing the other person's pain is a serious professional liability. Some counselors meditate before each session, bringing in an image of warm, protective light to surround them. Others image a protective suit which they "zip up" as a personal shield. Whatever method is devised, the counselor needs to be able to be fully present, or openhearted, without being a sponge for pain.

Dialogue Practices

In this afternoon session, we also used the Gestalt practice of dialoguing with the imagined mother. This useful verbal practice helps bring the absent person into the here-and-now through imagination and dialogue. In keeping with the person-centered philosophy, the structure I gave allowed the client to lead the way. Although I asked questions to stimulate Gail's dialogue, I had no predetermined notion as to right or wrong answers. Whatever she said to her mother, or her mother said to her, was okay. The goal is to help the client discover more of her feelings and attitudes, whatever they may be.

Being Fully Present

Being fully present always sounds relatively easy. But in reality, putting aside our usual tendencies to advise, share our own past griefs, or interpret or analyze the art takes a strong *intention* to be fully present for another. As friends, Gail and I make fun of each other's foibles and give advice as well as listen to each other. Here, the unspoken agreement was that I would intentionally focus on her world as she was viewing it, experiencing it, feeling it. The client-centered process holds a basic trust that the individual, if deeply understood, eventually finds her own right path. This brings with it a sense of personal strength, self-esteem, and empowerment. The vignette with Gail highlights part of the difference between being together as friends and being in a counseling session.

Physical Support

Touch was also an important aspect in our counseling session. With so many lawsuits regarding sexual advances on the part of therapists toward clients, many therapists are terrified to touch their clients at all. Although I loathe sexual harassment and the misuse of touch in counseling relationships, it is a pity that therapists have become so fearful of lawsuits that they no longer think they can use any kind of touch. People are touch-deprived in this fast-paced society. During the afternoon with Gail, I did not hesitate to use touch, but I am always concerned as to whether my touch is of help or is a hindrance. An easy way to find out: ASK! "Is putting my hand on your back helpful?" "Is it okay to touch your hair?" If in doubt, take your hand away.

Readers may say, "This is not a good example of a counseling session, since Gail was your friend. The relationship is different." In some respects that is true. Our trust was easy and mutual. We had no contract or commitment to continue. Yet much of the same process evolved, and it seems like an event from which we all can learn.

I also want to give an example of how one colleague can be of help to another. Wherever I live, I try to create my own support group of two or three people who, after establishing close friendships, are available to each other in a deep, personal way. Women, particularly, establish support circles. To me this is one of the things friends, particularly therapist friends, do for each other. And we choose each other carefully.

Transpersonal Aspects

This review of the Creative Connection process concludes by looking at the session's transpersonal qualities. The word *transpersonal* literally means "beyond the personal." Transpersonal and spiritual experiences are closely related. It seems that every time I am in this type of altered or nonordinary state of consciousness with someone—whether it is client, friend, or lover—very special things happen. They happen both internally and externally (if there *is* an "external"). These experiences invoke the spirit, whether that spirit comes from within or from another reality, or both. Who is to say whether a spirit is in the room with us? Or is it our own expanded consciousness that is filling the room? Who is to say whether a deceased person can return in another form to "fill the whole room"? What is helpful to the client is for you to accept these experiences in any way that fits with your belief system. What is nonhelpful or nonhealing is to reject the experiences completely.

Why is it that Gail, in going deep into her grief, comes up with a universal symbol of Christ—a depleted, suffering Christ with no body? Carl Jung would agree that here we have a religious symbol springing from the unconscious:

> religious symbols have a distinctly "revelatory" character; they are usually spontaneous products of unconscious psychic activity. They are anything rather than thought up; on the contrary, in the course of the millennia, they have developed, plant-like, as natural manifestations of the human psyche. Even today we can see in individuals the spontaneous genesis of genuine and valid religious symbols springing from the unconscious like flowers of a strange species, while the consciousness stands aside perplexed.[11]

One further point: when Gail suggested she draw an image, I wondered whether it would be of her lost heart, her fish, or her mother. How important it is to let the client choose the image to draw! The fish image came from deep within her unconscious and has continued to have significance for her. Again it is evident that psychological suffering, if deeply explored, brings forth a state of deeper consciousness. The process seems to put the individual in touch with the collective unconscious.

Stan Grof put it this way:

> Deep experiential encounter with birth and death is typically associated with an existential crisis of extraordinary proportions during which the individual seriously questions the meaning of his or her life and existence in general. This crisis can be successfully resolved only by connecting with the intrinsic spiritual dimensions of the psyche and deep resources of the collective unconscious. The resulting personality transformation and consciousness evolution can be compared to the changes described in the context of ancient death–rebirth mysteries.[12]

Although Stan is referring to reexperiencing one's own birth or eventual death, I believe the same is true when we deeply experience the birth of a child or the death of a beloved.

I compare my own experience with Gail's. From being with both my mother and father at their respective times of death, I know that the experience of feeling (and perhaps even seeing) them leave their bodies—yet stay in the room—has changed my perception of death. As a young woman I always thought of death as the absolute end. Death was like entering a black box: no life existed after this life. Now my experience has me seriously questioning that assumption. After my parents' deaths, I spent months of grief, release, and healing through art, movement, and sharing with close friends. All this led to important personal understandings of the meaning of death. As I try to accept death as a very different beginning (rather than a dead end), I find I become more totally present in life.

The Discovery Process

For some people, discovering higher (or deeper) consciousness and spirituality happens in a moment of revelation. For others it is a long, steady process of opening and unfolding, of becoming aware of forces beyond the self. As the examples in this chapter illustrate, some people discover a higher self for the first time. Others experience a new dimension of their spirits. It is also evident that the intense

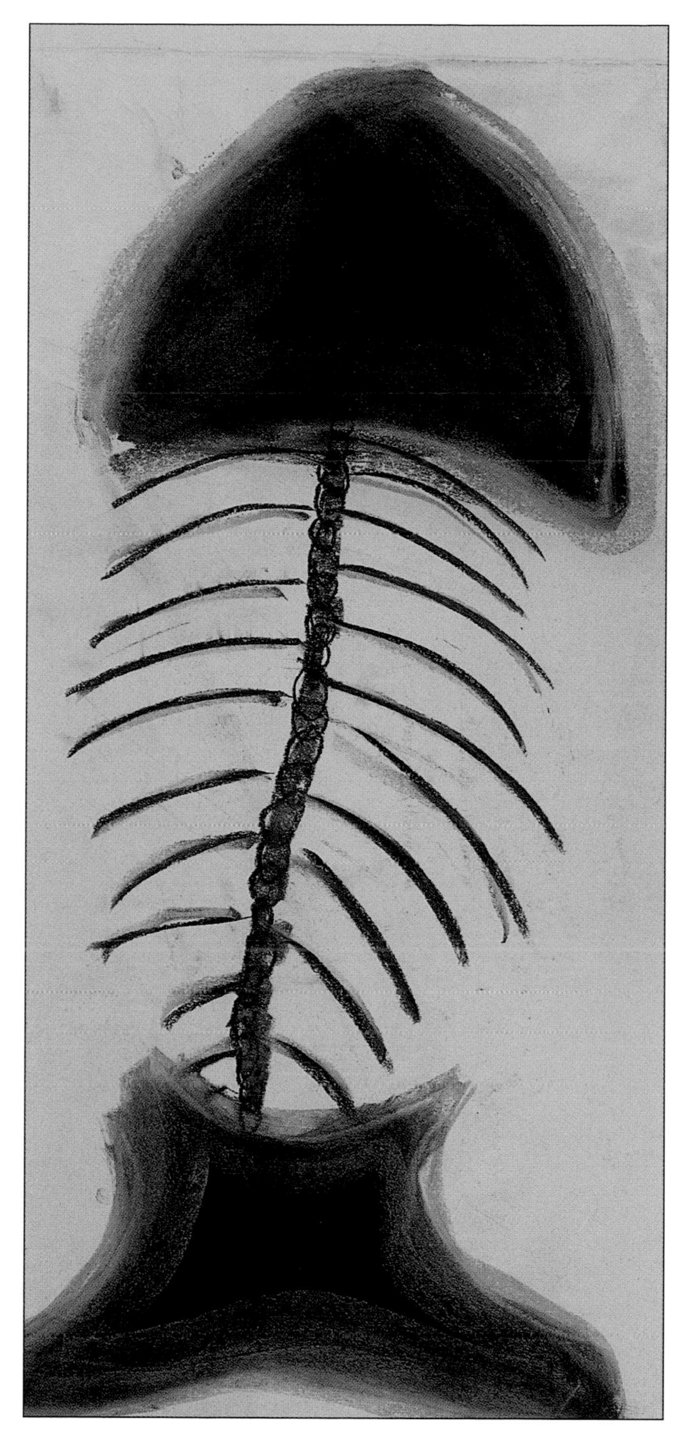

"How can it be? I'm no artist, and I used my left hand, and it came out exactly as I wanted. I love it."
—Gail Laird

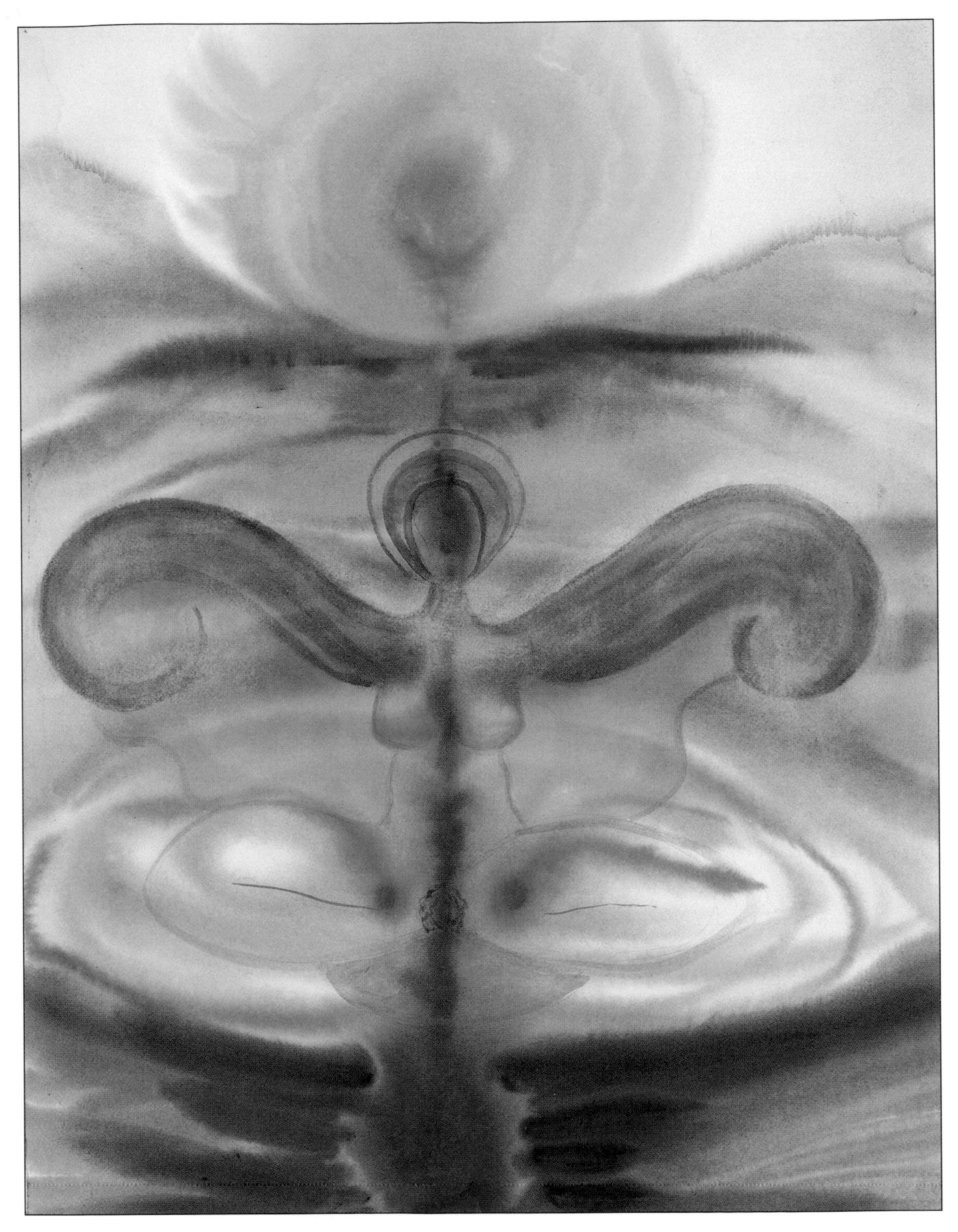

The Feminine: "A path to the divine self." —N. R.

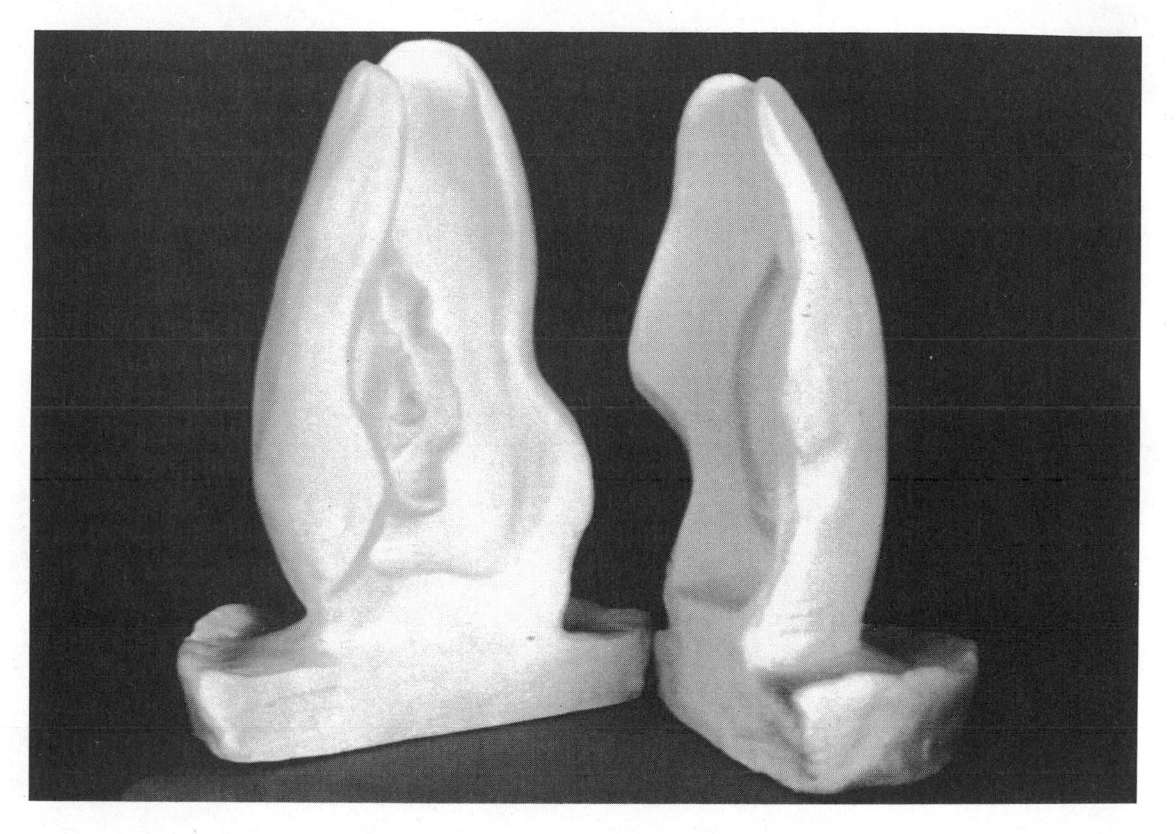

Magnolia Blossom: Sensuality as an opening to the spiritual. —N. R.

focusing and concentration on the creative process is, in itself, sacred. When we are in an environment of empathy and understanding, we use our creativity to journey inward to our deepest inner essence, bringing us a sense of peace. It seems miraculous that using movement, art, sound, writing, and drama opens a window of consciousness and gives us a new perspective on ourselves—but it happens. One student described her sense of the creative process:

> I have a sense of awe and a sense of it being something really sacred . . . as if I were an estuary and the waters happened to flow into me. My significance comes from the creative force, not the other way around. . . . I think being a creative person has also had an effect on me spiritually and politically in that I can't act without being conscious in some way of having an effect. The creative force has incredible amounts of power and it's up to me with my little piece of it how I'm going to direct it.[13]

Radiance: A sense of inner peace.—N. R.

I have often heard such statements. It is encouraging to know that discovering one's spirituality through the creative process activates a sense of personal responsibility in the world. Another student also connected the sacred nature of the self with others:

> Creativity is, to me, the act of "becoming." It is the unfolding of unique patterns of expression—the Universal Impulse manifesting Itself in an infinite variety of expressions. As we move into a conscious relationship with our own process of creativity, we begin to understand the sacred nature of ourselves and others.[14]

The creative process is a path to finding the divine self. Discovering our capacity to love is profound. Discovering our ability to receive love, whether it is from a particular individual or a universal source, can be so awesome as to be frightening to some people. However, opening to that ability or consciousness is both healing and revolutionary: it changes the lenses through which we view the world.

NOTES

1 Gary Lark, "Opening the Sacred Space" (Santa Rosa, CA: Person-Centered Expressive Therapy Institute, intern paper, 1989), p. 2.

2 Anonymous student, untitled paper (Orinda, CA: JFK University, 1988).

3 Frances Vaughan, *The Inward Arc* (Boston: Shambala, 1986), p. 87.

4 Ibid, p. 156.

5 Mukti Khanna, "A Phenomenological Investigation of Creativity in Person-Centered Expressive Therapy" (Knoxville, TN: The University of Tennessee, Ph.D. dissertation, December 1989).

6 Ibid, pp. 74–75.

7 Interview with Matthew Fox in *Creation Spirituality* (date unknown).

8 Frances Vaughan, "Spiritual Issues in Psychotherapy," *Journal of Transpersonal Psychology,* 23:2 (1991), p. 107.

9 David Whyte, *Where Many Rivers Meet* (Langley, WA: Many Rivers Press, 1990).

10 Edward F. Edinger, *Ego and Archetype* (Baltimore, MD: Penguin Books, 1973), p.258.

11 C. G. Jung, *Psychology and the Occult,* translated by R. F. C. Hull (Princeton, NJ: Princeton University Press, 1977), p. 131.

12 Stanislav Grof, *The Adventure of Self Discovery* (Albany, NY: State University of New York Press, 1988), p. 10.

13 In Mukti Khanna, op. cit., p. 74.

14 Anonymous student, op. cit., 1988.

10

Cross-Cultural Bridges

Should you really open your eyes and see, you would behold your image in all images. And should you open your ears and listen, you would hear your own voice in all voices.

—Kahlil Gibran, *Sand and Foam*

Although I have used the expressive arts in many situations—with children, teachers, artists, clients, health professionals, and organizations—my personal mission is to work cross-culturally to facilitate understanding within and between national and ethnic groups. I have had the privilege of working in most European countries, the former Soviet Union, Mexico, South America, Japan, and the Philippines.

Working with the expressive arts allows people to peel away their social masks. This enables me to glimpse the hearts and minds of people with differing religious, social, political, and ethnic beliefs. As is my custom, I also offer my own truths. The mutual sharing builds personal bridges that last a lifetime. Also, the international folks who join our training program add a richness to understanding ourselves and the world. As we go on our inner journey and share our concerns and hopes, interpersonal bonding occurs. In the process, we are helping to build an international network of people with humanistic and democratic values. Small as this network may be, every link of communication builds a stronger chain.

The nonverbal, symbolic, and mythic expressions that arise from our deeper selves when we express creatively are understood across cultures. Whether in Frankfurt, Moscow, Tokyo, or Buenos Aires, personal images are painted, dances are created, sounds are vocalized, and any of us can say, "Yes, I understand what you are feeling," or "I have had a similar experience." No words are necessary. Anguish is anguish in any culture. Celebration and delight are experienced everywhere. Color, movement, and sound express these feelings poignantly. One painting can reveal your inner experience to me regardless of your ethnic background. Your expressive movement can captivate me as I identify with your struggles and transformation.

Music performances and art exhibits have always linked nations because these expressions come from the heart and soul and speak directly to others. They do not need translation. Working with individuals and groups, the expressive arts bring this heart and soul connection to the personal level. When people gather together with no common language, there can be great awkwardness and distance. Offer them an expressive arts exercise using movement to get acquainted or using art to share a personal experience, and the barrier dissolves.

The same person-centered philosophy and guidelines apply to using the expressive arts cross-culturally as in any other situation. It is particularly important to respect and allow expression of individual and cultural differences. Creating an environment in which people can trust each other may take some special effort. What builds trust in the United States may be unacceptable in another culture. Before offering movement or sound exercises, it is wise to talk to your host in that country to understand the prevailing customs. Some cultures save touching one another for very intimate occasions. In other cultures, embracing and kissing are part of every meeting. The facilitator needs to be aware of the taboos and social habits as she offers expressive arts. If in doubt, ask your participants. They are always eager to share the customs of their homeland.

It takes added effort to understand a person from a different culture. Our sensitivities and listening skills need to be acute. I am particularly careful not to interpret or analyze the art, movement, sounding, or writing when in a foreign country. I am there as a learner to soak up knowledge about our similarities and differences, as well as the social and political conditions of that culture. Working and living in other countries has been the richest education of my life.

When I was first invited to work in Europe in the 1970s, my personal goal was to drop the stereotypes I had about people from other countries: stereotypes such as, "the French approach everything from the intellect," or "the Italians are extremely emotional," or "the

Swedes are quiet and reserved." As I worked in those countries, I discovered that some of those generalizations have truth to them. Climate, religion, and customs bring forth some qualities that many people exhibit in a given country. (Their generalization that Californians wear a permanent smile on their faces seems to hold some truth as well.)

My goal shifted to something more relevant: how can I understand these people, whose surface behavior is different from mine, and what can I do to facilitate mutual understanding? In Sweden I had to overcome my annoyance that people seem to take forever to say what is in their hearts or minds. I learned gentle and patient ways to allow them to drop their reserve and to experience their depth. In France it was a challenge to create an environment where people could express their feelings as well as their thoughts. In Italy the emotional outpourings were so powerful I needed all of my skills to help them ground and center themselves. And in the process of all of this, I discovered my own reserve, my own ways of intellectualizing, my own emotionality. In working with people of other cultures and different ethnic groups, I face my own prejudices, my own racism, my ethnocentrism. The richness comes in discovering the deep human qualities that connect us. It is profound and humbling.

I could tell many fascinating tales about my adventures in Europe and Japan that illustrate the facilitation of personal growth and awakening to innate creativity. For this discussion, however, I wish to focus on those countries that have been under the rule of dictators. I do this to point out, theoretically and with personal examples, that using the expressive arts in a person-centered environment is of particular value to nations emerging from despotic despair. The expressive arts involve people in their imaginations, metaphoric imagery, dance, and sound. This brings vitality and life back to their deadened spirits. Although I help people focus on the grief and despair, there is also the opportunity to reexperience the creative, childlike, playful, and hopeful aspects of self. *Where death and tragedy loom large, there is a need to dream, envision, and regain faith in the possible.*

Expressive Arts in Latin American Dictatorships

In November 1977 I told friends that I was cutting loose from all professional work at home to travel in Central and South America, letting my plans evolve as I went along. Remarkable experiences ensued with colleagues in Mexico, Chile, Argentina, and Nicaragua. Each gathering led me to people who wanted to create a workshop for me in another country.

These were times of tremendous political turmoil and unrest. I arrived in Managua, Nicaragua ten days after the national opposition hero, Pedro Joaquin Chomoro, had been assassinated. Evidence suggested that President Somoza's son had done it.

The women who had invited me to Nicaragua arrived at the airport to tell me a national strike had just been declared. Revolution against the corrupt government was in the air. As we drove through the empty city streets, military personnel were on every rooftop, automatic rifles cocked and ready. Each evening, our women's group met in secret in someone's home. The workshop had to end before curfew so these women could get home safely. They were admittedly scared to come and go, but they took the risk.[1]

Using the person-centered expressive arts group process with these women—a school principal, a university psychologist, a public relations expert, a communications executive, and housewives volunteering their talents—led to discussions of their struggle for equality and their concern for the rights of *all* people. As they discussed their own efforts to be treated equally with men, their hearts and minds expanded to include others who are oppressed. Although these were upper-class, college-educated women, many of whom were married to businessmen getting wealthy under Somoza's government, they were saying, "Human values are more important than financial wealth." I wondered if they understood the full implications of their proclamations—if, to support equality for all, they would really be willing to give up having servants and sending their children to North American universities. Meanwhile, at least this was their dream, their hope, their vision: that all peoples, including those who were rebelling against the government, would have equal opportunity. They were tired of living in a corrupt system. They argued with their husbands, who had more ego—as well as money—invested in the status quo.

I left Nicaragua thinking that as women discover the extent of their own oppression, they will become a very strong world force for human rights and human dignity. My experience in Nicaragua seemed like a powerful example that when we discover our own worth and dignity, we become concerned for those of others.

In Chile I phoned a couple who were members of the Association for Humanistic Psychology. They invited me to visit their home and, as we talked, the wife asked me to work with women therapists she knew. I agreed.

It was a new concept, for these women, to meet for personal-growth work without men. Again, as in Nicaragua, the women empowered themselves in the process and learned how to be a support group for each other. Through art, movement, and discussion, they peeled away their more formal natures to reveal the hidden essence of their beings.

A psychologist-parachutist-wife-mother took metaphoric sky-dives into her unconscious, discovering that she had assumed women would criticize her for perceiving herself as equal to or better than men. A well-established therapist who had a childish nickname raised her self-esteem by uncovering the meaning of that name in her life; she then asked her colleagues to address her by her full name. A beautiful woman feared aging, since attractiveness had been her ticket to acceptance. She had always wanted to dance. So we danced! She began to experience the joy of her whole body—more than just a face. And she decided to interview women in their sixties and seventies to discover how they maintain their vitality.

The workshop took on excitement as women acknowledged their strengths, verbalized them, and made action plans. I received touching feedback that gave me energy to travel on. One said, "Natalie, I feel you have deep respect for people with different life styles and values. It is not a therapeutic tool. It is you!"

My new therapist friend in Chile called a colleague in Argentina. By the time I arrived, another women's workshop had evolved. Here are excerpts from my notes:

> 1977, Argentina: I'm impressed with the courage of the psychologists I am meeting. Since they have lived in fear for years, they have become accustomed to it as a way of life. Here is a country ruled by the military where, during the last three years, 12,000 people have either disappeared or are dead or are in jail.
>
> I just returned from my first day facilitating a professional women's workshop. My god, I feel sad! The women are fantastic—intelligent, strong, beautiful, and courageous in facing many of the issues women must confront all over the world. But as I sit in my hotel room looking at the notes I have just written summarizing the problems they are facing, I am weeping. I am used to working with women who have severe emotional disturbances, but something else is occurring here. The emotional problems these women are having are exacerbated by or *created* by the political brutality and the fear-based structure in which they live.
>
> One woman says, "I'm still trying to get over the loss of my two children." She is a therapist. I ask if she wishes to say more about it.

"They died a few years ago. They were just teenagers, active in the fight for freedom." This statement led to another woman saying, "Two of my children are in Spain and they are having psychological difficulty because of their premature separation from home. I had to send them there to keep them alive. I can't afford to go see them and they can't come back here." On and on it went, the tales of tragedy, of loss, separation and torture due to the political situation. One therapist revealed how she and her family were taken to prison in the middle of the night and were kept there many months. She was suffering tremendous guilt because she and her family were released, while others were still in jail. She still hears the shouts and screams of torture in her dreams at night.

There were few tears. The women were just stating facts that had become part of their daily lives. What seems unthinkable to me has become a normal part of their daily lives. Deaths in the family, kidnaping, and the loneliness of one Jewish woman because all of her relatives had fled. She said, "I have no one with whom to spend the holidays."

I am realizing this is a different context in which to deal with psychological problems. Argentinians have become accustomed to the ongoing threat of sudden loss, but as I listen to it I get in touch with my own sense of powerlessness in the face of a dictatorship. *Such political impotence is my own dreaded nightmare.* To be repressed at gunpoint, to have no power to say openly what I believe, to have terror created daily by the powers in authority—that really hits me in the guts! I find myself crying *their* tears, wanting to shout out *their* rage. They have swallowed it, or worn themselves out crying and raging in private. They know they could lose their own lives or be imprisoned for shouting out loud or rebelling.

The last day: The results of this togetherness are overwhelmingly joyous and nurturing. These women need each other and are discovering the meaning of a support group. Trusting each other comes slowly in this environment where one neighbor can report another. As one person said, "Fear is under the skin."

Building cross-cultural bridges brings learning in both directions. It is second nature for me to create a trusting atmosphere in which people can communicate with each other, verbally and through art images. As I listen to them—to the "music" as well as the words—they start to truly hear each other. My genuine acceptance gives them permission to speak their fear and grief and allows them to comfort and support each other. They desperately need such support. My visit brings them together in new ways. They will continue meeting and giving each other courage.

And these people inspire me! To hear how they live under the oppressor's thumb, overcoming tragic losses and roadblocks to their professional work, gives me new energy. Their inner strength and courage are far greater than anything I have ever experienced. Although I tell them they inspire me, I am not sure they believe it. They are too close to their life-threatening situation to have perspective on their own fortitude.

Expressive Arts in the Soviet Union

My recent trips to the (then) Soviet Union have also been a two-way bridge for cross-cultural understanding.[2] As the coming examples show, the sustained efforts of many people have actually effected change. It is heartwarming to know that a few individuals can make a significant difference in the personal lives and political direction of a country. Our Russian friends tell us that the direction of psychology has dramatically changed with the input of humanistic psychologists, Carl Rogers and Virginia Satir being the first to visit in the mid 1980s.

Rich in cultural heritage of music, art, and literature, the Soviet Union had been sealed off from information about psychology and humanistic values. Psychotherapy had been outlawed for seventy years. Clinical training and supervision were not available. Mental hospitals were institutions in which to jail political prisoners. The situation was best described by the Russians themselves. A statement put out by Garmonia, a new nonprofit counseling and training center in St. Petersburg, reads:

> Ugly ideology which existed in our country for seventy years harmed our people. It spoiled their minds, erasing true human values and rejecting the sacred uniqueness of every human being.
>
> Reorienting people's minds towards humanistic ideals is the major goal of the reconstruction taking place now. . . .
>
> Not all changes in Soviet life have been positive. Political instability, national conflicts, and economical hardships have all increased human suffering, intensifying fears and feelings of hopelessness, igniting aggression and self-destructiveness. . . .
>
> To help people live through critical periods, to provide them not only with physical support but, even more important under present dramatic circumstances, to encourage their personal growth in the face of sudden devastating hardship. . . . Thus psychotherapy and psychological help acquire major importance. In the present circumstances they are hopelessly inadequate. Leningrad, for example, a city of five million people, has only a few dozen

> professional therapists, smaller cities have fewer, and most towns are likely to have none.
>
> It should be kept in mind that psychotherapy has been officially regarded as a kind of ideological tool mainly used to enforce the adjustment of a personality to the ugly way of life. Professional training conditioned psychologists and therapists to match psychology to Marxist philosophy. Even now, psychological education is far from satisfactory.
>
> In response to this crisis a group of Leningrad psychologists and psychotherapists organized an independent cooperative center, "Harmony."

I have been told many times by Russians that my father's trip to the USSR changed the face of psychology there. Sitting at her kitchen table, Moscow University professor Julia Gippenreiter told me:

> Before Carl Rogers came, psychology as a field drew little interest because we focused on things like measuring eye movement, or some other such irrelevant research. When we heard that Carl Rogers was coming, we couldn't actually believe it.
>
> When he did arrive we fought to get into his workshops and swarmed to his lectures. Having experienced the Person-Centered Approach from this genuine and rather humble man changed my focus in psychology, as it did many others. I am now teaching teachers how to relate to their pupils and am using the principles of facilitation in my University classes.

When Carl returned from this trip, he told me he had no idea Soviets had read his writings since none of his books had been translated into Russian. He was incredulous that people knew something about his work.

The visits of several humanistic psychologists to the Soviet Union in the late 1980s brought status and popularity to this field of study. It is certainly a much needed program since the people there have had no hotlines, no crisis intervention methods, and very little clinical training. In Communist days, people didn't have emotional problems —or so the government dictated.

After my father's death in 1987, Dr. Alexei Matyushkin invited me to continue with Carl's work in the USSR. I explained that I would want to teach my own work, which was quite different from my father's. I handed him literature to acquaint him with person-centered expressive arts therapy. After studying it, he sent me an enthusiastic invitation.

My two trips to the Soviet Union (in 1989 and 1991) left me a wiser human being. My efforts to understand something of the politics, the economics, and most of all the human condition of those who have experienced life under seventy years of a repressive, brutal system have touched me so deeply as to change my own outlook on life. When people ask me what I learned, I reply, "Courage and patience." Every time I walk into my huge neighborhood supermarket, filled to overflowing with produce, meats, and every imaginable food, I recall my visits to the state-owned markets in Moscow where people wait to get a few pounds of sausage and a slice of butter.

Indicative of the changing times, my first invitation in 1989 came from a powerful Soviet government body: the Academy of Pedagogical Sciences. The second trip was sponsored by two newly formed private nonprofit training institutes for psychotherapists: the Institute of Psychology and Psychotherapy in Moscow, and Garmonia ("Harmony") in Leningrad. During the year of writing this book, there have been dramatic changes: the Soviet Union has become the Commonwealth of Independent States; our Soviet colleagues are now called Russians; Leningrad has taken back its former name, St. Petersburg; and our Estonian colleagues have restored their national independence.

Both my trips included giving intensive training in person-centered expressive therapy for psychologists, educators, social workers, doctors, hotline workers, and researchers. In 1989 I invited colleagues Claire Fitzgerald and Fran Macy to work with me as a team. In 1991 Fran and I followed up this work. We offered expressive arts experiences for individuals and groups to enhance self-awareness, nonverbal communication skills, and higher states of consciousness. These experiences were integrated with clinical training in person-centered counseling.

Involving themselves in the Creative Connection process, the Russians eagerly opened to their creative, intuitive natures, delving into emotional pain and trauma by drawing pictures, making collages, or expressing themselves through dance. By exploring their inner worlds in metaphor, movement, and images, as well as in words, they transformed much of that pain into life learnings, joy, laughter, and new visions for their personal futures. Following are some poignant examples of how people used this opportunity to transform and empower themselves, enabling them to take strong and positive action in their lives.

Estonia: "All We Have Been Told Is False!"

In Tartu, Estonia (then part of the USSR), group participants created collages to depict their feelings about their present life. I ask "Peter" to tell me about his collage—a combination of photos cut from magazines and newspapers and original personal art work. He replies:

> Here is a night owl looking hopefully into the future. It is the hopeful part of me. However, the owl is also a symbol of the devil in each of us. In the upper left corner is a picture of Lenin—I placed a black eye on him because there is a blackness we are seeing now. We are very tired of him and all that he has been. He is not all bad but now that we are receiving information from other countries, we are facing the fact that all we have been told is false! Over here I placed a cartoon of a man trying to catch a butterfly, but you see this big foot is tripping him up.

A long sigh emanates from his chest as he continues explaining the symbolism of his collage.

> Here is an empty head of a man, with a bottle pouring into it. This symbolizes the way people have accepted false information as it has been poured into us. It is a tremendous shock to realize that so much we have learned for so long is false!

I ask Peter if he is willing to rephrase his statements, putting them into the first person. This method gets people to own their art and their feelings about it. He said: "I am like an owl looking hopefully into the future. Like many others, I have been filled with misinformation. Also, even if I am only trying to catch a butterfly, someone may try to stop me."

I then direct his attention to three orange hands cut from colored paper and glued to the edge of his collage. "What meaning do these have for you?" I asked. His reply: "I wish to reach out beyond the frame of my world into transcendence. From beyond my own borders, I can gain perspective."

I am amazed to see how quickly Peter gained insight into this personal and political trauma. Using imagery is a quick road to stripping away denial. The unconscious brings forth hidden truths, allowing the images to speak to their creator.

It was not easy for Peter to face the shocking reality that he had been fed misinformation for his thirty-four years. He uncovered a sense of betrayal as he studied his collage. Having found a new truth, his next step would be to face the feelings he experienced.

Moscow: "A Window of Hope"

In Moscow, another moving episode occurred during a counseling demonstration. First, the group broke into pairs to spend ten minutes interviewing each other about "something that is exciting in your life, and something that is disturbing." Following these interviews, each person took art materials to draw two pictures depicting his or her feelings about these life situations. When they were finished, I asked

"Sasha" (Alex) Orlov, a forty-year-old psychologist, if he would be willing to talk with me about his pictures as part of a counseling demonstration for the group. He accepted with appreciation. As the the other workshop members sat in a circle surrounding our two chairs, I explained that the concentrated energy of the group, with its quiet and focused attention, magnifies the experience for both the counselor and the counselee.

Sasha brought his two pictures depicting "elements of my life that are exciting and those that are disturbing" (see color plate following page 216). First he described the bright side—a series of concentric circles in blazing yellow—as the part of himself that is radiant, pushing forth, sunny. Then he gazed at the other half of the picture: jagged rocks, black birds on the horizon, an ocean, and at the bottom of the ocean a large fish with open mouth and menacing teeth. He described the ocean as tumultuous and the fish as all-consuming; a danger that was always lurking, that could grab him any time. He spoke of his childhood pain, his ever-present fears, and the potential danger, as represented in this fish. His tone was genuine and thoughtful. A heaviness was in the air.

I responded with warmth and acceptance, questioning him only when I needed further verbal clarification of his images. Then he looked into my eyes and remained quietly fixed in that gaze for almost two minutes. I was a bit puzzled by the long silence and the continued gaze but was also aware that silence can be one of the most fruitful times for the client. Gradually I began to feel some discomfort and curiosity, so I said, "I think I could accept this continued eye contact more easily if I had some sense of what is happening to you."

Sasha replied slowly: "Looking into your eyes is like looking into a window of hope—a window into another world."

Following this demonstration counseling session, Sasha took the opportunity to comment on the process as he had experienced it. "At first, I didn't want to go into my feelings about the ocean and the rocks and fish. But as I explored it, they didn't seem so awful after all. But the most important quality of this session was you allowing me to see a different world by entering your eyes."

During that workshop I had heard many personal stories about life in the Soviet Union under Stalin. Also, all of my senses had been soaking up the different colors, smells, food, faces, and ambience in Moscow. I felt both the pathos and the richness in spirit and culture. While the group participants were making their final collage, I moved to the oil pastels to put down my impressions of Russia spontaneously. After starting with the beautiful domes in Zagorsk, I then quickly drew

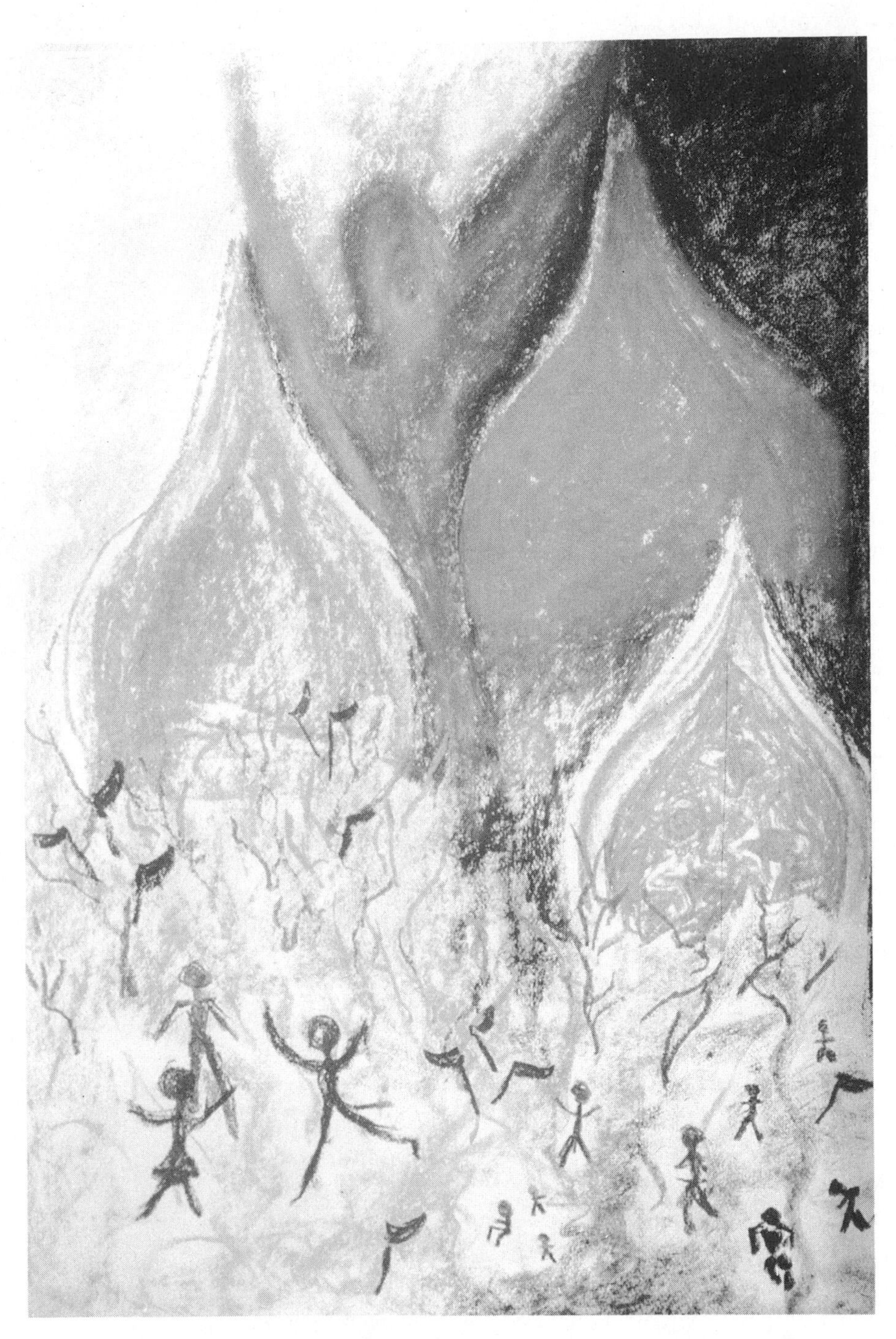

Moscow: My impression—beautiful Zagorsk domes dancing friends with a black angel hovering over.—N. R.

Estonian Collage: "All we have been told is false." An Estonian depicts the bleak past with hopeful hands reaching out "beyond the frame of my world into transcendence."

Alex and other Soviet psychologists and educators using expressive art for self-exploration.

My bright side is "radiant, sunny, pushing forth. The other side—a problem in my life—feels like a danger always lurking."
—Alex "Sasha" Orlov

Building cross-cultural understanding (Moscow).—N. R.

some stick figures dancing in the streets, as symbols of our group spirit. As I colored in the sky behind the domes, a dark figure seemed to appear. I looked at it and—as these things happen—realized it wanted to emerge. When finished with my impressionistic art, I shared it with the group. Some members were very concerned that the "black angel" was a foreboding of the future. They were curious about my own interpretation. I replied, "When I saw the figure emerging in the picture, I immediately thought of the black history you have experienced under Stalin. But now that you describe it as a 'black angel'—which really intrigues me—I am wondering if it is a protector of the future? Or something ominous? I really don't know."

Gleanings

The example of Sasha points up several aspects of person-centered expressive therapy as a means to creating an environment for peace.

When he depicted the awful fear he had been carrying since childhood, its overwhelming aspect began to disappear. Fear is paralyzing. It inhibits us from taking action. Certainly the Russians have been living in fear. Fear has been the appropriate response for survival. Imaging the fearful aspects and being able to share that dread with others begins the process of putting fear into a new perspective. Now that the totalitarian regime has fallen, there is less to fear. Old behaviors and attitudes are difficult to change, however. Here, Sasha could actually see and experience a shift in perspective.

Another very important aspect of the expressive arts is that they offer an avenue to express hope and delight. In this accepting atmosphere, Sasha was able to see, through my eyes, a world of hope. In one sense, he was seeing deep into my soul, since I was feeling extremely moved by the courage of the Soviets as they shared their personal and political history with me. I did have a very positive sense that these stalwart individuals would be part of the solution in their own country.

Sasha used the bright colors to express his awakening sense of light. The image speaks back to him as a message and a reminder. Therapy that stays verbal does not offer as much opportunity to *experience* hope, joy, and vision. Imagery through movement and art evokes a sense of what is possible.

Returning to Moscow in 1991, I met with the participants of our 1989 group to inquire how they had been using their training. I was amazed. Vera and Vitalia had started a group of seventy-six people—families—who have met one Sunday a month for two years. Vera's comment: "The children's natural curiosity and playful creativity with the art materials lead the way for the parents and teenagers. The parents say it has totally changed their way of communicating with their children. I never would have had courage to offer this before our training."

Victoria is working with neurotic gifted children. "They had been very frustrated trying to fit into the narrow academic mold. The expressive art and writing really heal their neuroses, rather than using direct verbal communication."

Yuri, an author and academician, used the expressive arts with the Russian military. "They need to get to know their associates as *humans.* Maybe we'll revolutionize the military!" he said, laughingly.

It was inspiring to see how quickly these Russians had taken their learnings and applied them to their work situations. Being hungry for approaches that work, they adapted the expressive arts to meet the needs of the populations they were working with.

Summary

Building bridges across cultures is citizen diplomacy at its best. Using the expressive arts can help us discover that we are all humans with hopes and aspirations, with suffering, anger, and love, and that we each have our own uniqueness and worth.

This chapter gives you many specific examples of using the creative process to foster international understanding. The following chapter puts forth the theory that developing our personal creativity is essential to promote democracy and offer peaceful solutions in the world.

NOTES

1 See also "A Traveler's Notes," *The Association of Humanistic Psychology Newsletter* (April 1979).

2 Much of this report on the Soviet Union is from Natalie Rogers et al., "Fostering Creative Expression in the Soviet Union," *New Realities* (March/April 1990).

II

WE ARE THE CURATORS OF LIFE ON EARTH
WE HOLD IT IN THE PALM OF OUR HAND
Helen Caldicott

Creativity and Consciousness for the Future

Creativity is like freedom: once you taste it, you cannot live without it. It is a transformative force, enhancing self-esteem and self-empowerment.

—Natalie Rogers

Earlier parts of this book speak of awakening our creativity through the expressive arts to find inner truth, personal integration, higher consciousness, spirituality, and connectedness to a universal energy source. The previous chapter also emphasized the creative process and the expressive arts as a bridge for cross-cultural understanding. This chapter pulls together my thoughts, feelings, and experiences about creativity as a path to a humanitarian, peaceful world. I believe that those of us who are midwives to the creative process play a crucial role in today's troubled world.

Where are we now? What can we envision? How can creativity and the expressive arts further our journey on this path? How can I be part of the solution? These are challenging questions.

Many outstanding individuals have documented that we are in a time of global crises. We have the ability to eradicate ourselves and all life forms through nuclear radiation, by allowing holes to develop in the ozone layer, by using toxic substances that enter the food chain, and through our own violent methods of trying to solve problems. The vast amounts of information about how we are destroying ourselves can be overwhelming. I am also exhausted and frightened by the rapidly escalating violence perpetrated by all elements of our society:

adolescents, children, the rich, the impoverished, the elderly, the powerful, and the oppressed. All of this must change. Indeed, there are many forces moving to create change.

Envisioning the Future

What can we envision? Perhaps this is the most crucial question of our time. Without engaging in the process of envisioning the possible, we are stumbling blindly on any path we create.

Imagine a rushing river leading to a large, clear, deep, calm, blue lake. The lake is our goal. It is where inner peace and outer peace become one. The devastating storms have ceased, although at times the wind whips up whitecaps. When calm occurs, the clouds, trees, and animals are reflected on the lake's mirrorlike surface. We can play in and drink the water. We can swim on the surface or dive deep.

As a world community, we will hold hands around this lake, seeing the reflections of old and young, of many tribes and clans, with various shades of color. We will dance, sing, paint, and drum. We will settle our disputes through listening, compassion, negotiation, and compromise. When our neighbor is hungry, we will say, "Here, please have some of mine. I have more than I need."

Personally, I long for such a world, in which cooperation and collaboration are the accepted values. I envision a world in which colleagues and nations help each other rather than trying to be "one up." The purpose of having power would be to share it rather than use it to dominate and control others. I envision a world in which women and minorities truly have equal opportunity and where materialism and greed are replaced by a larger vision—one in which self-fulfillment is accomplished by being a creative, caring person rather than accumulating things. I envision a world in which men are allowed to experience their sensitive, sensual, intuitive aspects and women are appreciated as they offer their ideas and empower themselves. And I envision a world where the animals, plants, and humans are toxin-free and can breathe deeply, knowing they have clean, fresh air. I envision a world without repression, hunger, or fear, and therefore without any need to be violent. We can use our creativity and technology to see to it that basic needs are met and that individuals are respected for their differences.

"Dream on!" you may say. Yes, I will dream on. We have proven we can do whatever it is we envision, whether it is sending people to the moon or splitting the atom. If we collaborate to dream, envision, discuss our needs, and share our feelings, our intuitions, and our expertise, we can manifest that dream. If we have some notion of where it is we want to go, we can create the necessary steps along the way.

If we are envisioning a better world, how do we get there? What does the riverway look like? How can creativity and the expressive arts play a role in evolving that world? To get to the calm lake, we must involve ourselves in a process that is ever flowing, ever changing. The riverway will have twists and turns, white waters and rapids, storms and sunshine.

As we board our river-raft to begin our journey, we have a general sense of what this trip will involve. It involves shedding our denial to become acutely aware. It involves acknowledging and integrating polarities to transcend duality, and becoming peaceful within in order to become whole people with self-esteem and self-empowerment. This journey will engage us in becoming creative people able to be responsive and responsible. We know that as we steer through the whitewater, we need to hold the ultimate vision—the expansive clear lake—in our hearts and minds.

The Signposts

As we push off, we can read specific signposts that point the way. At the entrance, the signpost says:

> To effect change takes the efforts of highly conscious, integrated, creative people who are responsive and willing to act on their beliefs.

As I look at the map of the riverway, these are some other markers I see that point the way.

- Trust in the human potential.
- Awareness must replace denial.
- Creativity awakens energy.
- Awareness results in global consciousness.
- Integrating polarities brings wholeness.
- Embody peace.
- Self-empowerment prepares us for action.
- Creativity overrides conformity.
- Seek resolution.

- Practice creative response.
- Creative vision is the guiding star.

As we allow the current to carry us on this river, we can explore the meaning of each of these signposts. Let me expand on the first statement, "To effect change takes the efforts of highly conscious, integrated, creative people who are responsive and willing to act on their beliefs." The philosophy, values, and process of person-centered expressive therapy are one avenue for fostering the development of such individuals. Committed citizens need skills in listening to others, in empathizing and being compassionate, while holding a hopeful vision. The expressive arts and the person-centered approach have true relevance in helping people come into such fullness.

We know from past experience that when a critical number of people change their perspective on world events, speak out, and take action, it can change the course of history. Such was the case in the anti–Vietnam War movement. This book demonstrates that self-awareness, self-empowerment, and action go hand in hand. The pages that follow summarize and give further examples of how going inward to what is deeply personal results in feeling connected to the universal. And when we feel connected to people on the other side of the globe, as well as to the plants and animals, we gradually change how we live to reflect that consciousness.

Although much of this chapter links the person-centered philosophy and creativity with social action—such as writing your congresspeople, or speaking out publicly for environmental and political causes—the most important change any of us can make is in our own perspective, in our own lifestyle, and in how we relate to our friends, family members, and employers. Adopting a person-centered approach to life changes how you listen to and speak with your children, your students, your partner or lover, your doctor or patient. When people feel respected and understood, they are more likely to create that safe space for others. The process can seep into all aspects of life, thus changing the personal and social environment in which we live. Add the Creative Connection process to any of those relationships and the depth of understanding and meaning increases.

Trust in the Human Potential

At the first turn in the riverway we pass the marker, "Trust in the human potential." Trusting in the human capacity for and drive toward its full potential is a simple statement, yet it represents the basic difference between those who believe in equality and shared power as a way of life and those who believe they must dominate and have power and control over people. It does not uphold the naive view that there is no evil in the world. It does mean that if given the proper environment for growth, each person seeks to find her fullest self. "The actualizing tendency can be thwarted or warped but it cannot be destroyed without destroying the organism."[1]

Trusting in the human capacity for self-actualization also means that we value the individual's personal exploration of her inner world. It means respecting efforts for personal growth, self-understanding, and insight. Some critics of the human potential movement have labeled individual efforts of self-awareness and self-understanding as narcissistic. Although it may be true that some individuals never go beyond self-investigation, those facilitators (teachers, therapists, parents, etc.) who continually emphasize a broader consciousness create the environment for global awareness. The image that comes to mind is one of concentric circles; the self being the core, with each surrounding circle embracing other people, other cultures, and the environment. It is essential, however, that individuals know and value themselves in order to actively empower themselves in the world. As Theodore Roszak, author of *Person/Planet,* says,

> There is political relevance to experiences of self-discovery that have carried people toward private and inward explorations in the quiet interstices of the world. Unlike many impatient critics and heavy radicals, I would not be quick to condemn these seemingly apolitical interludes as narcissistic or escapist. *I recognize their necessity as the seed time of a new culture.*[Emphasis added.][2]

Trusting that people will do their best if given the proper environment is not easy in a chaotic world. We tend to loose faith and discard the evidence that people who are loved, cared for, understood, and appreciated will choose to behave in socially acceptable ways. It may be important to limit unacceptable behavior until the individual is capable of self-regulation, but the desire to be one's fullest self is a very powerful inner force. This concept has enormous ramifications for childrearing, for teaching, for psychotherapists, for health providers, and even for business executives and administrators. The practice of this concept begins at home, at school, and in the workplace. If we approach people (including children) knowing that if they feel safe, cared for, and understood, they will strive to be their best selves, we will be doing a lot to improve the quality of life in this world.

Awareness Must Replace Denial

As we travel toward our destination, the next step is to become personally aware. You can make appropriate choices only if you are aware: aware of your feelings about your relationships, aware of feelings about events in the world, and aware of the deep pain and suffering happening globally. It is also important to be aware of each individual's ability to be courageous and loving. The expressive arts are powerful instruments for surfacing your feelings, thoughts, and perceptions of the world as you live in it. Letting the unconscious speak to you through your body, your images, and your sounds helps you become aware.

Denial is our biggest personal and global enemy. Awareness is its antithesis. To deny our grief and suffering over a personal tragedy or over the needless human tragedies of starvation, pollution, and war puts a lid on all of our feelings. This leads us to lethargy, depression, and apathy. To become aware, on the other hand, leads us into the fiery waters of emotions that need to be appropriately channeled into creative energy.

It is not surprising that so much denial exists in the world. With communication technology bringing us news of disasters around the globe, we are bombarded with massive amounts of anguish. Denial keeps us from being overcome by despair. Yet wearing a plate of armor tends to make us into technological robots, capable of producing quantities of goods but incapable of compassion and creative solutions.

It is important that we find emotionally safe ways to experience both sides of the coin: the massive suffering and the altruistic impulse in each of us. Much of the violence in our cities is due to our unwillingness to look at and take responsibility for its root causes: poverty, homelessness, unemployment, discrimination, poor education—all of which breed anger, fear, and insecurity. Our denial results in an explosion of hideous crimes, glorified by the media. Our national denial of root causes has us putting BandAids on the symptoms rather than addressing the needs of the people who act out the crimes.

We are also denying the humanitarian impulse within each individual. When a crisis occurs—a flood or earthquake, an abandoned child or maimed individual—people have the opportunity to respond by giving. And they feel rewarded as they provide for others. Yet our leaders seldom call on us to give of ourselves as a nation, for the highest good of all people. This denial by political leaders of the natural, generous response to human suffering leaves us operating on the lowest common human denominator. Throughout this book I have emphasized expressive arts as a path to self-awareness, showing that as we become deeply aware of self, we discover others. Being aware of your capacity to be compassionate and loving can lead you to a path of creative, cooperative endeavor with others.

It is also necessary to become conscious of what is happening in the world: with your neighbors, your community, the world community, the air you breathe, the water you drink, and the plants and animals that are intricate parts of the ecosystem. Ultimately this leads to expanding your consciousness to include *all.* As you educate yourself, you can use the arts to express how you feel about the knowledge you have acquired. By expressing your concern, your confusion, your sense of impotence or despair, you will discover a personal center: the core that is part of every living organism, the core that says, "I want to be my full potential, my empowered self!" When you are upset about the pollution in your local river, try drawing how you feel. Or do some free writing to explore your thoughts and outrage. When funding gets cut for your child's school, write, dance, and paint how you feel. You may be surprised at the outcome. It will help clarify your thoughts and feelings, and help you gain perspective. You may find yourself writing a letter to the editor or speaking up at the School Board meeting.

In the "Artist as Activist" section later in this chapter, I cite Connie Smith Siegel's awakening to the horrendous destructive power of nuclear radiation and her resulting use of art to speak out. The arts are powerful tools to help us shed our denial and bring forth new awareness. We can then manifest images of new societal forms.

Creativity Awakens Energy

Creativity is our vital life-force energy. Having some energy aids us in being creative. But it is not a prerequisite. If we allow ourselves to enter into the creative process even if we feel tired, bored, or stuck, that creative process opens the energy flow in our body/mind/spirit.

As we allow ourselves to dance, paint, sing, write, and improvise without concern for the product, we stimulate our childlike energy. We have vast resources of personal energy that we hold in tightly, fearing disapproval and judgment. Creativity is a dynamic energy source that anyone can tap at any time.

One form of energy that frequently gets blocked is anger-energy. As discussed in chapter 8, anger is an energy that we can channel constructively. If we are aware of our anger (rather than denying it), we can use it as a fuel to propel us up out of our chairs to do something constructive. Feeling upset and angry that our forests are disappearing through overcutting and neglect can be the fuel that gets us to take action, for example. Being aware of our feelings of despair that nuclear waste is radiating us into disease is a first step to becoming concerned or angry, which then propels us to do something about it. Being enraged that women are being harassed and raped can lead to constructive activism. Feeling incensed that minorities are blocked and frustrated at every turn helps us find ways to right those injustices.

I was teaching a multi-ethnic class the week after the Rodney King verdict and the Los Angeles riots. I dropped my agenda in order to spend time using the Creative Connection process. First I suggested we walk slowly in the room, paying attention to how we were feeling about any events of the week. (I did not mention the riots.) "Notice any messages your body may be giving you as you move. Experiment with some movement with your eyes closed to be in touch with any feelings." After five minutes of such movement, I suggested people put those feelings on paper using their nondominant hand. When we were finished with the art (after about fifteen minutes), I asked them to write a few words on the art. Finally we shared what we had experienced. It was an incredible afternoon as we listened to each other's anger, pain, sense of injustice, fears, and hopes. I will never forget one black woman expressing her feelings about the repeated injustices to her people: "Not again! Not again! No! No! Not again!" she moaned, reading the words on her art. As we listened, empathized, and understood some of our own racism, we learned at a very deep level. It was the kind of learning that is never forgotten.

Keeping a lid on all of our rage and pain would have invited blowing the fuse. Since we had built trust and a safe environment, we each began to shed our denial as we started to move. (I was particularly aware of my own denial during the week as I watched the horror of the riots and was aware that I had blocked my feelings.) By using art, movement, sound, and imagery, we vented our feelings and discussed ways we could personally make a difference. In one sense, we were already making a difference since the cross-ethnic understanding and caring grew within our own class.

I appreciate the way the Vietnamese Zen master Thich Nhat Hanh talks about anger:

> If I have a feeling of anger, how would I meditate on that? How would I deal with it, as a Buddhist, or as an intelligent person? I would not look upon anger as something foreign to me that I have to fight, to have surgery in order to remove it. I know that anger is me, and I am anger. Nonduality, not two. I have to deal with my anger

> with care, with love, with tenderness, with nonviolence. Because anger is me, I have to tend my anger as I would tend a younger brother or sister, with love, with care, because I myself am anger, I am in it, I am it. In Buddhism we do not consider anger, hatred, greed as enemies we have to fight, to destroy, to annihilate. If we annihilate anger, we annihilate ourselves. Dealing with anger in that way would be like transforming yourself into a battlefield, tearing yourself into parts. . . . If you struggle in that way, you do violence to yourself. If you cannot be compassionate to yourself, you will not be able to be compassionate to others. When we get angry, we have to produce awareness: "I am angry. Anger is in me. I am anger." That is the first thing to do.
>
> In the case of a minor irritation, the recognition of the presence of the irritation, along with a smile and a few breaths, will usually be enough to transform the irritation into something more positive, like forgiveness, understanding, and love. Irritation is a destructive energy. We cannot destroy the energy; we can only convert it into a more constructive energy. Forgiveness is a constructive energy. . . . *we have to convert anger into some kind of energy that is more constructive, because anger is you.* [Emphasis added.][3]

Thich Nhat Hanh is talking about meditation to relieve minor irritations. In the case of *major* irritations and dissatisfactions, we can use the arts to find self-insight and a powerful voice. Since anger is the fuel for violence, it is imperative that we find ways to hear it, understand its causes, and address underlying issues. The arts are also media through which our rage can be released and used to send a potent message.

Through creativity we also tap our lively, wondrous, and ecstatic energy. Using expressive arts to share those feelings brings pleasure and joy to others. Try some free writing after a hike in the woods. Create some art when you are feeling deeply in love. Art need not be professional to bring enjoyment to yourself and others. Rather than sitting in your chair, try using movement when you listen to music that you truly enjoy. You will find your vitality increasing as you enter into the mystery of the creative process.

Integrating Polarities Brings Wholeness

Although each of us struggles with integrating and transcending various personal polarities (see chapter 8), it is the masculine/feminine polarity that divides the world at this time. By this I do not mean men versus women, although that is part of the split. It is the masculine within women and the feminine within men that we must accept, integrate, and transcend.

> One of the most important and general polarities in the three kingdoms of organic life (vegetable, animal and human) is the sexual . . . the masculine element being the dynamic, initiating pole, while the feminine element is the receptive, "gestative," elaborative pole. This type of polarity extends far beyond the man-woman relationship to innumerable manifestations in life. It has been particularly and deeply emphasized by the Chinese, who regard these two principles as the foundation both of cosmic evolution and of every aspect of human life. The creative aspect, symbolized by the father and Heaven, they call Yang, while Yin is the receptive and elaborative aspect, symbolized by the mother and the Earth.[4]

Women are discovering their self-worth, personal strength, and power. As they define new roles for themselves, at home and in society, they exert their masculine or yang energy and bring it into balance with their feminine. As men discover their intuitive, nurturing feelings and their ability to cooperate rather than compete, they will accept their feminine energy and likewise come into balance. As each of us finds *internal* balance, we will become participants in co-creating peaceful solutions.

Individual and planetary well-being depend on the harmonious interaction of yin and yang—of receptive and assertive. Our culture has overemphasized the yang: the assertive, productive, logical, linear, competitive masculine energy. To bring ourselves and our world into balance, we must allow the feminine its proper place. It is time to bring forth the intuitive, receptive, cooperative, and visionary mode to correct the imbalance we have created. We need to integrate the yin and yang within each of us.

One student put it this way:

> My sad feelings are very much a part of me. I love those feelings. They are connected to my deepest feelings of love. . . . I am learning to embrace and cherish those feelings rather than to fear them. I did a sculpture of me in that grounded, sad, prayerful position, and when I look at my sculpture I feel my pain, but I feel protected and supported. This experience internalized for me a bondedness to the earth. It is a peaceful, safe feeling . . . I was able to experience myself as all that I am.
>
> *Creativity is a means by which we can come to the place of peace within ourselves.* It is what we are all looking for, the thing needed to bridge the gap between left and right, East and West, and . . . to stay informed about the whole, the bigger meaning of life which is togetherness, coming together, unity. [Emphasis added.][5]

The expressive arts are particularly suited to bring forth imagery, movement, sound, and writing that heighten our awareness of our polarities and to transcend them. By their natures, the creative arts help people approach their feelings and thoughts at a symbolic and metaphoric level. This level, in turn, makes it easier to integrate and transcend our dualistic patterns.

Awareness Results in Global Consciousness

As we change our consciousness, so will we change the world. Fully engaging in the creative process of self-expression awakens spontaneity and gives us fresh perspective on personal problems and world issues. Your initial awakenings may take place in your body: you may begin to notice when driving your car that you tend to hold your breath or grip the steering wheel tightly, for instance. You may begin to discover that your range of emotions is widening. Scenes that previously never touched your heart may now give you emotional nourishment. Perhaps you become aware of your feelings when someone is subtly putting you down. These personal awakenings to awareness are, amazingly, the prerequisites to global consciousness. Like concentric circles, the awareness eventually expands to include all living creatures. These personal awakenings are the data from which we make choices. I may know the statistics about women being sexually harassed in the workplace, but until I acknowledge my feelings about those incidents, I will most likely ignore them. Our emotions often become motivators for action.

To act constructively in the world, we need to broaden our consciousness to encompass the sufferings and joys of humankind and to find our connection to nature. The Creative Connection process fosters a consciousness that we are all connected, that we are all One. This broadening of consciousness happens as we become deeply aware of our inner essence. Finding our inner core brings us to a transpersonal state of awareness: an understanding of the interconnection and interdependence of all life forms.

At times, this seems like an overwhelming stretch of the heart and mind. I ask myself, "How can I possibly feel connected to or care about people very different from me, some of them in lands with strange cultures and beliefs?" Then, when an earthquake tumbles part of Mexico City, I feel close to those people. Or when a threatening world event occurs, such as the Persian Gulf War, and my *whole body* responds to the suffering of the innocent citizens we have bombed, I know I am connected to others. At that moment, there is no stopping the pain. It comes flooding in.

It bewildered me to experience the Persian Gulf War as though my own family were being maimed. While many Americans were cheering as the bombs dropped, I experienced tremendous guilt. While people were out celebrating a "victory," I was wracked with pain that we had killed 150,000 people, many of them women and children. I wondered, "How is it that I cannot hold up any personal wall against the suffering of people thousands of miles away?" But I also realized that the capacity to suffer with innocent victims brings with it the capacity to fully enjoy the celebration when the Berlin Wall came crumbling down, or to feel exhilaration when courageous Russians stood steadfastly in front of their "White House" to stave off a military coup, or when U.S. citizens demonstrated in front of our White House decrying conditions in Central America. An expanded consciousness allows for a life rich in emotional experience, which fuels responsible activism. (Later in this chapter, I describe this personal awakening more fully—how body consciousness brought me, via poetry, to political action.)

Embody Peace

Being silent and meditating are ways to return to the self, to listen to inner messages and receive guidance from your higher self. It is important to return to the self, not as an escape, but as a centering that allows you to be thoughtfully proactive in society.

My colleague Ben Hedges wrote:

> Words such as "explore, discover, journey, search" are common in accounts of creative processes. This process oriented way can be extremely tiring if there aren't rests, pauses, silences and moments to simply appreciate. Continually having to know, heal, work toward peace can be consuming and deadening in its goal orientation. Joy, play, silliness, spontaneity, are critical to the human spirit and heartbeat. They are also a foundation block of the creative process and all human endeavors. *One of the most profound ways of working towards peace is to embody and be peace.* [Emphasis added.][6]

I agree. Embodying peace manifests wholeness and empowerment. In our clock-oriented, production-minded culture, it is becoming more and more necessary to balance our lives with time to be quiet, receptive, and open to higher states of consciousness. Let us go back to our original image of our destination: the expansive, deep, clear blue lake. Imagine yourself as that lake with waves rising and falling, whipped by a storm. Then let the waves settle as on a calm, quiet day. Let yourself become still waters, peaceful, reflective. Take the time.

As facilitators, we also embody peace by being able to listen empathically to each side of a dispute, helping people to understand each other. The person-centered approach lends itself to mediation and solving disputes peacefully. A facilitator who listens to disputing parties with empathy and uses methods of clarification in response to each person creates a climate for them to hear each other at a profound level of understanding. It seems like an incredibly simple truth that when one person is heard at a deep level in the presence of another person, those two people are better able to hear each other. We know this from couples therapy, family therapy, and team development processes. In building a climate of trust, the facilitator helps the people who disagree to sift through the periphery discussion and arguments to get to the kernel of dispute, which often has many emotional as well as logical components. The emotional elements are just as important as the logical ones and need to be verbalized, listened to, clarified, accepted, and understood. When mutual understanding is achieved, the door opens to creative problem solving.

This process can be enhanced using visual arts for imagery and metaphor. Members in a dispute frequently lack the ability to identify and express their feelings regarding their differences. By using color and symbols, they can identify their feelings and any unconscious interpersonal dynamics. As they begin to recognize their feeling states, they can communicate them more accurately.

My father, in his later years, was particularly interested in experimenting with and applying the person-centered approach to international disputes. In a peace project designed by The Center for the Study of the Person and cosponsored by the University for Peace in Costa Rica and the United Nations, he and a staff met with fifty participants, many being high-level government officials from Central America and seventeen other countries. In the climate created through person-centered facilitation in the plenary session and in subgroups, the officials gradually became more trusting, more personal, and more open to hearing opponents' views. This resulted in their thinking through some possible creative solutions.[7]

I bring this project to your attention because my book strongly states that the foundation for trust is the climate or environment created by the person-centered philosophy. The expressive arts can become a powerful vehicle for growth within this environment. As we discuss the expressive arts process to be used as we work for peace, it is important to preserve this context.

Self-Empowerment Prepares Us for Action

As we travel on the flowing river of creative process, we are learning awareness, becoming expanded in our consciousness, integrating inner polarities, and practicing inner peace. We are becoming more whole, with new self-esteem. Valuing ourselves—not in an egotistical way but with genuine appreciation of our unique qualities—leads us to self-empowerment. Self-empowerment, in turn, translates into personal and social action.

Preceding chapters include many examples of the development of self-esteem and self-empowerment through the expressive arts. Often words are not enough in this self-exploration. Using all of our senses brings new awareness and confidence. Frequently, in a movement exercise, I ask people to walk "*as if* you feel self-confident and empowered." Amazing differences in posture, stride, and the sense of "presence" are evoked in such a way. Once people experience self-esteem kinesthetically, they begin to have a sense of what it will take to actually have more self-esteem. Esteem grows in mini-steps. It takes time and practice to value yourself. You may find your self-esteem developing quickly, but more likely you will learn to appreciate yourself more each year.

Self-esteem, self-empowerment, and action are all part of the same process. As we develop a sense of our worth, we feel stronger. As we take steps to improve our lives or the lives of others, we gain self-esteem. Such is the cycle to full maturity.

Creativity Overrides Conformity

As our river flows on, we come to a big fork and must choose our course. One fork leads us to conformity; the other to freedom of self-expression. The fork that leads to conformity is that ultimately chosen by those citizens who prefer to be ruled by (and political leaders who prefer to lead in) a totalitarian regime. Clark Moustakas points out:

> When the individual is conforming, following, imitating, being like others, he moves increasingly in the direction of self-alienation. Such a person fears issues and controversies. he fears standing out or being different. He does not think through his experience to find value or meaning, does not permit himself to follow his own perceptions to some natural conclusion. He avoids directly facing disputes and becomes anxious in situations which require self-awareness and self-discovery. . . .
>
> Cut off from his own real wishes and capacities, the individual experiences no fulfillment and no sense of authentic relatedness. . . .
>
> The conforming person does not use his own resources, his own experiences, but takes his direction from experts, authority figures,

> and traditional guides. Somewhere along the way he has given up his actual identity and submerged himself into acceptable group modes.[8]

This is precisely the reason we need to foster creativity in our society: to support individuals to become independent thinkers and doers. Such people use their own intellectual discriminating powers as to the appropriateness, the morality, and the ethics of any given situation. When people do not use their individual creativity and ability to discriminate, they become vulnerable to extremist leaders, which can result in such tragedies as the Jonestown mass suicide.

Some conformity is necessary, of course. When we abide by the law, we are, in a sense, conforming. We are consciously deciding that it is in our and society's best interest to obey the law. Such a decision is quite different from those who blindly follow a leader because they have lost the courage of their convictions or have lost their identity. The creative person stays open to options, is flexible, and values individual differences. The conformist is closed, rigid in her thinking, and follows the leader without using her self-knowledge or ability to discriminate. To maintain a democracy, we must be able to play with ideas, to look at options and alternatives.

Since creativity and self-expression bring forth independent thinking, spontaneity, self-esteem, and self-empowerment and also invoke our higher powers, they should be part of our regular educational diet. I was fortunate to have grown up in an educational system where creativity, whether it was in the art room or the social studies class, was encouraged and valued. Most schools stifle creativity. In the long run, this is devastating to our democratic system.

Creativity is threatening to those who demand conformity. Dictators squelch self-expression and the creative process. They do not want their citizens to think for themselves or to be spontaneous, imaginative, or self-determined. Dictators want conformity: unquestioning obedience. The creative process does not fit into any dogma. As we have seen, the creative process involves intuition, mystery, delving into the unknown; messing around with ideas, shapes, and colors; being willing to play and experiment. And part of the process is to allow feelings to be expressed through all media: the written word, speech, color, line, form, drama, music. Through this whole process, we find our individuality, self-esteem, and ability to act consciously.

Our democracy and our economic system seem to be fostering greed and violence these days. Although I feel fortunate in our relative freedom, when I contrast our system to oppressive regimes, I also realize we must use our creativity and heightened consciousness to avoid becoming an oppressive dictatorship ourselves. Tyrannical leaders create massive fear, which forces people to inhibit their creativity. That system also requires a type of personal inauthenticity to survive, in which each individual must put on a completely false face in public. What does it do to the soul to live a lie all day at work? Or to say what you really believe only within the confines of your own kitchen, worrying that the kitchen may be bugged? Having visited and talked in depth with people in such systems, I know they have had to lead two lives: a public life and a private one. It tears apart the human spirit.

It is not surprising, then, that people greet person-centered expressive arts with enthusiasm. Having an opportunity to rediscover their thoughts and feelings, and to permit themselves to share openly what is *inside*, allows them to experience personal congruence. What they experience inwardly is what is seen outwardly. This brings tremendous relief and a delight in reexperiencing authenticity. Once this authenticity is lived, it can be stifled only at gunpoint.

The issue of creativity and conformity was brought home to me when I was in Moscow in 1989. Hearing that Kandinsky was one of my favorite artists, some Soviets took me to a newly opened retrospective of his works. Kandinsky's art had been hidden in the basement of the museum for over thirty years! After two hours of viewing hundreds of his lavishly colored paintings, I came away feeling exhilarated, powerful, and high. I walked out into the Moscow avenue feeling I had the courage to be fully myself. I remarked to my Soviet colleagues, "I am not surprised that Stalin put these paintings under lock and key. They exemplify freedom of expression, creativity, and individuality!"

Seek Resolution

Creative people seek resolution. Riding along the river of creativity, you may look to the riverbanks to find individuals who model the kind of activism you seek. This activism can be as simple as respecting the different culture of your neighbor or giving your youngster the opportunity to scribble freely (without your judgment). It can be bringing some movement, art, sound, and free writing into your classroom or boardroom.

The following pages bring you two examples of letting the art be the message bearer. The first is from an artist who empowered herself. The second is a personal example, an experience from which I am still learning and which still mystifies me.

The Artist as Activist

My artist friend Connie Smith Siegel, longtime teacher and painter, has written an article in which she eloquently expresses many feelings that I hold dear. She describes her awakening to the nuclear madness that surrounds us—to the real possibility of human extinction.

> Feeling the wrongness of the world . . . work in the studio became impossible. I began to be inundated with ideas and schemes in which art could be used in speaking out, both in my work, and with other artists. These ideas spun out with vigor and intensity, and it was finally in acting on some of them that the sense of living in a nightmare diminished.[9]

Having previously painted and exhibited magnificent landscapes, Connie then created huge banners combining those landscapes with bold words of the noted physician Helen Caldicott. These words frame two of the large paintings: "Each of us must accept total responsibility for the earth's survival," and "We are the curators of life on earth. We hold it in the palm of our hand." Having used her art as a potent vehicle for communication, Connie took a stand. She says:

> There is a tremendous need for the arts in communicating emotional responses to the nuclear dilemma, and every style of art can become relevant. . . . I feel the process of making art is in itself a potent political activity. Of all the professions, the arts are the most vulnerable as they seem to have no practical function other than the expression of human uniqueness. And yet it is in this very function that the arts might be supremely practical, and most desperately needed at this time—to remind us we are living creatures, and that life is a miracle when really experienced. . . . Because the "art" of eliminating life has become so stunningly effective and prolific, our survival may depend upon embracing those activities which create life, on the utilization of the transformative process inherent in creative expression in all parts of living, in every vocation.
>
> Not only do the arts provide a vehicle for validating human uniqueness and affirming life, but they offer an important opportunity for expressing and transforming a whole range of human feeling, including anger and aggression. When grounded in color, movement or drama, even the most powerful rage can open into a larger, more

> elemental world: a greater reality which includes these feelings, but can transcend them. When anger is expressed in color, for example, red and black, it is possible to see it as a basic elemental force, such as fire, and to become energized by its power, rather than destroyed by it. All the arts offer this possibility.[10]

I particularly like the strength with which Connie discusses the channeling of anger and aggression into constructive art:

> The possibility of transformation, or sublimation of human energy through expression in the arts, is one of our most amazing human resources, and could have a far greater impact on problems such as sickness, crime and war than is commonly supposed. If the powers of sublimation were better known and utilized it would put most hospitals, law courts, prisons and armed forces out of business.
>
> In the dictionary sublimation is defined as "directing the energy (of an impulse) from its primitive aim to one that is aesthetically or culturally 'higher.'" I have experienced this qualitative change in myself and witness it in hundreds of students; whatever impulse might lead a person to creative expression—frustration, joy, or just curiosity, when translated into color, line, sound or movement, a shift of consciousness occurs. . . .

Connie concludes her article with:

> The rationale for creating nuclear weapons is based on a fear of this dynamic force, a belief that human nature is basically destructive, and must constantly be held in check. It is a thoroughly pessimistic viewpoint, but has a persuasive logic in the face of human atrocities already committed. Artists, along with therapists and healers of all kinds can supply important evidence of another rationale: that human nature is not destructive, but loving. At the base of human behavior is an urge toward life, and it is only in reclaiming and expressing this creative energy that healing can happen.[11]

The power of expression is not limited to professional artists. I have observed that expressive art that comes forth authentically from any gut-level, raw experience conveys a strong message. Exhibits created from this work have had a potent impact.

Poetry Speaks Out

In the foregoing example, Connie used her art as self-healing and as activism. She is but one of many artists, playwrights, film producers, and poets who use the power of imagery to change consciousness.

My experience of identifying with innocent victims on the other side of the world is an example of the potency of the connection

WE ARE THE CURATORS OF LIFE ON EARTH
WE HOLD IT IN THE PALM OF OUR HAND
Helen Caldicott

Artist as Activist: Connie Smith Siegel uses her art as a potent vehicle for communication.

Gut-level, raw experience conveys a strong message.—N. R.

between movement, poetry, and political action. I share it because the process by which the poetry evolved is a dramatic example of how messages come directly from the kinesthetic body uncorking the unconscious and letting creativity flow freely. The mystery as to how and why this happens fascinates me. I ask you to drop your judgment temporarily about whether our action in the Persian Gulf was right or wrong. I include this account so you can vicariously experience the universality of human connection.

In January 1991, as the advent of the Persian Gulf war was being spelled out on television and the front pages of the newspaper, my anxiety and anger mounted. At that time I was in a weekend program of "authentic movement" with Janet Adler in which we spent most of the day creating personal movement from the inner impulse of the body. There were empathic, caring witnesses sitting in a circle, holding the container, or consciousness, for the group. I joined a small group of individuals in the center of the room and moved with my eyes closed, letting the impulse from within guide my movements for more than an hour. Although I had no intention of opening myself to world events, my body felt like a sponge absorbing the buildup of tension that was the preparation for massive killings. The countdown for Desert Storm was like a countdown for my own inner time-bomb. Although my own life was unusually serene, my antennae to the world were bringing in messages of potential devastation.

After the movement experience, we had an opportunity to talk about it. Although I am usually very verbal about my experiences, this time I was so totally choked up about what had happened to me during that hour that I couldn't utter a word. It was too overwhelming.

That night, when I was unable to sleep, a poem poured out of me. I say "poured out" because that is exactly how it felt. I did not *think,* "What shall I write to release my feelings?" I sat in bed with my journal and the words came out exactly as you read them below. Poetry has never been a mode of expression for me. I have written perhaps three or four poems in my life. So, this event is one of the mysteries of the Creative Connection process.

Speaking the Unspeakable

I have a vision.
(I wish I didn't)
Blood soaked sand,
      bodies, flattened pancakes on the
            hot dry land.
Not a hundred, nor thousands
      but tens and tens of thousands,
            gone, forever.
(I just heard the Pentagon ordered
      sixty thousand body bags be made.
Singer sewing machines whirring at double speed.
      "Be prepared," they say.)
I see two massive lines, PEOPLE
      (not "troops" or "battalions")
Thousands of sons,
      daughters,
            fathers,
                  mothers,
                        lovers, and friends,
Creeping along the sifting sand, inching nearer and
      nearer to the Big Kill.

"Cut them off, and KILL," says General Powell with cool
calm addressing the world on public TV.
My vision SEES the kill—
like a madman stabbing a wounded dog who bites back
Again and again and again—neither side
willing to stop.
Then gas and germs, strewing folks like flies after
the flit gun sprays.
"Ghastly," we say. "This deserves more.
We must end it now! Flatten them all!"
"A nuke will finish it quick," they'll say.
The nukes finish it,
and the poison falls,
and spreads
Like thick oil on the Persian Sea.
Who needs sixty thousand body bags?
Why not bag it ALL?
Iraq, Iran, Saudi Arabia, Syria, Turkey, Jordan, Egypt, Kuwait,
Israel and a million Arab, English, French, Israeli and
American sons,
daughters,
fathers,
mothers,
lovers and friends.
Anyone got a Persian Gulf bag
big enough to hold it all?
Big enough to hold the precious sea, the desert blooms,
the ancient shrines,
and a million rotting souls?

****

Cry!
Shout!
Plea,
Beg,
Carry a banner,
Call,
Vote.
Does anyone HEAR?
Hey! You at the helm!
Can you *see* the BLACK HOLE?

I have a vision.
(I wish I didn't)

Writing this was like opening the steam vent on a pressure cooker. I wept as I wrote it, and I wept as I read it to my authentic movement group the next day. They were my support network and encouraged me to use the poem to take the next step: to send it to radio stations, to political leaders; to use it as a potent tool for antiwar action. My self-confidence as a poet was nil, so the validation by the group that the poem was worthy encouraged me to take the next step. After receiving that support, I went home and sent it to public radio. It was read several times, and I was called in to read it in person. I also mailed it to over thirty-five political leaders, asking them to take appropriate action.

My anguish had become an awareness through movement. That awareness translated itself into an art form that I could use as a political message. I felt a tremendous sense of relief as I took some action.

Whether or not you agree with my politics, I think you could agree that my transformation through the arts to action is a model for anyone. As you allow yourself to experiment and explore the creative process, you will also find moments of exquisite perception and understanding. Some of it will reflect the suffering in the world, some of it will reflect ecstasy. In either case, the potency of the message can be taken into the larger world.

I know I am not alone as a person who, at crucial moments in history, feels emotionally, kinesthetically, and spiritually connected to others. Many religions embrace the notion that we are all One. Yet opening to the actual experience of that kind of connectedness is rare. It can be cultivated by becoming *aware,* by tapping your *creative energy,* by finding your *personal core* or center, and by opening to the *universal energy force.* The sense of interconnectedness and compassion on the global level is the spirit that will eventually lead us to new methods of peacekeeping.

Practice Creative Response

To summarize: creative people are those who are able to respond; they seek resolution. We cannot wait for political leaders to show us the way. It takes creative populations that insist on negotiation and peaceful solutions to conflict, populations that insist on lifestyles that help sustain the planet. Creative people are the product of a safe and trusting environment where they feel free to be authentic: to be all of themselves, not just the facade or mask. *Creative response* refers to really hearing the needs of each party within a conflict without harsh judging. Creative response means staying open-minded, flexible, constructive, hopeful, and persistent in finding alternative solutions to our present crisis.

We need creative response to world events. Otherwise, violence and mass destruction are seen as a means to peace, and unlimited high technology is viewed as progress.

Although I am emphasizing using the person-centered approach to expressive arts as a form of social activism, I know that using these methods to foster awareness and changes in behavior in personal relationships is the hub from which all other changes are made. Finding new and creative ways to be open, honest, and communicative with your friend, partner, or child can have a ripple effect on many people.

Let's look at the profile of the conscious, creative person. This individual:

- has self-awareness and self-esteem
- is self-empowered, which means taking risks to think and act independently
- looks for new solutions to old problems, using intuition as well as logic, playing with ideas, being inventive, and thinking holistically
- can lead yet be cooperative
- listens to, understands, and empathizes with differences while maintaining her own value system
- facilitates communication between individuals of differing views by helping the parties involved hear each other at a deep emotional as well as intellectual level

As you look over this list, I hope you recognize yourself in many of these criteria. If certain qualities seem beyond your self-concept, look again. This book discusses the process of becoming aware, empowering ourselves, and transcending dualities as well as being facilitative listeners. You have undoubtedly recognized much of your creative self as you have been reading. The ability to be a conscious, creative person is available to each of us. We are all creative. We all have the ability to expand our awareness or consciousness. Our creativity has been layered over with years of cultural inhibition. Becoming our conscious, creative selves means taking the time to peel away those crusty layers to find our real selves and to open our hearts and minds to the world around us.

Creative Vision Is the Guiding Star

It is imperative that our relationships, our families, our educational systems, our corporations, and our political leaders stimulate, foster,

Touching the Heart of Life—Sadja Greenwood

and use the creative process to promote personal well-being and to bring about imaginative, enlightened collaboration for peaceful solutions to this troubled planet. The Creative Connection process—the person-centered philosophy and the expressive arts process—is one means of awakening creativity and allowing people to become authentic and empowered.

We can never expect that the peoples of the world will be of one mind—there will always be conflict and controversy—but we can expect people to respond creatively to find mutually beneficial solutions. If we are resolved, as a world community, to settle our disagreements peacefully, it can happen. We have all the technological resources and the brain power to solve our global crises. The clash seems to be between those who want to have control over others and those who want cooperation and collaboration. The hierarchical system has not worked. *For us to survive, our model must change from ladders and pyramids to circles.* We need a willingness and determination to look at the potential solutions creatively, cooperatively, and without greed. We might ask ourselves: "What would I be willing to give up if I were *guaranteed* that there would be no more war or hunger in the world?"

What *would* you relinquish to have peace and health for your children's children? I know I would not give up my freedom, my individuality, or my right to believe and say what I choose. I would definitely be willing to give up many material gains if I could be assured there would be no more needless starvation, destruction, or violence. What a magnificent world would evolve if we could actually love to our full potential! Imagine turning on the television news to see people cocreating affordable housing, or to view diplomats *listening* to each other across cultural and religious boundaries. Imagine watching real situations in which fear and greed are dispelled.

Imagine the excitement if we put as much creative energy, money, and determination into constructing a feasible future as we did in creating a Gulf War. We are capable of mustering incredible amounts of goods and technology to meet a targeted goal. All we need is to use the same spirit to target a goal that will bring quality living to the earth's inhabitants.

Nothing really holds us back from solutions to our world dilemmas, except the lid we have put on our creativity. Opening ourselves to the creative force within allows us to envision the possible. Envisioning the possible excites our will and determination to create it. Holding the vision is an important step in the creative process. We can be pioneers who light the candle.

Vaclev Havel, the imprisoned poet who later became president of Czechoslovakia, wrote this to his wife, Olga, from behind bars:

> Hope is a dimension of the spirit.
> It is not outside us but within us.
> When you lose it you must seek it again
> Within yourself
> and with people around you
> Not in objects
> Or even in events.[12]

To complete the circle, I repeat my statement from chapter 1: a connection exists between our life-force—our inner core, or soul—and the essence of all beings. As we journey inward to discover our essence or wholeness, we discover our relatedness to the outer world.

The inner and outer become one. Journeying down the river—reawakening our innate creativity—enables us to create and sustain the vision of a humanitarian, peaceful world.

NOTES

1 Carl Rogers, *A Way of Being* (Boston: Houghton Mifflin, 1980), p. 118.

2 Theodore Roszak, *Person/Planet* (New York: Doubleday, 1978), p. 318.

3 Thich Nhat Hanh, *Being Peace,* edited by Arnold Kotler (Berkeley: Parallax Press, 1987), pp. 40–41.

4 Ibid, p. 2.

5 Christine Wayne, "The Creative Connection" (Orinda, CA: JFK University, student paper, 1988), p. 3.

6 Ben Hedges, "Creative Confluence," (Orinda, CA: JFK University, unpublished paper, 1990).

7 *See* Carl Rogers, "The Rust Workshop: A Personal Overview," *The Journal of Humanistic Psychology* 26: 3 (Summer 1986), pp. 23–45.

8 Clark Moustakas, *Creativity and Conformity* (New York: Van Nostrand Reinhold, 1967), p. 35.

9 Connie Smith Siegel, "Artist as Activist," *Awakening in the Nuclear Age,* Issue 13 (Spring 1986), p. 9.

10 Ibid, p. 11.

11 Ibid, p. 12.

12 Vaclev Havel, quoted in *Noetic Sciences Review* (Spring 1990).

Appendix

Materials

This list is offered to help you find appropriate materials for expressive arts to use for yourself, with your family or friends, or with clients. Some of these things can be purchased at major drugstores. If you have a local art store, it should carry all of these materials.

Paper

Newsprint is good for beginning projects. Since it is inexpensive, it is easier to use it without feeling guilty about wasting paper. But it also turns yellow and disintegrates after a year or two. So consider the other suggestions as well. Also, try using felt-tip pens on newspaper for your experimental doodles or try recycling computer paper.

Newsprint pads

12″ × 14″

14″ × 17″

18″ × 24″

Drawing paper

(Morilla, Inc. puts out a good medium-weight paper that comes in pads.)

12″ × 14″

14″ × 17″

18″ × 24″

Art journal pad

Try a spiral-bound art pad about 8½″ × 11″

Construction paper (colored paper)

Comes in pads with a variety of colors included.

9″ × 12″

12″ × 18″

Watercolor paper

If you plan to use watercolors, it helps to get some watercolor paper. It comes in pads of various sizes. Strathmore makes a medium to high grade paper. Arches is the best but not necessary for beginners. I recommend 80-lb. to 130-lb. paper.

Bulk paper

If you plan to use paper often or with groups, there is a paper that if bought by the ream is the same price as newsprint (500 sheets for about $40) and is ten times better. It is satisfactory for drawing, tempera, oil pastels, and chalk. You can order it from Empire Distributing Company, 29A Maxwell Court, Santa Rosa, CA 95401. Telephone: (800) 995-1382 or (707) 579-1419. It is an 80-lb. sulfite drawing paper, product #4818. It comes in sheets 18″× 24″ and larger.

Colors

Pens

Felt-tip pens come individually or in sets of colors at discount stores, stationery stores, and art stores.

Oil pastels

Cray-Pas, Jumbo, 25 colors (about $7 or $8 per box). I recommend these since you get more for your money in the long run. The jumbo sticks don't break as easily as the regular Cray-Pas and last three times as long. Or you can start with the small box (about $1) or the box of 25 regular (about $3.) Grumbacher and Rembrandt are high-quality brand names that are more expensive.

Chalk pastels

Koss Pastels come in boxes of 12, 24, or 48 square sticks, ranging from approximately $3 for the smaller box to $9 for the largest box.

Tempera paint

I recommend buying tempera in plastic jars with pouring spouts. These bottles keep the paint from drying up and are easy to use. Tempera comes in pint bottles available at art stores or school supply stores (look in the Yellow Pages). Get your brushes there, too. (Tempera also comes in small jars at discount stores.) Buy primary colors—red, yellow, blue—and black, brown, green, and white. Prang is a good quality brand name, but BesTemp and most any other brand will do.

Watercolors

Watercolors come in tubes or in a box with 8 to 12 color blocks in little pans. For beginners, I suggest the paint-set box. Prang makes a good-quality set (about $7).

Collage material

Making a collage entails using a variety of materials glued onto paper, cardboard, or a hard surface such as masonite. Old magazines are the best source to begin with. Other materials can include: fabric, buttons, beads, colored tissue paper, feathers, and found objects such as bark, grass, sticks, and nails. Materials are limited only by your imagination.

Clay

Ceramic clay comes in 25-lb. bags (about $6 to $8) and is one of the least expensive, most satisfying, and often overlooked art materials. You can buy it at some art stores (or look in the Yellow Pages under "Ceramic Supplies"). Ask for clay that is appropriate for sculpting.

Miscellaneous supplies

For tempera painting (to mix paint with water):

old muffin tins, or aluminum foil muffin tins, or glass jars

For watercolor painting:

watercolor palette

For clay work:

You don't need tools other than your hands for clay work, but you may want to use: a few clay tools and/or a wooden rolling pin, wooden spoons or spatula, old table knife, fork, and spoon. A piece of lightweight wire or dental floss helps you cut chunks of clay off of the big 25-lb. chunk.

For general purposes:

masking tape

scotch tape

stapler

scissors

glue (Elmer's glue and glue sticks)

paper plates (The flat kind can be used under clay sculptures.)

lined pads for free writing

pens, pencils

poster board to use as backing for the art paper

plastic or cloth tarp to use under any or all of your art projects

Music/sound

tape deck or boom box

your favorite music cassettes, including classical, jazz, rock, and new age music

simple instruments for making sound, such as: drums, claves, tambourines, bells, gongs, triangles, simple flutes, xylophones. These can be purchased through school supply catalogs or at music stores.

Bibliography

This bibliography lists books that have influenced me as my work in person-centered expressive arts therapy evolved. My intention is to recommend books that will be particularly useful to those pursuing the new and expanding field of expressive arts therapy. These therefore include therapies in art, movement, music, sound, and writing as well as the principles of psychotherapy.

I apologize for leaving out the field of improvisational drama; it frequently brings together many of the expressive arts in an effective way. I hope to bridge that gap in the future. Dance and movement therapists and music therapists seem to write articles rather than books. This bibliography does not list articles; however, I recommend those of movement therapists Mary Whitehouse, Joan Chodorow, and Janet Adler and music therapist Frances Goldberg.

Some of the books are classics in humanistic psychology, including titles from authors Abraham Maslow, Carl Rogers, Rollo May, Clark Moustakas, and Sidney Jourard. These men were pioneers who changed psychology from a distrusting view of human nature that relied on outside authority and fostered dependence, to a philosophy and practice that trusted human nature and supported personal empowerment. This latter view is the basis for humanistic values and methods, which are much needed for the twenty-first century. Unfortunately, these important works are not featured in today's academic courses. If we are to change consciousness to affect future events in the world, we need to bring these important works to the foreground.

Achterberg, Jeanne. *Imagery in Healing: Shamanism and Modern Medicine.* Boston: New Science Library, 1985.

Adamson, Edward. *Art as Healing.* York Beach, ME: Nicolas-Hays, 1984.

Anderson, Harold H. *Creativity and Its Cultivation.* New York: Harper & Brothers, 1959.

Arrien, Angeles. *The Tarot Handbook: Practical Applications of Ancient Visual Symbols.* Sonoma, CA: Arcus Publishing, 1987.

———. *The Five Universal Shapes and How To Use Them.* Sonoma, CA: Arcus Publishing, 1992.

Assagioli, Roberto. *Psychosynthesis: A Manual of Principles and Techniques.* New York: Viking, 1965.

Barlin, Anne Lief and Greenberg, Tamara Robbin. *Move and Be Moved.* Los Angeles: Learning Through Movement (5757 Ranchito, Van Nuys, CA 91401), 1980.

Barron, Frank. *Creativity and Psychological Health.* Princeton, NJ: Van Nostrand, 1963.

———. *Creativity and Personal Freedom.* Princeton, NJ: Van Nostrand, 1968.

Benzwie, Teresa. *A Moving Experience: Dance for Lovers of Children and the Child Within.* Tucson, AZ: Zephyr Press, 1987.

Berman, Morris. *Coming to Our Senses.* New York: Bantam, 1989.

Bridges, William. *Transitions: Making Sense of Life's Changes.* Menlo Park, CA: Addison-Wesley, 1980.

Brown, J. et al. *Free Writing! A Group Approach.* Rochelle Park, NJ: Hayden Books, 1977.

Bugental, James F. T. *The Art of the Psychotherapist.* New York: W. W. Norton, 1987.

———. *Psychotherapy and Process: The Fundamentals of an Existential-Humanistic Approach.* New York: Random House, 1978.

Campbell, Don G. *The Roar of Silence: The Healing Powers of Breath, Tone, and Music.* Wheaton, IL: Theosophical Publishing House, 1989.

Campbell, Joseph. *The Mythic Image.* Princeton, NJ: Princeton University Press, 1974.

——— (Ed.). *The Portable Jung.* New York: Viking Penguin, 1971.

Cane, Florence. *The Artist in Each of Us.* Craftsbury Common, VT: Art Therapy Publications, 1953.

Capacchione, Lucia. *The Creative Journal: The Art of Finding Yourself.* Athens, OH: Swallow Press, 1979.

———. *Recovery of Your Inner Child.* New York: Simon & Schuster, 1991.

———. *The Power of Your Other Hand: A Course in Channeling the Inner Wisdom of the Right Brain.* North Hollywood, CA: Newcastle Publishing, 1988.

Chicago, Judy. *Through the Flower: My Struggle as a Woman Artist.* Garden City, NY: Doubleday, 1975.

Cornell, Judith. *Drawing the Light from Within.* New York: Prentice Hall, 1990.

Edwards, Betty. *Drawing on the Artist Within: A Guide to Innovation, Invention, Imagination and Creativity.* New York: Simon & Schuster, 1986.

———. *Drawing on the Right Side of the Brain: A Course in Enhancing Creativity and Artistic Confidence.* Los Angeles: J. P. Tarcher, 1989.

Feder, Elaine and Bernard. *The Expressive Art Therapies: Art, Music and Dance as Psychotherapy.* Englewood Cliffs, NJ: Prentice-Hall, 1981.

Feldenkrais, Moshe. *Awareness Through Movement: Health Exercises for Personal Growth.* New York: Harper & Row, 1972.

Fox, Matthew. *The Coming of the Cosmic Christ: The Healing of Mother Earth and the Birth of a Global Renaissance.* San Francisco: Harper & Row, 1988.

Gawain, Shakti. *Creative Visualization.* New York: Bantam, 1985.

———. *Living in the Light: A Guide to Personal and Planetary Transformation.* San Rafael, CA: New World Library, 1986.

Gendlin, Eugene T. *Focusing.* New York: Everest House, 1978.

Ghiselin, Brewster (Ed.). *The Creative Process: A Symposium.* Berkeley, CA: University of California Press, 1952.

Goldberg, Natalie. *Writing Down the Bones: Freeing the Writer Within.* Boston: Shambhala, 1986.

———. *Wild Mind: Living the Writers' Life.* New York: Bantam, 1990.

Grof, Stanislav. *The Adventure of Self-Discovery: Dimensions of Consciousness and New Perspectives in Psychotherapy and Inner Exploration.* Albany: State University of New York Press, 1988.

Gunther, Bernard. *Sense Relaxation: Below Your Mind.* New York: Macmillan, 1969.

Halprin, Anna et al. *Collected Writings.* San Franciso: San Francisco Dancers' Workshop, 1973.

Harman, Willis. *Global Mind Change: The Promise of the Last Years of the Twentieth Century.* Indianapolis, IN: Knowledge Systems, in cooperation with the Institute of Noetic Sciences, 1988.

——— and Rheingold, Howard. *Higher Creativity: Liberating the Unconscious for Breakthrough Insights.* Los Angeles: J. P. Tarcher, 1984.

Heider, John. *The Tao of Leadership.* Atlanta: Humanics Limited, 1985.

Heilbrun, Carolyn G. *Writing A Woman's Life.* New York: Ballentine, 1988.

Houston, Jean. *The Possible Human: A Course in Enhancing Your Physical, Mental, and Creative Abilities.* Los Angeles: J. P. Tarcher, 1982.

Ingerman, Sandra. *Soul Retrieval: Mending the Fragmented Self.* San Francisco: Harper San Francisco, 1991.

Jaffee, Aniela (Ed.). C. J. Jung: *Word and Image.* Los Angeles: J. P. Tarcher, 1982.

Jourard, Sidney M. *The Transparent Self.* New York: Van Nostrand Reinhold, 1971.

Jung, Carl G. *Man and His Symbols.* Garden City, NJ: Doubleday, 1964.

———. *Mandala Symbolism* [from *Collected Works of C. G. Jung,* Volume 9, Part I. Bollingen Series XX]. Princeton, NJ: Princeton University Press, 1959.

———. *Memories, Dreams, and Reflections.* New York: Pantheon, 1963.

Kenny, Carolyn. *The Mythic Artery.* Atascadero, CA: Ridgeview Publishing, 1982.

Keyes, Laurel Elizabeth. *Toning: The Creative Power of the Voice.* Marina del Rey, CA: DeVorss & Co., 1973.

Keyes, Margaret Frings. *Inward Journey: Art as Therapy.* London: Open Court Publishing, 1983.

Kiebert, Coeleen. *All of a Sudden.* Aptos, CA: self-published, 1980.

Kirschenbaum, Howard. *On Becoming Carl Rogers.* New York: Delacorte, 1979.

——— and Henderson, Valerie Land, eds. *The Carl Rogers Reader.* Boston: Houghton Mifflin, 1989.

Knill, Paolo. *Intermodal Learning in Education and Therapy.* Cambridge, MA: self-published, 1978.

LeShan, Lawrence. *How To Meditate: A Guide to Self-Discovery.* Boston: Little, Brown, 1974.

Levant, Ronald F. and Shlien, John M. *Client-Centered Therapy and the Person-Centered Approach: New Directions in Theory, Research, and Practice.* New York: Praeger, 1984.

Levine, Stephen K. Poiesis: *The Language of Psychology and the Speech of the Soul.* Toronto: Palmerston Press, 1992.

Lewis, Penny (Ed.). *Theoretical Approaches in Dance-Movement Therapy,* Volume II. Dubuque, IA: Kendall/Hunt, 1984.

London, Peter. *No More Secondhand Art: Awakening the Artist Within.* Boston: Shambhala, 1989.

Maslow, Abraham H. *Toward a Psychology of Being.* Princeton, NJ: Van Nostrand, 1962.

———. *The Farther Reaches of Human Nature.* New York: Viking, 1971.

Mathieu, W. A. *The Listening Book: Discovering Your Own Music.* Boston: Shambhala, 1991.

May, Rollo. *The Courage To Create.* New York: Bantam, 1975.

McMurray, Madeline. *Illumination: The Healing Image.* Berkeley, CA: Wingbow Press, 1988.

McNiff, Shaun. *The Arts and Psychotherapy.* Springfield, IL: Charles C. Thomas, 1981.

———. *Depth Psychology of Art.* Springfield, IL: Charles C. Thomas, 1989.

———. *Art as Medicine: Creating a Therapy of the Imagination.* Boston: Shambhala, 1992.

Mindell, Arnold. *Dreambody: Body's Role in Revealing the Self.* Boston: Sigo Press, 1982.

———. *The Year 1: Global Process Work. Community Creation from Global Problems, Tensions and Myths.* London: Penguin, 1989.

Moon, Bruce L. *Existential Art Therapy: The Canvas Mirror.* Springfield, IL: Charles C. Thomas, 1990.

Moustakas, Clark E. *The Self: Explorations in Personal Growth.* New York: Harper & Brothers, 1956.

———. *Creativity and Conformity.* New York: Van Nostrand Reinhold, 1967.

Nachmanovitch, Stephen. *Free Play: Improvisation in Life and Art.* Los Angeles: J. P. Tarcher, 1990.

Oaklander, Violet. *Windows to Our Children.* Moab, UT: Real People Press, 1969.

Pelletier, Kenneth R. *Mind as Healer, Mind as Slayer: A Holistic Approach to Preventing Stress Disorders.* New York: Dell, 1977.

Prinzhorn, Hans. *Artistry of the Mentally Ill.* New York: Springer-Verlag, 1972.

Progoff, Ira. *At a Journal Workshop: The Basic Text and Guide for Using the Intensive Journal Process.* New York: Dialogue House Library, 1975.

Purce, Jill. *The Mystic Spiral: Journey of the Soul.* New York: Avon, 1974.

Ray, Michael and Myers, Rochelle. *Creativity in Business.* New York: Doubleday, 1986.

Rhyne, Janie. *The Gestalt Art Experience.* Monterey, CA: Brooks/Cole, 1973.

Rico, Gabriele L. *Writing the Natural Way: Using Right-Brain Techniques to Release Your Expressive Powers.* Los Angeles: J. P. Tarcher, 1983.

Ristad, Eloise. *A Soprano on Her Head: Right-side-up Reflections on Life and Other Performances.* Moab, UT: Real People Press, 1982.

Robbins, Arthur. *The Artist as Therapist.* New York: Human Sciences Press, 1987.

Robbins, Lois. *Waking Up in the Age of Creativity.* Santa Fe, NM: Bear & Co., 1985.

Rogers, Carl R. *Client-centered Therapy: Its Current Practices, Implications, and Theory.* New York: Houghton Mifflin, 1951.

———. *On Becoming a Person.* Boston: Houghton Mifflin, 1961.

———. *Carl Rogers on Personal Power: Inner Strength and Its Revolutionary Impact.* New York: Delacorte, 1977.

———. *A Way of Being*. Boston: Houghton Mifflin, 1980.

———. *Freedom To Learn for the 80s*. Columbus, OH: Charles E. Merrill, 1983.

Rogers, Natalie. *Emerging Woman: A Decade of Midlife Transitions*. Santa Rosa, CA: Personal Press, 1980.

Rubin, Judith Aron (Ed.). *Approaches to Art Therapy: Theory and Technique*. New York: Brunner/Mazel, 1987.

Schoop, Trudi. *Won't You Join the Dance*. Palo Alto: National Press Books, 1974.

Stevens, John O. *Awareness: Exploring, Experimenting, Experiencing*. Moab, UT: Real People Press, 1971.

Thich Nhat Hanh. *Being Peace*. Berkeley, CA: Parallax Press, 1987.

Ueland, Brenda. *If You Want To Write: A Book about Art, Independence and Spirit*. St. Paul, MN: Graywolf, 1987.

Vaughan, Frances E. *Awakening Intuition: Greater Realization Through Your Intuitive Powers*. New York: Doubleday, 1979.

———. *The Inward Arc: Healing and Wholeness in Psychotherapy and Spirituality*. Boston: Shambhala, 1986.

Virshup, Evelyn. *Right Brain People in a Left Brain World*. Los Angeles: The Guild of Tutors Press, 1978.

Wadeson, Harriet. *Art Psychotherapy*. New York: John Wiley & Sons, 1980.

Walsh, Roger N. and Vaughan, Frances (Eds.). *Beyond Ego: Transpersonal Dimensions in Psychology*. Los Angeles: J. P. Tarcher, 1980.

Zweig, Connie and Abrams, Jeremiah (Eds.). *Meeting the Shadow: The Hidden Power of the Dark Side of Human Nature*. Los Angeles: J. P. Tarcher, 1990.

Index

Acknowledgments

A book of this kind can only be produced with the support and contributions of many individuals, many of whom I would like to acknowledge with a few words of appreciation. First, I am profoundly grateful to the author-educators whose works have been included here. They have done worthy service to biology education by developing, writing and sharing the wonderful activities included in this new resource for teaching evolutionary biology in the laboratory.

I am grateful to Dr. Wayne Carley, Executive Director of the National Association of Biology Teachers (Reston, VA) and publisher of *The American Biology Teacher* who enthusiastically permitted us to edit and include material that originally appeared in their publications. Readers of *Investigating Evolution in the Laboratory* are encouraged to subscribe to *The American Biology Teacher (ABT)*. ABT is published nine times per year and presents the results of research into the teaching, learning, and assessment of biology, laboratory teaching strategies, advances relevant to biology instruction and curriculum design, along with current opinion from practitioners and researchers alike. Information about *The American Biology Teacher* may be found at http://www.nabt.org.

To the production and marketing team at Kendall/Hunt, I offer my sincere thanks. Terri Schiesl for a thorough copyedit and an engaging and readable interior design and Jenifer Chapman for the elegant cover design. Project Manager, Jane Nielsen brilliantly shepherded the book through the publication process. It has been a joy working with all of you; I am already looking forward to our collaboration on the next volume in the series.

Finally, I would like to acknowledge current and former graduate students of the Program to Advance Science Education at the USC Rossier School of Education who contributed in many ways. Susan Zweip and Brian Alters reviewed the biology education literature and made suggestions for the activities to be included. Norm Brennan, Cassie Carter, Kim Henige, Jesse Kass, Joy Kobashi, Debby Lujan, Gail Ngo, Elaine Perez, Michelle Nickell-Ramos, and Barbara Shannon scoured the Internet searching for worthy activities. As the project reached its final stage, Jason Leong and Robert Stewart worked with me almost daily to edit each activity into a common style and format; their efforts were invaluable.

To our readers and the original authors, I alone take full responsibility for the editorial decisions that may have resulted in changes in meaning or style when the activities were modified, abridged, and molded into the final common format. Although the majority of the authors were not given the opportunity to review the changes made to their work, I hope that the efforts in producing this laboratory resource will meet with general approval from those whose interesting ideas have been included. For those activities which were previously published elsewhere, a complete reference is provided and readers are encouraged to consult the original source if any questions arise.

Contents

I

Foundations of Evolution Education

I-1 Investigating Evolutionary Biology in the Laboratory

William F. McComas

Introduction

Simply put, evolution is the most important unifying theme in biology. The basic idea that populations of organisms have changed through time along with the mechanism of natural selection have withstood the test of scientific scrutiny and have emerged as powerful tools in understanding and explaining the living world. Just as geneticist Dobzhansky stated that "Nothing in biology makes sense except in the light of evolution" (1973, p. 125), John Scopes, central player in the famous *Monkey Trial*, wisely adds ". . . you can't teach biology without teaching evolution" (1967, p. 59). Without a doubt an understanding of evolution is vital to students in order to properly appreciate and comprehend almost any aspect of the life sciences.

However, in spite of the importance of evolution in biology education, it has become one of the most controversial and difficult subjects to teach. It has been attacked by certain religious fundamentalists as immoral and wrong. There is confusion about whether evolution is a law or theory (actually, it is both). Some draw faulty implications from evolution about how humans should interact with each other (there are none) or about whether accepting evolution somewhat taints ones personal views regarding spirituality (it does no such thing). In addition, there are misconceptions regarding the historical development of the mechanism of evolution called natural selection that have created a mythology about the science of evolutionary biology. Finally, there is the challenge presented by evolution as an abstract and generally nonobservable phenomenon. Stebbins and Allen (1975, p. 206) stated, "Like the concept of the atom, evolution by natural selection is an abstract principle. [Evolution] . . . involves great reaches of time and processes dimly perceptible in ordinary sensation and experience." Many students have only marginally formed the mental structures necessary to conceptualize the complex topics associated with evolutionary biology.

These concerns have caused some such as Edwards (2002) to suggest that it would be better if evolution were removed from the K-12 science curriculum and placed solely in the higher education setting where, for instance, the "evolution-creation issue would mercifully fade away . . ." (p. 615). Such a suggestion, while expedient, is not the solution. Eliminating evolution would indefensibly improvise K-12 school science by removing the foundation that gives meaning to almost every topic in the life science curriculum.

What is clear is that evolution at any level must be taught in a more effective fashion that takes into account what learners already know about this important subject while providing instructional opportunities that engage students in firsthand experiences. These are the goals that guided the development of this book.

A New Kind of Laboratory Manual: An Enhanced Resource Guide

This unique laboratory guide is far more than the typical collection of laboratory activities spanning a variety of topics in the biology curriculum. This guide is focused on a single aspect of biology education and provides both activities and a series of essays designed to help teachers establish or enhance their foundation knowledge in the targeted field. The foundation material provided is not designed to replace the textbook but rather to build on what textbooks contain.

For instance, the introductory chapters in *investigating evolutionary biology in the laboratory* are designed to augment teachers' knowledge of evolution by focusing on a variety of related topics. One chapter provides a definition of evolution along with a discussion of the various ideas supporting the basic mechanism. A pair of chapters analyses the evolution misconceptions—both historical and cognitive—that hamper student understanding. Additional chapters examine ways that teachers can structure evolution learning experiences while reducing students' resistance to evolution. Final chapters provide teachers with perspectives into Darwin's experimental method and a discussion of the legal aspects of evolution education. The second aim of this book is to provide teachers with a diverse collection of resources that educators can use to engage learners of evolution theory at the most effective level available—the concrete, hands-on, laboratory experience. Every aspect of the Darwin-Wallace model of evolution by natural selection is illustrated by at least one laboratory activity, making a hands-on approach to evolution education practical, dynamic, and generally student-centered and investigative.

These exercises were either written exclusively for this book or were extensively modified from other sources and provide many options that are rarely available in one place. Most teachers have their textbook and a supplementary laboratory manual or a teacher resource guidebook as a source of activities. Not surprisingly, the number and kind of activities included in the laboratory manuals that accompany textbooks corresponds closely with the extent and coverage of evolution in the textbook itself. In many cases, evolution is included in only a chapter or two supported by a few laboratory activities in the accompanying manual. Few teachers have the luxury of reviewing dozens of manuals and choosing the one activity that features evolution appropriately for their curriculum and to support the interest level and ability of their students.

The laboratory activities have been edited into a common format and placed together in sections with other exercises illustrating a common evolutionary principle. These principles include the evidence of evolution, variation within the species, adaptation, simulations of natural selection and explorations of neo-Darwinism. Each activity begins with a brief overview so that teachers may judge the suitability of the exercise along with several of the specific evolutionary principles exemplified by the laboratory. The materials section is divided between those common materials necessary for the entire class and those needed for the individual laboratory group. As you will see in Table 2 on pages 14–15, this resource includes 32 different activities together exemplifying 35 different principles related to evolutionary biology including homology, natural selection, adaptation, competition, probability, the mode and tempo of evolution and fitness to name but a few.

The activities included here were chosen because of their relevance to the basic life science curriculum, creativity in design, the ease with which the activities might be modified to support instruction at a particular grade level, and availability of equipment. Some of the activities are new versions of well-known exercises, some overlap others, a few would make useful classroom demonstrations, and several require sophisticated equipment. However, as a group, these activities represent one of the most valuable teaching resources available for evolution eduction. Biology educators can now select an appropriate activity from each section of this resource and go into as much detail as they like in exemplifying aspects of the Darwin-Wallace model of evolution by natural selection.

Improving Laboratory Instruction

The laboratory is a place "where students can investigate natural phenomena in an immediate or first-hand experience and apply various cognitive skills toward an interpretation of these phenomena" (Anderson, 1976, p. 7) and has long been a featured element of the school science experience. Increased use of investigative teaching has been strongly endorsed by both the AAAS (1993) in *Benchmarks for Science Literacy* and the National Research Council (NRC, 1995) in the *National Standards in Science Education* and in many new state frameworks for science instruction.

During the past century many individuals (Lowry, 1921; Tamir, 1976; Hofstein and Lunetta, 1980; Blosser, 1981; Woolnough and Allsop, 1985) have voiced strong support for the role of laboratory instruction in science teaching. More recent research has substantiated the position earlier. When eighth graders completed laboratory work at least once a week they had significantly higher scores in a correlation study than those who did not (Stohr-Hunt, 1996). Freedman (1997) has shown that ninth grade physical science students who had laboratory experiences demonstrated increased achievement and a more positive attitude toward science than those lacking such experiences. In another study, Weaver (1998) found that students in the middle school environment report that the most enjoyable part of science class was the laboratory.

In spite of these strong recommendations for the inclusion of laboratory experiences in school science instruction, the actual application of hands-on instruction in the classroom often does not live up to its promise. The typical laboratory exercise is used simply to verify a previous classroom content lesson with students carrying out cookbook-like instructions. Such an orientation to laboratory teaching is contrary to the tenets of constructivist teaching and distinct from the way that scientists themselves use such procedures. Changes in the typical laboratory format are therefore necessary. However, most educators will agree that if breaking with tradition more fully involves the students, enhances their engagement with the laboratory, and positively impacts their attitudes toward the laboratory, then some rethinking of the role and nature of the laboratory experience is worthwhile.

Although the activities presented in this book are provided in a standard format, there is no intent that each exercise simply be copied and given directly to students. The laboratory experience itself should be orchestrated in such a way that students make as many decisions as possible regarding both the work they do and how they interpret results. This is also true of data tables. Although such tables have been included for your review, in most cases it would be advisable for students to develop their own models for reporting data. Models that make sense to students personally will be much more useful to them than any teacher-provided data reporting sheets.

What follows here is an overview of a number of research-supported suggestions for how laboratory teaching of any science content can be enhanced. It would be impractical, ill-advised and likely impossible to use all of these suggestions with every laboratory activity, but improving only a few elements of the laboratory experience is a worthy goal. Even with the kind of enhancement advocated here, there is no expectation that students will discover all of the essential ingredients for the Darwin-Wallace model of evolution by natural selection. However, with your help, the laboratory can be a much more useful and engaging ingredient of their understanding than it is presently.

The wide variety of unique and effective laboratory activities provided here should make a hands-on approach to evolution education practical. A careful choice of laboratory exercises can make evolution a dynamic experience for students as they study biology. It is the goal of this extended laboratory manual to help educators invigorate biology instruction by changing from the passive lecture to the dynamic investigation as they communicate the fascinating story of evolutionary biology.

Teaching and Learning in the Laboratory: Considering the Level of Challenge

An initial step in enhancing the laboratory experience is to recognize that not all laboratory activities are likely to have the same impact on learners. The "cognitive burden" imposed by the exercise on the students is one of the most potent variables worth considering in predicting how the activity will be viewed by students and what learning it might help foster.

Schwab (1962) was one of the first major science educators to consider the laboratory as a potential place for enquiry. He stated that "the . . . function of

TABLE 1 Schwab/Herron levels of openness for classifying laboratory activities.

Level	Problem	Investigative Methods	Answers
0	Given	Given	Given
1	Given	Given	Open
2	Given	Open	Open
3	Open	Open	Open

the enquiring laboratory is to provide occasions for and invitations to the conduct of miniature but exemplary programs of enquiry" (p. 55). He developed a taxonomy of laboratory activities based on "different levels of openness and permissiveness . . ." (p. 55) expressed by the laboratory. Herron (1971) took a related approach in his proposed laboratory classification plan with his addition of the zero-level. The Schwab/Herron classification scheme is shown in Table 1.

This plan for classifying laboratory exercises is based on an appraisal of how much information the students have before beginning the activity. The central questions in the taxonomy relate to who provides the laboratory problem, who provides the methods for solving the problem, and who provides the answer to the laboratory question. In a Level "0" laboratory, the teacher gives both the problem and method. In addition, the answer is known before the laboratory work begins because of prior knowledge on the part of the students gleaned from the textbook, lecture or laboratory manual itself. Level "1" activities are somewhat more challenging but do little more than give students an opportunity to follow a recipe in cookbook fashion and verify some preexisting facts. Students are given no authentic opportunities to make decisions about the nature of the procedure or choice of the problem. Only in Level "2" and "3" exercises are students really acting as scientists in the choices they make about procedures and problems.

No one should suggest that all laboratory work in a given course be at the highest level. Students do need direction with respect to some procedures and techniques, and they will need to gain experience in conducting high-level work. However, whenever the opportunity exists to "raise the bar" somewhat by increasing the level of challenge, teachers should do so. The first step in enhancing the laboratory experience is to determine the level of challenge that exists in the activities chosen. In reviews of laboratory manuals, researchers have consistently found that the vast majority of labs are at the "0" or "1" level of openness.

What Research Says about Teaching and Learning in the Laboratory

An extensive review of the research literature with respect to laboratory teaching reveals a number of suggestions to enhance the overall student experience. The dozen suggestions associated with high-quality laboratory instruction are grouped into one of three general categories: laboratory activity design issues, pedagogical considerations, and teaching practices. Although these issues do not address every potential variable that may impact the laboratory experience, they are among the most important and should prove useful in visualizing and potentially enhancing laboratory instruction.

Laboratory Activity Design Issues

1. Encourage Investigations at Sites Beyond the Classroom

The authors of Project 2061 (AAAS, 1989, p. 151) suggest that "science teachers should exploit the rich resources of the larger community . . ." in the design of lessons. This implication supports an earlier call from Penick and Yager (1986) who state that students should see the world as their laboratory by moving toward what they call *real* laboratory investigation in school science. The true investigative laboratory can be "in home, in nature, in [the students'] mind and any place students can investigate . . ." (p. 7). Both teachers and students should expand their definition and expectations of the laboratory experience and extend beyond the narrow confines of the traditional school laboratory. Scientists do not work exclusively in laboratory rooms, yet for many students, the classroom laboratory setting must seem like the only possible research site. Broadening the investigative arena to include parks, nature centers, the schoolyard, the students' home neighborhood, botanical gardens, zoos and museums will help students see that investigations can take place almost anywhere.

For example, teachers could refrain from telling students about the types of rocks in the area, but instead ask them to bring in a wide assortment of samples from the community for group identification and/or classification. Rather than asking students to memorize the parts of a flower, have students examine dozens of flowers at the local nursery. These flowers may appear unique but share many similar elements in their basic construction—as students may discover. Instead of having students read in their textbooks that there is variation within the species, a field trip to the zoo or a local pet store may demonstrate this important fact without a word being read.

2. Encourage Long-Term Investigations

The authors of *Criteria for Excellence in Science Teaching* (NSTA, 1987) suggest that "both long term and short term field work and laboratory studies should be both experiential and experimental" (p. 14). Hodson (1988) states that during open-ended work "children come closest to doing real science" and, therefore, "we should regard [such work] as the very pinnacle of science education" (pp. 63–4). Scientists rarely do investigations where the solution is assured within an hour or so. In contrast, students typically work in the laboratory with the expectation that an answer will be achieved quickly by simply following directions.

There are several ways to encourage long-term activities even within the tight time constraints of the school day. First, longer exercises might take place out of school. Students could make daily or weekly observations of a living thing such as a tree or a pet hamster, the pattern of moon phases, or the varying amount of daylight hours throughout the year. Allowing students to observe and discover patterns in nature is more effective than simply telling students that such patterns exist.

Another strategy for longer-term projects is to have students work on an extended activity for a few minutes each day. For instance, students could make observations of some phenomenon such as mold growth or crystal formation at the beginning of each class period. Alternately, student groups might work on part of a longer project that they will later share with each other to visualize the whole process. This suggestion could be facilitated by having students in a different part of the region or the country work together via the Internet on some project of interest such as an analysis of groundwater pollution or on a census of an ecologically sensitive organism. Given the demands of time in science instruction, teachers must be somewhat clever to facilitate labs of longer duration, but such exercises are possible and rewarding. These more detailed investigations may also serve as a source of renewal for teachers who likely tire of seeing the same activity with the same results year after year.

3. Ensure That Laboratory Experiences Are Developmentally Appropriate

In all cases educators should be aware of the developmental appropriateness of both goals and methodologies applied in school science. This issue is particularly important in laboratory instruction where the student must make personal sense of the process and product. If a particular activity requires thinking skills that the students do not possess, the students may become frustrated if they learn faulty lessons about the phenomenon in question. All teachers must remember that even adults do not function at the highest cognitive levels on every task.

The link between developmental readiness and laboratory task requirements has long been a feature of well-designed curricula. For instance, the hands-on project *Science—A Process Approach* (S-APA) from the 1960s and the new *Full Option Science System* (FOSS) were produced with reference to knowledge of student capabilities. In S-APA, for instance, skills such as observation, classifying, measuring, communicating, predicting, and inferring are applied for students in the primary grades. The integrated skills such as controlling variables, interpreting data, hypothesizing, and experimenting are reserved for students in the upper elementary grades. The FOSS curriculum (Lowrey, 1990) provides tasks that include observing, comparing, and communicating for primary students while upper elementary students are asked to propose relationships and organize their thoughts.

For the laboratory to be effective it must also be appropriate in terms of its cognitive demands. All those who provide laboratory experiences for learners must be aware of the learners' limitations and make suitable choices regarding the skills required by the activities involved.

4. Use Laboratory Activities and Practices Illustrating the Authentic Nature of Science

Accurate portrayal of the nature of the scientific endeavor stands at the core of all high-quality science teaching. Although the laboratory provides a unique opportunity for teachers to help students understand how scientists gain information, they must be used with care.

Misconceptions regarding the nature of science can occur in the school science laboratory just by the teachers' choice of language. Frequently teachers indicate that the results of a laboratory experience will *prove* scientific ideas in the way that proof is used in mathematics. Scientists do not prove ideas, but only fail to disprove them at that moment. Therefore, it is most correct to talk about the role of the laboratory in verifying and substantiating ideas. Another problem results when teachers refer to any work in the laboratory as experimental. Most scientists would label something an experiment only if it involves purposeful manipulations of nature with limited variables accompanied by an appropriate control for comparison. By this definition, little classroom laboratory practice is experimental. Activities, observations, or exercises are more suitable labels for the work done in school.

Another important philosophical issue presents itself when students fail to get the *correct* answer associated with the laboratory. When only one answer is expected or valued students may come to believe that this is also the case in science. In science, results deviating from what are expected are often among the most interesting and useful. In addition, when we ask students to accept an answer they did not see personally, what kind of message about real science are we expressing?

Pedagogical Considerations of Laboratory Instruction

5. Use the Challenge Question Approach

The best instructors usually frame the laboratory objective as a thought-provoking challenge question provided to students in the briefest fashion possible. Leonard (1991) provides a useful overview of what might be called the challenge lab approach with the following admonition. Teachers should give the students a task or goal providing only essential procedures, while refraining from telling students how to complete the investigation; students could work cooperatively using a list of resources from which they may choose to guide their investigation. By setting the goal but failing to provide step-by-step recipes that can sidetrack learning, students must think for themselves.

This technique may be used in all educational settings as long as the students and teacher are prepared for the experience. Students must know what is expected of them and realize what the teacher is prepared to provide them in terms of assistance. The teacher must avoid being too helpful in assisting students with problem solving since this can defeat the effectiveness of this innovation.

As an example of an elementary challenge question related to the properties of matter, students might be given a mixture of iron filings, salt, and sand and be asked to separate the three materials. One could provide instructions to help students meet the objective, but more learning will take place if students are challenged to suggest a solution to the problem that makes sense to each student personally.

6. Use the Laboratory to *Introduce* Not Just *Verify* Concepts

The majority of laboratory exercises offer no surprise to students. Typically, teachers discuss a phenomenon in a class lecture and then have students verify in the laboratory what has been said earlier in class. For years, laboratory reformers have stated that such work should have the characteristics of "experience-getting" (Powers, 1932) rather than simply being illustrative or confirmatory. Inductive methods should be used so that the laboratory work *precedes* rather than follows the classroom discussion of a topic or principle. Requiring percent error calculations—typical in many chemistry and physics classes—is just another way of telling students that there is a "right" answer they are to find. Although one could argue such calculations improve accuracy, such practices do not reflect the purpose of investigations in *real* science. The technique of performing laboratory work before extensive classroom discussions may be all that is necessary to raise the level of the laboratory on the Schwab/Herron scale.

Evidence supplied by Boghai (1978), Raghubir (1979), Bishop (1990) and Ivins (1985) reveals that the placement of the laboratory within the process of concept development is important. Ivins (1985) found that laboratory work that introduces rather than confirms discussion of ideas is most effective in helping students learn. Raghubir (1979) discovered that students exhibit higher levels of cognitive ability when they actually gained knowledge through the laboratory rather than simply using the laboratory to verify what teachers and textbooks have stated. These findings are not surprising given the constructivist view of learning that suggests students can only assimilate new information by generating personal understanding out of their own experiences. Making laboratory activities more interesting and challenging may be as simple as providing the hands-on experience before the lecture rather than with the order reversed as is frequently the case.

7. Give Students Opportunities to Make Personal Choices During the Investigation

Students rarely have much to say about the way in which an investigation is conducted despite the general acceptance of constructivism as an explanation of how learning occurs most effectively. The evidence is clear that when students are allowed a choice in the design and implementation of laboratory work they perform better and enjoy the experience more. Eggelston (1973) and Leonard (1980) found that cookbook-like laboratories frequently bore students, but "the more involved a student is in the laboratory the more productive the educational outcomes will be" (Leonard, 1980, p. 338). In empirical studies such as those by Cavana and Leonard (1985), students who were given more choices in the way they conduct investigations had higher scores on laboratory reports and quizzes and were able to work independently for longer periods than students not permitted such discretion.

8. Assess Laboratory Learning Using Authentic Means

Laboratory work would be more highly valued by teachers and more useful as a diagnostic tool by teachers if assessment were more authentic. The term *authentic assessment* means that progress is measured in ways that match the instructional method or are related to some real life task. The desired goal for all lab-related assessment must be that students are evaluated in ways related to the investigative methods with which they were taught.

For instance, many teachers require students to use a standard format to report the results of laboratory investigations. Although a standard format is easy for students to use and straightforward for teachers to evaluate, one might argue that this practice encourages a degree of dishonesty when students use such a report to discuss what is really the result of a creative process.

Medawar (1963) took this position when he criticized the reporting convention used by scientists in their formal journal entries. He believed that such a form hides the true nature of the experimental discovery process, with all of its inherent false starts and dead ends. The pathway appears to be straightforward and the researcher's steps unwavering, but this is rarely the case. Just as the path from problem to solution is poorly reported in professional journals, the case is the same in instructional laboratories. To avoid this problem, students could be asked to write a narrative report describing their individual process of investigation rather than a forced convention disguising their personal method.

Increasing the use of practical or hands-on exams would be another recommendation for enhanced assessment, but the inclusion of learning cycle-based activities would be even better. In the learning cycle, students first are encouraged to investigate on their own *before* moving onto the second stage during which the concepts are discussed more formally. In the final step of the cycle, the students are asked to apply what they have learned. Assessment is authentic only if students apply what they have learned by doing an additional related investigative activity that can be used to measure their progress.

Laboratory Teaching Practices

9. Engage Students in Cooperative or Collaborative Work

Cooperative learning has been widely touted as a general pedagogical tool by researchers such as Slavin (1991) who states that such learning schemes encourage "students to discover, debate, diagram and ultimately to teach one another" (p. 71). Linn and Burbules make this distinction between cooperative and collaborative learning (1993). Cooperative learning "involves dividing a task into parts and having each group member complete one of the parts" while in collaborative learning, "two or more students join together to work out a single solution to a problem" (p. 92).

There are two principal recommendations for using cooperative and collaborative learning strategies in laboratory instruction, one practical and the other philosophical. In a practical sense, group work is valuable because students will learn how to complete a team-based task by assuming various roles in ways that will prepare students as future employees (Cohen, 1986; Schoenfeld, 1989). Also, by having students work together, limitations on equipment and supplies as well as time constraints associated with laboratory tasks can be addressed effectively. Breaking down a large task into smaller parts as recommended in collaborative schemes give students the opportunity to complete their assignments within the limitations imposed by time and materials.

Philosophically, group work in the laboratory is important so that students can simulate what scientists do as they solve problems. Part of the scientific process involves the negotiation and discourse that accompanies the conclusion-making phase of research. Scientists as a community decide what knowledge is important, what techniques are useful, and what the results of investigations mean. This social construction of knowledge is rarely discussed in the science classroom, but the laboratory provides an ideal opportunity to assist students in their understanding of this important dimension of the process of science.

10. Use Indirect Verbal Behaviors When Responding to Students

Although the instructor orchestrates the laboratory experience, some teacher actions are more effective than others in supporting a high-quality laboratory experience. Facilitation, not just interruption, is one such supportive laboratory teacher behavior. Students are distracted and annoyed when teachers stop their work repeatedly during the class period to add a forgotten direction, explanation, or procedural note. Once students are working, an effective technique is to guide in such a way that students know that what they are doing is valued but that they are in control.

The foundation for the suggestion that responses should be indirect is found in the work of Collins and Stevens (1983) and other who have described an inquiry approach to instruction as an alternative to more didactic methods. Inherent in an inquiry mode is the strategy that the discourse between teacher and students should be an authentic conversation rather than based on an authoritarian structure in which the students see the teacher as the ultimate source of approval and information. An indirect style of response to inquiries causes the students to look within themselves or within the group for guidance. Dillon (1979) lists indirect questions and imperatives as alternatives to traditional questioning styles. Indirect questions such as "I wonder what makes you think that?" or "Have you considered . . . ?" or "How would you find out?" are more thought provoking than simply answering the question.

Students seem to respond well to such a technique, as evidenced by McComas (1991) who observed laboratory interactions. In one classroom, the teacher would routinely answer almost every laboratory question by saying,

"I don't know." This response was quickly followed by a statement from a student, "Yes he does, he just wants us to figure it out for ourselves" indicates that students understand what the teacher is trying to accomplish by being somewhat evasive.

11. Engage and Interact Briefly with Small Groups of Students

In practice, highly skilled teachers move from one group of students to another, monitoring, encouraging, and questioning, but generally avoiding long periods of contact with any single student group (McComas, 1991). While additional study of this technique must be completed to authenticate the relationship of this practice to student learning, it is still reasonable to assume that when the teacher is available to the student but not intrusive, students will appreciate the support and react in a positive way to the teacher's interest.

This technique is also valuable to the teacher in assessing student interest and concerns. Should one group of students discover something interesting or demonstrate a common problem, the instructor is in an excellent position to react appropriately and constructively. Rather than stopping the entire group of students to share a concern with the technique or an interpretation of the results — a typical response on the part of the teacher — the instructor can easily spread the word with each group she or he visits. Since this technique is based on frequent but brief visits with those in each student group, the message is quickly spread throughout the classroom.

This management mode can also be used as part of the assessment strategy. The instructor can use a formal checklist to ascertain how well each student is completing a technique or process or can make more general notes about the degree to which students are engaging in the laboratory.

12. Apply Short Prelab Discussions with Extensive Postlab Debriefing Sessions

There is evidence that laboratory instructors who spend minimal time on explanations and directions given *before* laboratory work are the most effective in encouraging their students to think for themselves. This is particularly true with the challenge-type activities advocated earlier. Of course, when serious safety or procedural issues play a role in the activity, the prelab conversation will be longer. However, whole-class prelab discussion generally should last just a few minutes and should deal mainly with procedural and safety issues or in the demonstration of apparatus while avoiding focus on the expected results of the activity.

Emphasis instead should be placed on the postlab debriefing. The function of the postlab discussion is to establish the link between the laboratory and lecture components of the lesson by having students pool data and discuss conclusions supported by the data. Frequently, students themselves establish the underlying generalization governing the phenomenon observed with minimal help from the teacher. This approach is difficult to implement if students are accustomed to step-by-step labs, but in time, students will come to expect and enjoy the challenge-lab approach that is a part of this strategy.

TABLE 2 List of Evolution Principles in *Investigating Evolutionary Biology in the Laboratory (Part I)*

	II-2	II-3	II-4	II-5	II-6	II-7	II-8	II-9	III-1	III-2	III-3	III-4	IV-1	IV-2	IV-3	IV-4
Homology	X						X									
Comparative Anatomy/Genetics	X						X									
Molecular Clock		X														
Phylogeny		X			X	X	X	X								
Mutations			X													
Microevolution			X													
Systematics & Classification				X	X	X		X			X					
Phylogenetics				X												
Convergence & Divergence		X		X	X							X	X			
Variation within Species													X	X	X	X
Age determination									X							
Geologic Time										X						
Transitional Forms											X					
Geographic Distribution																
Population Dynamics																
Competition																X
Adaptation													X			X
Isolation															X	
Overproduction																
Biotic potential																
Natural Selection																
Genotype and Phenotype																
Founder Principle																
Predator-prey																
Hardy-Weinberg																
Genetic Drift																
Carrying Capacity																
Populations																
Probability																
Selection Types																
Mode & Tempo of Evolution																
Founder Effect																
DNA Hybridization																
Fitness																
Punctuated Equilibrium																

TABLE 2 List of Evolution Principles in *Investigating Evolutionary Biology in the Laboratory (Part II)*

	V-1	V-2	V-3	VI-1	VI-2	VI-3	VI-4	VI-5	VI-6	VI-7	VI-8	VII-1	VII-2	VII-3	VII-4	VII-5
Homology																
Comparative Anatomy/Genetics																
Molecular Clock														X		
Phylogeny														X		
Mutations				X												
Microevolution															X	
Systematics & Classification																
Phylogenetics																
Convergence & Divergence														X		
Variation within Species												X				
Age determination																
Geologic Time																
Transitional Forms																
Geographic Distribution																
Population Dynamics			X													
Competition	X									X						
Adaptation						X		X			X	X				
Isolation																
Overproduction	X	X														
Biotic potential		X														
Natural Selection				X	X	X	X	X	X	X	X					X
Genotype and Phenotype																
Founder Principle				X												
Predator-prey				X						X	X					
Hardy-Weinberg				X				X								X
Genetic Drift					X	X										X
Carrying Capacity																
Populations							X									
Probability									X		X					
Selection Types										X						
Mode & Tempo of Evolution													X			
Founder Effect															X	
DNA Hybridization														X		
Fitness												X				
Punctuated Equilibrium													X			

References

Anderson, O.R. (1976). *The experience of science*. New York: Teachers College Press.

AAAS. (1989). *Benchmarks for science literacy*. New York: Oxford University Press.

Bishop, R.D. (1990). *The effect of laboratory activity ordering on achievement and retention*. (unpublished doctoral dissertation.) Southern Illinois University, Edwardsville, IL.

Blosser, P.E. (1981). *A critical review of the role of the laboratory in science teaching*. Columbus, OH: ERIC Clearinghouse for Science, Mathematics, and Environmental Education.

Boghai, D. (1978). A comparison of the effects of laboratory and discussion sequences on learning college chemistry. *Dissertation Abstracts International, 39*, 6045A.

Cavana, G.R. & Leonard, W.H. (1985). Extending discretion in the high school science curricula. *Science Education, 69*(5), 593–603.

Cohen, E.G. (1986). *Designing groupwork: Strategies for the heterogeneous classroom*. New York: Teachers College Press.

Collins, A. & Stevens, A. (1983). A cognitive theory of inquiry teaching. In C. Reigeluth (Ed.), *Instructional-design theories and models: An overview of their current status*. Hillsdale, NJ: Erlbaum.

Dillon, J. (1979). Alternatives to questioning. *High School Journal, 62*, 217–222.

Doran, R.L. (1992). Successful laboratory assessment. *The Science Teacher, 59*(4), 22–27.

Dobzhansky, T. (1973). Nothing in biology makes sense except in the light of evolution. *The American Biology Teacher, 35*(3), 125–129.

Edwards, J.S. (2002). Dobzhansky's dangerous epigram. *BioScience 52*, 614–615.

Eggelston, J.C. (1973). Inductive vs. traditional methods of teaching high school biology laboratory experiments. *Science Education, 57*(4), 467–477.

Freedman, M.P. (1997). Relationships among laboratory instruction, attitude toward science and achievement in science knowledge. *Journal of Research in Science Teaching, 34*(4), 343–357.

Herron, M.D. (1971). The nature of scientific inquiry. 79(2), 171–212.

Hofstein, A. & Lunetta, V.N. (1980). *The role of the laboratory in science teaching: Research implications*. National Association for Research in Science Teaching (ERIC Document Reproduction Service No. ED 188 912).

Hodson, D. (1988). Experiments in science and science teaching. *Educational Philosophy and Theory, 20*(2), 53–66.

Ivins, J.E. (1985). *A comparison of the effects of two instructional sequences involving science laboratory activities*. Unpublished doctoral dissertation, University of Cincinnati, Cincinnati, OH (ERIC Document Reproduction Service No. ED 259 953).

Leonard, W. (1991). A recipe for uncookbooking laboratory investigations. *Journal of College Science Teaching, 21*(2), 84–87.

Leonard, W.H. (1980). Using an extended discretion approach in biology laboratory investigations. *The American Biology Teacher, 42*(7), 338–348.

Linn, M.C. & Burbules, N.C. (1993). Construction of knowledge and group learning. In K. Tobin (Ed.), *The practice of constructivism in science education* (pp. 91–144). Hillsdale, NJ: Lawrence Erlbaum Associates.

Lowrey, H. (1921). The place of practical work in science teaching. *School Science Review, 9*(1), 26–28.

Lowrey, L. (1990). *The biological basis for thinking and learning*. Monograph. Encyclopaedia Britannica Educational Corporation/Lawrence Hall of Science.

Mayr, E. (1991). *One long argument*. Cambridge, MA: Harvard University Press.

McComas, W.F. (1991). *The nature of exemplary practice in secondary school science laboratory instruction: A case study investigation*. Unpublished doctoral dissertation, The University of Iowa, Iowa City, IA.

Medawar, P.B. (1963). Is the scientific paper a fraud? In Medawar, P.B. (Ed.). *The Threat and the Glory* 1990, (pp. 228–233). New York: Harper/Collins.

National Research Council. (1996). *National Science Education Standards*. Washington, DC: National Academy Press.

NSTA. (1987). Criteria for excellence. Washington, DC: National Science Teachers Association.

Penick, J.E. & Yager, R.E. (1986). Trends in science education: Some observations of exemplary programs in the United States. *European Journal of Science Education, 8*(1), 1–8.

Powers, S.R. (1932). A program for teaching science. *The Thirty-First Yearbook of the National Society for the Study of Education, Part I.* Bloomington, IL: Public School Publishing Company.

Raghubir, K.P. (1979). The laboratory investigative approach to science instruction. *Journal of Research in Science Teaching, 16*(1), 13–18.

Schoenfeld, A.H. (1989). Ideas in the air: Speculations on small group learning. Environmental and cultural influences on cognition and epistemology. *International Journal of Educational Research, 13*(1), 17–88.

Scopes, J.T. & Presley, J. (1967). *Center of the storm: Memoirs of John T. Scopes*. New York: Holt, Rinehart and Winston.

Schwab, J.J. (1962). The teaching of science as inquiry. In J.J. Schwab & P.F. Brandwein (Eds.), *The teaching of science* (pp. 3–103). Cambridge, MA: Harvard University Press.

Slavin, R.E. (1991). Synthesis of research on cooperative learning. *Educational Leadership, 48*(5), 71–82.

Stebbins, R. & Allen, B. (1975). Simulating evolution. *The American Biology Teacher, 37*(4), 206–311

Stohr-Hunt, P.M. (1996). An analysis of frequency of hands-on experience and science achievement. *Journal of Research in Science Teaching, 33*(1), 101–109.

Tamir, P. (1976). *The role of the laboratory in science teaching*. (Technical Report 10). Iowa City, IA: The University of Iowa, Science Education Center.

Weaver, G.C. (1998). Strategies in K-12 science instruction to promote conceptual change. *Science Education, 82*(4), 455–472.

Woolnough, B. & Allsop, T. (1985). *Practical work in science*. New York: Cambridge University Press.

I-2 What Evolution Is and Why We Should Accept It:

Definitions, Deconstruction, Evidence and Evolutionary Biology

William F. McComas

> . . . nothing in biology makes sense except in the light of evolution.
>
> Theodosius Dobzhansky (1973, p. 125)

> The theory of evolution by natural selection was certainly the most important single scientific innovation in the nineteenth century. When all the foolish wind and wit that it raised had blown away, the living world was different because it was seen to be a world in movement.
>
> Jacob Brownowski (1973, p. 308)

The views expressed in the quotes by Brownowski and Dobzhansky represent opposite ends of a philosophical-pragmatic continuum with respect to the place of evolution in human thought. Brownowski, a historian of science, reminds us that through the lens of evolution we gain both an accurate and dynamic picture of the natural world. Such a view is not possible in a world that is only a few thousand years old, populated by organisms unalterably designed for their specific individual places in the environment. At the other extreme are the utilitarian suggestions by the geneticist Dobzhansky.

The simplicity of Dobzhansky's assertion may at first glance mask its importance; evolution *is* the unifying framework for the science of biology. Evolution provides a level of understanding linking form and function, ethology, biogeography, genetics, and almost every other aspect of the life sciences. It provides for understanding in fields as diverse as biochemistry and taxonomy, it permits predictions, and it allows us to make sense of the fossil record with a stunning degree of clarity and elegance. Without evolution, biology would simply be little more than a kind of "natural history stamp collecting" in which individual species are discarded, examined, and identified as individual entities with no apparent link between them and anything else in the living world.

Holding a naturalistic view of change through time—evolution—takes nothing away from humanity. In fact, quite the opposite is true. Evolution as a conceptual framework has enabled us to define, explain, and explore the living world in ways that would be impossible without it. Kelly and Milling (in

Pojeta and Springer, 2001, p. v) of the American Geological Institute and Paleontological Society add:

> *Evolution is one of the most fundamental underlying concepts of modern science. This powerful theory explains such phenomena as the history of life preserved in the fossil record; the genetic, molecular, and physical similarities and differences among organisms today and in the past. Indeed, evolution forms the foundation of modern biology and modern biology and paleontology and is well documented by evidence from a variety of scientific disciplines.*

The place of evolution within the science of biology is of such importance that it likewise demands an equally dominant role in biology education. It is vital that students know that "change through time" has occurred and that the proposed mechanism for such change has withstood intense scientific scrutiny.

Evolution is a unique element in science instruction. Simultaneously it is the most important, most misunderstood, and most maligned concept in the syllabus—if it even appears in the syllabus. More has been written to support and condemn evolution than for any other scientific idea. Such a conclusion is supported by the AAAS Benchmarks for Science Literacy (1993, p. 122):

> *In the twentieth century, no scientific theory has been more difficult for people to accept than biological evolution by natural selection. It goes against some people's strongly held beliefs about when and how the world and the living things in it were created. It hints that human beings had lesser creatures as ancestors, and it flies in the face of what people can plainly see . . .*

The question remains as to why evolution is such a controversial subject even when the evidence is strong, the scholarship deep, and the implications so far-reaching. One explanation may lie in the way in which evolution is presented in classrooms and textbooks. Even though many biology teachers provide evolutionary explanations, include discussion of the mechanics of evolution, and use textbooks that contain entire chapters devoted to the subject, the way in which the subject is treated may be both the problem and the solution. Miller (1998) and the National Academy of Sciences (1998, 1999) agree that evolution challenges teachers and their students alike.

We will explore the range of misconceptions that confront educators. The list of misunderstanding is extensive and may best be discussed in three broad categories: philosophic, historical, and cognitive. However, no matter what they are called, these pervasive and complex errors in understanding and thinking may serve to block or confuse understanding.

What Is Evolution?

Ernst Mayr (2001), one of the most productive scholars in evolutionary biology for much of the 20th century, says simply that evolution is "the gradual process by which the living world has been developing following the origin of life" (p. 286). The National Academy of Sciences (1998, p. 13) further defines evolution as "changes in the hereditary characteristics of groups of organisms over the course of generations." With these two definitions we have both a description of what happens (change through time) and identification of the unit on which the change operates (groups of organisms or populations).

A central question is whether evolution is a law, a theory, "just a theory," or something else. Although these terms have unique meanings, only rarely in science classrooms and almost never in common language is the proper distinction between them made.

There are several distinct kinds of knowledge in science, including facts, laws, and theories. Facts are empirical data representing individual "peculiar events" (Carnap, 1995, p. 5) that are the raw material of science. Laws and theories develop from facts, but they are not the same kind of knowledge. In spite of the popular misconception, theories do not become laws even with increased evidence (McComas, 1996). A scientific law is a generalization, rule, principle, or pattern, while a theory is an explanation for why a particular generalization operates in the way that it does (Dilworth, 1994; Rhodes and Schaible, 1989; Trusted, 1979; Horner and Rubba, 1979; Campbell, 1953). Laws explain instances but theories explain laws.

In science a law is a generalization or pattern found in nature, while a theory is something quite different. A theory provides an explanation for why a particular law exists as it does (McComas, 1996, 1997, 2003). Theories and laws are equally important scientific ideas. Laws are not more "grown up" versions of theories nor are theories less secure ideas no matter how much people would like to make this distinction. Therefore, it is simply illogical to say that something is "only a theory," as if someday it will mature into something more acceptable.

The standard definition of biological evolution is that all living things have developed from some common ancestor through a long series of natural changes (Bowler, 1989). Gould states that ". . . evolution is . . . a fact of nature, as well established as the fact that the earth revolves around the Sun" (Gould, 1987, p. 65). Even if one rejects any particular explanatory mechanism, it would be hard to deny the reality of evolution as evidenced by the kinds of change and nature of the relationships of fossils preserved in the rocks. That is the fact or principle of evolution. As we shall see, in some instances it might be possible to consider evolution a law because of what it explains. This is admittedly a controversial stance since, even with its law-like character, evolution does not make the kind of predictions we have come to expect from laws in the physical sciences.

The mechanism of how evolution occurs is correctly called the theory of evolution by natural selection. Although we have both the fact of evolution and the theory of natural selection, few make the distinction as deliberately as they should. Gould addresses this issue in saying that, ". . . evolution is a theory. It is also a fact. And facts and theories are different things, not rungs in a hierarchy of increasing complexity" (1983, p. 254).

It is instructional to see how this difference between laws and theories plays out in the real world. Consider the issue of fossils preserved in rock layers throughout the world. On examination, one quickly concludes that there is a pattern found in these assemblages. Organisms that are more recent—higher up in the rock layers—are related to those below in many instances, but they are also different. Evolution as a natural principle accounts for the pattern, but intellectually, it is just not satisfying enough to say that the fossils appear as they do in patterns because of evolution, although this is perfectly true.

What is missing in this definition is a mechanism to explain *how* the general principle of evolution functions. For the explanation, we look to Charles Darwin and Alfred Rusell Wallace. Their model is correctly called a theory—the theory of evolution by natural selection. This explanatory framework—or theory—is one of the most useful and encompassing in all of biology.

The controversy regarding the distinction between fact, law, and theory is alive and well. In an ill-advised and marked anti-intellectual decision, Cobb Country School officials have joined Oklahoma and Alabama in adding a warning label in students' biology texts pointing out that evolution is a theory:

> *This textbook contains material on evolution. Evolution is a theory, not a fact, regarding the origin of living things. This material should be approached with an open mind, studied carefully and critically considered.*

In many ways such a statement is both silly and unnecessary. All material should be approached with an open mind and studied carefully and critically. In truth, evolution by natural selection *is* a theory—and a good one at that. Of course, the intention of the label is to diminish the standing of evolution as a legitimate scientific idea in the minds of students by trading on the long-discarded notion that theories are less useful than laws.

What's in a Name?

With the distinction between law and theory in mind it is easy to see how important it is to provide the context when using the word *evolution*. On one hand, evolution refers to the natural principle of change through time, and on the other, evolution is an explanation for how this process occurs.

Scientists accept the fact of evolution without debate. The basic model explaining how evolution occurred has remained substantially intact since its development. However, in his day, Darwin recognized that some elements of the model could not be satisfactorily addressed given the current state of scientific knowledge. For instance, the cause for the origin and mechanism for the inheritance of the variations so central to the model were not known nor would they be known during Darwin's life. In the succeeding century, scientists have evaluated and enhanced the explanation of evolution by natural selection. Any conflicts within the scientific community regarding evolution involve fine points of the explanation, not its ultimate validity or utility. Debate, rethinking, and a cycle of verification are important elements of the scientific endeavor and as such are inherent in healthy scientific discourse. Students, administrators and school board members must recognize this.

What many fail to understand is that there is virtually no argument among biologists that evolution has occurred. Even without a mechanism, evolution would still be the greatest unifying idea in the biological sciences in the same way that gravity, which still has no universally accepted mechanism, is central to physics. What debate there is regarding evolution is at the level of the theory, not the fact. Current scientific work in evolutionary biology is aimed at fine-tuning our understanding rather than rejecting the basic fact of evolution.

Biologist John Maynard Smith commented on just this issue by saying, "I have no doubt that, basically, Darwin got it right" (Campbell, 1996, p. 412). Those who choose to reject evolution because of some disagreement among scientists fail to note the focus of such disagreement. The fact of evolution is not debated; only the details of Darwin's mechanism—the theory—are really up for discussion.

Deconstructing Evolution and Its Mechanism

It may seem odd to use a postmodernist phrase in a science essay, but in this case, the label "deconstruction" is useful. The mechanism of evolution by natural selection is based on a number of related but independent suppositions that Mayr (1991) has described as "one long argument." He chooses this phrase wisely because, in fact, evolution by natural selection is composed of a series of interdependent assertions that work together to provide understanding and explanation. From a pedagogical perspective, it is vital and useful for students to isolate and understand the individual components that explain and drive the mechanism for evolution. In fact, a useful way to teach evolution is to focus on the elements of the theory as one discusses how the elements function together.

Lewis (1980, 1986) reminds us that at least five distinct ideas were contributed by Darwin and/or Wallace as part of their evolution revolution. These ideas include the discovery that evolution itself has occurred, the idea of common descent, the principle of speciation, a general pattern of gradualism, and the mechanism of natural selection. Lewis calls all of these notions *theories*, and while some (McComas, 1997; 2003) would argue against such widespread application of this label, the list is important because it helps to clarify the range and interrelatedness of the contributions of Darwin and Wallace.

Evolution and its mechanism have withstood the test of time. Only gradualism, which Darwin advocated as the standard model of evolution, has been modified. Increasing empirical evidence has shown in some lineages that evolution seems to have occurred in quick bursts interspersed by long spans of time during which no speciation takes place. This idea, called punctuated equilibrium (Eldredge and Gould, 1972), is explained by the same underlying Darwinian mechanism that accounts for evolution, but more adequately describes the mode and tempo of the process. Even though punctuated equilibrium does nothing to weaken either evolution or its mechanism, some have

TABLE 1 The major assumptions of descent with modification as described by Darwin. Modified from Lewis (1986, p. 344).

1. All life evolved from one simple kind of organism.
2. Each species, fossil or living, arose from another species that preceded it in time.
3. Evolutionary changes were gradual and of long duration.
4. Each species originated in a single geographic location.
5. Over long periods of time new genera, new families, new orders, new classes, and new phyla arose by a continuation of the kind of evolution that produced new species (this is known as adaptive radiation).
6. The greater the similarity between two groups of organisms, the closer is their relationship and the closer in geologic time is their common ancestral group.
7. Extinction of old forms (species, etc.) is a consequence of the production of new forms or of environmental change.
8. Once a species or other group has become extinct, it never reappears.
9. Evolution continues today in generally the same manner as during preceding geologic eras (related to the geologic idea of uniformitarianism).
10. The geologic record is incomplete.

pointed to the development of punctuated equilibrium as an assault on Darwin. The real lesson is that science is inherently a self-correcting enterprise.

The two most important evolutionary ideas are *descent with modification* (the evidence for and implications of evolution) and the *theory of natural selection* (the interrelated elements that frame a model for how evolution by natural selection can occur). In Table 1, Lewis (1986) provides a synthesis of the major postulates of *descent with modification*. This list may be used by teachers to show students the major assumptions of the fact of evolution.

The next aspect of evolution to be deconstructed is the mechanism or theory of evolution by natural selection. Each of these elements exists independent of the theory of which it is a part. When these five principles work together, a theory is developed to explain how descent with modification takes place. The differential survival or reproduction of favored variants, given sufficient time, can gradually transform populations.

As a model, it is clear that natural selection can produce changes both large and small in populations of organisms. While it is not possible to see macroevolution (speciation) in the laboratory, it is possible for students to investigate many of the ingredients of the Darwin-Wallace model through investigative laboratory activities, explore evidence in support of evolution, engage in simulations, and consider elements of neo-Darwinian discoveries.

TABLE 2 The five independent elements of natural selection that work together to explain how evolution occurs through natural selection. Modified from Huxley (1966).

1. All organisms show considerable natural variation within each species.
2. Much of this variation is heritable.
3. In nature, organisms tend to produce more offspring than can survive.
4. Accordingly, there is a "struggle for existence," the result of which is that not all the offspring (and their genes) will be able to survive and reproduce.
5. Some variants have a better chance of surviving and thus reproducing than others. These survivors live to produce offspring that are more like them than those individuals that died.

The Evidence for Evolution

Darwin's list of evidence in support of evolution was first presented to the public in his landmark book *The Origin of Species* in 1859 and grew continuously, culminating with the sixth edition in 1872. Since Darwin laid down his pen almost 150 years ago, legions of scientists have worked diligently to continue filling the evidentiary ledger. Noted science and nature author David Quammen (2004) summed up the state of support for evolution by dramatically stating that "the evidence for evolution is overwhelming" (p. 4). The evidence is awesome and no one who has studied even a fraction of the data can seriously doubt that evolution has occurred.

Virtually every biology text includes evidence in support of evolution, and even a quick review of the kind and range of evidence itself can be both instructive and convincing. Gould (in Zimmer, 2001) characterizes the evidence into three categories: direct human observation, the fossil record itself, and the "quirks and imperfections present in all modern organisms" (p. xi). Related lines of evidence may be found in investigations of coevolutionary relationships, convergent and divergent trends, artificial selection and modern genetics, and biochemistry. Entire books have been written to convey what will be presented here only briefly, and the record continues to grow with each passing year.

Direct Human Observation

Direct human observation includes the plant and animal breeding work that was featured so prominently in *Origin of Species* along with studies of the increase in resistance in bacteria to antibiotics and in insects to insecticides. Certainly most impressive is the decades-long study of finches on one of the Galápagos Islands by Peter and Rosemary Grant (Weiner, 1994). They have demonstrated the ebb and flow of beak structure in the finch population in response to climatic changes. Evolution has caused these changes in populations, and we have witnessed them.

Modern genetics and biochemistry also provide a huge body of evidence in support of evolution that may be observed. Consider the fact that many organisms, even those that share only superficial appearances, share a common biochemistry, long strands of the same DNA sequences, or even larval forms found in both the echinoderms and vastly different forms such as dogs—and humans. Scientist Max Delbruke (1949) makes this case effectively when he said that "any living cell carries with it the experience of a billion years of experimentation by its ancestors" (p. 174).

The Fossil Record

Perhaps the most important source of evidence in support of evolution comes from the fossils. The fossil record provides an impressive record of large-scale change through time. One can almost "watch" evolution occur by examining the sequence of forms preserved in the rocks and by examining the rich array of transitional forms discovered since Darwin's time. Particularly striking in this case is the evolution of the whale from land-living tetrapod to fin-propelled ocean dweller (Zimmer, 1998). Even now some whales carry a remnant of the pelvis as a now-useless arch of bone buried deep in their rear anatomy. How too would one make sense of the vestigial pelvic bones found in pythons? These anomalies would be impossible to explain without evolution.

Quirks and Imperfections

Gould wrote extensively about evidence for evolution demonstrated by the oddities of nature. In fact, it was this single domain of evidence that most enlightened and entertained the readers of his series of *Natural History* articles. One of his most cited evolutionary quirks is the panda's "thumb." This "thumb" is actually an extension of the wrist bone, not a real digit at all, even though it performs much the same function. Darwin was convinced of evolution in part by the uncanny resemblance of orchid flowers to the insects that pollinate them. Modern scientists have discovered that co-evolution in the Galápagos Islands explains why the cacti on some islands have stout spines while on other islands the cactus spines are more like hairs. The explanation is that the spineless cacti live only on islands which have never had cactus-eating reptiles. The lack of this selection pressure has reduced the cactus spines in these populations to shadows of their former selves, thus saving the energy that cacti typically spend defending themselves.

Students will find one of the most engaging examples of quirks and imperfections within their own bodies. As described by Selim (2004) with a nicely illustrated chart, the human body is a museum of our own evolution. The list of eighteen interesting human features includes remnants of a third eyelid, scant body hair still raised by erector pili muscles, wisdom teeth, an extra set of ribs (possessed by 8% of adults), the appendix, and ear muscles that formerly helped direct the ears toward sound but now do little more that enable some to wiggle their ears. Curiously, the author does not mention the human tailbone and the very rare appearance of an actual tail on some human newborns. Any explanation of these interesting occurrences could only be explained with "just-so" stories without evolution.

Additional Evidence

Evolution is also seen in unrelated species that possess very similar characteristics. This case can be explained by the concept of adaptive radiation—the decent with modification from a common ancestor. The descendants of this common ancestor would retain certain characteristics in common with each other while potentially becoming quite different from each other in many other ways. An example would be the various kinds of rodents in South America (capybara and coypu).

Evolution also accounts for the fact that members of different species may share common characteristics because they share a similar environment. For instance, deer and kangaroos have very similar heads, making them look much the same from the neck up even though no one would confuse the two standing side-by-side. Despite the difference in their overall appearance, convergent evolution has brought about structural similarities between them because these animals share a common food source and eating style. It is no surprise that organisms with almost identical food requirements have evolved a common set of chewing tools. Examples abound, including the common body plan found in penguins, fish, porpoises, and extinct ichthyosaurs. Again, there is no mystery. Evolution has molded these unrelated animals into a streamlined form necessary for success as a water living creature.

Geographic distribution is frequently cited as evidence of evolution. For instance, Darwin was struck by the fact that island forms invariably resembled their mainland counterparts even if the island on which these populations now live is quite different from the homeland of the island colonists. Consider the volcanic nature of the Galápagos archipelago. It would seem highly inefficient to take a tropical animal such as an iguana and modify it for life in such a new environment—why not start fresh? However, that is exactly what has happened. Iguanas from the tropics colonized the rugged lava flows of the Galápagos, and evolution molded these animals into new species better suited for their island lives.

Final Thoughts

Evolution is a complex, interesting, and necessary element of biology instruction; a topic that may confound students and challenge teachers. This chapter has explored the evidence for evolution and discussed the basic definition of both the principle of evolution and its mechanism. An important aspect of the discussion has been to examine the independent but interrelated elements of the "theory of evolution by natural selection," the explanation for how evolution occurs. It is this distinction, the separation of the fact of evolution from its theoretical explanatory mechanism, on which teachers should focus as they engage students in the most important unifying concept in the biological sciences.

References

American Association for the Advancement of Science (AAAS). (1993). *Benchmarks for Science Literacy: Project 2061*. New York: Oxford University Press.

Bowler, P.J. (1989). *Evolution: The history of an idea (revised edition)*. Los Angeles: University of California Press.

Brownoski, J. (1973). *The ascent of man*. Boston: Little, Brown and Company.

Campbell, N.A. (1996). A conversation with John Maynard Smith. *The American Biology Teacher, 58*(7), 408–412.

Campbell, N.R. (1953). *What is science?* New York: Dover Publications.

Carnap, R. (1995). *An introduction to the philosophy of science*. Mineola, NY: Dover.

Delbruke, M. (1949). A physicist looks at biology. *Transactions of the Connecticut Academy of Arts and Science, 33*, 173–190.

Dobzhansky, T. (1973). Nothing in biology makes sense except in the light of evolution. *The American Biology Teacher, 35*(3), 125–129.

Dilworth, C. (1994). On the nature of scientific laws and theories, from *Scientific Progress* (3rd ed.). Boston: Kluwer Academic Publishers.

Eldredge, N. & Gould, S.J. (1972). Punctuated equilibria: An alternative to phyletic gradualism. In T.J. Schopf, (Ed.), *Models in paleobiology* (pp. 82–115). San Francisco: Freeman, Cooper.

Gould, S.J. (1983). Evolution as fact and theory. *Discover, 8*(1), 64–70.

Gould, S.J. (1987). Darwinism defined: The difference between fact and theory. In *Hen's teeth and horses toes*. (pp. 253–262) New York: W.W. Norton.

Horner, J.K. & Rubba, P.A. (1979). The laws are mature theories fable. *The Science Teacher, 46*(2), 31.

Huxley, J. (1966). *The Galápagos*. Berkeley, CA: University of California Press.

Lewis, R.W. (1986). Teaching the theories of evolution. *The American Biology Teacher, 48*(6), 344–47.

Lewis, R.W. (1980, Summer). Evolution: A system of theories. *Perspectives in biology and medicine*, p. 551–72.

Mayr, E. (1991). *One long argument*. Cambridge, MA: Harvard University Press.

Mayr, E. (2001). *What evolution is*. New York: Basic Books

McComas, W.F. (1996). Myths of science: Reexamining what we think we know about the nature of science. *School Science and Mathematics, 96*(1), 10–16.

McComas, W.F. (1997). The discovery and nature of evolution by natural selection: Misconceptions and lessons learned from the history of science. *The American Biology Teacher, 59*(8), 492–500.

McComas, W.F. (2003). A textbook case: Laws and theories and biology instruction. *The International Journal of Science and Mathematics Education, 1*(2), 1–15.

Miller, J.B. (1998). An evolving dialogue: scientific, historical, philosophical, and theological perspectives on evolution. Washington, DC: American Association for the Advancement of Science.

National Academy of Sciences, Working Group on Teaching Evolution. (1998). *Teaching About Evolution and the Nature of Science*. Washington, DC: National Academy Press.

National Academy of Sciences, Steering Committee on Science and Creationism. (1999). *Science and Creationism: A View from the National Academy of Sciences* (2nd ed.). Washington, DC: National Academy Press.

Pojeta, J. & Springer, D.A. (2001). *Evolution and the fossil record*. American Geological Institute: Alexandria, VA.

Quammen, D. (2004, November). Was Darwin wrong? *National Geographic*, pp. 3–35.

Rhodes, G. & R. Schaible (1989). Fact, law, and theory: Ways of thinking in science and literature. *Journal of College Science Teaching, 18*(4), 228–32, 288.

Selim, J. (2004, June). Useless body parts. *Discover*, 41–45.

Trusted, J. (1979). *Theories and laws in the logic of scientific inference*. New York: Macmillan.

Weiner, J. (1994). *The beak of the finch: A story of evolution in our time*. New York: Knopf.

Zimmer, C. (1998). *At the water's edge: Macroevolution and the transformation of life*. New York: The Free Press, a division of Simon and Schuster.

Zimmer, C. (2001) *Evolution: The triumph of an idea*. New York: Harper Collins.

Philosophical Challenges in Evolution Education:

Darwin, Divinity, Religion, and Reason

I-3

 William F. McComas

Educational Challenges of Evolution

Even though evolution presents educational challenges more extensive than those associated with other scientific concepts, the root cause and solution to these challenges is much the same as with any difficult learning issue. As with other concerns in education, the problem with evolution education is a problem of faulty prior knowledge or misconceptions. Prior understanding is a powerful tool that aids students in making sense of new information by providing a scaffold for the incorporation of new ideas into already established schema. However, if prior understanding is incorrect, the misconceptions held can block or confuse learners' future understanding.

The range and nature of misconceptions encountered when teaching about evolution and its mechanism are vast. At least three domains of evolution-related misconceptions exist, including philosophical, historical, and cognitive misunderstandings. The philosophical misconceptions will be the focus of this chapter with the other two featured in succeeding chapters.

The basic philosophical notion discussed here will be the confusion regarding the implications of evolution that seem to flow from an odd religious interpretation almost unique to the United States. We will begin this discussion with an analysis of what Americans think about evolution even if it is not clear whether people distinguish the general principle from its explanation—evolution by natural selection.

American Views of Evolution

Through a remarkable series of polls conducted by the Gallup Organization[1] (Brooks, 2001) starting in 1982, we gain a snapshot view of what people

[1] A recent CBSNews (2004) poll found similar results, with 55% of adults reporting creationist views, 27% holding theistic evolution views, and 13% with atheistic views. The purpose of the CBS poll was to examine differences between those voting for Bush (the conservative) and Kerry (the liberal). For those expressing creationism views, 47% supported Kerry and 67% Bush. 28% of Kerry supporters and 22% of Bush supporters were theistic evolutionists. Finally, 21% of those with outlooks considered atheistic or agnostic supported Kerry, while only 6% supported Bush. There is a clear bias toward the more conservative candidate by those with more conservative, or at least traditional, religious opinions.

FIGURE 1 The Gallup poll (1982–2001) reports of Americans' views on human evolution as measured during the past 20 years (Brooks, 2001).

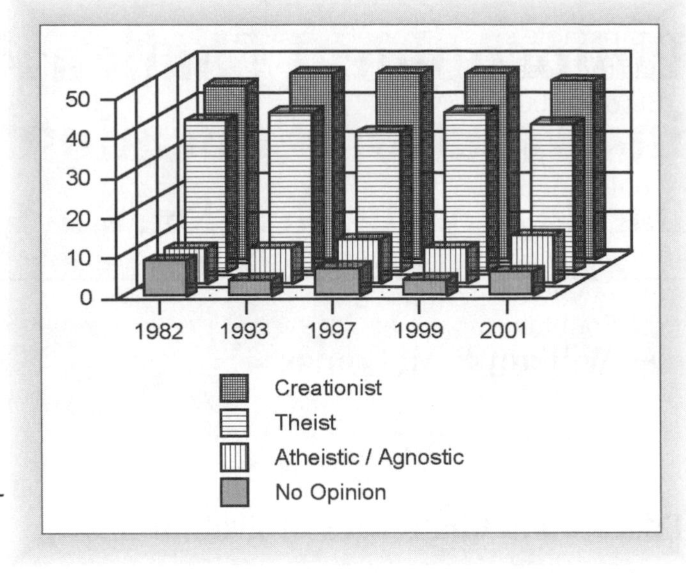

think about evolution. What the Poll (Figure 1) shows is that in 2001, 45% of Americans (1016 adults over 18 years of age) believed that "God created human beings pretty much in their present form at one time within the last 10,000 years or so." 37% chose "Human beings have developed over millions of years from less advanced forms of life, but God guided this process," and 12% felt that "Human beings have developed over millions of years from less advanced forms . . . but God had no part in this process." Those in the first group are likely to be creationists. Those in the next group are theistic evolutionists, while those in the last category might best be considered atheistic or agnostic evolutionists.

There is no surprise with the number of theistic evolutionists given the general level of religiosity in the United States. This view is logically tenable since these individuals accept the basic scientific principle but believe that this natural process is guided metaphysically. Science can neither confirm nor deny this point. It is surprising that such a high number of individuals (almost 50%) seemed to have responded from a non-evolutionist or creationist perspective. Even more sobering is the conclusion that given the nature of the questions, these may also be "young earth" creationists who believe that our planet is only 10,000 years old.

Although this poll reports one of the few measures of the publics' views of evolution, it is open to interpretation. Remember that Alfred Russel Wallace, the co-discoverer of natural selection, dismissed a role of evolution in the development of humans. Therefore, members of the public may share a similar perspective and perceive human evolution as distinct from the evolution of other organisms. If this is true, the survey questions about human evolution may not be the best proxy for the way in which Americans view evolution generally.

Of course, even if this is true, the problem deepens since evolution functions in the same fashion for all living organisms from fungi to fish, hyacinths to humans. The other surprise is that even with our increasingly standards-based science curriculum in which students study evolution in life science and biology, there has been no significant shift in understanding during the past two decades. If this survey is taken at face value, the state of evolution understanding, and by inference, evolution education is dire. We do not have a comparable survey for other regions of the world, but it is intriguing to note that the acceptance level of evolution among Europeans is around 80% (Brooks, 2001; Miller, 1987).

We might have hoped that understanding and acceptance of evolution would not be an issue for teachers charged with incorporating it into science class, but we might be disappointed. Eve and Dunn (1990) surveyed almost 400 secondary school biology teachers and discovered that 39% agreed with the statement, "There are sufficient problems with the theory of evolution to cast doubt on its validity." Of these individuals, 45% expressed belief that "Adam and Eve were the first human beings and were created by God" (p. 14). Weld and McNew (1999) substantiated the earlier finding of Eve and Dunn by showing that 33% of biology teachers do not believe that evolution is central to biology and place little to no emphasis on evolution in their classes. Astoundingly, 30% of these teachers would choose only creationism if they were required to choose one over the other. It is hard to imagine that roughly one-third of the nation's biology teachers somehow remain unconvinced of the reality, scientific utility, and pedagogical imperative of evolutionary biology.

Just as sobering is the issue of "equal time" put forward by many who suggest that students should be presented all sides of this issue and then be allowed to make up their own minds. Unfortunately, this confusion between accuracy and fairness is also evident in another finding by Eve and Dunn. They state that 43% of those high school biology teachers surveyed would opt for the inclusion of both evolution and nonscientific ideas such as creationism "regardless of the validity . . . of special creation and evolution . . ." (p. 15). Such a view might be expected of those in a democratic society that takes pride in honoring diverse opinions (Scott, 2000), but our science curriculum must not be based on the desire of special interests nor can we encourage students to think that one can vote on the truth. Students have the right to expect that what is discussed in science class is actually science.

A specific reason explaining this phenomenon is lacking, but we might start by looking at the extent of inclusion of evolution in college biology courses, the depth of focus on philosophy of science in preservice science teaching methods programs, and state content standards and exit examinations.

Why Some Reject Evolution

One of the most fascinating questions for science educators involves the reasons why almost half of Americans reject evolution. The 1925 Scopes trial had as its central feature a clash of titans with Clarence Darrow, an avowed agnostic, acting as defense attorney in a confrontation with fundamentalist William Jennings Bryan as prosecutor.[2] Bryan was personally drawn into the

[2] Both Darrow and Bryan were really guests in their roles in the trial and were associated with other attorneys who were licensed to practice law in the state of Tennessee. Although the trial was legitimate, it had its origin as a publicity stunt to garner attention for the town of Dayton, Tennessee. Were it not for the support of the American Civil Liberties Union and the passion of the cause generally, it would have been highly unlikely that national figures of the stature of Darrow and Bryan would have come together in the summer heat of a small town courtroom in 1925.

battle because he believed that it would give him a forum to demonstrate the errors of evolution. Bryan prepared a long and involved summative speech that he ultimately did not get to deliver; in it he articulated a number of notions why evolution was worthy of rejection. He thought that (1) evolution contradicts the Bible, (2) survival of the fittest destroys faith in God and love of others, (3) evolution diverts attention from spiritually and socially useful pursuits, and (4) a deterministic view [assumed as part of evolution] undermines efforts to reform society (Larson, 1997, p. 198). We might add to this list the consideration that some reject evolution because they fail to appreciate the kind of knowledge that evolution represents—law and theory. Finally, there are those who dismiss evolution because they think that the facts simply do not support it. In the following sections, we will examine these counterarguments to evolution in an attempt to explore why some students fail to accept evolution and why misconceptions about evolution exist widely across the nation.

Some Believe That Evolution Is "Just a Theory"

The preceding chapter focused on one of the most important and widespread philosophical misconceptions in evolution permitting some to say that evolution is "just a theory." Only those with a less than secure view of the nature of science—principally the distinction between fact, law, and theory—would say such a thing. What they mean, of course, is that evolution is not yet a law so there is no reason to accept it. This is exactly the faculty logic applied by the Cobb County Board of Education in Georgia which, along with Oklahoma and Alabama, has labeled all biology books with a warning that evolution is a theory. They clearly believe that theories are not to be trusted and in labeling evolution as such, they are attempting to discredit the utility and truthfulness of evolution itself.

Many have written about the distinction between laws and theories (Horner and Rubba, 1979; McComas, 1996, 2003; Rhodes and Schaible, 1989), describing laws as general principles and theories as explanations. One does not mature into the other. Unfortunately, the difference between laws and theories that is so clear to those with basic knowledge of the philosophy of science remains a misconception for most others. Those who believe that theories turn into general principles with more evidence would be wise to wait until a higher status is bestowed on evolution, but as we know, evolution is both a general principle (descent with modification) accompanied by a theoretical mechanism (the theory of evolution by natural selection) at the same time. The message is clear. Saying "evolution" is not enough; one must provide the context for how she or he is using the term.

Some Believe That Evolution Is an Incorrect Explanation

If an individual truly understands the distinction between laws and theories and has studied the evidence for evolution and its mechanism and sincerely finds the evidence lacking, then it is reasonable to reject evolution on intellectual grounds. However, this position is hard to accept. The evidence both in support of the principle and in support of the mechanism is overwhelming. Countless references, including most high school biology books, could be cited to support the evidence for evolution. One of the most succinct and comprehensive treatments is found in Hofmann and Weber (2003), while the history of evolution is well described in Larson (2004).

As science educators, we must make a more concerted effort to emphasize the distinction between principle and mechanism, law and theory in an attempt to eliminate potential misunderstanding. However, even if the proposed mechanism for evolution seems flawed to some, that does not mean that the principle of evolution itself is suspect. After all, we do not know the ultimate cause of gravity, but we still accept its existence. It is likely that those who reject evolution make no distinction between the principle and the explanation. Therefore, they deny evolution outright, not on the basis of evidence but because they simply do not want to accept it.

In reality, few who reject evolution have examined it thoroughly enough to understand much about it. During the Scopes trial, Williams Jennings Bryan stated frequently that he had not read the *Origin of Species* and had no interest in doing so. This view is unfortunate when expressed by one of the prosecution team, but even more intriguing when offered by one of the spectators at the trial. This witness, John Washington Butler (Potter, 1935), stated that,

> *The judge ought to give him a chance to tell what evolution is. 'Course, we got 'em licked anyway but I believe in being fair and square and American. Besides, I'd like to know what evolution is myself.*

This might be seen as a refreshing burst of honesty from one of the spectators at the trial, but such an utterance from this particular individual is particularly revealing for reasons that will soon become clear.

In January 1925, John W. Butler, then a Tennessee State Senator, proposed making it a misdemeanor for a public school teacher to "teach any theory that denies the story of the divine creation of many as taught in the Bible and to teach instead that man had descended from lower order of animals" (Larson, 1997, p. 50). This bill, called the Butler Act, was ultimately passed in the Tennessee House by a vote of 71 to 5 and was later signed by the governor. How ironic that Butler, the man responsible for the law itself, admitted that even he did not have a clear understanding of evolution. He just knew he did not like it. Unfortunately, this is still true today. Many who reject evolution have not taken the time to understand it yet they seem to have no reluctance in dismissing this central principle of biology.

Some Believe That Evolution Advocates or Supports Unacceptable Human Actions

Several of Bryan's concerns about evolution are addressed in this section. His view that evolution "destroyed faith in God and love of others" and "diverted attention from . . . socially useful pursuits" (Larson, 1997, p. 198) will be addressed here. In spite of the fact that evolution makes no philosophical implications, there are many who read into the idea of evolution a number of suggestions about how humans can, should, or do act.

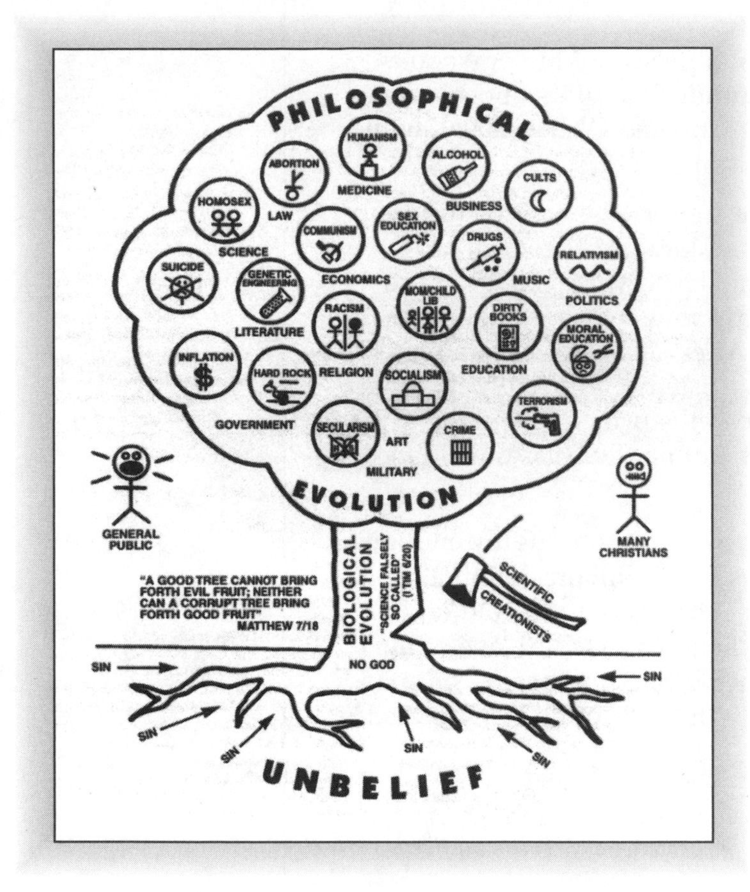

FIGURE 2 The "evil" tree of evolution as depicted in many creationist publications. This one appeared in an article critiquing creationism (Shermer, 1996, p. 88)

The creationist literature is replete with the implication that evolution tells us that we can act in less than altruistic, moral, and ethical ways. Drawing on a quote from scripture, that "[a] good tree cannot bring forth evil fruit, neither can a corrupt tree bring forth good fruit" (Matthew 7:18), creationists label evolution a corrupt tree and proceed to fill its branches with all sorts of societal ills they see as evil springing from that tree. Figure 2, which appears in one form or another in a variety of creationist brochures, concludes that evolution is responsible for everything from drug abuse, to abortion, to racism, to women's liberation, to pornography. They even blame inflation and hard rock on evolution! Another example of the misapplication of evolution to human affairs may be found in the Watchtower biblical tract which states, "[i]n the view of many who accept the theory of evolution, life will always be made of intense competition, with strife, hatred, wars and death" (Watchtower Bible and Tract Society, 1988, p. 8). Bryan said as much in 1925, and the intervening years have not dimmed the ability of fundamentalists to read into evolution interpretations unsupported by the facts.

For most it would be logically inconsistent to propose a link between evolution and the ills of society. However, such a connection was evoked by Representative Tom Delay (R, Texas) as he blamed schools rather than guns and troubled youths for the April 1999 shootings at Columbine High School in Littleton, Colorado. As reported in Lazare (1999), Delay quoted approvingly from a letter to the editor of a Texas newspaper by reading the following into the Congressional Record:

> *Our school systems teach the children that they are nothing but glorified apes who are evolutionized [sic] out of some primordial soup of mud.*

The view supported by Delay is wrong, misguided, unreasonable, illogical, and even dangerous since it shifts the focus away from the true root causes of tragedies such as Columbine. If anything, Delay's comment makes it clear that evolution—taught correctly—should be part of the school curriculum since even educated adults such as Mr. Delay clearly misunderstand it and its implications. In fact, perhaps he should be first in line to take the course.

There have been many instances in history when individuals have assumed a rationale of "survival of the fittest" in their dealings with others. Many of the industrialists of the early part of the 20th century seem to have operated with such an idea in mind. However, just because some have looked to evolution for justifications of their actions and opinions does not mean that such a stand is reasonable. Scientific concepts themselves are amoral (not immoral); we humans have to make moral or ethical sense of all ideas including evolution by natural selection. Evolution and its mechanism explain how nature works, but nothing about it provides guidance about how people should live or act. It is our challenge and responsibility to act morally and ethically. Even altruism is alive and well with most people supporting government programs designed to assist those who are less fortunate. Individuals who choose to live selfishly or who dispute the value of assistance schemes for others cannot logically claim support for their actions from science.

Thomas Henry Huxley (1902, p. 76), a contemporary and supporter of Darwin, said,

> *The question of questions for mankind, the problem which underlies all others, is the ascertainment of the place which man occupies in nature, and of his relations to the universe of things.*

Einstein (1949), speaking philosophically, correctly reminds us that there is an important role for science, but scientism (the idea that science can address all issues) is not appropriate:

> *. . . we should be on our guard not to overestimate science and scientific methods when it is a question of human problems . . .*

Huxley and Einstein are wisely reminding us that it is our responsibility to figure out how to live, how to act, and how to relate to the rest of nature and to each other. We can get no guidance from evolution or science for that matter in this task—no matter what Representative Delay might like us to think.

Some Believe That Acceptance of Evolution Demands Rejection of Religion

A final reason why some people reject evolution is that they believe that evolution and religion are simply incompatible and one view must be chosen over another. This inevitably leads to the false conclusion that if one accepts evolution they would therefore reject a creator or any other metaphysical entity.

There certainly are some who believe that a scientistic view negates religion and some who think that a life based solely on religion does not require science. However, many are satisfied to give both science and religion a place at the intellectual table, thinking it unlikely that either of these two great world views can answer all of our questions. Such individuals realize that science and religion are both explanatory domains but with very different rules and goals. Problems and conflicts come quickly when one asks a question of authorities in the wrong domain.

Creationists would like people to think that science and religion are incompatible, but that is an unreasonable conclusion. In his book *Darwin on Trial*, Lawyer-creationist Philip Johnson (1991, p. 8–9) states that

> *The literature of Darwin is full of anti-theistic conclusions, such as that the universe was not designed and has no purpose and humans are the product of blind natural processes that care nothing about us.*

Johnson is wrong. Although there is nothing about science or evolution that proves that the universe was designed or has a purpose, there is also nothing in science that can prove that the universe lacks design or purpose. An accurate view of the nature of science would make this abundantly clear. It is not reasonable to suggest that science has proven or disproved the existence of God or any other metaphysical entity for that matter. Some may conclude for themselves that science permits or suggests an antitheist perspective, but those who truly understand science and its limitations know that such views are not reasonable. This issue is discussed brilliantly by Kenneth Miller (1999) in *Finding Darwin's God*.

As a postscript, it is reasonable to concede that for those who demand a literal rather than figural reading of the Bible, a conflict with evolution may exist. This issue is discussed well in Skehan and Nelson (2000), but the most useful response that can be made is the reminder that religious texts were not written as books of science; likewise, science texts make no moral or spiritual recommendations. In the 1600s Cesare Cardinal Boronio drew an enlightened and proper distinction between science and religion in stating that "the Bible is a book about how to go to heaven not how heaven goes" (quoted in Sobel, 1999, p. 65).

Is There Really a Conflict Between Science and Religion?

For centuries there has been antagonism between science and religion, most based on the false premise that it is philosophically untenable to accept both. William Jennings Bryan (1925, p. 266) asked, "How can any teacher tell his students that evolution does not tend to destroy his religious faith? They [Christians] do not want their children to lose sight of the rock of ages while they study the age of rocks . . ." The rhetoric here is compelling, but the logic is not. Only for those who fail to understand the distinction between the roles, methods, and goals of science and religion would be threatened by either.

However, we can see evidence of the friction between religion and science almost daily on our highways with countless cars featuring bumper stickers and plaques with either the traditional *Ichthys* symbol (Figure 3) or the so-called "Darwin" fish (Figure 4).

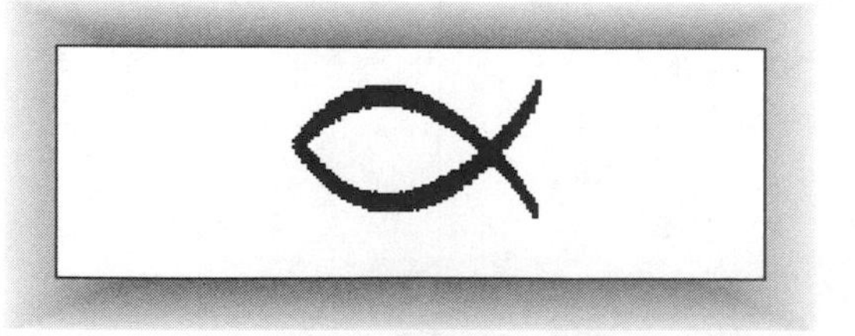

FIGURE 3 The *ICHTHYS* fish symbol from the days of early Christianity. The symbol had its origin in the expression that Christ was the "fisher of men" in his quest for disciples. Another interpretation is that in Greek the first letter in Jesus Christ Son of God and Savior spells out ICHTHYS.

Even though the original fish symbol is an icon of early Christianity where it was used as a secret code among believers, it has recently been co-opted by some who support evolution. All sorts of products from coffee mugs to key chains are available with the "Darwin fish." Of course, there is nothing wrong with announcing publicly one's acceptance of evolution. Unfortunately, those who use this symbol of evolution-acceptance seem not to have considered potential religious sensitivities. Perhaps those who display the "Darwin fish" simply fail to understand the historical nature of the symbol; maybe it really is a direct challenge. In either case, it seems unnecessary for those who support evolution to do so at the expense of others—either knowingly or unknowingly.

FIGURE 4 An assortment of "Darwin Fish" products based on the classic symbol.

The opportunity for religion and science to come together by defining their unique roles and domains is far more important than having one side win and the other side lose. The antagonism between evolution and religion is logically untenable but real. This view is shared by many, but few have written about it as effectively as evolutionary biologist Steven Jay Gould. Gould (1999) has provided abundant evidence for the view of nonoverlapping magisteria (NOMA), or ways of knowing. The NOMA view is deceptively simple; science and religion represent two different magisterial and as such these two great world views are not in conflict because they address two different domains with two distinct sets of rules.

Kipling's famous quip, "east is east and west is west and never the twain shall meet," could just as likely apply to science and religion if only individuals would take a mature philosophical view of the issues involved. We should not look to science for spiritual guidance and moral decision-making, just as we should not to religion to provide data and other forms of empirical evidence.

Not everyone feels that they need both science and religion, but the personal decision that either science or religion is not viable is a personal view, not one that is philosophically tenable. As a case in point, consider Darwin's views on this subject. In the latter half of his life, Charles Darwin came to a personal decision to exclude a deity but called himself an agnostic rather than an atheist. He knew full well that science could provide no evidence of the absence that atheists seek. As he said (Darwin, 1887/2002, p. 54),

> *The mystery of the beginning of all things is insoluble to us; and I for one must be content to remain an agnostic.*

Perhaps the Solution Is to Include "Religion" in Science Class

Just as there is a misunderstanding about the roles and impact on each other of science and religion, there is a misunderstanding about the place of religion in classroom discussions. It is generally believed that it is illegal to mention religion in school because of the "establishment clause" of the United States Constitution. However, what is prohibited is the explicit advocacy by the school or teachers for any particular religious view. There is nothing wrong with discussing religion from historical or philosophical perspectives in any class setting. This, of course, includes the perceived conflict between science and religion.

Therefore, rather than ignore the issue and potential misunderstanding, teachers must include aspects of the nature of science as a content goal of science instruction, just as biology teachers discuss the anatomy and physiology of the cell and chemistry instructors share strategies for balancing chemical equations. This logically would include discussions of the strengths and limitations of science and its relationship with any other explanatory models such as religion. It is time to be proactive rather than remain silent on this important issue.

Addressing the perceived misunderstanding and conflict between science and religion directly does not imply giving equal time to evolution and creationism. Such an idea is frequently recommended—usually by creationists—as reasonable in a democracy. However, creationism is a belief system, while evolution is born of data and tested by evidence. Creationism, in whatever form, is a religious notion, while evolution is firmly rooted in the realm of natural science. Science is guided by natural law and explains by references to natural law. It is tested against evidence from the empirical world; it has conclusions that are tentative and is potentially falsifiable.[3] These elements are not required by religion nor should they be.

Through instruction we must give students permission to accept evolution by removing the misconception that science and religion cannot coexist. The only way to provide this understanding is to engage students in the kinds of discussions advocated here. No less a scientist than Albert Einstein (1954 in Pais, 1982) said, "science without religion is lame, religion without science is blind." He apparently found a place for both religion and science in his life or at least recognized the logic of such a view from a philosophical perspective. It would not be legitimate to insist that students share Einstein's view, only that they understand the logic on which it is based.

In the final analysis, we see that much of the resistance to evolution is due to a misunderstanding of its principles, its history, and its implications. Unfortunately, the debate regarding the inclusion of evolution in the science curriculum is alive and well. Hardly a year passes without news of creationists in some state or school district trying to contrive a reason to omit evolution from school science or to demand some form of "equal treatment." The encouraging news is that along with the mounting defeats for the anti-evolution position, evolution as a scientific principle has been examined and tested in ways far in excess of almost any other idea in science. This scrutiny should encourage any reasonable individual to accept evolution as one of the most secure ideas in modern science.

What is regrettable is that the attacks against evolution continue; we seem to have made no progress in using the controversy as a "teachable moment" to engage and inform students. Perhaps some teachers are content to gloss over or even omit discussions of evolution and its mechanism, natural selec-

[3] These five characteristics of science come from Judge William Overton's (1985) opinion in the case of *McClain vs. the Arkansas Board of Education,* one of many courtroom creationism defeats.

tion. Evolution as a scientific principle must form the foundation of the biology curriculum just as it serves as the cornerstone of biology itself. What we must do as science educators is to anticipate misconceptions and accept alterative but philosophically consistent views from our students. We should address these views and misconceptions in proactive and supportive ways while providing the scientific background necessary for our students to understand, evaluate, and apply the powerful principles and explanations provided by evolution.

References

Bryan, W.J. (1925). Bryan's Last Speech. An appendix to *The World's Greatest Court Trial.* Cincinnati, OH: National Book Company.

Brooks, D.J. (2001). Substantial numbers of Americans continue to doubt evolution as explanation for origin. From the Gallup News Service. Retrieved on April 5, 2004 from http://www.unl.edu/rhames/courses/current/creation/evol-poll.htm.

CBSNews (November 22, 2004). *Poll: Creationism Trumps Evolution.* Retrieved on December 11, 2004 from http://cbsnews.com/stories/2004/11/22/opinion/polls/printable657083.shtml.

Darwin, C.R. (1887/2002). *Autobiographies.* London: Penguin Classics.

Einstein, A. (May, 1949). Why socialism? *Monthly Review 1*(1), Reprinted in May 1998, *Monthly Review 50*(1).

Henig, R.M. (2000). *The monk in the garden.* Boston: Houghton Mifflin.

Eve, R.A. & Dunn, D. (1990). Psychic powers, astrology & creationism in the classroom? *The American Biology Teacher, 52,* 10–21.

Gould, S.J. (1999). *Rocks of ages.* New York: Library of Contemporary Thought.

Horner, J.K. & Rubba, P.A. (1979). The laws are mature theories fable. *The Science Teacher, 46*(2), 31.

Hoffmann, J.R. and Weber, B.H. (2003). The fact of evolution: Implications for science education. *Science and Education, 12*(8), 729–60.

Huxley, T.H. (1902). *Man's place in nature and other anthropological essays* (p. 77). New York: Appleton and Company.

Johnson, P. (1991). *Darwin on trial.* Washington, DC: Regnery Gateway.

Larson, E.J. (1997). *Summer for the gods.* The Scope's trial and America's continuing debate over science and religion. New York: Basic Books.

Lazare, D. (1999, October). Your constitution is killing you. *Harpers Magazine.*

McComas, W. F. (1996). Myths of science: Reexamining what we think we know about the nature of science. *School Science and Mathematics, 96*(1), 10–16.

McComas, W.F. (2003). A Textbook Case: Laws and Theories and Biology Instruction. *The International Journal of Science and Mathematics Education, 1*(2), 1–15.

Miller, J. (1987, June). The scientifically illiterate. *American Demographics,* 26–31.

Miller, K.R. (1999). *Finding Darwin's God.* New York: Cliff Street Books/Harper Collins.

Overton, W. R. (1985). Memorandum opinion of United States District Judge William R. Overton in *Mclean v. Arkansas, 5 January 1982.* In L. Gilkey (Ed.), *Creationism on Trial: Evolution and God at Little Rock.* New York: Harper and Row.

Pais, A. (1982). *Subtle is the Lord: The science and the life of Albert Einstein.* New York: Oxford University Press.

Potter. (1935, September 28). *Liberty Magazine.*

Rhodes, G. & Schaible R. (1989). Fact, law, and theory: Ways of thinking in science and literature. *Journal of College Science Teaching, 18*(4), 228–32, 288.

Scopes, J.T. and Presley, J. (1967). *Center of the storm: Memoirs of John T. Scopes*. New York: Holt, Rinehart and Winston.

Scott, E. (2000). Not (just) in Kansas anymore. *Science, 288*, 813–15.

Shermer, M. (1996). Why creationists fear evolution. *Skeptic*, 4(2), 88.

Skehan, J.W. & Nelson, C.E. (2000). *The Creation controversy and the science classroom*. Arlington, VA: NSTA Press.

Sobel, D. (1999). *Galileo's daughter*. New York: Walker and Company.

Watchtower Bible and Tract Society (1988). *Life—How did it get here, by evolution or by creation?* Brooklyn, NY: Author.

Weld, J. & McNew J.C., (1999). Attitudes toward evolution. *The Science Teacher, 66*(9), 27–31.

Historical Challenges in Evolution Education:

Myths and Misconceptions from the History of Evolution and Natural Selection

I-4

 William F. McComas

Introduction

In addition to the philosophical challenges discussed in the previous chapter, students and teachers alike frequently hold incorrect views about the nature of evolution and the history of the discovery of the theory of natural selection. While these misconceptions may not be as pervasive or threatening as those classed as philosophical or cognitive, any faculty perspectives—particularly those transmitted by teachers and textbooks—are a source of concern.

Virtually all biology texts published in the past century discuss Charles Darwin, his voyage, and the subsequent discovery of the natural selection mechanism for evolution. Unfortunately, in most texts, the discovery and implications of evolution are presented so poorly that a veritable mythology has arisen regarding one of the most fundamental and interesting breakthroughs in the history of human thought. By minimizing or even ignoring the history and implications of the theory, even the best biology books provide little more than a caricature of what really happened and what it means.

As commonly presented, the discovery of evolution by natural selection is a somewhat ordinary story that is satisfying because it is both believable and conclusive. However, as Stephen Jay Gould said, typically "the most satisfying tales are false" (1996, p. 57). This is certainly the case here. Not only is the conventional textbook account incomplete and frequently incorrect, the true story is far more interesting than the typical fiction. Texts that omit a description of the fascinating history of the discovery of evolution miss a wonderful opportunity to acquaint students with the human dimension of science while correcting many of the misconceptions that now block a full understanding—and acceptance—of organic evolution.

Using history to enhance science instruction is strongly advocated by several of the new science education standards. Benchmarks for Science Literacy (AAAS, 1993) provide two principle reasons for including historical

This chapter is an expanded version of William F. McComas (1997). The Discovery and Nature of Evolution by Natural Selection: Misconceptions and Lessons from the Nature of Science. *The American Biology Teacher, 59*(8), 492–500.

perspectives. First, the history of science provides concrete examples of how the scientific enterprise really operates. Second, it is important that future citizens know how historical endeavors add to our cultural heritage. The National Science Education Standards assert that a historical approach in science will assist students "to elaborate various aspects of scientific inquiry, the nature of science and science in different historical and cultural perspectives" (National Research Council, 1996, p. 200). Finally, the New Standards Project (Learning Research and Development Center, 1995) suggests that for students to meet the "scientific connections and applications standard," they must "understand the historical and contemporary impact of science" (p. 336). While it is clear that science education is being asked to move toward the inclusion of historical approaches, we must tell the historical tales correctly. The lessons these stories teach when told accurately far exceed the examples provided by the inaccurate versions that so often accompany biology textbooks.

Evolution and Natural Selection: A Classic Account

Virtually all biology texts provide a version of the brief and incomplete picture of the discovery of evolution by natural selection. This means that teachers and students are forced to seek out a fuller account elsewhere—a task undertaken only by the most dedicated.

The typical textbook account is that young scientist and beetle-lover, Charles Darwin, having shunned a career in medicine and working hard to reject the ministry as a potential profession was recruited by Captain Robert Fitzroy to become the naturalist of the survey ship H.M.S. Beagle. During this five-year round-the-world voyage on the Beagle, Darwin gained important insights from the finches of the Galápagos Islands, culminating in a eureka-like discovery of the natural selection mechanism for evolution. Darwin returned home, wrote down his theory, and became famous for having solved one of science's great mysteries.

This is a good story, but what really happened and what it means will be recounted here in a description of several of the misconceptions typically held about evolution and its discovery.

Myth: Darwin Discovered Evolution

As we discovered in the previous chapter, the word *evolution* represents two different things—at once the term implies both a fact of nature and a theory of how the process occurs. A prevalent misconception exists regarding the distinction between evolution-as-principal and evolution-as-mechanism. Therefore, in the sense of evolution as a basic natural principle, Darwin did not discover evolution any more than Newton discovered gravity.

Evolution-like ideas were proposed by several of the ancient philosophers; as a principle, the idea of biological evolution has been around for millennia (Bardell, 1994). Many centuries ago the Ionian philosophers at work on what is now the West coast of Turkey developed the concept of the great chain of being linking all creatures on a scale of nature with one creature related to the next. Heraclitus of Ephesus (535–473 B.C.E.) and Anaximander of Miletus (611–547 B.C.E.) stated that animal species are mutable or changeable. Although these early Greek scientists did not have a mechanism for the process of evolution, it is clear that they added the concept of evolution to our intellectual heritage millennia ago. What Darwin did was to suggest how evolution operates with his invention of the theory of evolution by natural selection. By providing a mechanism to explain a natural pattern noticed for centuries, Darwin made it both possible and reasonable to accept that organisms change through time. Fossil evidence illustrates that organisms changed through time, the fact of evolution. Natural selection explains how evolution likely occurred.

Myth: Darwin was the Naturalist of the H.M.S. Beagle

Darwin is so frequently called the naturalist of the Beagle in biology textbooks that few would doubt it. It was the practice of the Royal Navy to gain maximum benefit from lengthy voyages. To accomplish this goal, naturalists and artists were commonly found onboard. In the case of the survey ship Beagle, as on many other such ships, the man officially assigned the task of collecting specimens and recording information about the natural world was the ship's surgeon. Robert MacCormick was the Beagle's surgeon who fully expected that he would be the chief collector (Gruber, 1968–69). So what was Darwin doing onboard during the 1831–36 voyage?

Darwin was actually listed on the ship manifest as a supernumerary who paid his own way and was not an official member of the crew. He was invited to travel with the ship primarily because he had the same social status as Captain Fitzroy, a man almost the same age as 22-year-old Darwin. As was the custom, Fitzroy would have been limited in his social interactions to the few officers onboard. Since there was a history of suicide in his family—unfortunately his ultimate fate—Fitzroy was apparently concerned that isolation might take its toll during the long voyage. With a few notable exceptions during the trip, both Darwin and Fitzroy got along well and engaged in a variety of spirited conversations.

However, the story does not end there. MacCormick, the real naturalist of the Beagle, felt that his role had been usurped by Darwin and apparently was not of the most agreeable disposition anyway. He left the ship in Rio de Janeiro in April of 1832 just a few months after the voyage began. At this point, Darwin became the de facto, but still unpaid, naturalist of the H.M.S. Beagle. The legend grew when Fitzroy, in his account of the expedition, described Darwin as the ship's naturalist and as a "young man of promising ability, extremely fond of geology, and indeed of all branches of natural history" (1839, pp. 18–19). Darwin was long appreciative that Fitzroy had extended the invitation to join the voyage. However, Fitzroy, who considered Darwin's work on evolution nothing less than heresy, later regretted that he had played such a pivotal role in the development of the theory of evolution by natural selection.

Myth: Darwin Developed the Idea of Natural Selection While on the Beagle Voyage

When Darwin embarked on the Beagle, he was a creationist as were most of his contemporaries—it was the prevailing view at the time. In brief, creationists believe that species were each created by the deity as individual, unchanging entities. This view, sometimes called special creation, was so widespread that even scientific arguments were framed with reference to it. Consider this selection from one of the standard works in zoology in the early 19th century:

> *It appears that various tribes of organized beings were originally placed by the Creator in certain regions, for which they are by their nature peculiarly adapted. (Swainson, 1835, p. 9)*

Darwin himself admits favoring religious explanations during the voyage. In his autobiography, he states that he was quite orthodox, "being heartily laughed at by several of the officers (though themselves orthodox) for quoting the Bible as an unanswerable authority of some point of morality" (1958, p. 85). When Darwin returned from the voyage, he was no longer a creationist since he rejected the prevailing view that each species was created by a supernatural force and is fixed and unchanging. However, that does not mean that he had discovered the mechanism by which evolution occurs. This is an important distinction that few texts make. One notable exception is found in Schraer and Stoltze (1995), in which the authors state, "although he recorded many observations that supported such a hypothesis [that species could change] he could offer no explanation of how evolution occurred" (p. 601).

Contrary to popular belief, there was no single "ah-ha" moment of discovery in which Darwin developed the theory of evolution by natural selection. In March of 1837, after arriving back in England, Darwin started his first notebook containing his speculations on the mechanism of what he called the mutability of species. By May of 1842, he had enough evidence to write his first formal essay on the subject and shared the news with his friend and colleague Joseph Hooker in January of 1844. In a letter to Hooker, Darwin states,

> *. . . I am almost convinced . . . that species are not (it is like confessing a murder) immutable . . . I think I have found out (here's presumption!) the simple way by which species become exquisitely adapted to various ends . . . . (Darwin, 1996, p. 80)*

Work continued toward an enlarged sketch of the theory early in 1844 but progressed only slightly until May of 1856. In mid-1856, Darwin began his major opus on speciation to be called *Natural Selection* or, in Darwin's own terminology, the *Big Book*. Of course, the book that eventually changed our thinking about the nature of evolution was the *Origin of Species* first published in November of 1859—decades after Darwin's return from the voyage.

Of course, the evidence Darwin collected on the voyage convinced him that species are not fixed and began the thinking process that eventually led to the development of a mechanism to explain how species could change through time. However, Darwin did not make that discovery while onboard the Beagle.

Myth: The Galápagos Islands Were Pivotal to Darwin's Discovery

It is a common notion that the Galápagos Islands, which Darwin visited between mid-September and mid-October 1835, played a vital role in the development of evolution by natural selection. This legend probably began early with ornithologist Osbert Salvin (1876) who called the islands "classic ground" in the history of biology. This notion was picked up by textbook authors who have consistently highlighted Darwin's time in the Galápagos Islands while ignoring virtually all of the other sites Darwin visited during his lengthy trip. The Galápagos Islands were important because they helped to substantiate observations that Darwin had already made elsewhere, but these islands, while fascinating, were hardly vital.

The Galápagos Islands provided more evidence of a recurring pattern Darwin observed rather than contributing a missing piece to the puzzle of evolution by natural selection. Remember that because Darwin was a creationist, it was first necessary for him to accept that species could change before he could consider the process by which species do change. Having visited the Galápagos Islands rather late in the trip, Darwin was already confronted with the reality of evolution with previous visits to other islands. The Galápagos Islands simply removed the final impediments to Darwin becoming an evolutionist.

Oceanic islands are interesting because their inhabitants are typically much more similar to those found on the closest mainland than they are to other creatures on other comparable islands. This makes the special creation of each organism highly suspect. If organisms were created especially for life in a particular environment, one would expect them to be quite specialized for that environment and to always be found in that environment.

Since the Galápagos Islands are a barren volcanic archipelago, one would expect that the species there would either be unique to Galápagos or at least be related to creatures on other volcanic islands. Rather, the majority of Galápagos species are most closely allied with those in the lush tropics of nearby South America. If one were going to make creatures specifically for life in Galápagos with a full compliment of characteristics for their existence there, why start with a body plan and lifestyle much more attuned to a tropical existence? What Darwin saw on the various islands during his voyage would make little sense when considered from a creationist frame of reference but is perfectly understandable when viewed from the perspective of evolution.

However, had Darwin's travels not taken him to both islands and the land, it is unlikely that he might have questioned his earlier creationist beliefs.

As Darwin wrote in the second edition of the *Voyage of the Beagle*,

> *Why, on these small points of land, which within a late geological period must have been covered by the ocean, which are formed by basaltic lava, and therefore differ in geological character from the American continent, and which are placed under a peculiar climate,—why were their aboriginal inhabitants . . . created on American types of organization? (1845, p. 416)*

He concludes by saying,

> *[I]t is probable that the islands of the Cape de Verd [sic] (Cape Verde) group resemble, in all their physical conditions, far more closely the Galápagos Islands, [which] physically resemble the coast of America, yet the aboriginal inhabitants of the two groups are totally unlike; those of the Cape de Verd Islands bearing the physical impress of Africa, as the inhabitants of the Galápagos Archipelago are stamped with that of South America. (1845, p. 417)*

The reality that organisms are related to preexisting forms helped to convince Darwin that evolution must have occurred. All that remained was to discover the mechanism—a process that began on the voyage but culminated 22 years later with the *Origin of Species*.

Myth: Finches Were Central to the Development of the Theory of Natural Selection

Certainly this notion must be true; after all, these birds have long been called *Darwin's Finches* and many biology texts feature these birds prominently in discussions of Darwin's discovery. Even the highly regarded book on evolution, *The Beak of the Finch* (Weiner, 1994), seems to suggest that these animals were important in the discovery of how evolution occurs. To be sure, the 13 species of finches with their highly specialized beaks do represent one of the finest examples of speciation and adaptive radiation. However, the significance of these birds was generally missed by the man for whom this group is so frequently named.

A careful reading of Darwin's notes, the *Origin of Species* (1859), and both editions of the *Voyage of the Beagle* (1839/1845) combined with the detective work of Sulloway (1982, 1984) show that had Darwin never seen the finches, we would still have evolution by natural selection in its traditional form. Darwin simply did not pay much attention to the finches. Not only did he fail to note the name of the islands where he collected his finch specimens, but he also did not realize that all of the birds now known to be finches were, in fact, finches. He called the warbler finch a "wren," the large finch a "grossbeak," and the cactus finch an "icterus" (a family including the orioles, meadow larks, and blackbirds). He collected only nine of the 13 known species of finches and properly identified only six *as finches*.

Sulloway points out that Darwin was not a poor taxonomist. He was simply misled by his prior assumption that islands so close together could not have distinct species and so he saw the finches only as varieties or as a completely different kind of bird. In his diary of the trip and in the first edition of the *Voyage of the Beagle*[1] (1839), Darwin mentions the finches only in passing. In his notebooks on transmutation of species and in the *Origin of Species*, these birds do not appear at all!

It seems likely that the finch legend grew for several reasons. First, the story is satisfying since the finches do represent a compelling example of evolution by natural selection. The name "Darwin's Finches" was chosen by Lack for the title of his famous book (1947) and article (1953) on evolutionary biology. Later he erroneously stated that the finches "provided one of the chief stimuli for their discoverer's theory of evolution" (1964, p. 178). In addition, a crucial error was made in the analysis of the finch specimens when Darwin returned to England and revised his own account of the voyage and its impact. These last two issues have caused such mischief that no biology text it seems has accurately sorted out the facts.

When Darwin returned from his voyage, many of Britain's top experts took charge of and analyzed his collections. The birds were given to preeminent ornithologist John Gould. It was Gould who pointed out to Darwin that some of the Galápagos birds, previously thought to belong to several groups were, in fact, all highly-variable species of finches. Gould classified Darwin's finch specimens into 13 species. Gould was quite correct about the importance of the finches but was wrong about the number of species Darwin collected. Subsequent studies found that Darwin collected only nine species of Galápagos finches. In fact, we now know that there are 13 species. The coincidence with respect to the number 13 has been unfortunate. Still, several current biology texts state that Darwin collected all 13 species; this is no easy feat since some of the birds are found only on islands that Darwin did not visit. The other major issue that has resulted in the finch myth was caused by Darwin himself. The first edition of the *Voyage of the Beagle* was published in 1839 and immediately became popular. Within a few years, Darwin was asked to make revisions for a second edition. What Darwin did was not just to enhance the narrative, but instead to rewrite the trip and its impact on his thinking. It is astounding that Darwin chose to add additional information relative to the development of his ideas that was not even available when he was originally

[1]There are three distinct versions of the *Voyage of the Beagle* written by Darwin, and it is useful to examine all three for insights into the development of his thinking. First, it is possible to examine the raw unedited notes that Darwin made in his diary during the voyage. Second, it is interesting to note the changes in the two published versions of his account of the voyage. The first edition, published in 1839, is called *Journal of researches into the geology and natural history of the various countries visited by the H.M.S. Beagle under the command of Captain Robert Fitzroy, R.N. from 1832 to 1836.* The second edition, published in 1845, was titled *Journal of researches into the natural history and geology of the various countries visited by the H.M.S. Beagle Round the World, under the command of Captain Robert Fitzroy, R.N.* In addition to the changes in title, it is fascinating to see that Darwin paid attention to the finches only in the 1845 edition after their significance was brought to his attention by ornithologist John Gould. One sure way to distinguish one edition from the other is to note the appearance of the finch etching in the second version.

onboard the Beagle. The revision was so complete that it seems as if there were two voyages of the Beagle. This has led to confusion about what Darwin knew and when he knew it. In the second edition of the *Voyage of the Beagle* (1845), Darwin includes discussion of the finches and a wonderful engraving showing the four major beak types. It is this second edition that has been widely reprinted so it is not a surprise that many believe that the finches were vital to his thinking. So, for these reasons, the legend took hold. Textbook authors continued to cite each other and spread the faulty idea that Darwin noted, collected, and based the theory of natural selection on "his" finches.

Had Darwin really formed his theory of natural selection with help from the finches, the story would be interesting enough, but the real tale is even more captivating. While on the islands, the vice-governor told Darwin that "the Spaniards [living in the Islands] can at once pronounce, from which Island any Tortoise may have been brought" (Darwin, 1963, p 262). This was the first clue that something interesting was happening in terms of speciation. The second major clue came in the form of the ordinary mockingbird. Darwin paid particular attention to the mockingbirds, stating the following:

> *I have specimens from four of the larger Islands . . . The specimens from Chatham and Albermarle Islands appear to be the same; but the other two are different. In each Island each kind is exclusively found: habits of all are indistinguishable. . . . The only fact of a similar kind of which I am aware, is the wolf-like Fox of East & West Falkland Islands. (Darwin, 1963, p 262)*

Reflecting on the tortoises and mockingbirds, Darwin concludes by saying, "if there is the slightest foundation for these remarks the zoology of the [Galápagos] Archipelagoes will be well worth examining; for such facts would undermine the stability of Species" (Darwin, 1963, p. 262). In his first notebook on the transmutation of species, Darwin returned to the examples of tortoises and the mockingbirds by saying, "According to this view animals of separate islands, ought to become different if kept long enough apart, with slightly different circumstances. Now Galápagos tortoises, mocking birds, Falkland fox, Chiloe fox—English and Irish Hare" (Darwin, 1960–61, p. 42). So Darwin, without a finch in sight, realized that species can change and began to consider the necessary elements permitting such change. The finches are a dramatic example of speciation, but textbooks do students a disservice by misrepresenting their role while neglecting the real examples that were central to Darwin's thinking.

Myth: Darwin Coined the Term Natural Selection

When Darwin concluded that evolution occurred through the process now called "natural selection," he did not immediately give it that label. In fact, he usually just referred to the idea as "my theory." What most do not know is that Darwin considered *Origin of Species* just an abstract or overview of his intended "big book" to be called *Natural Selection*. This proposed title gradually became the name of the theory itself. Almost immediately this label caught the eye of philosopher Herbert Spencer (1867) who thought that *survival of the fittest* was a better name for the process than natural selection. The problem with "natural selection" was in the potential interpretation. With that name it was too easy to assume that Darwin believed that nature purposefully chose which organisms would live and which would not. Scientists wisely disassociate the natural process of evolution from any guiding principle, metaphysical or otherwise.

This next issue might best be characterized as a potential myth. One might assume that the book *Origin of Species* addresses the question of how species arise. In two ways this is not the case. First, even taken at its word, the book deals with microevolution and through this initial process, suggests how macroevolution or speciation would take place. As to the question of where life came from in the first place, Darwin is quite reserved. His only known comment about the "origin" of species at the beginning of earth history is not in the book, but rather in a letter to Hooker (Darwin, 1871 in Calvin, 1969, p. 4):

> *. . . if (and oh what a big if) we could conceive in some warm little pond with all sorts of ammonia and phosphoric salts,—light, heat, electricity, etc. present, that a protein compound was chemically formed, ready to undergo more complex changes . . .*
>
> Letter to J. D. Hooker, February 1, 1871

Finally, even the word *evolution* is problematic. In its common Victorian usage, the word evolution did not have the same meaning that it has today. It basically meant to unroll or to uncover something that was already there, at least potentially. In Darwin's day it would have been correct to talk about a caterpillar "evolving" into a butterfly. Even then the word was gradually taking on its present—though no less problematic—definition. So we can see why he did not use the term "evolution" except as the very last word in *The Origin of Species* (Darwin, 1859):

> *There is grandeur in this view of life, with its several powers, having been originally breathed into a few forms or into one; and that, whilst this planet has gone cycling on according to the fixed law of gravity, from so simple a beginning endless forms most beautiful and most wonderful have been and are being evolved. (pp. 459 60)*

Myth: Evolution Is Progressive

The issue of progressivism is an interesting misconception because in one sense it appears to be true. When examining early evolution at the time of the first cells, it is unlikely that anything else could be any less complicated than some of these original creatures. So the apparent trend toward increasing complexity is due to the fact that there was really nowhere else to go. However, if increasing complexity were an evolutionary rule, we would not expect to find phyla such as *Porifera* and *Coelenterata* existing today. Phyla such as these are considered to be evolutionary dead ends, "simple" living things that have been around unchanged for millions of years. These phyla and others contain organisms well suited for the niches they occupy, and there is no environmental pressure for them to become anything beyond what they are.

Related to this misconception is the notion that there is some predetermined goal for evolution, with humans as the logical outcome of the process. One can find a vestige of this view contained in most charts picturing the tree of life. In almost every such case, humans (or mammals at least) are typically shown in some vaunted position or at least at the end of the long chain of living forms. In Hunter's *Civic Biology* (1914), the book used by John Thomas Scopes, the section on evolution discusses the lower and higher mammals and "man" is the very last example named at the bottom of the page. One would not predict, looking at the fossil record, that animals like humans would appear. Our evolutionary passage has been a circuitous one with many false starts and blind alleys and a good measure of what Gould frequently called contingency (1989). Perhaps it is best to say that we should count ourselves lucky to be here at all. In 1838, Darwin (Barrett, 1987, p. B214) reminded us of our relative insignificance:

> *It is absurd to talk of one animal being higher than another . . . People often talk of the wonderful event of intellectual Man appearing—the appearance of insects is more wonderful.*

Myth: Darwin Was the Sole Discoverer of Evolution by Natural Selection

Given the treatment of the history of evolution in biology texts, students may be surprised to find that Darwin was not the sole discoverer of the mechanism of evolution by natural selection. Through an interesting convergence of people and events, Darwin shares that honor with Alfred Russel Wallace, a young naturalist who was gathering insect specimens in the Spice Islands of Southeast Asia as Darwin was toiling away at Down House outside of London.

The early development of Darwin's theory is well known and usually represented correctly in biology texts. Darwin returned from his voyage, reviewed the conclusions of the experts analyzing his collections, read Malthus' work on population growth, and started his own notebooks (Darwin, 1960–61) on what he called the "species question." He wrote two manuscripts in 1842 and 1844 (Darwin, 1986) detailing his early thoughts about descent with modification.

The 1844 essay was a 231-page overview of natural selection emphasizing the importance of external conditions in accounting for variations but without discussion of the problem of why organisms of the same stock diverge as they become modified. This issue of divergence will later become important as the story continues. At this point, Darwin penned a now-famous letter to his wife in which he says that "I have just finished my sketch of my species theory. If as I believe that my theory is true and if it be accepted even by one competent judge, it will be a considerable step in science" (Darwin, 1996, p. 82). In this letter he instructs his wife to find someone to help edit and publish the essay upon his death. He even makes some suggestions as to who might assist in the process and provides a sum of money to facilitate the publication.

There has been much debate regarding why Darwin did not simply publish the essay in 1844. One explanation for the delay is that Darwin was anxious to avoid criticism about the theory. Although Darwin was no longer religious by the time he developed natural selection, his wife certainly was. Darwin may have hoped to spare his wife and family the adverse reaction that would likely follow the publication of his treatise on evolution. Darwin realized that his views on evolution pertained to humans and he knew that linking man to the animals would be a controversial idea in Victorian England. In addition, the last major book on evolution, *Vestiges of the Natural History of Creation* (Chambers, 1844), was widely criticized. Even though the book failed to include a mechanism for evolution, its central thesis that evolution had occurred was the subject of much critical and negative talk in the streets and from the pulpit. It is reasonable to assume that Darwin did not want to engage in a similar round of debate himself nor subject his family to the predictable public outcry.

On September 9, 1854, Darwin noted that he "began sorting notes for species theory" (Darwin, 1959, p. 13) in what he called his *Pocket Diary*. It was during this time that Darwin read a paper from a young naturalist working in Southeast Asia named Alfred Russel Wallace. In this paper, Wallace outlined his view that every species comes into existence with preexisting allied species closely related in both space and time (Wallace, 1855). This was an important clue to the nature of evolution by natural selection since it addressed the issue of divergence.

In May 1856, on the advice of colleague Charles Lyell, Darwin began work on his "big book" to be called *Natural Selection*. In October 1856, Wallace wrote to Darwin, requesting advice. In his response, Darwin stated:

> *". . . [b]y your letter and even still more by your paper in the Annals, a year or more ago, I can plainly see that we have thought very much alike and to a certain extent have come to similar conclusions. This summer will make the 20th year (!) since I opened my first note-book, on the question how and in what way do species and varieties differ from each other. I am now preparing my work for publication." (Darwin, 1996, p. 172)*

Many have viewed this statement as a way of telling Wallace that he had strayed into Darwin's territory. Darwin, for his part, continued work on his book, *Natural Selection*. Not long after receiving his first letter from Wallace, Darwin wrote to Asa Gray, a Harvard botanist. This letter was essentially the outline of the 1844 essay with an added paragraph on the important principle of divergence. What happened next is one of the most interesting stories in the history of science.

On the other side of the world Wallace had a flash of insight while recovering from a malarial fever in a hut on the island of Ternate. In February of 1858 Wallace wrote *On the Tendency of Varieties to Depart Indefinitely from the Original Type*, essentially Darwin's model for evolution by natural selection. He immediately sent his paper to Darwin, to gain advice and support from one of England's most esteemed biologists.

When the letter appeared at Darwin's house, Darwin was shocked and dismayed. He wrote to his friend Charles Lyell for advice:

> *He [Wallace] has today sent me the enclosed and asked me to forward it to you. Your words have come true with a vengeance that I should be forestalled. I never saw a more striking coincidence if Wallace had my M.S. [manuscript] sketch written out in 1842. He could not have made a better short abstract! Even his terms now stand as heads of my chapters. (Darwin, 1996, p. 188)*

Within days, with the support and insistence of colleagues Lyell and Hooker, what has been called a "delicate arrangement" (Brackman, 1980) was arranged. Darwin's 1844 essay and his letter to Gray were read along with the paper from Wallace at a meeting of the Linnean society in July. This occurred even though Wallace had no say in the compromise worked out regarding this joint publication. There really was no time to do so since Wallace was almost unreachable at his collecting station on the other side of the world.

Although the papers made little immediate impact, Darwin's priority was secured and he was finally inspired to complete what would become his landmark contribution to biology. Darwin dusted off his reams of notes and quickly got to work on his own decades-long project to fully explain the mechanism of evolution. He abandoned his big book, *Natural Selection*, but took sections from it to form the *Origin of Species* published at the end of 1859.

The story continues with contributions from recent scholars who have indicated that Darwin's original delay was due to the fact that he did not have all of the pieces in place to make his 1844 idea viable—particularly regarding the principle of divergence. Beddall (1986, 1988) believes that Darwin received some vital ideas directly from Wallace without acknowledging them, while Brackman (1980), Brooks (1984), and McKinney (1972) all cite evidence for a conspiracy if not outright fraud.

Brooks (1984) suggests that a 41-page addition on divergence was added to the 1844 manuscript just months after Darwin would likely have read Wallace's paper in the *Annals of Natural History*. Brackman (1980) believes this as well, but there is evidence in the 1857 letter to Asa Gray that Darwin had already grasped this principle. Darwin may have gotten some ideas from Wallace's published paper, but Darwin's own marginal notes on Wallace's article indicate that he did not see much new in the paper (Kohn, 1981).

Beddall (1988) makes the point that Lyell and Hooker deliberately arranged the order of the papers presented at the Linnean Society meeting to give Darwin what some consider undeserved precedence since Wallace's manuscript was in publication form while Darwin's was not. Darwin's modified 1844 essay and his letter to Asa Gray were read to the society before Wallace's paper. In addition, Beddall (1988) questions why Darwin added a note to his Linnean society papers that they were not intended for publication yet still made hundreds of changes to the 1844 sketch and to the letter sent to Asa Gray. Of course, Wallace was not able to make any changes to his part of the presentation at the Linnean society, nor did he even know for many months that the paper had been presented. Given her perspective that some collusion was involved regarding the presentation to the Linnean society, Beddall claims that in the end, the occasion of the reading of the joint papers was "not an occasion of 'mutual nobility' nor was it 'a monument to the natural generosity' of both the great biologists as is frequently claimed."

Finally, there is the issue of when the letter from Wallace arrived in Darwin's hands. Unfortunately, both the letter and its envelope are now missing, so circumstantial evidence is all that remains. By tracking historical records of the time it takes for letters during that period to travel from the Malay region to London, Brooks (1984) has suggested that the letter may have arrived up to a month earlier than Darwin reported. McKinney (1972) found a letter to another one of Wallace's correspondents in England with a postmark date of July 3, 1858. Given the limited mail service from Southeast Asia to England at the time, this letter presumably must have been mailed at the same time as the one to Darwin. If this is true, the question remains, was the letter from Wallace to Darwin delivered early in July or was it delayed until July 18th as Darwin claimed?

It was months before Wallace knew anything of the joint presentation and years before he realized exactly what had transpired in terms of the "delicate arrangement."

There is no conclusive proof for any of the assertions, but these are interesting speculations and the basis of a wonderful detective story. Even without an explicit link between Wallace and Darwin in terms of vital insights, it is quite clear that he was spurred to action by this challenge from a distinct island so far away. Wallace, it should be noted, was quite generous in supporting Darwin as the major force behind the development of natural selection, even writing a book called *Darwinism* (Wallace, 1889) and earlier in 1882 serving as a pall bearer at Darwin's funeral. Wallace continues to be denied credit for his role in the discovery of natural selection because of the poor historical treatment of evolution in biology texts. However, he became well respected as a naturalist in his own right and even without his role in the history of evolutionary thought he would become known as the father of the new science of biogeography.

Ultimately, Wallace and Darwin differed on one important evolutionary concept—the origin of humans. Darwin fully accepted that evolution by natural selection functioned to explain human development, but Wallace believed that humans had an origin distinct from the force of evolution by natural selection. Darwin (Darwin and Seward, 1903, p. 39), in keeping with his usual desire to avoid conflict, nudged Wallace in a letter by questioning him about the exclusion of humans from the mechanism of evolution by stating,

> *I hope you have not murdered too completely your own and my child.*

These issues of the human dimension of science and the role of ideas in scientific breakthroughs make a wonderful case study for students to explore the social dimension of how science operates in the real world in contrast to the purified version of discovery so common in textbooks. In this case, the evidence is clear that had Darwin not developed his particular explanation for how species change, we would still have evolution by natural selection, but it would not be called *Darwinian* but rather *Wallacian*.

Conclusions

There are many lessons to be learned from this new and more complete telling of the history of the discovery of evolution by natural selection. First, teachers must be careful not to rely solely on their textbooks as accurate and complete sources of information. In the case of the discovery of evolution by natural selection, texts are frequently replete with errors of omission and outright inaccuracies. Second, the real story of this discovery is far more interesting and enlightening than the commonly accepted version. How many students know that we would still have evolution by natural selection in much the same form without the Beagle, without the Galápagos Islands, without the finches, and even without Charles Darwin? The rich written documentation in the form of letters, diaries, public accounts, and commentary make natural selection perhaps the most accessible of all scientific discoveries.

Students who consult even a fraction of the available sources related to natural selection and its history will be treated to insights about the scientific process that are possible with few other discoveries. In the case of evolution by natural selection, it is almost possible to read Darwin's mind, getting a feeling for how half a lifetime of facts generated one of the most important theories of the past century. Finally, the history of science is replete with examples of simultaneous discovery with the work of one investigator informing and inspiring others. It is this human dimension that is generally missing in science instruction. We have traded people for facts. Nature does not do biology, people do. However, our students will come to know this only when we reinvigorate biology education by restoring the human dimension of science in an engaging and accurate fashion.

References

American Association for the Advancement of Science (AAAS). (1993). *Benchmarks for Science Literacy: Project 2061*. New York: Oxford University Press.

Bardell, D. (1994). Some ancient Greek ideas on evolution. *American Biology Teacher, 56*(4), 198–200.

Barrett, P.H., Gautrey, S., Herbert, Kohn, D. & Smith S. (Eds.) (1987). *Charles Darwin's Notebooks, 1836–44*. Ithaca: Cornell University Press.

Beddall, B.G. (1986). Wallace, Darwin and the theory of natural selection: A study in the development of ideas and attitudes. *Journal of the History of Biology, 1*, 261–323.

Beddall, B.G. (1988). Darwin and divergence: The Wallace connection. *Journal of the History of Biology* 21(1), 1–68.

Brackman, A. C. (1980). *A delicate arrangement: The strange case of Charles Darwin and Alfred Russel Wallace*. New York: Times Books.

Brooks, J. L. (1984). *Just before the Origin: Alfred Russel Wallace's theory of evolution*. New York: Columbia University Press.

Calvin, M. (1969). *Chemical evolution*. New York: Oxford University Press.

Chambers, R. (1844/1994). *Vestiges of the natural history of creation and other evolutionary writings.* Chicago: University of Chicago Press.

Darwin, C.R. (1839). *Journal of researches into the geology and natural history of the various countries visited by the H.M.S. Beagle under the command of Captain Robert Fitzroy, R.N. from 1832 to 1836.* London: Henry Colborne. (Note, this is the first edition of the *Voyage of the Beagle.)*

Darwin, C.R. (1845). *Journal of researches into the natural history and geology of the various countries visited by the H.M.S. Beagle Round the World, under the command of Captain Robert Fitzroy, R.N.* London: John Murray. (Note, this is the second edition of the *Voyage of the Beagle.*)

Darwin C.R. (1859/1968). *Origin of species.* London: Penguin Books.

Darwin, F. & Seward, A.C. (Eds.). (1903). More letters of Darwin (Vol. II, p. 39). London: John Murray.

Darwin, C.R. (1958). *The autobiography of Charles Darwin 1809–1882.* Edited by Nora Barrow New York: W.W. Norton and Company.

Darwin, C.R. (1959). Darwin's journal. Edited by Gavin de Beer. *Bulletin of the British Museum (Natural History) Historical Series,* 2(1), 1–21.

Darwin, C.R. (1960–61). Darwin's notebooks on transmutation of species. Edited by Gavin de Beer. *Bulletin of the British Museum (Natural History) Historical Series,* 2(2–6), 23–183.

Darwin, C.R. (1963). Darwin's ornithological notes. Edited by Nora Barrow. *Bulletin of the British Museum (Natural History) Historical Series,* 2(7).

Darwin, C.R. (1986). *The foundations of the origin of species: Two essays written in 1842 and 1844.* (Vol. 10 in The Works of Charles Darwin) Edited by P.H. Barrett and R.B. Freeman. Washington Square New York: New York University Press.

Darwin, C.R. (1996). *Charles Darwin's letters: A selection 1825–1859.* Edited by F. Burkhardt, Cambridge: Cambridge University Press.

Fitzroy, R. (1839). *Proceeding of The Second Expedition 1831–1836* (Vol. 2, pp. 18–19). London: Henry Colborne.

Gould, S.J. (1989). *Wonderful life.* New York: W.W. Norton.

Gould, S.J. (May, 1996). *The tallest tale. Natural History,* 18–23, 54, 56–57.

Gould, S.J. (1999). *Rocks of ages.* New York: Library of Contemporary Thought.

Gruber, J.W. (1968–69). Who was the Beagle's naturalist? *The British Journal for the History of Science.* 4, 266–82.

Hunter, G.W. (1914). *Hunter's civic biology.* New York: American Book Company.

Kohn, D. (1981). On the origin of the principle of diversity: A review of *A Delicate Arrangement. Science, 213,* 1105–08.

Lack, D. (1947). *Darwin's finches: An essay on the general biological theory of evolution.* Cambridge: Cambridge University Press.

Lack, D. (April, 1953). Darwin's finches. *Scientific American,* 66–72.

Lack, D. (1964). Darwin's finches. In A.L. Thompson (Ed.), *A new dictionary of birds* (pp. 178–79). London: Thomas Nelson and Sons.

Learning Research and Development Center. (1995). *First draft of new standards.* Washington, DC: Author.

McKinney, H.L. (1972). *Wallace and natural selection.* New Haven, CT: Yale University Press.

National Research Council. (1996). *National science education standards.* Washington, DC: National Academy Press.

Salvin, O. (1876). On the avifauna of the Galápagos archipelago. *Transactions of the Zoological Society of London, 9,* 373–418.

Schraer, W.D. and Stoltze, H.J. (1995). *Biology: The study of life.* Englewood Cliffs, NJ: Prentice-Hall.

Spencer, H. (1867). *Principles of Biology* (Chapter 12). London: Williams and Norgate.

Sulloway, F.J. (1982). Darwin and his finches: The evolution of a legend. *Journal of the History of Biology, 15*, 1–33.

Sulloway, F.J. (1984). Darwin and the Galápagos. *Biological Journal of the Linnean Society. 21*, 29–59.

Swainson, W. (1835). *Treatise on the geography and classification of animals*. London: Longman.

Wallace, A.R. (1855). On the law which has regulated the introduction of new species. *Annals and Magazine of Natural History*, 2nd series 16, 184-96.

Wallace, A.R. (1858). On the tendency of varieties to depart indefinitely from the original type. *Journal of the Proceedings of the Linnean Society: Zoology* 3, 53–62.

Wallace, A.R. (1889). *Darwinism: An exposition of the theory of natural selection with some of its applications*. London: Macmillan and Company.

Weiner, J. (1994). *The beak of the finch*. New York: Knopf.

Cognitive Challenges in Evolution Education:

Fundamental Misconceptions of the Science of Evolutionary Biology

I-5

William F. McComas, Linda Abraham-Silver, and LuLu Ma

This chapter concludes the discussion of the extensive range of prior conceptions related to evolution by focusing here on individuals' basic understanding of evolutionary biology. The issues discussed in this chapter join the historical and philosophical misunderstandings mentioned previously and together inform educators of the challenges ahead.

At a conceptual level, evolution has proven to be a particularly difficult topic for students at every level to grasp (Bishop & Anderson, 1990; Demastes, Good & Peebles, 1996; Ferrari & Chi, 1998; Rudolph & Stewart, 1998). Studies conducted in the K-12 environment show that students do not understand the mechanics or process of evolution even if they are able to articulate the basic tenets of the Darwin/Wallace model of natural selection (Deadman & Kelley, 1978; Samarapungavan & Reinout, 1997). Even students with several years of advanced biology coursework may hold deep-seated misconceptions about evolution and the mechanics that drive the process (Bishop & Anderson, 1990; Brem, Ranney & Schindel, 2003; Ferrari & Chi, 1998; Sundberg, 2003).

The challenges that are the focus of this chapter arise from the fact that evolutionary biology is based on a complex foundation requiring that students appreciate a range of scientific phenomena in order to make sense of evolution and its mechanism. As the authors of the *Atlas of Science Literacy* (AAAS, 2000) show, full understanding of evolutionary biology can only come when students comprehend a number of sophisticated and interrelated scientific ideas. These ideas fall into three large domains: evolution itself (evidence for change through time, geological processes resulting in fossilization and relatedness of organisms); natural selection (sexual reproduction, the chemical mechanisms and patterns of inheritance); and variation in inherited characteristics (mutations, DNA, etc.). The knowledge maps included in the *Atlas* provide a clear picture of how fundamental scientific principles link to each other and to evolution itself and should be taken into account in the design of evolution instructional plans.

Conceptual Challenges in Teaching Evolution: The Issue of Language

Many researchers have alluded to the problem of language when teaching evolution (Bishop & Anderson, 1990; Cooper, 2001; Wilkins, 2001). One of the main conceptual areas blocking understanding of evolution is found in the discrepancy between the way terms are used in the science of evolutionary biology and in vernacular speech.

Scientific vs. Everyday Theories

As has been mentioned elsewhere in this book, there is a mismatch between the everyday and scientific use of the word *theory*. In everyday conversation the word *theory* typically means a guess, speculation, or conjecture. However, scientists use the word much more specifically. Theories, according to the National Academy of Sciences, "are understandings that develop from extensive observation, experimentation, and reflection. They incorporate a large body of scientific facts, laws, tested hypotheses, and logical inferences" (1998, p. 6). When discussing the *Theory of Evolution*, those who apply the common use of the word *theory* may assign it less importance or dismiss evolution altogether by describing evolution as *just a theory*, meaning *just a guess*. This issue has been discussed at length in an earlier chapter along with the biology textbook disclaimer required in some states cited as an example of this linguistic misinterpretation in action.

Fitness and Adaptation

The difficulty with language and evolution becomes especially perplexing in the case of teaching about natural selection—the mechanism that explains evolutionary change. Specific issues arise with the terms *adapt* and *adaptation* as well as with the term *fitness* (Bishop & Anderson, 1990).

The term *adaptation* when used by evolutionary biologists means modifications achieved by natural selection operating on the natural variation found within populations of organisms (Whitfield, 1993). Members of the general public typically use the term *adapt* to apply to the willful ability of an individual to change to better fit the environment (Lucas, 1971). As an example of the latter, consider that many assume that a person moving from sunny Los Angeles to the windy and wintry city of Chicago would *adapt* to the change in climate by purchasing a warmer coat or at least by resisting the urge to complain about the weather.

Bishop and Anderson (1990) have shown that some students associate the meaning of evolutionary adaptation with the common definition. The disconnection between the scientific definition and the everyday use of the word *adapt* serves to reinforce the misconception that the environment causes the development of characteristics or traits in populations of organisms.

Similar problems result with the use of the word *fitness* (Bishop & Anderson, 1990). Often students will define natural selection as "survival of the fittest." The term *fit* when used by biologists relates to an individual's ability to procreate and produce viable progeny. When used in everyday conversation, *fit* is linked to an individual's overall health, strength, and, in an anthropomorphic sense, other physically desirable traits. Thus, the misconception that evolution means that only the stronger, faster, and smarter individuals in a population are selected to carry the population forward is reinforced by the everyday meaning of the term *fit*. This misconception would cause students to think that the strong, fast, and smart individuals are always more likely to survive when, in fact, even such generally desirable traits may not be those that permit survival in particular environments.

Evolution and Progress

Finally, the word *evolution* itself is often used in the vernacular to refer to *progression*. Such usage underscores a major misconception that many people hold about biological evolution—that evolution necessarily implies progression from less complex to more complex species in a hierarchical fashion with humans enjoying an "inherent superiority" over "less evolved" life forms (Gould, 2001, p. xii). Scientists use the term *evolution* to mean "change over time" or "descent with modification," not a process leading to perfection. The complexity of a species does not necessarily correlate with its long-term success on the planet. Dinosaurs, a group of animals that many would consider complex, are extinct, while seemingly less complex strains of bacterium have existed on the planet for billions of years. Thus a less complex (or what one might erringly consider a less evolved) form of life—bacteria—proliferates, while a more highly evolved form of life—the dinosaurs—has succumbed. Tackling the challenge of language remains a significant hurdle in overcoming student misconceptions about evolution.

Conceptual Challenges in Teaching Evolution: Naïve Explanations About Evolution and Natural Selection

In addition to the issue of vocabulary, studies conducted with K-12 and college students have shown an extensive list of more sophisticated cognitive misconceptions widely held about evolution. For instance, elementary and middle school students generally believe that species are unchangeable, a naïve conception that is deep-seated even before the children are introduced to concepts such as heredity and evolution in school (Keil, 1989). As shown in Table 1, this finding is supported by Samarapungavan and Reinout (1997) who studied children between the ages of 9

TABLE 1 Groups of evolution misconceptions found among secondary school students by Samarapungavan and Reinout (1997).

Students' misconceptions could be sorted into one of five groups:

- Those who believe that species have always existed and their characteristics do not change, but environmental factors can lead to extinction.
- Those who believe in a micro-evolutionary framework whereby all animals began as dinosaurs and have transformed into their modern-day exemplars (the "tiger" comes from a "dinosaur-tiger" ancestor, for example).
- Those who show a tendency to define evolution in Lamarckian terms. (These students believe that species become extinct when individuals are not able to adapt quickly enough to a changing environment, that new species are always preceded by less complex ancestors and become more complex as they evolve, and that a specie's characteristics change as a function of use and non-use.)
- Those who believe in a full-blown spontaneous generation event in which all species were created at one time.
- Those who subscribe to a creationist belief, citing all animals as created by God for a specific purpose.

and 12 and grouped their views about how species originate and change into one of five different belief pools.

In their frequently cited study with university students, Bishop and Anderson (1990) found that over 50 percent of the 110 students studied possessed naïve conceptions about evolution. They identified three major areas in which these students hold inaccurate views. These domains include issues related to the mechanism of evolution by natural selection, variation within populations, and the rise of new traits. Table 2 contains an overview of the results of this study along with examples of both the scientifically accepted view and the common misconception.

TABLE 2 Misconceptions about evolution held by university students (Bishop and Anderson, 1990).

Area of Misconception	Description
The Mechanism of Natural Selection	
Scientific View	Two processes influence trait change in populations: random changes in genetic material (either through random mutation or sexual recombination) and the survival or disappearance of traits due to natural selection.
Typical Misconception	A single influence causes trait change: the environment itself causes change, and organisms either recognize the *need* to develop new traits to survive, gain new traits through the use or disuse of appendages or abilities, or adapt to the environment. If the animal can't adapt, it goes extinct.
Example	Giraffes needed long necks to reach treetop leaves for food, so nature allowed them to develop longer necks. Because this trait was useful for survival, parents passed the trait onto their offspring.
The Role of Variation in Populations	
Scientific View	Variation of individuals within populations is an essential precondition for evolution to occur.
Typical Misconception	Populations may be made up of individuals, but evolution shapes the species.
Example	Cheetahs had to run fast to catch prey. Eventually all cheetahs developed specific muscle traits that allowed them to become fast runners.
The Rise of New Traits	
Scientific View	New traits arise through discrete genetic changes involving individual organisms.
Typical Misconception	Evolution occurs when the expressed traits themselves are enhanced or gradually lost over time.
Example	A cave salamander does not need to see, so each generation of salamander has weaker sight. Eventually only blind cave salamanders remain.

In a study of almost 400 university students, Lord and Marino (1993) revealed a similar set of unscientific conceptions. They report that "a large number [of students] . . . thought that traits acquired during the life of an organism could be inherited. Some felt that the use or disuse of an anatomical or physiological structure in the body was an important consideration in the evolutionary process. Many saw evolutionary advancement as a slow linear movement from a single cell to human being" (p. 353).

The alternative conceptions revealed by Bishop and Anderson (1990) among university students are similar to those held by students between the ages of 12 and 16 (Clough and Wood-Robinson, 1985). In addition to those students who have acceptable scientific ideas about the mechanism of evolution (11% in the Clough and Wood-Robinson study), the alternative views revealed can be identified as adaptationist (individuals need to change and so they do), anthropomorphic (individual organisms make changes based upon their observations of the environment), teleological (goal-directed), or Lamarckian (inheritance of acquired characteristics).

Evans (2000) and Ferrari and Chi (1998) conclude that some children seem to accept a hybridization model of evolution through which new species result from the mating of two unrelated ones. It should be noted that some of these categories are not mutually exclusive; an individual might accept both an adaptationist view and a Lamarckian mechanism. The misconceptions revealed for both precollege and college students parallel those identified in other studies and show that many students tend to perceive evolution in terms of goal-oriented progression (Ferrrari & Chi, 1998; Jensen & Finley, 1996; Rudolph & Stewart, 1998).

Evans (2000, 2001) adds to our knowledge of prior conceptions with the results of several studies probing students' views on the origin of species. In these interview examinations of school-age children, Evans (2001) found a strong correlation between the orientation of students' homes (religious fundamentalism vs. nonreligious and/or nonfundamentalist) and the likelihood that children possess a creationist or naturalistic notion regarding evolution. Not surprisingly, children from fundamentalist environments were likely to hold creationist views. She reports that young children are likely to have a combination of creationist and spontaneous generation views about the development of new species.

Of the difficulties inherent in evolution education, the issue of alternative conceptions of natural selection as the explanatory mechanism for evolution are the most pronounced. For instance, Brumby (1984) found a lack of understanding that natural selection explains both increasing resistance among insect populations to insecticide and bacterial resistance to antibiotics. Only 14% of students had a natural selection explanation for the situation in bacteria, while 67% saw the insecticide problem as one of natural selection even though both types of resistance are explained in the same fashion. Some students interviewed suggested that ". . . insects become more immune, rather than *more* insects become immune" (p. 499). Such explanatory frameworks demonstrate a lack of knowledge about the role of populations in evolution.

Cognitive Evolution Misconceptions: A Summary

It is interesting to note that many misconceptions about evolution held by students mirror the views offered by 18th and 19th century naturalists who proposed explanations for the diversity of life on Earth (Mayr, 1982; Costa, 2003; Rudolph & Stewart, 1998; Sundberg, 2003). The teleological interpretation that organisms change because of a specific goal—an idea originally proposed by Cuvie—is well represented both in the writings of early naturalists as well as in data of current naïve conceptions of evolution (Costa, 2003; Demastes, Good, & Peebles, 1996). The tendency toward progression—the idea that all organisms evolve from less complex to more complex forms—is also a commonly held misconception among college students, as is the Lamarckian assertion that characteristics acquired by individuals could be inherited or passed down to their progeny (Bishop & Anderson, 1990; Rudolph & Stewart, 1998; Sundberg, 2003).

General conclusions drawn from this review of the literature fall into two basic categories. First, evolution comprises a complex set of scientific phenomena that involves both a general principle and a mechanism. Knowledge of a number of underlying biological principles is necessary in order for students to fully understand either the principle or the explanation for how it may have occurred. This is clearly demonstrated by the web of interconnections found by those who have developed the *Atlas of Science Literacy* (AAAS, 2000). Unfortunately, as reported in Driver, Squires, Rushworth, and Wood-Robinson (1994), it is clear that students are likely to possess inaccurate views about variation, the sources of such variation, the mechanism of inheritance, and adaptation—all vital aspects of evolutionary biology. As evidence, consider the finding of Brumby (1984) who showed that even a few medical students who have years of training in the biological sciences believe that the children of light skinned parents were slightly more likely to be darker than expected if born in a sunny region. Not only does this suggest a common-sense use of the term *adaptation* but it also strongly suggests that these students seem not to understand the underlying mechanism of inheritance, the source of variation, and the role populations rather than individuals play in evolution.

Second, beyond the philosophical and historical misconceptions discussed in previous chapters, there exists a well established set of misconceptions that individuals hold about evolution and natural selection. The evidence is clear that many individuals harbor some or all of the misconceptions shown in Table 3, which provides a summary of the most widespread evolution misconceptions.

Evolution Instruction: Concerns and Strategies

As with other naïve views, prior conceptions related to evolution are both deep-seated and resistant to change (Bishop & Anderson, 1990; Demastes et al., 1996; Jensen & Finley, 1996; Sundberg, 2003). Efforts to correlate misconceptions with personal and/or religious beliefs or with previous instruction in science, specifically instruction in biology, have been of limited use in

TABLE 3 A summary of the most widespread misconceptions regarding evolution and natural selection revealed by a review of the literature.

Students' misconceptions typically center on the following faulty beliefs:

- Species are fixed and therefore do not evolve at all. (Evaluating this claim is important since it may be due to a creationist view or simply a lack of acceptance of the evidence supporting evolution.)
- Individuals *not* populations are the key to evolution. (In truth, populations evolve, individuals do not.)
- Evolution is goal-directed (teleological). (In fact, there is no evidence that evolution is goal directed, purposeful, or progressive.)
- Variations (the raw material of evolution) come from new mutations. (In actuality, variations occasionally do result from mutations, but it would be more accurate to recognize that variation is always resident in the population at some level; when there is a selective advantage associated with some variation, it may increase in frequency as a result of natural selection.)
- Individual organisms can adapt or change either at will or because they have to. (Of course, this is not possible.)
- The mechanism of evolution is Lamarckian and through *use or disuse* typically accompanied by ***inheritance of acquired characteristics*** species change through time. (The problem with this view is that there is no link between change in the phenotype and change in the genotype indicating a basic lack of knowledge about inheritance.)
- Evolution itself is a slow and consistent "advancement" from single cell to human being. (The discovery of punctuated equilibrium has shown that the mode and tempo of evolution is not typically steady. Also, the "target" or "purpose" of evolution is not the development of any specific form of life.)

improving evolution education. In the following sections we will consider some of the sources and potential solutions for evolution misconceptions.

The Nature of Science

In addition to lacking scientific foundation knowledge, another explanation for the persistent misconceptions regarding evolution may come from a faulty understanding of the nature of science (McComas, 1998; Solomon, Scott, & Duncan, 1996; Sundberg, 2003). For instance, Sinclair, Pendarvis, and Balwain (1997) report that many university students do not appreciate the distinction between a theory and a law and could not identify the mechanism of evolution in the context of a survey on evolution understanding. The first issue is a strong example of the possible misuse of language discussed earlier.

Studies also show that students do not tend to view science as a dynamic, human endeavor that requires creativity, but rather as an enterprise where a single scientific method is employed in an effort to discover the unchanging laws of nature (Abraham, 2002; Cooper, 2001; McComas, 1998). Evolutionary biology lies at the intersection of the historical and nonhistorical sciences by drawing on the disciplines of paleontology, geology, molecular cell biology, comparative anatomy, and other such fields. Rudolph and Stewart (1998) suggest that one of the greatest impediments to the effective evolution instruction is found in science teaching itself. They submit that teaching is typically "based on philosophical conceptions of science that are no longer viewed as adequately characterizing the diverse nature of scientific practice, especially in evolutionary biology" (p. 1069).

Cooper (2001) asserts that some students may see evolution as unscientific because it cannot be easily studied with the canonical scientific method that calls for the formulation of a hypothesis, the making of predictions, and the testing of hypotheses in the laboratory. In some ways this claim is unfounded since evolution and natural selection have been the study of many experimental investigations in recent years. Following a study investigating the relationship of knowledge and acceptance of evolution, Sinatra, Southerland, McConaughy, and Demastes (2003) advocate the incorporation of nature-of-science instruction into evolution education. This joins a similar earlier recommendation by Scharman and Harris (1992). Therefore, just as evolution is considered the unifying theme in biology, one could argue that evolution should be a key focus of nature of science instruction as a route to the improvement of students' understanding of evolution.

Science Teachers' Knowledge

Throughout this chapter, the focus has been on students' misconceptions as the dominant hurdle in effective evolution instruction. Unfortunately, Gregg, Janssen, and Bhattacharjee (2003) have shown that the knowledge base of many science teachers presents another serious challenge. They found that high school science teachers are not well prepared in either the theory or the evidence for evolution and therefore have difficulty conveying these complex ideas to students. Moore (2002) supports this assertion. His review of biology instruction shows that many teachers do not recall ever having taken college-level science coursework that incorporated evolution. Further, he reports that most of these teachers do not even recall hearing the word *evolution* in their college biology courses.

Even among biology teachers, where one would expect to find strong support of evolution, there remains doubt about the legitimacy of evolutionary theory. Researchers Eve and Dunn (1990) found that in their sampling of 387 high school biology teachers selected randomly from the membership list of the National Science Teachers Association (NSTA), 39% agreed with the statement, "There are sufficient problems with the theory of evolution to cast doubt on its validity" (p. 14). Of the same teachers surveyed, 45% agreed with the statement, "Adam and Eve were the first human beings and were created by God" (Eve & Dunn, 1990, p. 14). In their review of biology teachers across several states, Weld and McNew (1999) found that one-third (33%) of biology teachers do not believe that evolution is central to biology and place little to no emphasis on evolution in their classes. If these findings are representative of biology teachers generally, this fact alone can account for the lack of evolution knowledge generally among high school graduates. Coupling these findings with our general knowledge that teachers are poorly prepared to engage students in nature-of-science instruction, it should be no surprise that evolution education is imperiled.

Addressing the Problems of Evolution Education

The solution to the problem of how to teach evolution effectively is not an easy one. There are many targets in the battle to enhance understanding of this important scientific principle. First we must ensure that state standards contain appropriate and robust inclusion of evolutionary biology (such is not the case presently) (Lerner, 2000) while addressing widespread public misunderstanding and even fear of evolution. We must be aware of student misconceptions related to the history of evolutionary biology, and we must address illogical philosophical responses to evolution (typically based on inappropriate implications assumed for evolution because of religious interpretations). Of course, we must target conceptual misunderstanding related to evolution and the scientific foundation on which it rests.

Unfortunately, it is not enough to teach about evolution as if it were just another topic in biology, the range of misconceptions is simply too great even if one discounts the complication of creationist and other nonscientific counterarguments. Bishop and Anderson (1990) found that the amount of previous coursework in biology had little to no effect on student conceptions of evolution (even in cases where students had two or more years of college-level biology instruction). Their data indicate that student conceptions of evolution were not associated with their acceptance of evolution as true or untrue. Rather, students who accept evolution tended to make judgments based on their perception of science as powerful, prestigious, and reliable rather than basing their acceptance of evolution on their own understanding of the evidence for evolution. The medical students in the Brumby (1985) study similarly were not all competent in their understanding of evolution in spite of their high-level training in biology. In their replication of the Bishop and Anderson study, Demastes, Settlage, and Good (1995) also found that university students' current views of evolution were not linked to the amount of prior instruction. It seems reasonable to warn that in these cases we do not know if and how these students discussed evolution in their prior biology courses. There is growing evidence showing that some biology teachers either give minimal consideration to evolution or neglect it altogether.

It is clear that evolution must be addressed differently and more directly than other topics in biology. Several recently developed instructional methods are based on a conceptual change model of instruction through which students are given explicit opportunities to test for themselves the utility of evolution and its explanatory model natural selection. Conceptual change is based on the constructivist notion that students already have ideas about phenomena that must be evaluated personally in order to change minds. Lawson (in this volume) advocates such a plan, and Jensen and Finley (1995) applied a historical approach that directly targeted one of the most widespread misconceptions, that of the Lamarckian explanation for the mechanism of evolution. In their model, Jensen and Finley introduced students to the general nature of evolution, taught Lamarckian principles, focused on the evidence against such principles, and had students solve problems from both Lamarckian and Darwinian perspectives so that they might evaluate the effectiveness of each model. They found that this approach resulted in a 65% improvement in students' understanding (through reducing misconceptions). Blackwell, Powell, and Dukes (2003) used another constructivist approach and assessed students' knowledge of evolution in advance of instruction with a pretest. Although it was not made clear how the instructors would apply the results of such a test, one can assume that the students' responses would guide instruction and classroom discussion.

Passmore and Stewart (2002) report success with a similar curriculum that engages students "in developing, elaborating, and using one of the discipline's more important explanatory models . . . natural selection" (p. 185). While space here precludes inclusion of the full model, Passmore and Stewart began the development process with the end goal in mind and recognized immediately that communicating foundation topics such as "population thinking, the origin and role of variation in natural selection, differential survival and fitness" (p. 186) all play a role in the success of the curricular plan. In trying to help students test the usefulness and truthfulness of competing models (and common misconceptions), the curriculum had students explore "Paley's model of intelligent design, Lamarck's model of use [and disuse] inheritance, and Darwin's model of natural selection" (p. 191) while testing these models against facts such as the presence of fossils, the structure of the eye, and varieties of pigeons. Needless to say, when students' misconceptions are addressed proactively, students are likely to accept the scientific explanation, as was the case here.

As Rudolph and Stewart (1993) imply, teachers may be responsible for making poor choices about how to engage in instruction particularly with respect to evolution. They conclude that a "unit on evolution taught in a traditional science classroom may seem to students something of an entirely different kind, consisting of material describing a theory not subject to the usual rigorous test of scientific accountability" (p. 1078). This view is remarkably similar to that of Cooper (2001) who offered an explanation for some of the problems faced by students as they consider the topic of evolution. The recommendation is clear: school laboratory practice should be directed away from confirmation and toward authentic investigations so that students have an opportunity to explore rather than just reiterate vital ideas in science.

Settlage (1994), in his examination of the effectiveness of an evolution-specific curriculum, shows that the "teleological and Lamarckian explanations [that] accounted for over half of the students' explanations on the pretest . . . dropped to less than 20% on the posttest" (p. 449). This is powerful evidence that targeted teaching can impact understanding even with complex ideas like evolution. Of course, there remains the issue of whether learners who understand evolution actually accept it. Sinatra et. al (2003) give us much to consider with their finding that "there was no relation between [prior] knowledge and acceptance of animal or human evolution" (p. 510).

The research into learners' conceptual understanding of evolution is impressive and permits us to end this review on an optimistic note. It is probably no longer reasonable to consider evolution to be "biological education's underresearched unifying theme" (Cummins, Demastes, & Hafner, 1994, p. 445). We now know much about what must be done because the challenges are clear. We know what misconceptions students are likely to possess, and we have evidence that conceptual-change teaching, informed by references to the nature of science and accompanied by engaging laboratory activities, is likely to be effective in addressing these common misconceptions. However, this approach will require that educators give evolution education the prominence it deserves both as a foundation principle in biology and because evolution and natural selection are pedagogically complex topics. It is simply impossible and inappropriate to expect that teaching a unit on evolution in the way that one might engage students in studying cell anatomy will be effective. The centrality of evolution within the science of biology and complexity of evolution as a curriculum topic demand that we do much more, but there are many indications about where to begin.

References

Abraham, L.M. (2002). What do high school science students gain from research apprenticeship programs? *The Clearing House, 75*, 229–32.

American Association for the Advancement of Science. (2000). *Atlas for science literacy.* Washington, DC: AAAS Press.

Blackwell, W.H., Powell, M.J., & Dukes, G.H. (2003). The problem of student acceptance of evolution. *Journal of Biological Education, 37*(2), 58–67.

Bishop, B.A. & Anderson, C.W. (1990). Student conceptions of natural selection and its role in evolution. *Journal of Research in Science Teaching, 27*, 415–27.

Brem, S.K., Ranney, M., & Schindel, J. (2003). Perceived consequences of evolution: College students perceive negative personal and social impact in evolutionary theory. *Science Education, 87*(2), 181–206.

Brumby, M.N. (1984). Misconceptions about the concept of natural selection by medical biology students. *Science Education, 68*(4), 493–503.

Clough, E.E. & Wood-Robinson, C. (1985). How secondary students interpret instances of biological adaptation. *Journal of Biological Education, 19*(2), 125–30.

Cooper, R.A. (2001). The goal of evolution instruction: Should we aim for belief or literacy? *Reports of the National Center for Science Education, 21* (1–2), 14–18.

Costa, J.T. (2003). Teaching Darwin with Darwin. *BioScience, 53*, 1030–31.

Cummins, C.L., Demastes, S.S., & Hafner, M.S. (1994). Evolution: Biological education's under-researched unifying theme. *Journal of Research in Science Teaching, 31*, 445–48.

Deadman, J.A. & Kelley, P.J. (1978). What do secondary school boys understand about evolution and heredity before they are taught the subjects? *Journal of Biological Education, 12*, 7–15.

Demastes. S.S., Settlage, J., & Good, R. (1995). Students' conceptions of natural selection and its role in evolution: Cases of replication and comparison. *Journal of Research in Science Teaching, 32*(5), 535–50.

Demastes, S.S., Good, R.G., & Peebles, P. (1996). Patterns of conceptual change in evolution. *Journal of Research in Science Teaching, 33*, 407–31.

Driver, R., Squires, A., Rushworth, P., & Wood-Robinson, V. (1994). *Making sense of secondary science: Research into children's ideas.* London: Routledge Falmer.

Evans, E.M. (2000, April). The emergence of beliefs about the origins of species in school-age children. *Merrill-Palmer Quarterly, 46*(2), 221–54.

Eve, R.A. & Dunn, D. (1990). Psychic powers, astrology & creationism in the classroom? *The American Biology Teacher, 52*, 10–21.

Ferrari, M. & Chi, M. (1998). The nature of naïve explanations of natural selection. *International Journal of Science Education, 20*(10), 1231–56.

Gould, S.J. (2001). Introduction. In C. Zimmer (Ed.), *Evolution: The Triumph of an Idea*. New York: Harper Collins.

Gregg, T.G., Janssen, G.R., & Bhattacharjee, J.K. (2003). A teaching guide to evolution. *The Science Teacher, 70*(8), 24–31.

Jensen, M.S. & Finley, F.N. (1995). Teaching evolution using historical arguments in a conceptual chance strategy. *Science Education, 79*, 147–66.

Jensen, M.S. & Finley, F.N. (1996). Changes in students' understanding of evolution resulting from different curricular and instructional strategies. *Journal of Research in Science Teaching, 33*, 879–900.

Keil, F.C. (1989). *Concepts, kinds and cognitive development*. Cambridge, MA: MIT Press.

Lerner, L.S. (2000). *Good science, bad science: Teaching evolution in the states*. Washington, DC: Thomas B. Fordham Foundation.

Lord, T. & Marino, S. (1993). How university students view the theory of evolution. *Journal of College Science Teaching, 22*, 353–57.

Lucas, A.M. (1971). The teaching of 'adaptation.' *The Journal of Biological Education, 5*(2), 86–90.

Mayr, E. (1982). *The growth of biological thought: Diversity, evolution and inheritance*. Cambridge, MA: Harvard University Press.

McComas, W.F. (1998). The principle elements of the nature of science: Dispelling the myths. In W.F. McComas, (Ed.), *The Nature of Science in Science Education: Rationales and Strategies*. Dordrecht, Netherlands. Kluwer Academic Publishers.

Moore, R. (2002). Do standards matter? How the quality of state standards related to evolution instruction. *The Science Teacher, 69*, 49–51.

National Academy of Sciences. (1998). *Teaching about evolution and the nature of science*. Washington, DC: National Academy Press.

Passmore, C. & Stewart, J. (2002). A modeling approach to teaching evolutionary biology in high schools. *Journal of Research in Science Teaching, 39*(3), 185–204.

Rudolph, J.L. & Stewart, J. (1998). Evolution and the nature of science: On the historical discord and its implications for education. *Journal of Research in Science Teaching, 35*, 1069–89.

Solomon, J., Scott, L., & Duncan, J. (1996). Large-scale exploration of pupils' understandings of the nature of science. *Science Education, 80*, 493–508.

Samarapungavan, A. & Reinout, W.W. (1997). Children's thoughts on the origin of species: A study of explanatory coherence. *Cognitive Science, 21*(2), 147–77.

Scharman, L.C. & Harris, W.M. (1992). Teaching evolution: Understanding and applying the nature of science. *Journal of Research in Science Teaching, 29*, 375–88.

Settlage, J. (1994). Conceptions of natural selection: A snapshot of the sense making process. *Journal of Research in Science Teaching, 20*, 449–57.

Sinatra, G. M., Southerland, S.A., McConaughy, F., & Demastes, J. W. (2003). Intentions and beliefs in students' understanding and acceptance of biological evolution. *Journal of Research in Science Teaching, 40*(5), 510–28.

Sinclair, A.., Pendavis, M.P., & Baldwin, B. (1997). The relationship between college zoology students' beliefs about evolutionary theory and religion. *Journal of Research and Development in Education, 30*(2), 118–25.

Sundberg, M.D. (2003). Strategies to help students change naïve alternative conceptions about evolution and the natural selection. *Reports of the National Center for Science Education, 23*(2), 23–26.

Weld, J. & McNew, J.C. (1999). Attitudes toward evolution. *The Science Teacher, 66*(9), 27–31.

Wilkins, J. (2001). Defining evolution. *Reports of the National Center for Science Education, 21*(1–2), 29–36.

Whitfield, P. (1993). *From so Simple a Beginning: An Illustrated Exploration of the 4-Billion-Year Development of Life on Earth*. New York: Macmillan.

The Essential Role of the Nature of Science in Learning about Evolutionary Biology:

Strategies for Enhancing the Acceptance of Evolution

I-6

Michael P. Clough

> The citizens' appalling ignorance of the nature of science bodes ill for the future. And the more I think about this problem, the more I feel that the fault is mainly ours—we, the teachers in the schools, colleges, and universities of the nation, must accept much of the blame.
>
> John A. Moore (1983)

Introduction

Students of all ages possess a host of misconceptions concerning both the nature of science (NOS) and biological evolution and may be secretively or even openly hostile toward the idea of biological evolution. These misconceptions and apprehension exacerbate the challenges in teaching biological evolution. Therefore, before initiating activities designed to illuminate aspects of biological evolution, such as those provided in this monograph, teachers should first seriously consider the "conceptual baggage" that students bring to this topic. If students' misconceptions of the NOS and evolutionary theory are not addressed before, during, and after the laboratory activities provided here, desired outcomes will be seriously compromised. What teachers *do* with activities to engage students conceptually in wrestling with scientific argumentation will determine the value of this monograph's activities for understanding biological evolution! This paper suggests strategies that facilitate a more accurate portrayal of the NOS and diminish hostility toward evolution education, thereby promoting a deeper understanding of evolutionary theory.

The Public Evolution Education Controversy and the Nature of Science

While science education reform documents emphasize the importance of accurately conveying the NOS to students (AAAS, 1989; McComas & Olson, 1998; NRC, 1996), few teachers do so. Research has consistently documented science teachers' misconceptions regarding the NOS (Abd-El-Khalick & Lederman, 2000; Brush, 1989; Carey & Strauss, 1970; Eve & Dunn, 1990; Hodson, 1988; Rowe, 1976). Over 30 years ago Elkana (1970) stated that science teachers' views concerning the NOS trailed contemporary philosophical views by more than two decades, and DeBoer (1991), in his review of the history of science education, argues that problematic notions of the NOS from the last century still informs much classroom practice and pervades most available curriculum materials. Not surprising, therefore, are the numerous studies documenting science students' misconceptions concerning the NOS (Clough, 1995; Johnson & Peeples, 1987; Rowell & Cawthron, 1982; Rubba, Horner, & Smith, 1981; Ryan & Aikenhead, 1992). John Moore (1983) claimed that the public evolution education controversy is, in large part, a result of misunderstandings concerning the NOS:

> *. . . it becomes evermore important to understand what is science and what is not. Somehow we have failed to let our students in on that secret. We find as a consequence, that we have a large and effective group of creationists who seek to scuttle the basic concept of the science of biology . . . a huge majority of citizens who, in "fairness," opt for presenting as equals the "science" of creation and the science of evolutionary biology . . . . It is hard to think of a more terrible indictment of the way we have taught science.*

The importance of understanding the NOS takes on even greater urgency with recent attacks on evolution education. Past efforts to have "creation science" taught in public science classrooms were unsuccessful because the courts upheld the separation of church and state, and because even many citizens who personally doubt the ultimate truth of biological evolution find suspect the use of religious texts to mandate what should be taught in science classrooms. However, those sympathetic to the creationists' political agenda have become far more sophisticated in their efforts to bypass the scientific community and convince the general public and policymakers that biological evolution is an idea in crisis and that a viable scientific alternative, intelligent design (ID), exists. Terry (2004, p. 267) writes:

> *Not only is ID not about Biblical Literalism, but almost all talk of God has been carefully removed from the discussion. In an apparent nod to the failure of "scientific creationism," ID makes no reference to scripture and proudly proclaims that some of its advocates are nonbelievers. No proof of God's existence is offered—just that of an "Intelligent Designer." Students are not to be taught who this Designer is, just that the evidence shows that the Designer exists. Presumably, they can take it from there.*

Recently, biology teachers in Dover, PA were ordered by their school board to include "intelligent design" in their courses (Sappenfield & McCauley, 2004). Few biology teachers are prepared to argue effectively against such intrusions into the biology curriculum. To understand why ID is not science and why biological evolution is a sound scientific theory requires a sophisticated understanding of the nature of science.

Several studies (Bishop & Anderson, 1990; Johnson & Peeples, 1987; Rutledge & Warden, 2000; Trani, 2004) support the contention that those who understand the NOS are more likely to accept evolutionary theory as a sound scientific explanation. Especially disturbing, then, are the results from studies that biology majors and biology teachers have a poor understanding of important NOS issues relevant to biological evolution (Bybee, 2001; Johnson &

Peoples, 1987). Scharmann and Harris (1992) found that promoting science teachers' applied understanding of the NOS reduced anxiety toward the teaching of evolution, and several studies have linked teachers' understanding of the NOS to the likelihood they will teach biological evolution (Aguillard, 1999; Osif, 1997; Trani, 2004; Rutledge & Warden, 2000).

Not surprisingly, one widely accepted long-standing component of scientific literacy is the need for individuals to have a thorough understanding of the NOS (AAAS, 1989; ASE, 1981; Matthews, 1989; NAEP, 1989; NRC, 1996; NSTA, 2000). Many science educators have called for increased emphasis on the social studies of science in preservice and inservice science teacher education programs (Clough, 2004; Gallagher, 1984; Manuel, 1981; Matthews, 1989; 1994; McComas et al., 1998; Nunan, 1977; Summers, 1982). Understanding the NOS is crucial for comprehending why students often reject biological evolution and why many of Darwin's scientific contemporaries also rejected his theory. In both cases the issue is not about empirical evidence, but rather fundamental assumptions about the nature of reality and the origin and justification of scientific knowledge. As Rudolph and Stewart (1998, p. 1085) argued, conceptually understanding evolutionary biology, and science more generally, requires

> *students to become familiar with the metaphysical assumptions and methodological process that Darwin laid out. Theoretical context and scientific practice, in this view, are not just interdependent, but really two views of a single entity.*

For too long science educators have neglected these NOS issues as esoteric to scientific literacy, but they are fundamental to understanding what science is, how it works, why scientific creationism and ID are *not* science, and how to effectively teach biological evolution.

Suggestions for Reducing Resistance to Evolution Education

No single strategy will pacify all those who oppose the idea of biological evolution, but a large middle ground of students and parents exists who, while not having strong convictions for any one position, are sympathetic to the "fairness" issue and seriously believe a controversy exists in the scientific community concerning biological evolution. The following suggestions are intended to help science teachers decrease resistance to evolution education, avoid unnecessary controversy, and promote an understanding of the NOS and biological evolution.

Make Clear the Distinction between Biological Evolution and the Origin of Life

Much of the resistance to evolutionary theory arises from the mistaken notion that biological evolution and ideas concerning the origin of life are one in the same. This misconception is held by creationists, the general public, and, tragically, by Supreme Court Justices as evidenced by Justice Scalia's opinion in the Louisiana evolution/creation case. How life arose is an extremely interesting scientific problem. However, biological evolution *per se* does not involve the study of origins. "Evolution studies the pathways and mechanisms of organic change following the origin of life" (Gould, 1987). This single demarcation often eliminates much resistance to biological evolution. Of course, discussions of cosmology should not be avoided, but teachers should make clear that biological evolution explains the diversity and similarity of life on this planet—not how life first arose.

Use the Language of Science Correctly and Consistently

Science teachers must be very careful with significant language related to the NOS. Words such as "prove, true, theory, law and hypothesis" have different meanings in and out of science. If used incorrectly, these words have the potential to create misconceptions. For example, students often see scientific models and other ideas as exact copies of the natural world (Ryan & Aikenhead, 1992). Science teachers create needless trouble when they perpetuate this misconception. Many arguments can be made against the notion of "truth" or "certainty" in science, but Einstein and Infeld (1938, p. 31) provide an easily understood analogy:

> *In our endeavor to understand reality we are somewhat like a man trying to understand the mechanism of a closed watch. If he is ingenious he may form some picture of a mechanism which could be responsible for all the things he observes, but he may never be quite sure his picture is the only one which could explain his observations. He will never be able to compare his picture with the real mechanism and he cannot even imagine the possibility or the meaning of such a comparison.*

Because the "watch" can never be opened, asking whether ideas concerning the natural world are absolutely true (i.e., copies of reality) is to ask an unanswerable question. "Truth" in science does not refer to absolute certainty, but rather to ideas that work extremely well at explaining the natural world in naturalistic terms we can understand, making accurate predictions, and guiding further empirical research. Science teachers should acknowledge that all well-accepted scientific ideas (not just evolution) are judged by how well they work. So, while well-accepted scientific ideas are useful and durable, they remain open to revision.

As a second example, consider that outside of science, the word *theory* usually means "guess" or "speculation." Ryan and Aikenhead (1992), after collecting the responses of over 2,000 11th and 12th grade students, found that "The majority [of students] (64%) expressed a simplistic hierarchical relationship in which hypotheses become theories and theories become laws, depending on the amount of 'proof behind the idea.' Even science teachers make statements that convey this same misunderstanding (Bybee, 2001). When individuals bring this misconception to the evolution/creation controversy, nonsensical statements such as "evolution is *only* a theory" are often heard. The word "theory," however, has an entirely different meaning in science. Among other things, scientific theories predict, explain (Campbell, 1953), and provide conceptual frameworks for further research (Kuhn, 1970). Certainly some scientific theories are more speculative than others, but all must perform the functions just described.

Finally, due to the emotional response of many students toward evolutionary theory, what science teachers say and how they say it are especially critical. A fundamental tenet of constructivist learning theory is that students' views, whether they are alternate conceptions or misconceptions, must be treated with great respect. Dismissing or belittling students' views only exacerbates the difficulty of persuading them to build a functional understanding and acceptance of biological evolution.

Stress Functional Understanding Rather Than Belief

When students are faced with a choice between evolutionary theory and their personal religious convictions, science will almost always lose. Lawson and Worsnop (1992, p. 165) write:

> *. . . every teacher who has addressed the issue of special creation and evolution in the classroom already knows that highly religious students are not likely to change their belief in special creation as a consequence of relatively brief lessons on evolution. Our suggestion is that it is best not to try to do so, not directly at least.*

Students are more likely to consider and accept evolution if a functional understanding of the theory is stressed. This, once again, is accomplished by accurately addressing the NOS and showing how the theory of evolution works (i.e., explains, predicts, and provides a framework to conduct further research). *Science As a Way of Knowing* by John Moore (1993) does just this by providing a comprehensive list of deductions that follow from evolutionary theory and the evidence sustaining these deductions. These deductions represent propositions derived from and supported by evolution by natural selection. Students might be challenged to consider these deductions and then investigate them in the laboratory. Moore (1993) presented 15 deductions, including the following:

- The species that lived in the remote past must be different from the species today.
- The older the sedimentary strata, the less the chance of finding fossils of contemporary species.
- The simplest organisms would be found in the very oldest fossiliferous strata, and the more complex ones only in more recent strata.
- Demonstrating the slow change of one species into another must be possible.
- Demonstrating that forms between major groups (e.g., phyla, classes, orders) once existed must be possible.
- The age of the earth must be very great.
- If the members of a taxonomic unit share common ancestry, that should be reflected in their structure and embryonic development.
- If descent from a common ancestry is the basis for the unity of life, then this should be reflected in the structure of cells and in the molecular processes of organisms.

Another deduction of biological evolution—one that is at odds with intelligent design and particularly suited to student investigation—is that imperfections should be found in living organisms. Gould's prodigious writings provide a number of anatomical examples illustrating imperfections and makeshift developments in organisms (e.g., Gould, 1980). Behrman et al. (2004) provide six cases of biochemical imperfections in metabolic pathways and cite recent successes in the laboratory at directing biochemical evolution as an argument against the view that complexity in organisms could only arise through the work of a highly intelligent designer.

Another particularly effective approach to show the usefulness of evolutionary theory is to examine the implications of evolutionary theory for modern medicine. For example, an increasing number of biotechnology companies are using "applied" molecular evolution in the development of high-tech drugs (Bishop, 1992). At a macroevolution level, Gould (1988) writes a particularly biting attack showing how an ignorance of evolutionary theory resulted in a questionable heart transplant from a baboon to a human infant.

Some individuals will argue that emphasizing understanding and the utility of knowledge rather than expecting students to accept it as true is simply a form of avoidance. However, if we look to the history of science, well-known scientists took this same approach. Kekule, in 1867, reputedly wrote:

> *I have no hesitation in saying that from a philosophical point of view I do not believe in the actual existence of atoms . . . As a chemist, however, I regard the assumption of atoms as absolutely necessary. (cited in Post, 1968, p. 225)*

Students, when presented an instrumentalist perspective, not only are more likely to consider evolution, but also will learn a great deal about the history, philosophy, and sociology of science.

Well-Established Scientific Knowledge Is Not Fair, Nor Is It Decided Democratically

The public clamor for teaching both evolution and creationism in our nation's public science classrooms is, in part, an admirable, but sometimes inappropriate, belief in fair play. However, fair play doesn't mean giving credibility to every idea. We do not permit discredited views such as a flat earth, astrology, Aristotelian physics, and an earth-centered "solar" system into our science curriculum simply because a significant number of citizens may believe these ideas. A related problem is the way news media report science to the general public. Too many journalists believe that balanced science coverage means giving credibility to all ideas regardless of their standing in the scientific community. In a recent article in the *Columbia Journalism Review*, Mooney (2004) addresses how purported 'balanced' media coverage of science permits fringe groups to distort well-established knowledge. Students need to be made aware that the scientific community, not public opinion polls, individual scientists, or small groups of scientists decide what is good science! Moreover, when the scientific community has determined the veracity of particular scientific knowledge, fairness is not a satisfactory argument for continuing to advance ideas found wanting.

Science Provides Natural Explanations for Phenomena

Ryan and Aikenhead's (1992) research indicates that 46% of students hold the view that science, rather than being based on the assumption that the world is ordered and can be explained in solely naturalistic terms, could be based on the assumption of an interfering supernatural being. This misconception concerning a basic assumption of science has devastating consequences as students interpret the meaning of data gathered in evolution activities. This view may be confronted in the following way. A popular science cartoon by Sidney Harris (1977) has two scientists at a blackboard considering a lengthy series of mathematical computations interrupted by the written statement "then a miracle occurs," followed by another series of computations. The scientist in the foreground, pointing at the reference to a miracle, states, "I think you should be more explicit here in step two." In another cartoon an automobile mechanic, after having looked at a customer's engine, says to the owner, "It's either a demon or a clogged intake valve. It's almost impossible to tell without taking it apart." These cartoons convey an important message about science as well as the evolution/creation/ID education controversy. First, science deals with the natural world and, consequently, its explanations must be couched in naturalistic expressions. Explanations employing supernatural events and/or deities are beyond nature and, hence, beyond the realm of science to explore. Second, references to the supernatural or some intelligent designer, while being central to most people's lives, are not useful in science. Even if the evidence did suggest an abandonment of biological evolution, the scientific community would then attempt to explain the diversity of life in other naturalistic terms that would meet the criteria of a good scientific theory. This is the essence of science.

"Fitness" Is Not Just "Differential Reproductive Success"

Perhaps the most intuitive aspect of biological evolution is natural selection—the idea that organisms with advantageous characteristics in a given environment have a greater chance of survival and reproduction than organisms lacking these characteristics. Herbert Spencer coined the popular phrase "survival of the fittest" as a definition for natural selection. Many laboratory activities address this fundamental concept. However, when biological "fitness" is *defined* solely as "differential reproductive success," the phrase "survival of the fittest" becomes "survival of those who survive"—an empty tautology (Gould, 1977). Tautologies (e.g., my mother is a woman) are true by definition and hence not open to testing. Alert critics will, with good reason, attack evolution on the grounds that tautologies are not testable. The solution to this apparent problem is that "fitness," while often *expressed* as differential survival, is not defined by it (Gould, 1977). Rather, fitness is the state of being adapted or suited to the environment.

The Issue of Falsifiability

Critics often claim that evolutionary theory is not falsifiable, and hence not science by Popper's (1963) criteria. Yet in the next breath they will cite several pieces of evidence that supposedly falsify evolution. These two positions are self-contradictory because an idea cannot be both unfalsifiable and falsified. The testable deductions that follow from evolutionary theory make clear that it is science. The evidence in support of these deductions make clear that biological evolution has not been falsified.

Anomalies in Science

Perhaps the most counterintuitive notion that comes from the NOS is the well-supported view that unsolved puzzles and seemingly refuting evidence do not always result in rejection of a scientific idea. Kemp (1988 p. 80) writes:

> *Any theory of the scope of the theory of evolution will always be faced with anomalies, things that it cannot explain, or even things that seem to contradict it.*

The reasons for this are varied and detailed, but comprehensive theories are not discarded simply because several pieces do not fit. Many historical examples exist demonstrating that contradictory data did not result in abandonment of ideas accepted today as good science (Chalmers, 1982; Kitcher, 1982; Kuhn, 1970).

The debate surrounding punctuated equilibrium is a fairly recent example illustrating that anomalies do not always result in abandonment of well-supported ideas. Punctuated equilibrium states that for long periods of time most lineages remain constant with new species developing relatively infrequently but quickly. Darwin suggested that there was slow and steady change through time. Even if punctuated equilibrium does a better job of describing rates of change, it in no way diminishes the idea that evolution *has* taken place.

The Critical Role of the Nature of Science in Helping Students Make Sense of Their Laboratory Experiences

Making the most of laboratory experiences designed to teach about biological evolution demands that both students and teachers understand that science ideas do not follow simply from observing natural phenomena and "objectively" analyzing results from investigations. Philosophical presuppositions, implicitly shared in the scientific community, underlie laboratory work and the interpretation of results. What this means for effective school laboratory experiences is that teachers must help their students come to understand the epistemological (how knowledge is constructed and justified) and ontological (nature of reality) assumptions underlying scientific knowledge and the rationale for holding those assumptions while doing science.

Matthews (1994, pp. 188–89) points out that contemporary scientific knowledge is based on several assumptions that clash with ideas commonly held by students and the general public. Secondary and college students often hold to one or more of the following assumptions that interfere with their understanding biological evolution:

- ***Processes in the natural world bring about a suitable final state.*** Students holding this view often search for explanations that are unnecessarily teleological, thus interfering with their understanding the random character of evolutionary change and the improvised developments in organisms.

- ***Natural processes are activated and controlled by spiritual influences.*** This perspective is evident in many students' struggle to understand that the diversity of life can, or even should be, explained in naturalistic terms with no reference to the supernatural.
- ***Knowledge comes simply from observing phenomena in its natural state.*** This assumption is evident in students' difficulties reconciling the idea of biological evolution with what they observe in nature. Evolutionary understanding transcends observations of the natural world.
- ***Knowledge claims are validated by their successful predictions.*** Many people wrongly apply experimental methodologies and outcomes from some areas of physical sciences to all sciences. Rudolph and Stewart (1998) write, "Dependent upon the contingencies of the past and the indeterminacy of the future, [biological evolution has] little power to make predictions, much less have any specific prediction borne out by observation." Even in fields where accurate predictions are important, they are not the sole factor in determining the veracity of scientific knowledge.
- ***Knowledge is fixed and unchanging.*** Wrongly believing that good scientific knowledge should endure forever, students often struggle to understand bona fide disagreements within the scientific community regarding some aspect of biological evolution. When ideas are revisited and sometimes modified or abandoned by the scientific community, students working from this assumption can easily dismiss the entire theory of evolution.
- ***Acceptable knowledge is decided by authority figures.*** While well-respected scientists can and do influence science, in the end ideas in science are not accepted or rejected because of authority figures in or out of science. However, many people and cultures believe that particular authority figures (e.g., religious and political leaders and texts) cannot be questioned. This assumption is particularly problematic for understanding biological evolution when students' religious affiliations and/or parents take a strong stand against the idea of biological evolution.

Acknowledging that many of these assumptions were also held by scientists in Darwin's time and formed the basis of their opposition to biological evolution can be helpful in teaching students that scientific knowledge changes, but that it changes for good reasons. To promote intended learning in laboratory activities directed at biological evolution, the above everyday assumptions must be explicitly addressed to illustrate that contemporary scientific knowledge is built on a foundation that differs in significant ways from everyday thinking. Students should understand that while they need not abandon their personal views outside of science, to comprehend scientific knowledge they must work from different assumptions that have proven quite useful in understanding the natural world. Effective use of laboratory activities can help students and their teachers clarify the nature of science and how it differs from other ways of knowing. Relevant discussions about the nature of science in the context of laboratory work can help students make sense of their laboratory experiences and better understand important aspects of biological evolution.

Summary

Too many students graduate from high school and college without gaining a sufficient understanding of the NOS and biological evolution. Evolution must be taught in order to portray modern biology accurately and to help students understand its most comprehensive idea. Much of the resistance to biological evolution education by students, parents, *and* teachers can be attributed to a poor understanding of the NOS.

Science teachers at all levels convey an image of the nature of science whether or not that is their intent. Ever present in science content and teaching are implicit and explicit messages regarding how science works. Effectively teaching the nature of science requires that teachers become aware of the many ways they unknowingly convey an image of science and scientists, and implement strategies that will portray the nature of science more accurately (Clough, 1997 & 2004; Clough & Olson, 2004).

The suggestions made here are important because laboratory activities directed toward illuminating biological evolution are only as good as the teachers who implement them. The outcomes of model activities in this monograph will be severely compromised without explicit efforts to accurately teach students the nature of science and link that understanding to the methodological processes, interpretations, and conclusions regarding biological evolution.

Genuine acceptance of evolutionary theory first requires a functional understanding of the idea, and this is preceded by openness to learning about it. Science teachers, by utilizing strategies described here, can increase students' understanding of the NOS and significantly improve their attitudes toward evolution education. This will pave the way for full engagement in all instruction devoted to one of the most comprehensive and fascinating frameworks created by human intellect.

References

Abd-El-Khalick, F. & Lederman, N.G. (2000). Improving science teachers' conceptions of nature of science: A critical review of the literature. *International Journal of Science Education, 22*(7), 665–701.

Aguillard, D. (1999). Evolution Education in Louisiana public schools: A decade following *Edwards v. Aguillard. The American Biology Teacher, 61*(3), 182–88,

American Association for the Advancement of Science (AAAS). (1989). *Project 2061: Science for all Americans*. Washington, DC: Author.

Association for Science Education (ASE). (1981). *Education through science*. An ASE Policy Statement. Hatfield, UK: Author.

Behrman, E.J., Marzluf, G.A., & Bentley, R. (2004). Evidence from biochemical pathways in favor of unfinished evolution rather than intelligent design. *Journal of Chemical Education, 81*(7), 1051–52.

Bishop, B. & Anderson, C. (1990). Student conception of natural selection and its role in evolution. *Journal of Research in Science Teaching, 27*(5), 415–27.

Bishop, J.E. (1992). New way to develop high-tech drugs monkeys with Darwin's famed theory. *The Wall Street Journal*, 2/25.

Brush, S.G. (1989). History of science and science education, *Interchange, 20*(1), 60–71.

Bybee, R. (2001). Teaching about evolution: Old controversy, new challenges. *Bioscience, 51*(4), 309–12.

Campbell, N. (1953). *What is science?* New York: Dover.

Carey, R.L. & Strauss, N.G. (1970). An analysis of experienced science teachers' understanding of the nature of science. *School Science and Mathematics, 70*(5), 366–76.

Chalmers, A.F. (1982). *What is this thing called science?* (2nd ed.). Queensland: University of Queensland Press.

Clough, M.P. (2004). The Nature of Science: understanding how the "game" of science is played. In Jeff Weld (Ed.), *The Game of Science Education* (Chapter 8, pp. 198–227). Boston: Allyn and Bacon.

Clough, M.P. (1997). Strategies and activities for initiating and maintaining pressure on students' naive views concerning the nature of science. *Interchange, 28*(2–3), 191–204.

Clough, M.P. (1995). Longitudinal understanding of the nature of science as facilitated by an introductory high school biology course. *Proceedings of the Third International History, Philosophy, and Science Teaching Conference* (pp. 212–21). Minneapolis: University of Minnesota.

Clough, M.P. & Olson, J.K. (2004). The nature of science: Always part of the science story. *The Science Teacher, 71*(9), 28–31.

DeBoer, G. (1991). *A history of ideas in science education: Implications for practice*. New York: Teachers College Press.

Elkana, Y. (1970). Science, philosophy of science and science teaching. *Educational Philosophy and Theory, 2*, 15–35.

Einstein, A. & Infeld, L. (1938). *The evolution of physics*. New York: Simon and Schuster.

Eve, R.A. & Dunn, D. (1990). Psychic powers, astrology and creationism in the classroom? *The American Biology Teacher, 52*(1), 10–21.

Gallagher, J.J. (1984). Educating high school teachers to instruct effectively in science and technology. In R. Bybee, J. Carlson, & A.J. McCormack (Eds.), *Redesigning science and technology education—NSTA yearbook 1984*. Washington, DC: NSTA.

Gould, S.J. (1977). Darwin's untimely burial. *Ever Since Darwin*. New York: Norton.

Gould, S.J. (1980). The panda's thumb. In S.J. Gould, *The Panda's Thumb* (pp. 19–26). New York: Norton.

Gould, S.J. (1987). Justice Scalia's misunderstanding. *Natural History, 96*(10), 14–21.

Gould, S.J. (1988). The heart of terminology: What has an abstruse debate over evolutionary logic got to do with baby fae? *Natural History, 97*(2), 24–31.

Harris, S. (1977). *What's so funny about science?* Los Altos, CA: Kaufmann.

Hodson, D. (1988). Toward a philosophically more valid science curriculum. *Science Education, 72*(1), 19–40.

Johnson, R.L. & Peeples, E.E. (1987). The role of scientific understanding in college: Student acceptance of evolution. *The American Biology Teacher, 49*(2), 93–98.

Kemp, K.W. (1988). Discussing creation science. *The American Biology Teacher, 50*(2), 76–81.

Kitcher, P. (1982). *Abusing science: The case against creationism.* Cambridge, MA: The MIT Press.

Kuhn, T.S. (1970). *The structure of scientific revolutions.* Chicago: University of Chicago Press.

Lawson, A.E. & Worsnop, W.A. (1992). Learning about evolution and rejecting a belief in special creation: Effects of reflective reasoning skill, prior knowledge, prior belief and religious commitment. *Journal of Research in Science Teaching, 29*(2), 143–166.

Manuel, D.E. (1981). Reflections on the role of history and philosophy of science in school science education. *School Science Review, 62*(221), 769–71.

Matthews, M.R. (1994). *Science teaching: The role of history and philosophy of science.* New York: Routledge.

Matthews, M.R. (1989). A role for history and philosophy in science teaching. *Interchange, 20*(2), 3–15.

McComas, W.F. & Olson, J.K. (1998). The nature of science in international standards documents. In W.F. McComas (Ed.), *The nature of science in science education: rationales and strategies* (pp. 41-52), Dordrecht, The Netherlands: Kluwer Academic Publishers.

McComas, W.F., Clough, M.P., & Almazroa, H. (1998). The nature of science in science education: An introduction. *Science & Education, 7*(6), 11–532.

Mooney, C. (2004 November/December). Blinded by science: How 'balanced' coverage lets the scientific fringe hijack reality. *Columbia Journalism Review, 6.*

Moore, J.A. (1983). Evolution, education, and the nature of science and scientific inquiry. In J.P. Zetterberg (Ed.), *Evolution versus creationism: The public education controversy.* Phoenix, AZ: Oryx Press.

Moore, J.A. (1993). *Science as a way of knowing: The foundations of modern biology.* Cambridge: Harvard University Press.

National Assessment of Education Progress (NAEP). (1989). *Science objectives.* Princeton: Author.

National Research Council (1996). *National Science Education Standards.* Washington, DC: National Academy Press.

National Science Teachers Association. (2000). Position statement on the nature of science. http://www.nsta.org/positionstatement&psid=22 Also in *NSTA Reports!, 11*(6), 15.

Nunan, E. (1977). History and philosophy of science and science teaching: A revisit. *The Australian Science Teachers Journal, 23*(2), 65–71.

Osif, B. (1997). Evolution and religious beliefs: A survey of Pennsylvania high school teachers. *The American Biology Teacher, 59*(9), 552–56.

Popper, K.R. (1963). *Conjectures and Refutations: The growth of scientific knowledge.* New York: Harper & Row.

Post, H.R. (1968) & Kekule, F.A. (1867). Atomism 1900 I. *Physics Education, 3*(5), 225–32. September.

Rowe, R.E. (1976). Conceptualizations of the nature of scientific laws and theories held by middle school and junior high school teachers in Wisconsin. Unpublished doctoral thesis. The University of Wisconsin-Madison.

Rowell, J.A. & Cawthron, E.R. (1982). Image of science: An empirical study. *European Journal of Science Education, 4*(1), 79–94.

Rubba, P.A., Horner, J.K., & Smith, J.M. (1981). A study of two misconceptions about the nature of science among junior high school students. *School Science and Mathematics, 81*, 221–26.

Rudolph, J.L. & Stewart, J. (1998). Evolution and the nature of science: On the historical discord and its implications for education. *Journal of Research in Science Teaching, 35*(10), 1069–89.

Rutledge, M. & Warden, M. (2000). Evolutionary theory, the nature of science & high school biology teachers: Critical relationships. *The American Biology Teacher, 62*(1), 123–31.

Ryan, A.G. & Aikenhead, G.S. (1992). Students' preconceptions about the epistemology of science. *Science Education, 76*(6), 559–80.

Sappenfield, M. & McCauley, M.B. (2004, November 23). God or science? *The Christian Science Monitor.* http://www.csmonitor.com/2004/1123/p11s02-legn.html

Scharmann, L.C. & Harris, W.M. (1992). Teaching evolution: Understanding and applying the nature of science. *Journal of Research in Science Teaching*, *29*(4), 375–88.

Summers, M.K. (1982). Philosophy of science in the science teacher education curriculum. *European Journal of Science Education*, *4*(1), 19–27.

Terry, M. (2004). One nation, under the designer. *Phi Delta Kappan*, *86*(4), 264–70.

Trani, R. (2004). I won't teach evolution: It's against my religion. *The American Biology Teacher*, *66*(6), 419–27.

I-7

A Scientific Approach to Teaching about Evolution and Special Creation

 Anton E. Lawson

The purpose of this article is to present a lesson that deals with the scientific aspects of the so-called evolution versus special creation controversy for high school or introductory college biology courses. The lesson uses a "scientific approach to teaching," which means that it allows students to confront the evolution versus special creation issue largely in the way that scientists confronted the issue in the past. In other words, the teaching approach does not ignore the issue by pretending that some students do not take special creation seriously as an explanation for present-day species, nor does it simply "tell" students what to believe. Instead it raises the key scientific question and presents the major alternative explanations/theories that have been proposed in the past to answer the question. This approach then challenges students to gather evidence from the fossil record and analyze that evidence using critical thinking skills to decide for themselves which explanation (or explanations) represents the best answer to the question raised.

The lesson provokes students to inquire and engage in several elements of scientific reasoning. Those elements include:

1. *Raising causal questions.* In this case, the central causal question is: What caused present-day species diversity? (i.e., Where did all the different kinds of organisms come from?)
2. *Considering the major alternative explanations that have been proposed to answer the causal question.* In this case, the explanations involve spontaneous generation, special creation, and evolution.
3. *Deducing predictions (expectations) based on the assumed truth of one or more postulates of the explanations in question.* For example,

   If evolution is correct in claiming that present-day species arose through a gradual change/development of new forms through time (evolution theory),

   and . . . we compare fossils from older/lower rock layers with those from younger/higher rock layers (test conditions),

---

This activity is based on Anton E. Lawson's 1999 article, "A scientific approach to teaching about evolution and special creation," *The American Biology Teacher, 61*(4), 266–74. It has been adapted and reprinted with permission of the publisher.

then . . . the older layers should be less likely than the younger layers to contain fossils that look like present-day species (prediction, expected result).

4. *Gathering evidence* (i.e., fossils representative of the fossil record that were collected by the students on an imaginary hike through the Grand Canyon).
5. *Comparing the evidence from the fossil record with the deduced predictions to find out which explanation (or explanations) has been supported or contradicted* (e.g., because the older layers do not contain fossils that look like present-day species while the younger layers do, evolution theory has been supported).

The primary objective of the lesson is to not only enable students to discover evidence that generally supports evolution theory and fails to support the alternative explanations of special creation and spontaneous generation, but more importantly to improve students' understanding of the nature of science and to develop their critical thinking skills. Kemp (1988) has proposed a similar argument in favor of including alternatives to evolution in the biology curriculum. In Kemp's words:

> *A vigorous controversy is, to my mind, always worth a look. Such controversies provide a good context for cultivating critical thinking skills, which, like writing, should be emphasized across the curriculum. To ignore creation science is to miss a good opportunity. Further, it is not fair to students who may have heard something about creation science to dismiss it summarily without a word as to what is wrong with it. Surely there is something to be said about why it is bad. And understanding why scientists reject inadequate theories is part of what it is to be educated about science. (Kemp 1988, pp. 76–77)*

Details of the present teaching approach—sometimes referred to as the learning cycle—can be found in Lawson (1988, 1994, 1995). More recently, Lawson (1996) provided an example of how the approach could be used to introduce the theory of classical Mendelian genetics. That article also summarized research on the effectiveness of the learning cycle in promoting the development of thinking skills as well as in teaching important scientific concepts.

Most learning cycles, including the present one, include an initial "hands-on" instructional phase called exploration, in which students explore some new objects, events, or situations. The exploration phase is followed by a phase called term introduction in which the teacher introduces new terminology. Term introduction is followed by an instructional phase called concept application, in which students are given opportunities to deepen their understanding of newly constructed concepts by trying to apply them in new contexts. As mentioned, a key aspect of learning cycle lessons is that they attempt to engage students in meaningful inquiries with the aim of improving their abilities to inquire (i.e., improve their thinking skills) and with the aim of helping students construct new meaningful concepts (e.g., concepts such as evolution, fossilization, and adaptive radiation).

The present learning cycle is hypothetico-deductive in nature as it is initiated with the presentation of three major explanations, each advanced to account for the origin of present-day species diversity. Presentation of the explanations and their central postulates is followed by a challenge to students to gather evidence from the fossil record and use that evidence along with the postulates to generate hypothetico-deductive arguments for or against the alternatives. Generating hypothetico-deductive arguments will be difficult for some students, particularly in the sometimes emotionally charged context of evolution and special creation. Consequently, you will probably find the lesson more successful if it follows other lessons in which the hypothetico-deductive nature of science and scientific reasoning have already been introduced and used.

Details of the lesson will be presented in two sections. The first section, Student Material, includes an introduction, a set of lesson objectives, a materials list, a procedure to guide the student inquiry, and a set of application questions to extend the lesson. The second section, Teacher Material, includes content-related background and teaching tips for each phase of the lesson. Lesson success depends in large part on having a representative collection of fossils for student exploration. Obtaining such a set is no simple matter, but Platt (included in Section II of this book) provides some useful strategies.

Teacher Section

What Caused Present-Day Species Diversity?

The theory of organic evolution (i.e., the idea that species change across time) represents a cornerstone of modem biology as it conceptually ties together numerous and varied observations. The idea that species evolved had been suggested by others prior to publication of Charles Darwin's *The Origin of Species* in 1859, yet Darwin was the first to spell out major postulates of evolutionary theory—as extracted by Lewis (1986)—and listed as follows:

1. All life evolved from one simple kind of organism.
2. Each species, fossil or living, arose from another species that preceded it in time.
3. Evolutionary changes were gradual and of long duration.
4. Each species originated in a single geographic location.
5. Over long periods of time new genera, new families, new orders, new classes, and new phyla arose by a continuation of the kind of evolution that produced new species (= adaptive radiation).
6. The greater the similarity between two groups of organisms, the closer is their relationship and the closer in geologic time is their common ancestral group.
7. Extinction of old forms (species, etc.) is a consequence of the production of new forms or of environmental change.
8. Once a species or other group has become extinct, it never reappears.

9. Evolution continues today in generally the same manner as during preceding geologic eras.

In the *Origin of Species*, Darwin recognized that he was proposing two theories: "Evolution or Descent with Modification" and "Natural Selection." In general, you can expect that the fossil record will provide evidence to support evolution theory and not support spontaneous generation and special creation theories. *Note:* The term *theory* is used here as a general explanation for a broad class of related phenomena. This definition does not require that evidence has been gathered in the theory's favor. Although this is not the definition found in several recent texts, it is the sense used by many authors, including Darwin himself. For example, after mentioning natural selection in the introduction of *The Origin of Species* (6th ed., New York: D. Appleton and Company, 1898, p. 5), Darwin wrote ". . . the most apparent and gravest difficulties in accepting the *theory* [italics added] will be given." Many other authors use the term *theory* in this way, including Lewis (1986, 1988), Gibbs and Lawson (1992), Clough (1994), and—as quoted above—Kemp (1988).

Although space does not permit a discussion of all the relevant arguments, this is a preferable definition to the common textbook definition. It is preferable to differentiate hypotheses from theories based on generality and complexity rather than by degree of support. Clearly there is no scientific tribunal that meets periodically to decide when particular hypotheses have acquired enough support to be elevated to the status of the theory.

Some of the hypothetico-deductive arguments that students (or you) may generate to test evolution theory are as follows:

If . . . *Evolution theory is correct*

and . . . *we compare fossils from the oldest layers at the bottom of the canyon to fossils from the younger/higher layers and to present-day species (test conditions),*

then . . .

1) *species that lived in the remote past (lower layers) should be different from those living today (expected result 1);*
2) *the older (lower) the layer, the less likely that it should contain fossils similar to present-day species (expected result 2);*
3) *only the simplest organisms should be found in the oldest layers containing fossils and the more complex ones should be only in the more recent layers (expected result 3);*
4) *a comparison of fossils from layer to layer should show gradual changes in fossil forms (expected result 4);*
5) *fossils of intermediate forms (i.e., between major groups) should be found (expected result 5). Note: Due to the rarity of such intermediates, none is contained in typical fossil collections, however, casts of some intermediates such as Archaeopteryx, which is a classic intermediate showing both reptile and bird-like characteristics, are available for purchase from supply companies.*

No fossils appear in the bottom layer (layer F) but some very simple fossils do appear in the next higher layer (layer E). Students may recognize that evolution theory does not offer an adequate account for this apparent "spontaneous" appearance of simple life forms in layer E. Therefore, some support can be claimed for either spontaneous generation theory or special creation theory at this time.

Although some evidence may be consistent with spontaneous generation theory, students may generate arguments, such as the following, that fail to support the theory:

If . . .	*Spontaneous generation theory is correct,*
and . . .	*we compare fossils from the oldest layers at the bottom of the canyon to fossils from the younger/higher layers and to present-day species (test conditions),*
then . . .	*no particular patterns should be found because new kinds of organisms are presumably being generated all the time (expected result).*
But . . .	*clear patterns are seen from layer to layer (actual result),*
Therefore . . .	*spontaneous generation theory is not supported (conclusion).*

Likewise, special creation theory is not supported when actual observations are compared to the expected results/observations based on the following arguments:

If . . . *special creation theory is correct,*

and . . . *we compare fossils from the oldest layers at the bottom of the canyon to fossils from the younger/higher layers and to present day species (test conditions),*

then . . .

1) *species that lived in the remote past (lower layers) should be similar to those living today (expected result 1);*
2) *the older/lower layers should be just as likely to contain fossils similar to present-day species as the younger/higher layers (expected result 2);*
3) *the simplest as well as the most complex organisms should be found in the oldest layers containing fossils as well as in the more recent layers (expected result 3);*
4) *a comparison of fossils from layer to layer should not show gradual changes in fossil forms (expected result 4);*
5) *fossils of intermediate forms (i.e., between major groups) should not be found (expected result 5);*
6) *fossils of land plants should be found in lower/older layers than fossils of sea creatures because land plants presumably were created before sea creatures (expected result 6).*

Advanced Preparation for Teaching This Lesson

The fossil collection you put together should represent a minimum of four time periods (i.e., Cenozoic, Mesozoic, "Upper" Paleozoic [defined here as the periods following the invasion of the land by plants, i.e., Silurian through the Permian], and "Lower" Paleozoic [defined here as the periods when only marine animal and plant life was evident, i.e., the Ordovician and Cambrian]). In addition, a Pre-Cambrian "stomatolite layer" with accompanying photomicrographs of the microfossils found in the layer should be included along with an "empty layer" representing rocks devoid of fossils. Although the selected fossils are a very limited subset, they will demonstrate the following patterns characteristic of the fossil record (from oldest to youngest):

- An initial stage with only simple forms present
- Among the more "complex" fossils, a progression from those that are strikingly unlike living species to those which are more similar to living species
- A general increase in size and diversity of types
- A shift from exclusively marine organisms to a combination of aquatic and terrestrial types

Distribute the fossils among 10 stations around the lab (two stations for layer A, as well as two stations for each of the layers B, C, and D; one station for layer E and one for layer F). If you are concerned that some fossils may "disappear" during the lab, you can glue them to pieces of wood or sturdy cardboard. Another possibility is to trace fossil outlines on pieces of wood or cardboard and have students return them to their respective places after their observations. This way you can quickly account for all the fossils before students leave the lab.

Engagement

Draw a diagram of the Grand Canyon rock strata on the board and explain that the fossils and rocks were collected from the six corresponding layers (labeled A–F) during a class field trip (see Figure 1 in Student Material).

Review the three explanations and their postulates and challenge students to observe the fossils and use their observations to generate one or more "if . . . and . . . then . . . therefore" arguments for or against the explanations. An example of such an argument appears in the Student Material section, but you may need to offer a more familiar example to get students started on the right track. Consider, for example, the following argument that can be used to test the hypothesis that grass fails to grow under a tree because the tree shades the ground:

If . . .	*grass fails to grow under a tree because the tree shades the ground (hypothesis),*
and . . .	*several branches are cut off the tree (test conditions),*
then . . .	*the grass should start to grow better (expected result).*
But . . .	*after several weeks the grass still fails to grow (actual result).*
Therefore . . .	*the shade hypothesis has not been supported (conclusion).*

Exploration

Assign students to work in teams of two to make their observations.

When student teams have completed their observations, have them return to their seats and join another team. Ask the groups of four to discuss their observations and arguments. Challenge each group of four to decide on one or two of their "best" arguments to be presented during a class discussion. For teaching tips on how to encourage effective group work, see Johnson and Johnson (1987).

Hold a class discussion in which one member of each group presents the group's best argument. Invite comments on those arguments from other students. Continue the discussion of arguments and evidence as long as interest remains high. The intent of the discussion should be to have students evaluate the quality of the arguments and evidence and attempt to determine which explanation, or combination of explanations, best accounts for the evidence. There should be no need for you, as teacher, to interject your views (i.e., conclusions), although you should feel free to offer arguments and evidence that students may have missed. Also, you should not be compelled to tie up loose ends. Rather, the main points to leave students with are:

a. Science is primarily an alternative theory/hypothesis testing enterprise.
b. Alternative theories/hypotheses are tested using an "if . . . and . . . then . . . therefore . . ." form of hypothetico-deductive reasoning.
c. This form of reasoning can be used to test theories/hypotheses about past events as well as about present-day and future events. In other words, alternative explanations can be tested even when experiments cannot be conducted.

Term Introduction

At some point during the discussion you should ask students which rock layer they believe to be the youngest, oldest, and why. When a student presents the argument that the lowest layers must be the oldest because they must have been formed first, you have an opportunity to discuss the process of sedimentary rock formation and the way fossils are formed. You should introduce terms such as *sediments* (i.e., fragmental matter that settles to the bottom of a liquid), *sedimentation* (i.e., the deposition or accumulation of sediments), *sedimentary rocks* (i.e., rocks formed by the compaction and cementation of sediments, or by the precipitation of material from solution), *relative time scale* (i.e., a "before-and-after" scale for a series of events), and *fossilization* (i.e., the formation of fossils through processes such as imprinting, mineralization, and replacement). Imprinting occurs when organisms make traces of themselves on wet mud. If these traces are partly dried, then quickly buried, they may be preserved as fossils. Mineralization occurs when porous bones or shells are altered by having minerals deposited in them by percolating water. Replacement occurs when the original parts of an organism simultaneously go into solution and deposition of a new material occurs.

At this time you may want to introduce the names and some interesting details of some of the more unusual fossils such as the trilobites, ammonites, brachiopods, blastoids, and stromatolites (see Platt in this volume).

Terms such as *phyletic evolution* (i.e., a type of evolution in which an entire species is changed over time into a new species) and *divergent evolution* (i.e., the evolution of one or more new species from one ancestor) and *extinction* (i.e., the permanent loss of all members of a species) can also be introduced at this time. To introduce these and the previous terms, begin by mentioning the relevant observation(s), then present the definition, and finally introduce the term or terms. For example, to introduce the terms *extinct* and *extinction*, say something like the following:

> *You have noticed that several types of fossils such as the trilobites and the ammonites are found in the lower layers but do not appear in the higher layers, nor have they been found living today. This implies that all members of these fossil species have died and that the particular species has not reappeared. When this happens biologists say that the species in question has become extinct and the process of becoming extinct is called extinction.*

You may also wish to discuss how scientists use the rate of radioactive decay of materials in fossils or in the materials in which they are embedded to determine absolute ages. The term *radioactive dating* can be introduced and a discussion of how this is done might be appropriate at this time.

Concept Application

To extend and expand student understanding of the introduced concepts, you may want to show a relevant video or film and/or discuss some of the other areas of evidence that support the theory of organic evolution, notably comparative anatomy, comparative embryology, comparative biochemistry, chromosomal similarities, and so on. Also, you may want to have students consider predictions concerning what one should find based on evolution theory, special creation theory, or spontaneous generation theory regarding experiments conducted in new areas (e.g., a comparison of the proteins, DNA, or internal anatomy, etc. of closely related organisms and distantly related organisms). If you do not choose to discuss other areas of evidence at this time, you may want to have your students research the evolutionary sequence of an organism that is living today (e.g., horse, man, or elephant). You could also arrange for a field trip to a local fossil bed or museum.

Assign the Application Questions that appear in the Student Material as well as any relevant textbook readings. Additional application activities appear in Lawson (1994) as do two learning-cycle investigations that would be good follow-up labs to the present investigation. The first lab, Have Humans Been on Earth a Long Time?, explores the concept of geologic time, while the second lab, How Do Species Adapt to Environments?, allows you to introduce the theory of natural selection.

Biological Terms

sediments
sedimentation
sedimentary rocks
relative time scale
fossilization (imprinting, mineralization, replacement)
phyletic evolution
divergent evolution
extinct
extinction
radioactive dating

Thinking Skills

accurately describe nature
state causal questions
generate alternative theories
generate logical predictions
organize and analyze data
data draw and apply conclusions

Student Section

Where Did All the Kinds of Organisms Come From?

Introduction—Where Did All the Kinds of Organisms Come From?

People have long been impressed with the tremendous number and variety of living things on Earth. Quite naturally the question of where they all came from has been asked repeatedly over the centuries. Although countless answers have been offered, most attention and debate has centered on three general explanations.

The first of these explanations, called spontaneous generation theory, consists of the following three postulates:

1. Living things arise spontaneously from nonliving materials when acted upon by a special vital force.
2. Different sorts of nonliving materials give rise to different sorts of living things.
3. Spontaneous generation has occurred in the past and still occurs today.

The second explanation is called special creation theory. Relevant postulates of special creation theory, as they appear in the Bible's book of Genesis, are as follows:

- On the third day, God gathered the water below the sky into one place to produce land and seas and created seed- and fruit-bearing plants to inhabit the land, according to their kinds.
- On the fifth day, God created all the creatures of the sea, according to their kinds, and every bird, according to its kind.
- On the sixth day, God created all the creatures of the land, according to their kinds, including a man in God's own image and a woman. (*Note:* Although there are a number of special creation theories, this version was selected because it was the one widely accepted in Europe when Charles Darwin proposed an alternative theory.)

Relevant postulates of the third explanation, called evolution theory, as they first appeared in Charles Darwin's book *Origin of Species* in 1859 are as follows:

- All life arose from one simple kind of organism.
- Each species, fossil or living, arose from another that preceded it in time.
- Changes in living things were gradual and of long duration.
- Over long periods of time, new genera, new families, new orders, new classes, and new phyla arose by a continuation of the same kind of formation and development (i.e., evolution) that produced new species.
- Evolution continues today in generally the same manner as during preceding geologic eras.

The primary purpose of this activity is to gather evidence and generate arguments to test these alternative explanations. The evidence will come from

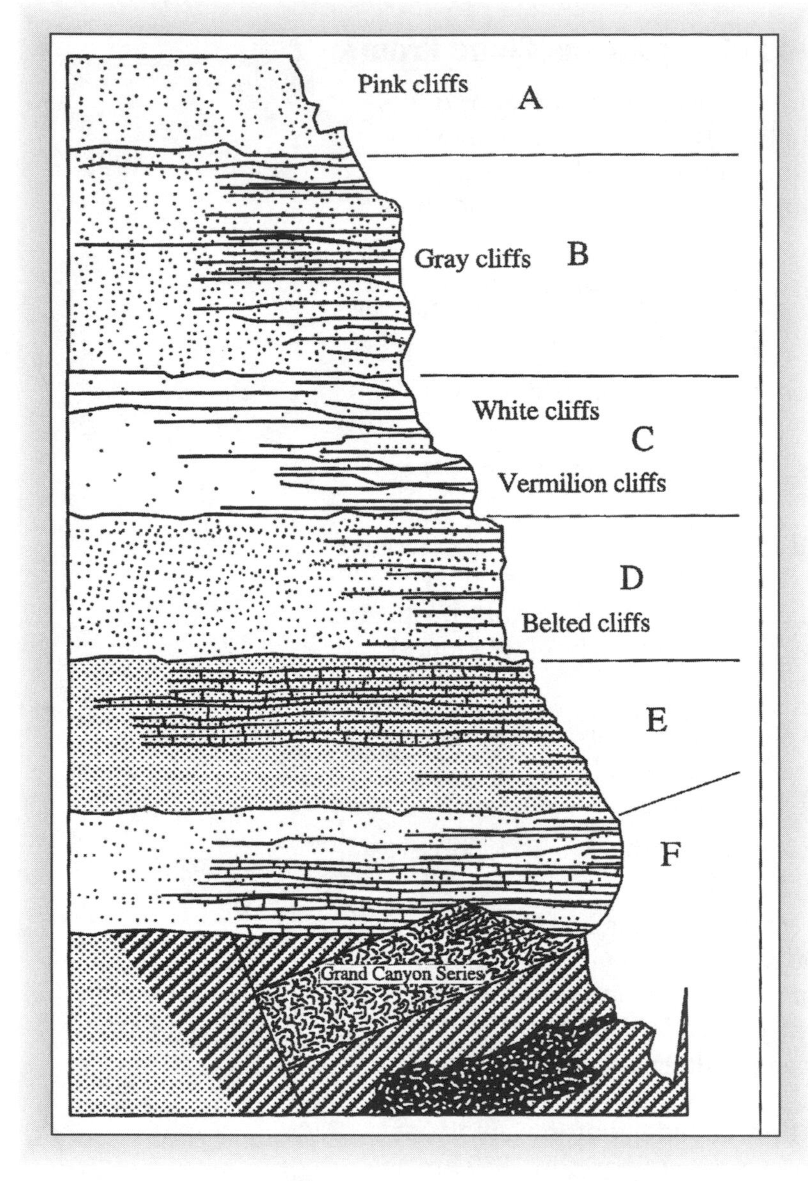

FIGURE 1 ■ Generalized rock layers in wall of Grand Canyon.

fossils collected from the Grand Canyon, a huge gorge in Northern Arizona. You will use this evidence to generate your arguments and draw conclusions. The gorge was formed by the Colorado River over hundreds of millions of years as it cut through several rock layers. A diagram of those rock layers appears in Figure 1. Imagine that while hiking in the Grand Canyon you observe what looks like a fossil embedded in a rock. As you may know, fossils are the remains of organisms that lived in the distant past and were buried in materials such as mud, sand, volcanic ash, or frozen ground. As you continue hiking, you stop occasionally, observe, and collect fossils from several of the rock layers.

Your observations raise many questions, including the following: Are different kinds of fossils found in different rock layers? Are certain fossil forms found only in certain rock layers? Are any fossil forms found in all rock layers? What patterns, if any, are revealed by a comparison of fossils (or lack of fossils) from one layer to the next? Do any fossils resemble an organism you might find living today? If so, what is the organism? Where does it live? What conditions might have been necessary for fossil formation? What might the environment have been like in which the fossilized organism lived?

Obviously, you have generated more questions than can be answered during your hike. In today's investigation you will examine several fossils collected from six of the Grand Canyon's rock layers and search for relationships and patterns in this fossil record. As mentioned, the primary objective is to use your observations as evidence to test the three explanations.

Objectives

1. To observe representative fossils from several rock layers of the Grand Canyon and discover patterns of variation in organisms through time.
2. To use the discovered patterns to test the theories of spontaneous generation, special creation, and evolution as satisfactory explanations for present-day species diversity.

3. To generate hypotheses about the environments in which the fossilized organisms lived.

Materials

- Representative fossils and/or rocks from six sedimentary layers of the Grand Canyon
- Hand lenses/microscopes
- Metric rulers

Procedure

Fossils from the six canyon layers are distributed at 10 "stations" in the lab/classroom. Fossils collected from layer A (the top layer) are located at two of these stations. Layer B fossils are located at two stations as are fossils from layers C and D. Fossils/rocks from layers E and F are each located at only one station.

Working with another student, start at any station. Carefully observe the fossils at that station, noting the layer from which they were collected and enough fossil characteristics to enable you to compare fossils with those from other layers. Record notes and make sketches to help you remember your observations and thoughts. Respond to the following questions as you observe the fossils at each station:

- What might the environments of the fossilized organisms at this station have been like when they were alive? How can you tell?
- How similar are the fossils at this station to present-day organisms?
- Which fossilized organisms, if any, are found in more than one layer?
- Which fossilized organisms, if any, are found in only one layer?
- What similarities and differences are revealed by a comparison of fossils from one layer to the next?
- Which explanation best accounts for your observations at each station? Explain.
- Which explanation best accounts for patterns revealed by a comparison of fossilized organisms from one layer to the next?

Go to another station and repeat your observations, data collection, and recordings.

After you have visited each station, join another pair of students and discuss your observations and interpretations. As a group, try to generate one or more arguments that either support or do not support one or more postulates of the three theories. Your arguments should be of the standard "if . . . and . . . then . . . therefore . . ." form that scientists use to test hypotheses and theories. For example,

> *If special creation theory is correct in claiming that land was created before any living things were created (special creation theory),*

and . . . rocks and fossils of several layers are compared (test conditions),

then . . . the lowest/oldest rock layer or layers (i.e., the layer or layers created before any living things were created) should contain no fossils (expected result).

Result . . . The lowest/oldest rock layer (i.e., layer F) contains no fossils while the higher/younger layers do contain fossils (actual result).

Therefore . . . special creation theory has been supported (conclusion).

Write down your group arguments and evidence in the space below, and be prepared to share them during a class discussion.

During the class discussion, give careful consideration to the arguments and evidence presented by other students. Which of the arguments/evidence did you find most/least convincing? Explain. What questions remain? How might answers to these questions be found?

Application Questions

1. Why is it reasonable to suspect that fossilized organisms found in the rock layers at the bottom of the Grand Canyon lived before those found in progressively higher layers?
2. Some fossils found in the lower layers are not found in the upper layers. Propose two possible explanations for this observation.
3. Some fossils found in upper layers are not found in lower layers. Propose two possible explanations for this observation.
4. In most locations on Earth, fossils are relatively rare. Propose two possible explanations for this observation.
5. Coal, which was formed from fossil plants, has been discovered in Antarctica. Propose a possible explanation to account for this discovery.
6. Suppose someone advances the claim that all kinds of organisms were created at essentially the same point in time and that they have not changed across time. If this claim is correct, state two predictions (expected results/observations) about what the fossil record should look like.
7. Suppose someone advances the counterclaim that organisms have changed and developed across vast periods of time. If this claim is correct, state two predictions about what the fossil record should look like.
8. The data in Table 1 were gathered by the geologist Charles Lyell and were reported in 1854. Which, if any, of the three theories do the data support? fail to support? Explain.
9. Do intermediate forms of organisms (i.e., those that appear not to fit into one kind or another) actually exist today? If so, how common are they? What are the implications of such organisms for the evolution and special creation explanations?

TABLE 1 Percentage of fossil species still alive today from four sedimentary rock layers that vary in age (from Lyell, 1854).

Rock layer	Fossil species	Alive today	Percent of fossil species still alive
Youngest	226	216	96%
Next Youngest	569	238	42%
Next Oldest	1,021	176	17%
Oldest	1,238	42	3%

10. What are vestigial structures? Does the existence of such structures support evolution theory or special creation theory? Explain.

References

Clough, M.P. (1994). Diminish students' resistance to biological evolution. *The American Biology Teacher, 56*(7), 409–15.

Darwin, C. (1898). *The origin of species by means of natural selection* (6th ed.). New York: D. Appleton and Company.

Gibbs, A. & Lawson, A.E. (1992). The nature of scientific thinking as reflected by the work of biologists & by biology textbooks. *The American Biology Teacher, 54*(3), 137–52.

Johnson, D. & Johnson, R. (1987). *Learning together and alone.* Englewood Cliffs, NJ: Prentice Hall.

Kemp, K.W. (1988). Discussing creation science. *The American Biology Teacher, 50*(2), 76–81.

Lawson, A.E. (1988). A better way to teach biology. *The American Biology Teacher, 50*(5), 266–78.

Lawson, A.E. (1994). *Biology: A critical thinking approach.* Menlo Park, CA: Addison-Wesley Publishing Company.

Lawson, A.E. (1995). *Science teaching and the development of thinking.* Belmont, CA: Wadsworth Publishing Company.

Lawson, A.E. (1996). Introducing Mendelian genetics through a learning cycle. *The American Biology Teacher, 58*(1), 38–42.

Lewis, R.W. (1986). Teaching the theories of evolution. *The American Biology Teacher, 48*(6), 344–47.

Lewis, R.W. (1988). Biology: A hypothetico-deductive science. *The American Biology Teacher, 50*(6), 362–67.

Lyell, C. (1854). *A manual of elementary geology: Or the ancient changes of the Earth and its inhabitants, as illustrated by geological monuments* (4th ed.). New York: Appleton.

Platt, J. (1999). Putting together fossil collections for "hands-on" evolution laboratories. *The American Biology Teacher, 61*(4), 275–81.

I-8 Charles Darwin:

Evolutionary Biology's Most Important Experimenter

Robert Dennison

Our understanding of the living world owes much to a scientist described as possessing "a brilliant mind, great intellectual boldness, and an ability to combine the best qualities of a naturalist-observer, philosophical theoretician, and experimentalist . . . " (Mayr, 1991, p. 11). According to Ernst Mayr, "the world has so far seen such a combination only once, and it was in the man Charles Darwin" (Mayr, 1991, p. 11). Most who are acquainted with his work would readily agree that Darwin was a great observer of nature and possibly the single greatest thinker/theoretician the discipline has ever known. Most biology teachers know of the astounding observations Darwin made, such as his noting of the similarities between organisms of neighboring geographic locales and between organisms of similar geologic age and location. As he stated in the opening lines of *The Origin of Species*, he was "much struck with . . . the distribution of organic beings . . . and in the geological relations of the present to the past inhabitants of continents" (Darwin, 1872, p. 11). Of course, virtually all biology textbooks discuss his observations of the striking anatomical similarities between the animals of the same class, such as his famous comparisons of the forelimbs of mammals. However, few teachers are aware of Darwin's voluminous and equally impressive experimental work. It is this experimental work and its relevance to biology teaching that will be addressed herein.

Darwin's experiments covered a wide variety of topics in biology, each of which ultimately related to his evolutionary work. His works can provide teachers with a rich source of experiments with which to teach evolution and, by example, the nature of science.

In reading Darwin's descriptions of his experiments in his books and papers, one is struck by the many paths his mind took as he thought through the far-reaching implications of his evolutionary theories. In hindsight, one can almost read his mind, imagining him thinking, "If I am to show that common descent and natural selection are true, then I must also be able to show that _______ is true," with the blank continually being filled in and tested via both experiments and observations. For example, he hypothesized that oceanic islands had been populated by immigrants from the nearest mainland, with the descendants of those original colonists having been modified into new species by selection pressures which differed from those encountered by the mainland inhabitants. He knew that for this idea to be possible, colonizing plants and/or their seeds had to be able to cross expanses of ocean to get to the islands in the first place. This meant they must be able to survive lengthy exposure to salt water in order to float from the mainland to the islands. In order to test the plausibility of his hypothesis, he soaked many different kinds of seeds in salt water for months at a time and then attempted to germinate them. To his delight, many of the seeds retained their viability, successfully germinating at the end of the experiment, lending support for his views. This is a classic example of the hypothetico-deductive method often favored by Darwin, wherein he would arrive at a hypothesis based on his observations, make testable deductions based on that hypothesis, then test those deductions experimentally. The more deductions he could support with his experimental results, the more confident he became in his hypothesis.

Darwin used a blend of such observations and experiments throughout his career. For instance, he was surprised to observe iguanas swimming off the coast of the Galápagos. He hypothesized that, unlike any known lizards, these creatures must regularly enter the ocean to feed. He then "opened the stomachs of several [iguanas] and found them [full of] a sea weed that grows at the bottom of the sea, some distance from the coast. The nature of this lizard's food, as well as the structure of its tail and feet absolutely prove its aquatic habits" (Darwin, 1845, p. 391).

Back home in England years later, while thinking of the interrelationships between species that his theory implied, he noticed bumblebees moving from flower to flower and hypothesized that both the bees and the flowers benefited from, indeed depended upon, this relationship. He put his ideas to the test by covering some experimental kidney bean plants with gauze, while leaving others uncovered. As expected, none of the covered plants produced seeds, whereas most of the uncovered ones "set fine pods with good seeds," leading him to conclude that "if every bee in Britain were destroyed, we should not again see a pod on our kidney beans" (Darwin, 1857).

Darwin used the results of over 20 years of such trials to help convince his audience of the validity of his arguments, confidently stating in *The Origin of Species*, "It can hardly be supposed that a false theory would explain in so satisfactory a manner as does the theory of natural selection, the several large classes of facts . . . specified" (Darwin, 1872, p. 367). Darwin continued performing observations and experiments in support of this claim, adding to the list of "large classes of facts," as he called such evidence long after first publishing *The Origin of Species* in 1859.

Earthworms in the Service of Science

Darwin knew that for his theories to be valid, it must also be true that small, minute changes could result in significant, major changes over time. He returned to this theme often throughout his life. In fact, his final book, on the seemingly insignificant topic of earthworms, reinforces and supports the truth of this crucial concept of gradualism.

Fortunately for biology teachers, the observations, deductions, and experiments in the "earthworm book" are easily understood and enjoyed by students. The book provides an easy to follow example of Darwin's methods, with the potential to inspire students to believe they, too, can think like great scientists. For example, you might have students consider the following quote from Darwin:

> *A field . . . was last ploughed in 1841 . . . and left to become pasture land. For several years it was clothed in extremely scant vegetation, and was so thickly covered with small and large flints (some of them half as large as a child's head) that the field was called by my sons 'the stony field'. [However] the smaller stones disappeared before many years had elapsed, as did every one of the larger ones over time; so that after thirty years (1871) a horse could gallop over the compact turf from one end of the field to the other and not strike a single stone . . . the transformation was wonderful. (Darwin, 1881, p. 143)*

Suppose we ask "Where did the stones go?" and invite the students to brainstorm in small groups to derive possible answers. All of the answers are then posted for discussion by the whole with the list being narrowed to a few reasonable explanations (common ones are erosion, human activity, etc.). The students are then given Darwin's further observation that the rocks were actually still present, but "lying at a depth of some inches beneath the turf." After considering the implications of this "new" data for their hypotheses, students are given Darwin's hypothesis that "the apparent sinking of superficial bodies is due . . . to the large quantity of fine earth continually brought up to the surface by worms in the form of castings. These castings are sooner or later spread out and cover up any object left on the surface" (Darwin, 1881, p. 3).

Darwin's hypothesis is added to the list for discussion, and the students are challenged to show how we can decide which answer is most likely to be correct (i.e., in which can we have the most confidence?). This leads to the formation of lists of deductions based on each hypothesis. The students quickly realize that these deductions must be able to be tested against the evidence. For example, if the apparent sinking of the stones is due to the action of small earthworms, there must be very many worms in the soil and they must pass through tremendous amounts of soil through their bodies!

Such properly constructed deductions are certainly testable, and that is exactly what Darwin did. For example, he describes the following:

1. evidence that a typical acre of land contains 53,767 worms;
2. experiments in which individual worm castings were counted and weighed, with the results extrapolated to show that worms move as much as 18 tons of earth to the surface per acre per year; and
3. trenches which he dug to find that the buried objects were still in a uniform layer beneath the surface, just as one would expect if the objects were simply covered up by castings being spread out over time. (Darwin, 1881)

As a result of examining Darwin's evidence and comparing it to any support for competing ideas, students become convinced that worms did indeed cause the disappearance of the rocks. Of course, that is not the point of the exercise. Instead, the purpose is two-fold: first, the students will come to realize the power of the hypothetico-deductive method, especially if teachers explicitly discuss that method while working through Darwin's simple example; and second, students will appreciate the cumulative power of small events occurring continuously over a long period of time.

Darwin gives us a clue that making this second point was the true reason for publishing the earthworm book. He had actually presented the basic ideas of the book in papers going back to 1837, but his claims were met with skepticism by some who doubted the power of such small creatures to do so much work. He describes and answers such criticism in the 1881 book's introduction: "Here we have an instance of that inability to sum up the effects of a continually recurrent cause, which has often retarded the progress of science, as formerly in the case of geology and more recently in the principle of evolution" (Darwin, 1881, p. 6). (For an excellent discussion of the significance of the earthworm book as Darwin's final publication, see Gould's essay, "A Worm for a Century," in *Hen's Teeth and Horse's Toes*, 1983).

Flowering Plants Provide Abundant Evidence for Evolution

In addition to gradualism, another common theme of Darwin's which was crucial to the arguments presented in *The Origin of Species* was that of variation among the individuals of a species. Darwin looked for and found variation among the members of all species he studied. He further sought to understand and explain the functions of those variations. As one example, let us consider Darwin's observations of and experiments on flowering plants. He published eight books and many papers dealing exclusively with various aspects of plant biology, and he stated in his autobiography that "It has always pleased me to exalt plants in the scale of organized beings" (Darwin, in Barlow, 1958 , p. 135). In fact, the experiments to be described below, though rarely discussed in biology books, were possibly Darwin's personal favorites. He describes his experiments on "heterostyled plants" in these terms: "I do not think anything in my scientific life has given me so much satisfaction as making out the structure of these plants" and "no little discovery of mine ever gave me so much pleasure as making out the meaning of heterostyled flowers" (Darwin, in Barlow, 1958, p. 134).

One might ask why the reproductive habits of these flowers could be so important to Darwin. In both *The Origin of Species* and his *Various Contrivances by which Orchids Are Fertilised by Insects* (the "orchid book"), Darwin maintained that "it is an almost universal law of nature that the higher organic beings require an occasional cross with another individual" (Darwin, 1877, p. 1). He goes on to conclude that "It is hardly an exaggeration to say that Nature tells us, in the most emphatic manner, that she abhors perpetual self-fertilization" (Darwin, 1877, p. 293). In *The Different Forms of Flower on Plants of the Same Species*, we find ample experimental evidence to support both this claim and the important postulate that there is variation among the individuals of a species.

Once again, the experiments described below are easily understood by students. These botanical experiments can be used to show both the importance of controls and to again stress the convergence of diverse lines of evidence in support of evolution by natural selection.

The species of plants collectively known as "heterostyled" have flowers that come in either two (dimorphic) or three (trimorphic) forms. In each case, the pistil is of a different length than the stamens. As a result, self-fertilization is less likely than it would be if the stamens were the same length as the pistil, allowing easy transfer of pollen within the same flower. For example, in the dimorphic flowers, "the long-styled plants have a much longer pistil . . . standing high above the anthers [while] the short-styled plants have a short pistil [and] the stamens are long" (Darwin, 1880, p. 12). Even more diverse are the trimorphic species which have three possible lengths of pistils and stamens: short, medium, and long. Each flower has one length of pistil accompanied by stamens of the two lengths which do not match that pistil. In other words, flowers with long pistils have only short and medium stamens, and so on. Observations of these flowers led Darwin to hypothesize that the arrangement of flower parts helped ensure cross-fertilization by insects. Taken from *Flowers*, Figure 1 illustrates the hypothesized pollination patterns he desired to test experimentally.

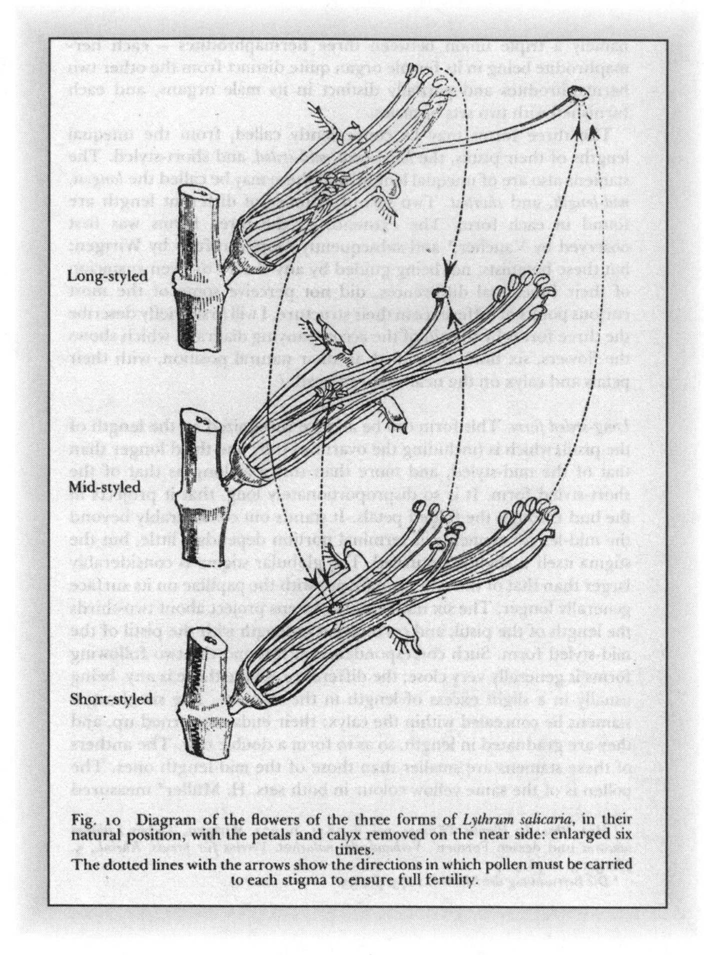

Fig. 10 Diagram of the flowers of the three forms of *Lythrum salicaria*, in their natural position, with the petals and calyx removed on the near side: enlarged six times.
The dotted lines with the arrows show the directions in which pollen must be carried to each stigma to ensure full fertility.

FIGURE 1 Pollination patterns which ensure maximum fertility (Darwin, 1880, p. 139).

Students can be asked to propose experiments to test the hypotheses he formed based on his earlier observations. They can then be given Darwin's descriptions of his own experiments and results and asked to evaluate whether or not he successfully supported his hypotheses.

In discussing the trimorphic flowers, Darwin states that "nothing shows more clearly the extraordinary complexity of the reproductive system of this plant, than the necessity of making eighteen different unions in order to ascertain the relative fertilization power of the three forms. Thus the long-styled form has to be fertilized with pollen from its own two kinds of anthers, from the two in the mid-styled and from the two in the short-styled" (Darwin, 1880, p. 107). He then goes on to describe the 223 experimental unions he performed, transferring pollen from stamen to pistils by means of camel hair brushes, and the controls he used, such as protecting the flowers from insects by covering them with large nets.

In each case, the most successful matings (i.e., good seeds produced) resulted when the length of the pistil matched the length of the stamen from which the pollen was taken (e.g., pollen taken from the long stamens of a short-styled flower would successfully fertilize the pistil of a long-styled flower, and so on). Since these flowers never have pistils and stamens of the same length on a single plant, cross-fertilization is strongly favored by natural selection.

Interested teachers may even consider providing students with the detailed data tables shown in Figure 2, in which Darwin reported his results (Darwin, 1880, pp. 150–57).

TABLE 23 *Long-styled form*

I

Legitimate union

13 flowers fertilized by the longest stamens of the mid-styled. These stamens equal in length the pistil of the long-styled.

Product of good seed in each capsule

36	53
81	0
0	0
0	0
0	0
	0
—	
45	
41	

38 per cent of these flowers yielded capsules. Each capsule contained, on an average, 51·2 seeds.

II

Legitimate union

13 flowers fertilized by the longest stamens of the short-styled. These stamens equal in length the pistil of the long-styled.

Product of good seed in each capsule

159	104
43	119
96 poor seed	96
103	99
0	131
0	116
—	
114	

83 per cent of these flowers yielded capsules. Each capsule contained, on an average, 107·3 seeds.

III

Illegitimate union

14 flowers fertilized by the shortest stamens of the mid-styled

3	0
0	0
0	0
0	0
0	0
–	0
0	0
0	

Too sterile for any average

IV

Illegitimate union

12 flowers fertilized by the mid-length stamens of the short-styled

20	0
0	0
0	0
0	0
—	0
0	0
0	

Too sterile for any average

V

Illegitimate union

15 flowers fertilized by own-form mid-length stamens

2	–
10	0
23	0
0	0
0	0
0	0
0	0
0	0

Too sterile for any average

VI

Illegitimate union

15 flowers fertilized by own-form shortest stamens

4	–
8	0
4	0
0	0
0	0
0	0
0	0
0	0

Too sterile for any average

FIGURE 2 Tables showing Darwin's results (Darwin, 1880, pp. 150–57).

FIGURE 2 ■ *Continued*

TABLE 24 *Mid-styled form*

I

Legitimate union

12 flowers fertilized by the mid-length stamens of the long-styled. These stamens equal in length the pistil of the mid-styled

Product of good seed in each capsule

138	122
149	50
147	151
109	119
133	138
144	0

92 per cent of the flowers (probably 100 per cent) yielded capsules. Each capsule contained, on an average, 127·3 seeds.

II

Legitimate union

12 flowers fertilized by the mid-length stamens of the short-styled. These stamens equal in length the pistil of the mid-styled

Product of good seed in each capsule

112	109
130	143
143	124
100	145
33	12
104	141

100 per cent of the flowers yielded capsules. Each capsule contained, on an average, 108·0 seeds; or, excluding capsules with less than 20 seeds, the average is 116·7 seeds./

III

Illegitimate union

13 flowers fertilized by the shortest stamens of the long-styled

83	12
0	19
0	85 seeds small and poor
—	0
44	0
44	0
45	0

54 per cent of the flowers yielded capsules. Each capsule contained, on an average, 47·4 seeds; or, excluding capsules with less than 20 seeds, the average is 60·2 seeds.

IV

Illegitimate union

15 flowers fertilized by the longest stamens of the short-styled

130	86
115	113
14	29
6	17
2	113
9	79
132	128
	0

93 per cent of the flowers yielded capsules. Each capsule contained, on an average, 69·5 seeds; or, excluding capsules with less than 20 seeds, the average is 102·8.

V

Illegitimate union

12 flowers fertilized by own-form longest stamens

92	0
9	0
63	0
	0
136?[26]	0
0	0
0	

Excluding the capsule with 136 seeds, 25 per cent of the flowers yielded capsules, and each capsule contained, on an average, 54·6 seeds; or, excluding capsules with less than 20 seeds, the average is 77·5.

VI

Illegitimate union

12 flowers fertilized by own-form shortest stamens

0	0
0	0
0	0
—	0
0	0
0	0
0	

Not one flower yielded a capsule.

Students could perform statistical analyses of the results, and they may also enjoy reading the accompanying text and footnotes in which Darwin frankly admits two "blunders" in his experiments in order to explain some anomalous results. Teachers who stress the importance of including accurate and honest error analyses in lab reports will especially appreciate Darwin's

FIGURE 2 *Continued*

TABLE 25 *Short-styled form*

I		II	
Legitimate union		*Legitimate union*	
12 flowers fertilized by the shortest stamens of the long-styled. These stamens equal in length the pistil of the short-styled		13 flowers fertilized by the shortest stamens of the mid-styled. These stamens equal in length the pistil of the short-styled	
69	56	93	69
61	88	77	69
88	112	48	53
66	111	43	9
0	62	0	0
0	100	0	0
—		—	0
83 per cent of the flowers yielded capsules. Each capsule contained, on an average, 81·3 seeds.		61 per cent of the flowers yielded capsules. Each capsule contained, on an average, 64·6 seeds.	

III		IV	
Illegitimate union		*Illegitimate union*	
10 flowers fertilized by the mid-length stamens of the long-styled		10 flowers fertilized by the longest stamens of the mid-styled	
0	14	0	0
0	0	0	0
0	0	0	0
0	0	0	0
—	0	—	0
23		0	
Too sterile for any average		Too sterile for any average	

V		VI	
Illegitimate union		*Illegitimate union*	
10 flowers fertilized by own-form longest stamens		10 flowers fertilized by own-form mid-length stamens	
0	0	64?[7]	0
0	0	0	0
0	0	0	0
—	0	—	0
0	0	21	0
0		9	
Too sterile for any average		Too sterile for any average	

admissions and his statement that "The erroneous numbers, however, are entered in the tables, that it may not be supposed that I have in any one instance tampered with the results" (Darwin, 1880, p. 150).

Another deduction which follows from the concepts of common descent and natural selection is that one should be able to see evidence of both when studying the anatomical structures of organisms. Closely related organisms should have structures which reveal homology due to their inheritance in a modified form from a common ancestor. To that end, he devoted large sections of *The Origin of Species* and, later, entire books to the study of variations and the homologies they revealed.

To ascertain the truth of this doctrine, he engaged in both extensive, detailed observations of and experiments on both plants and animals. Some of his most interesting observations and experiments are described in *The Various Contrivances by which Orchids Are Fertilised by Insects* (Darwin, 1877). Consider, for example, his statement that

> *In my examination of orchids, hardly any fact has struck me so much as the endless diversities of structures—the prodigality of resources—for gaining the very same end, namely, the fertilization of one flower by pollen from another plant. This fact is to a large extent intelligible on the principle of natural selection. (Darwin, 1877, p. 284)*

Students will enjoy learning of Darwin's and his sons' careful observations of insects as they visited flowers and became carriers of pollen masses from each flower. How could they be sure the insects were actually transferring pollen? He repeatedly describes catching and examining bees, butterflies, moths, flies, and other insects and finding pollen adhered to their heads. As just one example, on pages 30–31, he provides a list of 23 species of Lepidoptera "with the pollinia [the mass of pollen grains transferred as a whole during pollination] of this orchid . . . attached to their proboscides." He even provides a detailed drawing of the head of a particular moth found to have seven pairs of pollinia attached to it. Darwin goes on to tell the reader that "These facts show how well moths and butterflies perform their office of marriage-priests" (Darwin, 1877, p. 34). The book is filled with detailed descriptions of insects visiting flowers, crawling in and emerging with pollen firmly attached.

Of course, he was not satisfied with mere observations, but instead conducted numerous experiments to test the validity of his hypothesis that insects are instrumental in the cross-fertilization of orchids. Once again, these experiments are suitable for inclusion in high school biology classes via reenactments or simple descriptions combined with student analyses of Darwin's work, results, and conclusions.

As one example, consider challenging students to design experiments to determine whether or not insects are needed for the process of fertilization in a particular group of flowers. This exercise can then be followed by providing the following excerpt from Darwin:

> *. . . to prove that insects are necessary for the fertilization of flowers, [Darwin] covered up a plant . . . under a bell-glass, before any of its pollinia had been removed, leaving three adjoining plants uncovered; [he] then looked at the latter every morning, and daily found some of the pollinia removed, till all were gone . . . [he] then looked at the perfectly healthy plant under the bell-glass, and it had, of course all its pollinia . . . and did not set any seed. (Darwin, 1877, p. 29)*

While students may not immediately know the term *pollinia*, they will certainly understand Darwin's experiment, which in all likelihood will be similar to their own designs. As a result, students come to realize they really can think like a great scientist, with the added benefit of their learning the concepts being tested by the experiment.

Darwin also describes many simple experiments in which he manipulates flower parts in order to determine the functions of those parts. In reporting his findings, Darwin sprinkles his writing with phrases that indicate his enthusiasm for his work and for nature. Consider the following as just a few examples from the orchid book (Darwin, 1877): "At last I understood the mechanism of the flower" (p. 98); "We thus see how beautifully everything is contrived that the pollinia should be withdrawn by insects" (p. 112); "it was really beautiful to see how . . . accurately the [pollen] struck my finger" (p. 215); and finally,

> *The more I study nature, the more I become impressed with ever-increasing force, that the contrivances and beautiful adaptations . . . transcend in an incomparable manner the contrivances and adaptations which the most fertile imagination of man could invent. (p. 286)*

This last quote, of course, echoes a theme found throughout *The Origin of Species*, namely, the power of natural selection to explain the myriad structures found in the living world. The idea was so important to Darwin that he was still stressing it here in the 1877 edition of the orchid book. Once again, Darwin's experiments, such as those on orchids, present teachers with subtle, yet convincing, ways of reinforcing this important theme with students.

Another message from *The Origin of Species* that Darwin reiterates in the orchid book is that organisms in nature are interdependent, with one or more species often influencing the evolution of other species—the concept now called co-evolution. For instance,

> *From the observations . . . it is a safe generalization that species with a short and not very narrow nectary [nectar producing portion of the flower] are fertilized by bees and flies; whilst those with a much elongated nectary . . . are fertilized by butterflies and moths. . . . We thus see that the structure of the flowers . . . and that of the insects are correlated in an interesting manner. (Darwin, 1877, p. 30)*

In other words, flowers require insects for their survival and vice versa. With that conclusion in mind, students can then be asked to describe the insect(s) or other animals which must exist in nature based on the description of a particular flower. For example, if an orchid were discovered which had a nectary 12 inches deep, there must also be an insect with a tongue 12 inches long that feeds on and fertilizes that flower. Darwin found just such an orchid and deduced the existence of a butterfly with a 12 inch tongue. Though met with much skepticism, a butterfly matching Darwin's prediction was discovered years later in the same forest from which that orchid had been collected.

Conclusions

The several works described here barely scratch the surface of Darwin's experimental work. The reader is encouraged to consult other Darwin books on topics of interest in order to expand the repertoire of material to use in teaching not only evolution but all of biology. Fortunately, the great majority of Darwin's writings are available in their entirety on the World Wide Web. One excellent site is called "The Writings of Charles Darwin on the Web" and may be found at http://pages.britishlibrary.net/charles.darwin/.

By using Darwin's experimental works when teaching evolution, many benefits are gained. First, students will learn about the interplay of observations and experiments that converge to support Darwin's most important ideas, namely, descent with modification and natural selection. Students can learn much about the range of scientific methods from exploring Darwin's examples, including the hypothetico-deductive approach and the value of well-designed experiments. Finally, students using this approach will learn that scientists are not dull and dry, but instead are creative, enthusiastic individuals interested in furthering our understanding of the natural world. With luck, that enthusiasm will be contagious and will inspire the emergence of the next generation of scientists.

References

Barlow, N. (Ed.). (1958). *The autobiography of Charles Darwin 1809–1882, with original omissions restored.* New York and London: W.W. Norton.

Darwin, C. (1845). *Journal of researches into the natural history and geology of the countries visited during the voyage of H.M.S. Beagle round the world* (2nd ed.). London: John Murray.

Darwin, C. (1857). Bees and fertilisation of kidney beans. *Gardeners' Chronicle and Agricultural Gazette, 1857*(43), 725. [as found in Barrett, Paul, 1977. *The Collected Papers of Charles Darwin,* v. 1, p. 276]

Darwin, C. 1872. *The origin of species by means of natural selection, or the preservation of favoured races in the struggle for life* (6th ed.). London: John Murray.

Darwin, C. (1877). *The various contrivances by which orchids are fertilised by insects* (2nd ed.). London: John Murray.

Darwin, C. (1880). *The different forms of flowers on plants of the same species* (2nd ed.). London: John Murray.

Darwin, C. (1881). *The formation of vegetable mould, through the action of worms, with observations on their habits.* London: John Murray.

Gould, S.J. (1983). *Hen's teeth and horse's toes.* New York: W.W. Norton.

Mayr, E. (1991). *One long argument: Charles Darwin and the genesis of modern evolutionary thought.* Cambridge: Harvard University Press.

Cans and Can'ts of Teaching Evolution:

The Legal Issues

I-9

 Eugenie C. Scott

Introduction

High school teachers are in a quandary about teaching evolution. Sometimes they are pressed to teach creation "science," or "intelligent design theory," or "evidence against evolution"; sometimes they are pressed just to forget about teaching evolution. What should a teacher do? **What, legally, can and can't a teacher do?**

The "should" part is easy. Both teachers and scientists say, "Teach evolution." Students will not be properly educated unless they learn about evolution and its very important place in biology, geology, and astronomy.

But what does the law say about evolution and creationism? There have been a number of legal cases concerning this sticky issue, and the law is quite clear on several matters. But first a caveat: "Never depend on legal advice from a physical anthropologist!" Although I work with lawyers and for a layman am knowledgeable about the legal issues surrounding the creation and evolution controversy, I do not give legal advice, and anyone with a legal problem should contact a lawyer. (If only lawyers who make proclamations about science had similar disclaimers!)

Legal decisions concerning creationism and evolution rely upon the First Amendment of the U.S. Constitution. In part, it states, "Congress shall make no laws regarding the establishment of religion, or inhibiting the free exercise thereof." The Establishment and Free Exercise clauses taken together require that public institutions be religiously neutral: schools can neither promote nor inhibit religious expression. So it is perfectly legal for a teacher to teach about religion, although it has to be in a nondevotional context. One can describe a religion, or religious views, but it is not constitutional to say, "Buddha was right!" Similarly, one can discuss controversies involving religion, but it would not be proper to take sides (such as, "The Pilgrims were right to burn witches because witches are evil"). Let's look at what a teacher can't do.

This chapter is modified from *Cans and Can'ts of Teaching Evolution* by Eugenie C. Scott (2000). It was originally published on *PBS Online* (May 2000) and has been reprinted with permission of the author.

A State/District/School CAN'T Ban the Teaching of Evolution

The 1968 Supreme Court decision *Epperson v. Arkansas* struck down antievolution laws such as that under which John T. Scopes was tried in 1925 in Tennessee. Noting that antievolution laws were passed because they offended certain religious views, the court wrote,

> *. . . the First Amendment does not permit the state to require that teaching and learning must be tailored to the principles or prohibitions of any religious sect or dogma . . . the state has no legitimate interest in protecting any or all religions from views distasteful to them.*

Teachers who tell me that their principal has told them not to teach evolution have a principal who is breaking the law.

Some antievolutionists claim that evolution is a religion, and that its teaching is therefore unconstitutional. Alas for this view, the courts have been quite clear that evolution is science, and therefore to teach it does not violate the First Amendment. The 9th Circuit Federal Appeals Court wrote in a California case (*Peloza v. Capistrano*, 1994):

The Supreme Court has held unequivocally that while belief in a Divine Creator of the universe is a religious belief, the scientific theory that higher forms of life evolved from lower ones is not.

A State/District/School CAN'T Require Equal Time for Creationism or Creation Science

Creation "science" is the view that a literal interpretation of Genesis—special creation of all things at one time about 10,000 years ago—can scientifically be supported. Rejected by both scientists and teachers, creation science also has been rejected by the courts. In the 1982 District Court *McLean v. Arkansas* case, the judge wrote that creation scientists

> *. . . cannot properly describe the methodology used as scientific, if they start with a conclusion and refuse to change it regardless of the evidence developed during the course of the investigation.*

Creation science should not be taught, because our students deserve better than to be taught bad science. But bad science is not unconstitutional. However, the Supreme Court in 1987 (*Epperson v. Arkansas*) struck down laws that would require "equal time" for evolution and creation science by noting that even if the word "science" were used, creation science really was religion in disguise, and therefore it is illegal to teach it.

The act impermissibly endorses religion by advancing the religious belief that a supernatural being created humankind. The legislative history demonstrates that the term *creation science*, as contemplated by the state legislature, embraces this religious belief.

> *. . . Because the primary purpose of the Creationism Act is to advance a particular religious belief, the Act endorses religion in violation of the First Amendment.*

A Teacher CAN'T Teach Creationism on His or Her Own as a "Freelance"

Some teachers teach creationism or creation science even though their district does not (and legally cannot) have a policy requiring it. Such "freelancing" is illegal. Schools should be religiously neutral, and, as a Federal District Court stated (in *Webster v. New Lennox,* a case involving a "freelancing" teacher):

> *If a teacher in a public school uses religion and teaches religious beliefs or espouses theories clearly based on religious underpinnings, the principles of the separation of church and state are violated as clearly as if a statute ordered the teacher to teach religious theories such as the statutes in Edwards did.*

A State/District/School CAN'T Have a Disclaimer That Singles Out Evolution

An evolution disclaimer that singles out evolution from all other scientific theories for special treatment (for example, as "theory, not fact") has been declared unconstitutional by a Federal District Court and its associated Appeals Court. The case of *Freiler v. Tangipahoa Board of Education* (1997) involved a local Louisiana school board's antievolution disclaimer. Teachers were instructed to read a disclaimer to students stating that instruction in evolution is "not intended to influence or dissuade the Biblical version of creation or any other concept." The specific reference to the Bible was a major reason this disclaimer was struck down. The judge wrote:

> *While encouraging students to maintain their belief in the Bible, or in God, may be a noble aim, it cannot be one in which the public schools participate, no matter how important this goal may be to its supporters.*

So, in summary, a teacher can teach about religion (though not advocate it), and a teacher can teach evolution. A state, district, or school cannot ban evolution, require equal time for creationism, or require a disclaimer on evolution. An individual teacher cannot teach creationism or creation science "freelance."

If you are a teacher and you have any questions about these "cans and can'ts," feel free to check with me or your local school district counsel. Remember that our students deserve the best possible science education, which ultimately depends on you and your colleagues.

I-10 Teaching Evolution

The National Association of Biology Teachers Position Statement

As stated in *The American Biology Teacher* by the eminent scientist Theodosius Dobzhansky (1973), "Nothing in biology makes sense except in the light of evolution." This often-quoted declaration accurately reflects the central, unifying role of evolution in biology. The theory of evolution provides a framework that explains both the history of life and the ongoing adaptation of organisms to environmental challenges and changes.

While modern biologists constantly study and deliberate the patterns, mechanisms, and pace of evolution, they agree that all living things share common ancestors. The fossil record and the diversity of extant organisms, combined with modern techniques of molecular biology, taxonomy, and geology, provide exhaustive examples of and powerful evidence for current evolutionary theory. Genetic variation, natural selection, speciation, and extinction are well-established components of modern evolutionary theory. Explanations are constantly modified and refined as warranted by new scientific evidence that accumulates over time, which demonstrates the integrity and validity of the field.

Scientists have firmly established evolution as an important natural process. Experimentation, logical analysis, and evidence-based revision are procedures that clearly differentiate and separate science from other ways of knowing. Explanations or ways of knowing that invoke non-naturalistic or supernatural events or beings, whether called "creation science," "scientific creationism," "intelligent design theory," "young earth theory," or similar designations, are outside the realm of science and not part of a valid science curriculum.

The selection of topics covered in a biology curriculum should accurately reflect the principles of biological science. Teaching biology in an effective and scientifically honest manner requires that evolution be taught in a standards-based instructional framework with effective classroom discussions and laboratory experiences.

Adopted by the NABT Board of Directors, 1995. Revised 1997, 2000, and May 2004. Endorsed by: The Society for the Study of Evolution, 1998; The American Association of Physical Anthropologists, 1998.

NABT endorses the following tenets of science, evolution, and biology education. Teachers should take these tenets into account when teaching evolution.

The Nature and Methods of Science

- Scientists do science by asking questions, proposing and testing hypotheses, and designing empirical models and conceptual frameworks for research about natural events. Scientists use both observations and inferences to gather evidence and draw conclusions respectively; inferences are logical conclusions based on observations. Conclusions generate additional hypothesis testing, which yields further observations and inferences. Theories are ultimately proposed to explain observations and inferences, predict consequences, and solve scientific problems.
- In science, a theory is an extensive explanation developed from well-documented, reproducible sets of experimentally-derived data from repeated observations of natural processes. Science does not base theories on untestable dogmatic proposals or beliefs.
- Scientific theories can be—and often are—modified and improved as new empirical evidence is uncovered. Science is a constantly self-correcting endeavor to understand nature and natural phenomena.
- The scientific study of evolution has both contemporary and historical aspects. Scientists study contemporary processes directly through observation and experiment. Scientists infer past processes though the study of the historical record (for example, fossils and rock strata) and contemporary results (for example, inferring past evolution from the features of modern organisms.)
- Evolutionary theory holds a unique prominence in biology and science for its unifying properties and predictive features, the clear empirical testability of its models, and the richness of new scientific research it fosters.

Essential Concepts of Biological Evolution

- The diversity of life on earth is the outcome of biological evolution—an unpredictable and natural process of descent with modification that is affected by natural selection, mutation, genetic drift, migration and other natural biological and geological forces.
- Natural selection is the primary mechanism for evolutionary changes and can be demonstrated both in the laboratory and in the wild. A differential survival and reproduction of some genetic variants within a population under an existing environmental state, natural selection has no discernable direction or goal, including survival of a species.
- Biological evolution refers to changes in populations, not individuals. Changes must be successfully passed on to the next generation. This means evolution results in heritable changes in a population across

many generations. In fact, evolution can be defined as any change in the frequency of alleles within a gene pool from one generation to the next.

Evolution in the Classroom

- Evolution should be a recurrent theme throughout biology courses.
- Teaching the principles and mechanisms of evolution across the biology curriculum—from molecular and cellular to organismal and ecological levels—promotes a rational and coherent scientific account of biology.
- Science and religion differ in significant ways that make it inappropriate to teach religious beliefs in the science classroom. To contrast science with religion is not the role of science or science education.
- Teachers should respect diverse beliefs. Science teachers can, and often do, hold devout religious beliefs, accept evolution as a valid scientific theory, and teach the theory's mechanisms and principles. Students can maintain their religious beliefs and learn the scientific foundations of evolution.

Legal Issues and Evolution Education

Teachers should teach good science with the acknowledged support of the courts. For example, in Epperson v. Arkansas (1968), the U.S. Supreme Court struck down a 1928 Arkansas law prohibiting the teaching of evolution in state schools.

In McLean v. Arkansas (1982), the federal district court invalidated a state statute requiring equal classroom time for evolution and creationism. Edwards v. Aguillard (1987) led to another Supreme Court ruling against so-called "balanced treatment" of creation science and evolution in public schools. Subsequent district and state court decisions in Illinois, Minnesota and California have supported the right of a district to prohibit an individual teacher from promoting creation science in the classroom. A Louisiana district court has struck down a disclaimer on evolution that teachers had been required to read to students before evolution was taught.

After the demise of "equal time" for creationism laws, teachers began to be pressured to teach evolution and "evidence against evolution". The "No Child Left Behind" (NCLB) education bill signed into law in 2002 is presented by antievolutionists as requiring that evolution be "balanced" with "weaknesses in evolution" or "scientific evidence against evolution". In the supporting documentation that accompanies the bill, the NCLB contains a suggestion that "*...the curriculum should help students to understand the full range of scientific views that exists, why such topics may generate controversy, and how scientific discoveries profoundly affect society.*" Called the "Santorum Language" named after the Senator who proposed an earlier version of the statement, this recommendation refers generally to controversial issues, with evolution only presented as an example of a controversial issue. There is nothing in NCLB that requires the teaching of any specific subject, or that evolution or any specific subject be taught in any particular way. There is no warrant for teaching "weaknesses in evolution" because of the NCLB.

All teachers and administrators should be mindful of these legal issues, remembering that the law, science and NABT support them as they appropriately include the teaching of evolution in the science curriculum.

Suggested Readings

Aguillard, D. (1999). Evolution education in Louisiana public schools: a decade following Edwards V. Aguillard. *The American Biology Teacher,* 61, pp. 182-188.

Dobzhansky, T. (1973). Nothing in biology makes sense except in the light of evolution. *The American Biology Teacher,* 35, pp. 125-129.

Freeman, S. and Herron, J.C. (2000). *Evolutionary Analysis,* 2nd ed. Englewood Cliffs, NJ. Prentice Hall.

Futuyma, D. , Meagher, Tom, et. al. (2000) Evolution, Science, and Society, Evolutionay Biology and the National Research Agenda. http://www.rci.rutgers.edu/~ecolevol/fulldoc.pdf

Futuyma, D. (1998). *Evolutionary Biology,* 3rd ed. Sunderland, MA: Sinauer Associates, Inc. Futuyma, D. (1995). *Science on Trial.* Sunderland, MA: Sinauer Associates, Inc. Gillis, A. (1994). Keeping creationism out of the classroom. *Bioscience,* 44, pp. 650-656. Gould, S. (1994, October). The evolution of life on earth. *Scientific American,* 271, pp. 85-91.

Kiklas, K. (1997). *The Evolutionary Biology of Plants.* Chicago: The University of Chicago Press.

Matsumura, M. (Ed.). (1995). *Voices for Evolution.* Berkeley, CA: The National Center for Science Education.

Mayr, E. (2001). *What Evolution Is.* New York, NY: Basic Books.

Moore, J. (1993). *Science as a Way of Knowing~The Foundations of Modern Biology.* Cambridge, MA: Harvard University Press.

Moore, R. (1999). Creationism in the United States: VII. The Lingering Threat. *The American Biology Teacher,* 61, pp. 330-340. See also references therein to earlier articles in the series.

National Academy of Sciences. (1998). *Teaching About Evolution and the Nature of Science.* Washington, DC: National Academy Press.

National Academy of Sciences. (1999). *Science and Creationism—A View from the National Academy of Sciences.* Washington, DC: National Academy Press.

National Center for Science Education. P.O. Box 9477, Berkeley, CA 94709. Numerous publications including *NCSE Reports.*

National Research Council. (1996). *National Science Education Standards.* Washington, DC: National Academy Press.

Pennock, R.T. (1999). *Tower of Babel: The Evidence Against the New Creationism.* Cambridge, MA: MIT Press.

Weiner, J. (1994). *Beak of the Finch~A Story of Evolution in our Time.* New York: Alfred A. Knopf.

Zimmer, C. (2001). *Evolution: The Triumph of an Idea.* New York: Harper Collins Publishers.

Adopted by the NABT Board of Directors, 1995. Revised 1997, 2000, and May 2004. Endorsed by: The Society for the Study of Evolution, 1998; The American Association of Physical Anthropologists, 1998.

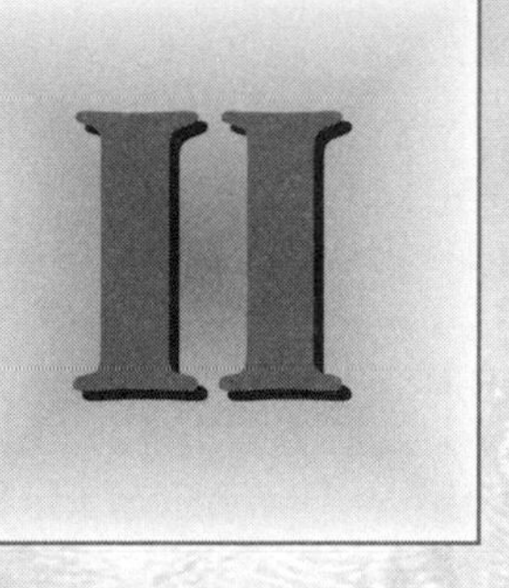

Examining the Evidence for Evolution

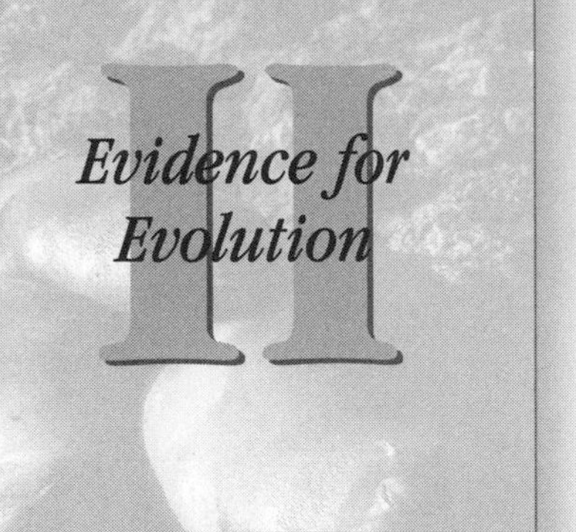

The conclusion that evolution has occurred is not intuitively obvious. However, as curious individuals began to explore the natural world, a number of intriguing observations led to the inescapable conclusion that all living things are related to each other. Evolution as an idea has roots that may be traced to ancient Greece, and the evidence that has accumulated since that time in support of the reality of evolution is abundant.

Many laboratory manuals include activities in which students compare fossils with living forms or in which they study, compare, and contrast apparently unrelated organisms (such as sea stars and humans) as evidence of evolution. Several activities in this section also take this approach by providing opportunities for students to visualize the principle of homology—the presence of structures or biochemicals that developed from those in a common ancestor and are now found within two distinct living forms. Comparative anatomy is frequently cited as support for the idea that evolution has indeed occurred.

Coler demonstrates the concept of structural homology as students look for commonalities in the anatomy of various vertebrates. The next activity, Antigen-Antibody Interaction, provides students an opportunity to examine the degree of molecular similarity between various species of hoofed mammals, the ungulates. Students investigate this by testing to see where there is any antigen-antibody interaction across species, the presence of which would be an example of homology. In both cases, evolution is the explanation for the existence of common structures and chemicals in otherwise unrelated species.

One of the goals of taxonomy is to provide an outline of "descent with modification" or, in common language, to produce family trees. Taxonomists use a wide variety of evidence to produce natural groupings of organisms that share a recent common ancestor. In doing so, they are proposing phylogenies that they will continually reexamine and refine as new evidence is gathered.

Students develop the ability to classify quite early in their intellectual development but, for the most part, use superficial or unimportant characteristics in developing their personal taxonomies. This type of artificial classification explains why whales and fish are seen as close relatives even by many adults. Once students can look past superficial characteristics, such as color or basic shape, they can begin to "weight" some traits or characteristics as more important than others in their proposals of relationships and lines of descent.

Various activities in this section afford teachers wonderful case studies of classification. Students examine nuts, bolts, nails, and screws in the Illustrating Phylogeny and Classification activity and imaginary creatures called "Caminalcules" in activities by Gendron and Smith to propose classification schemes. In addition, following each proposal of a "relationship" with any of these objects, students are asked to defend their choices to help them become more familiar with the notion of natural vs. artificial classification plans. Using the method outlined above, students will become much more familiar with the actual process of classification, which at its core, is a human construct.

The recent revolution in molecular genetics has given evolutionary biologists a previously unimaginable wealth of data to work with when determining the degree of relatedness between species and proposing phylogenies. Four lab activities give students the opportunity to use this molecular data in their comparison of different species and to use this type of evidence in their construction of phylogenetic trees. In the first of these, Hypothesis Testing and Phylogentic Analysis, students will compare the molecular data along with other data (skeletal anatomy, physiology, behavior, etc.) in proposing and testing the phylogeny of various mammals. In the next activity, by Kramer, students will learn how to conduct chromosomal analysis before using this process to compare humans and chimpanzees, discovering in the process how remarkably related the two species are indeed. Then, in Investigating Evolutionary Questions Using On Line Databases, students learn how to access and use powerful resources such as an online molecular database to help them to answer a variety of interesting evolutionary questions such as, "Should birds be included in the vertebrate class, Reptilia?" and "From which type of terrestrial four-legged hoofed mammal did whales evolve?"

In contrast to the relatively recent appearance of evolutionary genetics, fossil evidence has been available since the dawn of humankind. No examination of the evidence in support of evolution would nearly be complete without the opportunity to learn about fossils, their significance, their diversity, and their limitations. Included in this section is a wonderful article by Platt that guides the classroom teacher through the process of putting together a fossil collection that is both economical and representative for the purposes of teaching important concepts in evolution.

Finally, it is often said that one of the great challenges of evolution education is the fact that evolution itself occurs over a timescale that humans are not used to dealing with—deep, geologic time. The fact that we generally cannot observe evolution taking place often makes conceptualizing it difficult. One activity in this section, Biocide Resistance in *E. Coli* gives students the unusual opportunity to see evolution in action. In it, the commonly known bacteria *Escherichia coli* will actually mutate and evolve to develop a resistance to a biocide.

This section contains a wide variety of activities, giving students multiple opportunities to learn about and to apply different types of evidence in support of evolution. Also, as in other sections, the large number of exercises gives the teacher the option of using some activities for instruction and others for authentic assessment.

Fossils as Evidence of Evolution:

Designing Fossil Collections for "Hands-On" Evolution Laboratories

James E. Platt

Introduction

One of the most important sources of evidence both in support of evolution as a principle and of its mechanism, natural selection, is the fossil record. Lawson in his article earlier in this volume provides a conceptual framework for doing a laboratory that uses fossils to test ideas about the origins of organic diversity using a "learning cycle" approach. The success of such investigative laboratories hinges not only on the conceptual organization of the laboratory but also on the nature of the fossils used. The intent of this chapter is to share strategies with teachers to encourage the use of fossils in the laboratory environment. Such laboratories are sorely needed to address both the general lack of understanding of the meaning of fossils and the misinformation about evolution that continues to be spread by "scientific" creationists.

First, a comment or two is needed about what the fossil record can and cannot show. The fossil record does not directly "show" evolution happening. The evidence is indirect but exceptionally strong. Lawson documents the hypothetico-deductive patterns of reasoning that lead to predictions about what we should expect to find in the record if evolution has happened. Further, the record can effectively contradict certain versions of other explanations (e.g., a special creation explanation based upon a "young Earth" and "flood geology") as has been effectively pointed out (e.g., see Milne, 1981; Miller, 1982; Hopson, 1987; see also Moore, 1993 for a more extensive discussion of the issues). Of course, the proponents of these explanations will simply invent ad hoc postulates to accommodate such contradictions, but some students will be thoughtful enough to see through this ploy. What are some patterns that can be relatively easily seen in the fossil record and provide support for evolutionary theory and contradict alternative explanations? Here is a working list (a similar version was presented by Lawson):

- In the oldest fossiliferous sedimentary rocks (represented by stromatolites) only microfossils of prokaryotes are present; thus, the simplest known life forms appear first.

This article is based on "Putting together fossil collections for "hands-on" evolution laboratories" by James E. Platt (1999), in *The American Biology Teacher 61*(4), 275–76, 278–81 and is modified and reprinted with the permission of the publisher.

- From the beginning of the Paleozoic, macrofossils show a progression from those that are strikingly unlike any living species (i.e., most Paleozoic forms) to those that are very similar to living species (i.e., most Cenozoic forms) observed as one moves upward in time.
- There is a relative increase in diversity and size of fossils as one moves upward in time.
- There is a continuity of many types over several time periods with gradual changes accumulating throughout these intervals.
- Some groups appear, persist, and then go extinct (e.g., ammonites and trilobites).
- In the Paleozoic, there is a shift from exclusively marine organisms to a combination of aquatic and terrestrial types; vascular plants appear in the record for the first time.

While paleontologists generally agree that overall species diversity has increased across time (e.g., see Sepkoski, 1981, 1993), this should not be interpreted as a linear, progressive trend. At least in part, the net increase in diversity reflects the increased diversity of habitats open to new types of organisms. However, large drops in diversity have also occurred, precipitated by periodic mass extinction events.

Note that all of these patterns are reflective of relatively "large-scale" evolutionary phenomena. There are other, smaller-scale phenomena (e.g., morphological changes within specific lineages such as Mesozoic oysters) that can be documented with fossils, but the materials required for such demonstrations are acquired only with somewhat greater difficulty and expense. They are probably best left to upper-level courses. The point here is that all of the patterns described above support predictions derived deductively from an evolutionary theory and—not coincidently—fail to support similar sets of predictions derived deductively from various versions of special creation explanations.

Proponents of young Earth, flood geology-type creationism may object that such "predictions" are only being made a posteriori, but this is not true from the cognitive perspective of students. Furthermore, it is possible to take the above set of patterns and make real predictions about newly discovered fossil beds. For example, I will "bet the farm" that any newly discovered layer that is tentatively identified as Eocene, based upon initial examination of its fossil fauna or flora, will not be found to contain any trilobites, blastoids, seed ferns, dinosaurs, horn corals, or any number of other groups known to be extinct by the end of the Mesozoic, nor will it contain any hominid material. I'll also predict that, if any well-trained paleontologist is given a radiometrically determined date for a rock layer (determined by an independent investigator who is not allowed to look at the fossils that are present in the layer), then this paleontologist will also be able to predict the general kinds of fossils that will and will not be found in the layer before seeing these fossils.

So how can a teacher put together a collection of fossils that will effectively illustrate the patterns described above? Ordinarily, one would order the materials from one of the traditional scientific supply houses. However, I have found that I can get very high-quality items at a reasonable cost by buying from independent, wholesale dealers instead. I have discovered most of these dealers while attending fossil shows at several locations. Some of the best and largest shows occur annually in Denver and Tucson. To give some idea of the comparison between this approach and ordering from supply companies, consider the recent purchase of 100 Moroccan trilobites for a total of $65. All 100 of these are easily identified, complete or nearly complete individuals that are usually an inch or more in length. These same Moroccan trilobites were listed in a supply company catalog at the same time for almost $70 each. They may be better specimens, but hardly worth the 100-fold difference in price. While this is an extreme example, it is not uncommon to find price differentials between 2- and 10-fold when the wholesale dealer prices are compared to supply house prices. The dealer specimens are usually as good or better in quality. However, the intent of this article is not to heap criticism on the scientific supply companies. In many cases, they provide teachers essential goods and services that cannot be obtained elsewhere. In this case, however, we believe that a persuasive economic argument exists for exploring the options described here.

Before describing the kinds of fossils that we recommend for purchase and before providing a dealer list, some ground rules need to be spelled out. Because these dealers are wholesalers, they normally sell only to businesses, institutions, or agents acting on behalf of such entities. Therefore, when purchasing materials, you must make it clear that you are buying items for educational use, not for personal use. In most cases, you will also have to provide the dealer with an institutional tax identification number. Further, you should be prepared to purchase most items in bulk quantities if you expect to pay wholesale prices. You should think in terms of putting together a large collection that can be used in a number of science classrooms in your department or school, perhaps even throughout the district. Most items will be purchased in flats (i.e., flat, cardboard boxes about the size of soft drink cases) and will typically have from 10 to 100 fossils of the same type per flat.

One more note of caution should be considered. Fossils, especially vertebrate material, should not have been collected from public lands. You should request the assurance of the dealer that this was not done. Fortunately, the materials we recommend for purchase are generally available from privately owned sources or, in some cases, from foreign sources.

The descriptions that are provided are of the fossils that are part of the teaching collections at the University of Denver and Arizona State University. Both collections are used in introductory courses at these institutions. At the University of Denver, parts of the collection have also been used for K-12 outreach laboratories. The collections are put together to illustrate the patterns in the fossil record described here and in the Lawson article.

Cenozoic Fossils

Cenozoic fossils should be selected to illustrate the point that most Cenozoic fossil species are quite similar to living species. In particular, it is important to select fossils that students can observe and interpret. This is not always possible with materials that:

1. Are of such poor quality or small size that the student cannot identify them.
2. Represent species that fall outside of the range of organismic diversity which is likely to be familiar to at least some students (e.g., bryzoans and many corals fit into this "unfamiliar" category).

The items in the list that follows reflect the above considerations:

Teleost fishes—Usually from the Green River Formation which is Eocene in age.

Sand dollars—Usually Pleistocene or Pliocene.

Assorted mollusk shells—Materials from the Pleistocene to the Eocene are generally available.

Mammal jaw fragments with teeth or single horse teeth—The most abundant materials are from Oligocene deposits in western North America.

Shark teeth—Usually Miocene; available from both North American and Moroccan sources.

Angiosperm leaves—Most commonly from the Eocene Green River Formation.

Fly maggots—These large fly larvae are also from the Eocene Green River Formation. Unlike some insect fossils, they are easily recognized. But we recommend having a jar of preserved blowfly larvae available for comparison. Other Eocene insect larvae may be even better but will be somewhat more expensive.

Mesozoic Fossils

Mesozoic fossils will illustrate that there is a considerable departure from those forms that are familiar to most students, but most forms are still recognizable at a more general level (e.g., an ammonite is usually recognized as some kind of shelled sea creature, but it does not look quite like anything still living). For those few students who are familiar with the chambered nautilus, this provides a link to the present. Be aware, however, that the nautilus is probably no more closely related to ammonites than it is to living squids and octopuses. Other forms (e.g., belemnites) will be even less familiar. The replicas of dinosaur teeth and claws will illustrate the point that the dominant land animals were not mammals. Likewise, the nonangiosperm plant fossils (i.e., ferns, cycads, and gymnosperms) will illustrate that the dominant land plants were not angiosperms. Two groups, sea urchins and oysters, are generally similar to living relatives but still have an "archaic" appearance.

Ammonites—The Moroccan material is generally the most economical and is often sold by the pound; some good but relatively inexpensive specimens are also available from Texas.

Belemnites—These are essentially the internal shells of squid-like animals. Modern squid generally lack shells.

Sea urchins—A variety of forms is available from Cretaceous formations in Texas and Jurassic strata in Morocco.

Oysters—Available in large quantities from Texas, they can also be used for more advanced laboratories.

Nonangiosperm plants—Available from Jurassic deposits in China, this material is not always well characterized, but it does illustrate the point that the Mesozoic flora was not dominated by angiosperms.

Replicas of dinosaur teeth and claws—Make sure you get high-quality reproductions; these will look like the real things (which are rare, generally unavailable, and very expensive), and they are probably the only practical way to bring dinosaur "fossils" into the laboratory. Many dealers will sell fragments of dinosaur bone, but students are unable to identify these fragments as such; because of this, I would not use them.

Paleozoic Fossils

In contrast to Cenozoic and Mesozoic fossils, common Paleozoic materials represent many groups that are entirely extinct. Horn corals, blastoids, trilobites, and seed ferns are common, inexpensive Paleozoic fossils representing entirely extinct groups. Nautiloids are extinct except for the chambered nautilus; brachiopods, another common Paleozoic fossil, are greatly reduced in number and diversity today. It is probably desirable to subdivide this collection of materials into "upper" and "lower" Paleozoic sets if possible. (Note: This division will not correspond to the same definition of these time intervals used by geologists; the use here is strictly pedagogical.) By dividing the Paleozoic into material from the Silurian onward and Ordovician and Cambrian material, you can allow students to discover the transition of life from water to land (i.e., no vascular plants or terrestrial animals are found prior to the Silurian). This is another prediction of evolutionary theory, while special creation theory would not predict this (i.e., it predicts that all species, terrestrial and aquatic, should appear at the same time at the base of the record). The bottom line here is that Paleozoic life is distinctly less like life in the contemporary world than either Cenozoic or Mesozoic life, as predicted by evolutionary theory.

Horn corals—You can probably obtain both upper and lower Paleozoic types. If you live in parts of the country with the appropriate strata exposed, you can collect these on your own.

Blastoids—These are members of an extinct class of echinoderms; Mississippian species are commonly available, either as isolated pieces or attached to a larger piece of matrix. The latter type of material is a bit more expensive but much more difficult for someone to remove from your laboratory without being noticed. Blastoids will usually not be identified as echinoderms unless you point your students in the right direction by suggesting that they examine the type of symmetry these fossils show; the five-part radial symmetry is apparent when they are viewed from bottom of the calyx.

Trilobites—These are extremely interesting fossils and will usually be the hit of the laboratory. Considering both cost and quality, the best buys are probably Ordovician trilobites from Morocco, usually designated by the genus name *Diacalymene*, although other generic names are also applied. If you can spend a bit more, consider getting several species to illustrate the diversity of this extinct group. The least expensive trilobites are a group of very small Cambrian animals called agnostids; however, their small size and unusual morphology are distinct disadvantages in this type of laboratory.

Seed ferns—This extinct group of plants is very abundant in Pennsylvanian deposits, and several types are available; they also represent an "intermediate" stage in plant evolution (i.e., they bridge a "gap" between true gymnosperms and seedless, spore-bearing plants). We often forget about plant evolution, which is well documented by the fossil record.

Nautiloids—Again, both upper and lower Paleozoic versions of these predatory invertebrates can be obtained. Most of the Paleozoic genera have straight shells, but they will be difficult for students to identify because there is nothing comparable alive today—a point which needs to be made. You might consider having several "artist reconstructions" of these creatures for students to look at along with the fossils themselves.

Brachiopods—Most students will incorrectly identify these as mollusks, probably as some type of clam. While both clam and brachiopod shells have two valves, their symmetry is fundamentally different: Clams have a right valve and a left valve, while brachiopods have a dorsal valve and a ventral valve. These two types of "sea-shells" are classified in different phyla. The diversity and abundance of brachiopods is great in the Paleozoic and reduced in the Mesozoic and Cenozoic, while the mollusks show an increasing diversity and abundance in these later time periods. Both upper and lower Paleozoic collections of brachiopods can be obtained.

Precambrian Microfossils

This will probably be the most difficult part of the collection to obtain. Ideally, you should try to get several pieces of stromatolite (i.e., layered sedimentary rock containing microfossils, preferably of Precambrian age). You can also purchase thin sections of these rocks that can be examined microscopically to allow students to observe the actual microfossils. Oil immersion should be used, since these are microfossils of prokaryotic cells. Alternatively, you can use photomicrographs of microfossils. Despite the difficulties, it is strongly recommended that this element be included in the collection. The scientific creationists do not want to acknowledge the Precambrian fossil record, since it defeats their claim that the Cambrian "explosion" somehow provides the evidence for a single creation "event" (a claim which completely ignores the fact that the Cambrian fossils used to document this event are all marine and are all extinct). Furthermore, the use of the stromatolite material in the classroom confirms the prediction of evolutionary theory that the simplest fossils should occur in the oldest rocks. Thus, this piece of the laboratory is very important.

A Note About Fossil Dealers

In the original article a number of wholesale dealers were listed, including The Sahara Sea Collection (Sarasota, FL), Paleo Impressions (New Meadows, ID), Dan Ryder Fossils (Mineral Wells, TX), Potomac Museum Group (Golden Valley, MN), Extinctions (Clarita, OK) and Dino Productions (Englewood, CO). These and other such outlets for inexpensive fossils can easily be located through an Internet search.

References

Hopson, J.A. (1987). The mammal-like reptiles. *The American Biology Teacher, 49*, 16–26.

Lawson, A.E. (1999). A scientific approach to teaching about evolution and special creation. *The American Biology Teacher, 61*(4), 266–73.

Miller, K.R. (1982). Special creation and the fossil record: The central fallacy. *The American Biology Teacher, 44*, 85–89.

Milne, D.H. (1981). How to debate with creationists—and "win." *The American Biology Teacher, 43*, 235–45.

Moore, J.A. (1993). *Science as a way of knowing*. Cambridge, MA: Harvard University Press. 530 pp.

Sepkoski, J.J. (1981). A factor analytic description of the Phanerozoic marine fossil record. *Paleobiology, 7*, 36–53.

Sepkoski, J.J. (1993). Ten years in the library: New data confirm paleontological patterns. *Paleobiology, 19*, 43–51.

Comparative Anatomy as Evidence of Evolution

II-2

 Robert A. Coler

Overview

Many aspects of anatomy of various animals can be used to demonstrate evolutionary relationships and provide evidence relating to morphological adaptations. In the example provided in this activity, the skeletons of a variety of animals are compared as a concrete demonstration of evolution. The fact that numerous animals share similar anatomical structures with slight variations is a major piece of evidence for evolution. Anatomical features that were inherited from common ancestors are called homologous.

Evolutionary Principles Illustrated

- Homology
- Comparative anatomy

Background Information

In this activity, comparative anatomy is presented as strong evidence of evolution. Organisms in the same basic group are studied side-by-side to show how changes in anatomical features have occurred as adaptive responses to changes in the environment in which ancestral populations of those organisms lived. Structures that now may appear quite distinct and even have different functions (hand of a human and the wing of a bat, for instance) at an underlying anatomical level share many features because of their common heritage. Such structures are called homologous. Homology is a specific explanation of similarity of form in the biological world. Although the arms of four-limbed vertebrates (Figure 1) may appear quite different externally, they all have the same underlying basic pattern of skeleton and muscle.

This activity is based on "An evolutionary approach to a comparative anatomy laboratory" by Robert A. Coler (1966) in *The American Biology Teacher, 28*(4), 305–6. It has been adapted and reprinted with permission of the publisher.

FIGURE 1 ■ Comparative anatomy: Homologous bones in the forelimbs of several vertebrates.

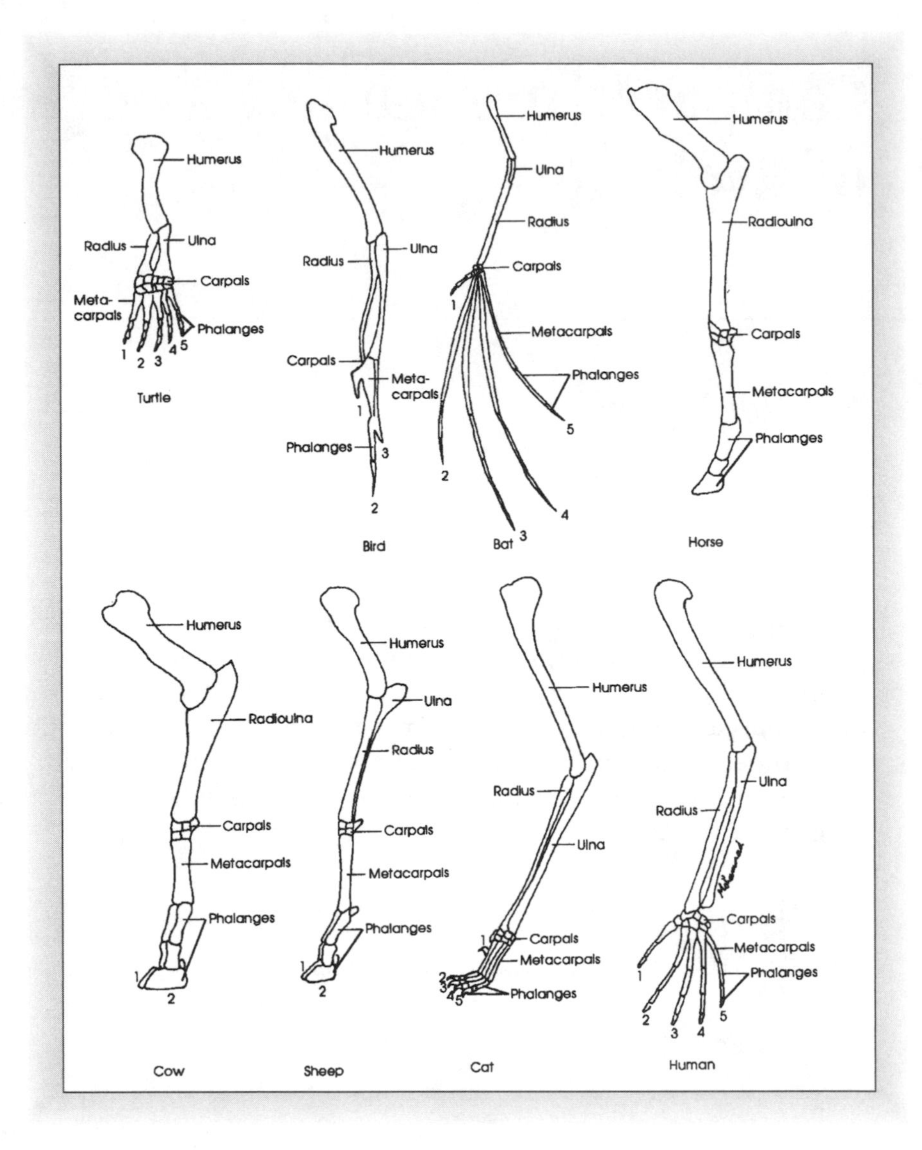

The best way to explain these shared characteristics is the inheritance from a common ancestor that also had such characteristics.

Materials

Per student group:

- Fine-point permanent markers (5 colors)
- Tie-on tags or stickers (optional)
- Clear nail polish
- Skeletons of various animals in related groups such as a frog, lizard, bird, bat, and human

Procedures

It is important to note that many groups of organisms—not just those listed here—could be used in this activity either as actual specimens or as drawings or photographs. The activity could involve having students examine a group of organisms externally and produce a matrix of similarities and differences. Another strategy (Example #1) would be to have students look at drawings or specimens and label homologous structures. Finally, a sophisticated technique might be used (Example #2), where students trace the evolution of specific structures throughout a group of organisms. In all cases the basic message is the same: common ancestry is reflected in shared characteristics.

Example #1

In comparing structures in the forelimbs of various organisms, students could be asked to label the phalanges or "finger bones" of each animal and note the changes that have occurred through time.

Example #2

To accomplish this task, students will number the homologous features on various skeletons with fine-pointed markers. One color will be used for bones and other colors for foramina (openings in or passages through bones), fossae (depressed areas), tuberosities (bumps or elevations), and processes (projections). Cover the labels with clear nail polish to prevent smudging. In the case of wet cartilaginous skeletons, color-coded cloth laundry tags with piercing clamps may be used. Tie-on tags or removable stickers may be used to avoid permanent labeling if the skeletons are to be used with other student groups.

Use the same numbers to label homologous features on the skeletons of related animal groups. If a bone is found with no homology in another group, give it a new number as has been done in the example below.

Using actual animal skeletons or labeled diagrams, students might trace the evolution of the mandibular suspensorium among terrestrial animals in its transition from sound detection through bones and ligaments of the mandibular arch (suspensorium) to detection of sound through air. These refinements in sensitivity involve the *hyomandibular* (numbered 2a, for example) of the *hyoid arch* (2), which gave rise in the post placoderms to the *urodele eucolumella* (2a1), the reptilian *paracolumella* (2a2, 3), which is also formed from the *quadrate* (3), and the mammalian *stapes* (2a3). Similarly, the *quadrate* (3) and *articular* (4) in amphibians gave rise to the *incus* (3a) and *malleus* (4a), respectively, in mammals.

Additional Considerations

As students identify and observe homologous structures in different groups of animals, help them to see that their differences arose as a result of gradual change over time. Homologous structures in amphibians, birds, reptiles, and mammals, for example, developed over hundreds of millions of years—the time it took for each of the respective groups of animals to evolve.

II-3

Antigen-Antibody Interaction:

Application of the Ouchterlony Method for Determining Evolutionary Relationships

 Mary Culp

Overview

The purpose of this experiment is to illustrate how antigen-antibody interactions can be applied to the study of evolution. Using the Ouchterlony test, students will test to see whether antigens and antibodies across several species react with each other. Using these data, evolutionary relationships between the chosen species will be constructed.

Evolutionary Principles Illustrated

- Divergence
- Molecular clock theory
- Phylogeny

Background Information

Antigens are substances that stimulate an immune response from the body. There are two general categories of antigens: pathogens and allergens (Karp, 1996). Pathogens include viruses, bacteria, fungi, protozoan parasites, and toxins. Allergens include pollen, spores, and food additives. Antibodies are globular proteins produced by B lymphocytes that bind to an antigen and target the antigen for destruction. Antibodies are located in interstitial fluid and plasma and are mostly effective against pathogens that have not invaded host cells.

The Ouchterlony test is a double diffusion method on an agar plate that clearly shows any reaction between antigens and antibody (Ouchterlony & Nilsson, 1973). Antigens and antibody are inoculated into separate wells on an

---

This activity is based on "Antigen-antibody interaction" by Mary Culp (2000) in *The American Biology Teacher, 62*(9), 658–63. It has been adapted and reprinted with permission of the publisher.

agar plate, where they diffuse through the medium. As long as the pore sizes within the agar are large enough, the assumption is that the diffusion of randomly moving particles can freely occur. The agar must consist of inert material that does not react with the antigens or antibodies. If the antibody recognizes and binds to an antigen on the plate, a white precipitate will form. The precipitate itself is too large to continue to diffuse—once a precipitate is formed, it is stationary.

The antigens for this experiment are albumins from various ungulates: horses, pigs, cows, and sheep. Albumins are small globular proteins that are isolated from blood. Albumin is produced by the liver and participates in homeostasis by influencing the osmotic balance of plasma. Antiserum is a liquid containing antibodies that have been exposed to a specific antigen. For example, anti-horse serum includes antibodies that will react against antigens isolated from a horse.

Students learn in lecture and laboratory that an outstanding characteristic of antibodies is their property of specificity. The general hypothesis being tested is: a specific antigen will react with a specific antibody that has been formed against it and will form a precipitate. Therefore, horse albumin should react only with anti-horse serum, pig albumin with anti-pig, and so on. The results can be used to support the current classification of the ungulates at the order and suborder level. To accomplish this, students must become familiar with the following subjects:

1. The specificity of antibodies.
2. The taxonomic relationship between the animal groups whose albumins are being tested.
3. The molecular clock theory.

The Specificity of Antibodies and How Antisera Are Produced

The property of antibodies that makes them a valuable tool in molecular biology is their specificity for a particular antigen. A reaction between an antibody and an antigen will occur only if the variable regions of the antibody recognize and bind to a compatible region of the antigen (Karp 1996). Some antibodies are so specific that a single amino acid substitution will result in an unrecognized antigen.

The antibodies used in this experiment are isolated by the traditional method (Karp, 1996). A host animal, typically a rabbit, goat, or donkey, is repeatedly injected with a protein, the antigen. After a few weeks, blood from the host is drawn that contains the antibodies the animal host made against the antigen. To isolate the antibody, whole blood and clotting factors are removed. The resultant serum or plasma contains all the animal's antibodies, including the ones made specifically against the injected protein. The plasma product is called antiserum because it contains known antibodies to a specific antigen. This method is used by manufacturers to make antisera against specific proteins, such as whey (mammalian milk protein), albumin, and others.

TABLE 1 Classification of representative ungulates (after Vaughan, 1986).

Classification
Order Perissodactyla
Family Equidae
Genus Equus (domestic horse)
Order Artiodactyla
Suborder Suina
Family Suidae
Genus Sus (domestic pig)
Suborder Ruminantia
Family Bovidae
Subfamily Bovinae
Tribe Bovini
Genus Bos (cattle)
Subfamily Caprinae
Tribe Caprini
Genus Ovis (domestic sheep)
Genus Capra (goat)

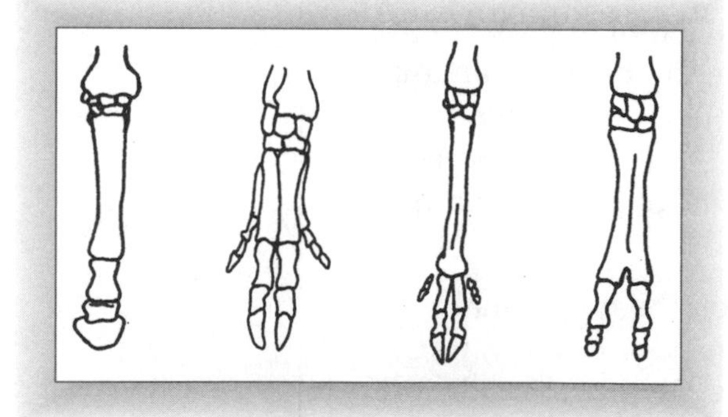

FIGURE 1 Lower front legs of representative ungulates showing even and odd toes. From left to right: horse (one), pig (four), elk (two), and camel (two) (after Vaughan, 1986).

Background and Relationships of the Ungulates

Ungulates are mammals that have evolved to stand on their toes, resulting in toenails that have been modified into solid hoofs. They are quadrupeds that primarily graze or browse on vegetable matter. Taxonomists have divided the ungulates into categories (Table 1) based mainly on foot anatomy, digestive tract anatomy and physiology, and dentition/tooth morphology (Vaughan, 1986). The initial division of this very large mammalian group is two subgroups based on the animal's number of toes (Figure 1). Table 2 contains a summary that describes the characteristics of the animal groups used for this study.

The order Perissodactyla contains ungulates with an odd number of toes (either one or three). Perissodactyls include horses, zebras, rhinoceroses, and tapirs. Horses have a large side pocket (cecum) attached to their intestine that acts as a fermentation chamber and absorptive surface for extracting nutrition from plant material (Nowak, 1991). Horses have strong jaws that include an upper and lower set of incisors for biting abrasive grasses, a back set of incisors for biting abrasive grasses, and a back set of molars for chewing (Figure 2). Male horses possess a set of reduced canines. The canines are vestigial or absent in female horses. The development of a single toe (hoof) on modern horses is an adaptation to running on hard, dry grasslands and prairies.

The order Artiodactyla contains ungulates with an even number of toes (either two or four). This group is further subdivided into the suborders Suina and Ruminantia based mostly on the anatomy of their digestive tracts.

The suborder Suina, animals with four toes, includes pigs, peccaries, and hippopotami. These animals possess simple nonruminant stomachs, and their digestive tracts do not contain large ceca (Vaughan, 1986). Pigs are in the family Suidae, which also includes warthogs and the babirusa. These animals possess upper and lower incisors and well-developed canines used as tusks for mating display or digging (Figure 2). Most suids are omnivorous and inhabit some form of scrubland, woodland, and/or marshland.

TABLE 2 Summary of major characteristics of horses (order Perissodactyla) and pigs, cows, and sheep (order Artiodactyla).

Animal	Number of toes	Dentition	Type of stomach
Horse	One	Upper and lower incisors, canines reduced or absent	Simple stomach with an enlarged cecum
Pig	Four	Upper and lower incisors, large ever-growing canines	Simple stomach without a cecum, nonruminating
Cow and sheep	Two	Upper incisors lacking, canines lacking	Complex, four-chambered stomach, ruminating

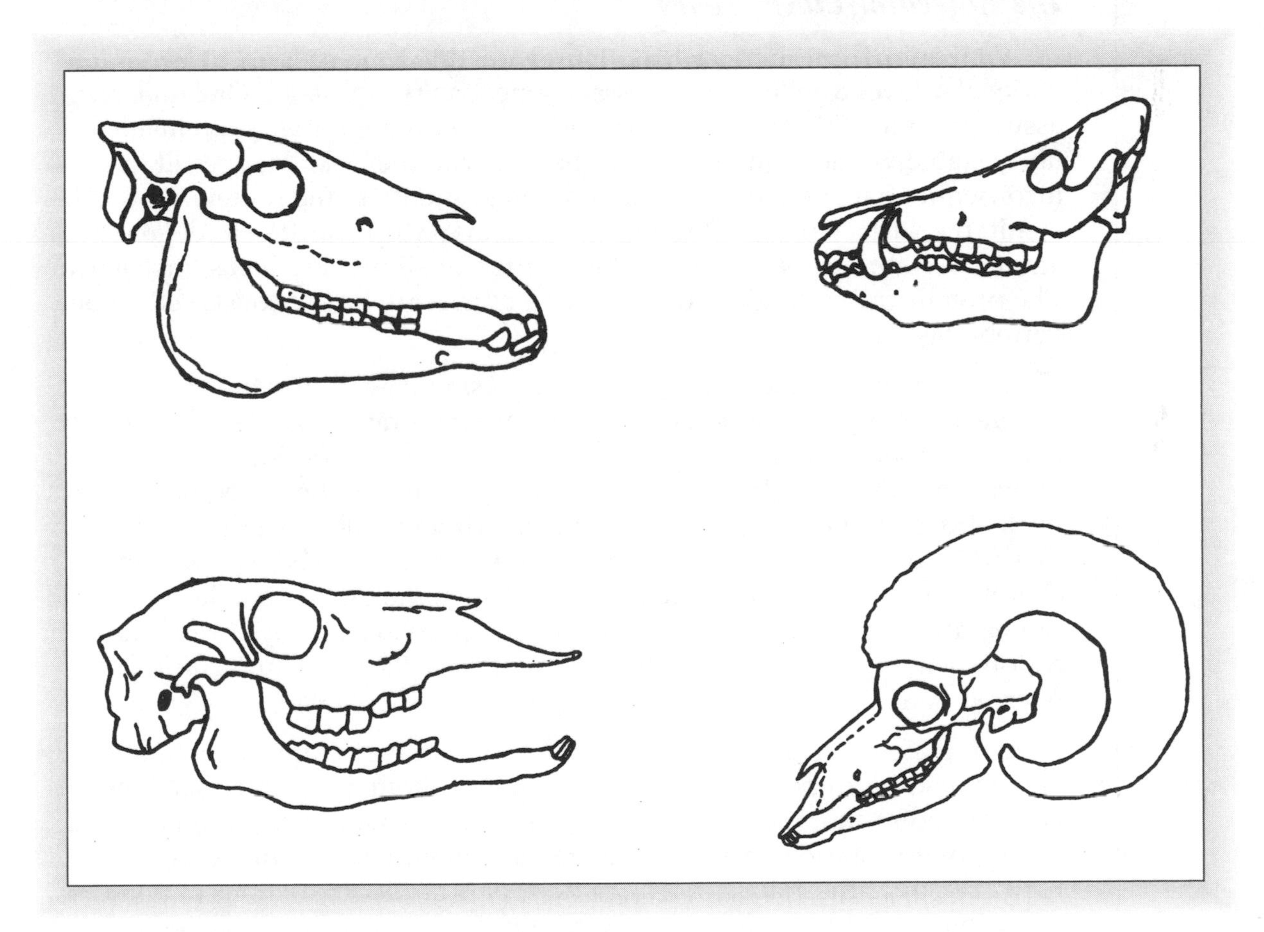

FIGURE 2 Skulls of representative ungulates showing variations in dentition. Horse (upper left), pig (upper right), cow (lower left), and bighorn sheep (lower right) (after Vaughan, 1986).

Two-toed representatives of the suborder Ruminantia are cattle, sheep and goats, along with giraffes, antelope, deer, and bison. These animals are ruminants, which means they have a four-chambered stomach (Nowak, 1991). Ruminants have a complex anatomy and physiology well suited for digesting plant matter. The animal chews and swallows vegetation that then enters the stomach's first chamber. Bacteria and protozoa decompose the plant matter, which is regurgitated back to the mouth. The partially digested food, cud, is chewed at length then swallowed again to the second chamber for more bacterial digestion. Eventually the food moves through the other two chambers, undergoing initial true digestion by digestive enzymes produced by the gastric lining of the fourth chamber. Ruminants can quickly consume vegetation and digest it at leisure. Ruminant jaws lack upper incisors and lack canines, thus their mouths are used mainly for eating, not for display or aggression (Figure 2). Most cattle live in grasslands and plains. Bovids are fast and usually escape predation by running. Sheep are adapted to mountainous habitats with cloven hoofs that appear to adhere to steep inclines with ease.

The Molecular Clock Theory

Vital animal proteins such as albumin tend to be conserved at the molecular level due to their necessary functions (Karp, 1996). One underlying assumption for this exercise is that the DNA coding for albumin remains fairly stable. Some point mutations that occur in the DNA may result in inconsequential changes in the amino acid sequence of the protein. As a result, the surface of the albumin molecule may vary to different degrees among vertebrate species, while the function of albumin remains unchanged. The protein-coding regions of DNA for albumin are highly conserved among vertebrates.

The molecular clock theory infers that a single gene over time should evolve at an invariant rate if the neutral mutation rate is constant. The molecular clock theory is based on the genetic code. The genetic code that determines albumin, as well as that for all other proteins, is composed of nucleotides of nucleic acids arranged in 64 triplet sequences called codons that code for 20 different amino acids. Three nucleic acid bases make up a codon that determines a single amino acid. In some cases, a single amino acid can be directed into place on the developing protein chain by several different codons. The usage of multiple triplets coding for the same amino acid is referred to as "degeneracy" of the genetic code (Karp, 1996).

Using albumin as an example, the role of mutations affecting evolutionary outcome now can be explained. Most mutations found in coding sections of a gene are point mutations. Owing to the repetitious nature of the genetic code, a few point mutations may not change the function or structure of albumin. However, over the course of long periods of time, accumulations of point mutations can change the sequence of nucleotides on a length of coding DNA. Mutations that affect the function of necessary proteins are unlikely to persist in the gene pool. Only neutral changes, those that do not alter function, are tolerated so that the activity of albumin is not compromised.

As animal groups separated and independently evolved from ancestral stock, one would expect accumulations of point mutations in the coding regions of their DNA. Eventually, the nucleic acid differences lead to amino acid differences ultimately resulting in an albumin molecule that "looks" different from the other group. The closer the relationship between two groups, the fewer mutations, and the more similar their albumin molecular configuration. Conversely, the more ancient the original split, the more changes in protein structure, which results in albumins that have different amino acid sequences. It is important to emphasize at this point that although the albumin molecules are somewhat different, the protein still maintains the same function.

Materials

For teacher preparation:

- Noble agar (Sigma, under microbial media)
- $NaH_2PO_4 \cdot H_2O$ (Sodium phosphate, monobasic)
- NaH_2PO_4 (Sodium phosphate, dibasic, anhydrous)
- NaCl (Sodium chloride)
- NaN_3 (Sodium azide)
- Polyethylene glycol (PEG)
- Petri dishes, plastic 10 × 35 mm
- Albumins (1 mg/ml): horse, pig, bovine, sheep; Fraction V powders, 1 gm bottles (Sigma)
- Antisera: anti-horse, anti-pig, anti-bovine, anti-sheep; liquid whole serum, 2 ml bottles (Sigma, under Additional Antibodies to Animal Proteins in the Immunochemicals section)
- Water baths: 100° C and 56° C
- Incubator, set at 37° C (optional) Agar punches (disposable transfer pipets, polyethylene, thin-stem 2-mm bore diameter, cut so that only the bulb and approximately 0.5 cm of bore remains; see Figure 3)
- Micropipettes

Per student group:

- Permanent marker
- Sealable plastic bags
- Kimwipes

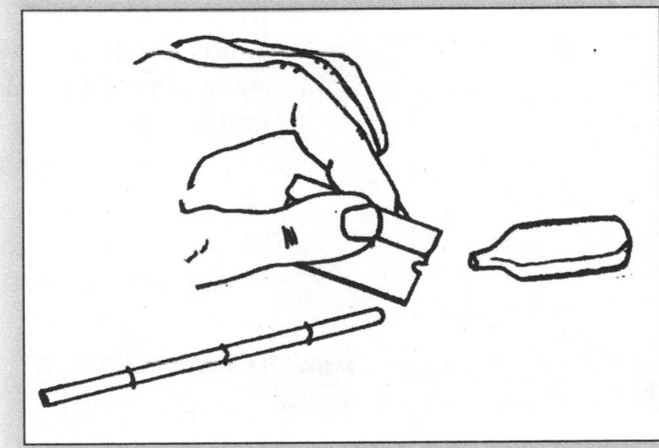

FIGURE 3 Illustration showing how to cut a transfer pipette to make an agar punch. The stem of the pipette is discarded, and the bulb section is used.

Procedures

Preparation of Materials (modified from Hornbeck, 1991)

1. Phosphate Buffered Saline (PBS), 1 liter

   Weigh out the following into a 1-liter beaker: 0.23 gm Na_2HPO_4, anhydrous (1.9 mM), 1.15 gm Na_2HPO_4, anhydrous (8.1 mM), 9.0 gm NaCl (154 mM). Add deionized H_2O to 900 ml; adjust pH to 7.2–7.4 using 1 M NaOH or 1 M HCl. Add deionized H_2O to 1 liter.
2. PBS with approximately 0.05% sodium azide (PBSN), 100 mL

   IMPORTANT NOTE: **Wear a mask, gloves and goggles when handling sodium azide to reduce exposure. This chemical is a respiratory chain inhibitor and is very dangerous!** The addition of sodium azide to the PBS buffer will inhibit the growth of contaminants such as fungi and bacteria on the plates. Add sodium azide (NaN_3) to100 ml PBS in the following manner: Take a glass rod, wet the tip in PBS, dip it into NaN_3 to collect a tip-full of granules, and mix into the PBS.
3. 4% polyethylene glycol (PEG), 100 mL

   Wear a mask. Weigh 4 grams of PEG into a 100-ml volumetric flask, add deionized H_2O to the 100 ml mark, and stir on plate. PEG can be made ahead and stored at room temperature. If using right away, place flask in a 56° C water bath.
4. Agar medium (makes enough for about 100 plates)

   Measure 2 gms Noble agar into a 250-ml flask, add 100 mL PBSN. Place the flask in boiling water bath for 15 minutes. Swirl the flask contents every 5 minutes. Solution will become translucent. Place flask in the 56° C water bath and allow the temperature of the agar to equilibrate. Combine the PEG and PBSN-Noble agar solutions together (total volume = 200 ml). Swirl until thoroughly mixed. Keep the solution in the water bath while making the plates. If desired, the agar medium can be made ahead of time and kept in the refrigerator. It can be microwaved to liquefy the agar, then placed in the 56° C water bath to equilibrate.
5. Pouring plates (flask contents will make 100 plates)

   Pipette 2 mL of the agar media into each petri plate. Let it set. Place the plates into a tray, cover with plastic wrap, and store in the refrigerator. Plates will stay usable for several weeks.

Student Procedures

Obtain the needed number of agar plates. Using a permanent marker, mark the top and bottom of each petri dish so that they can be aligned. Figure 4 is a template that approximates the actual size of the petri dishes. The template can be reproduced so each student/group has one to use. The template prevents variability among the distances between the wells. Center each petri plate bottom over the template. Using the modified transfer pipette punch, punch the wells as indicated on the template, expelling the agar plugs after each punch. Orientate the punch so that the wells are vertical and smooth; avoid cracks. Because of the small size of the petri dishes, label the top of the plates according to the pattern shown in Figure 5, using the following abbreviations:

HA = horse albumin
AHS = anti-horse serum
PA = pig albumin
APS = anti-pig serum
BA = bovine albumin
ABS = anti-bovine serum
SA = sheep albumin
ASS = anti-sheep serum

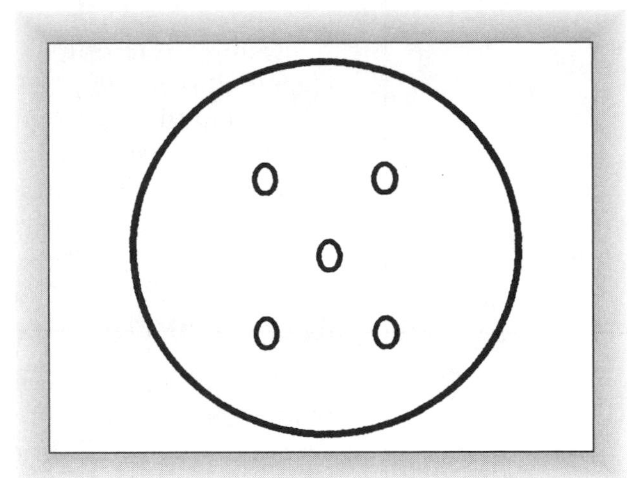

FIGURE 4 Template for alignment of punches of wells on the agar plate. Reproduce the template and give to each group to place under their petri dishes so the distance between the wells is standardized.

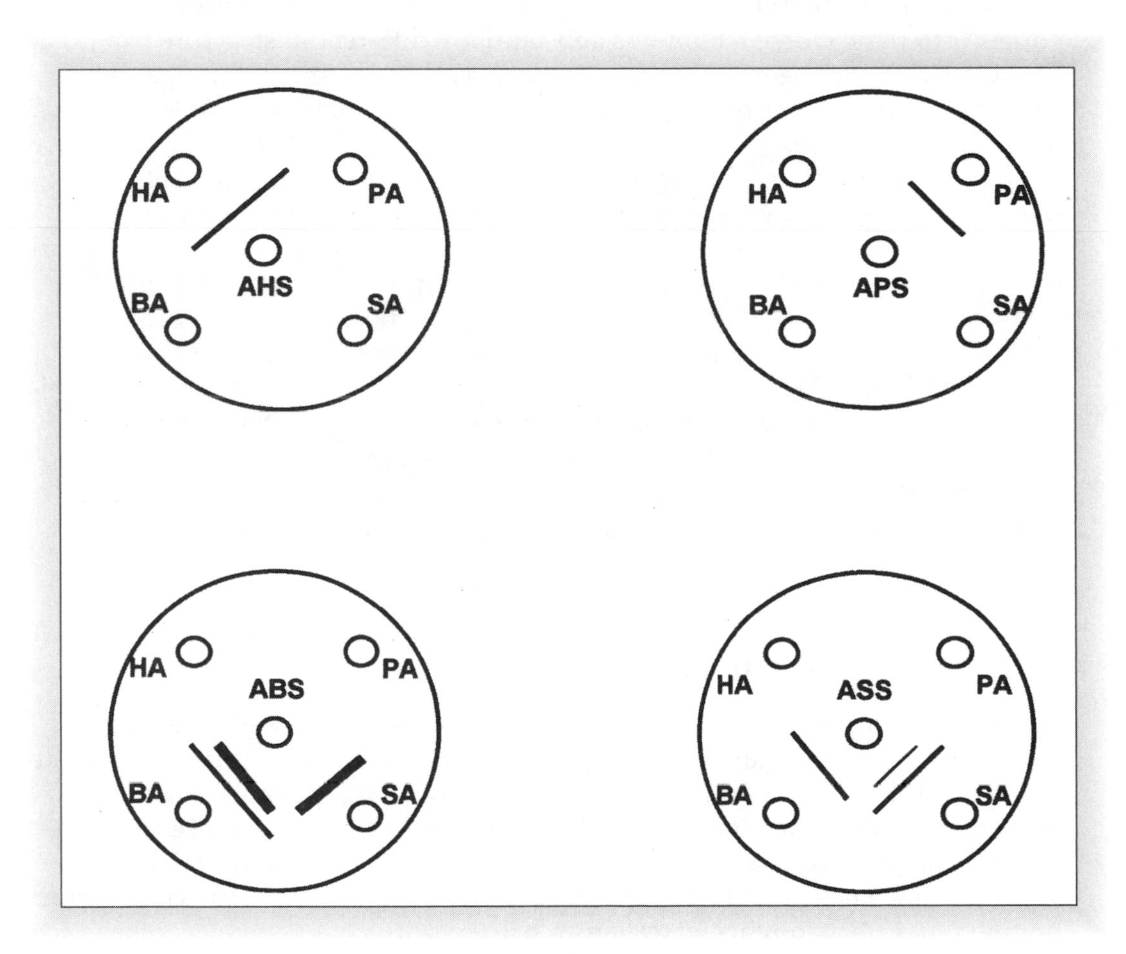

FIGURE 5 Typical results of the Ouchterlony test. Darker lines and double lines indicate a stronger reaction (more precipitate). Abbreviations are as follows: HA = horse albumin; PA = pig albumin; BA = bovine albumin; SA = sheep albumin; AHS = anti-horse serum; APS = anti-pig serum; ABS = anti-bovine serum; ASS = anti-sheep serum.

Using a micropipette, pipette the albumins and serums into the wells until each well is full (5 µL–10 µL). Use clean pipette tips after each different antigen and antibody. Cover each dish with the appropriate lid, slide into a resealable plastic bag, add a moistened Kimwipe, and seal. Plates should be kept on a flat surface, either at room temperature or in a 37° C incubator. The reaction will take up to two days at room temperature or overnight in the incubator.

Additional Considerations

Typical results, in the form of a precipitate (Figure 5), show antibodies made specifically against horses reacted with the horse albumin. Anti-horse serum antibodies did not react with pig, bovine, or sheep albumins. Anti-pig antibodies reacted with pig albumin but not with horse, bovine, or sheep albumin. Anti-sheep and anti-bovine sera both cross-reacted with sheep and bovine albumins but did not react with horse or pig.

Although reactions between horse-antihorse, pig-antipig, bovine-antibovine and sheep-antisheep occurred as expected, reactions across species lines were also evident. Information from the molecular clock theory now comes into play. Horse albumin is substantially different in structure from that of pig, bovine, or sheep. These results support the placement of horses into their own order (Perissodactyla), indicating the ancestral ungulate split from the Artiodactyla took place a very long time ago. Pig albumin also was shown to be structurally distinct from horse, bovine, and sheep, since the antibodies formed specifically against pig protein did not react with any other group. These molecular data support the pig group's placement into their own suborder and the view that the suids split from the ruminants fairly long ago. The cross-reactions between the bovine and sheep can be owing to their more recent common genetic ancestry and so their coding DNA sequences are nearly the same. The albumin from each ruminant group may share very similar DNA and nearly identical amino acid sequences—the latter being due to the degenerate genetic code. As a result, the albumin structure of the cow and sheep initiated a reaction (precipitate) between antibodies and their nearly similar antigens, supporting the inclusion of ruminants into their own suborder.

Ideas for Further Studies

One can further separate the ruminants (bovine, sheep, and goats) using anti-whey sera. React anti-whey antibodies with whey (milk) protein mixed at exactly the same concentration as the albumins. All components can be obtained from Sigma. Results from this experiment showed cross-reactions between sheep and goat whey and anti-sheep whey serum and anti-goat whey serum. There was no reaction between goat and sheep anti-whey sera to bovine whey. Anti-bovine whey serum reacted with bovine whey protein and not with sheep or goat whey. These data support the taxonomist's view that sheep and goats are more closely related to each other than either is to cattle. The data indicate that many mammalian milk proteins may not be as highly conserved as blood proteins. The function of milk is not as dependent on the molecular conformation of the protein content as is albumin. Changes in the DNA coding may alter amino acid sequences to a much greater degree without compromising the milk's nutritional function. The split between the sheep and goat groups from the ancestral bovine group is relatively recent and supports their inclusion into tribe Caprini, whereas cattle are in tribe Bovini (Table 1). This makes intuitive sense as well, because sheep and goats (particularly the wild members of the groups) appear to share many common physical features.

Troubleshooting the Ouchterlony Test (Ouchterlony & Nilsson, 1973; Small et al., 1976)

A. *Observation:* More than one line of precipitate occurs when only one was expected.

   Reason: The reactants were injected into the wells in a high concentration. The density of the reactants is too great and a reaction occurs only where the concentration is lessened—at the leading and trailing fronts.

   Solution: Two lines on the plate between a single antigen-antibody indicate a single reaction.

B. *Observation:* Sometimes two days are required in order to get a visible reaction.

   Reason: Each set of reactants has an optimal diffusion rate based mostly on temperature. Albumins usually take two days at room temperature (22° C). One day will suffice if plates are placed in a 37° C incubator.

   Solution: Precipitate formation, in general, will increase as temperature is increased.

C. *Observation:* No precipitate formed where it should be forming—no reaction between the antigen and the antibody specifically formed against it.

   Reason: For optimal results, the reactants should be in balance, usually a 1:1 ratio. Too much antigen to antibody or vice versa will result in no binding either due to not enough antigen available or not enough antibody available. The small amount that may react is not enough to be seen on the plate.

   Solution: Have a variety of plates made so that most will show the desired reaction.

D. *Observation:* The lines of precipitate between two adjacent and different antigens form a continuous arc between them and the antibody.

   Reason: The reaction of the antibody to the two antigens is equivalent. The antibody recognized the antigen's topography in spite of the two different sources of the antigen.

   Solution: The antigens in question are very similar, possibly identical, to each other. If the antigen is a protein, this implies a close relationship between the proteins and their parent DNA. Their amino acid sequences are nearly identical.

E. *Observation:* The lines of precipitate intersect (crisscross) between adjacent antigens.

Reason: There are two antibodies in the center well, not one.

Solution: The two reactions are independent of each other.

F. *Observation:* Nothing occurs on any plates.

Reason: Problems probably are related to preparation of materials, sera older than two years, improper mixture of antigens, and so on.

Solution: Make sure that the sera are still active ahead of time. Make sure that the phosphate buffer was properly made. The pH of the buffer is important. PBS provides electrolytes that are essential for precipitate formation. The optimal pH range insures that the precipitate will not form except as a result of the interaction of the reactants and that the precipitate is not inhibited.

References

Hornbeck, P. (1991). Double-immunodiffusion assay for detecting specific antibodies. *Current Protocols in Immunology.* 2.3.1.

Karp, G. (1996). *Cell and molecular biology*. New York: John Wiley and Sons.

Nowak, R.M. (1991). *Walker's mammals of the world* (5th ed., Vol. II). Baltimore: Johns Hopkins University Press.

Ouchterlony, O., & Nilsson, L.A. (1973). Immunodiffusion and immuno-electrophoresis. In D.M. Weir (Ed.), *Immunochemistry* (2nd ed.). Oxford, London, Edinburgh, and Victoria, Australia: Blackwell Scientific Publications.

Small. P., et al. (1976). Immunology as an analytical tool. *Carolina Tips, 39*(9). Burlington, North Carolina.

Vaughan, T.A. (1986). *Mammalogy* (3rd ed.). Philadelphia: Saunders College Publishing.

Evolution in the Laboratory:

Biocide Resistance in *E. Coli*

II.4

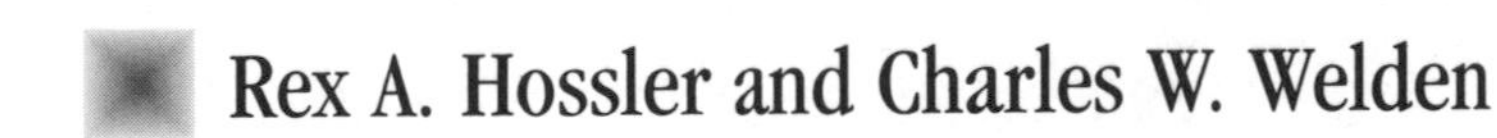

Rex A. Hossler and Charles W. Welden

Overview

Students will culture *Escherichia coli (E. coli)*, a bacterium normally found in the gut of humans and other mammals; expose the bacteria to triclosan, a biocide used in many consumer products; and discover that the bacteria evolve resistance to this compound with surprising rapidity. In this exercise, students will observe the occurrence of evolution and will be introduced to the issues of misuse of anitimicrobial compounds and the consequent spread of resistant bacteria.

Evolutionary Principles Illustrated

- Mutation
- Microevolution

Background Information

More than 40,000 cases of food-borne infection by the bacteria *Campylobacter*, *Staphylococcus*, *Salmonella*, and *E. coli*, resulting in about 500 deaths, occur every year in the United States (Cohen & Tauxe, 1986). These infections result from contact with contaminated beef products, poultry, eggs, or water. In response to consumer concern about unsafe foods and other sources of infection, manufacturers have incorporated biocides, or antimicrobial compounds, into an astonishing variety of products, ranging from hand soaps to plastic toys to kitchen cutting boards (Henderson, 2000a; Henderson, 2000b; Stix, 1998; Travis, 2000). One of the most widely used compounds is triclosan (2,4,4′-Trichloro-2′-hydroxydiphenyl ether, or 5-Chloro-2-[2,4-dichlorophenoxy] phenol, also marketed as Irgasan DP300).

This activity is based on "Evolution in the lab: biocide resistance in *E. coli*" by Charles W. Welden and Rex A. Hossler (2003), in *The American Biology Teacher 65*(1), 56–61. It has been adapted and reprinted with permission of the publisher.

The possibility that pathogenic bacteria may evolve resistance to triclosan is a source of escalating concern among microbiologists and public health officials (Levy, 1998; Stix, 1998; Travis, 2000). If consumers think themselves protected by triclosan-containing products, they may become lax in their food-handling practices, and expose themselves to greater risk of food-borne disease (Levy, 1998). By killing susceptible, nonpathogenic bacteria, triclosan may also remove competitors that normally prevent pathogens from colonizing household surfaces, increasing the risk of dangerous infections by other routes.

Triclosan has been classed as a biocide (a substance toxic to cells in general) or antimicrobial agent (a substance toxic to bacteria, fungi, and protistans) because it kills or inhibits the growth of a wide spectrum of microbes. It is not considered an antibiotic (a microbial product that kills or inhibits the growth of susceptible microbes) because of its origin and its broad spectrum of toxicity.

Bacteria and fungi are well known for evolving resistance to antibiotics (Levy, 1998), but are thought to be less likely to evolve resistance to biocides because these compounds often act by different mechanisms. However, recent research into the mechanism of action by triclosan (McMurray, Oethinger, & Levy, 1998; Levy et al., 1999) indicates that it may act more like an antibiotic than a true biocide. Bacteria may, therefore, be more likely to evolve resistance to triclosan than previously thought.

This laboratory exercise can serve as a springboard for further investigation and discussion of biocide and antibiotic resistance and likely consequences; the relevance of evolution to medicine, public health, and students' lives; and the observability of evolutionary processes in a laboratory setting. The exercise also introduces students to techniques of bacterial culture that they can apply to other experiments.

Materials

Instructor materials:

- Tryptic soy broth stock (500 mL)
- 99% pure triclosan (a white crystalline powder)
- *E. coli* culture (strain K-12)
- Tryptic soy agar plates
- Ethanol (17.5%)
- Distilled water

Per group of three to five students:

- 20 sterile petri dishes of tryptic soy agar
- 20 tubes of sterile tryptic soy broth

One workstation per two student groups (eight students) containing:

- A screw-top jar containing sterile cotton swabs
- A covered dish containing sterile 8 mm disks of filter paper (any diameter from 5 to 10 mm would work as well)
- Forceps labeled "Water," "Ethanol," and "Triclosan" sterilized by soaking in ethanol and air-dried before use (we simply laid these out on paper towels, but covering them may reduce contamination of petri dishes)
- Waste disposal buckets for used swabs, petri dishes, and culture tubes (filling these with enough disinfectant to cover the ends of the swabs may be a wise safety precaution)
- A rack for culture tubes and a tray for petri dishes
- A box of Parafilm® and scissors for cutting Parafilm®
- Indelible pens for labeling culture tubes and petri dishes
- Labeled container of distilled water
- Labeled container of Ethanol (17.5%)
- Labeled container of Triclosan (500 mg/mL)
- A capped tube containing about 10 mL of sterile water, labeled "*E. coli*"

Per lab class:

- Incubator cabinet set at 35 to 37° C

Procedures

Several days before the exercise, it is necessary to transfer *E. coli* (strain K-12) from stock cultures to tryptic soy agar plates, making a bacterial lawn (a more-or-less uniform sheet of bacteria covering the agar surface). Prepare one plate per lab section, with a few extras in case of contamination.

Pour approximately 20 sterile petri dishes of tryptic soy agar and 20 tubes of sterile tryptic soy broth per team of three to five students. Also prepare a working solution of triclosan by dissolving the powder in a solution of 17.5% ethanol and 82.5% distilled water to a final triclosan concentration of 500 milligrams per milliliter.

Immediately before the first lab meeting, rub a sterile cotton swab across the surface of one of the prepared dishes with a lawn of E. coli and swirl the swab in the tube of distilled water (second-to-last item in the list above) for each workstation. This will provide students with a dilute, spreadable suspension of *E. coli*.

Divide students into teams of three to five, and assign each team to start one petri dish for each treatment: water, ethanol, and triclosan. Alternatively, one could allow students to work alone, or assign each team a single treatment.

In outline, the experiment consisted of seven steps, repeated up to six times.

1. Transfer bacteria from a liquid culture to an agar plate.
2. Apply one of three paper disks soaked in water, ethanol, or triclosan.
3. Incubate 24 hours at 37° C.
4. Measure the width of the zone of inhibition (explained below).
5. Isolate from each plate the bacteria most resistant to the treatment applied (explained below).
6. Transfer these bacteria to liquid culture.
7. Incubate for 24 hours at 37° C.
8. Repeat.

To begin the experiment, students from each team transfer bacteria from the *E. coli* suspension provided by the instructor to petri dishes containing tryptic soy agar. They do this by swirling sterile cotton swabs in the bacterial suspension and spreading a lawn of bacteria on the agar surface of three petri dishes, using a separate swab for each dish. In subsequent rounds of the experiment, they transfer bacteria from their own liquid cultures, rather than from the initial suspension provided by the instructor.

To apply the treatments to their plates, students dip separate sterile disks of filter paper into distilled water, 17.5% ethanol, and 500 milligrams per milliliter triclosan, and place them, using the appropriate forceps, in the center of the agar surfaces of three petri dishes. After allowing a minute or so for the disks to adhere to the agar surfaces, students seal the edges of the petri dishes with parafilm, label them with a team identifier and the treatment applied, and place them in the incubator. If parafilm is unavailable, students could seal their dishes with transparent tape.

Incubate cultures (both liquid and plate) at 35 to 37° C for 24 hours. To maintain uniformity of treatments, teacher (or lab personnel) may move students' cultures into a refrigerator (approx. 5° C) over weekends, either before or after the 24 hour incubation at 35 to 37° C.

After the incubation period, students measure the width of the zone of inhibition. This is the distance from the edge of the paper disk to the inner margin of the bacterial lawn (Figure 1). Because the concentration of the applied compound decreases with distance from the paper disk, the width of this zone is inversely correlated with the degree of resistance in the most resistant members of the bacterial population.

Students next isolate the most resistant bacteria in each dish by rubbing a sterile cotton swab across the inner margin of the zone of inhibition. If no zone of inhibition is apparent, they swab bacteria from the area adjacent to the paper disk. If isolated bacterial colonies are visible within the zone of inhibition, they swab those.

Next, students transfer the bacteria collected from their dishes to liquid culture by swirling each cotton swab in a separate tube of tryptic soy broth.

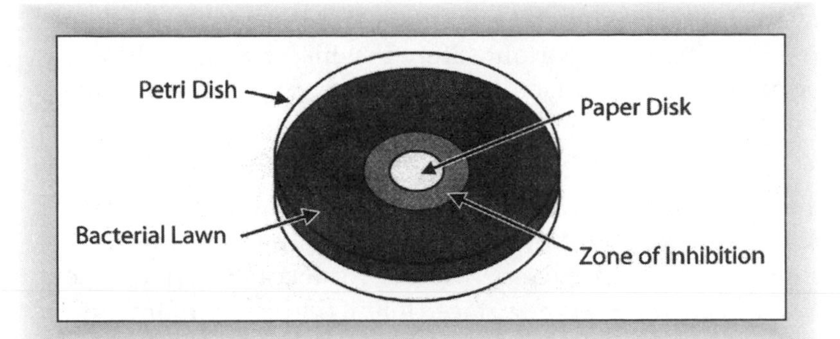

FIGURE 1 Experimental setup, showing placement of filter paper disk in the center of a petri dish of tryptic soy agar. Students measured the width of the zone of inhibition from the edge of the paper disk to the inner margin to the bacterial lawn.

They label the tube according to the treatment applied to the dish from which the bacteria are taken, and incubate the capped tubes at 35 to 37° C for 24 hours. This step allows the putatively resistant bacteria to multiply in preparation for the next round of selection.

Students repeat the above process of liquid culture, transfer to petri dish, treatment, measurement of zone of inhibition, isolation of the most resistant bacteria, and transfer to liquid culture for up to six rounds. They discard used petri dishes, liquid cultures, and cotton swabs after each round.

Thus, each team of students cultures three separate lineages of bacterial populations subjected to repeated episodes of the same treatment: triclosan, ethanol, or water. After each round of exposure to treatment, students record the width of the zone of inhibition in each dish in a common database, which the instructor later distributes to all students.

The instructor provides the compiled raw data from all student teams in a spreadsheet data file via the campus computer network (or hard copy). Students then compute the mean (average) width of zone of inhibition for each treatment on each measurement date and graph means against time.

Have the students determine whether zones of inhibition were wider initially on triclosan plates and whether widths of zones of inhibition in any treatment changed during the course of the experiment.

Additional Considerations

By applying the treatment in the center of the agar surface, students create a concentration gradient as the compound in the paper disk diffuses out into the agar. That is, the concentration of water, ethanol, or triclosan is highest adjacent to the disk and progressively lower farther from it.

We have found that using paper disks to apply the treatments is preferable to applying the liquids directly onto the agar. Liquids do not soak into agar immediately, but run irregularly across the surface, especially if the dish is tilted or jostled. This creates a very irregular distribution of concentrations, and students cannot see where the treatment was applied. The paper disk holds the liquid in place and allows students to apply a larger volume. It also provides a visual landmark to show where the center of the concentration gradient is located.

Using cotton swabs instead of inoculating loops allows us to avoid flame sterilization. We consider this an important safety benefit because it allows students to transfer bacteria without faculty supervision. Swabs also make spreading bacteria onto agar easier and less likely to puncture the agar surface.

Students may have problems in recognizing *E. coli* and in distinguishing it from contaminants. *E. coli* forms light gray-brown, glistening, smooth-surfaced colonies and lawns. Other bacteria usually form colonies of different colors (often yellow) or textures (rough-surfaced). Fungi grow in filaments (hyphae) and often resemble white, gray, green, or black fuzzy masses of cottony threads.

To reduce contamination, instruct students in sterile technique:

- Do not allow cotton swabs to touch any surfaces or solutions other than the bacterial cultures as directed. Do not touch agar or culture broth with fingers or anything other than cotton swabs.
- Keep petri dishes closed at all times except during the actual transfer of bacteria, and then open them as briefly and as narrowly as possible.
- When opening petri dishes for transfer, hold the lid over the agar surface and as close to it as possible.
- Make a uniform bacterial lawn on an agar surface by swirling a sterile cotton swab in a liquid *E. coli* culture and gently rubbing the swab back and forth over the entire surface of the agar. Rub gently to avoid puncturing the agar surface.
- Students should place used swabs, liquid cultures, and petri dishes in designated waste containers. These materials should be sterilized before disposal and should be treated and labeled as biological waste.
- Students should wash their hands with soap (preferably triclosan-free) and water after handling bacterial cultures.

Sample Results with Discussion

Our students began with 73 culture lines (25 exposed to triclosan, and 24 each exposed to ethanol and water). Of these, 71 culture lines completed four rounds of treatment exposure, 48 completed five rounds, and 22 completed six rounds. Other culture lines were lost due to miscommunication among lab instructors regarding the intended duration of the experiment. Much to our surprise, neither students nor lab instructors noted any contamination in the cultures.

Triclosan cultures had wider zones of inhibition initially than other treatments (triclosan: 2.7–15.0 mm, = 10.6, ethanol: 0.0–1.0 mm, water; all 0.0 mm), and the difference was statistically significant ($F = 372$, d.f.= 2, $p < 0.0001$). Mean width of zones of inhibition in triclosan treatments shrank progressively throughout the experiment, reaching a mean of 3.1 mm after six rounds of treatment (Figure 2). The difference between initial mean zone width and mean zone width after six rounds of treatment was statistically significant

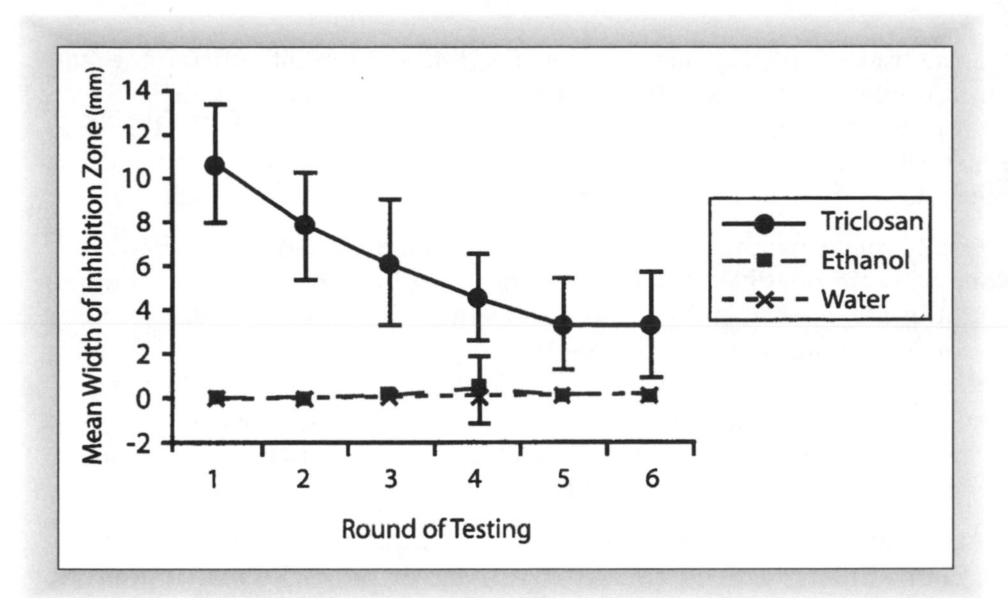

FIGURE 2 Mean widths of zones of inhibition. Treatments were water, 17.5% ethanol, and triclosan (500 milligrams per milliliter). Round of testing refers to the number of exposures to treatment. Error bars encompass 95% confidence intervals on each mean.

(paired $t = 6.3$, two-tailed $p < 0.002$). Differences between initial mean zone width and mean width after four and five rounds, although smaller, were also statistically significant. Zones of inhibition in other treatments showed no trend.

Although we show 95% confidence intervals (Figure 2) and report statistical tests, we did not ask students to carry out these statistical analyses. However, these analyses are relatively easy to do using spreadsheets or statistical programs, and more advanced students should be capable of carrying them out.

As shown by the initial widths of zones of inhibition in the three treatments, triclosan killed *E. coli* or inhibited their reproduction, whereas water and 17.5% ethanol did not. We were somewhat surprised that the ethanol treatment did not inhibit bacterial growth or reproduction, but it may be the case that the ethanol evaporated from the paper disk rather than diffusing into the agar, obviating any concentration gradient, and perhaps even diffusing (in the gaseous state) out of the petri dish entirely.

The bacteria apparently evolved resistance to triclosan rapidly, as shown by the rapid reduction in the width of the zone of inhibition (Figure 2). The continuing reduction in the width of the zone of inhibition may indicate that the bacteria accumulated several resistance mutations during the course of the experiment. McMurray, Oethinger, and Levy (1998) found five point mutations in different lineages of triclosan-resistant *E. coli*, and it is intriguing to speculate that our bacteria may have accumulated several of these.

The results reinforce several key concepts of evolutionary biology and can help combat some common misconceptions. Contrary to the claims of some, microevolution can be observed in the laboratory under controlled conditions. Also, notable evolutionary change can occur rapidly, especially in organisms with short life spans and rapid reproduction, such as bacteria. Finally, note that some triclosan dishes had very narrow zones of inhibition from the start (2.7 mm in one case). This indicates that triclosan-resistant mutations were present in the bacterial population before exposure to triclosan. In other words, triclosan resistance arises by normal random mutation, not in a direct response to the presence of triclosan in the environment.

Despite the apparent conclusiveness of these results, some alternative explanations are possible. Because students used the same triclosan solutions throughout the experiment, if the concentration of triclosan decreased over time, zones of inhibition would have shrunk as observed. This reduction in concentration may have occurred by breakdown of triclosan in solution (unlikely), or by precipitation of triclosan out of solution. However, lab instructors recognized the latter possibility partway through the experiment and began stirring the triclosan solutions before each lab.

These concerns may be met by altering the experimental design in two ways. First, students will be instructed to shake or stir triclosan solutions thoroughly before each use. Second, we will test the original stock culture of *E. coli* for resistance to the triclosan solution at the end of the experiment. If the solution retains the original concentration, we should see the same degree of resistance (or lack thereof) at the end of the experiment as at the beginning.

We also plan to control the amount of water, ethanol, and triclosan applied more carefully. In future labs, we will instruct the students to pipette uniform volumes of liquid onto the filter paper disks.

Although triclosan is not considered an antibiotic, this exercise is nonetheless relevant to the evolution of antibiotic resistance. The evolution of resistance to antibiotic drugs by pathogenic bacteria is nothing new (Levy, 1998). Some bacteria that cause life-threatening disease are already resistant to all of the more than 100 antibiotic drugs in use today. These multi-drug resistant strains are untreatable. Other bacteria, such as some strains of *Staphylococcus aureus* (which causes blood poisoning, wound infections, and pneumonia), have recently shown resistance to vancomycin, the antibiotic of last resort, and are considered likely to evolve multi-drug resistance in the near future. Some strains of *S. aureus* are already resistant to triclosan (Sasatusu, 1993).

Triclosan has been classed as a biocide or an antimicrobial compound, rather than an antibiotic, because it was presumed to inhibit bacterial growth and reproduction by a variety of mechanisms. Antibiotics, in contrast, usually interfere with a specific metabolic pathway. However, the mechanisms of triclosan's action were unknown until recent research (McMurray, Oethinger, & Levy, 1998; Levy et al., 1999) showed that it blocks a single step in the synthesis of fatty acids. Triclosan-resistant *E. coli* strains were shown to differ from susceptible strains by single base-pair substitutions in the DNA (McMurray, Oethinger, & Levy, 1998). Thus, triclosan appears to act more like an antibiotic than previously thought, and resistance to triclosan, like antibiotic resistance, can arise by point mutations. These findings imply that the evolution of triclosan resistance may be more likely than previously thought, and more likely than implied by manufacturers of triclosan-containing products (Larkin, 1999).

The enzyme blocked by triclosan is also the target of an antibiotic used to treat tuberculosis (Travis, 2000). Because bacteria frequently exchange drug-resistance genes via small loops of DNA called plasmids (Davies, 1994), some microbiologists have become concerned that triclosan-resistant bacteria could transfer a plasmid to *Mycobacterium tuberculosae* that would make it resistant to the antibiotic. This scenario is made more likely by the use of triclosan-containing gloves and soaps in hospitals treating tuberculosis patients.

The applicability of these results to real-world evolution is a matter for fruitful discussion with students. Resistance genes typically carry costs as well as benefits. Energy invested in circumventing the action of an antimicrobial compound is not available for reproduction, and therefore resistant bacteria usually reproduce at a slightly slower pace than susceptible strains. In an environment devoid of the antimicrobial, susceptible bacteria will out-reproduce and replace resistant ones. Only in an environment where the antimicrobial is prevalent will the benefit of resistance outweigh its cost.

Procter & Gamble, makers of several household products containing triclosan, criticized similar studies for this very reason. "These were not real world conditions. In the real world [germs] have to compete with a host of other organisms. We're really not worried about [triclosan use] leading to superbugs or resistant organisms," said a Procter & Gamble spokesperson (quoted in Hellinghausen, 1998).

The increasing prevalence of triclosan in household products calls this optimistic position into question. A recent survey of national and regional supermarkets in the U.S. found triclosan (or another antimicrobial, triclocarban) in 76% of liquid soaps and 29% of bar soaps (Henderson, 2000b). You might assign your students to visit local supermarkets and grocery stores to compile their own triclosan statistics, and ask themselves whether triclosan has become a normal part of the environment.

Note: We have now repeated this experiment with a new class of students, with an additional control. At each round of plate culture, students exposed previously unexposed and unselected *E. coli* from the original stock culture to the triclosan solution, using the same methods as for the selection treatment. The zone of inhibition in this control remained about 10 mm wide throughout the experiment, and the results from the other treatments were nearly identical to those of the original experiment, indicating that the decreased width of the zone of inhibition in the selection treatment was not due to chemical breakdown or precipitation in the triclosan solution.

References

Cohen, M.L., & Tauxe, R.V. (1986). Drug-resistant Salmonella in the United States: An epidemiological perspective. *Science, 234*, 964–69.

Davies, J. (1994). Inactivation of antibiotics and dissemination of resistance genes. *Science, 264*, 375–81.

Hellinghausen, M.A. (1998). Wash out: Could antibacterial soaps create new bacterial strains? Available: http://www.nurseweek.com/features/98-10/soap.html.

Henderson, C.W. (Ed.). (2000a). Use of triclosan in household products may increase harmful microbial resistance. Tuberculosis & Outbreaks Week, August 15, 2000.

Henderson, C.W. (Ed.). (2000b). Soaps containing potentially harmful antibacterial agents commonly available in the U.S. Tuberculosis & Outbreaks Week, September 19, 2000.

Larkin, M. (1999). A close look at triclosan raises questions. *The Lancet, 353*, 1160.

Levy, C.W., Roujeinikova, A., Sedelnikova, S., Baker, P., Stuitje, A., Slabas, A., Rice, D.W. &

Rafferty, J.B. (1999). Molecular basis of triclosan activity. *Nature, 398*, 383–84.

Levy, S.B. (1998). The challenge of antibiotic resistance. *Scientific American, 278*, 46–55.

McMurray, L.M., Oethinger, M., & Levy, S.B. (1998). Triclosan targets lipid synthesis. *Nature, 394*, 531–32.

Sasatusu, M. (1993). Triclosan-resistant Staphylococcus aureus. *The Lancet, 341*, 756.

Stix, G. (1998). The *E. coli* are coming. *Scientific American, 279*, 29.

Travis, J. (2000). Popularity of germ fighter raises concern. *Science News, 157*, 342.

The Classification and Evolution of *Caminalcules*

II-5

 Robert P. Gendron

Overview

The lab described here uses "organisms" with a fossil record, the *Caminalcules*. The activity consists of three related exercises through which students can develop a classification scheme for "living" *Caminalcules*, use the classification plan to develop a tentative phylogenetic tree, and construct a phylogenetic tree based on the fossil record.

Evolutionary Principles Illustrated

- Systematics
- Phylogeny
- Convergence

Background Information

The difficulty of teaching evolution arises, in part, because evolutionary processes are slow and generally cannot be observed, even over the course of an entire year. One way to circumvent this problem is by using simulations. Another approach is to teach evolutionary concepts by constructing phylogenetic trees. This lab has been developed in the latter category. The idea for this lab came from an exercise written by Vogel and Ewel (1972) in which students developed a classification of fasteners (nails, screws, and bolts).

Caminalcules (Figure 1) are imaginary organisms invented by Joseph H. Camin (Sokal, 1983). According to Sokal (1983), Camin created his organisms by starting with a primitive ancestor and gradually modifying the forms

---

This activity is based on "The classification and evolution of caminalcules" by Robert Gendron (2000), in *The American Biology Teacher, 62*(8), 570–76. It has been adapted and reprinted with permission of the publisher. Permission to reprint the Caminalcule drawings was granted by the noted biologist R.R. Sokal, a colleague of Joseph H. Camin (1922–1979) of the Department of Entomology at the University of Kansas, who originally developed them.

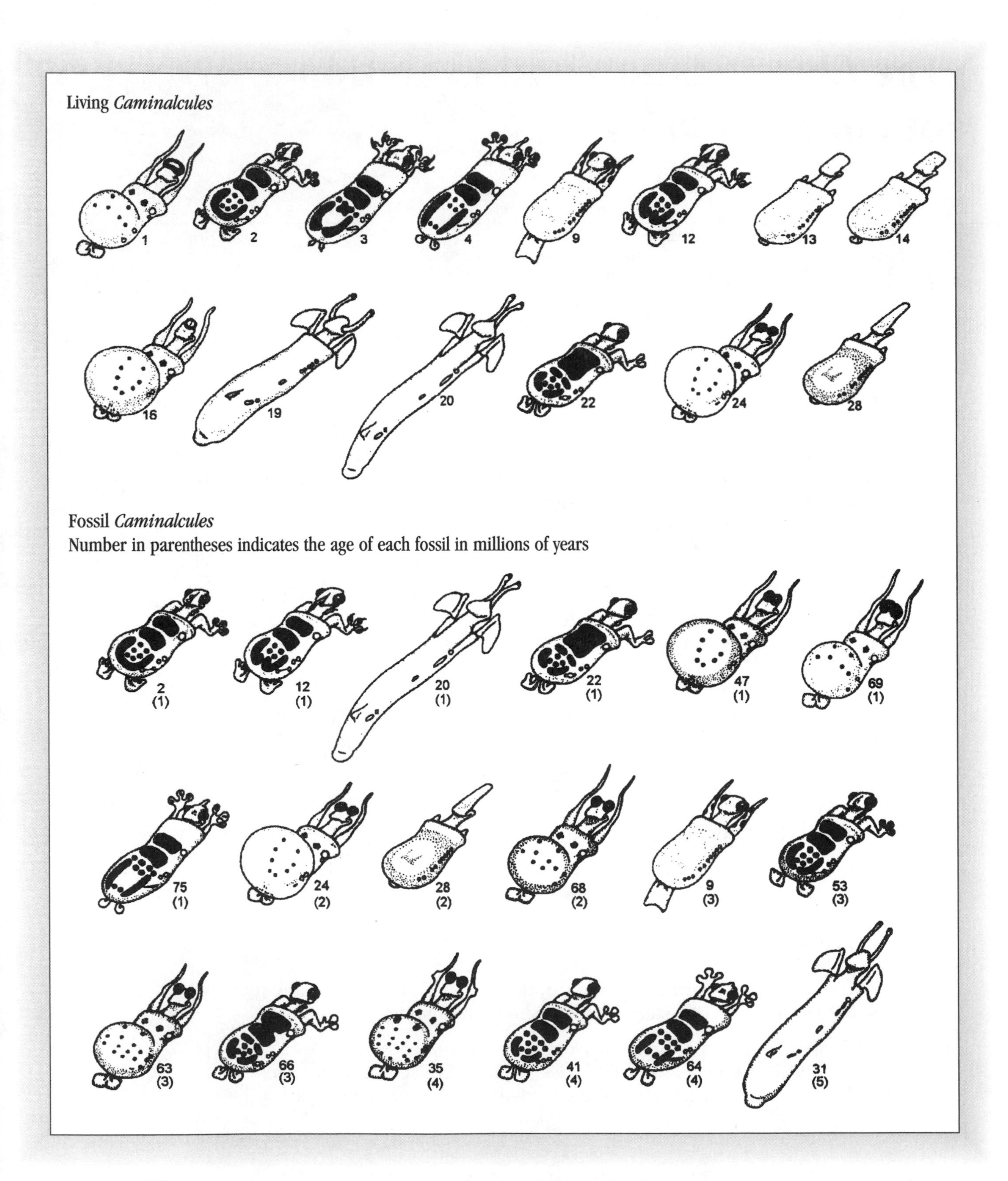

FIGURE 1 Fourteen living and 57 fossil *Caminalcules*. A number is used to identify each species in lieu of a name.

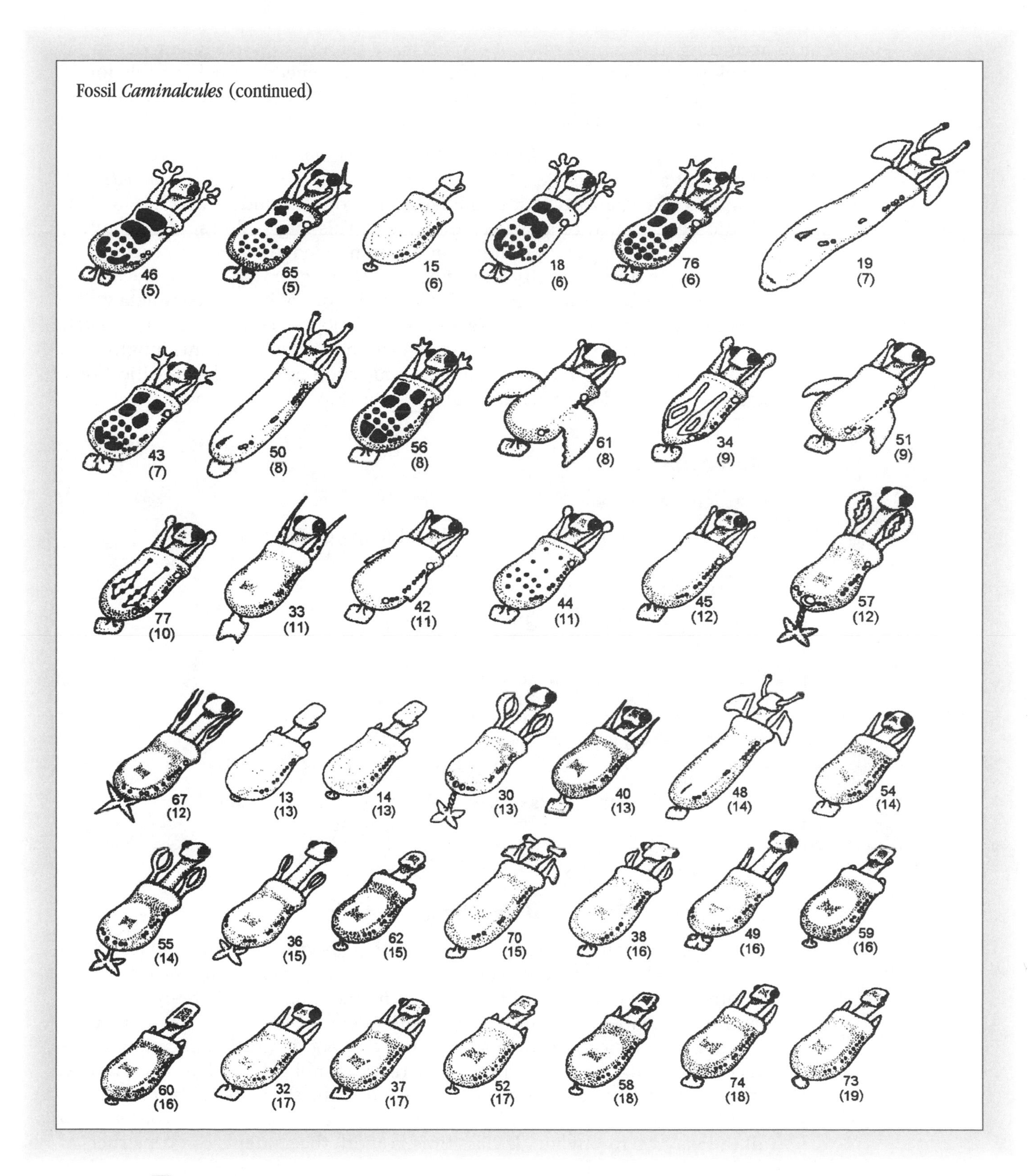

FIGURE 1 *Continued*

according to accepted rules of evolutionary change. Camin's intent was to develop a known phylogeny (something that is generally unobtainable for real organisms) that could be used to critically evaluate different taxonomic techniques such as phenetic and cladistic analysis.

For the purpose of teaching evolution, the *Caminalcules* offer several important advantages (McComas & Alters, 1994). First, because *Caminalcules* are artificial organisms, students have no preconceived ideas about how they should be classified or how they are related. This means that students have to concentrate on principles rather than prior knowledge when constructing a phylogenetic tree or classification. Second, unlike everyday objects such as fasteners, the *Caminalcules* have a "real" evolutionary history, complete with a detailed fossil record. With these fossils, students can construct a phylogenetic tree from the bottom up in a way that they find conceptually meaningful. Finally, this lab illustrates the intimate connection between the classification of living species and their evolutionary relationships.

Materials

Instructor materials:

- Overhead transparencies of the 14 living *Caminalcules*

Per student:

- Figure 1: Living and Fossil *Caminalcules*

Per group of two to four students:

- Scissors
- Meter stick
- Glue
- Large square sheets of paper about 28 inches on a side

Procedures

Part 1: Classification of the Living Caminalcules

Students begin by arranging the 14 living species into a hierarchical classification (Table 1). First, they combine species into genera using the criteria that members of a genus should resemble each other more closely than they resemble members of other genera. (With *Caminalcules*, as with many real organisms, physical resemblance is usually a good indication of common ancestry.) Using the same criteria, genera are combined into families, families into orders, and so on. Depending on whether the students are taxonomic "splitters" or "lumpers," their classification scheme might stop at order or go all the way up to phylum. If class time is short, the students can construct their preliminary classification at home. Another way to speed things up is by having the entire class work on it together, with the instructor acting as moderator and facilitator.

TABLE 1 Example of a hierarchical classification of the living *Caminalcules*. If one looks at the true phylogenetic tree in Figure 2, it is apparent that this is not the best classification scheme. Specifically, Genera 3 and 4 are more closely related to Genus 5 than they are to Genus 2. Without first looking at the fossil evidence, however, students are much more likely to come up with something like this.

Class	*Caminalcule*													
Order	01											02		
Family	F1		F2						F3			F4		
Genus	G1		G2	G3		G4			G5			G6		
Species	19	20	9	4	3	22	12	2	16	24	1	14	13	28

This exercise teaches several important concepts, beginning with the idea of hierarchical classification itself. Teachers of more advanced classes may wish to discuss theories of classification (Vogt, 1995; Ridley, 1996). The concept of convergent evolution is also introduced, as described below.

Once the students have completed their classification, lead a class discussion with the aid of an overhead projector and transparent images of the 14 living *Caminalcules*. Begin with *Caminalcule* 2 and ask what other species belong in the same genus. Most students want to put 2, 3, 4, 12, and 22 together (Figure 1). If so, ask them to split the five species into smaller genera. The most common mistake at this point is to put 3 and 12 in a genus by themselves because they both have claws. This provides an opportunity to point out that the classification should be based on all available characters. When the students consider characters such as color pattern, body shape, presence of elbows and head ornamentation, they quickly decide that 3 and 4 belong in one group (genus), and 2, 12, and 22 belong in another. Some would put 22 into its own genus, which is acceptable. Having classified the five species to everyone's satisfaction, one can then discuss convergent evolution, using 3 and 12 as an example. (The two *Caminalcule* cyclopes, Species 1 and 16, are also convergent.) Point out that convergent evolution is said to occur when a similar trait evolves independently in two separate lineages. For example, fish and whales both have the same shape, but based on their skeletal structure, endothermy, lactation, and so on, whales clearly belong with the mammals. The characteristics they share with fish evolved independently as an adaptation to an aquatic environment. Another way to identify convergent evolution, though not available to the students until later in the lab, is to determine if the character in question was absent in the most recent common ancestor. This is equivalent to saying that the characters are analogous rather than homologous.

I encourage the students to be taxonomic "splitters" rather than "lumpers" for heuristic reasons; it makes it easier to introduce the concept of convergent

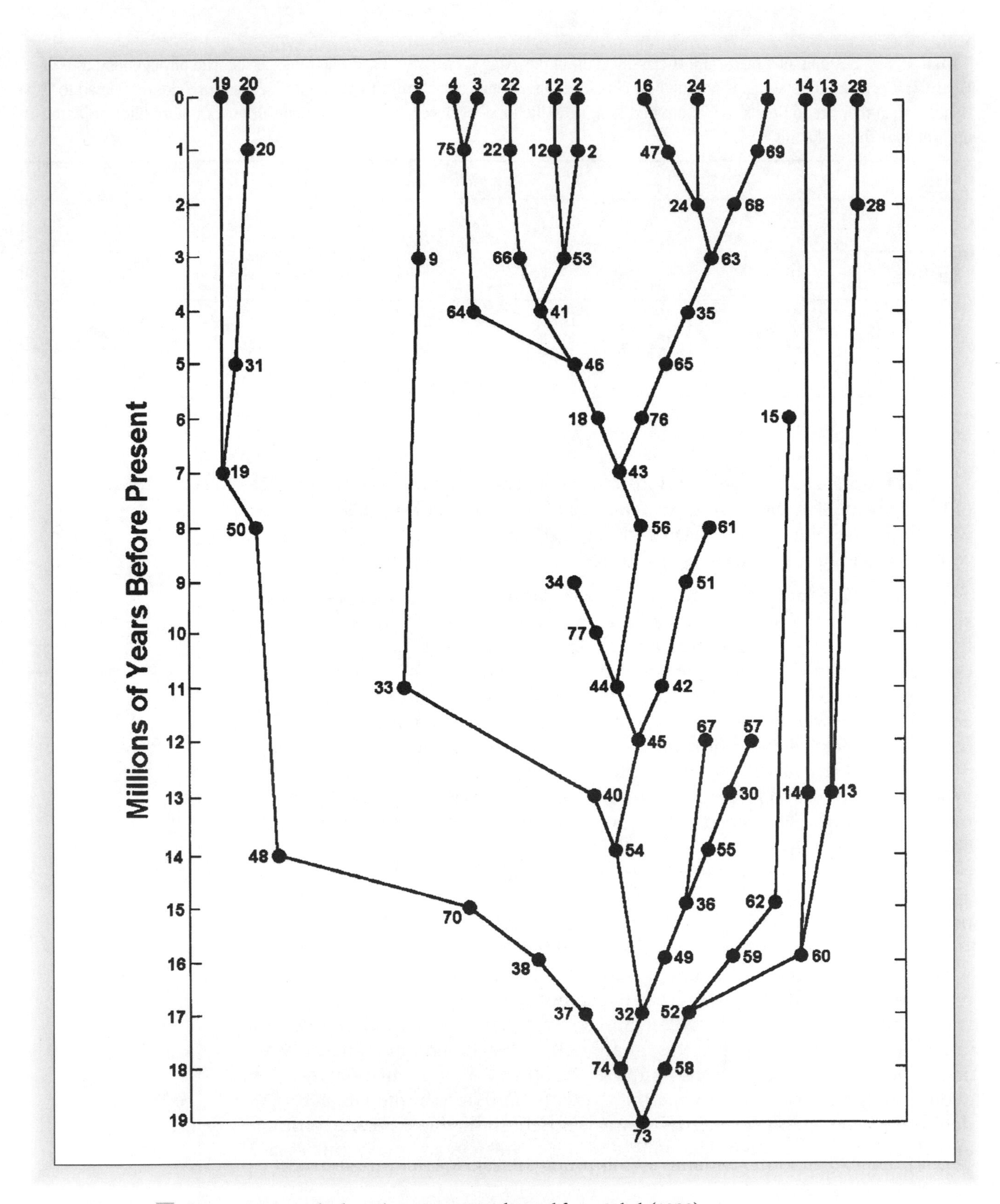

FIGURE 2 ■ The true *Caminalcule* evolutionary tree. Adapated from Sokal (1983). *Note:* some of the branches in the original tree have been removed.

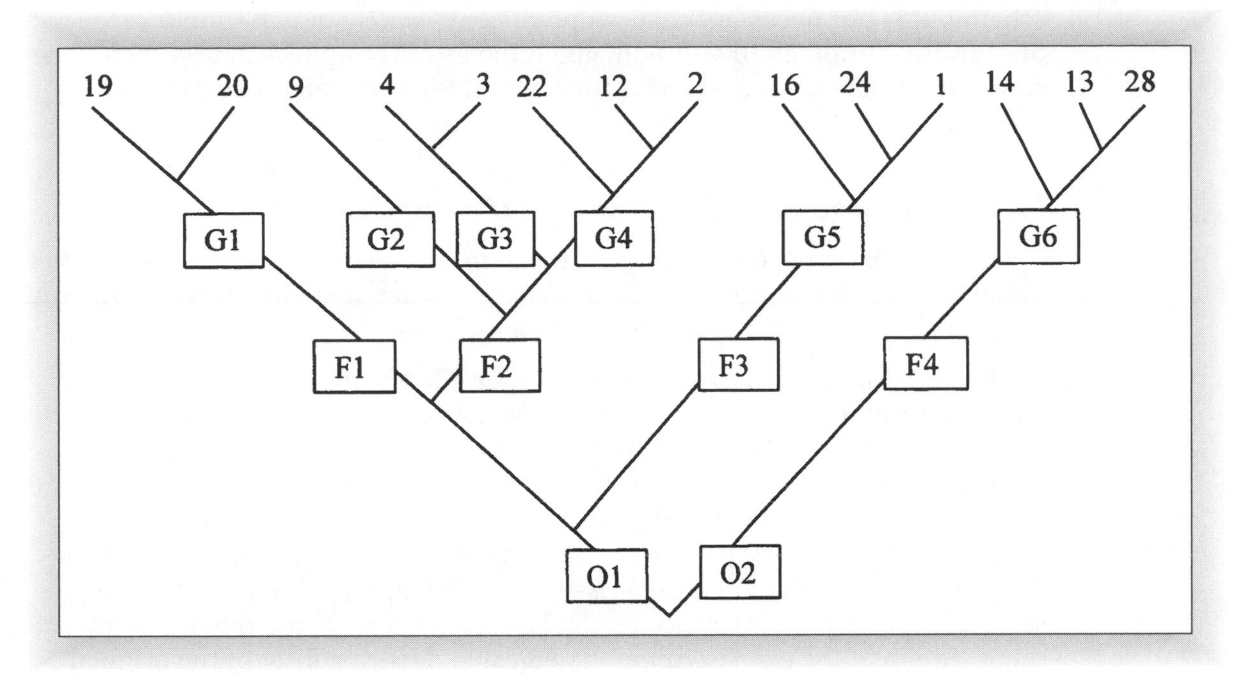

FIGURE 3 This phylogenetic tree is based on the classification of living species shown in Figure 2. The members of each genus share a common ancestor not shared by other genera. The same is true for each of the four families and two orders.

evolution as well as to emphasize the need to examine all available characters very carefully. In contrast, Sokal (1983) lumps species 2, 3, 4, 12, and 22 into one genus.

Part 2: A Phylogenetic Tree Based Only on Living Species

In the second exercise, students use their classification of the living *Caminalcules* to construct a phylogenetic tree. The classification shown in Table 1, for example, would suggest the tree in Figure 3. One of the key concepts here is that of the most recent common ancestor. Students learn that when they put two species, say 19 and 20, in the same genus, this implies that these species share a common ancestor not shared by other genera (the phylogenetic principle of classification). When there are three or more species in a genus, students must decide which two of those species are most closely related (Figure 4).

The same procedure is applied through the higher classification levels. For example, if two genera resemble each other more closely than they do other genera, this is presumably because they share a unique common ancestor. Thus, students learn that even in the absence of a fossil record, it is possible to develop a tentative phylogenetic tree that corresponds to the classification

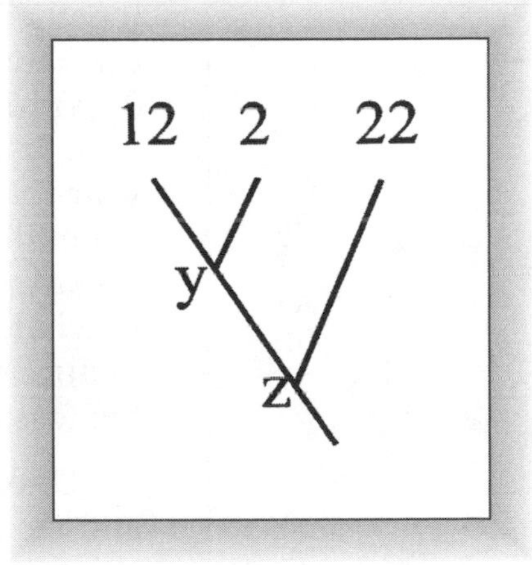

FIGURE 4 When a genus is made up of three (or more) species, students must decide which two of the species share a common ancestor not shared by the other. This diagram indicates that Species 2 and 12 are more closely related to each other than either is to 22. We hypothesize that 2 and 12 have a common ancestor (y) that is not shared by 22.

scheme. It is not necessary that the phylogeny exactly match Camin's true one, and it is unlikely that it will, given the intuitive approach used here. The students can discover any errors for themselves after completing the final exercise.

Part 3: A Phylogenetic Tree Based on the Fossil Record

For this exercise, each group of two to four students needs a large sheet of paper, scissors for cutting out *Caminalcules*, a meter stick for drawing lines on the paper, and glue for attaching the *Caminalcules*.

Each fossil *Caminalcule* (Figure 1) is identified by its species number and its age (in millions of years) in parentheses. Make sure the students do not cut off these numbers. Since the oldest fossil (Species 73) is 19 million years old, students draw 20 horizontal lines on the sheet of paper and label them from 0 (present time) at the top to 19 at the bottom. I usually show the class how to begin the phylogenetic tree by placing Species 73 in the middle of the 19 million-year line. This species gave rise to two new species (58 and 74) represented by 18-million-year-old fossils. The students continue the tree from there. To make the exercise more manageable, I use a subset of the original *Caminalcules*. I pruned some of the branches from Camin's original tree, leaving 14 living and 47 extinct species (Figure 2). For the complete set, see Sokal (1983). Note that some species are represented by both living and fossil specimens.

Students enjoy this exercise and generally do a good job of piecing together *Caminalcule* evolution. There are, however, several pitfalls that may catch even the most careful among them. These pitfalls provide an excellent opportunity to discuss concepts such as gaps in the fossil record and evolutionary stasis (Figure 2). For example, when they get to Species 67 (12 million years old), most students assume it must have branched off from Species 30 (13 million years). This would require an unlikely scenario in which an evolutionary trend toward heavy crushing claws is suddenly reversed to give rise to what look like forked tentacles. Once this is pointed out, students will deduce correctly that 67 branched off further down and that there is a gap in the fossil record.

Once their tree is complete, the students compare it to Camin's phylogeny and reconcile any discrepancies. Then ask them to identify the following, either in lab or as an assignment:

1. The most recent common ancestor of any two species.
2. Additional examples of convergent evolution.
3. Examples of vestigial structures (e.g., the inner toe of Species 66 at 3 million years).
4. Examples of evolutionary stasis (e.g., Species 14 and 13 remain unchanged for 13 million years).
5. An example of rapid adaptive radiation (e.g., the many lineages that arise from Species 43 at 7 million years).

These observations can easily be applied to real world examples and lead to interesting discussion questions such as the following:

How do vestigial structures provide clues about a species' evolutionary history?

What ecological conditions might result in the rapid diversification of some lineages (e.g., the mammals at the beginning of the Cenozoic) or the long-term stasis of others (e.g., horseshoe crabs and other "living fossils")?

Some *Caminalcule* species became extinct. What factors might increase or decrease the probability of extinction in the real world?

Teachers should also use the tree to emphasize the important principle that evolutionary change occurs through the modification of preexisting structures.

Additional Considerations

One reason for this lab's success is that students enjoy the group problem-solving aspect of the exercises. It is important, however, that the instructor monitor each group's progress in order to identify problems as they pop up. This provides an opportunity for the instructor to discuss with each group some of the concepts mentioned with this activity.

References

McComas, W.F., & Alters, B.J. (1994). Modeling modes of evolution: Comparing phyletic gradualism and punctuated equilibrium. *The American Biology Teacher, 56*(6), 354–60.

Ridley, M. (1996). *Evolution* (2nd ed.). Cambridge, MA: Blackwell Science.

Sokal, R.R. (1983). A phylogenetic analysis of the *Caminalcules*. I. The data base. *Systematic Zoology, 32*, 159–84.

Vogel, S., & Ewel, K.C. (1972). *A model menagerie: Laboratory studies about living systems*. Reading, MA: Addison-Wesley.

Vogt, K.D. (1995). Demonstrating biological classification using a simulation of natural taxa. *The American Biology Teacher, 57*(5), 282–83.

II-6 The *Caminalcule* Family Tree

D.J. Smith

Overview

This simulation involves studying drawings of members of an imaginary phylum of animals, called *Caminalcules*, developed by J.H. Camin. The use of these creatures can lead to an understanding of some of the basic principles of evolution and variation with species as reflected in students' proposals of a taxonomy for the *Caminalcules*.

Evolutionary Principles Illustrated

- Phylogeny
- Variation within species

Background Information

Caminalcules are members of a phylum of imaginary organisms as the basis for a series of advanced exercises in numerical taxonomy as described by Sokal (1966). These "organisms" are useful for teaching aspects of taxonomy and evolutionary biology for a number of reasons, including the following:

They are completely hypothetical, so that any problems involving them must be solved by rational processes rather than by chance acquaintance with a particular specimen.

They can be custom-made to suit the requirements of a particular exercise.

This activity is based on "Simulation in taxonomy: The use of Caminalcules" by D. J. Smith (1975), in *Journal of Biological Education, 9*(3/4), 155–57. It has been adapted and reprinted with permission of the publisher. Permission to reprint the Caminalcule drawings was granted by the noted biologist R.R. Sokal, a colleague of Joseph H. Camin (1922–1979) of the Department of Entomology at the University of Kansas, who originally developed them.

A restricted range of characteristics can be displayed, so that the amount of information available to students may be controlled.

They have been found to be engaging and amusing for students across a wide range of ages and abilities.

Materials

Per student group:

- Set of *Caminalcule* drawings
- Scissors (optional)

Procedures

In developing a series of *Caminalcules* for school use, no attempt was made to follow Sokal's rather advanced treatment or to apply the strict rules of design originally suggested by Camin. Instead, six basic forms were drawn (Figure 1). They represent some body plans appropriate to life on land, in water, and in the air. From these basic types, new forms were designed along what seem to be biologically consistent lines to represent various evolutionary sequences.

Members of the complete set of *Caminalcules* (Figure 2) may be presented to students as a set or each on an individual card for ease of sorting. Each depicts one organism which is numbered at random within the sequence. Five different types within each evolutionary line are figured.

Exercises using the set have aimed to present a series of open-ended problems in evolutionary biology and taxonomy. These start from an investigation of some of the basic principles of classification. The lack of any definite relationships between the different evolutionary lines means that any hypotheses which seems to accord with the data may be considered valid. By careful analogy with real situations and problems, care can be taken to prevent the exercise from becoming too abstract.

Proposing Biological Names

We give things names in order to be able to describe them more easily. For example, the word *pig* saves us having to give a very long description every time we want to talk about that animal.

Have the students examine the six cards that have been provided. Each card shows a completely imaginary organism. Pretend that each one occurs near where the students live. Have students invent suitable names for

FIGURE 1 The six main *Caminalcule* forms: A. squid; B. snail; C. flirt; D. parasite; E. generalized land; and F. generalized aquatic.

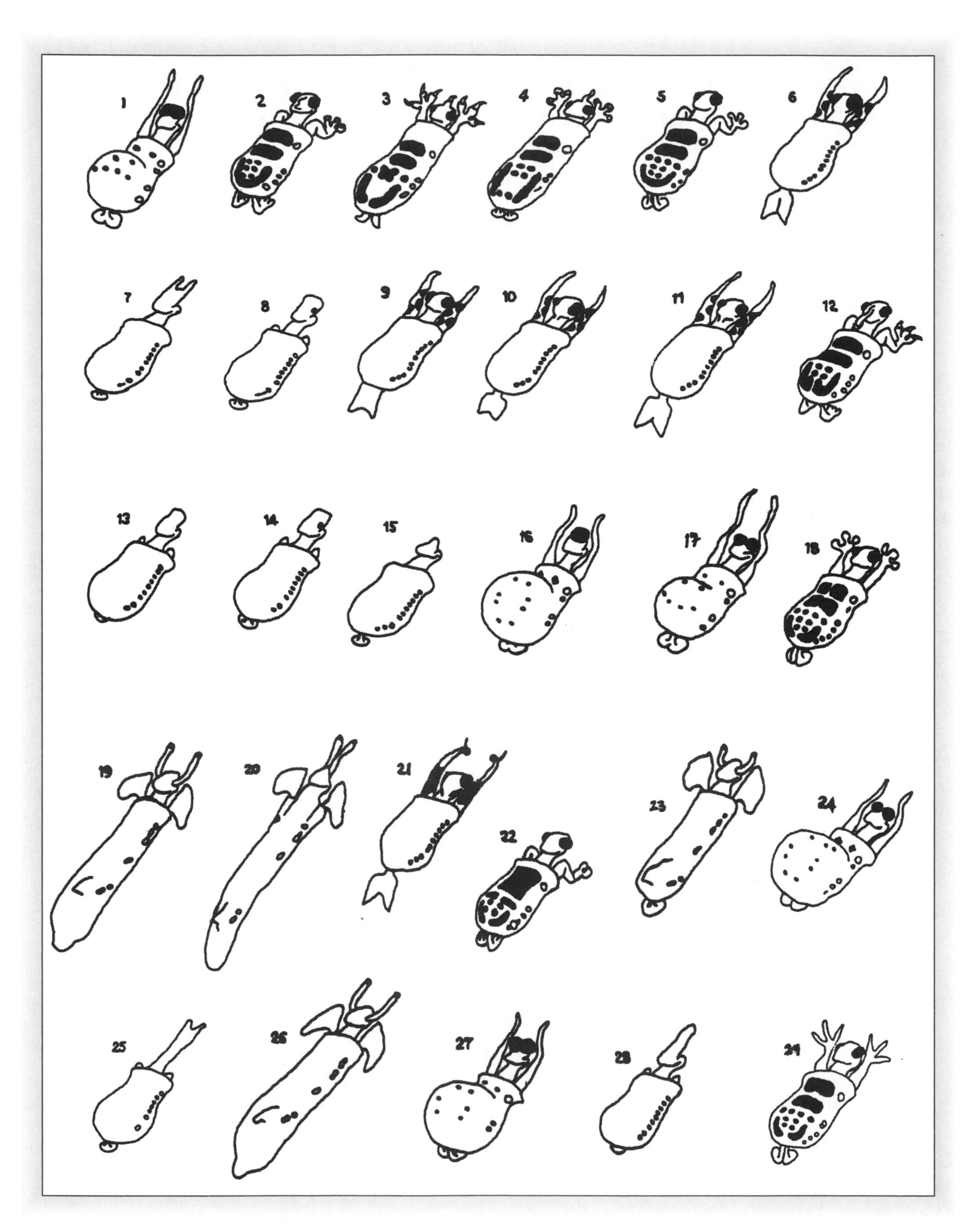

FIGURE 2 Various types of *Caminalcules*.

each organism. See how many people in the class can recognize which name goes with which organism. Did anybody else in the class choose the same names as you?

People try to give names to everything they see around them, but different people living far apart often give totally different names to exactly the same thing. For example the names *king cat, ghost cat, catamount, panther, puma, cougar,* and *mountain lion* all refer to one and the same animal.

This particular exercise proceeds from the uncertainty of common names to the need for a systematic nomenclature. The unwieldiness of the descriptive names used by the early classifiers is contrasted with the simplicity of binomial names. For example, the carnation was originally described as 'Dianthus floribus solitariis, squamis calycinis subovatis brevissimis, corollis crenatis' or by the Linnaean binomial *Dianthus caryophyllus.*

Students are asked to invent suitable binomial names for the six *Caminalcules* presented. Rival binomial names provide a very good area for discussion about precedence and other taxonomic conventions. For more advanced students, reference may be made to discussions regarding precedence in taxonomic papers in learned journals. See, for example, the taxonomic review in Higgins (1974).

This stage of the exercise ends with the general acceptance of definitive binomial names for the original six organisms. The names are retained throughout the rest of the study.

Proposing Phylogenies

The question of relationships and classification arises when students are asked to derive names for the whole set (Figure 2) of *Caminalcules* while retaining those agreed upon for the original six. It becomes necessary to consider how similar looking organisms may be related, and how these relationships may be referred to sets and subsets. The scientific cards' inadequacy of descriptive information soon becomes apparent to most students. This means that the students must try to decide for themselves what and how much information is necessary for realistic classification. The question of how many distinct types of organisms are represented among the 29 different pictures in the set necessitates some discussion of natural variation and polymorphism. Some students realize that there is no way of telling whether the *Caminalcules* are sexually dimorphic, and the value of field studies in elucidating problems of this kind can be stressed. Bird study has been found to be helpful here because, as in the case of the "LBJs" (little brown jobs) such as sparrows, only close and careful observation will reveal the true pattern of relationships. This is an example immediately available for study by students. The aim of this part of the exercise is to investigate some of the basic ideas of taxonomy and to establish the need for much detailed information.

At a fairly advanced level, consideration of polymorphism and variation leads fairly directly on to the subject of evolution, and the *Caminalcules* offer good scope for treatment of this topic. At the upper end of the school and beyond, students who are asked to sort the cards into putative evolutionary lines will generally notice a degree of coincidence between these and their taxonomic sets and subsets, though with a monolithic taxonomy it is difficult to ensure that this is not merely a restatement of the classification. In the absence of a clear ancestral type, a number of parallel arguments will be advanced. When rival groups are asked to defend their positions, a hardening of opinion tends to be seen, with students taking great exception to opposition, even in the face of a generally agreed inadequacy of information. This has been found to be a suitable point to introduce discussion of the evolutionary debates of the last century and a consideration of the relative status of different evolutionary ideas which are not amendable to empirical investigation.

References

Higgins, R.C. (1974). Specific status of Echinocardium cordatum, E. australe and E. zealandicum around New Zealand. *Journal of Zoology, London, 173*, 451–75.

Sokal, R.R. (1966). Numerical taxonomy. *Scientific American, 215*(6), 106–16.

The Comparative Method, Hypothesis Testing, and Phylogenetic Analysis

II-7

Fred Singer, Joel B. Hagen, and Robert R. Sheehy

Overview

In this laboratory activity, students will use various types of evidence to construct multiple phylogenetic hypotheses for a group of mammals. Students will compare the skeletal anatomy, physiology, behavior, ecology, and molecular data of the different mammals in forming and testing their phylogenetic hypotheses. In doing so, students will come to understand that scientists often depend on nonexperimental techniques—such as comparative methods—for testing hypotheses and that the data do not necessarily support one clear-cut hypothesis.

Evolutionary Principles Illustrated

- Systematics
- Phylogenetics

Background Information

Textbook discussions of scientific methodology often focus almost exclusively upon controlled experiments, but biologists also use many nonexperimental techniques for testing hypotheses. Particularly important are the comparative methods developed for phylogenetic analysis by biologists who study systematics. Today, these comparative methods can be applied at multiple levels of organization, from behavior and ecology, to more traditional levels of gross anatomy and development, and downward to information-carrying macromolecules (DNA, RNA, and proteins). Phylogenetic analysis is

---

This activity is based on "The comparative method, hypothesis testing and phylogenetic analysis" by Fred Singer, Joel B. Hagan, and Robert R. Sheehy (2001), in *The American Biology Teacher* 63(7), 518–23 and is modified and reprinted with the permission of the publisher.

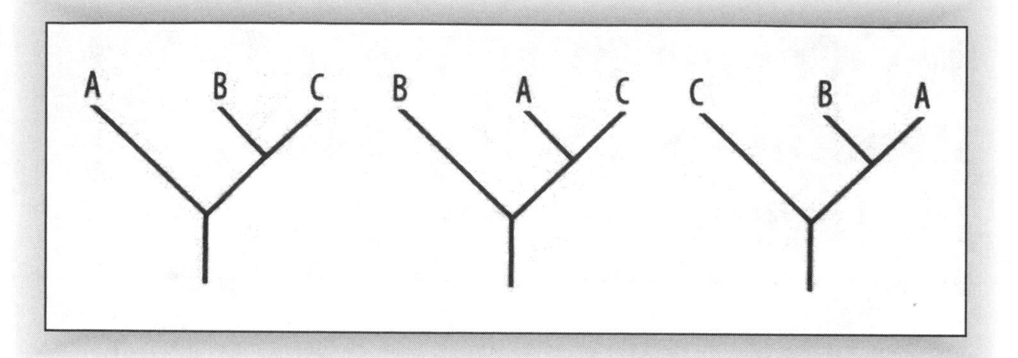

FIGURE 1 Alternative phylogenetic hypotheses. For three taxa—A, B and C—there are three unique hypotheses. As more taxa are included in the phylogenetic analysis, the number of possible hypotheses rapidly increases. For t taxa, there are $(2t-3)!/[2^{t-2}(t-2)!]$ unique phylogenetic hypotheses (Quicke 1993).

important not only for evolutionary biology, but also for applied fields of biology from conservation to medicine (Harvey et al., 1996). Because such analyses have become so fundamental to modern biology, we feel that all students should have a basic understanding of them. Practicing phylogenetic analysis can also strengthen students' logical and mathematical abilities (Bilardello & Valdes, 1998), and their general problem-posing and problem-solving skills.

Consider three taxa—A, B and C—that hypothetically can be related in three different ways, as represented by the phylogenetic trees in Figure 1.

The choice among the alternative hypotheses is based upon shared characteristics, but in most real cases the systematic biologist encounters conflicting evidence (Table 1). Some data may support one hypothesis, some another. On what basis can a rational decision be made? This dilemma is a real problem in systematics, but it also provides a useful basis for problem-solving exercises in biology courses.

We have developed a laboratory sequence allowing students to investigate such problems by making preliminary observations, posing alternative hypotheses, gathering a variety of data, analyzing these data in various ways, and drawing tentative conclusions. We consider this to be a nontrivial exercise

TABLE 1 Example of conflicting data that do not unambiguously support any of the alternative phylogenetic hypotheses presented in Figure 1. A "+" indicates that the taxon has the character; a "–" indicates that the taxon lacks the character in question.

Character	Taxon A	Taxon B	Taxon C
1	+	+	–
2	+	+	–
3	–	+	+
4	+	–	+
5	+	+	+

TABLE 2 Software and databases for phylogenetic analysis that can be accessed from the World Wide Web.

Readily Available Software for Phylogenetic Analysis	
PAUP	http://onyx.si.edu/PAUP/
Phylip	http://evolution.genetics.washington.edu/phylip.html
McClade	http://phylogeny.arizona.edu/macclade/macclade.html
Molecular Databases on the World Wide Web	
Genbank	http://www.ncbi.nlm.nih.gov/Entrez/
Protein Information Resource (PIR)	http://pir.georgetown.edu
Swiss-Prot	http://www.expasy.ch/sprot/

because, although we stress rigorous critical thinking, there is no obvious or unambiguous correct answer. We also favor this approach because it can be easily modified for use by students at a variety of levels.

For this exercise, we chose to use specimens drawn from several orders of mammals. Mammals offer a number of attractive advantages. They are generally familiar to students. They offer a large number of anatomical, physiological, behavioral, and ecological characteristics that students can easily identify from skeletons, diagrams, or readily available reference books. Extensive molecular data exist for a wide variety of mammals and can be easily obtained from data banks on the World Wide Web (Table 2). Finally, although mammals have been extensively studied, there remain several unresolved phylogenetic relationships. For example, the placement of rabbits on the mammalian phylogenetic tree is unresolved (Graur et al., 1996; Halanych, 1998). These features and considerations provide the basis for students to pose evolutionary problems and investigate alternative hypotheses.

Materials

Per group of four students:

- Skeletons of a dog, cat, rat, opossum, and rabbit
- Internet access to gather molecular databases and to access software for phylogenetic analysis
- Drawings of *Megazostrodon*
- Protein sequence of hemoglobin A of each mammal for comparison
- Nucleic acid sequence of the mitochondrial gene that codes for the 16S subunit of rRNA of each mammal for comparison

Procedures

Part 1: Forming Preliminary Hypotheses

To begin the exercise, groups of students studied five skeletons: dog, cat, rat, opossum, and rabbit. Students made informal comparisons of the mammals, looking for particularly striking similarities and differences during this initial brainstorming period. At the end of this time, each group generated a preliminary character table summarizing its observations and including any previous knowledge it had about other characteristics of the different species. Using this information, each group constructed a phylogenetic tree and verbal statement of its primary hypothesis. Given five taxa, there are 105 possible rooted phylogenetic trees. There was a great deal of variation among each group's preliminary hypothesis.

Each group was required to display its phylogenetic tree and defend it to the class. During these presentations, the class debated which characters were useful for discriminating evolutionary relationships and which characters seemed trivial. We suggested that students consider how difficult it would be from a genetic and developmental standpoint for a character to change from character state A to state B. For example, the evolution of the placenta probably required considerable genetic and developmental changes. The independent evolution or loss of such a complex organ in two different lineages is unlikely; therefore, most students soon realized that a reasonable phylogenetic tree had to have the opossum isolated by the first major branch. On the other hand, evolution of sociality in a nonsocial animal (or vice versa) probably requires relatively minor genetic and developmental changes. On this basis, sociality was not considered a very useful character for discriminating between phylogenetic hypotheses.

Part 2: Testing Hypotheses with Comparative Anatomy, Physiology, Behavior, and Ecology

After this first brainstorming session, students had several competing hypotheses to evaluate. We then presented students with background information on the physiology, behavior, and ecology of each species and explained to them that these characters could also be used to construct and test phylogenetic trees.

To aid students with their analysis, we presented them with accurate line drawings of *Megazostrodon*, a presumed common ancestor of present-day mammals (Colbert & Morales, 1991). These drawings included several views of the skull and an artist's reconstruction of the body. We explained that *Megazostrodon* is an outgroup—a species that diverged from a group of other species (the ingroup) before the ingroup species diverged from each other (Futuyma, 1998; Maddison et al., 1986). Another way of looking at it is that *Megazostrodon* is equally related to each of the ingroup species and that all ingroup species are more closely related to each other than they are to *Megazostrodon*.

TABLE 3 Sample character table.

Character	Megazostrodon	Opossum	Dog	Rat	Cat	Rabbit
Placenta	–	–	+	+	+	+
Prehensile tail	+	+	–	–	–	–
Solitary lifestyle	?	+	–	+	+	*
Number of teeth	52	50	42	16	28	28
Large canine teeth	+	+	+	–	+	–
Large incisors	–	–	–	+	–	+
Expanded metatarsals	–	–	+	–	+	+
Hopping locomotion	–	–	–	–	–	+

*Indicates variation within the group that precludes categorizing rabbits as solitary or social.

Students incorporated the additional information on physiology, behavior, and ecology to generate a character table, which included the outgroup (Table 3). For outgroup comparisons, systematists assume that character states shared by the outgroup and members of the ingroup are ancestral, and that alternative character states found in the descendent species are new character states derived from the ancestral state. Our students were instructed to test the alternative hypotheses based on whether species shared derived characters. They were asked to give higher weight to characters that seemed more useful for discriminating between evolutionary hypotheses and to include the physiological, behavioral, and ecological characters in their analysis.

Students wrote brief essays to defend their preferred hypotheses and to justify each node of their trees. In some cases, students chose to reject all of the original hypotheses and constructed new trees that had not been proposed in the initial session.

Part 3: Protein and Nucleic Acid Sequences

The instructor must go through a number of steps to prepare protein or nucleic acid sequences for analysis. First, the appropriate sequences must be selected (see Parts 3A and 3B). Second, the sequences must be extracted from the database (e.g., Genbank). Third, the sequences must be aligned, so homologous regions of the molecule can be compared. Lastly, aligned sequences must be converted into the appropriate format for importing into the phylogenetic analysis program.

Part 3A: Testing Hypotheses with Molecular Data—Amino Acid Sequences for Hemoglobin A

The use of various kinds of molecular data has become increasingly important in systematics. We chose to use a protein molecule with which students had some familiarity: hemoglobin A. This molecule is relatively small and contains both variable and invariable (conserved) regions.

Analyzing large data sets, such as the molecular data that we presented to the students, usually requires a computer, but we did not want students to treat this part of the exercise as a "black box." Therefore, we started with a highly simplified exercise in calculating the overall similarity of the amino acid sequence of hemoglobin A in the five species of mammals.

Students calculated percent similarity for each species pair by dividing the number of positions where the amino acids are identical by the total number of amino acids:

% Similarity = (number of identical amino acids / total number of amino acids) * 100

This allowed students to construct a similarity matrix (Table 4).

Students built an evolutionary tree based on the similarity of hemoglobin A molecules using the following set of instructions:

1. Cluster the two most similar species.
2. Find the species that is most similar to the two clustered species. Calculate the mean similarity between this species and the first two species.

3a. If the mean similarity of the third species to the original two is greater than its similarity to any of the remaining species, it is added to the first cluster.

3b. If, on the other hand, the third species is more similar to one of the remaining species than it is to the first cluster, then form a new cluster at the appropriate level of similarity.

4. Continue this clustering process until all species have been added to the tree (Figure 2).

TABLE 4 Matrix for constructing evolutionary tree based on the similarities calculated for the hemoglobin A molecule.

	Dog	Cat	Rat	Opossum	Rabbit
Dog	100%	X	X	X	X
Cat	85.8	100%	X	X	X
Rat	81.6	81.6	100%	X	X
Opossum	67.4	66.7	66.7	100%	X
Rabbit	80.9	78.0	82.3	64.5	100%

Part 3B: Testing Hypotheses with Molecular Data—DNA Sequences for 16S Subunit of rRNA

After generating a similarity tree for hemoglobin A, students used a computer program (Table 2) to aid in finding the shortest phylogenetic tree(s) for DNA sequence of the mitochondrial gene which codes for the 16S subunit of rRNA. We chose this molecule because students should be familiar with ribosome structure and function and because data are available for each of the five species.

Students were asked to choose the two best evolutionary trees based on the unweighted DNA sequence of the mitochondrial gene for the 16S subunit of rRNA (Figure 3). Students selected two trees rather than one because we wanted to emphasize that, like morphological and behavioral data, DNA sequencing does not necessarily reveal the "correct" answer. In fact, several different hypotheses may be supported, depending on the assumptions that are made in the selection of the sequence and its alignment.

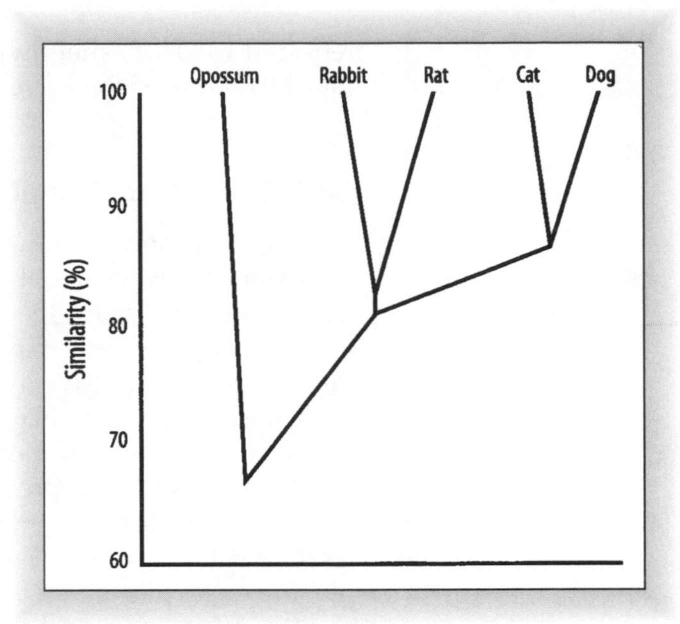

FIGURE 2 Evolutionary tree constructed from similarity data in Table 4.

Part 4: Putting It All Together

By now students had several sources of information:

1. Their intuition based on initial observations of skeletal anatomy.
2. A more sophisticated hypothesis based on outgroup analysis of comparative anatomy, physiology, behavior, and ecology.
3. Molecular similarity of hemoglobin as calculated by hand.
4. Phylogenetic analysis of rRNA using MacClade.

Each of these sources of information may have supported a different hypothesis. The capstone assignment asked students to reevaluate the initial hypotheses and to decide which hypothesis was most strongly supported. Students could also propose a new hypothesis that was different from any initial ones. They were

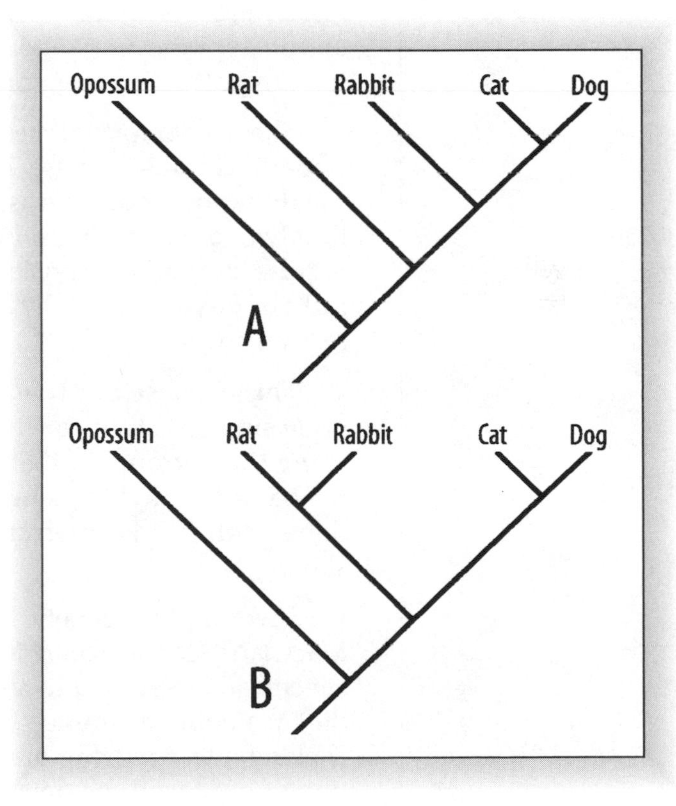

FIGURE 3 (A) Shortest tree and (B) second shortest tree based on the mitochondrial gene for the 16S subunit of rRNA.

required to justify their hypotheses with the data that they had collected during the course of the exercise.

Additional Considerations

This laboratory requires each student to understand and apply several important concepts about science in general and evolutionary biology in particular. Students learn that scientific hypotheses are tentative statements that are open to being tested and revised. Scientists explore a problem by considering multiple alternative hypotheses and use data to evaluate the validity of each alternative. Data may be collected in several different ways other than experiments. Scientists gain greater confidence using larger data sets and greater diversity of approaches. By comparing conclusions of different groups, students learn that even when given the same data, it is possible to draw different conclusions. However, not all conclusions are equally valid. For example, the exact placement of the rabbit on the tree was open to question, but the position of the opossum was not.

Students also learn that phylogenetic trees are in reality graphical representations of hypotheses about evolution. Organisms are classified on the basis of their evolutionary relationships, and more closely related species will tend to share more characters in common. Many students are surprised to learn that evolutionary hypotheses can be tested in ways similar to other scientific hypotheses. We found this exercise to be an effective way of showing how hypothesis testing can take forms other than a controlled experiment.

The instructor will need to be vigilant about several misconceptions that can arise in this exercise. For example, it is easy for students to lapse into linear thinking, under the assumption that complex characters imply more highly evolved animals. Instructors may exacerbate this problem if they require students to consider characters that are more complex either genetically or developmentally as being more useful for discriminating evolutionary relationships.

This exercise can be easily modified to work with other taxa. We have done similar activities with insects, various algae, and plants. An advantage to using these groups is that students can collect their own specimens to use as the basis for phylogenetic analysis. Additionally, these groups provide students with good opportunities to improve their measurement and microscopy skills.

Several phylogenetic analysis programs are readily available. We chose MacClade (Maddison & Maddison, 1992) because it is easy to learn and specifically designed to allow the user to test various hypotheses about how the taxa being examined evolved. Tree topology can be easily manipulated by clicking and dragging branches. Additionally, MacClade provides an indication of how well the data fit the tree in a way that minimizes total tree length.

In general, parsimony methods select trees that minimize the total tree length, or the number of evolutionary steps (transformation of one character state to another) required to explain the data. Steps might be changes in anatomical, physiological, behavioral, or molecular characters. Examples could include the change from nonplacental to placental, the change from a poikilotherm to a homeotherm, the change from a migrant to a nonmigrant, or the substitution of one nucleotide for another. MacClade, by default, allows any state to transform directly into another and considers back (reverse) mutations to be as likely as forward mutations. Initially, all mutations are assumed to have equal weight, so that the development of an amnion is as likely as a neutral nucleotide substitution. These default assumptions can be modified in the program.

Due to time constraints, we limit this exercise to considering only two molecules with unweighted character states. As a result, the conclusions based on molecular data are particularly suspect. However, students may become enamored with the simplicity of the MacClade program and tend to accept the best tree based on the one molecule analyzed with this program. The instructor must stress that even though a particular tree is most parsimonious, that doesn't mean that it reflects evolutionary reality. We are constantly reminding students that they need to be looking for common themes in their evaluation of the data; thus, if two animals are similar based on a variety of characters, then we have much greater confidence that they are closely related.

Challenge Exercises and Points of Departure

This lab can be enhanced in many different ways. Below we list a few questions and activities that can generate further investigation.

1. Would it be better to use protein or nucleic acid sequences for these analyses? Why?
2. Go to a database and find another molecule that has been sequenced for your group of species. Do the sequences support your hypothesis? Reevaluate your hypothesis in light of these new sequences.
3. What would be another potential outgroup for the analysis based on anatomy, physiology, ecology, and behavior? Find as much information as you can about your new outgroup and reevaluate your tree in light of what you've learned about this new outgroup. In general, how many outgroup taxa should you have, and what criteria should you use for outgroup selection?
4. The hemoglobin A molecule contains 141 amino acids. Should each of these amino acids be considered an individual character, or should the entire molecule be considered one character? Defend your answer.

References

Bilardello, N., & Valdes, L. (1998). Constructing phylogenies. *The American Biology Teacher, 60*, 369–73.

Colbert, E.H., & Morales, M. (1991). *Evolution of the vertebrates*. New York: John Wiley.

Futuyma, D.J. (1998). *Evolutionary biology* (3rd ed.). Sunderland, MA: Sinauer Associates.

Graur, D., Duret, L., & Gouy, M. (1996). Phylogenetic position of the order Lagomorpha (rabbits, hares and allies). *Nature, 379*, 333–35.

Halanych, K.M. (1998). Lagomorphs misplaced by more characters and fewer taxa. *Systematic Biology, 47*, 138–46.

Harvey, P.H., Leigh Brown, A.J., Maynard Smith, J., & Nee, S. (1996). *New uses for new phylogenies*. Oxford: Oxford University Press.

Maddison, W.P., Donoghue, M.J., & Maddison, D.R. (1986). Outgroup analysis and parsimony. *Systematic Zoology, 33*, 83–103.

Maddison, W.P., & Maddison, D.R. (1992). *MacClade analysis of phylogeny and character evolution*. Sunderland, MA: Sinauer.

Quicke, D.L.J. (1993). *Principles and techniques of contemporary taxonomy*. New York: Blackie Adademic and Professional.

Comparing Human and Chimpanzee Chromosomes:
Evidence of Common Ancestry

II-8

 Beth Kramer

Overview

This laboratory activity will enable students to become familiar with the terminology used when geneticists examine chromosomes. Students then can simulate the work of evolutionary biologists and compare a set of human chromosomes to a set of chimpanzee chromosomes to explore the evolutionary relationship between the two species.

Evolutionary Principles Illustrated

- Comparative genetics
- Phylogeny
- Homology

Background Information

Chromosomes are microscopic strands found in the nuclei of living cells on which the genetic code for the organism's characteristics are located. Similarities between the characteristics in the members of a particular species (humans, for example) are due to the similarities in the information on their chromosomes. This is also true for similarities between members of different species (Yunis, Sawyer, & Dunham, 1980).

Biologists known as evolutionary geneticists compare the chromosomes of different species to determine evolutionary relationships. Evolution predicts that two species having a recent common ancestor should have chromosomes that are more similar than two species having a common ancestor further back in time. In other words, species that are more closely related should have more similar chromosomes.

This activity was written expressly for *Investigating Evolutionary Biology in the Laboratory* by Beth Kramer.

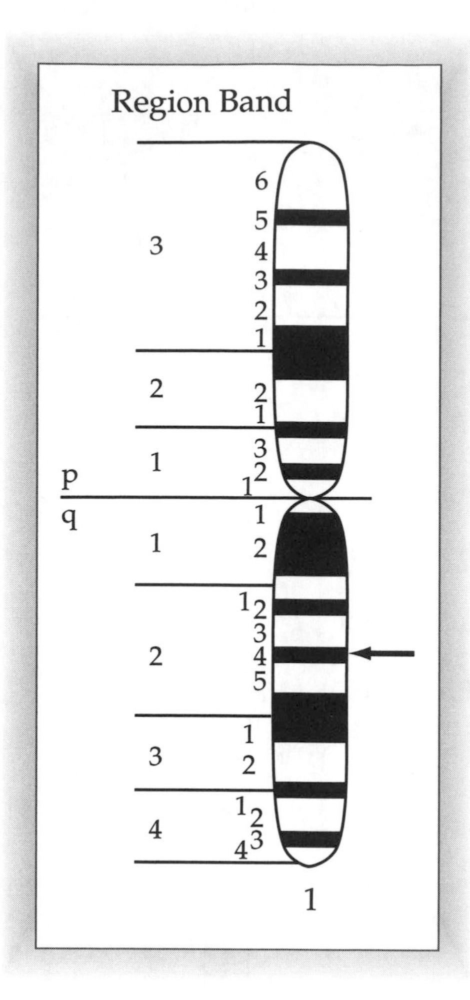

FIGURE 1 Human chromosome #1, with its characteristic light and dark banding patterns.

It is possible to directly compare the chromosomes of two species and make inferences based on the degree of similarity. Cells are obtained from members of each of the two species and the chromosomes in those cells are photographed through a microscope. The picture that results is called a karyotype showing the pairs of chromosomes lined up next to each other. In humans, there are 23 pairs of chromosomes (23 of which look identical in the karyotype for females, but in the males 22 look identical with one "mismatched" pair representing the X and Y sex chromosomes).

An important technique has been added to the process of kayotyping making it easier to distinguish one chromosome from another. Rather than simply relying on length and other physical characteristics to identify chromosomes, it is possible to stain the chromosomes, resulting in a unique pattern of dark and light bands. This staining procedure uses a chemical called Giemsa resulting in bands called "G bands." When chromosomes are stained in this fashion, areas where the chromatin is highly condensed form dark bands and areas where the chromatin is less densely condensed form light bands. The light bands are believed to be areas where the genes are more active, while genes in the dark bands are thought to be less active. Particular chromosomes within a specific species absorb the stain in the same way. In Figure 1, notice the detailed diagram (karyogram) of human chromosome #1 that shows these bands. All #1 chromosomes in humans will have this same pattern.

When comparing the chromosomes from two species, it is necessary to use only one of each pair. A chromosome from one species is lined up next to the corresponding chromosome from the second species based on the physical characteristics of the chromosomes such as length, location of the constriction in the middle (the centromere), and the banding pattern. The similarities and differences of the two chromosomes can then be carefully noted.

One way to determine how closely related two species are is to compare their characteristics. Humans are most similar in their characteristics to orangutans, gorillas, and chimpanzees (called the great apes). However, orangutans, gorillas and chimpanzees are very similar to each other. Therefore, determining which of these animals may be most closely related to humans and to each other is difficult. In making a determination of the relationships, chromosome comparison is very helpful.

Materials

Per student:

- Colored pencils (red, purple, yellow, orange, blue, green)
- Two handouts: Part 1 and Part 2

Procedures

Students should complete Part 1 of this activity in order to gain an understanding of the terminology geneticists use when examining chromosomes. This may be assigned as an in-class or homework assignment and should come only after students have been introduced to the concept of chromosomes.

Next, discuss student answers from Part 1 and clarify any misconceptions. Then, introduce to the students how evolutionary geneticists compare chromosomes from different species before assigning Part 2. Follow up this assignment with a class discussion.

Teachers are advised to get a copy of the dramatic diagram comparing human, chimpanzee, gorilla, and orangutan chromosomes originally reported in Yunnis and Prakash (1982) and reprinted in Strickberger (1990).

Additional Considerations

If genetics and evolution are taught as distinct units within the biology course, the teacher would need to decide when during the school year it would be most effective to use this teaching activity. It may be used when the first topic is taught, as a way of previewing the second, or it may be used when the second topic is taught, as a way of reviewing the first.

References

Strickberger, M.W. (1990). *Evolution*. Boston: Jones and Bartlett.

Yunis, J.J., Sawyer, J.R., & Dunham, K. (1980). The striking resemblance of high-resolution G-banded chromosomes of man and chimpanzee. *Science*, 208, 1145–48.

Yunis, J.J., & Prakash, O. (1982). The origin of man: A chromosomal pictorial legacy. *Science, 215*, 1525–30.

Chromosome Analysis: Student Section (Part 1)

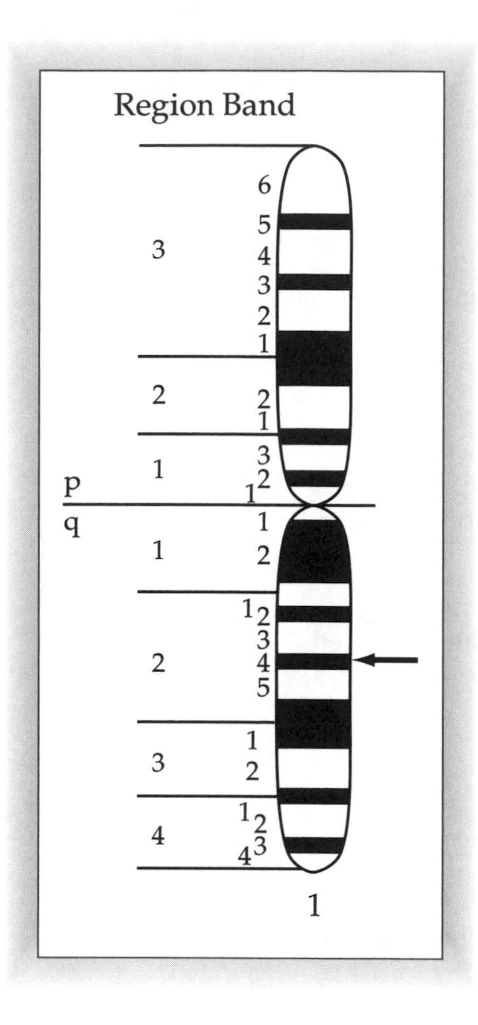

FIGURE 1 Human chromosome #1, with its characteristic light and dark banding patterns.

1. _____ How many bands are on the chromosome in Figure 1?
2. _____ How many bands are there with highly condensed chromatin (dark bands)?
3. _____ How many bands are there with less condensed chromatin (light bands)?

Notice that the chromosome in Figure 1 has a narrow area in the middle. This is called the **centromere.** The centromere can be located in the center of the chromosome, as it is in Figure 1, or it may be far off center. The centromere is an important physical characteristic for matching chromosomes.

4. Using the chromosomes in Figures 2a–2d as a guide, draw examples of the four types of centromere location in the space below. Label each drawing with its type of centromere location.

Chromosome banding patterns and centromere location have been used as the basis for a system of identifying specific chromosome **regions** on each chromosome. Notice in Figure 1 that the centromere divides the chromosome into two **arms**. In this system, the short arm of each chromosome is designated the **"p"** arm.

5. _____ What is the long arm designated?

Now, notice that each arm is subdivided into numbered regions beginning at the centromere and moving toward the ends.

6. _____ How many regions on the chromosome are on the "p" arm?

7. _____ How many regions on the chromosome are on the "q" arm?

Within each region, the bands are also identified by numbers.

8. _____ How many bands does the third region on the "p" arm have?

In this manner, any region in the human karyotype can be identified by an **"address"** such as 1q2.4. The address consists of the chromosome number (1), the arm (q), the region (2), and the band (4).

9. _____ Find this band (1q2.4) on the chromosome of Figure 1. What do you find pointing to this band?

These banding and centromere markers allow the geneticist to identify clearly each of the different human chromosomes. The development of banding techniques and related methods has provided researchers with a powerful tool for chromosome studies and comparisons. Chromosome analysis has many important applications in the studies of genetics and evolution.

Chromosome Analysis: Student Section (Part 2)

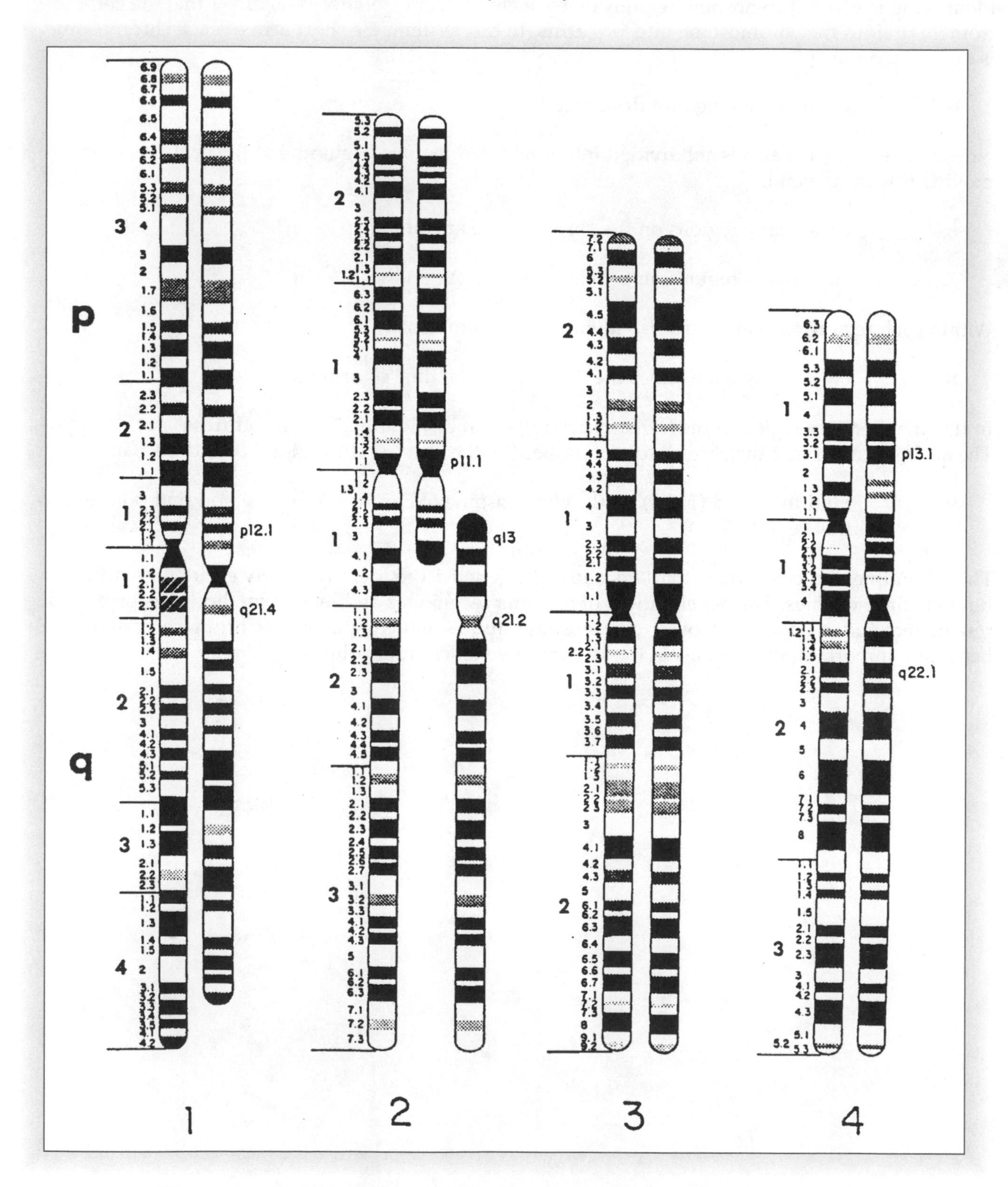

FIGURE 2A Human (left) and chimpanzee (right) chromosome numbers 1–4. Note that chimpanzees have two of chromosome number 2.

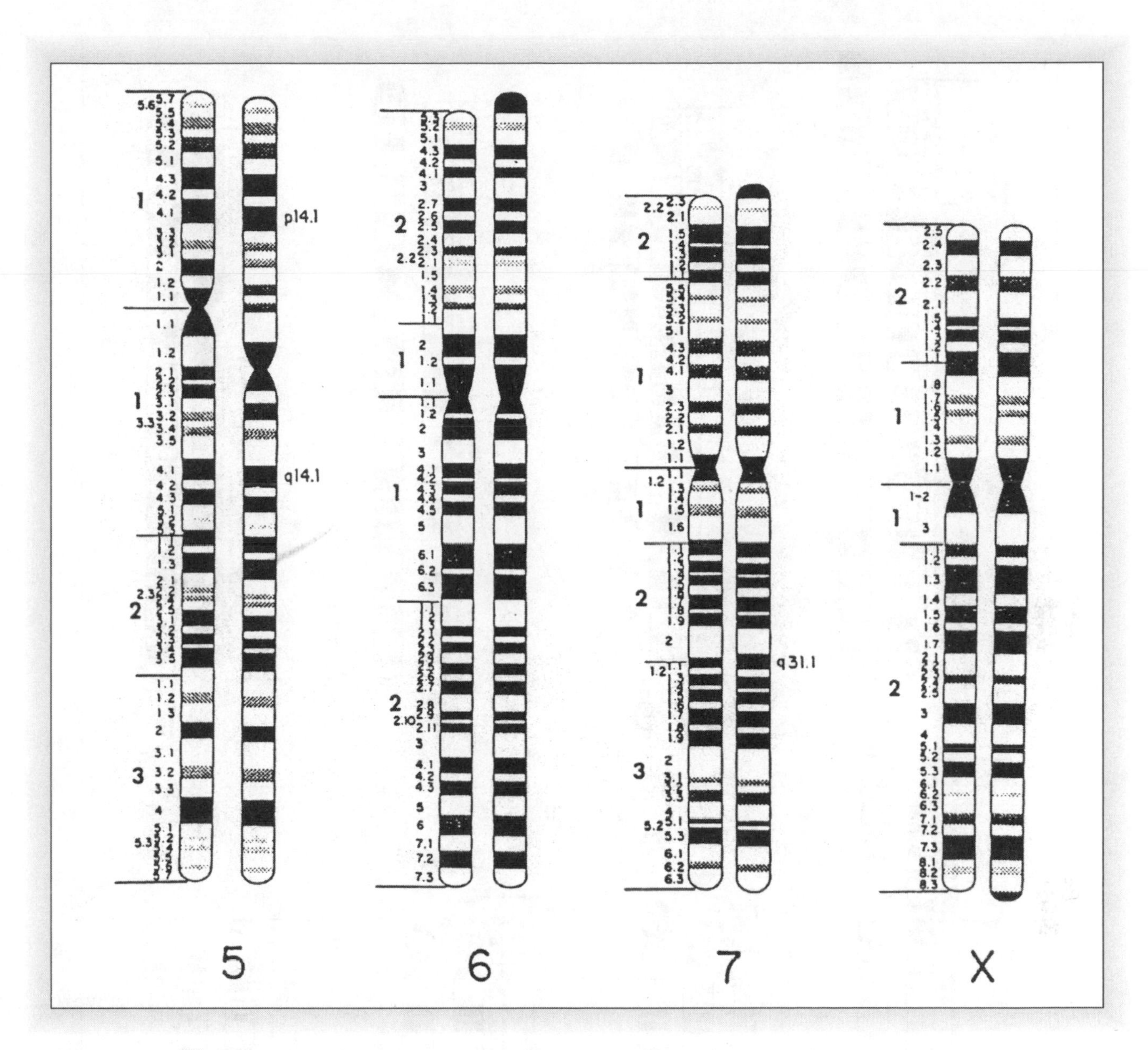

FIGURE 2B Human (left) and chimpanzee (right) chromosome numbers 5–7 and "X."

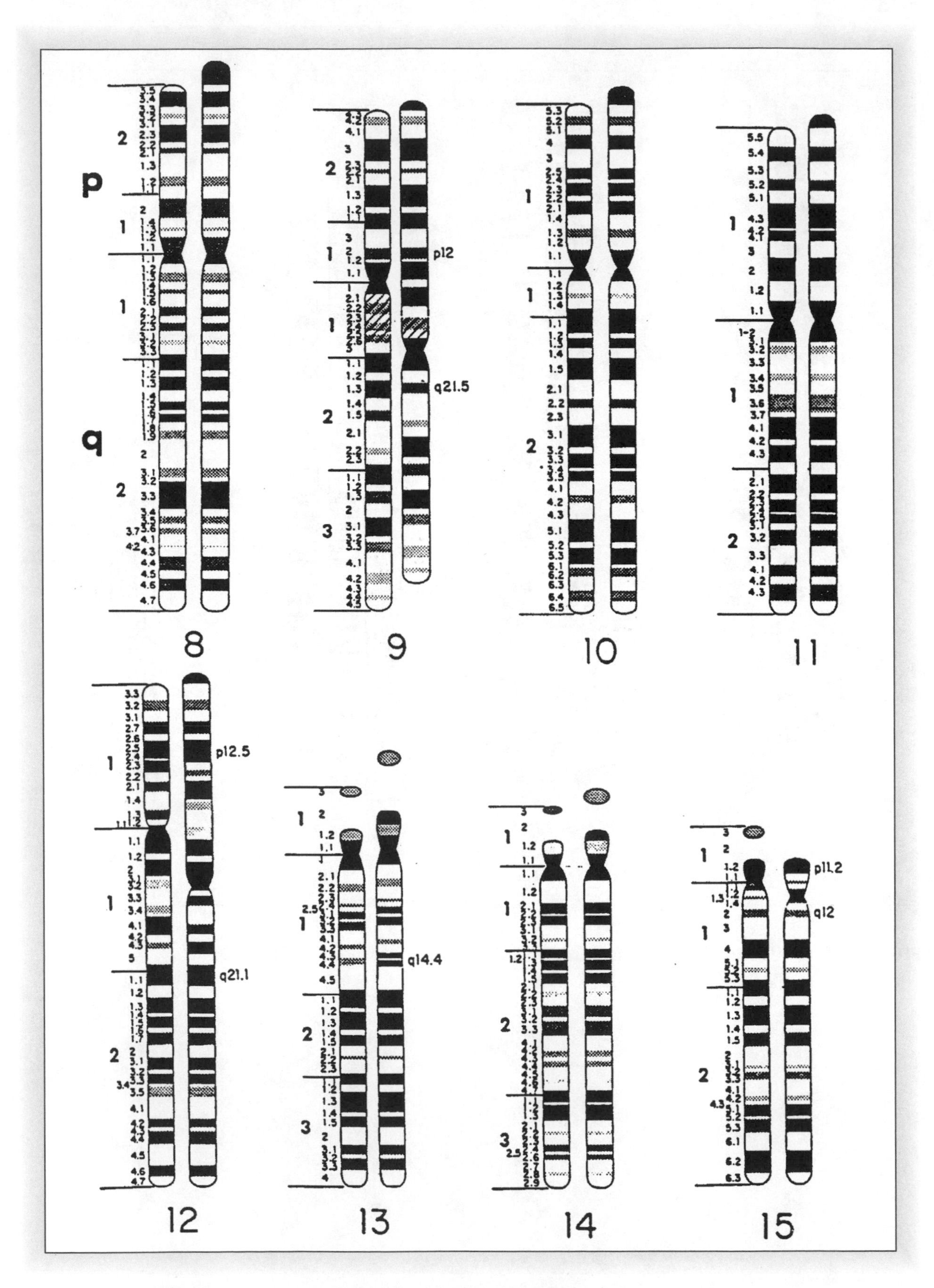

FIGURE 2C Human (left) and chimpanzee (right) chromosome numbers 8–15.

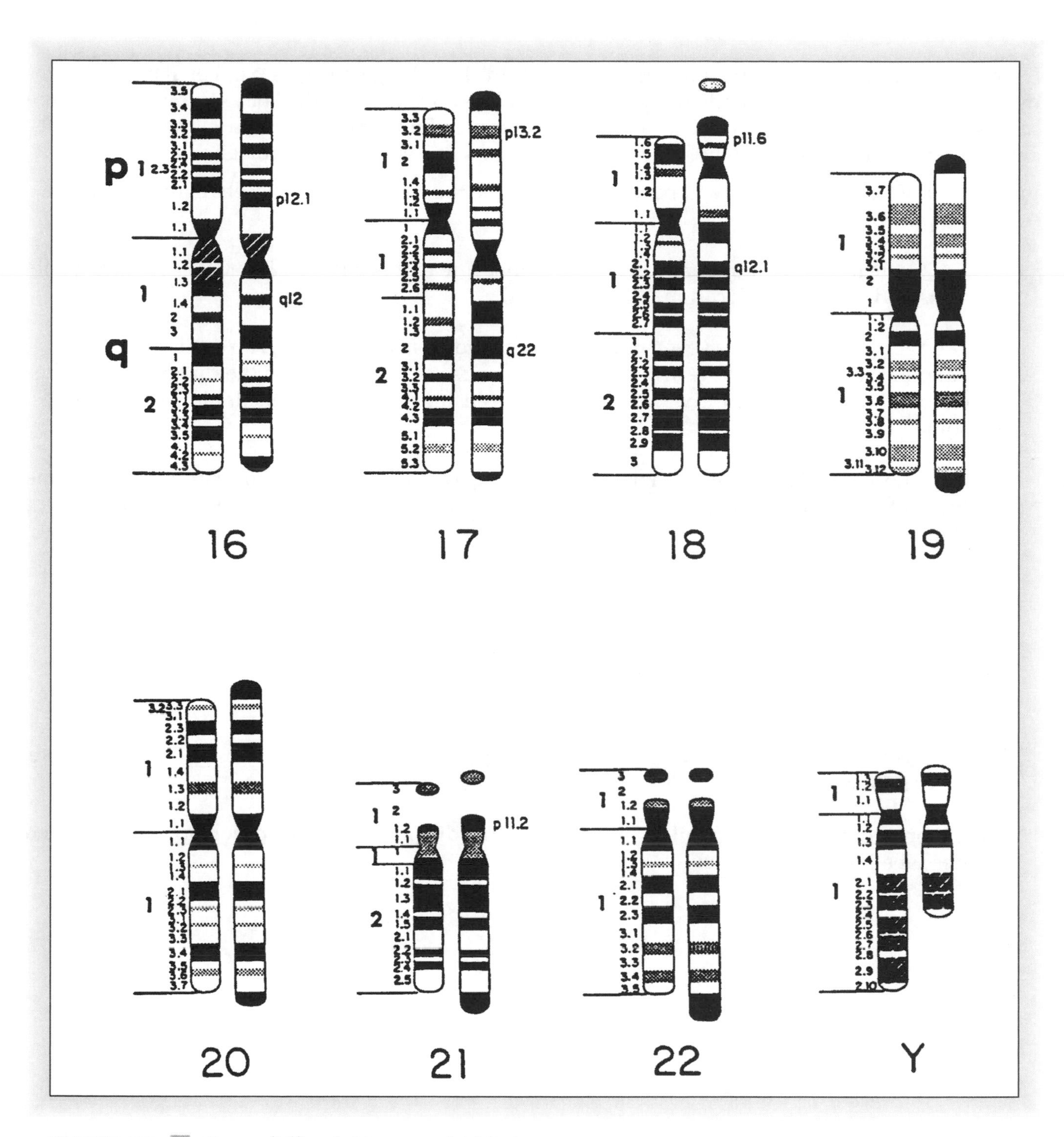

FIGURE 2D Human (left) and chimpanzee (right) chromosomes.

Examine all of the chromosome pairs in Figures 2a–2d. This diagram shows pairs of G banded chromosomes from human (left) and chimpanzee (right) lined up side by side. For example, the chromosomes marked as #1 show human chromosome #1 next to chimpanzee chromosome #1. Notice that chromosome #2 has three chromosomes. We will discuss this interesting occurrence later.

In this part of the activity, you will be asked to examine the chromosomes closely in order to make some comparisons.

10. _____ What is the number of the one chromosome that is virtually identical in banding patterns and centromere location in both species?

11. ____________ There are seven chromosomes whose *only* difference is an additional dark band at the tip of *one* of the arms of the chimpanzee chromosome. On the diagram, circle the extra bands on these chimpanzee chromosomes using red colored pencil. List the chromosome numbers here.

12. Chromosome #7 has an extra dark band at the tip of one arm of the chimpanzee chromosome too, but it also has another very slight difference. In the space below, describe the other difference.

13. Circle the difference in #7 with purple colored pencil and give the address of the band where this difference occurs.

14. Chromosome #13 has a similar difference. On the diagram, circle the difference in orange and describe it in the space below.

15. ___________ Give the address of the band where this difference occurs.

16. There are three chromosomes that differ *only* in that there are two additional dark concentrated bands at the tips of the arms of the chimpanzee chromosome. Circle the extra bands on these chimpanzee chromosomes in blue.

    List the chromosome numbers here: ______________

An **inversion** is a segment of a chromosome that is reversed in the order of the bands. It looks as if a piece of the chromosome had been cut out, inverted, and put back in the chromosome in reverse order. A **pericentric inversion** is an inversion that contains the centromere and has break points in both arms.

17. There are nine chromosomes that differ *mostly* in the presence of a pericentric inversion. Chromosome #5 is one of them. Find the section in chromosome #5 that is reversed between the two species. The segments that are inverted in these chromosomes vary in size. Designate the inverted section on all nine chromosomes by drawing a green arrow on both chromosomes that shows the inverted section.

    List the other eight chromosomes with pericentric inversions here: ____________________

18. As you were answering question 17 above, you might have noticed that some of the chromosomes also had differences *within* the sections that were inverted.

    List these chromosomes here: ________________________

19. On the diagram, circle (in yellow) the feature in the Y chromosome that is different between the two species and describe the difference in the space below.

20. Overall, would you say that there are more similarities or more differences between the two sets of chromosomes? Give reasons for your answer below.

21. You may have heard about a human condition called Down Syndrome. This condition is caused by an extra chromosome #21 in a person's cells. Recently, a baby chimpanzee in a zoo was born with characteristics similar to those found in humans with Down Syndrome. When a karyotype prepared from the baby chimpanzee's chromosomes was examined, it was discovered that there was an extra chromosome #21 also. What does this finding tell us one way or the other about the relationship between humans and chimps? Explain your answer.

22. Examine both the chimpanzee and human chromosome #2. The left chromosome is human and the other two are from the chimpanzee. Assuming that chimpanzees and humans had a common ancestor approximately 5.5 million years ago, give two possible scientific explanations for why there are two chimpanzee and one human chromosomes here while there are only one of each of all of the other chromosomes.

23. Assuming the two species (human and chimp) had a common ancestor, do you think the change in chromosome number occurred before or after the human line split from the ape lines? What physical evidence in the chromosomes supports your conclusion?

24. Studies similar to this one were conducted where the chromosomes of humans were compared with those of gorillas and orangutans. There were more differences in both of these comparisons than there were in the human-chimpanzee comparison. What would this indicate about which of these ape species is most closely related to humans? What physical evidence supports your conclusion?

25. The chromosome comparisons in this study were done between regular chimpanzees and humans. There are actually two known species of chimpanzees. The most recently discovered of these two species is known as the Pygmy Chimpanzee or the Bonobo. The Bonobo is more like humans in its appearance and behavior than the regular chimpanzee. Thus by appearances alone, it appears that the Bonobos are more closely related to humans than are the regular chimpanzees. If this is the case, what would you predict you would find if you did a chromosome comparison between Bonobo chimpanzees and humans? Give scientific reasons for your predictions.

Answer Key / Comparing Human and Chimpanzee Chromosomes: Evidence of Common Ancestry

Part 1

1. There are 24 bands all together. **Note:** On the "p" arm, region 1 has 3 bands, region 2 has 2 bands, and region 3 has 6 bands. On the "q" arm, region 1 has 2 bands, region 2 has 5 bands, region 3 has 2 bands, and region 4 has 4 bands.
2. There are 11 bands (dark) with highly condensed chromatin.
3. There are 13 bands (light) with less condensed chromatin.
4. An example from Figure 2a of a chromosome with the centromere slightly to one side of center is #4. An example from Figure 2d of a chromosome with the centromere near the end is #18. An example from Figure 2d of a chromosome with the centromere on the end is #21.
5. The long arm is designated the "q" arm.
6. There are three regions on the "p" arm.
7. There are four regions on the "q" arm.
8. The third region of the "p" arm has six bands.
9. An arrow points to band 1q2.4 on the chromosome.

Part 2

10. The chromosome that shows no differences is #3.
11. The seven chromosomes that differ only in an additional dark band at the tip of *one* of the arms of the chimp chromosome are: #6, 8, 10, 11, 14, 22, X.
12. The other difference in chromosome #7 is that one band in the "q" arm is slightly wider in the chimp.
13. The address of the above band is 7q31.1.
14. On the chimp chromosome there is an extra dark band that humans do not have.
15. 13q14.4 is the address of the additional band in the chimp chromosome #13.
16. The chromosomes that have two additional dark bands at the tips of the arms are #19, 20, and 21.
17. In addition to chromosome #5 discussed in the question, chromosomes #1, 4, 9, 12, 15, 16, 17, and 18 have pericentric inversions.
18. Of the chromosomes with pericentric inversions, chromosomes 1, 9, and 12 also have differences within the inverted section.
19. In the Y chromosome, the "p" arms are homologous and much of the "q" arm is too. However, there are additional bands on the "q" arm of the human chromosome.
20. There are many more similarities than differences when you look at the total number of bands, lengths, and so on. According to Yunis and Prakash (1982), there are more than 1200 bands that were compared. The differences noted in this activity are minor compared to the similarities. There is virtual homology in all of the nonheterochromatic bands (the light ones). Remember, these are the bands where the chromatin is less condensed and the genes are more active. Every band seen in human chromosomes is also found on the chimp chromosomes. There are also precise locations of the break-points in the inversions.

21. The extra chromosomes (#21) are homologous in chimps and humans; that is, the chromosome lengths, banding patterns, and centromere locations match. Since the bands indicate areas of active (light) and inactive (dark) genes, this would seem to increase the likelihood that at least some of the genes on the two chromosomes are homologous also. While this is not direct evidence of homologous genes, the fact that the syndromes in two species are also very similar lends a high degree of probability to this conclusion. This is an indication that the extra chromosome had very similar effect (through actions of genes) on both organisms. The evidence is consistent with humans and chimps being closely related.
22. It is clear that the two chimp chromosomes are homologous to the one human chromosome. Since we do not know how many chromosomes the common ancestor of 5.5 million years ago had, there are two possible explanations. The two chromosomes might have joined together to form the one human chromosome and the organism that this happened in is a human ancestor but not an ape ancestor. The other possibility is that in an ape ancestor one chromosome broke into two.
23. The change probably occurred after the human line split from the ape line since the apes have the same number of chromosome #2 and humans are different. Orangutans, gorillas, and chimps all have two of chromosome #2 (actually they have four since we are only looking at one of each pair here). A fusion of the two chromosomes in the human line most likely happened after the human line split from the apes. (See the diagram in Yunis and Prakash, 1982.)
24. These data seems to indicate that humans are more closely related to chimpanzees than to gorillas and orangutans since there are fewer differences between humans and chimps than there are with the gorilla and orangutan.
25. If Bonobos are more closely related to humans than regular chimpanzees, then there should be fewer differences between Bonobo and human chromosomes than there are between human and regular chimpanzee chromosomes. *Additional note:* Perhaps just as intriguing would be to determine whether the differences between the two chimpanzees is greater than the difference between humans and either chimpanzee species!

Investigating Evolutionary Questions Using Online Molecular Databases

II-9

 Mary N. Puterbaugh and J. Gordon Burleigh

Overview

This laboratory activity is designed to introduce students to the public molecular databases while encouraging them to address morphological evolutionary questions with molecular data.

Evolutionary Principles Illustrated

- Phylogeny
- Systematics

Background Information

Although the morphological diversity of animals can generate student excitement, it is often harder to interest students in the use of molecular diversity to examine evolutionary relationships (molecular phylogenetics and systematics). The molecular revolution and the advent of computers give us greater power to assess relationships between organisms than just examining morphology. For this reason, we are in an exciting period of change in our understanding of relationships among organisms, and accordingly, it is worth the effort to persuade students that molecular systematics is an interesting field of study. Most scientific journals require that authors submit the molecular sequences reported in their scientific papers to public databases such as Genbank. The databases are therefore a rich source of data from thousands of studies performed throughout the world. These databases also have a great potential as a teaching tool.

This activity is based on "Investigating evolutionary questions using online molecular databases" by Mary N. Puterbaugh and J. Gordon Burleigh (2001), in *The American Biology Teacher 63*(6), 422–31 and is modified and reprinted with the permission of the publisher.

In the first exercise, students attack Calvin's (of the cartoon series) report on "Bats are Birds" by comparing the amino-acid sequences of hemoglobin molecules from bats, birds, and non-bat mammal species. In the second exercise, students consider the evolution of whales from terrestrial animals. Scientists believe that whales evolved from ungulates (hooved mammals), which subsequently became entirely aquatic (Novacek, 1992). Students investigate whether the most recent land-dwelling hooved ancestor of the whales was more likely an artiodactyl ("even-toed," like sheep, hippos, cows, deer, and pigs), or a perissodactyl ("odd-toed," like horses, tapirs, zebras, and rhinos) ungulate. Lastly, the students use BLAST (Best Local Alignment Search Tool) to help them understand why some molecular systematists argue that the vertebrate class Reptilia should include birds. The term "paraphyletic" can be difficult to grasp, and in our opinion, this exercise illustrates the paraphyletic nature of the class Reptilia more clearly than any explanation. In other words, the exercise illustrates that Reptilia does not include all relatives of the most recent common ancestor of the group.

The exercises require some computer savvy to download the sequences from the Internet, but the evolutionary questions are fun and easy for advanced high school students or introductory college biology students to grasp. The exercises do not involve constructing phylogenetic trees since we wanted students to grasp the excitement of the questions without getting mired in the details of the methods.

Collaborative Science: Public Databases

Most scientific journals require that authors submit any sequences they use in a paper to a public, online database. Two frequently used online sequence databases are Genbank and Swiss-Prot. Genbank contains nucleotide data and is associated with the National Center for Biotechnology Information (NCBI), a part of the National Institutes of Health (NIH) (Benson et al., 1999). Swiss-Prot contains only protein amino-acid sequences and is sponsored by the European Molecular Biology Laboratory (EMBL) and the Swiss Institute of Bioinformatics (SIB) (Bairoch & Apweiler, 2000). You can search these databases with descriptive words, scientific or common names, or with the special sequence identification numbers. In the exercises described here, students will search for amino-acid sequences of the hemoglobin beta chain from the Swiss database Swiss-Prot.

The Hemoglobin Genes

Before one begins to make molecular comparisons among species, one must first choose a molecule to compare. The public databases such as GenBank and Swiss-Prot contain data on many different genes. In all the exercises, we use the beta chain of the hemoglobin molecule. We encourage teachers to develop their own exercises using other molecules as well. What makes the beta chain useful for teaching the comparative method? First, it is probably a molecule that students have encountered already. Second, the beta subunit is usually close to 146 amino acids long, and hence there are fewer problems aligning sequences from different animals than with proteins that vary more in length. Third, the public databases contain sequences from more than 100 different animals, including some bizarre and rare animals that may intrigue the students. For example, the Swiss-Prot database contains sequences from the Antarctic dragonfish, the electric eel, the yellow baboon, and the thick-tailed galago. If you do not know what the last animal is, try Part 4 of this lab.

Students may already know that there is variation in the hemoglobin molecule among humans. Individuals who are carriers for sickle-cell anemia have one allele that makes a normal beta subunit and one allele that makes the sickle-type subunit. The sickle subunit differs by only one amino acid from the normal subunit. You may wish to begin these exercises by having students tell you what the percent similarity is between a normal and a sickle beta subunit. Because 145 amino acids are the same between the sickle-type beta hemoglobin and the normal-type beta hemoglobin, and one amino acid is different, the percent similarity is (145/146)*100, or 99.3%.

Limitations of the Comparative Method

In the process of completing these exercises, students are likely to see that using the comparative method to evaluate evolutionary questions is no simple task. When the molecular and computer revolutions were in their infancy, many scientists hoped that the entire tree of life, describing the relationships of all organisms, might eventually be reconstructed. The scientific community is now more aware of the limitations of molecular phylogenetics. Some of these limitations are as follows:

1. Lateral (or horizontal) gene transfer can confound our ability to use molecular data to predict relationships between organisms. Lateral gene transfer occurs when a gene is passed to an unrelated individual. A purely hypothetical example would be a case in which a retrovirus infected a coyote, moved from the coyote to infect a black bear, and in the process transferred coyote DNA to the black bear. In this hypothetical example, the DNA traveled laterally rather than vertically from parent to offspring. Lateral gene transfer is a serious problem for identifying relationships among bacteria that share genes regularly through conjugation, transduction, and transformation; however, it is also potentially a problem among multicellular organisms.
2. Convergent evolution occurs even in molecules. Two molecules may be similar not because two species are related but because of selection. For example, the lysozyme proteins of leaf-eating langur monkeys and cows have some similarities. These similarities arose not because cows and langur monkeys share a recent common ancestor but rather because they both eat leaves and selection has acted on both species in a similar way. The form of lysozymes in the langurs and cows enhances the digestion of plant matter and is characteristic of animals that digest their food in a foregut (Stewart et al., 1987). The comparative method lacks the power to assign cause in the same way experimental methods can. The comparative method can determine if certain predications are

upheld, but it cannot determine why two species have similar sequences.

3. If the same gene or protein is different lengths in different species, difficulties can occur in trying to align those sequences. You may make different conclusions about the similarity of the sequences, depending on how you align the two sequences.
4. Comparisons can be hampered if molecules are either too variable or not variable enough. Different molecules are needed for comparing animals that diverged long ago than for those that diverged more recently. You might consider this particular limitation in Part II because a more variable molecule than the hemoglobin beta chain would be more useful for determining relationships of whales with perissodactyl and artiodactyl ungulates.

Materials

Per student or pair of students:

- One computer with access to the Internet and with a word-processing program and an Internet browser running simultaneously
- Specimens or pictures showing morphological features of bats, birds, whales, fish, crocodiles, and perissodactyl and arteriodactyl mammals (*Hint*: a field trip to the zoo with a list of animals that you will eventually download hemoglobin sequences from would be a great way to prepare for this exercise!)
- Student handout (see Appendix A)

Procedures

This laboratory activity is divided into four parts. In the Appendix, there are reproducible student handouts which will guide them through the required steps for each part. Depending on the students' level, the teacher may prefer to have the class complete Part I as an entire class, in pairs, or individually for homework. Students generally feel more comfortable attempting Parts 2, 3, and 4 of this lab, as there are repeating elements in each part. It is important to provide students with the opportunity to discuss and share their findings after each part of the lab.

Additional Considerations

The teaching value of public online databases depends greatly on the quality of the questions that students use the databases to answer. Our experience is that the questions chosen for these exercises generate student interest. Even though the exercises are online and make use of molecular data, students walk away with a greater understanding of organismal biology, better appreciating, for example, the differences between artiodactyl and perissodactyl and the concept of convergent morphological evolution.

References

Bairoch, A., & Apweiler, R. (2000). The SWISS-PROT protein sequence database and its supplement TrEMBL in 2000. *Nucleic Acids Research, 28*, 45–48.

Benson, D.A., Boguski, M.S., Lipman, D.J., Ostell, J., Ouellette, B.F., Rapp, B.A., & Wheeler, D.L. (1999). GenBank. *Nucleic Acids Research, 27*, 12–17.

Gingerich, P.D., Smith, B.H., & Simons, E.L. (1990). Hind limbs of Eocene Basilosaurus: Evidence of feet in whales. *Science, 249*, 154–57.

Novacek, M.J. (1992). Mammalian phylogeny: Shaking the tree. *Nature, 356*, 121–25.

Shimamura, M., Yasue, H., Ohshima, K., Abe, H., Kato, H., Kishiro, T., Goto, M., Munechika, I., & Okada, N. (1997). Molecular evidence from retroposons that whales form a clade within even-toed ungulates. *Nature, 388*, 666–70.

Stewart, C.-B., Schilling, J.W., & Wilson, A.C. (1987). Adaptive evolution in the stomach lysozymes of foregut fermenters. *Science, 330*, 401–04.

Investigating Evolutionary Questions Using Online Databases: Student Materials

Introduction

How does an evolutionary biologist decide how closely related two different species are? The simplest way is to compare the physical features of the species. This method is very similar to comparing two people to determine how closely related they are. We generally expect that brothers and sisters will look more similar to each other than two cousins might. If you make a family tree, you find that brothers and sisters share a common parent, but you must look harder at the tree to find which ancestor the two cousins share. Cousins do not share the same parents; rather, they share some of the same grandparents. In other words, the common ancestor of two brothers is more recent (parents) than the common ancestor of two cousins (grandparents), and in an evolutionary sense, this is why we say that two brothers are more closely related than two cousins. Similarly, evolutionary biologists might compare salamanders and frogs and salamanders and fish. More physical features are shared between frogs and salamanders than between frogs and fish, and an evolutionary biologist might use this information to infer that frogs and salamanders had a more recent common ancestor than did frogs and fish.

This methodology certainly has problems. Two very similar looking people are not necessarily related, and two species that have similar features also may not be closely related. Comparing morphology can also be difficult if it is hard to find sufficient morphological characteristics to compare. Imagine that you were responsible for determining which two of three salamander species were most closely related. What physical features would you compare? When you ran out of physical features, is there anything else you could compare?

Many biologists turn next to comparing genes and proteins. Genes and proteins are not necessarily better than morphological features except in the sense that differences in morphology can be a result of environmental conditions rather than genetics, and differences in genes are definitely genetic. Also, there are sometimes more molecules to compare than physical features. In these exercises, you will use data in a public protein database of gene products (proteins) to evaluate evolutionary relationships.

Choosing a molecule to compare is not always simple. In all these exercises, you will work with the hemoglobin beta chain. You will obtain your data from a public online database that contains the amino-acid sequences of proteins coded for by many genes for many different organisms. Hemoglobin, the molecule that carries oxygen in our bloodstream, is composed of four subunits. In adult hemoglobin, two of these subunits are identical and coded for by the alpha hemoglobin gene. The other two are identical and coded for by the beta-hemoglobin genes. The hemoglobin genes are worthy of study themselves, but today we will just use the protein sequences as a set of traits to compare among species.

Part 1

Calvin, from the Calvin and Hobbes' cartoon series, is trying to convince you that because bats have wings, they are really birds. Help convince Calvin that bats share more features with mammals than with birds.

Procedure

What morphological features do bats share with mammals? With birds? Complete Table 1. What other morphological features could you compare? Based on morphology, are bats more similar to birds or mammals?

Generate a distance matrix for the beta-hemoglobin chain for two bird species, two bat species, and two non-bat mammal species into a word processing worksheet. Complete the following steps to do this:

Step 1. Swiss-Prot is a Swiss database of amino-acid sequences of many proteins from many species. Begin by going to the website for the Swiss-Prot database at: http://expasy.proteome.org.au/sprot/.

Step 2. Using the right-hand scroll bar, scan down the screen until you see a section titled "Access to Swiss-Prot and TrEMBLE." Use the mouse to click on "by description or identification." A new screen will appear (Figure 1). You can also go directly to the description search site: http://expasy.cbr.nrc.ca/cgi-bin/sprot-search-de.

Step 3. Under "Enter search keywords," type the phrase *beta hemoglobin* and mouse click on "submit." The computer will retrieve many entries.

Step 4. Use the right-hand scroll bar to scroll through the names of the many entries. Find one for either a bird, a bat, or some other mammal. When you find one, check to make sure that it is the hemoglobin beta chain (preferably without a number after it) and not the alpha or gamma or other hemoglobin subunit. If the sequence is for the beta chain and it is for an appropriate species, click on it and the computer will retrieve the sequence.

TABLE 1 Morphological comparison of birds, bats, and other non-bat mammals.

Feature	Birds	Bats	Other Mammals
Presence of hair			
Presence of feathers			
Presence of mammary glands			
Presence of wings			
Homeothermy			
Four chambers in heart			

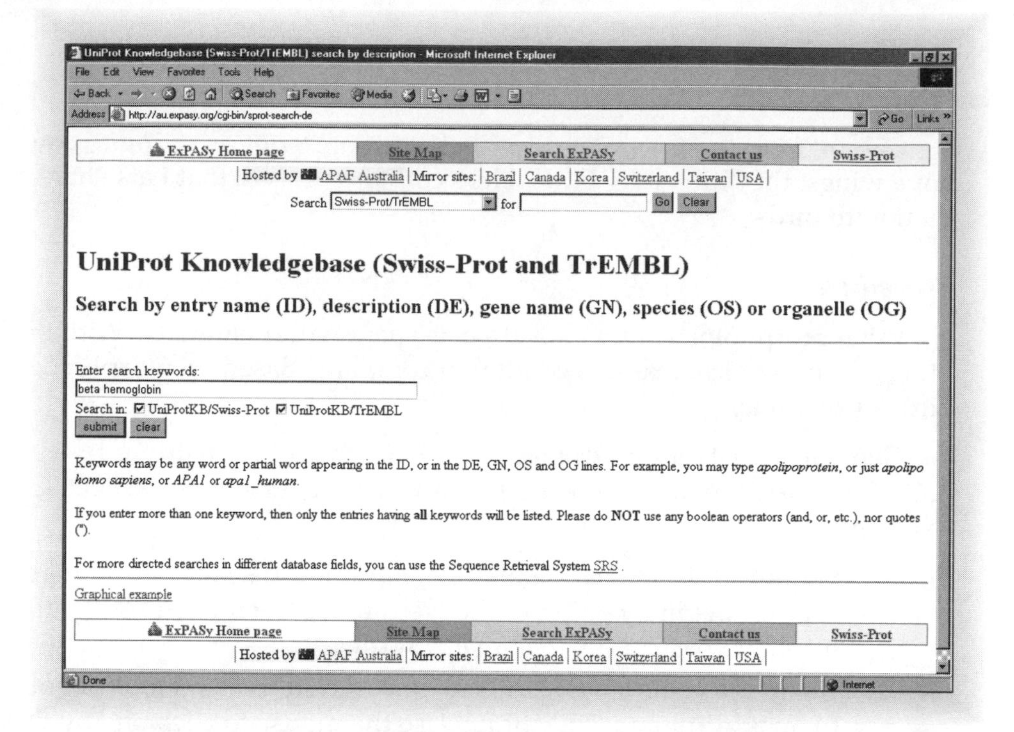

FIGURE 1 The search page for the Swiss-Prot database with the phrase "beta hemoglobin" entered.

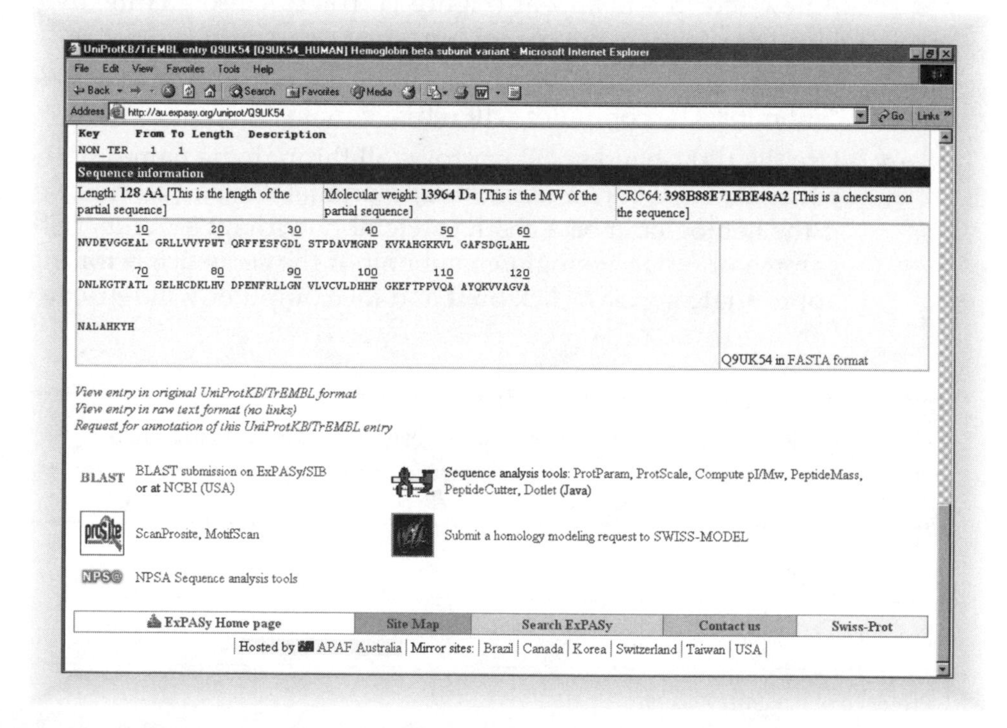

FIGURE 2 The hemoglobin sequence information retrieved for a particular species.

Step 5. This screen contains a lot of information. The protein sequence is at the very bottom of the information sheet in the "Sequence information" section (for an example, see Figure 2). Using the right-hand scroll bar, find the amino-acid sequence. The amino acids are abbreviated by single letters (see Table 2 for the full names).

Step 6. At the lower right of the sequence (Figure 2), click on "FASTA format."

TABLE 2 Amino-acid abbreviations used in Swiss-Prot.

One-letter abbreviation	Three-letter abbreviation	Full name
A	Ala	Alanine
R	Arg	Arginine
N	Asn	Asparagine
D	Asp	Aspartic acid
C	Cys	Cysteine
Q	Gln	Glutamine
E	Glu	Glutamic acid
G	Gly	Glycine
H	His	Histidine
I	Ile	Isoleucine
L	Leu	Leucine
K	Lys	Lysine
M	Met	Methionine
F	Phe	Phenylalanine
P	Pro	Proline
S	Ser	Serine
T	Thr	Threonine
W	Trp	Tryptophan
Y	Tyr	Tyrosine
V	Val	Valine
B	Asx	Aspartic acid
Z	Glx	Glutamine
X	Xaa	Any amino acid

Step 7. Use your mouse to copy the information, and paste this into your word-processing sheet. The copied information will look something like the following:

>sp | P02140 | HBB_CARAU HEMO GLOBIN BETA CHAIN - Carassius auratus (Goldfish).

VEWTDAERSAIIGLWGKLNPDEL GPQALARCLIVYPWTQRYFATFGNLSS
PAAIMGNPKVAAHGRTVMG GLERAIKNMDNIKATYAPLSVMHSEKL
HVDPDNFRLLADCITVCAAMKFGPS GFNADVQEAWQKFLSVVVSALCRQYH

Step 8. Repeat steps 1–7 until your word-processing sheet contains the FASTA formatted sequence for two bird species, two bat species, and two non-bat mammal species. Write the names of the species you chose in Table 3.

Step 9. Save your word-processing sheet but do not close it.

Step 10. To align the sequences and determine how similar they are, go to the following Internet site: http://fasta.bioch.virginia.edu/fasta/lalign.htm. (Other online alignment programs exist; we like the simplicity of Lalign.)

Step 11. Copy and paste one sequence from your word-processing sheet into the first sequence box and another sequence into the second sequence box as shown in Figure 3. For simplicity's sake, just copy the protein sequence and not any of the identification information. However, make sure you keep track of which two species' data you have entered.

Step 12. Click on "Align Sequences."

Step 13. The computer will return a set of information including "the percent identity in the 146 aa overlap." Record that piece of information in Table 4. This value is essentially the percent of amino acids that are similar. If all the amino acids were the same, the percent would be 100%. Not only does Lalign give you the percent similarity, but it also shows you the actual alignment of the two sequences. Identical amino acids are marked with two dots between them (:). If there is one dot, the change in amino acid is conservative (both amino acids

TABLE 3 List of species used for Part 1.

Species	Common name	Scientific name
Bat species #1		
Bat species #2		
Bird species #1		
Bird species #2		
Mammal species #1		
Mammal species #2		

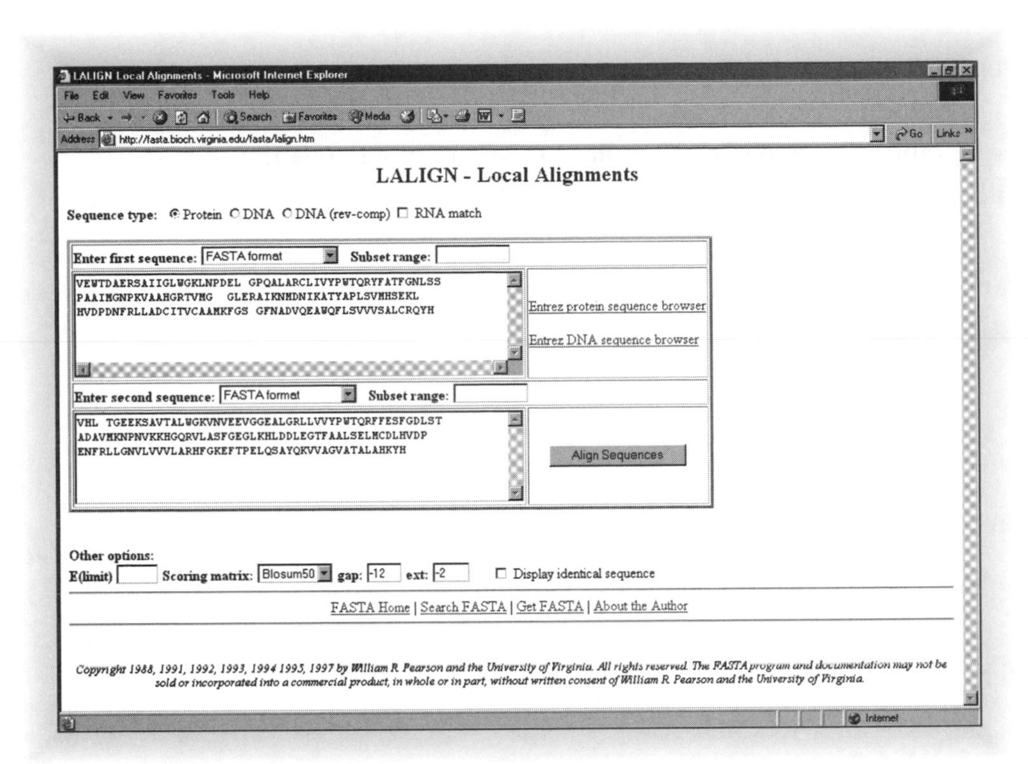

FIGURE 3 ■ Two sequences ready to be compared by Lalign.

have similar properties and charge), and if there are no dots, then the two amino acids have different biochemical properties.

Step 14. A distance matrix is a table that shows all the pairwise comparisons between species. Continue to make all pairwise comparisons until Table 4 is complete. For each comparison, use the percent identity for the overlap of all the 146 amino acids.

TABLE 4 ■ The distance matrix for Part 1.

	BAT #1	BAT #2	BIRD #1	BIRD #2	MAMMAL #1	MAMMAL #2
Bat #1	100%					
Bat #2		100%				
Bird #1			100%			
Bird #2				100%		
Mammal #1					100%	
Mammal #2						100%

Step 15. Use Table 4 to answer the following questions:

- Which two species in Table 4 have the most similar beta-hemoglobin chains?
- Which two species in Table 4 have the least similar beta-hemoglobin chains?
- For Bat #1, make a list of species that have the most similar beta-hemoglobin sequence to the least similar:

  1. (most similar)
  2.
  3.
  4.
  5. (least similar)

- For Bat #2, make a list of species that have the most similar beta-hemoglobin sequence to the least similar:

  1. (most similar)
  2.
  3.
  4.
  5. (least similar)

Does this information seem consistent with the hypothesis that bats are mammals? Are bats more closely related to other mammals than to birds?

Part 2

Help a graduate student figure out what the feet of the ancestors of whales were like. She knows that whales are mammals and that they evolved from terrestrial four-legged hooved mammals (ungulates) which somehow moved and adapted to the life at sea. She heard that whales evolved either from perissodactyl (odd-toed) or from artiodactyl (even-toed) ungulates. Unfortunately, whales do not have feet so she cannot examine the morphology of whales to figure out which is the more likely scenario. Help her use hemoglobin beta chain sequence data to evaluate these two hypotheses.

Procedure

Examine some specimens or pictures of whales, fish, and perissodactyl (odd-toed) and artiodactyl (even-toed) mammals, and take note of the morphological differences of these. Repeat the process used in Part 1, but this time construct a distance matrix for one whale, one fish, two perissodactyl mammals, and two artiodactyl mammals. Describe the morphological distinctions between perissodactyls and artiodactyls. What are some examples of perissodactyl ungulates? What are some examples of artiodactyl ungulates?

Complete and use Tables 5 and 6 to answer the following questions:

1. Is the whale hemoglobin more similar to the fish hemoglobin or the mammal hemoglobin? (Are you convinced that whales are not fish?)
2. Is the whale hemoglobin more similar to the hemoglobin of odd-toed mammals or even-toed mammals?
3. Was the hemoglobin of the whale much more similar to the hemoglobin of mammals of one type of foot than the other or just a little more similar? With this in mind, what problems do you see with using your answer in Step 2 to conclude from which type of four-footed mammal whales evolved?

TABLE 5 Species used for Part 2.

Species	Common name	Scientific name
Whale species		
Fish species		
Odd-toed mammal #1		
Odd-toed mammal #2		
Even-toed mammal #1		
Even-toed mammal #2		

TABLE 6 Distance matrix for Part 2.

	Whale species	Fish species	Odd-toed mammal #1	Odd-toed mammal #2	Even-toed mammal #1	Even-toed mammal #2
Whale species	100%					
Fish species		100%				
Odd-toed mammal #1			100%			
Odd-toed mammal #2				100%		
Even-toed mammal #1					100%	
Even-toed mammal #2						100%

4. The graduate student's advisor suggested that she examine published paleontological and molecular studies to see what other researchers have concluded about the closest relatives of whales. Examine the two papers in the references that follow and determine whether your conclusion is the same as their conclusions regarding the feet of the ancestors of whales. If your conclusion is different, propose some reasons why.

References

Gingerich, P.D., Smith, B.H., & Simons, E.L. (1990). *Science, 249,* 154–57.

Shimamura, M., Yasue, H., Ohshima, K., Abe, H., Kato, H., Kishiro, T., Goto, M., Munechika, I., & Okada, N. (1997). *Nature, 388,* 666–70.

Part 3

Some phylogenetic systematists (scientists who work to make the classification of organisms match their evolutionary history) complain that the vertebrate class Reptilia is improper because it should include birds. In technical terms, the vertebrate class Reptilia is paraphyletic because it contains some but not all of the species that arose from the most recent common ancestor to this group. Just how similar are reptiles and birds in terms of the beta-hemoglobin chain? Should birds be considered a type of reptile? You will evaluate this question in this exercise using a BLAST (Best Local Alignment Search Tool) search.

Procedure

Step 1. As in the previous two exercises, start by going to the Swiss-Prot database (http://expasy.proteome.org.au/sprot/).

Step 2. Find a beta-hemoglobin chain for any type of crocodile. You can do this just as in the previous two exercises or you can type in *hemoglobin beta chain* for the search keywords or you can type in *crocodile* instead.

Step 3. A BLAST (Best Local Alignment Search Tool) search takes a particular sequence and then locates the most similar sequences in the entire database. A BLAST search will result in a list of sequences with the first sequence being most close to the one entered and the last sequences being least similar. The easiest way for us to do a BLAST search is using links within Swiss-Prot as follows. Once you have found and clicked on a crocodile entry for the beta-hemoglobin chain, you will enter the screen with the amino-acid sequence as you did before (Figure 2). This time, do not mouse click on FASTA format as in the previous exercises. Instead, look below the sequence at the very bottom of the web page (you will need to scroll down the page), and mouse click on either BLAST submission on ExPASy/SIB or NCBI (USA). On the screen that appears next, you will see the crocodile sequence pasted into the BLAST search screen. All you need to do is mouse click on "Run Blast" at the bottom of the page. The default options are appropriate for our search. It may take a few minutes for the results to appear.

Step 4. The next screen will have a list of sequences in order of similarity. Mouse click on the first 10 sequences to determine their species. List those species in Table 7, beginning with the first most similar species that is not a crocodile. Were any of those species birds? An unusual reptile is the tuatara (*Sphenodon punctatus*). How similar is the tuatara to the crocodile? Does it appear in your list of 10? If not, how far down on the BLAST search list does it occur (15th, 20th, etc.)? (*Hint: Sphenodon punctatus* is abbreviated as "sphpu" in the NCBI blast search list.) Most important, which species are more similar to the crocodile—birds, or other reptiles? Many phylogenetic systematists believe that the names of taxa should include *all* the relatives of the most recent common ancestor of that group (in technical terms, they believe that the group should be "monophyletic"). If Reptilia is monophyletic, then all reptiles should be more closely related to the crocodile than any other nonreptilian group. If any other nonreptile is more closely related than a reptile, then the group is paraphyletic. Do the molecular data suggest that Reptilia is paraphyletic or monophyletic? Explain.

TABLE 7 ■ Results of a BLAST search on the crocodile beta-hemoglobin sequence.

Similarity	Species name and name of protein
First most similar (do not use crocodile)	
Second most similar	
Third most similar	
Fourth most similar	
Fifth most similar	
Sixth most similar	
Seventh most similar	
Eighth most similar	
Ninth most similar	
Tenth most similar	

Part 4

What in the world is a spectacled caiman? A red gurnard? A northern gundi? A Gray francolin? A slender loris? A European suslik? Any other animal in Prot-Swiss that you do not know?

Procedure

Obtain the beta-hemoglobin sequence for one of the animals listed (or any other animal you do not know). Use a BLAST search to determine who is most closely related to one of the animals above or any other animal in the database that you do not know. What animal came up that was most similar and that you recognized? Look up your unknown animal in a textbook or at the library. What type of animal was it? Did the BLAST search help you predict what type of animal it was? How important and of what use is it that the taxonomy and classification of organisms reflect the evolutionary relationships of organisms?

III

Using the Tools and Principles of Evolution

Using the Tools and Principles of Evolution

A study of the history of life on earth reveals the unmistakable reality that evolution has occurred. The impact of this principle, particularly the theory that explains its mechanism, remains the defining moment in biology as a discipline. Today, evolution provides the frame of reference through which seemingly disparate facts—such as mutation, the unique genetic component of chloroplasts and mitochondria, the apparently useless tailbone still found in humans, and analogous structures such as the wings of a bird and a bat—can all be tied together. The activities in this section offer variety in terms of both content and instructional strategies. They can be used as is or modified to suit the needs of your audience and instructional goals.

This section provides students opportunities to explore and use some of the tools by which evolution is investigated. Particularly useful is radiometric dating, a technique that is based on the regular decay of certain elements permitting scientists to determine the age of fossils. This permits us to construct an accurate picture of life in the past. In the Date a Rock activity, students use peanuts and M&M's to simulate the application of radiometric dating on various geologic samples and in doing so understand why we have so much confidence in our picture of the past.

Other activities yield deeper insight into the various principles at work in the process of evolution. Two activities tackle in unique fashion the often difficult to comprehend principle of geologic time. In How Long Is a Long Time, students can visualize the incredible length of time that has passed since the dawn of earth's history by considering time as if it were distance. This exercise further permits students to make connections between major geologic and biologic events in earth's past.

Hazard provides a model for teaching about intermediate forms to give students an interesting glimpse into how classification may conceal intermediate forms in the fossil record. By showing that transitional forms *do* exist, this activity addresses a common challenge posed by those who continue to question the fact of evolution.

One of the major tools of evolutionary biology is the exploration of convergence where two or more unrelated species resemble each other because they share a common environment and have developed similar tools to assure success in that environment. Bardell uses the microscopic examination of the structures of leaves and lichens to give students a clear example of convergence. Through observation as well as careful consideration of the evolutionary history of lichen and plants, students will grasp this important principle.

Date a Rock! Age Determination by Radioactive Decay

Karen E. Kalumuck

Overview

Radiometric dating is a powerful technique used to determine the age of rocks and fossils. In this simulation, students act as "mass spectrometers" to determine the age of sample rocks by calculating the proportion of a hypothetical parent radioisotope "Peanutium-128" and its radioactive decay product "Emmanemmium-128."

Evolutionary Principles Illustrated

- Radiometric dating

Background Information

Radiometric dating revolutionized the study of the earth and fossils by providing an "absolute" number for dating, rather than the relative values obtained from earlier methods. Scientists often use two or more pairs of radioactive isotopes in radiometric dating, and only use the values when the results agree within less than one percent of each other. A wide range of materials are dated using these methods, ranging from geologic layers of the earth, to fossils, primate skeletons, archeological sites, and even meteorites!

Materials

Per group of two students

- Peanuts in the shell
- Tape and marker for bag labels
- Plain M&M's
- One sealable plastic bag

This activity was written expressly for *Investigating Evolutionary Biology in the Laboratory* by Karen E. Kalumuck.

TABLE 1 The contents of student sample bags of "geologic material."

Sample	Number of peanuts	Number of M&M's
A	96	32
B	64	64
C	32	96
D	16	112
E	8	120
F	4	124
G	2	126
H	1	127
I	0	128

Procedures

Prepare and label the sample "geologic material" from different strata of a study site according to Table 1. Assemble duplicate bags so that there is one sample for each group. Also, prior to the start of the activity, you may wish to review the concepts of radioactive decay and half-lives.

Explain to the class that they have been selected by a group of geologists to help them determine the age of rocks from various geologic areas of a new study site. Each group will be given a sample bag from a particular geologic layer. To determine the age of the sample, scientists normally use a tool called a *mass spectrometer* that identifies elements by measuring the relative masses of atoms and molecules present in a sample. In this case, the students will perform the role of the mass spectrometer.

Distribute the sample bags randomly to each group. Tell the students that the radioisotope Peanutium-128 (peanuts in the shell) decays into the more stable element Emmanemmium-128 (M&M's) with a half-life of 100 million years. Remind the students that when the geologic samples were first formed they would have contained only Peanutium-128 and no Emmanemmium-128.

To determine the age of their sample, students will:

1. Establish the amount of each element present in their sample by counting and recording the number of atoms of each element (individual peanuts and M&M's).

TABLE 2 Radiometric dating of geologic samples: Peanutium-128 (Pe-128) → Emmanemmium-128 (Em-128); half-life = 100 million years.

Sample	Pe-128	Em-128	# Half-Lives	Age (Millions of Years)
A	96	32	0.5	50
B	64	64	1	100
C	32	96	2	200
D	16	112	3	300
E	8	120	4	400
F	4	124	5	500
G	2	126	6	600
H	1	127	7	700
I	0	128	8	800

2. Determine the number of half-lives the sample has undergone by examining the ratio of the originating element (Peanutium-128) and decay product (Emmanemmium-128).
3. Calculate the age of the sample using the following equation:

$$\text{Age of sample} = \text{Number of half-lives} \times \text{half-life}$$

Collect and display student data using a data table similar to Table 2. Post all answers, including those from duplicate samples.

Additional Considerations

As a variation to using peanuts and M&M's, you may wish to use macaroni (macaronium) and unpopped popcorn kernels (cornium). You can count 50 popcorn kernels into a 10 ml graduated cylinder, and use that volume to measure approximate amounts for the samples.

Expected Results

The data in Table 2 illustrate the expected results if all sample counting, in both preparation and analysis, were executed perfectly. If you record numbers that deviate slightly from these simply round the results to the nearest possibility. "Incorrect" numbers help illustrate that even expensive, state-of-the-art equipment such as mass spectrometers need to be calibrated regularly, and that minor deviations can be expected due to "experimental error."

What's Going On?

The total number of "atoms" in each bag is 128. We assume that, when the rock formed, radioactive decay had not yet occurred. The mass spectrometer would detect only the parent radioisotope, Peanutium-128. During each subsequent 100 million years—the half-life of Peanutium-128—50% of the atoms of Peanutium-128 would release energy and decay into the more stable element, Emmanemmium-128. After one half-life, there would be equal numbers of peanuts and M&M's (sample "B"), after two half lives, 25% of the atoms would be Peanutium-128 (sample "C"), and so on. Because radioactive decay is a continuous process, genuine samples will include fractions of half-lives, as illustrated by sample A, which has undergone 0.5 half-lives.

When the half-life of a radioisotope is known, it is a simple matter to multiply the number of half-lives undergone by a sample by the number of years per half-life to determine the age of a sample.

Going Further

- Encourage your students to graph the amount of Peanutium-128 and Emmenemmium-128 versus time. What does the shape of the curve suggest about the rate of decay? (Answer: It's exponential.)
- Investigate some genuine elements used in radiometric dating to see how scientists actually date rocks and fossils. Are some elements more appropriate for dating certain types of samples? Can all rocks be dated by radiometric methods? Why or why not? What other information do scientists use in determining the age of rocks or fossils?
- To provide a connection to advanced mathematics, have the students calculate the age of the sample using the following equation:

$$t = 1/\lambda \ln (1 + D/P)$$

Where: t = age of specimen
D = the number of atoms of the decay product today
P = the number of atoms of the originating isotope
ln = the natural logarithm (logarithm to the base e)
λ = decay constant*

---

* The decay constant of each originating isotope is related to its half-life, $t^{1/2}$ by the following expression:

$$t^{1/2} = (\ln 2)/\lambda$$

URL's for more information about radiometric dating:

http://pubs.usgs.gov/gip/geotime/radiometric.html
http://www.gpc.edu/~pgore/geology/geo102/radio.htm

How Long Is a Long Time?

Constructing a Scale Model of the Development of Life on Earth and Events That Have Shaped Earth History

III-2

 William F. McComas

Overview

This activity gives students the opportunity to construct a scale model of geologic time labeled with significant biologic and geologic events. This exercise will allow students to gain some perspective of the magnitude of geologic time while exploring and inferring relationships between events.

Evolutionary Principles Illustrated

- Geologic time

Background Information

The vast amount of time that has passed since the origin of the earth has permitted a wide variety of events to occur. However, it is difficult for students to conceptualize the passage of time itself and to visualize the relationship of the important biologic and geologic events that have framed evolution on the earth.

It is common practice for a teacher or textbook to state that the first living cells appeared on earth about 3.5–3.8 billion years ago, but few can really visualize the size of a number measured in the billions. To further complicate the issue, it is practically impossible to illustrate the expanse of geologic time to scale in a textbook diagram since a division even as small as a centimeter—used to represent one of the geologic periods—would result in a chart many meters long. For instance, on most textbook geologic timetables it appears as if the Pleistocene epoch and the Devonian period lasted the same length of time because they take up the same amount of space. The Devonian lasted

---

This activity is based on "How long Is a long time? Constructing a scale model of the development of life on earth" by William F. McComas (1988), in *The American Biology Teacher, 52*(3), 161–67 and is modified and reprinted with permission of the publisher.

63 million years, in comparison with the Pleistocene which lasted only 1.8 million years making, the Devonian 35 times longer in extent! Such is the problem of scale when billions of years are reduced to a single page. This activity will result in the construction of a scale model that helps to tie various events together and to permit a leisurely stroll through the enormous expanse of time.

Materials

Per student:

- Geologic timetable (Table 1)
- Chart showing significant geologic events (Table 2)
- Chart showing significant biologic events (Table 3)

Per class:

- 65 or more 5 × 7 inch cards
- Several metric tape measures
- Three colors of marking pens (perhaps black, green, and red)
- Cards on wooden stakes on which students may illustrate various events

Procedures

Decide on the length of the space in which you will set up your scale model of geologic time. Please note that depending on the space available, you can use almost any area for your model, but you will likely have to change the scaling calculations. The example here is based on a football field that is 100 yards (91.44 meters) in length. To encourage the use of the metric system, 91.44 meters will be used throughout this example.

Calculate the scaling factor for your model by referring to the sample calculation.

In this model the length of a football field is used to represent the length of time that has passed since the formation of the earth. In the metric system the 100-yard-long football field measures 91.44 meters. The calculation below reduces 1 million years to a distance of 0.01988 meters (1.988 cm). Therefore, a marker placed on the far goal line representing the origin of the earth would be 91.44 meters away, representing 4,600 million (4.6 billion) years.

$$91.44 \text{ meters} / 4{,}600 \text{ million yrs} = 0.01988 \text{ meters per million years}$$

This calculation may be used to convert into meters the number of years that have passed from any past event. For instance, using the knowledge that multicelled plants and animals arose about 700 million years ago, it is possible to determine the proper placement for the marker as follows:

$$(700 \text{ million})\ (0.01988 \text{ meters/yr}) = 13.92 \text{ meters}$$

The marker for this event should be placed 13.92 meters from the time zero goal line, the one that represents the present. The boundaries of the geologic periods would be determined in exactly the same manner. The Devonian period began about 408 million years ago, or approximately 8.1 meters from the closest goal line.

With some of the recent events, time intervals are represented in units of less than one meter. This is no problem in the metric system since units can be easily converted from one into another—a feat not so easily accomplished in the English system of measurement. To use the Pliocene epoch as an example, the marker would be placed 0.11 meter (11 cm) from the closest goal since the Pliocene began only 5.3 million years ago.

Use colored markers to label the 5 × 7 inch cards. Label geologic eras, significant aspects of biology, and significant aspects of geology, each with a different color.

Fold the 5 × 7 cards as indicated in Figure 1 to form "tent" shapes. They will then stand up by themselves on the ground.

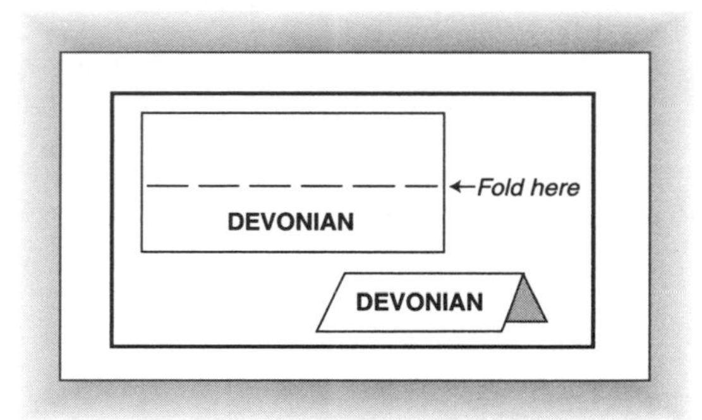

FIGURE 1 Example of folded "event" card.

Refer to the geologic time scale (Tables 1a and 1b) and use the scaling factor to calculate the distance for placing markers for the geologic periods.

Refer to the charts of the significant geologic (Tables 2a and 2b) and biologic (Table 3a and 3b) events and calculate positions for the placement of the markers.

Use the measuring tapes to determine the distance from the nearest goal line for the placement of each card.

You are now ready for a walk through an accurate scale model of geologic time.

Additional Considerations

It would be possible to adapt this idea to show the even longer period of time since the development of the universe itself, but the scale would have to be recalculated to allow all the events to fit into the football field. This may not be as effective, since the markers of significant events will now be much closer together. This approach is best reserved for a longer area.

Depending on the nature of the group, students could work independently on the calculations or the teacher could provide them. The list of events could be made longer or shorter to suit specific instructional purposes, and the marker cards could be made by the students or prepared in advance by the instructor. With younger or less able students, it may be possible to communicate the point with just a few cards on the scale model. Students should be encouraged to draw signposts for the most interesting events. A picture of a fish representing the Devonian attached to the model or a dinosaur indicating the Cretaceous can make this quite a colorful activity.

Two references that are strongly recommended to help fill in the details for both students and teachers are *Life on Earth* by David Attenborough (1979) and *The Rise of Life* by John Reader (1986). These books are both well written and contain beautiful illustrations to tell the story of life's development in an engaging and intelligent way. The chronological treatment used makes both books quite useful for the purposes of extending this activity. For a visual representation of this approach, you might want to show a videotape of the episode titled *One Voice in the Cosmic Fugue* from Carl Sagan's classic *Cosmos* television series.

Finally, a narrative of the major geologic and biologic events in earth history is included in support material following this activity and may be used to supplement this lab activity.

References

Attenborough, D. (1979). *Life on earth.* Boston: Little, Brown and Company.

Reader, J. (1986). *The rise of life: The first 3.5 billion years.* New York: Knopf.

Sagan, C. (1980). *Cosmos.* New York: Random House.

How Long Is a Long Time: Student Materials

TABLE 1A Student worksheet/geologic eras.

Era	Period	Epoch	Beginning (MYA)	Duration (MYA)	Number of meters	Major events
Cenozoic era	Quaternary	Recent	Began 10,000 years ago			Human civilization spreads as humans become the dominant life form.
		Pleistocene	1.8	1.8		The "Ice Age." Modern humans present. Mammoths and other such animals become extinct.
	Tertiary	Pliocene	5.3	3.5		Fossil evidence of ancient humans near the end of the epoch. Many birds, mammals, and sea life similar to modern types. Climate cools.
		Miocene	23.8	18.5		Many grazing animals. Flowering plants and trees similar to modern types.
		Oligocene	33.8	10		Fossil evidence of primitive apes. Elephants, camels, and horses develop. Climate generally mild.
		Eocene	54.8	21		Fossil evidence of a small horse. Grasslands and forests present. Many mammals including primitive whales, rhinos, and monkeys.
		Paleocene	65	10		Flowering plants and small mammals abundant. Many climate types exist.
Mesozoic era	Cretaceous		144	79		Fossil evidence of flowering birds and trees. Small mammals. Non-avian dinosaurs are extinct by the end of the period.
	Jurassic		206	62		First fossil evidence of mammals and feathered birds. Many types of dinosaurs.
	Triassic		248	42		Beginning of the "Age of Dinosaurs." Insects plentiful. Cone-bearing plants present.
Paleozoic era	Permian		290	42		First evidence of seed plants. Fish, amphibians, and giant insects present.
	Carboniferous	Pennsylvanian period	323	33		First evidence of reptiles. Many amphibians and giant insects present. Many large fern trees. Swamps cover low land areas.
		Mississippian period	354	31		
	Devonian		417	63		"Age of Fish." First fossil evidence of amphibians and insects. Many different kinds of fish in the earth's waters. The first forests grow in swamps.
	Silurian		443	26		First evidence of land plants. Algae, trilobites, and armored fish plentiful. Coral reefs form.
	Ordovician		490	47		Jawless fishes, algae, and trilobites plentiful. Great floods cover most of North America.
	Cambrian		543	53		Fossil evidence of trilobites, clams, snails, and seaweed. Seas spread across North America.
Precambrian		Proterozoic era	4.6 billion	Almost 4 billion		Earliest fossils of bacteria and algae (3.5 byrs). Earliest chemical evidence of life (3.8 billion). Earth forms.
		Archeozoic era				

TABLE 1B ■ Student worksheet/geologic eras with answers.

Era	Period	Epoch	Beginning (MYA)	Duration (MYA)	Number of meters	Major events
Cenozoic era	Quaternary	Recent	Began 10,000 years ago		0.2 cm	Human civilization spreads as humans become the dominant life form.
		Pleistocene	1.8	1.8	0.04	The "Ice Age." Modern humans present. Mammoths and other such animals become extinct.
	Tertiary	Pliocene	5.3	3.5	0.11	Fossil evidence of ancient humans near the end of the epoch. Many birds, mammals, and sea life similar to modern types. Climate cools.
		Miocene	23.8	18.5	0.47	Many grazing animals. Flowering plants and trees similar to modern types.
		Oligocene	33.8	10	0.67	Fossil evidence of primitive apes. Elephants, camels, and horses develop. Climate generally mild.
		Eocene	54.8	21	1.09	Fossil evidence of a small horse. Grasslands and forests present. Many mammals including primitive whales, rhinos, and monkeys.
		Paleocene	65	10	1.29	Flowering plants and small mammals abundant. Many climate types exist.
Mesozoic era	Cretaceous		144	79	2.86	Fossil evidence of flowering birds and trees. Small mammals. Non-avian dinosaurs are extinct by the end of the period.
	Jurassic		206	62	4.09	First fossil evidence of mammals and feathered birds. Many types of dinosaurs.
	Triassic		248	42	4.93	Beginning of the "Age of Dinosaurs." Insects plentiful. Cone-bearing plants present.
Paleozoic era	Permian		290	42	5.77	First evidence of seed plants. Fish, amphibians, and giant insects present.
	Carboniferous	Pennsylvanian period	323	33	6.42	First evidence of reptiles. Many amphibians and giant insects present. Many large fern trees. Swamps cover low land areas.
		Mississippian period	354	31	7.04	
	Devonian		417	63	8.29	"Age of Fish." First fossil evidence of amphibians and insects. Many different kinds of fish in the earth's waters. The first forests grow in swamps.
	Silurian		443	26	8.81	First evidence of land plants. Algae, trilobites, and armored fish plentiful. Coral reefs form.
	Ordovician		490	47	9.74	Jawless fishes, algae, and trilobites plentiful. Great floods cover most of North America.
	Cambrian		543	53	10.79	Fossil evidence of trilobites, clams, snails, and seaweed. Seas spread across North America.
Precambrian		Proterozoic era	4.6 billion	Almost 4 billion	91.44	Earliest fossils of bacteria and algae (3.5 byrs). Earliest chemical evidence of life (3.8 billion). Earth forms.
		Archeozoic era				

TABLE 2A Student worksheet/significant geologic events.

Event	Millions of years ago	Meters from closest goal
Worldwide glaciations (average)	1.6	
Linking of North and South America with land bridge	5.7	
Formation of the Himalaya Mountains	15	
Collision of Indian and Asian Plates	35	
Separation of Australia and Antarctica	50	
Formation of the Alps	65	
Formation of the Rocky Mountains	70	
Opening of the Atlantic Ocean as the Eastern Hemisphere splits from the West	100	
Formation of Supercontinent—Pangaea II	200	
Formation of coal deposits	340	
Oxygen reaches 20% (present level)	380	
Development of the Appalachian Mountains	575	
Breakup of the Early Supercontinent	580	
Free oxygen reaches 2% in the atmosphere	600	
Formation of the Early Supercontinent	1250	
Free oxygen begins to build up	2500	
Period of no free oxygen	3700	
Oldest known earth rocks	3800	
Origin of the earth as a solid mass	4600	

TABLE 2B Student worksheet/significant geologic events—answer key (scaled to a 100 yard or 91.44 meter long football field).

Event	Millions of years ago	Meters from closest goal
Worldwide glaciations (average)	1.6	0.03
Linking of North and South America with land bridge	5.7	0.11
Formation of the Himalaya Mountains	15	0.30
Collision of Indian and Asian Plates	35	0.70
Separation of Australia and Antarctica	50	0.99
Formation of the Alps	65	1.29
Formation of the Rocky Mountains	70	1.39
Opening of the Atlantic Ocean as the Eastern and Western Hemispheres Split	100	1.99
Formation of Supercontinent—Pangaea II	200	3.98
Formation of coal deposits	340	6.76
Oxygen reaches 20% (present level)	380	7.55
Development of the Appalachian Mountains	575	11.43
Breakup of the Early Supercontinent	580	11.53
Free oxygen reaches 2% in the atmosphere	600	11.93
Formation of the Early Supercontinent	1250	42.85
Free oxygen begins of build up	2500	49.70
Period of no free oxygen	3700	73.56
Oldest known Earth rocks	3800	75.54
Origin of the Earth	4600	91.45

TABLE 3A Student worksheet/significant biologic events.

Event	Millions of years ago	Meters from closest goal
Anatomically modern humans *(Homo sapiens)*	0.05	
Early *Homo sapiens* develop	0.3	
Development of *Homo erectus*	1.2	
Australopithecines and *Homo habilis* develop	3.2	
Development of early primates	35	
Extinction of the dinosaurs—"Great Extinction"	65	
Flowering plants develop	140	
Dinosaurs are abundant	175	
First birds	180	
First mammals	220	
First dinosaurs	235	
Rapid diversification of living things—"Permian Explosion"	250	
First reptiles	300	
Development of the self-contained egg	340	
Trees appear	350	
First amphibians	360	
Insect-like creatures appear	400	
Earliest fishes	500	
Early shelled organisms	570	
Marine invertebrates abundant	600	
Multicelled plants and animals	700	
Advanced single cells	1000	
Development of eukaryotic cells	1400	
Early algae (blue-green) Gunflint formation	2200	
First life (single-celled prokaryotes)	3500	

TABLE 3B Student worksheet/significant biologic events—answer key (scaled to a 100 yard or 91.44 meter long football field).

Event	Millions of years ago	Meters from closest goal
Anatomically modern humans *(Homo sapiens)*	0.05	0.001
Early *Homo sapiens* develop	0.3	0.006
Development of *Homo erectus*	1.2	0.01
Australopithecines and *Homo habilis* develop	3.2	0.06
Development of early primates	35	1.29
Extinction of the dinosaurs—"Great Extinction"	65	1.29
Flowering plants develop	140	2.78
Dinosaurs are abundant	175	3.48
First birds	180	3.58
First mammals	220	4.37
First dinosaurs	235	4.67
Rapid diversification of living things—"Permian Explosion"	250	4.97
First reptiles	300	5.96
Development of the self-contained egg	340	6.76
Trees appear	350	6.96
First amphibians	360	7.16
Insect-like creatures appear	400	7.95
Earliest fishes	500	9.94
Early shelled organisms	570	11.34
Marine invertebrates abundant	600	11.93
Multicelled plants and animals	700	13.92
Advanced single cells	1000	19.88
Development of eukaryotic cells	1400	27.83
Early algae (blue-green) Gunflint formation	2200	43.74
First life (single-celled prokaryotes)	3500	69.58

The Development of Life Through time

The following narrative of events across geologic time was developed by Robert P. Wright and Eugene L. Chiapetta of the University of Houston and can be used as is or modified to fit the objectives of your activity. It is structured to provide the reader with some understanding of what the planet was like during the time of certain events. Again, the included distances are based on a 91.44 meter-long (100-yards) football field.

Precambrian History (4.5 billion to 550 million years)

1. The earth forms by a process of accretion of cosmic dust and meteorites some 4.5 billion years ago. The Apollo space program studies show that crater impact was in great abundance at that time. Heat generated by impacts and from radioactive decay of radioactive elements such as Uranium resulted in earth's interior heating up. . . *(91.28 meters from present). . .*

2. Earth differentiates into core, mantle, and early crust. Heat convection from the core and mantle resulted in volcanic activity and the beginning of an early atmosphere. The early atmosphere was probably a composition similar to volcanic gases or carbon dioxide, and nitrogen with smaller amounts of methane, ammonia, and sulfur dioxide. The amount of isotopes of rare gases on earth (argon 40 and xenon 129, measured from mantle rocks collected along mid-oceanic ridges) indicates that 85% of the atmosphere was outgased in the first million years. The rapid outgasing liberated water from the mantle, creating the oceans . . . *(also about 91.44 meters from present)*

3. The oldest rocks dated and evidence of continental crust are 3.8 billion years from West Greenland. It is thought that the origin of life had occurred by this time and consisted of anaerobic Archaebacteria and Eubacteria. Oxygen, after all, is a product of photosynthesis and there is no evidence of aerobic metabolism until later. *(75.40 meters)*

4. Some of the oldest fossils are coccoid and filamentous microfossils found in weakly metamorphosed 3.5 billion year old sedimentary rock from South Africa and Western Australia. They resemble cyanobacteria. At present they are considered the oldest single-celled prokaryotes, and biologic diversity was probably greater than this oldest record. This was probably a time of no free oxygen. *(63.62 meters)*

5. It is suggested that by 2.5 billion years aerobic metabolisms of prokaryotes and possibly the symbiotic acquisition of mitochondria and chloroplasts by prokaryotes (to become eukaryotes) occurred during this time (though this is speculative). *(49.61 meters)*

6. Fossils resembling photoautotrophs (cyanobacteria) that indicate that biologic diversity was well established at this level are found in the cherts of the 2 billion year old Gunflint Iron Formation of Ontario. Filaments and cocci abound. They are associated with layers of stromatolites that resemble modern stromatolites forming in the intertidal range at

Shark Bay Australia. Oxygen generated at this time was utilized in the oxidation of minerals such as iron. The world-famous Precambrian banded iron deposits of commercial value were now deposited. Iron was transported unoxidized as sediment because there was no oxygen in the atmosphere. The sediment was deposited in the oceans, where it was then oxidized by the oxygen derived from the cyanobacteria. *(39.68 meters)*

7. Oxygen bloom probably began after deposition of the banded iron formations and eukaryotic cells shortly thereafter because mitochondria in such cells are oxygen users. The eukaryotic cells are represented by fossils called Acritarchs that appear 1.8 billion years ago. The present level of oxygen in the atmosphere (20%) is a result of photosynthetic activity. The presence of oxygen in the atmosphere is important because it filters UV radiation that allows life to live on land. The rapid evolution of life from pro to eukaryotic to metazoans was during this period of oxygen and ozone growth. *(35.71 meters)*

8. Multicellular life (metazoans) is found in the Late Precambrian. At this time the world's continents were together as a single land mass called Rodinia. This was a time of glaciers formed by the rapid depletion of carbon dioxide in the atmosphere by photosynthesizers that would have lowered temperatures. The metazoans are called the Ediacaran fauna after the Ediacaran Hills in South Australia. Fossils possibly include annelids, arthropods, and others. The time is about 580 million years. *(11.50 meters)*

Summary Statement: This is the end of the Precambrian. Five-sixths of the story of life has taken place. Life has remained almost exclusively unicellular but the transition from pro to eukaryotic cells occurred followed by multicellularity by 600 million years. Bacteria have persevered and we await the soon-to-follow Cambrian explosion of life that represents the beginning of the first geologic period of the Paleozoic era.

The Paleozoic Era (550 to 245 million years)

The race of man shall perish,
but the eyes
of Trilobites eternal be in stone,
And seem to stare about in mild surprise,
At changes greater than they have yet known.

T.A. Conrad

9. The Paleozoic era means ancient life and was a time when trilobites, corals, crinoids, jawless fish, the first insects, and many more different kinds of animals and plants evolved. It began nearly 4 billion years after the birth of our planet and represents a time when mineralization of calcium phosphate and calcium carbonate into skeletal hard parts resulted in fossil preservation.

10. The famous Cambrian explosion in life diversity occurred about 530 million years ago. At this time, most all of the modern phylum made their first appearance. Strange-looking creatures, many being arthropods, were preserved as fossils by undersea mud slides now represented by the famous Burgess Shale fauna found in the Rocky Mountains in British Columbia. Among the strange-looking animals called Opabinia, Anomalocaris, Marella, and Hallucigenia, was one of particular interest; it is called Pikaia with preserved zigzag muscle bands and visible backbone that indicates it to be the oldest chordate. *(10.52 meters)*

11. The supercontinent Rodinia had rifted apart along oceanic ridge spreading centers, and North America would start a 500-million-year trek during which it would collide with South America and northeastern Europe and unite as another supercontinent, Pangaea, in the Early Permian (the last geologic period in the Paleozoic) by 260 million years ago. Let's place this Pangaea event at the beginning of Permian time (5.15 meters), and then we will go back and fill in several important events that happened during the Paleozoic era.

12. Invertebrates flourished in the earliest Paleozioc, and some early jawless fish (agnathans) are found as fossils. By the Devonian, fish had diversified in the seas and freshwater. Jaws had been acquired, as well as pectoral and pelvic girdles (important if land mobility is to evolve) and bony (not just heavy armor) and cartilaginous (the sharks are here!) skeletons. Fossil collectors since the 1820s have known of the famous sandstone fossil fish deposits in northern Scotland called the Orcadian Basin lake sediments. The famous Swiss naturalist Louis Agassiz spent 12 years publishing five volumes on fossil fish (the study of fossil fish is called *paleoichtyology*). (*Orcadian fossil beds are placed at 408 million years or 8.09 meters.*)

13. The Devonian was a busy time. By the end of the period, the Appalachian Mountains were forming as a result of collision between North America and parts of South America and Africa. Lobe-fin fish had evolved as well as the Amphibians themselves. Ichthyostega of the Late Devonian in Greenland were present (evolved from lung fish that reached their peak in the Devonian). Forests of giant club mosses (Sigillaria and Lepidodendron), horsetails (Calamites), and tree ferns appeared as well. The gymnosperms were flourishing. Also, there were bugs, but we will hold their story until the next event! (*Place a marker at 360 million years, or 7.14 meters.*)

14. Ah! The bugs! Imagine dragonflies as large as seagulls hunting luscious, juicy cockroaches, all present in the Carboniferous forests of Nyrany, the Czech Republic, where the climate was warm, soils were rich, and vegetation was thick. Also, watch out for spiders, scorpions, millipedes, and centipedes, and primitive reptiles (where did they come from?). There were three major continents at this time: Gondwanaland in the Southern Hemisphere (South America, Africa, Antarctica, Australia, India), Laurussia in the north (North America and Europe), and Siberia. There were major climatic belts: glacial deposits in southern continents and humid warm coal forming climates in the north. Living things had quite a selection! (*286 million years ago, or 5.67 meters*)

15. The greatest of all extinctions (there were many throughout earth's history) ended the Paleozoic era. By the end of the Permian period (245 million years ago), major groups of land and ocean dwellers were gone. It has been estimated that only 5% of all species survived into the Mesozoic era (the next major block of time). What was the earth like and what happened? The continents were fused together into one called Pangaea, huge deserts formed, mountains were high, seasonality showed hot to cold extremes, and sea levels fell. Was there a single cause of this crash or an interplay of many environmental causes? What do you think and why? Go ahead! No one really knows for sure! (*Place this event at 4.86 meters.*)

Let's take a breather and look back at the busy Paleozoic. Think of it. All major phyla of metazoans had evolved and the land was green with vegetation. Yet, where were the birds, dinosaurs, mammals, man himself? Look to the future.

The Mesozoic Era (245 through 65 million years ago)

The "terrible ones" have finally arrived along with the flowering plants.

16. The Jurassic world saw the breakup of Pangaea as North America rifted from North Africa and the North Atlantic Ocean. The South Atlantic would open a bit later. Climates were like today, but there was no polar ice. Tropical and subtropical belts were wide; forests were aplenty. (*208 million years ago, or 4.12 meters*)

17. The Age of the Dinosaurs was underway on land supported by abundant vegetation and warm climates. The seas swarmed with marine reptile-like, dolphin-like Ichthyosaurs, and long-necked Plesiosaurs—all in pursuit of fishes, mollusks, and other sea life. The dinosaurs were as successful as warm-blooded animals and rapidly filled all available ecologic niches; the Pterosaurs even flew. Also present were the first feathered birds (Archaeopteryx found in the Solnhofen Limestone that formed in a lagoon in an area that is now Germany). First discovered in 1860, Archaeopteryx was about the size of a pigeon, and like the Therapod reptile that it was, it had a long bony tail, claws, teeth, and beautifully preserved imprints of feathers. (*150 million years, or 2.97 meters*)

18. Near the end of the Mesozoic, the planet looked different than at the end of the Paleozoic. For one thing, the Atlantic Ocean had formed as most continents had separated from Pangaea; flowering plants (angiosperms) and hardwood trees spread quickly as well as low-level feeding herbivorous dinosaurs such as ankylosaurs, ceratopsians, and others. Along with the spread of flowering plants were insects such as butterflies, moths, ants, and bees. They arose and spread quickly. Know why? (*100 million years, or 1.98 meters*)

19. Not again! Probably the most talked about major extinction by the end of the Mesozoic (the end of the Cretaceous period), possibly due to the impact of a large asteroid many

kilometers in diameter (Alvarez Hypothesis, 1979). Is it possible that such an event caused the great extinction near the Cretaceous Tertiary boundary 65 million years ago? Imagine, an impact so great the dust cloud generated from it blocked sunlight for several months or longer and cooled the Earth long enough to upset the ecologic balance, killing off most of the dinosaurs. Think of it! Photosynthesis suppressed, food chain disruption, temperatures below freezing point. *(65 million years ago, or 1.29 meters)*

20. Let's tabulate who did not survive: dinosaurs gone (except the birds), many reptiles (pterosaurs, plesiosaurs), many fish and mollusks, and over half the plankton of the seas. Survivors include: most land plants and land animals—insects, frogs, snails, turtles, lizards, snakes, crocodiles, placental mammals, and most invertebrates. (*Place this at 1.29 meters as well.*)

Take a breather. Let's look at this impact hypothesis. An impact from an asteroid did you say? Any evidence? How about iridium (rare on Earth but common in meteorites)? Did you know that levels are 100 times higher in rocks at the Cretaceous-Tertiary boundary? And what about those large meteor impact craters like the one on the coast of northern Yucatan? Perhaps there was a swarm of meteors! Others say no. Fossil plants tell us that the world climates were cooling by the end of the Cretaceous and ecosystems were changing. The cooling may have been a result of continents moving more toward higher latitudes. What do you think? Why?

The Cenozoic Era (65 million years to the present)

So far this has been a long and wonderful time excursion. Place the beginning of the Cenozoic at 65 million years, or 1.29 meters. Not much room is left there; but a lot happened. We will just mention a few things. During this time, the earth became more like the present; mammals evolved to what we see today, grasslands appeared, and with them the herding grazers such as buffalo, antelope, zebra, horses, and wart hogs! And with them came carnivores such as hyena, dogs, and cats. Cool and dry climates often prevailed as continents moved to where they are now (are they still moving?). Oh yes. India made its long trek from the southern hemisphere to collide with Asia to form the Himalayas by 35 million years ago, or 0.69 meters. Place this event.

Only two events remain that we should remember, and they happened in quick succession.

21. First, the early primates developed in the tropics. These tree dwellers had opposable thumbs, binocular vision, larger brains than other mammals, fewer offspring, and possessed a social organization. We are interested in the Hominidae for they include the great apes and us. Specifically, the ape/human split was probably in the region of 4 to 6 million years ago. (Did you know that DNA studies show that the chimpanzees show a closer kinship to humans than they do to the gorilla?) The base of the hominid tree is *Ardipithecus ramidus*, whose teeth and arm bones were discovered recently by anthropologist Tim White in Ethiopia. *(4.4 million years, or 0.08 meters!)*

22. From *Ardipithecus*, the transition through *Australiphthecine* to *Homo sapiens* (essentially us) took place in a short time. The rapid evolution occurred during the Pleistocene or ice ages. The Neanderthals (200,000 to 35,000 years ago) followed by and coevolved with early modern people or Cro-magnons. We have arrived—30,000 years ago or so!

Teaching About Intermediate Forms

III-3

 Evan B. Hazard

Overview

This activity explores the process by which biologists classify transitional forms in the fossil record. Students will come to see that the fossil record is rich in transitional forms despite the fact that the rules of Linnaean classification tends not to label them as such.

> ***Evolutionary Principles Illustrated***
>
> - Transitional forms
> - Systematics

Background Information

A common objection to a naturalistic understanding of the history of life is the supposed universal lack of intermediate, or transitional, forms. For example, Morris (1963) writes of "clear-cut 'gaps' between species, genera, families, etc." And Gish (1985) claims there are no transitional forms in the fossil record. Note that, for this objection to be valid, there must be no intermediates, either fossil or recent, between what these and many other special creationists regard as supernaturally created "kinds" of organisms. *Note*: I follow the definition provided by Bailey (1993) who distinguishes special creationists from those who acknowledge a creator but believe the created universe has worked, and continues to work, naturally.

Many transitional forms are known, although special creationists refuse to recognize them as such. Intermediates are more common between species and genera than between higher categories (Simpson, 1949) but also occur between families, orders, and classes (see the following examples). However,

This activity is based on "Teaching about intermediate forms" by Evan B Hazard (1998), in *The American Biology Teacher, 60*(5), 359–61 and is modified and reprinted with permission of the publisher.

intermediates are rare enough that many otherwise reliable texts uncritically repeat the story of their absence. I suspect many professional biologists also accept this notion. Further, the supposed lack of intermediates is in part an artifact of the rules of Linnaean classification. At Bemidji State University we use the following exercise to illustrate this.

Materials

Per class:

- Overhead transparency of Figure 1
- Illustrations or models of vertebrate organisms

Procedures

Prepare Figure 1 as an overhead transparency. A washable overhead pen will allow you to continually reuse it. Modify the following scenario to suit your own taxonomic tastes. Section *a* represents 11 species of birds found in the forests of the tropical island Barataria. (Keep sections *b–e* covered with a sheet of paper.) The numbers indicate the chronological order of the published descriptions of these species. The distances between the 11 species roughly indicate degree of morphological similarity, not geographic separation. The species occupy different niches, and many of their geographic ranges overlap. A 1925 expedition collected species 1, 2, 3, 4, and 5. An experienced taxonomist put them in two genera, X and Y. She described the species of X in a 1926 paper and those of Y in a 1927 paper. Two subsequent expeditions collected species 6–11; experienced taxonomists in the 1960s found that these also fit comfortably in genera X and Y.

On last summer's expedition to Barataria, you (the students) collected several specimens that morphologically fall at position 12, shown in sections *b–e*. (Now, uncover the whole transparency.) Morphologically, species 12 is intermediate between genus X and genus Y. How do you classify it? The rules of biological nomenclature allow only four choices. First, you evaluate your data; all important science involves judgment (Bronowski, 1965), and it is important that students and teachers know that. If you decide that species 12 fits better into X than Y, label it X12 in section *b*, circle the species of X and of Y, and you still have two genera. If you decide that species 12 fits better into Y than X, label it Y12 in section *c*, circle the species of X and of Y, and again you still have two genera. If you decide that species 12 confirms what you (a "lumper") have known all along, that X and Y are enough alike to be one genus, label it X12 in section *d*, and circle all 12 species as one genus, X (the name X has priority). If you (a "splitter") decide that species 12, despite its similarity to X11 and Y10, is pretty special, create a new genus for it, label it Z12 in section *e*, and circle X, Y, and Z as three genera.

These are the only four options under the rules of biological nomenclature. Then someone comes along and says there are no intermediate species between genera. Here you may want to make a nice philosophical point. If asked, the class will generally agree that, in Figure lb, you have redefined X

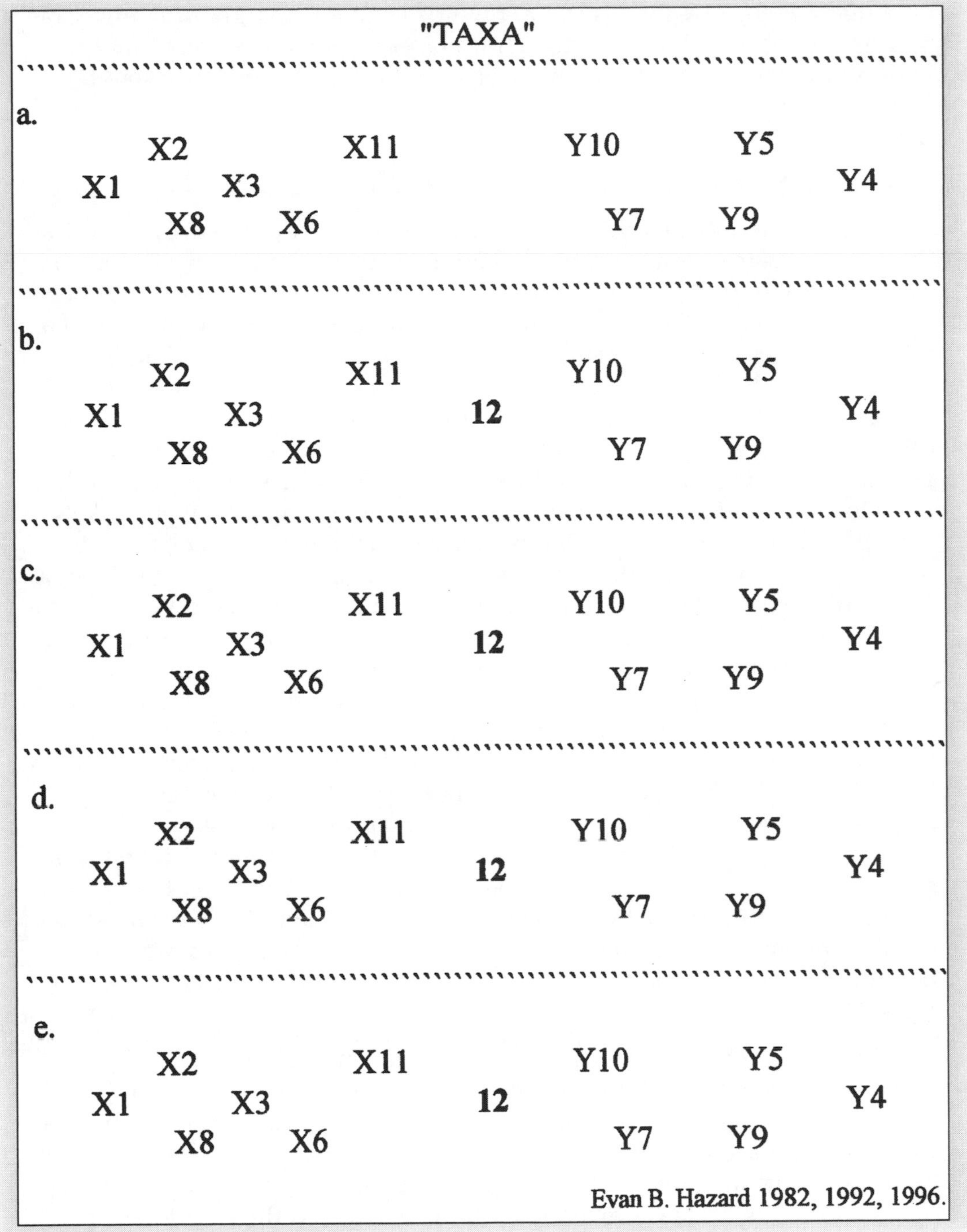

"TAXA"

a.

X2 X11 Y10 Y5
X1 X3 Y4
X8 X6 Y7 Y9

b.

X2 X11 Y10 Y5
X1 X3 12 Y4
X8 X6 Y7 Y9

c.

X2 X11 Y10 Y5
X1 X3 12 Y4
X8 X6 Y7 Y9

d.

X2 X11 Y10 Y5
X1 X3 12 Y4
X8 X6 Y7 Y9

e.

X2 X11 Y10 Y5
X1 X3 12 Y4
X8 X6 Y7 Y9

Evan B. Hazard 1982, 1992, 1996.

FIGURE 1 An exercise targeting intermediate forms.

but not Y; in Figure 1c, you have redefined Y but not X; in Figure 1d, you have redefined both; and in Figure 1e, you have redefined neither. Wrong! In each, you have redefined both X and Y. Every time you define something new, here species 12, you implicitly redefine all other categories as "not 12." Perhaps only a few will take delight in this insight, but that is enough.

I made Figure 1 with an ordinary word-processing program. Comparable figures could be made using geometric shapes, caminalcules, or plantoids, variously marked with stripes, dots, or shading, perhaps even without the help of a computer.

Vertebrate Examples at the Levels of Family, Order, and Class

Once you establish that intermediate species exist despite their classification into discrete genera, you can extend the principle to higher categories. Evolutionary theory predicts that, as we follow related families back through time, their fossils will resemble one another more and more closely. The evolution of horses and their relatives provides a nice example (MacFadden, 1992). Hyracotherium ("Eohippus"), classified as the earliest equid, resembles its early Cenozoic contemporaries that are classified as the earliest rhinocerotids and tapirids. The three are put in the horse, rhino, and tapir families because we have a good fossil record of their descendants. Had these three lineages gone extinct without issue, paleomammalogists would likely have put them in one family, and probably not in a distinct order, Perissodactyla. They are enough like the condylarth Phenacodus to be considered a family in the extinct order tCondylarthra. Nobody claims that tPhenacodus is the ancestor of Hyracotherium and other early perissodactyls; finding fossil genera that are actual ancestors of later forms is unlikely (though Hyracotherium and other later genera are likely actual ancestors within Equidae). But Hyracotherium and friends are clearly transitional between two orders, the condylarths and the perissodactyls. These Eocene genera occupy position 12 in Figure 1, with respect to three extant mammalian families, and with respect to an extinct and an extant mammalian order. The Jurassic Archaeopteryx is probably not ancestral to modem birds, and bird fossils are rare enough that we may never find such an ancestor. But it and the more derived Cretaceous fossil Sinornis (Sereno & Chenggang, 1992) are mosaics of reptilian and avian characters and thus transitional between dinosaurs (or possibly thecodonts) and birds. They, too, occupy position 12, between two classes, in Figure 1.

The much richer fossil record of the Permian and Triassic synapsids ("mammal-like reptiles") documents the transition from reptiles to mammals (Carroll, 1988; Halstead, 1968; Kemp, 1982). In those synapsids that gave rise to mammals, various characters (e.g., secondary palate, heterodont dentition, phalangeal formula, rib-free lumbar vertebrae plus diaphragmatic breathing, dentary/squamosal jaw articulation, diphyodonty, and three middle-ear bones) show up at different times. What you decide to call the earliest mammal depends on which character or character suite you choose as definitive. These advanced synapsids occupy position 12 in Figure 1 with respect to two classes, reptiles and mammals. (Cladistic taxonomists advocate different taxonomic levels for some of the above categories, but that procedural argument does not change the transitional nature of the organisms involved.)

Considering the restricted geographic and chronological distribution of fossil beds, restricted geographic areas of fossilization and outcropping, chance of preservation of a given species as fossils, and likelihood of loss (especially of older fossils) by erosion, the fossil record is reasonably rich in transitional forms. Since the animal phyla probably differentiated over half a billion years ago as soft-bodied forms, it is not surprising that we have no clear record of transitions between phyla.

References

Bailey, L.R. (1993). *Genesis, creation, and creationism*. New York: Paulist Press.

Bronowski, J. (1965). *Science and human values* (Rev. ed). New York: Harper and Row.

Carroll, R.L. (1988). *Vertebrate paleontology and evolution*. New York: W.H. Freeman.

Gish, D.T. (1985). Evolution: *The challenge of the fossil record*. El Cajon, CA: Creation-Life Publishers.

Halstead, L.B. (1968). *The pattern of vertebrate evolution*. New York: W.H. Freeman.

Kemp, T.S. (1982). *Mammal-like reptiles and the origin of mammals*. New York: Academic Press.

MacFadden, B.J. (1992). *Fossil horses: Systematics, paleobiology, and evolution*. New York: Cambridge University Press.

Morris, H.M. (1963). *The twilight of evolution*. Grand Rapids, MI: Baker Book House.

Sereno, P.C., & Chenggang, R. (1992). Early evolution of early flight and perching: New evidence from the lower Cretaceous of China. *Science, 255*, 845–48.

Simpson, G.G. (1949). *The meaning of evolution*. New Haven, CT: Yale University Press.

III-4

Microscopic Examination of a Leaf and Lichen to Show Convergent Evolution

 David Bardell

Overview

In this activity, students will examine the structures of relatively unrelated organisms—a plant leaf and lichen. In doing so, students will come to find that the organisms have accumulated similar structural adaptations over time, beautifully illustrating the concept of convergent evolution.

Evolutionary Principles Illustrated

- Convergent evolution

Background Information

Before 1859, the year Charles Darwin published his book *On the Origin of Species*, it was generally believed that the biological world was unchanging. All of the many species of organisms were believed to have been created at the same time and had remained unchanged since their creation. According to the Darwinian theory of evolution, species change over long periods of time, and this leads to the creation of new species. As explained by Darwin, changes are due to natural selection of variant individuals of a species. Those variants with characteristics that allow them to better cope with natural phenomena in their environment will have a greater chance of surviving, reproducing, and passing on their characteristics to their offspring. Consequently, beneficial characteristics will accumulate over many generations, whereas there will be a tendency for characteristics that are either harmful or of no benefit to be lost. Thus, the characteristics of a species change as time goes by, and such changes can eventually give rise to new species.

This activity is based on "Microscopic examination of a leaf & a lichen to show convergent evolution" by David Bardell (1995), in *The American Biology Teacher, 57*(3), 99-100 and is modified and reprinted with permission of the publisher.

Natural selection often leads to species that are markedly different from each other and from their ancestors; this process is called divergent evolution. For example, modern horses and zebras are different species of the genus *Equus*. They not only differ from each other in several ways, but also from their common ancestor, a member of the extinct genus *Pliohippus*. It is generally divergent evolution that comes to mind in students, and the population at large, when giving their attention to evolutionary change.

In contrast to divergent evolution, organisms with dissimilar ancestors sometimes come to resemble each other—a process called convergent evolution. For example, cetaceans (whales, dolphins, and porpoises), like fishes, have a streamlined body to reduce resistance to movement through water, stabilizing fins, and a powerful muscular tail to bring about movement. Be that as it may, the ancestors of cetaceans were land-dwelling mammals that moved on four legs.

A convenient way of observing convergent evolution in the classroom can be achieved by microscopic study of a leaf and lichen.

Materials

Per student group:

- Microscope
- Slides of leaf cross sections (*Ligustrum vulgare* or similar species)
- Slides of lichen cross sections (*Physcia sp.* or similar specimen)

Procedures

The following descriptions of plant and lichen physiology may be addressed with students prior to their observation of the prepared slides. Alternatively, students may first observe the slides and be asked to describe what similarities exist between the two. Then, the students can research the physiology of plant leaves and lichen for themselves or be given the information and asked to draw conclusions on their own, explaining why plant leaves and lichen share structural similarities.

The primary function of leaves is photosynthesis: a series of actions by which light energy is converted to chemical energy, which is then used to synthesize organic molecules from inorganic molecules taken in by the plant from its environment. Thus, plants can make their own food from simple chemicals. The leaf has evolved into a remarkably well-constructed structure, with its different constituent cells positioned in a way that allows for efficient photosynthesis.

In addition to its necessity for plants, photosynthesis is basic for the existence of virtually all other forms of life; exceptions include photosynthetic and chemosynthetic bacteria, and animals living in the vicinity of deep ocean vents that are the beneficiaries of chemosynthetic bacteria inhabiting the same environment. The products of photosynthesis are used directly or indirectly by animals, fungi, and most species of bacteria as a source of energy, without which they could not exist.

Lichens are composite organisms consisting of a fungus and certain species of unicellular plants belonging to either the cyanophyta or chlorophyta groups of algae. This relationship allows the two organisms to live in places where neither of them could exist alone—for example, on bare rock. The fungus obtains organic nutrients from the photosynthesizing algal partner. It is not a one-sided relationship, since the fungus supplies water and provides a habitat for the algae. The fungus forms the bulk of a lichen, and protects the algae from wind, excessive light, and desiccation—conditions the algae would be vulnerable to as free-living organisms in the kinds of harsh environments where lichens are usually found.

Although a leaf is an organ of a higher plant and a lichen is an association of a fungus and algae, both the leaf and lichen have a similar arrangement of cells (Figures 1 and 2). This reflects the photosynthesizing activity of leaves and lichens, and the requirement for photosynthetic cells to be in a position that allows them to receive optimal light for photosynthesis. The photosynthetic cells, in turn, need to be protected and supported by other cells.

The upper surface of a leaf is a protective layer of epidermal cells, with cuticle covering its outer surface. The waxy cuticle provides additional protection and also prevents loss of water from the leaf. The cuticle and epidermis are transparent so that light can reach the cells beneath. Immediately below the epidermis are palisade cells protecting the spongy mesophyll and photosynthetic cells which contain numerous chloroplasts. The loose arrangement of cells in the mesophyll provides air spaces that permit the uptake of carbon dioxide from the environment and the release of oxygen from the plant itself.

Carbon dioxide is essential for photosynthesis. Oxygen is a waste product of the process and must be eliminated from the cells. Movement of materials into and out of the photosynthetic cells would be less efficient if, instead of being loosely arranged, the cells in this part of the leaf were closely packed. The lower surface of the leaf, like the upper surface, is a protective layer of epidermal cells. Carbon dioxide and oxygen move into and out of the leaf through the stomata, microscopic openings that are usually more abundant in the lower epidermis than in the upper epidermis.

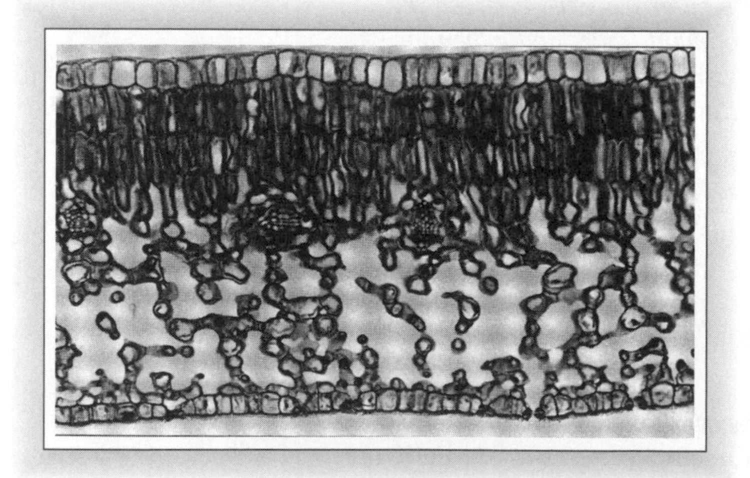

FIGURE 1 The microscopic appearance of a cross section of a privet leaf. The main photosynthetic cells are the elongated cells below the upper surface. See the text for a full description.

Most kinds of lichens have a similar organization of their cells. There is an upper cortex of fungal cells, beneath which the algal cells are located. Below the algal cells is an area of loosely organized fungal cells called the medulla. Beneath the medulla is a lower cortex of fungal cells.

Cortices are often covered with cuticle or some other protective material.

The descriptions provided reveal striking similarities between a leaf and lichen. The epidermal layers of the leaf and the cortices of the lichen provide protection. The photosynthesizing cells are just below the upper surface in both leaf and lichen. Furthermore, the spongy mesophyll of the leaf and the medulla of the lichen consist of loosely arranged cells, which allow for a ready exchange of carbon dioxide and oxygen between the photosynthesizing cells and the atmosphere.

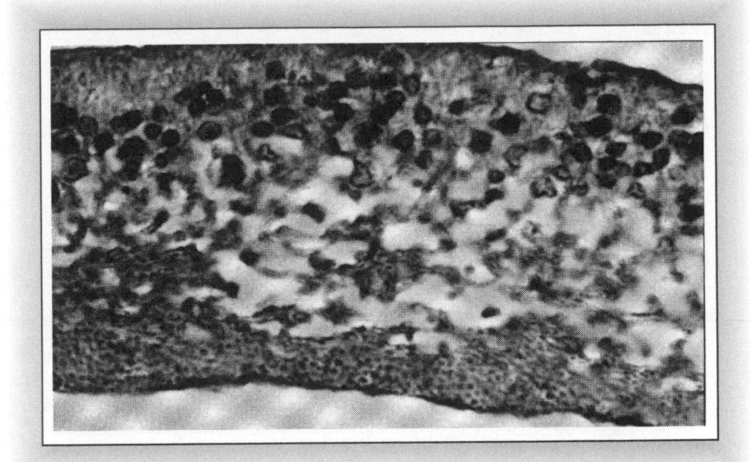

FIGURE 2 The microscopic appearance of a cross section of a member of the lichen genus Physcia. The photosynthetic algal cells are the dark-staining oval to round cells below the upper surface. See the text for a full description.

Additional Considerations

Microscopic slides showing cross sections of leaves and lichens are available from biological supply companies. Thus, good and long-lasting materials can easily be obtained that show convergent evolution. The leaf described herein was that of *Ligustrum vulgare*, commonly called privet. The lichen was of the genus *Physcia*. Since lichens are made up of organisms from two different kingdoms, they are a problem with respect to classification and are named after the fungal component.

IV

Variation and Adaptations within Species

Variation and Adaptation within Species

IV

This section features several activities designed to help students explore the vital role played by variation within the species as the raw material of evolution by natural selection. Although neither Darwin nor Wallace could explain the source of the variation, both recognized that something in the physical, behavioral, or biochemical makeup of some members of a population permitted survival while others failed to survive.

Darwin viewed variation within the population to be so important that he frequently discussed the diversity found in pigeons and other species. Darwin reasoned that if pigeon breeders could produce countless varieties intentionally by selecting desirable traits from the normal variation within the pigeon population, nature could be capable of almost anything over millennia.

These activities target the basic concept that, although there is a range of variation within natural populations, sometimes one must look for it. The first exercise takes place at the zoo, where students examine groups of animals for subtle variations while they hypothesize about why some groups of traits are common in animals living in the same environment.

A second activity provides instructions for students to examine variation at a higher level by studying different, closely-related species of fruit flies. The unique aspect of this procedure is that students are able to gauge the amount of variation after speciation has already occurred.

Taking a harder look at the often overlooked is the theme once again in Demonstrating Variation within the Human Species, an activity in which students record the range of variation that exists among their classmates. Variation in morphology, reaction times, and short-term memory may be investigated.

When a small group of individuals possess variation that provides some advantage it is said to have an adaptive trait. Unfortunately, adaptation as a biological term is almost universally misunderstood by students. In common language, the term represents something over which an individual has control. In the world of living things the term "adaptation" means a trait or set of traits already possessed by an individual that gives it an advantage over others in the struggle for survival. Organisms cannot choose to adapt; they must already possess the raw materials for such adaptation.

Two activities in this section enable students to see how a particular trait or adaptation can be of value. In The Birds and the Beaks, students use a variety of instruments such as drinking straws, tweezers, and pliers as if they were beaks to pick up various types of seeds. Obviously, some "beaks" will be better adapted than others for certain kinds of seeds.

Finally, students can revisit the zoo activity and have the opportunity to consider the adaptive traits that have allowed their chosen organism to survive and perhaps even to thrive in its particular environment. Students can also consider the fact that sometimes members of different species will possess similar adaptations because of convergent evolution due to a shared environment.

Illustrating and Exploring Variations and Adaptations in Animal Species at the Zoo

IV-1

 William F. McComas

Overview

During a visit to the zoo, students investigate variation within species and have an opportunity to visualize and explore the link between physical and behavioral characteristics possessed by organisms and the environment they inhabit. On an accompanying set of worksheets, the students will record their observations and reflections, providing a raw material for enhanced classroom discussion.

> ***Evolutionary Principles Illustrated***
>
> - Variation within species
> - Adaptation
> - Convergent evolution

Background Information

One goal of this exercise is to illustrate variation within a species. Students are given the opportunity to study a single type of organism and establish that even members of the same species will show some differences when one individual is compared with another. Such variations are the raw material on which evolution by natural selection operates.

Variations in domestic species and in humans may be hard to miss, but many students would likely be surprised to find that variation—no matter how subtle—exists throughout the living world. In addition, while advantageous physical characteristics are generally thought of by students to be the principal factors that enable some individuals to survive, differences in physiology, behavior, and reproductive success must also be considered. Although

This activity is based on "Variation, adaptation and evolution at the zoo" by William F. McComas (1988), in *The American Biology Teacher, 50*(6), 379–83. It is modified and reprinted with permission of the publisher.

these factors may not be as apparent to the casual observer, they play just as big a role in the process.

In addition, this activity illustrates the principle of convergent evolution. In its most general form, convergent evolution is a trend that produces similarities between more distantly related forms because they share a common environment. Whales and fish both have fin-like structures that move them within their watery environment, but this is not evidence of close relationship, just an indication that in many instances the "tools" needed to survive in a particular environment are the same.

Environmental pressure has dictated that in order to be a contender within a given environment, even distantly related animals living there must share many common tools. Organisms coexisting in a given environment will often have a number of characteristics in common as a result of the processes of change working on both populations at the same time. This concept of similar traits due to living in a similar environment is called *analogy*.

Finally, this activity primarily illustrates aspects of the Darwin-Wallace model of evolution by natural selection; issues of rate or patterns of changes that one might see with punctuated equilibrium are not featured here.

Materials

Per group of students:

- Photocopy of each worksheet

Procedures

This lab is divided into four parts, each with a corresponding worksheet to be used by students. The worksheets are generally self-explanatory but some notes for the teacher are included here. It is expected that classroom discussion following data collection will help students understand the implications of what they are seeing.

Part A: Variation within a Species

This first section is designed to illustrate the principle of variation within a species. Each student should choose a different animal species on exhibit at the zoo. These animals are studied as a group; therefore, several representatives of the animal should be available. A quick look at the individual animals may reveal nothing special, but a more detailed examination of many individuals will quickly reveal subtle differences between them.

Attention should be paid in this section to sexual differences within a species. The students should be aware that in those species where such differences are common, they should examine a variety of animals of the same species and of the same sex. Sexual differences can, of course, be an interesting discussion topic. Additional differences that might confuse students include those such as size and other age-related factors.

Part B: Adaptations with Respect to the Environment

Next, the students will examine in detail the environment in which the animal naturally lives. The student will try to see what characteristics seem to allow the animal to thrive in that setting. This exercise is not meant to imply that there is a single perfect form for a species in any situation. The form that finally arises as being best suited is defined as that which is best relative to the other types with which it is in competition within the population.

Part C: Convergent and Divergent Evolution

Students in this section are asked to find another animal that shares a similar environment with the animal selected in the section addressing variation within a species. In this case the environment can be a large physical environment (i.e., desert, forest, grassland, etc.) or a smaller scale nutritional environment (i.e., seed eaters versus fruit eaters in the same general area).

Some students may be lucky enough to have found two organisms that live in similar environments in different parts of the world. An example using animals that may be familiar to students would be the gerbil and the kangaroo rat. Both of these rodents live in the same type of desert environment, but the gerbil is native to the dry, sandy areas of Africa and Asia, while the kangaroo rat is found only in the deserts of North America. These animals resemble each other in a number of ways and have almost identical food requirements. If they lived in the same area they would be in direct competition for resources.

It would be an interesting project to concentrate on the differences between the two rodents and see how each has features that help it survive in its environment. This would take some research, but from this information it might be possible to predict which animal would survive if both lived together in either the southwest desert of North America or in Asia.

In another example, the student might choose the deer and the kangaroo. Both have very similar nutritional requirements and, upon close inspection, are seen to have almost identical construction of their skull and teeth. The head of a kangaroo and the head of a deer are very much the same, not because of close relationship, but as a result of convergent evolution. Deer, of course, are placental mammals and carry their young inside their bodies until birth, while the marsupial kangaroos raise their young primarily in an external pouch. There are many other examples of placental mammals and their marsupial counterparts which students may discover.

Examples such as these show why an introduced species may effectively out compete the native occupant of an environment. The transplanted or introduced organism may find itself well suited for the new environment but lacking the population controls provided by its own natural enemies.

Part D: Predicting Future Evolutionary Trends

Note: This section is included only because it is entertaining; it is impossible to predict future evolutionary trends. However, teachers might profit from seeing how students react to this creative challenge—however fanciful—and apply evolutionary principles and make use of knowledge about environmental change and variation with species to propose some alternative future forms of life.

Ask students to imagine what evolutionary changes might result in a group of animals if their present environment slowly changed. This part of the exercise represents a simplistic view of a complex process, but is useful in encouraging students to apply what they have learned. Furthermore, it may be possible to discern more about the students' understanding of evolution from this creative exercise than any number of typical objective test questions.

Students should keep in mind that even if a small group of individuals in a population possesses an advantageous characteristic, this characteristic may not be easily passed on to the next generation. This concept of heritability is poorly understood, but it is central to any discussion of future evolutionary ends.

With these cautions in mind, we could suppose that a desert environment became woodland over a long period of time. Students might logically predict that those desert toads that already have a slight green coloration might be "selected" by the environment since they would be more effectively hidden in the green of the forest. At the same time, those tan-colored animals might not be able to hide as effectively and would be removed by predators.

Teachers may find it useful to consult the book *After Man* by Dixon (1981). This fascinating book makes predictions of what future creatures may look like based upon the present evolutionary trends coupled with projections from the study of continental drift.

Additional Considerations

The accompanying worksheets each target a major principle pertaining to evolution by natural selection. The worksheets have not been designed to discuss fully or explain evolutionary theory, but to foster classroom discussion by providing exciting illustrations of the principles involved. The individual sections may be modified for specific student groups or may be used independent of each other.

One major consideration relative to the potential success of this activity is the size and diversity of the collection at the zoo itself. It is very important that the zoo have a large variety of animals, preferably from different geographic areas, with at least three representatives of each animal to be investigated. This may be easier now with the new emphasis in zoos on having more examples of some species but fewer total species.

For the first activity, it would be possible to use farm animals or the inhabitants of a large local pet store or animal shelter. Advanced students might also be able to examine the plants found at an arboretum or large nursery, but admittedly this will be more difficult since the differences are harder to discern given our "animal-centric" perspectives. In any case, it is important to point out that the basic principles illustrated in this activity pertain to all living things since evolution is a unifying concept.

Reference

Dixon, D. (1981). *After man*. London: Harrow House Editions.

Evolution at the Zoo: Student Materials

Part A—Variation within a Species

1. Choose an animal in the zoo that is represented by at least three (3) different individual specimens. Write the common and scientific names of the animals on the lines below:

Animal A

_______________________________ _______________________________

Common name Scientific name

2. What is the specific location of the animal in the zoo?

3. Examine your animals in detail and list as many individual differences as possible for the species in question. Example: hair (long, short, or medium); light brown vs. dark brown fur color, etc.

Characteristic *Variation seen*

a.

b.

c.

d.

e.

f.

4. In the space below, discuss the role of variation within a species in the process of evolution by natural selection.

Part B—Adaptations with Respect to the Environment

In this section, you are to examine the environment in which the animal you have chosen naturally lives. Try to see what general characteristics make the animal thrive in a specific setting and suggest what other characteristics, if present, would make the animal less adapted to that particular environment.

5. Write a short paragraph that discusses the environment in which the type of animal you have chosen lives. Be very specific. *Note*—you may need to do some additional research here!

6. Select and list those characteristics that you believe will help the animal fit into its environment. Example: long fur to help the animal stay warm in cold temperatures, etc.

	Characteristic	*Why does the characteristic help the animal survive in its environment?*
a.		
b.		
c.		
d.		
e.		
f.		

7. List a few general characteristics that would make the animal poorly suited to its normal environment.

	Characteristic	*Why would this characteristic be harmful?*
a.		
b.		
c.		

8. In the space below, discuss the advantages and disadvantages of having particular characteristics in relation to the process of evolution by natural selection.

Part C—Convergent and Divergent Evolution

In this section, you are to find another animal that lives in the same type of environment as Animal A. *Note*—the two animals chosen may both live in the desert, but they do not necessarily have to live in the same desert.

9. Choose a new animal that lives in the same type of environment as Animal A. Write the common and scientific names of the animal on the lines below:

Animal B

______________________	______________________
Common name	Scientific name

10. What is the specific location of the animal in the zoo?

11. Examine Animal B and list the characteristics that it has in common with the organism you chose at the beginning (Animal A).

    Both animals have:

    a. d.

    b. e.

    c. f.

12. Define and discuss the term *convergent evolution.*

13. Why do you think two animals that share a common environment have so many characteristics in common? How could this similarity have occurred?

14. What do you think might happen if the two animals you have identified lived in not only the same type of environment but also in the same area?

Part D—Divergent Evolution Due to Geographic Separation

15. To further illustrate the idea of convergent evolution, identify yet another animal that shares a high percentage of the same characteristics with Animal A. Write the common and scientific names of this new animal on the lines below:

Animal C

_______________________________ _______________________________

Common name Scientific name

16. What is the specific location of the animal in the zoo?

17. Examine this animal and list the characteristics that it shares with the organism you chose at the beginning.

a. d.

b. e.

c. f.

18. State and discuss the relationships, if any, between the two organisms that you have identified. Relationships include predator-prey, competitors, helpers (mutualism/symbiosis), amensalism (no relationship), etc.

19. Define and discuss the term *divergent evolution.*

Part E—Predicting Future Evolutionary Trends

Finally, go back to the animal you chose first (Animal A) and try to imagine what evolution would do to this species if its environment slowly changed toward one quite different from that seen at present. For example, you might examine an animal in a desert environment and predict what would happen to its species evolutionarily if the environment slowly became more like woodland. Please note that this activity is designed for fun only; there is no way of predicting future evolutionary trends in this fashion.

20. Restate the common name of Animal A and the type of environment in which it now lives.

21. Suppose that for some reason the animal's normal environment slowly changes, and choose a new environment into which the old one will change. Describe this new environment. Specifically, what will be different about it?

22. Choose eight (8) characteristics seen in the animal at present and show how those characteristics will have to change (if they must) as the environment changes in order for the species to survive. Example, if woodland slowly becomes a desert, the green coloration of a population of toad in a species might "shift" to brown so that it could hide more effectively.

	Present characteristic	*Future characteristic*	*Reason*
a.			
b.			
c.			
d.			
e.			
f.			
g.			
h.			

23. Do you think that the animal in question will be able to live in the new environment proposed for it? To help you answer the question, think about the normal variation within the species. Do any of the individuals that you have observed have any of the characteristics that would enable it to survive and reproduce as the environment changes?

IV-2

Demonstrating Variation within the Human Species

D. H. Keown

Overview

Through this exercise students can come to see the variability that exists in a population by carrying out several simple, fun classroom activities. By considering such variation in its multiplicity of forms, students will develop a deeper understanding of the raw material upon which natural selection operates.

Evolutionary Principles Illustrated

- Variation within species

Background Information

The definition of evolution is sometimes given as change in the genetic makeup of a population over a period of time. This definition is not without criticism for it is the total organism with all of its systems and behaviors that passes on the genetic code. In the case of humans, who have developed cultural evolution, it may not only be the genetic code per se that predicates survival. Nonetheless, the definition is applicable to most organisms. It is the genetic blueprint that expresses the anatomy, physiology, and behavior of the organism. Thus, there is a need to know the genetic material in order to gain an understanding of evolution.

The ties that bind the mechanics of genetics to the process of evolution, however, are often presented without proper emphasis. For instance, it is at the time of synapsis that the variability made possible in sexual reproduction is accomplished. Without it the variability that appears in the offspring is limited to mutations and chromosomal aberrations. In fact, these are the only

This activity is based on "Teaching evolution: Improved approaches for unprepared students" by D.H. Keown (1988), in *The American Biology Teacher, 50*(7), 407–10. It is modified and reprinted with permission of the publisher.

factors creating variation within the species in asexually reproducing populations.

Darwin discovered the mechanism of evolution without the kind of genetic knowledge provided by Mendel's laws. Though he had never heard of genes, mutations, or DNA, he was well aware of the variability of offspring in sexual reproduction. In discussions with plant and animal breeders of the area, he became acquainted with the knowledge of genetics of this time. Experiences similar to those that led Charles Darwin and Alfred Wallace to their discovery of evolution through natural selection are an important foundation for preparing students for studies of organic change.

Materials

Per group of students:

- 5″ × 8″ index cards
- Cloth tape measure

Procedures

Students might study variation by examining many species of plants and animals. For instance, students may examine a type of cloning by vegetatively propagating flowers such as geraniums to see the lack of diversity in the offspring when compared with the "parent" and contrast this finding with plants produced from crossing hybrids. In addition, a litter of kittens or puppies will readily illustrate the variability in mammals quite well. Students can analyze "personal" characteristics such as height, weight, color, length of tail, and behavior.

The variability of features expressed by a population of humans in the biology class is interesting and may show the variation that natural selection might work upon, were we a species exposed fully to the pressures of nature. It is important to point out that survival of individual humans is determined much less by these physical characteristics than for organisms exposed to pressures in the natural world. Here are some activities that can be useful in demonstrating variation within the human species:

- Hand shapes can be analyzed by having the students trace the outlines of their hands on paper. Post the papers on the wall and compare them.
- You may also try using such features as head circumference, foot length, and other morphological features that are mainly genetically controlled to show the variation in the classroom population. With a large enough sample, the classic bell-shaped curve will result if the data for one of these characteristics are graphed.
- It would be instructive to have students compare other characteristics such as the ability to play a musical instrument or engage in sports accompanied by a class discussion of the role played by "nature"

(genetics) vs. "nurture" (experience) in performing these activities successfully.

- Another activity shows the variety of reaction time among students. From a uniform height, drop a 5 x 8 file card between the outspread thumb and index finger of each student while he/she tries to grab the card. Make a mark on the card at the point where each student catches the card.
- Illustrate the varying ability to memorize by giving each student a verse of an obscure poem that none of the students has seen. Place it facedown on their desks and have them all turn it over at the same time and begin to memorize the verse. Tell them to raise their hands as soon as they have the verse memorized and record the times.

Additional Considerations

Care must be exercised with any of these activities to make sure that students with slow reaction time or poor memorization skills are not embarrassed. One way to do this is to make the process a team event so that groups of two students work together to memorize the passages or engage in a determination of reaction time.

IV-3

A Species Approach to Evolution Education

 Dorothy B. Rosenthal

Overview

In this activity students investigate a species within a single genus and observe and appreciate the tiny but significant differences that provide the raw material of evolution by natural selection. This strategy focuses not only on the final results of evolution but also has the advantage of showing students the small, intermediate steps that must occur in the early stages of evolution by natural selection.

> ***Evolutionary Principles Illustrated***
>
> - Variation within species
> - Reproductive isolation

Background Information

Members of the genus *Drosophila* are used to demonstrate aspects of evolution theory. *Drosophila* are ideal for this purpose because many species are available that can be easily reared in the laboratory.

The species approach to evolution education can demonstrate the following:

- Diversity is found at the genus level as well as at higher, more obvious taxons.
- Evolution occurs in small steps.
- Reproductive isolation is a significant factor in speciation.
- Species are usually, but not always, morphologically distinct.

This activity is based on "Using species of Drosophila to teach evolution," by Dorothy B. Rosenthal (1979), in *The American Biology Teacher, 41*(9), 552–55. It is modified and reprinted with permission of the publisher.

- Organisms that do not naturally interbreed and/or those that mate and fail to produce fertile offspring are in different species, no matter how similar they appear.
- Different species are frequently adapted to different ecological niches.

Teachers should note that there are several goals associated with this laboratory, including learning worthwhile techniques such as preparing insects for a collection, making permanent whole mounts of insects, writing a species description, constructing a dichotomous key, and maintaining fruit flies under laboratory conditions. In addition, students may investigate the life cycle of a holometabolous insect (those with a pupa stage between the larval and adults forms), the morphology of insects in general, the importance of objective and quantitative descriptions of observations, and the significance of details related to those observations. The activity is included here primarily as a rich example of variation within species and within a genus. It is possible for students to gain much by completing the examination exercise only while leaving the actual breeding activities for more advanced groups or for those classes with extended laboratory periods.

Materials

Per group of students:

- Cultures of *Drosophila virilis, D. melanogaster, D. mojavensis, D. pseudoobscura*, and *D. persimilis*
- Ethyl alcohol (10 ml)
- Mounting pins (40)
- Small fly-rearing vials (10)
- Foam plugs
- *Drosophila* media, food, and anti-mite paper
- Xylene
- Mounting fluid

Procedures

The laboratory project outlined here is designed for a month of laboratory work by advanced placement students (two 90-minute periods per week). Students are divided into teams of four, and each team is given cultures of *one* of the following species of *Drosophila*: *D. virilis, D. melanogaster, D. mojavensis*, and *D. pseudoobscura* (and its sibling species, *D. persimilis*). Cultures may be obtained from scientific supply companies.

The stock cultures should be maintained by the instructor, but each group should be responsible for maintaining cultures of their own species and observing the stages in the life cycle. Cultures are held at room temperature and ambient light in plastic vials with foam plugs and anti-mite paper using standard techniques.

Initially, all five species are just "fruit flies" to the students, but as the flies are examined more closely students will find that all except *D. pseudoobscura* and *D. persimilis* are quite distinctive. *Drosophila pseudoobscura* and *D. persimilis* are sibling species, indistinguishable on the basic of gross morphology alone. The differences to be noted in these sibling species include indistinct aspects of behavior, chromosome arrangement, and habitat (Dobzhansky and Epling, 1944; Prakash, 1977). The process of learning to recognize the four morphological groups of flies is a valuable experience in observation.

After the students learn to recognize the flies easily, they are given the following assignments:

- Preserve specimens for later study.
- Describe their own species using accepted scientific terminology and quantitative characters whenever possible.
- Devise a key for the species under study.
- Experiment with breeding and competition experiments using two or more of the species in the same habitat.

Preservation of Specimens

Students can preserve their specimens by three methods: dry insect mounts, in 75% alcohol, and in permanent whole mounts on microscope slides.

For the dry mounts, etherized flies are mounted on entomological "points," labeled and pinned to the bottom of the box.

Etherized specimens are easily preserved in 75% alcohol, placed in tightly closed vials, and saved for future observation.

Flies are prepared for permanent mounts by first dehydrating them in 95% and 5% alcohol and then clearing in xylene. The flies are then mounted in piccolyte, using regular or depression-type slide.

Species Descriptions

Each student should be provided a drawing and anatomical information on insects in general through sources such as Borror and White (1970) and for *Drosophila melanogaster* in particular (Sturtevant, 1921). Students should also be provided with an outline of the significant anatomical features of *D. melanogaster*. With this material and their preserved specimens, the students are then asked to write a description of their own species using scientific terminology, measurements, and illustrations.

Although the work is somewhat painstaking, students gain insight into both the degree of attention to detail and the rigor that is the basis for much scientific research. Because of the amount of work involved, team members found it useful to specialize in the different regions of the fly's body. Each team produced a paragraph or two describing its own species, along with a number of drawings. These descriptions could then be compared with standard descriptions of each species such as may be found in classic references such as Sturtevant (1921), Patterson and Wheeler (1942), or Dobzhansky and Epling (1944) or in newer works.

Constructing a Key

In the process of describing its own species, each team will find it necessary to borrow specimens from the other groups for comparison. When all of the species descriptions are complete, it will be possible for the class as a whole to construct a dichotomous key to the species. Models of taxonomic keys are available in a number of sources.

Breeding and Competition Experiments

The breeding experiments consist of placing males of one species and females of a second species in a single culture vial (with the reciprocal cross in another vial) and observing the behavior and reproduction (Dobzhansky and Epling, 1944). By contrast, mutant forms of one species (*D. melanogaster*) can be used to demonstrate that some obvious differences, such eye color, are not isolating mechanisms.

For the competition experiments, known numbers of two or more species are placed in a "drosophila habitat" and allowed to reproduce. At the end of the experiment, reproductive success can be measured by counting the number of each species.

References

Borror, D.J., & White, R.E. (1970). *A field guide to the insects*. Boston: Houghton Mifflin.

Dobzhansky, T., & Epling, C. (1944). *Contributions to the genetics, taxonomy and ecology of Drosophila pseudoobscura and its relatives*. Washington, DC: Carnegie Institution.

Patterson, J.T. & Wheeler, M.R. (1942). *Description of new species of the subgenus* Hirtodrosophila *and* Drosophila. Austin, TX: University of Texas Press.

Prakash, S. (1977). Gene polymorphism in natural populations of *Drosophila persimilis*. *Genetics*, *85*, 513.

Stewart, I. (1990). Representación matematizada de las species, de sus aptitudes y del curso de su evolución. *Investigación y Ciencia*, *168*(1), 85–91.

Sturtevant, A.H. (1921). *The North American species of* Drosophila. Carnegie Institution of Washington Pub. 301. Washington, DC: Carnegie Institution.

The Birds and the Beaks

IV-4

Roxie Esterle

Overview

This activity aims to demonstrate the principles of natural selection by showing that different adaptations (usually physical structures) have value in a specific environment or for a specific purpose.

In this activity, students simulate the usefulness of bird beaks by trying to pick up particular types of seeds with various "beak-like" tools such as pliers, knives, spoons, and so on. It is possible to make this activity quite sophisticated by having students use many seeds and tools and then calculate the ratios of various seed types "captured" with particular tools. This activity may also be useful as a simple and effective illustration of adaptive structures.

Evolutionary Principles Illustrated

- Adaptations
- Variation
- Competition

Background Information

One of the basic principles of evolution championed by Darwin and Wallace is the idea that organisms tend to adapt to their environment due to characteristics they innately possess. The need to adapt to environments can be a result of competitive environments where resources are scarce and survival is predicated upon whether a niche can be carved out. The result over time of this competition and adaptation is a diverse population of similar organisms that do not depend on the same resources for survival. A good example is Darwin's finches on the Gálapagos Islands. Darwin hypothesized that the

---

This activity, originally titled "All About the Birds and Beaks," was contributed by Roxie Esterle, a science consultant specializing in evolution education.

finches developed differences in beaks because the birds had to adapt to an environment where the competition for food was great. Therefore, over time, some birds would develop beaks that could be utilized for seeds, fruit, insects, and so on. With more niches and adapted tools (i.e., beaks), the environment could support more finches, thereby allowing more finches to reproduce and contribute their adaptive genes to offspring.

Materials

Per group of students:

- Assorted tools of varying design, including pliers with different tip configurations, knives, spoons, straws, forks, and so on.
- Two flat dishes (one will contain the mixed seed and one to contain the "eaten" seeds)
- Four types of beans or seeds of varying sizes such as sunflower seeds, kidney beans, and flax seeds (a mixed bag of commercial bird seed may be useful)

Procedures

1. Assemble an assortment of beans for each student group consisting of approximately one teaspoon of each type of seed mixed together.
2. Instruct students that they are to use their "tool" to pick up as many seeds as possible and put them into the now-empty flat dish.
3. Pliers will be used to represent the beaks of various birds, and the student using the pliers will represent the bird. Students should be instructed to use both hands to manipulate the pliers.
4. Each "bird" (student) is instructed to forage for seeds in the flat dish for one minute.
5. After one minute, all birds are asked to stop eating. Other members of the flock can then sort and count the beans, and then record their data in an appropriate chart.
6. Return all beans to the flat dish and repeat as necessary until all the "birds" (students) in the laboratory group have had a chance to feed.
7. Depending upon the goals of the instructor or the nature of the learners, the data may be entered into a table similar to Table 1, or may simply be discussed qualitatively.
8. For those who would like to have students make graphs, the following relationships might prove illustrative:
   - Seed type versus number of seeds eaten
   - Tool type versus total number of seeds eaten
   - Tool type versus weight of seeds eaten

TABLE 1 The relationship between the number of seeds collected (eaten) by various tool types.

Name of tool	Type of seed eaten				
Averages:					

Additional Considerations

Suggested Discussion Questions

1. Which type of bird beak do you feel is the best adapted? Why?
2. Which type of seed do you feel is best adapted to avoid being eaten? Why?
3. Which bird beak (tool) functioned best as a "generalist"? This may be determined by looking at the data for your lab group. Did your bird beak catch an equal number of each type of seed, or was it more successful with a specific type?
4. Which bird beak (tool) was the most specialized?
5. What would happen to a bird in a natural situation if it was unable to catch an adequate number of seeds? What will happen to the bird that

can catch the most seeds? (What will happen to the genes of each of these two birds?)

6. Are some of the "birds" in this activity more skilled than others in gathering seeds? Does this happen in nature?
7. Are all offspring from the same parents identical in their physical appearance? In their ability level? Give some examples to support your answer.
8. Identify an example from real life experience where competition occurs among living things.
9. Do you think that all of the seeds are equal in nutritional value to the birds? Should this be a consideration in experiments such as this?
10. What factors influence exactly how much food a bird eats?
11. What are some of the sources of error in this activity?
12. How does this activity relate to the Darwin/Wallace explanation of how evolution occurs?

V

Biotic Potential and Survival

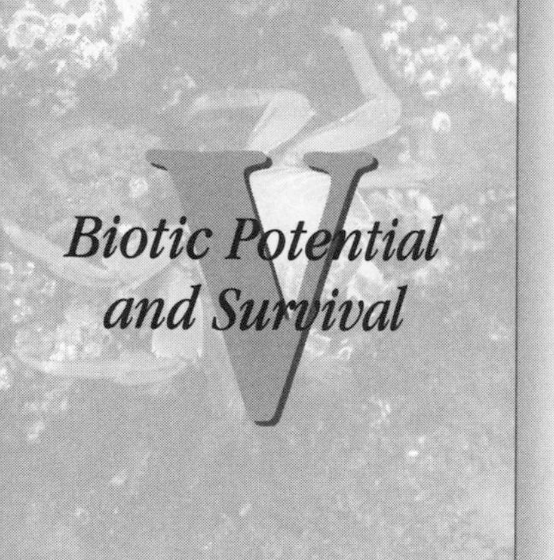

Darwin and Wallace both read Thomas Malthus' book, *An Essay on the Principle of Population*, and were intrigued by the central idea that "populations increase geometrically, but food supplies increase only arithmetically." Although he was speaking about humans, Malthus made a valid point about all populations: they grow very quickly and soon outpace available food sources. Wallace and Darwin inferred that natural populations would always produce offspring in excess of what the environment could support. As a consequence, there would be a struggle for survival to be won only by the best suited individuals. Those individuals surviving would, of course, be the ones permitted by nature to reproduce, moving the traits that made them successful into the next generation. Without overproduction, competition would be significantly reduced and along with it the impact of natural selection.

The activities presented in this section all demonstrate overproduction and competition, key elements in the theory of evolution by natural selection. In Demonstrating Biotic Potential students can examine the growth of a worm population and consider the roles of competition and overpopulation in evolution. The other two exercises in this set simulate population growth. In The Arithmetic of Evolution students may examine unchecked growth of plant and animal populations while Simulating Population Dynamics adds a random effect by rolling dice to show that the population growth is not always without limits.

Demonstrating Biotic Potential

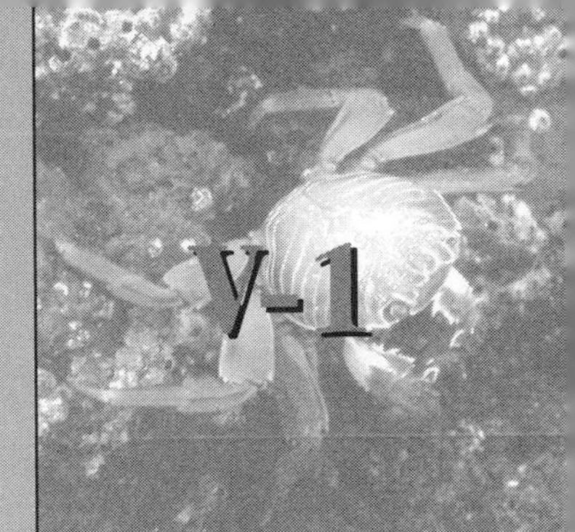

D. H. Keown

Overview

This activity demonstrates the phenomenon of overproduction by using fishing worms to study population dynamics. Students can count and graph worm numbers on a daily basis to visualize population growth. Students will realize the dynamics of population growth by use of counting and graphing techniques while realizing the relationship between overproduction and competition for resources.

Evolutionary Principles Illustrated

- Competition
- Overproduction

Background Information

This activity graphically and concretely shows students the potential for species to overpopulate. Because of this potential in natural populations, most of the offspring do not survive to reproductive age and there is the "struggle for survival" that became the focal point of Darwin and Wallace's discovery. The survivors of the "struggle" would then live long enough to contribute advantageous genetic characteristics to their offspring, thus contributing to the population. Because the losers of the "struggle" usually do not survive, then the population maintains a delicate balance with the available resources. Furthermore, in a given space, waste accumulation (assuming there was no alternative way to dispose of waste) will also affect the dynamics of the population.

This activity is modified from "Teaching evolution: Improved approaches for unprepared students," by D. H. Keown (1988), in *The American Biology Teacher, 50*(7), 407–10. It is modified and reprinted with permission of the publisher.

Materials

Per group of students:

- 4 red wigglers (worms) (purchased from a local bait dealer)
- 1 quart-sized container (cottage cheese carton) filled with peat moss and rich soil
- 1 box of Total or Wheaties breakfast cereal (used as worm food)

Procedures

The concepts of biotic potential are illustrated concretely by culturing some fast-reproducing organisms in a closed environment. Commercial fishing worms called red wigglers, which are purchased from bait dealers, are great for this purpose. Place four worms in quart-sized cottage cheese cartons filled with a media of peat moss and rich soil. A finely ground breakfast food provides a good diet for the worms. Sprinkle the cereal on top of the media and keep the culture moist and cool.

At two-week intervals, the students count the number of worms in the cartons. The students then record and graph the elapsed time versus the number of worms present, perhaps graphing this relationship to show the growth of the population. Students can also measure the average size of 10 worms at each counting since there is another serendipitous outcome to be seen. Students will notice that as the population peaks, the worms begin to diminish in size and numbers until there are none left. Through this exercise students can see a real example of the earthworm's biotic potential and a stark example of the result of overcrowding resulting in depletion of resources and accumulation of waste.

The Arithmetic of Evolution

V-2

Roxie Esterle, Susan Black, and Paul Narguizian

Overview

These activities will acquaint students with the notion that organisms have the ability to produce vast numbers of offspring. This overproduction helps insure the survival of the species, but also sets in motion a competition for survival between the offspring. With the use of various references including books and websites, along with examples of the reproduction rates of various organisms, students can readily understand the relationship between population size and limited resources and the possible consequences of that situation.

> ***Evolutionary Principles Illustrated***
>
> - Overproduction
> - Biotic potential

Background Information

A major influence on both Darwin and Wallace was the work of Thomas Malthus, an English clergyman and economist. Malthus showed that populations tend to increase and that if humans continued to reproduce at the current rate, they would eventually run out of food and other essential resources necessary for survival. Malthus concluded that there would be a "struggle for survival" between those who had sufficient resources and those who did not. Darwin and Wallace both applied this idea of a "struggle for survival" to their theory of evolution by natural selection.

This activity was written expressly for *Investigating Evolutionary Biology in the Laboratory* by Roxie Esterle and enhanced by Susan Black and Paul Narguizian.

Materials

Per group of students:

- World population data
- Individual data table
- Graph paper (semi-logarithmic optional)
- Various types of plants and fruits for dissection
- Tools for the dissection of various plants and fruits
- Natural history reference books and Internet websites

Procedures

Part 1: Species Growth Potential in Plants

1. Students can dissect an assortment of plant parts bearing seeds and count the number of seeds, on average, in each. Such examples might include string beans, apples, tomatoes, pears, or pinecones.
2. Using an appropriate reference book and/or website, students should determine the average number of fruits per adult plant.
3. If one assumes that all of the seeds from a given plant germinate, it is a simple task to calculate how many offspring a single plant will potentially produce in one growing season. In addition, one could calculate how many offspring a given plant would produce in a lifetime. Clearly, there are limits in accuracy with this technique since the average life span of a particular plant is somewhat variable. Therefore, the actual germination rates and survival rates will not be a part of the projection made by students; however, they do play an important role in the real world. Finally, the point of this exercise is to investigate potential rates of production rather than actual ones so it will not be necessary to consider other factors (although mention of them could be helpful).

Botanical Examples:

A single fern plant produces 50,000,000 spores per year.

A mustard plant produces 730,000 seeds. If they all matured, the adult plants would cover an area 2000 times the land surface of the Earth in just two years.

Note: Data for plants are highly variable because, unlike in animals, there are frequently more reproductive structures as the plant increases in size.

Part 2: Species Growth Potential in Animals

1. Using an appropriate reference book or Table 1, students can compare the average litter size of various animals.
2. As in the plant activity, if one assumes that all of the offspring survive, the total number of offspring per adult could be determined.

TABLE 1 Reproductive data for various animal species.

Name	Litters/year	Number in litter (average)	Maximum life span
Bear, Brown	1	1–2 (1.5)	30
Cat, Domestic	2	3–6 (4.5)	20
Elephant, African	1 every other year	1 (1)	70
Fox	1	5–10 (7.5)	14
Lion	1	2–4 (3)	40
Goat	1–3	2–3 (2.5)	10
Mole	1–2	3–7 (5)	3
Rabbit, Wild	3–4	4–10 (7)	6
Seal	1	1–2 (1.5)	30
Weasel	1–2	3–8 (5.5)	8
Whale, Blue	1	1 (1)	3

Adapted from the *Larousse Encyclopedia of Animal Life* (1967).

For example, students might calculate mouse population growth based on four offspring per litter, 21 days of gestation, 21 days to sexual maturity, and a life span of about one year.

Zoological Examples (adapted from Otto and Towle, 1973, p. 207):

An oyster produces 114,000,000 eggs at a single spawning. In five generations, there would be more oysters than the estimated number of electrons in the visible universe!

Although an elephant produces only six young per lifetime, if all of these offspring lived, in 750 years 19,000,000 elephants would be produced from the first mated pair.

A sea hare (a marine annelid worm) produces 14 billion eggs during its lifetime. If all hatch and mature, the earth would be many feet deep in sea hares in a few generations. (Note: In actuality, only five offspring from each generation ever reach maturity as a result of survival of the fittest caused in part by the incredible reproductive potential exhibited by this species.)

TABLE 2A Worksheet for population growth calculation.

Year	# of pairs of individuals	×	Avg. # of breeding time/year	×	Avg. # of offspring per pair	=	# of offspring	+	# of original individuals	=	TOTAL (rounded)
1		×		×		=		+		=	
2		×		×		=		+		=	
3		×		×		=		+		=	
4		×		×		=		+		=	
5		×		×		=		+		=	
6		×		×		=		+		=	
7		×		×		=		+		=	
8		×		×		=		+		=	
9		×		×		=		+		=	

The point of this calculation is to demonstrate the impact of maximum population growth. It is important that students understand that a number of assumptions are made to make the calculations easier. It is assumed that organisms reproduce in the year in which they are born (this is not the case with many larger animals). It is assumed that there is no emigration (individuals leaving the region), no immigration (individuals entering the region), and no mortality (death). This last factor could be factored in by removing individuals from the breeding population each year based on the maximum life span of members of that species as indicated in the table.

3. A blank chart to facilitate this calculation is provided as Table 2a and a worked example of unchecked population growth in weasels is shown in Table 2b.

Part 3: Human Population Growth

Using the data from Table 3, students can plot the growth of the world-wide human population. Label the x-axis "Time" and the y-axis "Population." Graphs of these data on standard graph paper will result in a J-shaped curve. This is a classic finding in populations that are increasing at a logarithmic or exponential rate. However, graphs of the same data on semi-logarithmic paper will result in a straight line. Semi-logarithmic paper is often used when one value (population size) changes much faster than the other (years).

TABLE 2B Example of the population growth calculation for weasels using the data from the *Larousse Encyclopedia of Animal Life.*

Year	# of pairs of individuals	×	Avg. # of breeding time/year	×	Avg. # of offspring per pair	=	# of offspring	+	# of original individuals	=	TOTAL (rounded)
1	1 pair	×	1.5	×	5.5	=	8	+	2	=	10
2	5 pair	×	1.5	×	5.5	=	41	+	10	=	51
3	26 pair	×	1.5	×	5.5	=	215	+	51	=	266
4	133 pair	×	1.5	×	5.5	=	1097	+	266	=	1363
5	682 pair	×	1.5	×	5.5	=	5627	+	1363	=	6990
6	3495 pair	×	1.5	×	5.5	=	28,834	+	6990	=	35,825
7	17,912 pair	×	1.5	×	5.5	=	14,774	+	35,825	=	183,598
8		×	1.5	×	5.5	=		+		=	

Additional Considerations

Suggested Discussion Questions for Human Population Growth Data

1. On a piece of graph paper, plot the logarithmic growth of the human population based on Table 3. It will be useful to use semi-logarithmic graph paper because one of the two values (population size) changes so much faster than the other (years). Teachers should note that the typical J-shaped curve seen on typical graph paper will appear more like a straight line with semi-logarithmic paper.
2. Use the graph data from question 1 to calculate the **Doubling Time** for human populations between 1950 and 2000. (*Note*: Doubling time refers to the number of years required for a given population to increase its size by doubling it.) How much time elapsed before the human population of 1950 doubled the first time? Is the amount of time needed for the human population to double increasing or decreasing? What does that indicate about the rate of human population growth?

TABLE 3 Estimated world population (1950–2005).

Year	Population
1950	2,518,629,000
1955	2,755,823,000
1960	3,021,475,000
1965	3,334,874,000
1970	3,692,492,000
1975	4,068,109,000
1980	4,434,682,000
1985	4,830,979,000
1990	5,263,593,000
1995	5,674,380,000
2000	6,070,581,000
2005	6,453,628,000

Source: Population Division of the Department of Economic and Social Affairs of the United Nations Secretariat, *World Population Prospects: The 2002 Revision and World Urbanization Prospects: The 2001 Revision,* http://esa.un.org/unpp.

3. Lengthen your graph to 2040. What do you think the human population will be in 2010? 2020? 2030? 2040? What information can you find on estimates of future population numbers?

Using the following equations, estimate the doubling time for the current population based on the rate of growth from 1990 to 2000. In what year will the present population double?

$$\text{Rate of growth (in percent)} = \frac{(\text{Population in 2000} - \text{Population in 1990})}{\text{Population in 1990} \times \text{Number of years}} \times 100\%$$

$$\text{Doubling time} = \frac{70}{\text{Rate of growth}}$$

$$2000 + \text{Doubling time} = \text{Year}$$

5. Is "natural selection" in the Wallace/Darwin sense working in any human populations? Provide support for your answer.

References

Biological Science Curriculum Study (BSCS). (2002). *Biology: An ecological approach* (9th ed.). Dubuque, IA: Kendall-Hunt.

Larousse encyclopedia of animal life. (1967). New York: McGraw-Hill.

Otto, J.H., & Towle, A. (1973). *Modern biology*. New York: Holt, Rinehart and Winston.

Website

Population Division of the Department of Economic and Social Affairs of the United Nations Secretariat, *World Population Prospects: The 2002 Revision and World Urbanization Prospects: The 2001 Revision*, http://esa.un.org/unpp

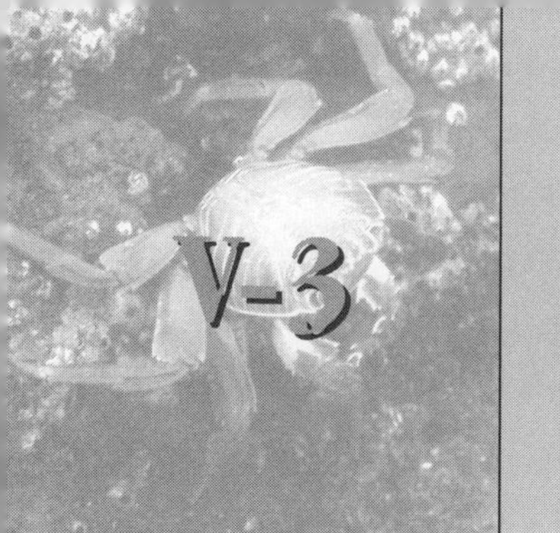

Simulating Population Dynamics

Brian J. Alters

Overview

This activity symbolically and graphically allows students to experience the impact of several important variables on population growth. Furthermore, this activity will model such concepts as carrying capacity, exponential growth, patterns of population growth, zero population growth, and possible extinction. Some effects of chance, immigration, emigration, competition, disease, pollution, and seasonal changes are also involved. Student groups run probability experiments, in which inanimate populations grow and level off due to multiple factors, after which students construct population curves that are different for almost every population (student group) due to chance. This is accomplished using dice and plastic or paper chips (other items may be used instead of chips).

Evolutionary Principles Illustrated

- Population dynamics

Background Information

Organisms have the ability to reproduce vast numbers of offspring in ideal conditions such as abundant food and living space, no competition for resources, and no predators or disease present. However, this biotic potential is rarely realized in nature. Consequently, most organisms do not survive to reproduce fully or reproduce at all due to the "struggle for survival." This concept became the focal point of Darwin and Wallace's evolutionary discoveries.

This activity was written expressly for *Investigating Evolutionary Biology in the Laboratory* by Brian J. Alters.

Materials

Per group of students:

- 1 pair of dice
- 100 paper chips of any color (or anything small with which to keep tallies)
- 200 paper chips of an other color (or anything small with which to keep tallies)
- 1 sheet of graph paper (optional)

Procedures

Population Dynamics Using a Student Niche

Each student group should have a pair of dice, 100 of one colored item and 200 of another colored item (for example, 100 red chips and 200 green chips). The dice introduce the element of chance. Each red chip represents an individual organism that has the potential to reproduce. In population activities, only organisms with the potential to reproduce "count"; therefore, there is no need to mention nonreproducing organisms. Each green chip represents the resources necessary (consumed) per individual per year.

Each individual has the capability of reproducing once a year. A year is defined as the time required for each individual *already* in the population that year to roll the dice once. For example, if the population has five individuals, and the third roll of the dice reads "4" (meaning "one immigration," from dice values below), the population would still only have two more dice rolls for that year. The immigrated individual will not have the chance to roll the dice until the following year.

At the beginning of each year, the population receives 20 resource chips. During each year, each individual will use up one resource chip, to be surrendered at the end of the year (after all roles of the dice have been made for the year). In addition, as above, if a new individual joined the population that year, then there is no need to give up a resource chip for that person (that new individual will eat and drink next year).

If there are not enough resource chips for each individual (not counting the newly joined or born individuals), then those individuals, without resource chips, leave the population (die and, to a much lesser extent, emigrate).

Most Important: If an individual joins the population within the year, the individual *is not* considered for rolling the dice or using up resource chips for that year. However, the individual *is* counted as part of the total population count at the end of the year.

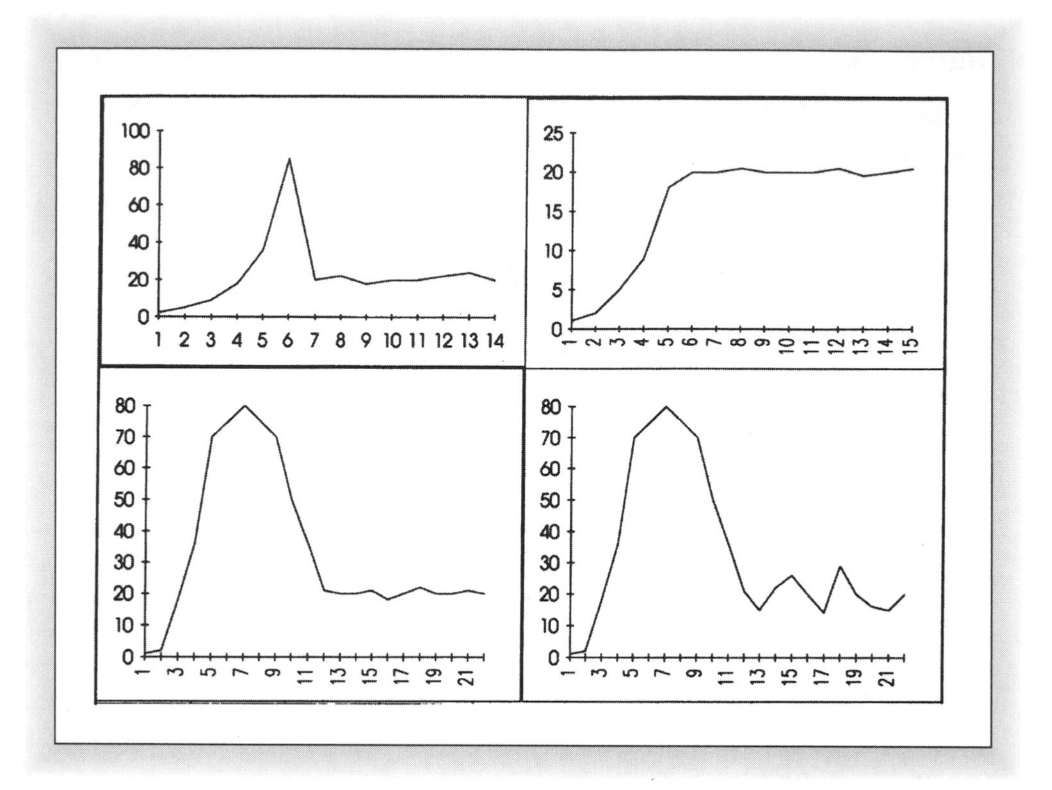

FIGURE 1 Graph possibilities.

Additional Considerations

Figure 1 shows some possible graphs for this exercise (years versus population) that can be used by students. Notice, in each case, a carrying capacity was established. Although each student group will have a different graph for its population, each probably will have established a carrying capacity (except for extinctions).

After completion of the activity, the teacher could lead a discussion with the entire class, to share the experiences of the various student group populations. Furthermore, the teacher should discuss topics such as biotic potential and extinctions and their relationship to the idea of "survival of the fittest."

Simulating Population Dynamics: Student Materials

Stepwise Instructions for Students

First Year

1. Start with five individuals in the population and 20 resource chips.
2. Roll the dice once for each of the five individuals. Move individuals and resource chips in and out of the population depending on what is rolled on the dice:

   If the total is:

   - 2, then forfeit 5 resource chips (due to a nonfavorable seasonal change)
   - 3, then record one birth
   - 4, then record one immigration
   - 5, then record one birth
   - 6, then record one birth
   - 7, then record one birth
   - 8, then record one death (due to competition)
   - 9, then record one death (due to disease)
   - 10, then record one emigration
   - 11, then record one death (due to pollution)
   - 12, then receive 5 resource chips (favorable seasonal change)
3. After the five rolls, the year has ended. Take away one resource chip for each of the individuals that were in the population at the *beginning of the year* (newcomers do not eat or drink until next year).
4. Count the total number of individuals now in the population. Record the number and the year on paper. You are now ready to begin the following years.

Following Years

5. Give your population 20 resource chips.
6. Roll the dice once for each of the individuals that are in the population at the *beginning of this year* (new births and immigrants will roll next year). Move individuals and resource chips in and out of the population depending on what is rolled on the dice.
7. After the dice have been rolled once for each individual that *started the same year*, the year has ended. Take away one resource chip for each of the individuals that were in the population at the *beginning of the year* (newcomers do not eat or drink until next year). If there are more individuals than resource chips, those individuals die or, to a lesser extent, emigrate out of the population.

8. Count the total number of individuals now in the population and record the number and the year on paper.
9. Repeat steps 5–8 until the population has struggled through 20 years.
10. From your chart of year and number in population, graph years vs. number of individuals in the population, assuming an extinction of your population has not occurred. Try to derive a population rate formula by filling in A or B:

A: (Population growth rate) = ( ) + ( ) – ( ) + ( ) ***or***

B: (Population growth rate) = ( ) – ( ) × ( ).

From your population experiences define 1–3 below:

1. Exponential growth (*Hint*: J-shaped curve)

2. Carrying capacity (*Hint*: resources)

3. Zero population growth (*Hint*: where [ ] – [ ] = 0)

4. What is the population growth rate for your own population?

5. What things limit population growth?

6. How does all of the above relate to Darwin and Wallace's "struggle for survival"?

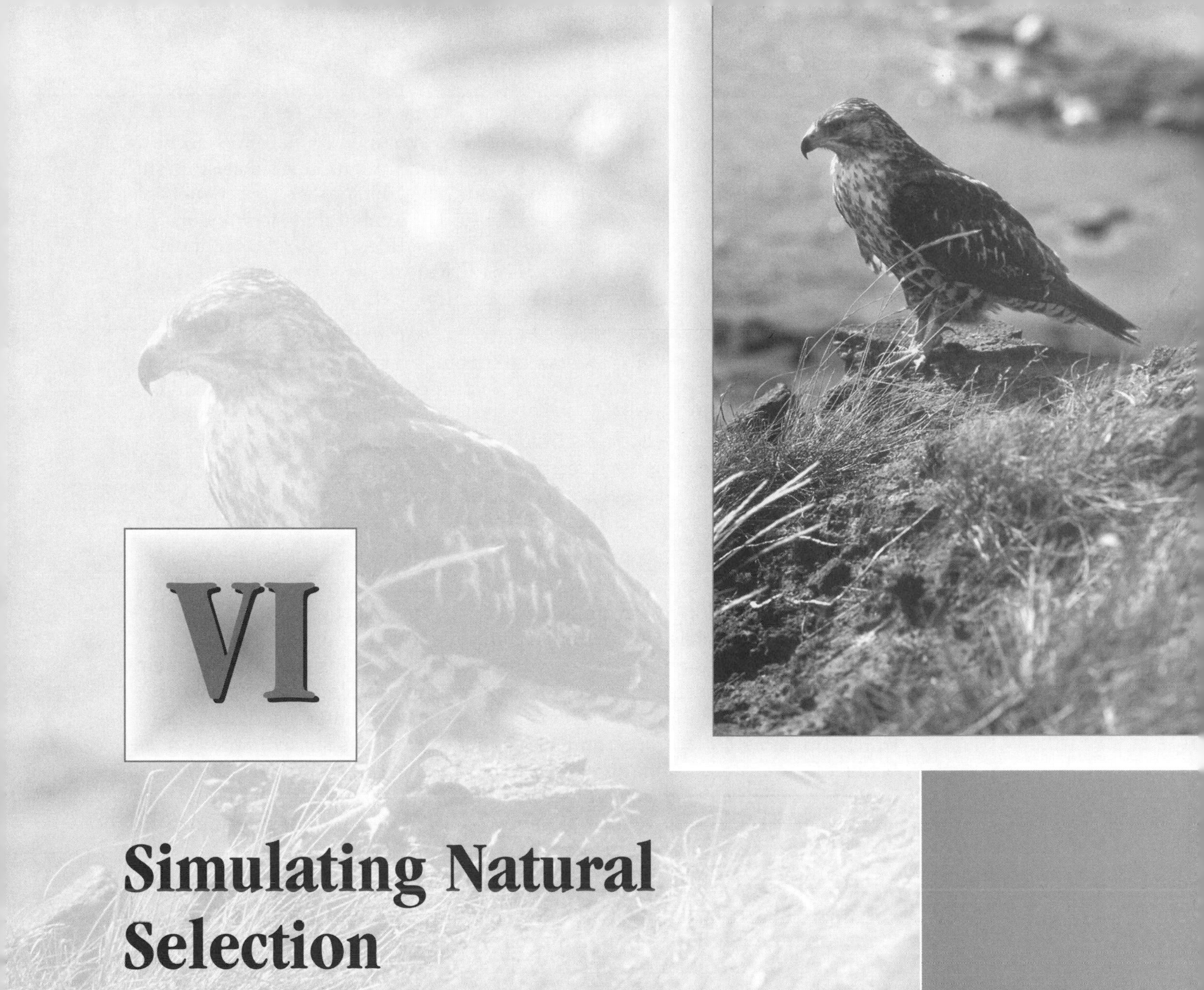

VI

Simulating Natural Selection

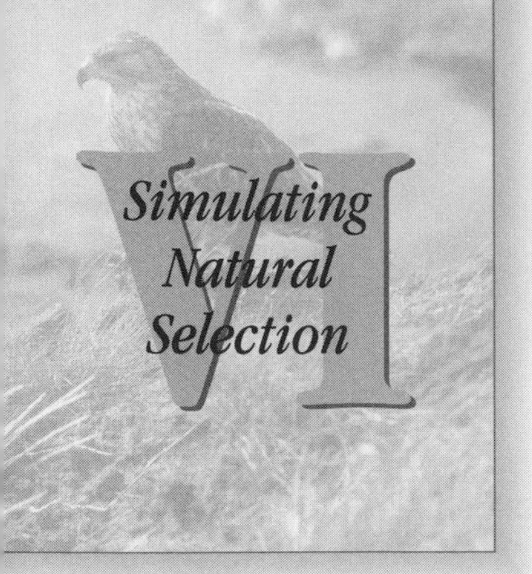

When the Darwin-Wallace model of evolution by natural selection was presented to the scientific community, it represented a seismic shift in our discipline. Not only did evolutionary biology become widely accepted from that point onward, but a unifying theme for modern biology had just emerged—that life has evolved. Natural selection, beautifully simple yet remarkably intricate at the same time, was central to all of this, and it is the focus of this section.

This section of the manual features a variety of exercises that simulate the Darwin-Wallace model of evolution by natural selection, giving students an opportunity to "see" evolution in action. Students will be challenged by complex concepts at the foundation of natural selection and at the same time be engaged in fun and exciting hands-on activities designed to capture their attention. Each of these activities permits students to experience the dynamics of changing populations due to various selection pressures while providing authentic opportunities to gather, record, interpret, and present data.

These exercises represent a synthesis of many of the important aspects of natural selection along with simulations of natural selection itself. These simulations of natural selection are offered in several of the activities, each of which highlights different aspects of this process. Stebbins and Allen in their classic exercise demonstrate through the 'hunting' of colored dots why variants within a population have different fitness levels. Lauer's activity illustrates directional, disruptive, and stabilizing selection as students prey on jelly beans of their preferred flavors. Jelly beans are once again the prey of choice in Smitley's *Predators as a Selection Force: The Jelly Bean Lab*, which demonstrates various concepts related to natural selection, including Batesian mimicry, divergence, and convergence.

Simulations of natural selection continue with an exercise by Maret and Kissing, which explores the link between natural selection and genetic drift by reenacting the plight of a population of mussels inhabiting a rocky shoreline. Finally, the toothpick organisms in Simulating Natural Selection offer a simulation of natural selection that illustrates the concepts of carrying capacity as well as the benefits of having morphological adaptations.

One of the common misconceptions regarding evolution is that natural selection operates with end goals in mind. Instead, much of evolution involves pure chance; mutations leading to variation with populations, for example, are random events. Chance, however, is not the only player in this evolutionary game. Natural selection describes the process by which relatively useful variants are saved, based on the environment in which they are found. This interplay between chance and even the smallest of selective pressures can lead, over time, to highly complex structures that chance alone would likely not produce. Dickinson uses a popular children's game to explore the important aspect of natural selection.

A logical extension of understandin the process of natural selection is to learn how to quantify the resulting changes in a population over time. This can be done through the use of the Hardy-Weinberg equations. The Hardy-Weinberg equilibrium principle is introduced to students by Welch, an activity that builds on the familiar activity in which students "capture" simulated prey using knives, forks, and spoons by subjecting the resulting data to spreadsheet analysis with reference to the Hardy-Weinberg equilibrium. Then, students have the opportunity to work in detail with the equations in the population genetics exercise from Thomerson.

This section features a diverse assortment of natural selection activities, not because any teacher would likely use them all, but to provide the widest possible range of options so that each student group can experience, investigate, and appreciate the principles and implications of the mechanism of evolution by natural selection.

With several of these simulations appropriate for students of the same ability, it might be interesting to run a variety of labs in the same classroom with students from different groups reporting on conclusions reached after completing different simulations. Likewise, as with other sections, one simulation could be chosen for use as a class exercise, and another could be used later to assess authentically what students have learned.

Simulating Evolution

Robert C. Stebbins and Brockenbrough Allen

Overview

This simulation of natural selection uses dots of different colored paper scattered on various cloth backgrounds. Students act as predators to remove the paper dots they are able to find. In a unique step, the remaining dots are collected and arranged by color into a histogram on graph paper to help students visualize what has happened to the species variants. The survivors may be subjected to another bout of predation, thus producing another histogram. Other ideas include having the students wear different colored cellophane glasses to test the effects of color vision on predation. Suggestions for outdoor trials with toothpick "caterpillars" with pipe cleaner bodies.

Evolutionary Principles Illustrated

- Natural selection
- Founder principle
- Predator-prey relationships
- Mutations
- Hardy-Weinberg equilibrium

Background Information

In our simulation, a population of individuals of ten different colors (punched out of paper strips) is distributed over an imitation habitat of colorful, patterned fabric. Predators (humans) prey upon the population and remove 75%. The survivors reproduce asexually, producing three offspring like themselves, thus returning the population to its former size. Asexual

---

This activity is based on "Simulating evolution" by Robert Stebbins and Brockenbrough Allen (1975), in *The American Biology Teacher, 37*(4), 206–311. It has been adapted and reprinted with permission of the publisher.

reproduction is used for simplicity. The process of predation and reproduction is repeated once or twice, after which most survivors blend with their surroundings, and the population is adapted to the color of its background. If 100 animals are used, it is easy to calculate percentages of surviving color types.

Obviously the demonstration greatly oversimplifies what happens in nature. However, it should provide a clearer understanding of natural selection than can be acquired from reading alone. The participants are involved personally in the dynamics of the population changes. Since they are themselves the predators, they can appreciate more fully the nature of the changes that take place. Basic factors involved in natural selection are encompassed by the demonstration even though only asexual reproduction is employed. Asexual reproduction must have preceded sexual reproduction in the evolution of life on earth, and many organisms now living reproduce in this way. Some higher vertebrates such as certain species of fish, amphibians, and lizards reproduce by pathogenesis.

The visual drama of coloration in animals makes it a particularly suitable vehicle for the introduction of evolutionary principles. Yet it should be remembered that the principles of natural selection set forth in the demonstrations to follow probably apply to the evolution of the most far-reaching and profound details of living things.

Materials

Per group of students:

- 1 quarter-inch paper punch, preferably with a compartment to hold punched-out chips
- Construction paper, including different shades of the same color (10 to 20 colors, including black, gray, brown, and white)
- Two (or more) pieces of fabric (3 by 6 feet), each of various designs and differing in basic colors
- 1 clear plastic vial or other transparent container with lid
- Cellophane tape (scotch tape)
- Graph paper (four squares/inch)
- 1 black waterproof felt pen
- 3 small bowls

Procedures

Punch out 500 paper chips, 50 each of ten different colors. Use a wide variety of colors, such as red, orange, yellow, green, blue, violet, brown, gray, black, and white. To speed preparation, fold the paper to four thicknesses and punch out four chips at a time. Put chips of each color in separate plastic vials and shake well to prevent clumping.

Choose fabric patterns that simulate natural environments, such as floral, leaf, or fruit prints. The patterns should be of varied colors and intricate design. Test colored chips to be used against the patterns to make sure that at least some of them blend. Select several designs, each with a different predominant color. It will then be possible to demonstrate the evolution of different adaptive color types from the same kind of starting population. To do so, conduct several demonstrations simultaneously and compare the surviving populations.

Conducting the Basic Simulation

Remove ten chips from each of the ten vials, and create a population of 100 animals of ten different colors. Assign participants to the care and handling of chips. If there are five persons, for example, each one might be responsible for counting out the colored chips. It is important to double check all counts at this time and on all later occasions in the simulation. If this is not done, exponential growth can lead to unmanageable population sizes. Place all chips in a single vial and mix well by shaking. Spread out the fabric habitat on a table top and dim room lights if chips appear overly conspicuous. Empty the vial in the center of the fabric and achieve a roughly uniform distribution of chips by moving them throughout the habitat with a sliding motion of the hand. Then go over the habitat, separate the chips that may be clumped, and place them in gap areas.

Participants should stand with their backs toward the habitat to prevent locating particular chips in advance. At a signal, each predator picks up one chip at a time. After each chip is grasped, the predator should place it in a container (bowl) nearby. This forces the participant to simulate common predatory behavior in which attention is centered on the prey as it is killed or carried off. Chips may be taken from any part of the habitat, by sliding the hands over the habitat.

In order to ensure the survival of 25% of the chips, a quota is prescribed for each predator. The quota is determined by dividing the number of predators into the total number of chips removed. In the present example, each participant would take 15. Arbitrarily adjust counts when multiples are uneven.

The 25 surviving chips are removed from the habitat and grouped according to color type. To remove the survivors, lift the two long sides of the fabric simultaneously and shake the chips into the trough to be sure all chips have been removed. Alternatively, fold one half of the fabric over on top of the other half, spread out the fabric close to the table top with chip surface down, then lift the fabric by its four corners, a few inches above the table, and shake to free adherent chips. If more than 25 chips have survived, redistribute the survivors on the habitat, and remove the excess by predation in a manner described previously. If there are fewer than 25, make up the difference by random selection from among those chips captured. Minor variation in numbers of survivors (two or three chips) can be accepted and the survivor count need not be corrected if selection proceeds for only a few generations.

Arrange the survivors in a horizontal row, about one-half inch apart, placing those of each color type together. Each surviving chip produces three offspring. Place the offspring in a vertical column below each print, using chips from the reserve supply punched out earlier. (Once participants are fully aware that each chip is reproducing, they can simply determine the number of offspring by multiplication.) When all survivors have reproduced, mix them and their offspring thoroughly and distribute them as before throughout the habitat. Repeat the entire process of selection one or more times to achieve a population that closely matches its surroundings.

Preparation of Graphs

Although a colorful record of population changes can be kept through photographs or colored drawings, it is desirable to have someone graph results as they are obtained. Place the graph paper on a firm surface and line up the chips within appropriate squares. Representatives of the starting population can be placed in order of spectral colors (red to violet) in a horizontal row at the bottom of the graph. Cover all at once with a single piece of scotch tape, then arrange survivors a row at a time in columns. Cover with vertical strips of tape. If you wish to save time and chips, use X's to show frequency of survivors.

To carry selection through two generations of survivors requires approximately 20 minutes if all "props" have been prepared in advance.

Simulations of Other Phenomena

Adaptive Radiation

The simulation can be used to show how, from same genetic stock, differently adapted groups of organisms may arise in different environments. There are many examples among living organisms. Notable are the adaptive radiations that took place among Australian marsupials and Darwin's finches of the Galápagos Islands.

Use three or more different fabrics and start a population of identical composition on each. After two or three generations, compare the populations derived in each of these habitats. If a pale fabric (desert habitat) is included, adaptation to simple and complex environments can also be compared.

Selection for Two or More Characteristics Simultaneously

In natural populations, survival frequently is a matter of chance and occurs regardless of any seemingly useful traits possessed by the individual. Often, however, survival is greatly influenced by the individual's total array of attributes. However, at any given time and place one or a few attributes may be particularly important. In the basic simulation, selection was based on only one characteristic: color. To make the selection model more realistic, traits in addition to color can be introduced. Selection then has an opportunity to work on two or more characteristics simultaneously. In addition to color, characteristics of pattern, size, shape, and thickness may be used. These traits can

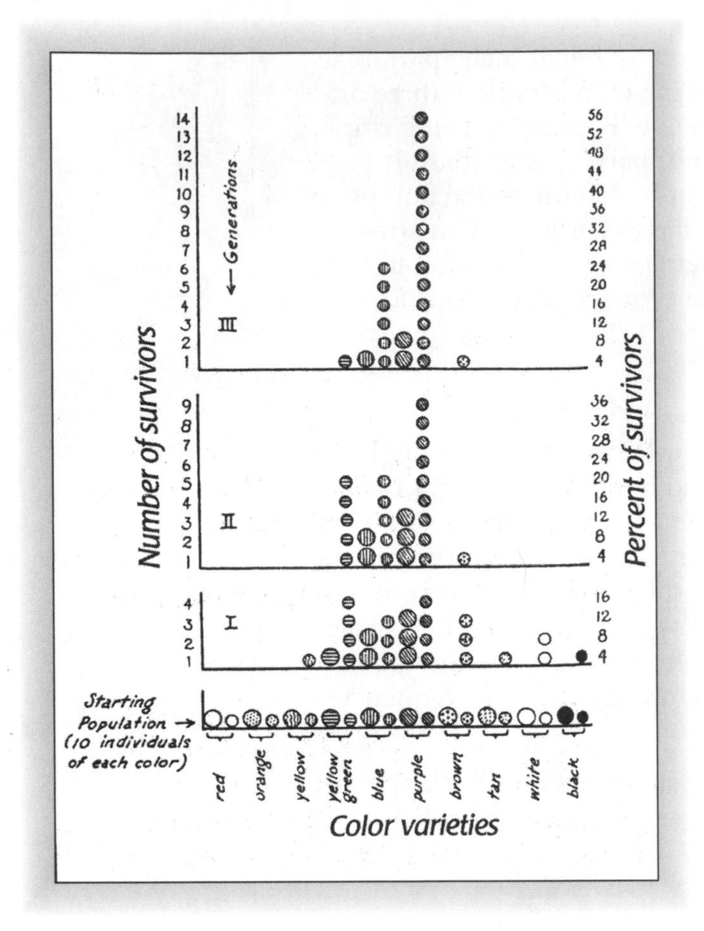

FIGURE 1 Color varieties.

be combined in various ways. Figure 1 illustrates results obtained when each of the ten color varieties used were of two sizes: five small and five large. On the habitat chosen, selection favored small size, and purple and blue colors.

Patterned chips can be made by placing black felt pen markings on both sides of colored paper and punching chips from the marked strips. Half the chips of each color can be patterned and the remainder left plain. The pattern can be of ruled lines 1/8 inch apart or closely set dots. Colors other than black can be used for patterns; felt pens come in many colors. Shape variation can be introduced by comparing half chips with round ones. Thick chips may also be used. The latter can be made by gluing together two pieces of the same colored paper. Use rubber cement or hot-press photographic ready-mounted tissue. On smooth cloth backgrounds, selection often works against thick chips even though they are a precise color match, perhaps because the slightly more conspicuous shadow they cast may reveal them. This demonstrates the problem of shadow concealment that faces otherwise-camouflaged animals in nature.

Selection for a Precise Color Match to Backgrounds

Many camouflaged animals match colors present in their habitat with remarkable precision. In this simulation, an opportunity can be afforded for the evolution of a precise color match. Included in the starting population are several shades of each of the predominant colors present in the habitat. An experiment conducted on a pale background, simulating a snow or desert habitat, may be of interest. Include in the chip population pale yellow and several shades of white (newsprint, construction paper, and so on) and make sure offspring of survivors are the proper shade.

The Founder Principle

The particular course of evolution followed by a population is greatly influenced by the hereditary composition of the original founding group. The "founder principle" is exemplified by the rare accidental transport of a few members of a population from a mainland region to a remote island where they establish themselves and achieve a stable colony. If the parent stock is highly variable genetically, it offers a reservoir of many different possibilities for evolutionary development on the island. The characteristics of the population that evolves there will be greatly influenced by the heredity of the particular individuals that happened to reach the new frontier. Assuming that no additional colonists arrive, it will be the heredity of these founders alone that will provide the genetic material upon which natural selection will work.

To illustrate the principle, place chips (perhaps 50, no two alike) in a container. The container represents the ancestral habitat occupied by this highly variable population. Remove ten chips at random without looking at them. These are the colonists. Replace those removed with an identical set. Distribute the "founding" ten individuals on a fabric representing the new environment. Increase each of the color types to ten, making a population of 100. Conduct two or three generations of selection, keeping a record of population changes as described earlier. Remove a second random sample from the parent population on the mainland habitat and repeat the process. Compare the final population obtained in each of these experiments. Differences resulting from the accident of initial sampling will be present. This simulation can be made more realistic (but more time consuming) by throwing a handful of chips from the parent population toward the "island" habitat, allowing them to fall short on the floor nearby. Assume that the closest ten individuals would have reached the island and use them in starting a population. Pick up the remaining chips and return them to the container. Add replacements for those removed to restore the ancestral population for the second trial.

Predator Vision

Changes in habitat and in the variability of a population are not the only factors that can influence selection in our simulations. One can experiment with changes in the predators. Provide one group of predators with colored cellophane masks and the other with clear masks as a control. To make a mask, cut a rectangle of cellophane approximately 8 by 4 inches and attach a 12-inch strip of masking tape along one of its long sides. Tape the mask to the forehead. Red is an effective color. Greatly limited color vision appears to be quite common among animals. The masked predators will experience great restriction in color vision and will see the world presumably as do certain animals, in varying tones of a single hue. It is thought to occur in such well known predators as wolves, foxes, dogs, lions, tigers, and domestic cats. On the other hand, there are animals such as lizards, many fish, and birds that have good color vision. The subject of animal color vision, however, has not been studied sufficiently to provide conclusive answers. Conduct two natural selection simulations simultaneously, using the same starting populations on separate backgrounds but of the same pattern. In one habitat you might use predators with restricted color vision (red cellophane masks) and in the other those with normal vision (clear cellophane masks). Alternatively, use one group of predators and do the simulation twice, using first control and then red masks. Compare the populations evolved after two generations. This demonstration often yields surprising results.

Possibilities for Further Simulations

We wish to stress the open-ended nature of the basic simulation and the collateral activities that have grown out of it. Actually these simulations are experiments with variables that can be manipulated. Students should be invited to innovate and explore new avenues to understanding. Once the basic natural selection demonstration has been experienced, many people find ways to use the physical materials of the demonstration to illustrate other population phenomena.

Mutation

To simulate mutations, add a number of new chips to an "adapted" population and continue the selection process. In most cases it can be expected that all the mutants will quickly die out, simulating what happens in nature. Occasionally, however, one can expect that one or more mutant(s) will take hold and expand in the population. To obtain a "take" in the short time usually available for conducting simulations, a high mutation rate may be required. It may also be necessary to introduce each mutant in sets of three or four chips. In order that the viability of the several mutants can be compared, each set must be composed of the same number of chips. Often in classroom trials, several selection simulations are conducted simultaneously on different backgrounds. It would be interesting to introduce the same kind and number of mutants into each of the adapted populations at the same stage of their evolution (for example, after the second generation). By introducing these mutants into several populations simultaneously, the chances of mutants becoming established would be greatly increased. One could also experiment with changing the habitat of an adapted population and noting the contribution that mutants might make to adaptation in the new surroundings. Experiments with habitat change would be desirable whether mutants are introduced or not. For example, a population evolved to match a "desert" background may be transferred to "jungle" and subjected to selection in the new environment.

Sexual Reproduction

Trials indicate that the model is capable of demonstrating dihybrid and trihybrid crosses and that it shows promise of demonstrating such phenomena as the Hardy-Weinberg equilibrium and genetic drift. Special laminated chips may be used to represent homozygous and heterozygous individuals. Heterozygote chips contain a colored inner layer which serves to code for hidden genotypic information. Special dice allow determination of offspring genotypes. The dice generate a precise simulation of the probabilities and ratios of chip genotypes resulting from any given cross between individuals. If natural selection in a sexually-reproducing population can be demonstrated, the pedagogic value of the simulations will be greatly increased. Presently these simulations do not show the great importance of sexual reproduction in providing the genetic variation so essential in the selection process. A sexual version could reveal how hidden variability (heterozygosity) can be made available to natural selection through the process of genetic recombination.

Selection in Predators

The effects of foraging success on the size of the population of predators can be investigated. Reproduction in predators can be geared to capture of prey. For example, a predator is required to capture a specified number of prey for the production of each offspring. If it fails to reproduce in a prescribed time, it is eliminated. In such simulations each predator feeds as rapidly as possible until a monitor calls a halt. Successful hunters increase in number. Success fluctuates with ease in detection of prey. Each predator can be represented by different colored chips kept together at one side of the habitat. An event selector (dial with spinning arrow) can provide for random genetic changes and environmental factors affecting both predator and prey populations. For example, a predator may inherit or have an accident causing a change in vision and be required to wear a red cellophane mask or search for prey with one eye covered.

Additional Considerations

In designing these simulations of natural selection, an effort has been made to provide students with a greater understanding of the relationship between an organism's characteristics and its environment, and how adaptive changes can take place in natural populations.

Questions arise as to the source of the variability present in the starting populations. The role of mutations is discussed, as they are the only source of new genetic information in our asexually reproducing populations. It is pointed out that mutations that are disadvantageous under one set of environmental conditions may be advantageous under another and that traits selected in one environment may be selected against in another. Do the terms superior or inferior (good or bad) in reference to a characteristic have any meaning if no environmental or situation context is given? Might this also be true of things other than animals such as cars or books? What is represented by the several kinds of colored chips in the starting population? Are they varieties within one variable species or are they separate species? We have deliberately avoided classifying them. How the color types are viewed does not affect the demonstration of the natural selection principle. However, if the population is considered to be a variable species, the color variants present (if genetic) must be viewed as having arisen solely by mutation.

It is important to make clear to students the shortcomings of the present basic simulation. In particular, the lack of the great contribution to variability made by sexual reproduction and the rapidity of the simulation generation time should be noted. Students should realize that in humans and other complex organisms with a slow generation rate, vast periods of time, measured in hundreds or even thousands of years, have been involved in the processes we have simulated quickly. This simulation of natural selection is more nearly comparable in its rate to that in bacteria and some fungi. Furthermore, predation is merely one of many factors in natural selection. To broaden the conceptual base of the simulation, one might view the removal of chips as the decimating effect of disease, moisture, temperature extremes, or environmental contaminants. Chip color variation should then be thought of as the range in tolerance for the factor in question.

Simulating Genetic Drift and Natural Selection

Timothy J. Maret and Steven W. Rissing

Overview

In this module, students explore the concept of genetic drift. In this exercise, students simulate changes within a population of mussels inhabiting a rocky shoreline. There are two sources of mortality: oystercatchers (large shorebirds) that hunt for mussels visually and drifting logs that slam into the rocks and crush mussels randomly. Since oystercatchers are visual predators, the color of a mussel will affect its survival. Color will have no effect on whether or not a mussel is crushed by a drifting log. By monitoring changes in the population over several generations, students can explore the simultaneous effects of natural selection (due to mortality from oystercatchers) and genetic drift (due to random mortality, at least in terms of color, from drifting logs) on their population. Students will gain an increased understanding of the roles of genetic drift and natural selection in affecting change in a population and come to see that both hypotheses (change through natural selection versus change through drift) can be valid.

Evolutionary Principles Illustrated

- Genetic drift
- Natural selection

Background Information

During the 1960s and early 1970s, the theory of natural selection as a mechanism for evolution was at its heyday. Other mechanisms of evolution such as genetic drift were regarded as being of minor importance relative to

This activity is based on "Exploring genetic drift and natural selection through a simulation activity" by Timothy Maret and Steven W. Rissing (1998), in *The American Biology Teacher 60*(9), 681–83. It has been adapted and reprinted with permission of the publisher.

natural selection. Textbooks of the time echoed that sentiment, and genetic drift received little more than a passing mention that it could conceivably be a factor in evolution in populations of extremely small size.

> *. . .major evolutionary changes would be unlikely to occur by chance alone in any except very small populations (Keeton, 1967).*
>
> *It is certainly fair to say, however, that in the evolution of average animal and plant populations, genetic drift is usually a negligible factor (Baker & Allen, 1971).*

Since that time, the potential role of genetic drift in evolution has received considerable theoretical attention. The growing acceptance of Wright's (1931) shifting balance theory and Mayr's (1954, 1963) theory of peripatric speciation provided genetic drift a major role, along with natural selection, in evolution and speciation. Eldridge and Gould's (1972) theory of punctuated equilibrium relies heavily on genetic drift in isolated populations. In Kimura's (1983) neutral theory, genetic drift is the principal factor in the evolution and divergence of species.

The implications of genetic drift are also of increasing concern to conservation biologists (Meffe & Carroll, 1994). As populations of many species decrease in size, genetic drift may cause a significant loss of genetic diversity, potentially reducing a species' capability for adaptive change in current or future environments. Genetic drift is a concept that an educated public must understand in order to make informed decisions on issues of species preservation and biodiversity. The disclaimer made in old introductory biology textbooks (and courses) that genetic drift is not important because it only occurs in small populations is no longer appropriate.

Materials

Per group of two to four students:

- Habitat (piece of fabric 3 X 3 feet) with a complex pattern
- Standard hole punch
- Construction paper of various colors (at least ten different colors)
- 10 vials
- Graph paper
- Masking tape

Procedures

We present the laboratory exercise using a learning cycle approach, with exploration, discussion/term introduction, and concept application phases. To begin the exercise, have each group of students spread out a habitat (piece of fabric) and scatter 10 mussels (paper dots) of each of the 10 colors randomly over the habitat (for a total of 100 mussels). Assign each group to act either as an oystercatcher or a log.

Students who act as oystercatchers are to hunt visually for the mussels. Each group should catch 75 of the 100 mussels. To do this, students should look at the fabric habitat, pick up the first paper dot they see, remove the dot, look back at the habitat, pick up the first paper dot they see, and so on, until only 25 paper dots are left.

Students who act as logs slamming into the rocky shore should not hunt visually, but rather should remove 75 paper dots in a random fashion. We have found that an effective way to do this is to wrap masking tape around a pencil sticky side out and drop the pencil onto the habitat at random until all but 25 dots are stuck to the pencil. An alternative method is for students to wrap the tape (sticky side out) around the tips of their fingers and randomly touch their fingers to the habitat.

The 75 mussels that were removed from the habitat are dead; they can be returned to the appropriate vials. The 25 mussels that are left on the habitat survived the first selection episode. They should be removed by gently shaking the habitat. The next step is to have each survivor reproduce by adding three paper dots of the same color as the survivor. The new population of 100 mussels will consist of the 25 survivors and 75 offspring. Randomly scatter this new group of mussels on the habitat and repeat the selection and reproduction processes two more times (for a total of three rounds). Each group should have 100 living mussels at the conclusion of the simulation.

The next step is to have the students tally up the number of survivors of each color and display their results using a bar graph, with "number of mussels" on the vertical axis and "color of mussels" on the horizontal axis. To facilitate the comparison of results among groups, have all groups list the color of mussels in the same order along the horizontal axis. When the graphs are complete, each group should attach its graph to the front board grouped with the other results for oystercatchers or logs.

The exercise appears to work best when students work in small groups of two to four. Each group will need a piece of fabric (about 3 by 3 feet). The fabric should have a complex pattern with a variety of colors. (Note: the choice of fabric is not critical; any fabric with a pattern of several colors will suffice.) All groups should have the same color pattern on their fabric. Each group will also need paper dots punched out of construction paper with a standard hole punch. We provide each group of students with 10 vials, each containing about 100 dots of a certain color (we use black, white, blue, red, yellow, purple, green, orange, pink, and gray or brown). Other necessary materials are graph paper and masking tape.

Starting with the results for the oystercatcher groups, have students discuss similarities and differences among the graphs. While no two graphs will be identical, if all groups used the same color and pattern of habitat fabric, the graphs should all be similar. Mussels that matched the habitat survived and reproduced whereas those that didn't became extinct. Next, discuss the graphs for the log groups. Many of the colors of mussels will have gone extinct, but each group will probably have different colors that survived. If some extinctions occurred through this random process (logs), might there be a random and "directed" component to the extinction patterns observed in the oystercatcher groups? Why do all of the oystercatcher graphs look similar and the log graphs look so different? What other factors might affect the outcome of the simulations? What might happen if color was not heritable (i.e., offspring did not resemble parents)? How would population size and mortality rate affect the outcome for the oystercatchers? For the logs?

Now you are ready to introduce the terms *natural selection* for the process seen with the oystercatchers and *genetic drift* for the process seen with the logs. Natural selection results in adaptation, whereas genetic drift does not.

Additional Considerations

The above exercise usually fits well into a two-hour laboratory period. If time permits, allow students to modify the basic procedure to explore the role of various factors in affecting changes in the population. What happens if the population size is larger or smaller, or if mortality is higher or lower? Can sexual reproduction be simulated? What if both selection and drift are operating in a population? Can you predict ahead of time which colors will survive on a habitat with a new color pattern? What if mussels varied in size rather than color (you can even add in differences in reproduction, with larger mussels having higher numbers of offspring)? Different laboratory sections can be provided with different color backgrounds, and the oystercatcher results from those sections can be compared.

To reinforce the concept of natural selection, well known examples such as speciation of Galápagos tortoises, iguanas, or finches can be shown and/or discussed. Generally, such species assemblages appear to have risen after an initial "founder population" colonized an area. By what process might such similar species, each differently adapted to its habitat, arise? In addition to natural selection, how might genetic drift, immigration, emigration, and mutation have played a role?

Consider the problems conservation biologists face in the design and management of nature preserves. How will the processes of genetic drift, migration, and natural selection be influenced by management choices, and how, in turn, will these processes affect organisms in the preserve? Do organisms in a nature preserve evolve? Do they do so adaptively? It is the tendency for genetic drift to reduce genetic variance, potentially increasing the likelihood for small populations of organisms (or those descended from small populations) to go extinct, that concerns conservation biologists today? Imagine if an economically important species were becoming rare and that you were charged with a breeding program to guarantee its persistence. The individuals you might preserve in a natural sanctuary or use to establish a captive breeding population likely will not represent the full range of genetic variation found in the entire species now, much less before it became endangered. Not only do you not know what range of genetic variance is currently adaptive in some parts of the species range, but also you have no hope of knowing if some genetic variants that are currently neutral, or even maladaptive, may be strongly favored by some future natural selective forces. As more species become endangered and their ranges fragmented, concerns of small population size and genetic drift will become paramount in efforts to preserve them.

Note: A complete copy of this exercise is available from Steve Rissing at srissing@asu.edu.

References

Baker, J.J.W. & Allen, G.E. (1971). *The study of biology*. Reading, MA: Addison-Wesley.

Eldridge, N., & Gould, S.J. (1972). Punctuated equilibria: An alternative to phyletic gradualism. In T.J.M. Schopf (Ed.), *Models in paleobiology*. San Francisco: Freeman Cooper.

Keeton, W.T. (1967). *Biological science*. New York: W.W. Norton.

Kimura, M. (1983). *The neutral theory of molecular evolution*. Cambridge, UK: Cambridge University Press.

Mayr, E. (1963). *Animal species and evolution*. Cambridge, MA: Harvard University Press.

Mayr, E. (1954). Change in genetic environment and evolution. In J.S. Huxley, A.C. Hardy, & E.B. Ford (Eds.), *Evolution as a process*. London: Allen and Unwin.

Meffe, G.K., & Carroll, R.C. (1994). *Principles of conservation biology*. Sunderland, MA: Sinauer Associates.

Wright, S. (1931). Evolution in Mendelian populations. *Genetics*, 97–159.

Simulating Natural Selection

 Robert Patterson, T. Custer, and Bayard H. Brattstrom

Overview

This activity presents a model for natural selection simulation including color-matching by prey (crypsis), morphologic adaptation to habit (beak length versus prey size), flock versus individual feeding success, and the concept of environmental carrying capacity.

> ***Evolutionary Principles Illustrated***
>
> - Natural selection
> - Adaptation
> - Carrying capacity

Background Information

The laboratory simulates natural selection in several ways and although it may be used as written, teachers are encouraged to consider building on the various options provided. The first option incorporates the use of toothpicks of various colors to represent prey organisms scattered against backgrounds which permit some prey to hide better than others. This demonstrates the ideas of camouflage in creating or reducing selection pressure from predators. In another version of the basic simulation, short and long wooden matches serve as prey as students holding tongs of various types attempt to collect their "prey" items while exploring the adaptive value of predators' feeding mechanisms. Toothpicks again represent prey while students explore the efficiency of working alone and together in gathering them. Finally, students may engage in an activity investigating how many predators may be supported by a plot of land with various levels of food supply.

This activity is based on "Simulations of natural selection" by Robert Patterson, T. Custer, and Bayard H. Brattstrom (1972), in *The American Biology Teacher 34*(2), 95–97. It has been adapted and reprinted with permission of the publisher.

Materials

Per group of students:

- 100 green toothpicks
- 100 red toothpicks
- Tongs or tweezers (enough for half of the students)
- 100 wooden matches (long stemmed)
- 100 wooden matches (short stemmed)
- Pictures of various Galápagos finches

Procedures

Concealing Coloration

The class is divided into two equal groups, each including a person who acts as recorder. The group is taken to a preselected habitat, which consists of two large lawns or weedy fields. Each group walks onto one of the lawns or weedy fields. The students close their eyes while 100 red and 100 green toothpicks (cocktail or food-color-dyed) are scattered at random in each of the habitats (this can be done before class). The toothpicks represent insect prey. The students then open their eyes. Pretending to be birds, they collect as many of the toothpick prey as possible in a 30-second trial (size of plots and amount of time spent feeding can be varied, with interesting results). They close their eyes again, and the recorder tallies and collects the toothpicks from each person. The trials are repeated until each group has collected most of the 200 toothpick-prey. The red toothpicks are very obvious and are picked up rapidly, but eight or more trials may be required to find all of the green toothpicks. This agrees with and supports the findings of Kettlewell (1959) on the selective advantage of habitat-matching in moths.

The class is next taken to a brown dirt habitat, where 200 red and green toothpicks are distributed and the hunt for them is repeated. Both colors of prey (toothpicks) are easily seen here and are selected against by the birds (students). Usually fewer than four trails are needed to collect most of the toothpicks.

Morphologic Adaptation

To show morphologic adaptation within a habitat, beak length in birds as seen in the Galápagos Islands finches (Lack, 1953) can be easily investigated. Two groups of students are taken to the grassy or weedy plots as before. Half of each group is provided with kitchen tongs or long forceps; these students act as the long-beaked birds. The other half of each group is asked to pick up prey with only one hand; they are acting as the short beaked birds. Wooden matches are scattered over the two plots—long-stemmed matches on one plot and short-stemmed matches on the other. In either case, the matches are to be picked up with the hand or tongs and transferred to the other hand, for holding. The data show the disadvantage of using tongs (long beaks) to pick up the short-stemmed matches (small prey) but not the long-stemmed matches (larger prey).

Feeding Efficiency

Flock vs. individual feeding efficiency can be studied by using 200 green matches on the grassy plots. Half the class "feeds" as individuals; the other half feeds as a flock or herd, each student remaining within 30 cm of his neighbor. The flock or herd usually will collect more food items because of its greater efficiency in finding prey in a restricted locality, its cooperative strategy in hunting, and its social facilitation, as was noted by Etkin (1967) in both mammals and birds.

The effect of injury on feeding efficiency can be studied by using 100 red toothpicks on the green plot. In one group the students cover one eye with a hand, simulating an eye injury; in the other group the students simply place the unused hand on top of the head. The data usually show higher efficiency in the binocular birds than in the injured, monocular birds. The role of injury and illness in decreasing the chances of survival is well known for both individuals and groups of animals. Washburn and DeVore (1961) noted this in baboon troops.

Carrying Capacity

Carrying capacity can be illustrated on two grassy plots of equal size. Scatter 200 toothpicks on each plot. Start with only six people (birds) to a plot. After each trial, while the number of prey items captured is being tallied, cast 26 new toothpicks onto the plot selected for prey growth. The birds on the other plot, which has no prey growth, are soon observed to "starve"; but the competition for prey becomes rigorous on the plot with prey growth. The model can be amplified and altered by changing the numbers of birds on each plot. Data can be suggested to the class for consideration. For example, to survive a species of longspur, a tundra bird requires three prey items every 15 minutes for eight hours every day, on average (Custer, 1971).

Additional Considerations

Figure 1 illustrates a sample data sheet completed by one of the recorders. The data can be cumulated and graphed after the recorder returns to the laboratory. A graph could show the cumulative number of prey removed from the habitat under a given condition of predation (Figure 2). Additionally, a graph could be designed to show the number of prey removed under two conditions: the number of prey remaining in the habitat per trial and the number of prey still to be removed from the habitat. The students can also tally the data for each individual and then rank the birds as to their efficiency in each habitat. Usually students will discover that a bird is more efficient in one habitat than in another. Data on sex can also be tallied; usually males will have collected more prey items than most of the females.

Condition:	Bird no.	1 R	1 G	2 R	2 G	3 R	3 G	4 R	4 G	5 R	5 G	6 R	6 G	7 R	7 G
Grass		*R*	*G*	*R*	*G*	*R*	*G*	*R*	*G*	*R*	*G*	*R*	*G*	*R*	*G*
	1	12	14	7	8	7	3	1	1	0	2	0	0		
	2	9	4	8	5	5	4	0	2	0	1	0	1		
	3	5	2	6	5	3	1	3	1	0	1	0	1		
	4	4	4	3	4	2	3	0	2	0	0	0	0		
	5	4	5	5	3	1	2	0	0	0	0	0	0		
	6	7	6	3	6	1	4	4	4	0	1	0	0		
	Sum	41	35	32	31	19	17	8	10	0	5	0	2		
	Cum f	41	35	73	66	92	83	100	98	—	98	—	100		

FIGURE 1 Abbreviated data sheet used by the recorder.

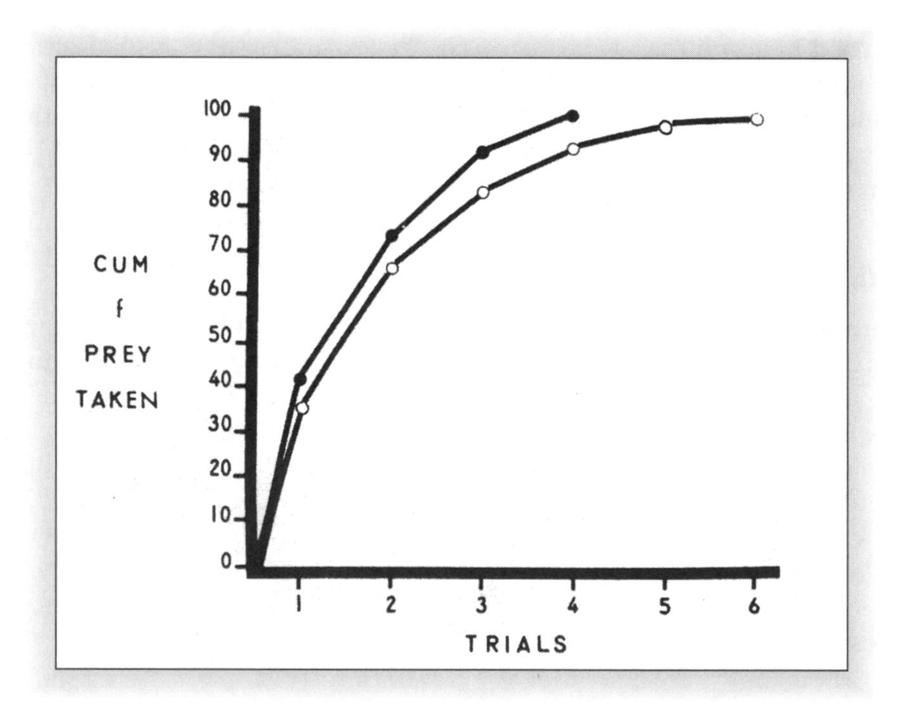

FIGURE 2 Plot of captured red and green prey found in a green grass habitat.

References

Custer, T. (1971). Breeding biology of the Alaskan longspur. Unpublished master's thesis, California State College, Fullerton, California.

Etkin, W. (1967). *Social behavior from fish to man*. Chicago: University of Chicago Press.

Kettlewell, H.B.D. (1959). Darwin's missing evidence. *Scientific American, 200*(4), 48–53.

Lack, D. (1953). Darwin's finches. *Scientific American, 188*(4), 66–72.

Washburn, S.L., and Devore, I. (1961). The social life of baboons. *Scientific American, 204*(6), 62–71.

Demonstrating the Effects of Selection

 Jamie E. Thomerson

Overview

In this population genetics experiment, beans represent genes in the population gene pool. This simulation introduces students to the idea of predictable changes in gene frequency as a result of selection pressure. Furthermore, the exercise presents the idea that individuals homozygous for a certain recessive allele will die before they are able to reproduce, thus causing the reduction in the frequency of the gene in question. Finally, students learn that individuals not selected against and that are able to successfully reproduce will contribute more often to the gene pool of a given population, thus resulting in the maintenance of deleterious alleles in the gene pool.

Evolutionary Principles Illustrated

- Population genetics
- Natural selection

Background Information

The students should have had some introduction to population genetics concepts, perhaps a general treatment of the Hardy-Weinberg law, and some explanation of the concept of selection before they meet this experiment. The experiment requires 45 to 60 minutes to complete, is inexpensive, requires no special facilities, generates student participation, and introduces the student to the idea of predictable change in gene frequency as a result of selection. Pinto beans are used to represent the dominant gene (R) of a pair of alleles and red beans to represent the recessive allele (r). Other items such as beads, marbles, or corn grains could be used instead of beans, but the two different alleles should not be identifiable by touch.

This activity is based on "Demonstrating the effects of selection," by Jamie Thomerson (1971), in *The American Biology Teacher, 33*(1), 43-45. It has been adapted and reprinted with permission of the publisher.

Materials

Per class:

- Small pinto beans (1 lb)
- Small red beans (1 lb)
- 2 coffee cans

Procedures

The original gene pool is established by pouring a pound each of red and pinto beans into a coffee can and thoroughly mixing them. This gives an original gene pool with about equal numbers of both alleles. Students in the lab are divided into 10 groups, and the coffee can is passed from group to group. One member of each group, with eyes closed, picks out at random 10 pairs of beans to represent 10 diploid individuals. The first coffee can is returned to the instructor and set aside.

Each student records the genotype of his or her group's 10 individuals (10 pairs of genes) on a tally sheet (Figure 1) and then reports the results to the instructor. The instructor tallies the results for the whole class and computes the gene frequency for the whole population of 100 individuals (Figure 2). These are recorded by the class as the original frequencies (O.F.) (Figure 1). The instructor has each group set aside all the individuals that are homozygous recessive (two red beans) and return the rest of the genes to a second, empty coffee can. (A remark to the class about not dropping any of the genes is appropriate at this time.) The instructor explains that the homozygous recessive individuals have been selected against, and that they have been removed from the breeding population. The instructor then computes the new gene frequency, after the removal of the homozygous recessive individuals. The new frequencies are recorded by the class as the first generation (Figure 1).

The instructor then adds enough genes to the second can to bring the number of genes in the gene pool back up to 200 (Figure 2). Dominant and recessive genes are added after each round in proportion to the gene frequencies after selection in that round. This addition is necessary to the mechanics of the experiment and does not seem to confuse the students.

It may be most expedient to have a student from each table come to the front of the room with a paper cup. The instructor divides the 200 genes between the various lab groups. The division is by eye, and the students quickly understand that excess genes in the cup go to those groups that are short. This does not have much effect on the randomness of drawing the genes, and the mechanics of this step can be adjusted for a wide range of situations.

As soon as each group has recorded and reported the genotypes of its 10 individuals, the student groups set aside their homozygous-recessive individuals and return the rest of the genes to the second coffee can. The instructor

Generation	Your Group # (7)			Class Total				
	RR	Rr	rr	RR	Rr	rr	%R	%r
O.F.	5	5	0	21	61	18	51.5	48.5
1	1	6	3	40	46	14	63	37
2	5	2	3	52	42	6	73	27
3	10	0	0	58	38	4	77	23
4	7	0	3	68	24	8	80	20
5	9	1	0	80	14	6	81	19

FIGURE 1 Sample tally sheet completed by student. Each student records the group's results and the pooled class results.

Group	RR	Rr	rr
1	5	3	2
2	1	6	3
3	1	7	2
4	0	10	0
5	3	2	5
6	0	9	1
7	5	5	0
8	5	4	01
9	1	9	0
10	0	6	4
Total	21	61	18

RR=21 x 2=42R } =103
Rr= 61R }
61r
164

%R= 103/164 = 62.8%

%r= 61/164 = 37.2%

add 18 x 2=36 beans
.63 x 36=23± Pinto (R)
.37 x 36=13+ red (r)

FIGURE 2 Instructor's tally for the class results for Generation 1. The instructor would add red and pinto beans to make 200 for the next generation.

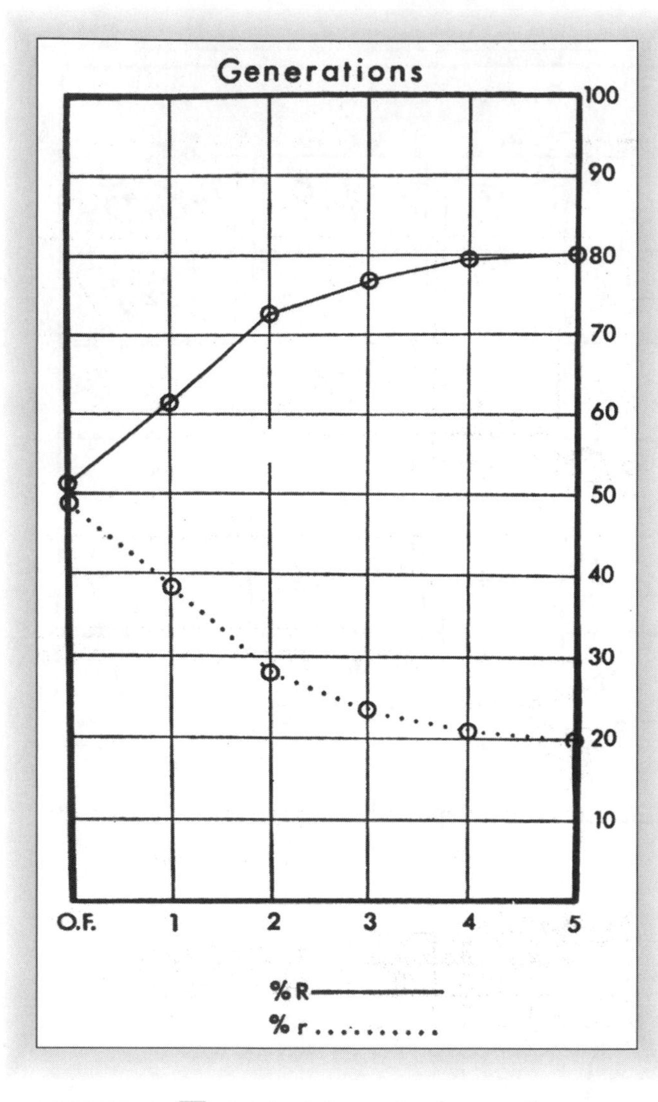

FIGURE 3 Graph of the results shown in Figure 1; note flattening of curves. The graph's coordinates were reproduced on the same sheet of paper as the student's tally form.

computes the gene frequency for the population after selection, which are then recorded by the students as the second generation (Figure 1). The instructor then takes the population back to 200 genes in proper proportion, and the procedure is repeated for the third generation. In 45 to 60 minutes five generations beyond the original population can easily be run.

Students may plot the values for each generation on the graph (Figure 3) as they are obtained, or they may wait until the end of the experiment. We have run this experiment more than 100 times and have obtained results similar to those shown in Figure 3 each time. As would be expected, the frequency of the recessive gene drops rapidly at first, but after two or three generations the curve flattens out. After participating in this experiment, students easily grasp the point that there is an initial rapid shift of gene frequency in response to strong selection, but that deleterious recessive genes are very difficult to completely remove from the gene pool.

Additional Considerations

Even after participating in this experiment, students may not immediately appreciate the results of selection when the dominant gene is lethal. Picking 10 individual pairs out of the gene pool and then removing the individuals having the dominant genes demonstrates the point that dominant lethals are immediately removed from the population.

The experiment outlined here demonstrates a very simple situation, but the procedure could easily be modified to simulate more complex situations—for example, the effects of mutation, partial lethality, or selection against the heterozygote. However, the population seems to be too small to guarantee a reliable, convincing demonstration of the Hardy-Weinberg law. Doubling the size of the gene pool might help. We cover Hardy-Weinberg in some detail in lecture and have not had great interest in further treatment in the laboratory.

A Model of Microevolution in Action

Larry A. Welch

Overview

The following activity is designed to help students understand the precepts of the Hardy-Weinberg principle and simultaneously permit observation of a model of evolution through natural selection. This activity uses students as predators equipped with a variety of prey capturing structures, such as knives, forks, spoons, forceps, and hands, in much the same fashion as the related activity, Birds and the Beaks, also included in this volume. The prey "organisms" in this activity are ordinary dried beans of several colors. When these "prey" are distributed around the "environment," the "predators" begin capturing them quickly. The optional use of a spreadsheet can enhance the impact of this activity.

Evolutionary Principles Illustrated

- Adaptations
- Hardy-Weinberg equilibrium
- Natural selection

Background Information

Prior to this activity, it is important to discuss the Hardy-Weinberg principle. Students need to understand that sexual reproduction alone will not result in a change in gene frequency. (Note: genetic drift may occur in small isolated populations.) Knowledge of the Hardy-Weinberg equilibrium will help insure that students have the background to establish that microevolution (change in gene frequencies) is occurring in the population and is caused

---

This activity is based on "A model of microevolution in action" by Larry Welch (1993), in *The American Biology Teacher*, *55*(6), 362–65. It has been adapted and reprinted with permission of the publisher.

by some force (selection) other than sexual reproduction. The Hardy-Weinberg expression is:

$$(p + q)^2 = p^2 + 2pq + q^2$$

where:

p = the frequency of allele A
q = the frequency of allele a, and
p + q = 1

Hardy and Weinberg independently arrived at the same conclusion when they established the principle that gene frequencies will not change in a population if there is:

1. Absence of random mating.
2. No migration (in or out).
3. No mutation (or equal mutation).
4. No natural selection.
5. No genetic drift (random changes of allele frequencies as occurs in small populations).

Biologists know that all of these phenomena can and do act on populations. Therefore, an evaluation of changes in gene frequency becomes a mechanism for evaluating evolutionary direction and rate.

Materials

Per each group of students:

- Disposable cups
- Capturing device (such as a plastic spoon, fork, knife, forceps, or a hand) for each student
- Packages of dried beans of the following colors: white, red (brown), spotted, and black
- Data tables and graph paper

Procedures

1. Count out exactly 100 dried beans of each of the four colors. Mix these together thoroughly in a single container and spread them evenly over the "habitat" surface.
2. Issue each student a capturing device (spoon, fork, knife, forceps). Of course, the hand "predators" already have their capturing device.
3. Upon an established signal, predators are permitted to begin capturing prey, but they must observe the following rules:
   - At the instructor's signal, predators are to begin hunting and continue for three minutes. During this time, the predators will attempt to capture as many prey items as possible, without regard for color.

- Predators must use their capturing devices to capture prey. Those issued spoons, knives, forks, and forceps may *not* use their fingers to "trap" the prey on the assigned device.
- Predators may not scoop prey from the ground with their cup. (The cup must not touch the ground.)
- At the sound of the "stop" signal, the class must stop the hunt. Prey in the capturing device but not in the cup must be released.

4. Each predator determines the number of prey of each color captured. All predators using the same capturing device aggregate their total, and the total number captured is entered on the data sheet (see Table 1 for a sample) or entered on a computer spreadsheet (see Table 2 for a sample to be used with values included in the Supporting Materials).
5. The average number of prey captured for each type of capturing device is determined, and those predator types not capturing at least the mean number of prey are now "extinct." (These students may return to the activity as the offspring of those predators who captured more than the mean number of prey.)
6. From the totals of each color of bean captured, natural selection may be observed directly. That is, there will be a natural tendency for one of the colors to be more commonly captured and others to be less frequently captured.

Sample data sheet—Number captured. Generation ______

	White	Black	Red	Spotted	Total	Percent Captured
Forceps						
Hand						
Spoon						
Fork						
Knife						
Total Kills						
Survivors						
% Surviving						

TABLE 1 ▪ Sample table for manual data recording and analysis.

Sample Data Sheet* - (Enter Number of Prey Captured) Generation _______								
Beginning Population	100	100	100	100	400			
Prey Color	White	Black	Red	Spotted	Total	Percent		
Forceps					0	0.00%		
Hand					0	0.00%		
Spoon					0	0.00%	Mean =	
Fork					0	0.00%		
Knife					0	0.00%		
Total Kills					0			
F1 Survivors					400			
% Surviving					100%			

TABLE 2 Sample table for spreadsheet-based recording and analysis of data. The spreadsheet may be created using the cell values provided on page 306.

7. From the number of beans of each color captured, determine the number of beans or each color still remaining in the habitat. The computer spreadsheet will calculate this information for you.
8. Assume that each prey specimen remaining in the environment will reproduce. Count out one bean of the appropriate color to be added to the hunting area as offspring. If 65 red beans were captured, you would know that there are 35 still remaining in the habitat that can reproduce. In this mode, we are ignoring other forces that tend to decrease populations. Therefore, count out 35 additional red beans to be added to the habitat before the next hunt begins.
9. Repeat this procedure for each of the colors of prey. Record the new "beginning" population sizes (the spreadsheet will perform this calculation automatically), and return the predators to the field for another 3-minute hunt.
10. Repeat as many times as the class period permits, and keep accurate records of changes in population numbers of both prey and predators.
11. Divide the class into groups to analyze and report to the rest of the class what happened to each kind of predator and prey. A master data form displayed on the board or on an overhead transparency provides

an opportunity for the students to enter their contributions in the appropriate grid and gives the entire class access to the data.

12. You may wish to construct a "super graph" on which you plot the ascension of successful populations and the demise of unsuccessful populations. Examples of such graphs are provided as Figures 1 and 2.
13. Ask your students to prepare a written report of what happened in this mock predator/prey interaction. Be sure to ask them to explain their understanding of why some creatures became more numerous and others became less numerous.

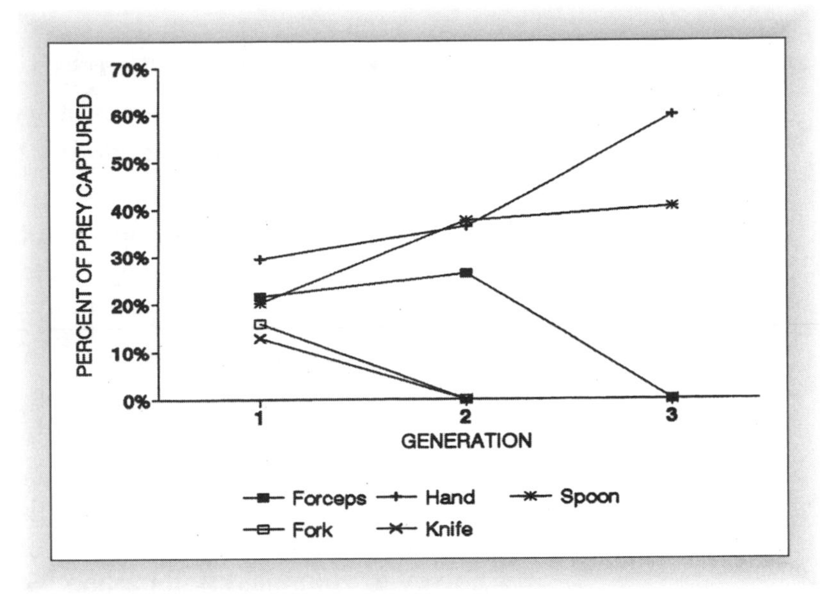

FIGURE 1 Sample graph of population changes with selection among predators.

Students will begin to grasp the concept that populations—not individuals—evolve through time. This activity will open doors for discussion of topics in genetics, population biology, competition and natural selection. It also presents evolutionary concepts in a nonthreatening fashion and stimulates discussion and interaction among students and between students and the instructor.

If possible, run the laboratory procedure for one class from a lawn environment and a second one from a snow-covered area. The differing results emphasize the significance of environment in survival of organisms and underscore the fact that each organism lives or dies based on its inherited characteristics and the environment in which it is found—Microevolution in action!

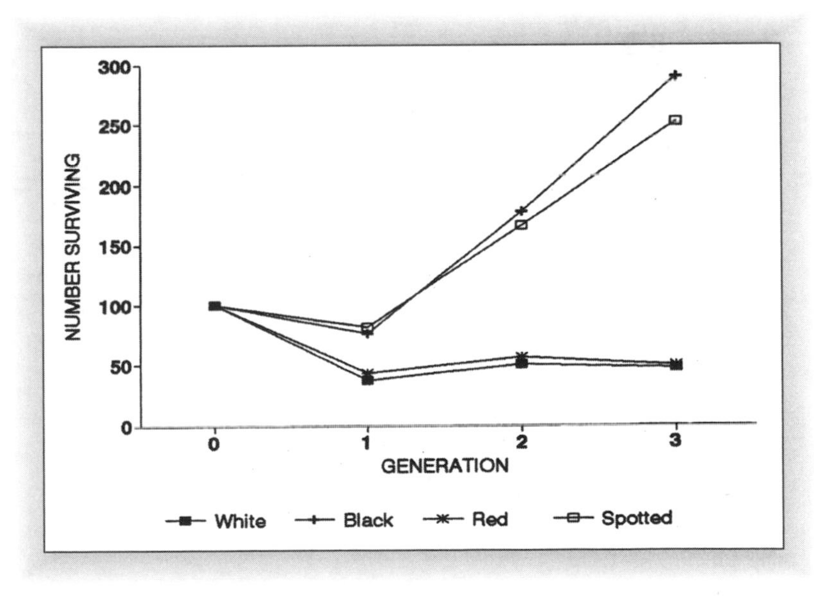

FIGURE 2 Sample graph of population changes with selection among prey.

Additional Considerations

The activity works well with classes of up to 24 students. Above that number, it may be necessary to modify the procedure to compensate for the large number of "predators."

The time required is approximately two hours. If your class periods are shorter, consider conducting the hunts during one class period, organizing the data in a second period, and analyzing data in a third period.

Space requirements are minimal and, if class size permits, can be as small as an area 20′ X 20′. Grassy lawn is the preferred surface but almost any type of surface (grass, concrete, asphalt, etc.) will do.

Students may use a form similar to that in Table 1 to record the number "kills" following each hunt. Calculated cells within the table are best left to the computer. Hand calculations are good practice for the student. If used, however, your class will probably run out of time before achieving your teaching objectives.

Completed copies of data tables are shown as Tables 3–5.

Population Prey Color	*100 White*	*100 Black*	*100 Red*	*100 Spotted*	*400 Total*	*Percent Captured*
Forceps	15	5	13	2	35	21.47%
Hand	22	9	15	2	48	29.45%
Spoon	11	2	11	9	33	20.25%
Fork	10	3	8	5	26	15.95%
Knife	5	5	10	1	21	12.88%
Total Kills	63	24	57	19	163	
Survivors	37	76	43	81	237	
% Survived	37.00%	76.00%	43.00%	81.00%	59.25%	

TABLE 3 Sample data. Predator prey interactions. Generation 1.

Population Prey Color	*111 White*	*228 Black*	*129 Red*	*243 Spotted*	*711 Total*	*Percent Captured*
Forceps	21	18	12	18	69	26.34%
Hand	22	13	31	29	95	36.26%
Spoon	18	20	30	30	98	37.40%
Fork	0	0	0	0	0	0.00%
Knife	0	0	0	0	0	0.00%
Total Kills	61	51	73	77	262	
Survivors	50	177	56	166	449	
% Survived	45.05%	77.63%	43.41%	68.31%	63.15%	

TABLE 4 Sample data. Predator prey interactions. Generation 2.

Population Prey Color	*100 White*	*354 Black*	*112 Red*	*332 Spotted*	*898 Total*	*Percent Captured*
Forceps	0	0	0	0	0	0.00%
Hand	32	42	38	44	156	59.54%
Spoon	21	23	25	37	106	40.46%
Fork	0	0	0	0	0	0.00%
Knife	0	0	0	0	0	0.00%
Total Kills	53	65	63	81	262	
Survivors	47	289	49	251	636	
% Survived	47.00%	81.64%	43.75%	75.60%	70.82%	

TABLE 5 Sample data. Predator prey interactions. Generation 3.

Model of Microevolution: Spreadsheet Cell Values

A1: [W11] 'Predator/Prey Interaction
- Generation One
A3: [W11] 'Population
B3: [W8] 100
C3: [W9] 100
D3: [W8] 100
E3: [W8] 100
F3: [W7] @SUM(B3 . . . E3)
G3: 'Percent
A4: [W11] 'Prey color
B4: [W8] 'White
C4: [W9] 'Black
D4: [W4] 'Red
E4: [W8] 'Spotted
F4: [W7] 'Total
G4: 'Captured
A5: [W11] 'Forcepts
B5: [W8] 15
C5: [W9] 5
D5: [W8] 13
E5: [W8] 2
F5: [W7] @SUM(B5 . . . E5)
G5: (P2) (F5/F11)
A6: [W11] 'Hand
B6: [W8] 22
C6: [W9] 9
D6: [W8] 15
E6: [W8] 2
F6: [W7] @SUM(B6 . . .E6)
G6: (P2) (F6/F11)
A7: [W11] 'Spoon
B7: [W8] 11
C7: [W9] 2
D7: [W8] 11
E7: [W8] 9
F7: [W7] @SUM(B7 . . . E7)
G7: (P2) (F7/F11)
A8: [W11] 'Fork
B8: [W8] 10
C8: [W9] 3
D8: [W8] 8
E8: [W8] 5
F8: [W7] @SUM(B8 . . E8)
G8: (P2) (F8/Fll)
A9: [W11] 'Knife
B9: [W8] 5
C9: [W9] 5
D9: [W8] 10
E9: [W8] 1
F9: [W7] @SUM(B9 . . E9)
G9: (P2) (F9/Fl1)
A11: [W11] 'Total Kills
B11: [W8] @SUM(B5 . . B9)
C11: [W9] @SUM(C5 . . C9)
D11: [W8] @SUM(D5 . . D9)
E11: [W8] @SUM(E5 . . E9)
F11: [W7] @SUM(F5 . . F9)
A12: [W11] 'Survivors
B12: [W8] (B3-B11)
C12: [W9] (C3-C 11)
D12: [W8] (D3-D11)
E12: [W8] (E3-E11)
F12: [W7] (F3-F11)
A13: [W11] '% Survived
B13: (P2) [W8] (B12/B3)
C13: (P2) [W9] (C12/C3)
D13: (P2) [W8] (D12/D3)
E13: (P2) [W8] (E12/E3)
F13: (PS) [W7] (F12/F3)

Using Yahtzee to Explore Evolutionary Concepts

 W.J. Dickinson

Overview

This exercise seeks to show students that achievement of evolutionary change due to chance alone is an extreme improbability—selection is the key. Using dice or cards, the simulation reveals that the addition of selective forces greatly enhances the probability that evolutionary change will occur much faster than if it were due to chance alone.

Evolutionary Principles Illustrated

- Natural selection
- Probability theory

Background Information

The extreme improbability of obtaining complex structures by chance is a major stumbling block to student understanding (and acceptance) of evolution. Moreover, this problem frequently is exploited by "scientific creationists" and others seeking to prevent meaningful discussion of evolution in our classrooms. Difficulties arise primarily from failure to appreciate three important points:

1. Chance does not work alone; natural selection operates on products of random processes (e.g., mutation) to "save" useful variants.
2. This process is cumulative; complex structures evolve through many small steps, not in a single incredibly unlikely event.
3. Post-hoc probability calculations (formal or intuitive) usually treat an observed structure as a preordained "target" to be reached.

This activity is based on "Using a popular game to explore evolutionary children's concepts," by W.J. Dickinson (1998), in *The American Biology Teacher, 60*(3), 213–15. It has been adapted and reprinted with permission of the publisher.

However, evolution is opportunistic and has no goals, so the observed end point is only one among an enormous number of possibilities.

Few people have any intuitive feeling for how drastically these considerations change probabilities (Dawkins, 1986, 1995). Nolan and Ostrovsky (1996) describe a model using dice to illustrate the power of cumulative selection. They recognize, however, that it does involve a fixed target.

Materials

- Yahtzee game
- Deck of playing cards

Procedures

The Yahtzee Model

The game of Yahtzee is familiar to many students (over half in recent sections of my introductory biology class) and is available in most game or toy stores. Students experiment with the factors mentioned above by varying rules that they already know or quickly learn. Basically, players roll five dice and score points by obtaining specific combinations (three of a kind, four of a kind, full house, straight, etc.). Two rules are relevant: First, there is no set target at the beginning of a turn; the combination achieved can be applied (opportunistically) to any category on the scorecard. Second, each turn consists of up to three rolls, and any combination already obtained can be saved (selected). For example, a player with the combination 2, 3, 3, 3, 6 could save the threes (already good for points as three of a kind) and roll the other two dice to try for a better combination (e.g. four of a kind or a full house). In other words, one can accumulate a good combination in steps that alternate chance (rolling the dice) and selection (choosing what to save).

To illustrate the power of these factors to affect outcomes, students play several games with modified rules. For example:

1. One roll per turn; fill in scores strictly in the order on the scorecard (no accumulation, fixed target).
2. One roll per turn; fill in scores in any order (no accumulation, flexible target).
3. Three rolls per turn; scores in strict order (accumulation allowed, fixed target).
4. Three rolls per turn; scores in any order (accumulation and flexible target both allowed).
5. More rolls per turn (e.g., 5 or 10); scores in any order (more extensive accumulation).
6. Unlimited rolls per turn; scores in any order. How many rolls are needed to get a perfect score?

Yahtzee® PLAYER'S NAME ____________

SCORE CARD

UPPER SECTION	HOW TO SCORE	GAME #1	GAME #2	GAME #3	GAME #4	GAME #5	GAME #6	
Aces ⚀ = 1	Count and Add Only Aces	1	1	4	2	4	5	6
Twos ⚁ = 2	Count and Add Only Twos	2	2	2	2	8	10	5
Threes ⚂ = 3	Count and Add Only Threes	3	6	9	9	9	15	11
Fours ⚃ = 4	Count and Add Only Fours	8	8	4	16	20	20	18
Fives ⚄ = 5	Count and Add Only Fives	0	10	20	10	25	25	29
Sixes ⚅ = 6	Count and Add Only Sixes	0	12	18	12	30	30	9
TOTAL SCORE	→	14	39	57	51	96	105	
BONUS If total score is 63 or over	SCORE 35	0	0	0	0	35	35	
TOTAL Of Upper Section	→	14	39	57	51	131	140	
LOWER SECTION								
3 of a kind	Add Total Of All Dice	0	26	0	23	28	30	6
4 of a kind	Add Total Of All Dice	0	17	20	29	30	30	5
Full House	SCORE 25	0	0	0	25	25	25	3
Sm. Straight Sequence of 4	SCORE 30	0	0	30	30	30	30	1
Lg. Straight Sequence of 5	SCORE 40	0	40	40	40	40	40	2
YAHTZEE 5 of a kind	SCORE 50	0	0	0	0	50	50	7
Chance	Score Total Of All 5 Dice	15	22	21	14	25	30	14
YAHTZEE BONUS	✓ FOR EACH BONUS					✓✓✓✓	✓✓✓✓✓✓✓✓✓	
	SCORE 100 PER ✓	0	0	0	0	400	900	
TOTAL Of Lower Section	→	15	105	111	161	628	1135	
TOTAL Of Upper Section	→	14	39	57	51	131	140	
GRAND TOTAL	→	29	144	168	212	759	1275	116

FIGURE 1 Trial runs of Yahtzee under different rules. For games #1–#6, the rules were modified as follows (see text): #1—one roll, fixed order; #2—one roll, flexible order; #3—three rolls, fixed order; #4—three rolls, flexible order (standard rules); #5—ten rolls, flexible order; #6—unlimited rolls, flexible order. The numbers entered in the right margin record the rolls actually used for each turn in game #6.

A representative set of trials is illustrated in Figure 1. Note that the score improves dramatically with either cumulative selection or flexible target, and we can achieve incredibly improbable results when the two are combined. Even my perfect game took only 116 rolls, just about three times the 39 allowed by standard rules. I point out to students that billions of games must have been played by millions of children (and parents) over many years, but it is certain that no one has ever approached a perfect score. Yet we can achieve the result in a few minutes with a modest increase in the cumulative selection over that allowed by standard rules!

Some Probability Calculations

Advanced students might like to evaluate the probability of achieving a perfect score. This is very complex under standard rules, but manageable for the most restrictive rules (one roll, fixed order). For that case, the probability of a perfect game is about 4.9×10^{-43}. In other words, we should expect to get one perfect game in about 2×10^{-2} tries. Assuming it takes a minute to play one game (a little over a half million per year), the expected time to obtain one perfect game is about 3.9×10^{36} years, or a billion times the age of the Earth!

With some guidance, students may be able to reproduce these probability calculations. For each scorecard entry except "full house," "small straight," "large straight," and "YAHTZEE" there is only one way to earn the maximum score. The probability of achieving that specific target in a single roll is, of course, $(1/6)^5$ or 1/7776. For the four exceptions, this figure can be corrected by determining the number of ways in which equally valuable combinations can be obtained (a good exercise in careful reasoning) and multiplying that number times 1/7776. For example, any of six combinations counts for "YAHTZEE," so the probability of getting one of them in a single try is 6 × 1 / 7776 = 1/1296. Finally, the individual probabilities for the 13 different entries on a scorecard must be multiplied together.

A Poker Model

An extended version of "draw" poker also illustrates cumulative selection, and the associated probability calculations are easier. The probability of getting any specific combination of five cards (e.g., an unbeatable royal flush in spades) in a single try (five consecutive cards drawn from a well-shuffled deck) is 5/52 × 4/51 × 3/50 × 2/49 × 1/48 = 1/2,598,960. Allowing only 15 seconds per hand to shuffle and deal, we expect on average to get one such hand in a little over a year of continuous trials (2,102,400 hands per year). However, we can get our perfect hand relatively quickly if we are allowed a series of turns in which we save what we like, shuffle the remaining cards, and draw to fill out a five-card hand. To calculate the expected time, we can break the process down to a series of five steps, determine the time expected for each step, and total those numbers. Thus, in the first step, any one of five cards is acceptable, so our probability in any try is 5/52. Inverting that, we need an average of 52/5 = 10.4 tries to find the first card we want to keep. By similar reasoning on subsequent steps, our total expected number of tries is 52/5 + 51/4 + 50/3 + 49/2 + 48 = 112.3. With our 15-second time allowance per deal, we can do that in under 30 minutes.

Draw poker also allows us to appreciate one other important aspect of evolution. Some potential phenotypes that would be highly adaptive may never be achieved because each intermediate step along an evolutionary pathway must itself be an improvement. That is, natural selection is a blind process that operates without plan or foresight, so there is no way to take steps that have no immediate benefit even if they could open up future possibilities (Kauffman, 1987; Dickinson, 1988). Within the poker model, this amounts to a requirement that one save only combinations that are themselves playable poker hands, and that each newly saved card improves on what you already had. Students will find that they can still draw four of a kind, but drawing four aces is hard. Furthermore, straights and flushes are almost impossible.

Additional Considerations

Probability calculations are not feasible for complex biological structures, but are relatively straightforward for linear polymers like DNA and proteins. For example, the probability of assembling a specific sequence of 100 amino acids in a single random try is $1/100^{20}$ (because any of 20 different amino acids can occupy each position) or $1/10^{40}$ (rather close to our chance of a perfect Yahtzee game). It is sometimes claimed that this proves the impossibility of evolving even one protein, let alone a living cell. Comparison to our models reveals the fatal flaws in that argument. First, the present sequence of any protein was not formed in a single chance event; it accumulated through many rounds of mutation and selection. Second, that sequence is only one among an enormous set that might have evolved. To begin with, we know from comparing homologous proteins in different species that a wide range of amino acids can be substituted at many positions with essentially no effect on function. An even greater number of modifications produce less efficient proteins that still would be useful (and possible steps along a cumulative selection pathway). Finally (and most importantly), remember that the function was not preordained; the DNA that encodes our protein might have taken on any of an almost infinite variety of other useful functions (the opportunistic aspect of our models).

For more complex structures, we can still help students see how cumulative selection makes the seemingly impossible merely time consuming. The eye is a favorite subject for creationists; they like to claim that it is useful only if all parts are perfectly developed, so evolution in gradual steps would have been impossible. This is obvious nonsense, as students can prove to themselves. Even with eyes closed, they can tell when a bright light is switched on or when something passes between them and the light. Can they think of organisms and situations for which that limited ability would be advantageous (relative to being totally blind)? They also can experiment with different degrees of visual acuity by having a partner move things to different positions within their visual fields (while fixing their gaze at a target in front of them). At the very periphery, you detect motion but can't identify objects. As things are moved closer to the center of the field, more and more detail is seen. Is peripheral vision useful even though not very clear? Would an eye with a best image comparable to our peripheral vision be advantageous in a world where everyone else was blind or could detect only light and dark? Could each small step from fuzzy to sharp be favored by natural selection?

For another example, have students compare adaptations across the following series: mink, otter, sea lion, seal, and dolphin. This is not a real evolutionary progression, but it helps us imagine how a transition between two very different lifestyles can be accomplished through a smooth series of steps, each well adapted to its own way of life. For more detail on the eye as well as other examples of cumulative selection, see Dawkins (1986) Chapter 4 or (1995) Chapter 3.

While it often is possible to connect very different states by way of plausible intermediates, the requirement that each step have immediate selective advantage sometimes imposes constraints akin to those noted in the poker model. In the real world, this may account for adaptations that we can imagine but never actually observe. Why, for example, are there no winged monkeys like the imaginary ones in the *Wizard of Oz* (with both arms and wings)? That would seem to be a nifty adaptation. Perhaps it is because selection can convert a leg (as present in ancestral mammals) into either an arm or a wing (as in bats) through multiple small steps, each advantageous relative to what came before, but the earliest steps in "sprouting" a whole new pair of appendages (e.g., stumps sticking out of the back) would confer no advantage. However, it is difficult to rule out alternative explanations. It is possible that appropriate mutations never occurred or even that wings aren't such a good idea for monkeys after all.

We can see the effects of constraint with more confidence in the failure of evolution to correct some rather glaring flaws. The eye again provides a good example. That wonderful organ is "wired" wrong; the nerves that carry signals from the light sensitive rods and cones toward the brain are in front of the retina, right in the light path! We even have a blind spot in each eye where the optic nerve passes through the retina. Why can't this be "fixed"? We argue that once the "choice" was made to put nerves in front (probably in a light detector so crude that it didn't really matter), there was no way back. As vision gradually improved, any mutation tending to undo this initial "bad design" would produce an eye that didn't work as well as the one already achieved. Natural selection can produce weird and wonderful things, but it is completely incapable of taking the long way around even if the ultimate product would be better. The resulting examples of less-than-optimum design provide some of the most vivid evidence that organisms indeed are products of blind natural selection.

References

Dawkins, R. (1986). *The blind watch-maker*. New York: W.W. Norton.

Dawkins, R. (1995). *River out of Eden*. New York: BasicBooks.

Dickinson, W.J. (1988). On the architecture of regulatory systems: Evolutionary insights and implications. *BioEssays, 8*, 204–08.

Kauffman, S.A. (1987). Developmental logic and its evolution. *BioEssays, 6*, 82–87.

Nolan, M.J., & Ostrovsky, D.S. (1996). A gambler's model of natural selection. *The American Biology Teacher, 58*(5), 300–01.

Investigating Evolutionary Principles:

A Jelly Bean Approach

VI-7

Thomas E. Lauer

Overview

This exercise uses the students' sense of taste in investigating aspects of selection. Taste can be used as an effective learning tool in the classroom, particularly when illustrating the ecological significance of predation. Additionally, students make great predators and can be counted upon to eat at almost any time. Taste can also be incorporated with sight and sound to enhance the learning experience. Students clearly have taste preferences, and this can be used when illustrating any number of ecological concepts, particularly when food, foraging, predator or prey species are discussed. Finally, this activity gives students an opportunity to identify how directional, disruptive, and stabilizing selection occurs in phenotypes using predation as the selection pressure and to consider how two species competing for the same food resources exhibit niche partitioning, thereby enabling coexistence.

Evolutionary Principles Illustrated

- Competition
- Types of selection
- Predator-prey relationships
- Natural selection

Background Information

The prey species used for this exercise is the Jelly Belly jelly bean. Two specific examples of how Jelly Bellies can be used in the classroom are listed below as well as some other less detailed examples of applications to other teaching concepts. You can find a more complete description of the ecological principles discussed in this presentation by referring to Smith (1995), Begon et al. (1996), or Krohne (1997).

This activity is based on "Jelly Belly Jelly beans and evolutionary principles in the classroom: Appealing to the students' stomachs," by Thomas Lauer (2000), in *The American Biology Teacher, 62*(1), 42–45. It has been adapted and reprinted with permission of the publisher.

Jelly Bellies not only come in different colors, but also they have a wide range of distinctive and unique flavors (40 in all) that can be counted upon to entice or discourage predatory students. These two features can be used to illustrate specific biological adaptations whenever taste or color (e.g., mimicry, camouflage) choices are made by predators or prey. Both features can be combined to extend the concept to a more complex interaction. Among those flavors used successfully are licorice, toasted marshmallow, margarita, root beer, orange juice, tangerine, cantaloupe, jalapeno, lemon, blueberry, and sizzling cinnamon. The "best" flavors are those that some but not all students prefer. A complete listing of Jelly Belly jelly beans can be found at sales locations or by contacting the company on the Internet.

Materials

Per class:

- 3–8 bags of assorted Jelly Bellies characteristic of those described below

Procedures

Exercise #1—Illustrating the three fundamental modes of natural selection.

Limit distribution of jelly beans to fewer than six students in any given class. Although only a limited number of students directly participate, anticipation is great among all students in the class. In addition, students chosen for the testing usually share with those around them, expanding the direct student involvement. This technique has been used successfully in classes of 70 students with no apparent loss of attention by those not directly involved.

1. The procedure requires three bags (minimum) of Jelly Belly jelly beans with an assortment of colors, one bag for each of three selection types (directional, stabilizing, and disruptive). Typically one should use six colors from light (yellow) to dark (black) as shown below, but many combinations work equally as well. Always include licorice as most students either really like or dislike the flavor and it is at the extreme end of the color range. The number of beans used is a compromise between minimizing the cost of the jelly beans and obtaining a "normal" or "bell-shaped" distribution of color frequencies. Colors represent the array of phenotypes found within a population of a single prey species.

Color/Flavor	Number of Beans
Yellow / Lemon	5
Green / Margarita	14
Orange / Cantaloupe	31
Red / Very Cherry	28
Blue / Blueberry	16
Black / Licorice	6
Total per bag	100

2. At the beginning of class, solicit volunteers to eat the Jelly Bellies. Depending on the selection process, you may or may not choose those who like or dislike certain flavors, such as licorice. (If students don't like licorice and you want them to eat these beans, they may not follow your instructions.) Included with each bag of jelly beans is an instruction sheet that students must follow. Do not tell the rest of the class what the instructions say. Examples of the instructions for each of the three selection types are given in the following paragraphs. Remember to give instructions that do not allow students to eat more than about half of the beans (at least initially).

Instructions Given to a Student for Directional Selection

In the next 15 minutes, you must eat between 40 and 60 jelly beans. However, you don't like licorice or anything that resembles it. Don't eat any of those beans. You may allow consumption participation from the students around you, provided the instructions are not violated.

Instructions Given to a Student for Stabilizing Selection

In the next 15 minutes, you must eat between 20 and 30 jelly beans. You love licorice and anything that looks like it, as well as the color of the noonday sun. Eat these beans first. You may allow consumption participation from the students around you, provided the instructions are not violated.

Instructions Given to a Student for Disruptive Selection

In the next 15 minutes, you must eat between 40 and 60 jelly beans. You always eat the most common beans, because you hate searching for the ones that are few in number. However, you must eat one color at a time until it is gone. You may allow consumption participation from the students around you, provided that instructions are not violated.

3. During the period of student predation on the jelly beans, cover the ideas of directional, stabilizing, and disruptive selection. Included in this discussion is the theory of fitness, or the ability of organisms to pass on their genetic character to the next generation. Selection, of course, takes place over a number of generations and this should be emphasized. You may want to include discussion of changes in phenotypes under various kinds of selection pressure (see Figure 1 for examples).
4. Check with the students who were eating the jelly beans and then ask students to tell the class what directions they were given to limit their consumption of jelly beans, followed by the number and kinds of jelly beans they have left in their jelly bean prey populations. The distribution should be similar to the theoretical "new" frequencies shown earlier in the graphs for each of the three selection types.

Exercise #2—Illustrating competitive exclusion and how competition structures communities.

Limit distribution of jelly beans to four or five students. This number parallels the number of flavors used in the examples. Students usually share with

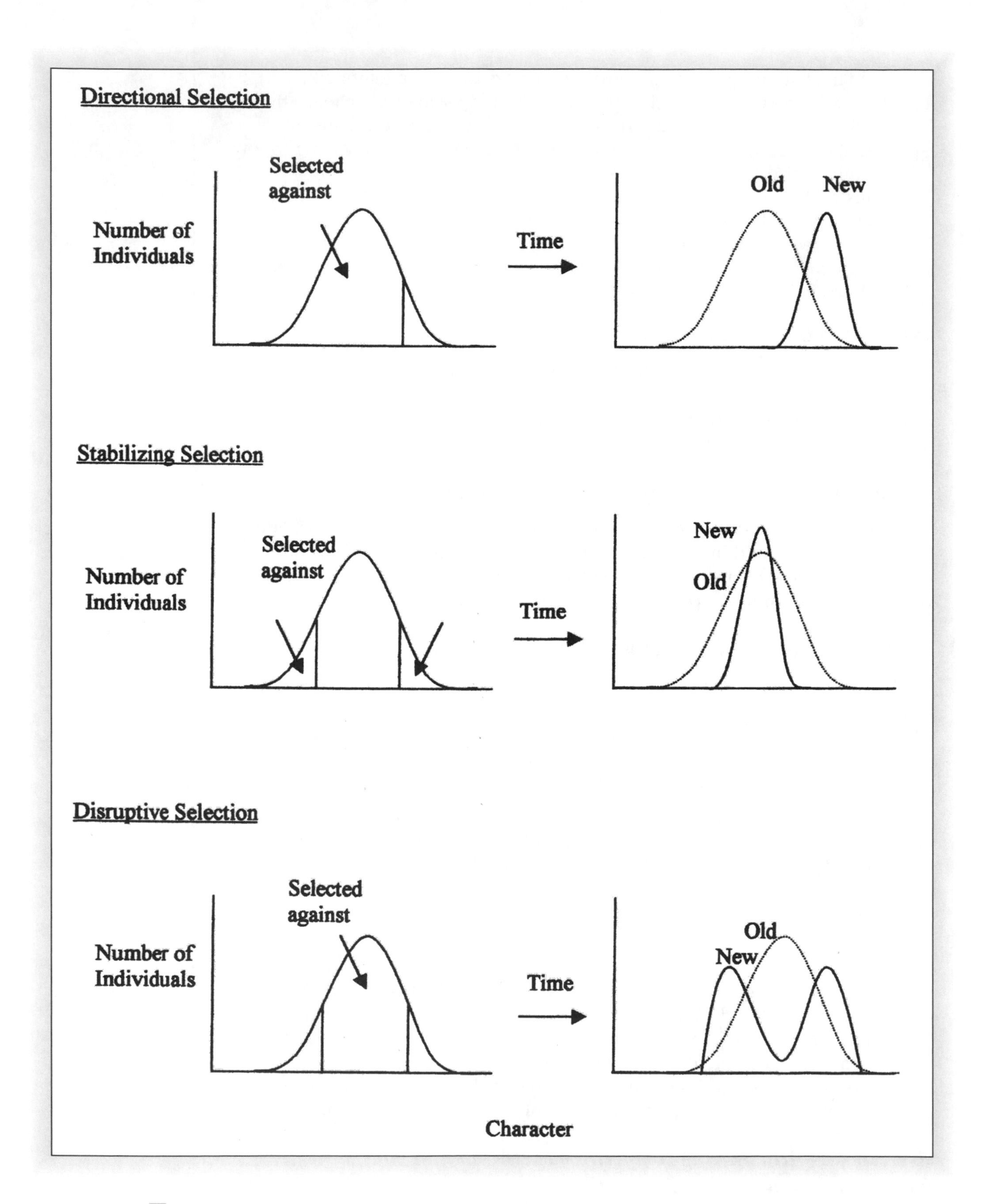

FIGURE 1 Changes in phenotypes under directional, stabilizing and disruptive selection pressures over time.

those around them in these exercises, thereby directly involving more than those initially chosen. Although only 15 or 20 students may become directly involved, this technique has been used in classes of 70 students with no apparent loss of attention by those not directly involved.

1. Five bags of Jelly Bellies are needed, each with about 100 beans. One bag should be of a mixed variety of all types of beans. A second bag should contain an unusual or distinctive flavor that not all students would eat, such as licorice, root beer, or sizzling cinnamon. Bags three, four, and five should contain beans of the same color, but different flavors, such as cantaloupe, orange juice, and tangerine, or Hawaiian Punch, very cherry, and cinnamon.
2. Identify a student who will eat a wide variety of jelly beans, but will not eat the distinctive flavor in the mixed bag. Identify a second student who likes, or even prefers, the distinctive flavor. Have the two students discuss with each other which bag they want to eat, and stipulate they cannot mix beans between bags. Most likely, the student who prefers the distinctive flavor will end up with it, and the student with the cosmopolitan taste will end up with the mixed bag. These students can be thought of as generalist and specialist consumers. Make the class aware of this distinction. Use the licorice flavor for the specialist because some students really don't like it, and refer to it as "black" rather than "licorice." Students readily recognize the black color as the licorice flavor. The acceptance of one student's choice of only licorice and the other student's choice of everything but licorice illustrates one of the ecological forces structuring communities, that is, decreasing niche breadth under competition. Limiting food items to licorice jelly beans represents a realized niche for one student. Both students are able to coexist due to partitioning of food resources and the avoidance of competitive interactions that may be detrimental for each.

You may carry this ecological principle one step further by finding students who like orange jelly beans, while holding up the cantaloupe, orange juice, and tangerine flavors in three separate bags. Most cannot tell that they are different flavors by looks alone. After letting students taste the three different flavors, discuss the continued specialization and narrowing of niche breadth with the resulting increases in competition intensity. The further specialization by student predators to flavor preferences within a single color provides this example.

These classroom examples can easily be tied to empirical data of sympatric species coexistence (organisms living in the same area) for a number of resource parameters. These would include bird bill speciation in Darwin finches on the Galápagos Islands, and tree feeding positions of warblers in coniferous forests (MacArthur, 1958).

Additional Considerations

Other Uses of Jelly Belly Jelly Beans

Sexual Selection by Females

I have had students select favorite colors or flavors to "mate" with. Sexual selection suggests that a female will choose a mate that possesses certain characteristics she finds appealing. In the case of the Jelly Belly jelly bean, this may be color or flavor. You should note that Jelly Bellies have a logo on most of the beans, and this also can be a selective trait. After all, if you were a Jelly Belly looking for a mate, you would want one that was labeled as such!

Optimum Foraging Theory

The theory of maximizing energy or time while foraging is not a concept that is difficult to grasp. However, it is easily illustrated by placing a given number of beans (e.g., n = 100) in each of two separate groups. The first group has them all in a single bag, while the second has them in a number of bags. The group with a single bag of beans demands less handling time and energy expended for the energy returned to the predator.

Hardy Weinberg Theory

In addition to using Jelly Bellies for natural selection as shown previously, they can be used to demonstrate other pressures placed on a population. In a particular population of beans with four or five color/flavor alleles, place a single bean of a different color/ flavor, representing immigration of a new allele. Students then have to make a decision whether it will be lost (eaten), or successfully invade the population.

Most of the demonstrations of ecological principles and theories in the classroom using Jelly Bellies take 10 to 15 minutes. You will likely find that student retention of information presented in this manner is extensive, and concepts become lucid. They seem to easily remember eating different flavors and colors long after the information is presented (like at test time!).

References

Begon, M., Harper, J.L. & Townsend, C.R. (1996). *Ecology: Individuals, populations, and communities*, (3rd ed). London: Blackwell Science.

Krohne, D.T. (1997). *General ecology*. Belmont, CA: Wadsworth.

MacArthur, R.H. (1958). Population ecology of some warblers of north-eastern coniferous forests. *Ecology, 39*, 599–619.

Smith, R.L. (1995). *Ecology and field biology* (5th ed). New York: Harper Collins.

Predators as a Selection Force:
The Jelly Bean Lab

David Smitley

Overview

The selection force of predators on prey and some of the escape mechanisms can be explored in a laboratory exercise using jelly beans as prey for students' predators. This activity will enable students to explore how predator-prey relationships can derive the natural selection process.

Evolutionary Principles Illustrated

- Natural selection
- Predator-prey relationships
- Adaptation (cryptic coloration and mimicry)

Background Information

Predators are a driving force in insect communities, keeping populations of prey under control and exerting powerful selection pressures on herbivorous insects. Predators and parasites are constantly removing a large proportion of insect herbivores in most habitats. The most palatable and easily discovered prey items are removed first, leaving behind the most inconspicuous individuals.

Over time, plant-feeding insects and predators that are prey for other predators have evolved appearances and behaviors to escape predation. Every insect species has some form of protection from predators. Some of the more common strategies are cryptic coloration, noxious taste, cryptic behavior, intimidating appearance or behavior, production of chemicals toxic to predators, or mimicking noxious or dangerous prey.

This activity is based on "Predators as a selection force: The jelly bean lab" by David Smitley (1998), in *Michigan Science Teachers' Association Journal* (Fall), 50–51. It has been adapted and reprinted with permission of the author.

Materials

Per class:

- 600 jelly beans (100 each of six different colors)

Procedures

Purchase approximately 600 jelly beans: 100 each of six different colors. Before starting an experiment, show your students the different colors of jelly beans you will be using and ask them to predict what will happen. Take your students outdoors to an area where you can compare thin turf to dense turf, short grass to tall grass, or sand to grass. Select four students to position themselves in the corners of a 20-foot by 20-foot square. Direct the remaining students to stand between them to outline your first test arena. Select four students as predators. Ask them to close their eyes as you scatter 20 of each color of jelly beans around the arena. Allow the predators two minutes to collect as many jelly beans as they can. At this point more jelly beans can be added or other arenas selected in many different ways, depending on what principles you want to investigate.

Refugia or Cryptic Behavior

Scatter the first batch of jelly beans for a standard round of predation. Collect and record the number of each kind of jelly bean found by predators. Select another group of four predators and have them close their eyes while you scatter the recovered jelly beans around the arena for a second round of 2 minutes. Record the number of jelly beans found, and disperse them for a third round of predation. Keep the final round of jelly beans that were found in a plastic bag. Record the results and return to the classroom where the results may be put on the board for discussion or put in table form and photocopied for a discussion the next day. The number of jelly beans found after each round of predation will go down. Ask your students to develop several hypotheses to explain these observations. Name each hypothesis after the student that developed it. The following concepts can be discussed in support of different hypotheses:

1. A dark gray moth is difficult to see on a dark tree trunk but is easily discovered on a white tree trunk. The turf arena is not one color; grass blades are green, thatch and dead grass are straw colored, and exposed ground other colors depending on soil type and moisture. Light and shadows are critical. Dark jelly beans are difficult to see in dark shadow. Jelly beans that land in a protected site and on a substrate that matches their color are less likely to be found than exposed ones. Each round of predation selects the exposed individuals and leaves the cryptic ones, until hardly any jelly beans can be found.
2. The movement of predators in the arena may push jelly beans under thatch or make them more cryptic from clinging soil or plant debris. Examine the recovered jelly beans and compare them to fresh ones. Could an experiment be devised to test the hypothesis that trampled

jelly beans are more difficult to find because they are discolored? Consider using the class to trample one arena and not another after scattering the jelly beans and before predators begin collecting, or collect trampled jelly beans and compare their visibility to predators with fresh jelly beans by tossing them into an adjacent arena for a round of predation.

Extirpation and Stability of Prey Populations

After the first round of predation, record the number of each type of jelly bean found. Calculate the number of surviving jelly beans and allow each pair of survivors to have two offspring for the next generation. For example, when starting with 20 jelly beans, if 4 black jelly beans were found, 8 pairs survived to produce 16 offspring, so add 16 more black jelly beans to the test arena. Select another four predators for a second 2-minute round of predation. Record the results and add the appropriate number of offspring again. Repeat this process for four or five generations. It is likely that one or two colors will have every individual removed (extirpated) at some point in the experiment. Some colors may have about the same population each generation while other will increase rapidly initially, then level off. Have the students generate hypotheses to explain why. If one type of jelly bean became abundant because of its cryptic coloration, predators begin to find more of them, providing an upper threshold for the population. Predators can also become overwhelmed when the number of prey exceeds their ability to collect them.

Cryptic Coloration

The best way to demonstrate cryptic coloration is to compare jelly bean survival in two different arenas. You may want to compare long grass with short grass, bare or thin grass with thick grass, or sandy areas with grass. Another way to change the arena is with shadows. Start with 20 jelly beans of each color in an arena completely surrounded by students. Small arenas (20 feet x 20 feet) will be mostly covered by the shadows of the students standing on the periphery of the arena, particularly early in the morning when shadows are long. For the next round of predation scatter the same number and color of jelly beans in a adjacent arena, but this time have the students stand on three sides only, allowing full sunlight on the arena.

Diverging and Converging Gene Pools

Start with five or more different shades of the same color of jelly bean and select two arenas that are very different in ground cover vegetation. Start with the same mix of jelly beans at each site and go through five rounds of predation, allowing the surviving shades of jelly beans to reproduce as in the "extirpation and stability" experiment. Graph the results and compare the abundance of each shade of jelly bean at the end of the experiment in the two different habitats. Now find side-by-side arenas of the same habitat, begin with the individuals at the end of the first experiment, and run through five more rounds of predation. Now compare the shading of individuals in the two separate populations after five generations in the same habitat.

Batesian Mimicry

Some noxious-tasting insects are brightly colored (aposematic coloration) to warn predators, thereby reducing the amount of "mistaken" predation on their species. Other species of insects may mimic the pattern of bright colors worn by a noxious insect to escape predation even though they actually have an acceptable taste to predators. The best known example of this is the viceroy butterfly that mimics the foul tasting monarch butterfly. Without explaining the principle of Batesian mimicry, have your student predators collect jelly beans of six to eight different colors as before, only this time identify one bright color as being poisonous and instruct the predators not to pick it up. When selecting jelly beans for this experiment, find a jelly bean similar in color to the poisonous color but easily distinguished in your hand.

Search Images

Predators learn to find prey more efficiently by developing a search image that they can recognize quickly. Start with two adjacent arenas. In one, scatter 20 jelly beans each of colors A, B, C, D, E, and F; in the second arena use colors D, E, F, G, H, and I, so that three of the colors are used in both arenas and three are unique to each arena. Allow the predators to go through two rounds of collecting prey, then mark off a third arena nearby where all nine colors are used. Have the same eight predators search for prey together in the new arena. Compare the color of prey caught by each original group of four predators.

Additional Considerations

Unexpected Results

In order to look at how predators select for size of prey we cut two colors of jelly beans in half and compared recovery of those to whole ones of the same colors. After tallying the results we immediately saw that more of the half-jelly beans were found than the whole jelly beans. I was surprised by the results and asked the class for some ideas. It was the predators themselves who gave the best explanation. When the jelly beans were cut in half, the center contrasted with the outside in a way that left a target pattern readily spotted by predators. In the same experiment we unexpectedly found that bright yellow jelly beans survived better than any color except black. After some discussion it was hypothesized that the yellow jelly beans survived well because of the small yellow leaves of the golden rain tree that had fallen over the turf in our arena. There were not enough fallen leaves to make the ground appear yellow, but evidently enough to interfere without predators' ability to find yellow jelly beans. The final lesson of the jelly bean experiment: Many important discoveries have been made by following up on experiments with unexpected results.

Size, Color, and Unexpected Results

In one experiment bright yellow jelly beans survived surprisingly well, until we realized that small yellow leaves had fallen into the test arena. The half-size pink and yellow jelly beans were unexpectedly easier to find than the whole beans of the same color because of the target pattern left where the jelly bean was cut in half.

Mimicry and Unexpected Results

In another trial, red jelly beans were poisonous and could not be handled by predators. Dark pink survived better in this experiment than in other experiments in which red jelly beans were not considered poisonous.

Sample data from various trials are shown in Table 1 and illustrated in Figure 1.

TABLE 1 Sample data collected from various jelly bean exercises discussed previously.

Color	Start	Final Population		Color	Start	Final Population
Purple	20	7		Green	20	22
Yellow	20	22		Yellow	20	15
Red	20	3		White	20	16
Pink	20	11		Orange	20	17
White	20	7		Dark Pink	20	23
Orange	20	3		Purple	20	20
Green	20	17		Red (Poisonous)	20 (no predation)	20
Black	20	42				
Pink	20	5				
Yellow	20	1				

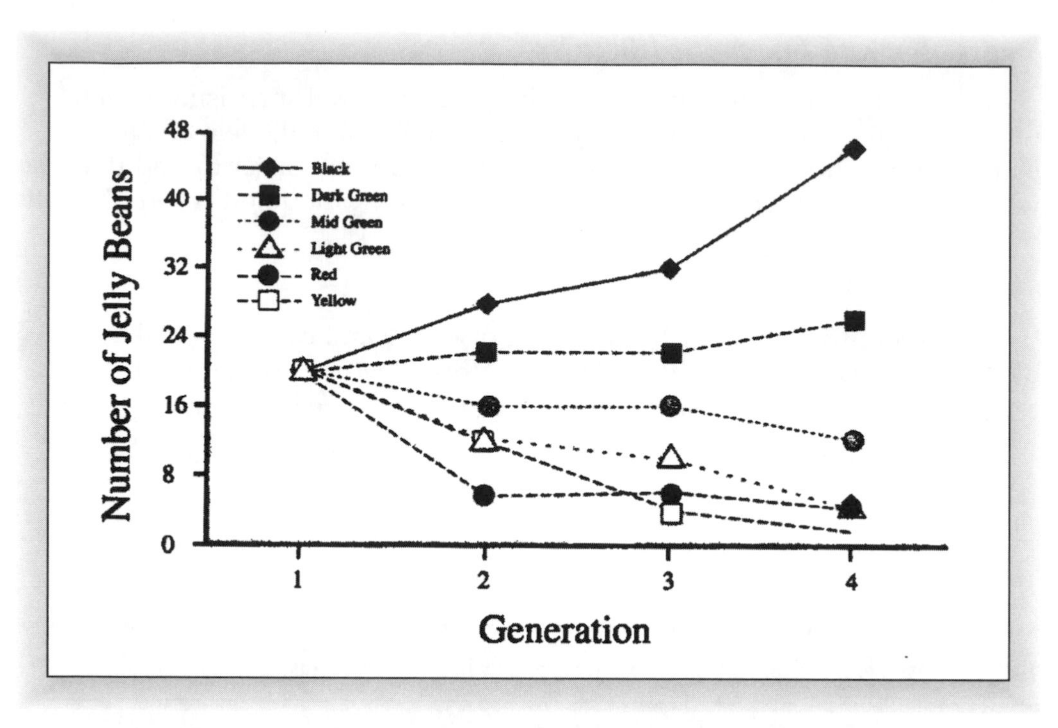

FIGURE 1 Graph showing population patterns after four simulated "generations" of various colored jelly beans were tested for fitness against visual student predators.

References

Cott, H.B. (1940). *Adaptive coloration in animals*. New York: Oxford University Press.

Eisner, T. (1970). Chemical defense against predation in arthropods. In E. Sondheimer & J.B. Simeone (Eds.), *Chemical ecology (pp.157–217)*. New York: Academic.

Keiper, R.R. (1969). Behavioral adaptations of cryptic moths IV. Preliminary studies on species resembling dead leaves. *Journal of the Lepidoptera Society* 23, 205–10.

Portmann, A. (1959). *Animal camouflage.*. Ann Arbor, MI: University of Michigan Press.

Price, P.W. (1984). *Insect Ecology*. New York: John Wiley & Sons.

Rettenmeyer, C.W. (1970). Insect mimicry. *Animal Review of Entomology, 15*, 43–74.

Thayer, G.H. (1909). *Concealing-coloration in the animal kingdom: An exposition of the laws of disguise through color and pattern*. New York: Macmillan.

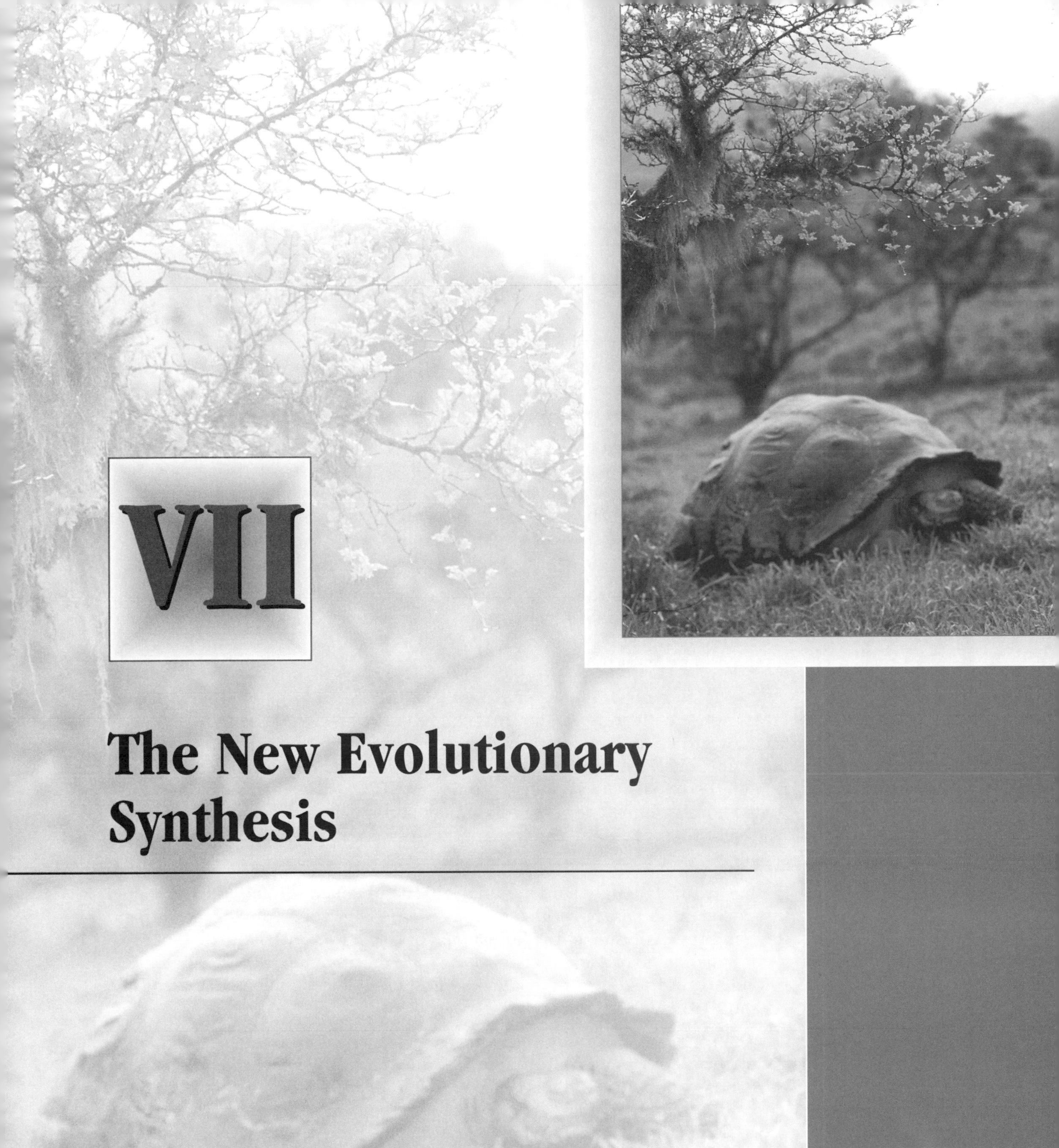

VII

The New Evolutionary Synthesis

Even though Darwin and Wallace provided the mechanism for evolution with the development of natural selection, countless questions remained unanswered and many discoveries regarding biological evolution remained which would build on their work. For instance, Darwin and Wallace could not explain the source of the variation so central to natural selection. Full understanding of the gene as the unit of inheritance coupled with DNA as the underlying biochemical mechanism of heredity was unknown to these pioneers in the study of evolution. The explosion of work in evolutionary biology in the century or more since Darwin and Wallace has come to be known as neo-Darwinism or the new evolutionary synthesis. Rather than threatening the validity of descent with modification established in the 19th century, the new synthesis has added to our store of knowledge about the details of evolution while affirming the central tenets established so long ago.

This chapter contains several strategies focused on aspects of descent with modification unknown to Darwin and Wallace. New discoveries in genetics, the nature of mutation, new tools for the analysis of DNA, and innovative ideas about the rate and tempo of evolutionary change have ushered in a period known as the new evolutionary synthesis.

In the first activity, students use quantitative data to evaluate two alternative hypotheses regarding the evolution of two related flowering plants. Both of the proposed hypotheses involve neo-Darwinistic ideas—the concept of speciation as a result of inbreeding as well as the effect of a co-evolved species on the evolution of the first.

Next, students examine simulated data discovered from two mythical creatures: one illustrating a gradualistic evolutionary sequence and the other the new punctuated equilibrium. In the latter, sudden changes (punctuation) interrupt otherwise long periods of time in which the form of the creatures remains essentially unchanged (equilibrium). For many organisms, this punctuated equilibrium style of evolution may be a much more accurate characterization of their ancestral history than the gradualism previously advocated by scientists.

In the third activity, students analyze data obtained through the technique known as DNA-DNA hybridization in order to construct a phylogenetic tree detailing the evolution of the human and ape superfamily. The use of such data, which have become available only with the advent of new technologies, provides multiple layers of evidence—most of which were unavailable to Darwin and Wallace—in support of proposed phylogenies.

The innovative use of mathematics to determine gene frequency data for a given population is a tool introduced to students in the Leonard and Edmondson activity. Students will collect and analyze hairline data from the class population and then apply the Hardy-Weinberg equations to determine probable genotype and allele frequencies for the group. Furthermore, students will consider the factors (other than natural selection) that can lead a population's allele frequencies to change over time, particularly migration which can result in a phenomenon known as the Founder Effect, a type of genetic drift.

Genetic drift is explored in the final activity of this chapter. Here students attempt to explain the apparent randomness in change observed for a group of related fish. In this same activity, students will also consider the various effects that natural selection can have on a population, including disruptive, directional, and stabilizing selection.

As essential as it is to recognize the role of natural selection in evolution, student understanding and appreciation of descent with modification will become richer through the use of activities such as those provided here, as they illustrate the many facets of change through time.

Investigating Evolution with Living Plants

Mark A. Schlessman

Overview

This chapter provides details of two activities that may be done with inexpensive equipment and quantitative data analysis to illustrate evolution and the consequences of inbreeding, or mating among relatives in living plants. In the first lab, students evaluate alternative hypotheses for the evolution of different floral sizes in two species of monkey flowers, the genus Mimulus in the snapdragon family, Scrophulariaceae. For this activity, one can use *M. guttatus*, which has relatively large flowers, and *M. laciniatus*, which has much smaller flowers (Figures 1 and 2). The ultimate purpose is for students to evaluate two hypotheses for the evolution of small flowers in *M. laciniatus*: the "smaller pollinator" hypothesis and the "selfing" hypothesis.

In the second lab, students explore the effect of self-incompatibility on inbreeding depression. For this second activity, the students use two "stocks" of rapid-cycling Brassica. One stock has the normal self-incompatible phenotype and is thus cross-pollinated and relatively outbred. The other is a specially developed self-compatible stock that is partially self-pollinated and presumably more inbred. Students cross- and self-pollinate individuals of both stocks in order to make predictions on the frequency of inbreeding depression.

Evolutionary Principles Illustrated

- Variation within species
- Fitness (impact of inbreeding)
- Adaptation (deleterious)

This activity is based on "Investigating evolution with living plants" by Mark A. Schlessman (1997), in *The American Biology Teacher*, *59*(8), 472–79. It has been adapted and reprinted with permission of the publisher.

Background Information

Monkey Flower Business: The Evolution of Flower Size in Mimulus

Because the reproductive success (Darwinian fitness) of an individual plant often depends on its success at attracting pollinators, floral characters are relatively constant within species (This is one reason why flowers are usually necessary to identify plants). On the other hand, differences in floral morphology among species help prevent nonproductive interspecific pollinations, and it is not unusual to find that closely related species have distinctly different flowers. Such differences may evolve for a variety of reasons.

The **smaller pollinator** hypothesis is based on the idea that floral structure has evolved to promote efficient pollination. Essentially all general biology textbooks cover the relationship between variation in floral structure and variation in kinds and behaviors of pollinators, and also the different mechanisms that promote cross-pollination. *Mimulus guttatus* is excellent for illustrating these concepts. The showy yellow flowers are bilaterally symmetrical, just as we are (Figures 1 and 2). The enlarged bottom "lip" of the corolla tube (the five fused petals) serves as a landing platform for bumble bees. Red dots and yellow hairs may help guide bees to nectar inside the flower. Some botanists see a monkey's face in the pattern of red dots, hence the common name for *Mimulus*. As the bee enters the flower, pollen on its back will be deposited on the stigma, which protrudes beyond the two pairs of stamens. In many monkey flowers, the two-lobed stigmas are sensitive to touch. They will close whether pollen is deposited or not, but may reopen if no pollen is present. As the bee moves further inside, it contacts the anthers and receives new pollen on its back. Although *Mimulus* is capable of self-fertilization (i.e., it is genetically self-compatible), the spatial separation of stigma and anthers and the sensitive stigma lobes both promote cross-pollination. Closed stigma lobes prevent self-pollination as the bee backs out of the flower.

The smaller pollinator hypothesis assumes that *M. laciniatus* (small flowers) is cross-pollinated in much the same way as *Mimulus guttatus* (large flowers), but that the former just has a smaller pollinator (i.e., a solitary bee versus a bumble bee). Under this hypothesis, we can envision an ancestral population in which floral size varied and in which larger bees became less abundant while smaller bees became more abundant. Those flowers that just happened to be the appropriate size for effective pollination by the smaller bees would be more likely to produce fruits than other flowers, thus selection would favor those plants with flowers that "fit" the smaller bees. In its simplest form, this hypothesis predicts that in order to retain the appropriate spatial and functional relationships among floral parts,

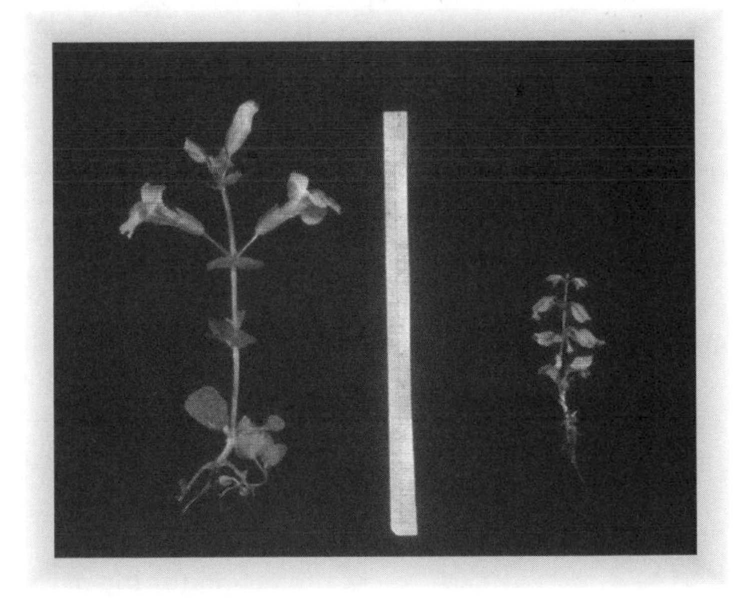

FIGURE 1 Monkey flower plants (Mimulus, Scrophulariaceae): right, *M. guttatus;* left, *M. laciniatus.* The ruler is 15 mm long.

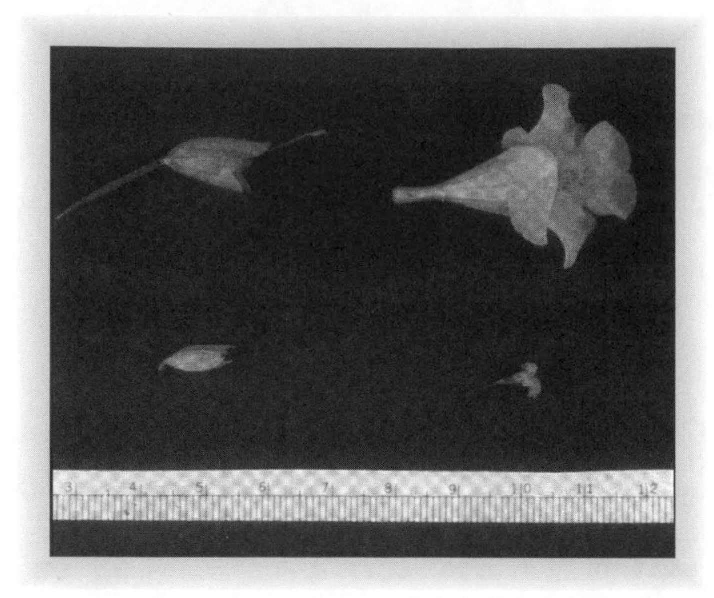

FIGURE 2 Monkey flowers with corollas (right) separated from calyces and pistils (left). Mimulus guttatus is shown above, and M. laciniatus below. All are viewed from the side, except M. guttatus corolla, which is seen from above.

all the parts (sepals, petals, stamens, and carpels) of the *M. laciniatus* flower should be equally reduced versions of those in *M. guttatus*. This hypothesis also predicts that in both *M. laciniatus* and *M. guttatus* the stigma should protrude beyond the anthers in order to promote self-pollination.

In contrast to the smaller pollinator hypothesis, the **selfing** hypothesis is based on a phenomenon that most high school and general biology textbooks do not address: the evolution of self-pollinating, self-fertilizing, and consequently inbred species from cross-pollinating, outbred ancestors. Some students may remember that Mendel's peas could self-pollinate and self-fertilize, but you'll probably have to provide some background for this idea. Ask your students what would happen if a plant's pollinators became rare or extinct, but no new pollinator was available or workable as a replacement. Would the plants become extinct, too? Perhaps. But what if the plants were able to self-fertilize, and a few individuals had some flowers that self-pollinated? Those flowers would produce more fruits than flowers that could only be cross-pollinated. If the offspring of self-pollinating plants resembled their parents, sooner or later a new, self-pollinating species might evolve. Now, some students may object to this scenario on the grounds that self-pollination and self-fertilization result in inbreeding, and inbreeding is "bad" (see background on *Brassica* lab below). You might respond by asking them to consider which plant has the higher fitness, one that self-pollinates and self-fertilizes or one that produces no offspring at all.

Another question to ponder is: how would the flowers of the new, self-pollinating species differ from those of its cross-pollinating ancestor? The flowers would probably be smaller, simply because a smaller and narrower corolla tube would tend to bring the anthers closer to the stigma, which would promote self-pollination. But would the reduction in floral size be equal for all floral parts? What are the consequences, in terms of Darwinian fitness, of having smaller flowers? Smaller corollas might be less attractive to pollinators, but that is not likely to affect the fitness of self-pollinating individuals. Smaller anthers with fewer pollen grains would also have little effect, as long as there were enough pollen grains to fertilize all of the ovules (potential seeds) in the ovary of the flower. In contrast, smaller ovaries and calyces (sepals) might reduce fitness, because smaller ovaries with fewer ovules would lower the number of seeds produced, and smaller calyces would afford less protection for the developing fruits. Following this reasoning, and noting that in a self-pollinating species relative sizes of floral parts do not have consequences for pollinator behavior and effectiveness, the selfing hypothesis predicts that relative to *M. guttatus*, the petals and stamens of *M. laciniatus* will be more reduced than the sepals and ovaries. Lastly, under the selfing hypothesis, the stigma of *M. laciniatus* should not protrude beyond the anthers, but rather should be located next to them in order to facilitate self-pollination.

Thus, the selfing hypothesis differs from the smaller pollinator hypothesis in three ways. First, it assumes that while *M. guttatus* is cross-pollinated, *M. laciniatus* has lost its pollinator and evolved self-pollination. Second, it predicts that some parts of the *M. laciniatus* flower (petals and stamens) will be more reduced relative to those of *M. guttatus* than others (sepals and ovaries). Third, it predicts that in *M. laciniatus*, there will be no spatial separation between the stigma and anthers.

Effects of Self- and Cross-Pollination in Genetically Self-Compatible Versus Self-Incompatible Rapid-Cycling Brassica

Many students know that inbreeding, or mating among relatives, is "bad" because it increases the frequency of loci that are homozygous, and thus the expression of recessive, often deleterious alleles. But there's much more to inbreeding depression than that. What if a population, such as a plant that is losing its pollinators, becomes inbred and remains so for a long time? If the inbreeding depression is not so devastating that the population becomes extinct, natural selection will tend to eliminate the deleterious alleles. In fact, the deleterious recessive alleles that cause inbreeding depression will remain in a population only if they frequently arise by mutation, or if regular outbreeding keeps them "hidden" from selection in heterozygous genotypes. Thus, evolutionary geneticists predict that regularly inbred populations will exhibit less inbreeding depression than regularly outbred ones.

Because they are often capable of self-fertilization, flowering plants are excellent experimental organisms for testing this prediction. Self-fertilization, mating with one's self, is the most extreme form of inbreeding. It is genetically equivalent to a mating between identical twins. A quick Punnett square will show that if an Aa heterozygote self-pollinates, one-half of the offspring will be homozygotes (25% AA, 25% aa). Assuming that "a" is a recessive deleterious allele, one-fourth of the offspring may exhibit inbreeding depression due to homozygosity at this locus. Since individuals from a regularly cross-pollinating population should be heterozygous at many loci, self-pollinating them should produce marked inbreeding depression. On the other hand, individuals from a regularly self-pollinating population should be mostly homozygous for nondeleterious alleles, and self-pollination should produce a lower level of inbreeding depression. Students can test this prediction by comparing the results of self- and cross-pollinations of regularly outbred and inbred plants.

In many ways, the large- and small-flowered *Mimulus* described previously would be ideal for this activity. You might want to try it with your students (see Carr & Dudash, 1996). However, *Mimulus* has very small seeds that are relatively easy to count but hard to weigh. For this and other reasons, instead of *Mimulus* one can use rapid-cycling "stocks" of *Brassica rapa*

(= B. campestris). The commercial cultivars of this species include turnips, pak choi, and Chinese cabbage (Figure 7).

Geneticists working on the improvement of mustard family (Brassicaceae or Cruciferae) crops (Williams & Hill, 1986) developed rapid-cycling *Brassicas* (Rcb's). Rcb's have fairly large flowers that are easy to work with, extremely short generation times, high fruit production, and seeds that are large enough to handle individually. You may be familiar with their educational offshoot, Wisconsin Fast Plants™, which are marketed by the Carolina Biological Supply Company. In contrast to *M. guttatus*, which has morphological features that limit self-pollination, *Brassica* exhibits self-incompatibility, a genetic mechanism that prevents self-fertilization if self-pollination occurs.

Although the basic genetics of self-incompatibility are fairly clear, its cellular and molecular mechanisms are still poorly known. The phenomenon is somewhat analogous to self-recognition and non-self rejection by our immune system. If pollen is recognized as self, it will either not germinate at all, or the pollen tube will stop growing soon after germination. Pollen germination often requires hydration by stigmatic secretions, and uptake of nutrients from the style is essential for pollen tube growth. Self-incompatibility mechanisms can block one or both of these processes. Self-incompatibility is governed by a supergene commonly known as the "S-locus," which may have several alleles. In *Brassica*, pollen will not grow if it carries an S-allele that is also present in cells of the stigma. Thus, S1 pollen will not grow on stigmas with the genotypes S1S1, S1S2 or S1S3; but it will grow on stigmas with these genotypes: S2S2, S2S3 or S3S3. This system is called "gametophytic" incompatibility, because the incompatibility phenotype of each pollen grain (male gametophyte) corresponds directly to its genotype.

Materials

Per Group of Students:

- Rulers
- Dissecting microsope
- Fine point forceps

Procedures

Specific Procedure 1

Monkey Flower Business: The Evolution of Flower Size in *Mimulus*

In the lab, students can use measurements of floral part (Figure 3) to test the predictions of the two hypotheses. They can make three kinds of comparisons: sizes of the same floral parts, such as *M. laciniatus* corollas versus *M. guttatus* corollas (Figure 4); ratios of sizes of different floral parts, such as calyx: corolla of *M. laciniatus* versus calyx: corolla of *M. guttatus* (Figure 5); and stigma-anther separation (Figure 6). Using these data as an example,

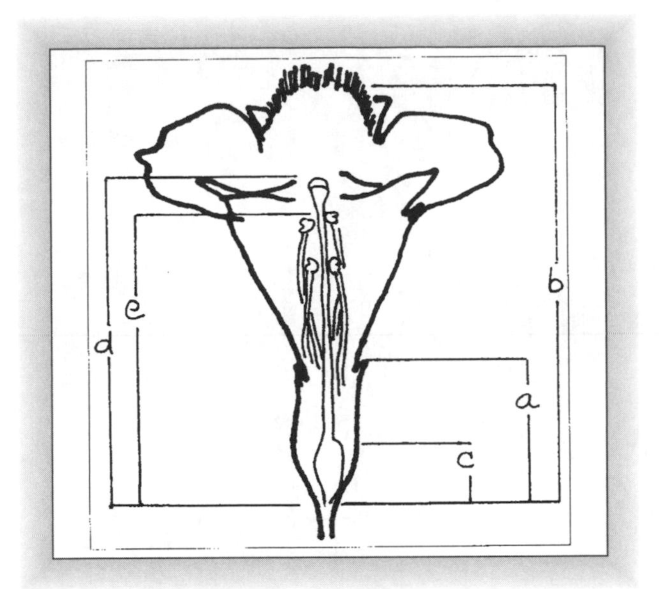

FIGURE 3 Illustration of measurements of monkey flowers (after Ritland & Ritland, 1989). Stamens are attached to the corolla and will remain with it when it is removed. Measurements taken to the nearest mm are: a = calyx length, b = corolla length, c = ovary length, d = pistil length, e = distance from base of corolla to tips of longest stamens. Stigma-anther separation relative to floral size = (d – e)/b. Students also measure the width of an anther of one of the long stamens, estimating to the nearest 0.5 mm.

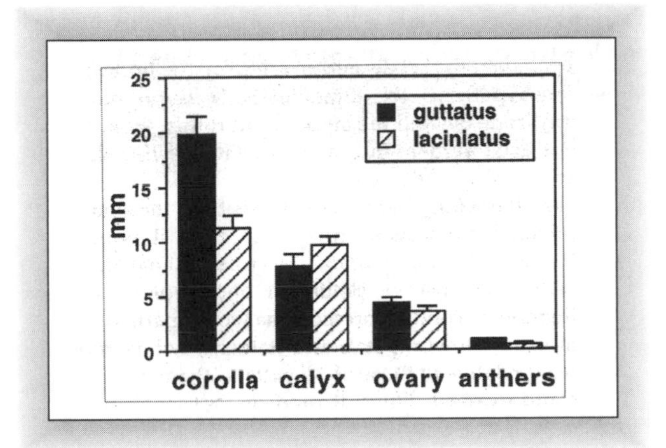

FIGURE 4 Class data from "Monkey Flower Business." Means plus 95% confidence limits for corolla length, calyx length, ovary length, and anther width.

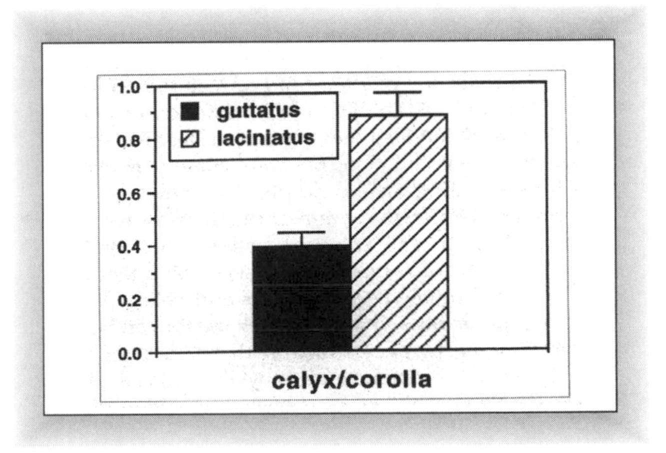

FIGURE 5 Class data from "Monkey Flower Business." Means plus 95% confidence intervals for calyx length/corolla length ratios.

students could conclude that the smaller pollinator hypothesis for the evolution of small flowers in *M. laciniatus* could be rejected.

Mimulus is annual, so plants must be grown from seed. Any of the species listed in Table 2 of Ritland and Ritland (1989) should work well. *M. guttatus* is available from commercial seed suppliers (such as Abundant Life Seed Foundation, P. O. Box 772, Port Townsend, WA 98368). The less showy species are more difficult to obtain. You can find your own, check with native plant seed suppliers. Seeds can be sowed in small peat pots containing commercial potting soil, and they can be germinated in a growth chamber with 14-hour days (but a growth chamber is certainly not necessary!). *M. laciniatus* should bloom in three to four weeks and produce flowers for at least three weeks. *M. guttatus* should bloom in about five weeks and produce flowers for two to three weeks.

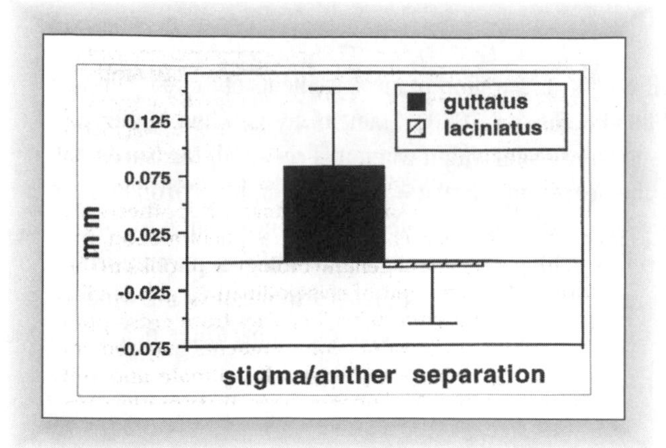

FIGURE 6 Class data from "Monkey Flower Business." Stigma-anther separation relative to floral size.

FIGURE 7 Rapid-cycling *Brassica rapa* in flower (left) and in fruit (right). The white Styrofoam pot on the left is 4.4 cm tall.

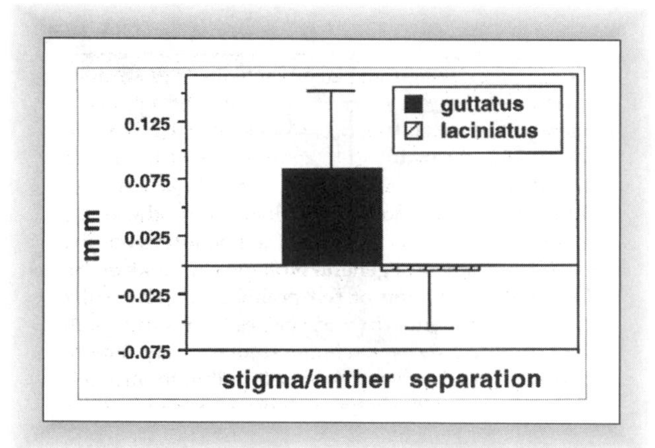

FIGURE 8 Data from a group project on inbreeding depression in rapid-cycling *Brassica*. Means plus 95% confidence intervals for seed set (numbers of seed per fruit). The difference between self- and cross-pollinated fruits for the outcrosser (self-incompatible stock CrGC 1-1) is statistically significant (t test, $P < 0.05$), but for the selfer (self-compatible stock CrGC 1-8) it is not.

It is recommended that you plant two or three groups of seeds at two-week intervals to increase the likelihood that you will have enough flowers when you want them. Rulers and dissecting microscopes are the only necessary equipment. Dissecting points and fine-pointed (watchmakers) forceps can be helpful. It is wise to have students practice on one or two flowers before they start recording measurements. Try it yourself so you can show them the best way to proceed. It is recommended to give students a handout on this lab at least three days ahead of time, and ask them to prepare a chart contrasting the assumptions and predictions of the two hypotheses before they come to lab.

Students take measurements (a total of at least 20 flowers for each species—each student measures only a few flowers), record their data on paper, enter them in a statistical software package, perform statistical analyses, and prepare tables and figures in one afternoon lab. Data can be discussed in class the following morning.

Specific Procedure 2

Effects of Self- and Cross-Pollination in Genetically Self-Compatible Versus Self-Incompatible Rapid-Cycling *Brassica*

Carolina Biological Supply Company markets a wide variety of rapid-cycling *Brassica rapa* stocks (Wisconsin Fast Plants), all of which are presumably self-incompatible. However, students have found that these stocks occasionally self-fertilize, so you may want to obtain both stocks directly from the Crucifer Genetics Cooperative (CrGC). Ask for CrGC stocks 1-1 (self-incompatible) and 1-8 (self-compatible). Carolina Biological also sells supplies for growing rapid-cycling *Brassicas*, instructors' manuals, and activities booklets. Their Wisconsin Fast Plants Manual contains a wealth of useful information, including clear diagrams of floral morphology and detailed instructions on how to grow and pollinate the plants.

Rapid-cycling *Brassica* will germinate within two days, and if grown under continuous light they will flower after two to three weeks and set fruit in about five weeks. The flowers have two green sepals, four yellow petals, six stamens (four long and two short), and a single pistil composed of two fused carpels (see Figures 9–12 and the Wisconsin Fast Plants Manual). Making effective hand-pollinations requires sound knowledge of floral structure and the process of floral maturation, so it's a good idea to have your students familiarize themselves with *Brassica* flowers and practice pollinating them before the actual experiment.

Cross-pollinations can be made by removing an anther of the pollen donor with watchmakers' forceps and dusting pollen on recipients' stigmas, or you can purchase or make "bee sticks" (see Wisconsin Fast Plants Manual) for this purpose. For cross-pollination of the self-compatible stock, the anthers of recipient flowers should be removed before maturation so that unintended self-pollination cannot occur. It's a good idea to emasculate the recipients of cross-pollen in the self-incompatible stock, too, just to make sure. For self-pollination of the self-incompatible stock, you need to circumvent the genetic incompatibility. This can be done by making self-pollinations of floral buds that have not fully opened (Figures 9–12). You might also try using a salt solution to overcome genetic incompatibility (Monteiro et al., 1988).

Students usually propose to self-pollinate several flowers on one group of plants and cross-pollinate several flowers on a different group of plants. A better experimental design is to make both cross- and self-pollinations on the same individuals. Flowers can be marked with different colors of permanent ink, white correction fluid, or thread. This design allows use of more powerful statistical analyses (i.e., paired tests rather than unpaired tests).

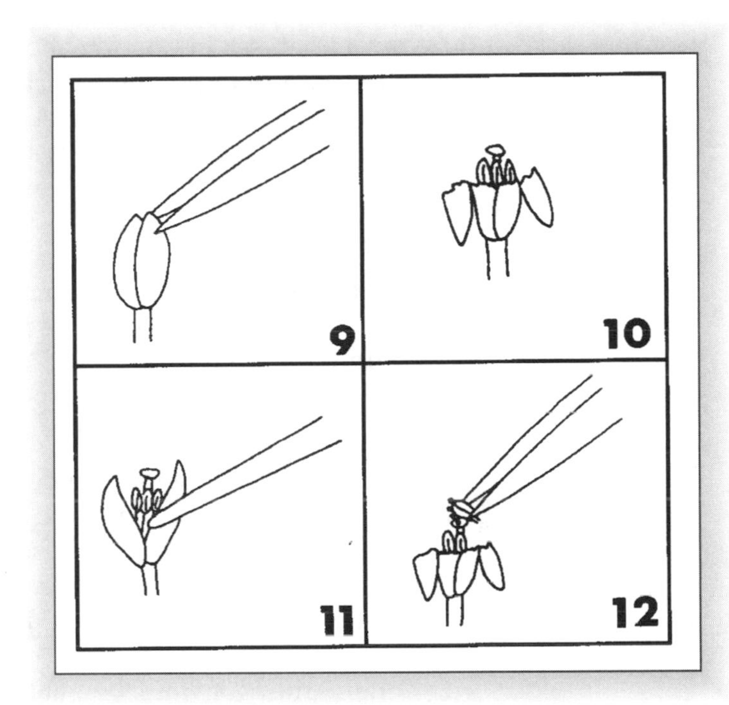

FIGURES 9–12 Procedure for self-pollination of self-incompatible rapid-cycling *Brassica* when the flowers are in bud. Figure 9. With watchmakers' forceps, gently part the sepals of a bud one to three days before it would open on its own. Figure 10. With forceps, crimp and lay back sepals to expose stigma and anthers. Figure 11. With forceps, remove a recently dehisced anther from another flower on the same plant. Figure 12. Place pollen from the recently dehisced anther on the stigma of the bud. (These figures were reproduced for the original article with the permission of Carolina Biological Supply Company, Burlington, NC 27215 and Wisconsin Alumni Research Foundation, Madison, WI 53707.)

This activity is a semester-long group project. The group usually divides itself in two groups: one subgroup works with the self-incompatible stock and the other handles the self-compatible stock. The students are given a minimal amount of background information and are asked to design their own experiments.

Additional Considerations

These activities allow the teacher to demonstrate the value of plants as experimental organisms, illustrate some sophisticated concepts, and link lab activity with current research. Each exercise also reinforces knowledge of floral biology by helping students think about the functions of flowers, not just the names of floral parts.

Although students enjoy working with *Mimulus* flowers, especially *M. guttatus*, they are often rushed to complete their measurements, data entry, and analyses in one four-hour lab period. If you can, introduce the plants and discuss the hypotheses in class before the lab, and save discussion of the data for the class after the lab. As given here, "Monkey Flower Business" will work for large classes as well as small. In fact, the version featured here is adapted from one used for a large introductory class at the University of Maryland. With more time or smaller classes, the exercise can become open-ended where students can generate their own hypotheses and tests. Students could determine fruit and seed production when cross-pollination is prevented (e.g., by enclosing flowers or entire plants in fine mesh). Students might also want to compare the results of self- and cross-pollinations, or ask whether fruits can be produced without any pollination at all (i.e., remove the anthers before pollen is released and prevent cross-pollination).

Students have responded that group research projects, such as the *Brassica* activity described here, are the most valuable part of their evolution course. The *Brassica* activity can also be adapted to large labs; one simply needs to grow more plants. The numbers of flowers pollinated and the ways your students measure inbreeding depression can be adjusted to your own time constraints and equipment. If your students can weigh seeds as well as count them, they may ask you about a trade-off between seed number and seed weight. This could lead to further investigation of the effects of seed weight on germination and seedling vigor. You might also get into an interesting discussion on whether traits such as fruit set, seed number, and seed weight are characteristics of the mother plant or its offspring.

Several general biology texts have good discussions of inbreeding, self-fertilization in plants, or both. Raven and Johnson (1989) mention genetic self-incompatibility in plants, self-fertilization as a departure from random mating that increases homozygosity, and the possible detrimental effects of inbreeding in small, often rare or endangered, populations. Curtis and Barnes (1980) give an extended discussion of mechanisms that promote outbreeding, including genetic "self-sterility." Levine and Miller (1992) also briefly mention self-incompatibility. Campbell (1993) briefly discusses the effects of inbreeding on allele frequencies in populations using wildflowers as an example, and also explains self-incompatibility in plants. Purvis, Orians, and Heller (1995) have a nice section on plant reproduction and mention self-pollination in several contexts. A discussion of the evolution of self-pollination and self-fertilization may raise some very interesting questions, such as whether regularly self-fertilizing organisms fit into our concepts of what a species is, and whether "not needing" a structure is an appropriate explanation for the evolutionary reduction or loss of that structure.

References

General references on floral biology, pollination, and mating among plants, including the general biology texts cited above

Barth, F.G. (1985). *Insects and flowers: The biology of a partnership*. Princeton, NJ: Princeton University Press.

Campbell, N. (1993). *Biology* (3rd ed.). Redwood City, CA: Benjamin Cummings.

Curtis, H., & Barnes, N.S. (1980). *Biology* (5th ed.). New York: Worth.

Faegri, K., & van der Pijl, L. (1980). *The principles of pollination ecology*. New York: Pergamon Press.

Levine, J.S., & Miller, K.R. (1992). *Biology: Discovering life*. Lexington, MA: D.C. Heath & Co.

Percival, M. (1965). *Floral biology*. New York: Pergamon Press.

Purvis, W.K., Orians, G.H., & Heller, H.C. (1995). *Life: The science of biology*, (4th ed.). Sunderland, MA: Sinauer Associates, Inc.

Proctor, M., & Yeo, P. (1972). *The pollination of flowers*. New York: Taplinger.

Raven, P.H., & Johnson, G.B. (1989). *Biology*, (2nd ed.). St. Louis: Times Mirror/Mosby.

Richards, A.J. (1986). *Plant breeding systems*. London: George Allen & Unwin.

Wyatt, R. (1983). Pollinator-plant interactions and the evolution of breeding systems. In L. Real (Ed.), *Pollination biology* (pp. 51–95). New York: Academic Press.

Monkey Flower Business (including research papers that instructors may wish to read and assign)

Bell, G. (1985). On the function of flowers. Proceedings of the Royal Society of London, B Series, 224, 223–65.

Bradshaw, H.D., et al. (1995). Genetic mapping of floral traits associated with reproductive isolation in monkeyflowers (Mimulus). *Nature, 376*, 762–65.

Carr, D.E., & Dudash, M. (1996). Inbreeding depression in two species of Mimulus (Scrophulariaceae) with contrasting mating systems. *American Journal of Botany, 83*, 586–93.

Carr, D.E., et al. (1997). The relationship between mating-system characters and inbreeding depression in Mimulus guttatus. *Evolution, 51*, 363–72.

Coyne, J.A. (1995). Speciation in monkeyflowers. *Nature, 376*, 726–27.

Cruden, R.W., & Lyon, D.L. (1985). Patterns of biomass allocation to male and female functions in plants with different mating systems. *Oecologia, 66*, 299–306.

Dole, J.A. (1992). Reproductive assurance mechanisms in three taxa of the *Mimulus guttatus* complex (Scrophulariaceae). *American Journal of Botany, 79*, 650–59.

Dudash, M.R., et al. (1997). Five generations of enforced selfing and outcrossing in *Mimulus guttatus*: Inbreeding depression variation at the population and family level. *Evolution, 51*, 54–65.

Lovet Doust, J., & Cavers, P.B. (1982). Biomass allocation in hermaphroditic flowers. *Canadian Journal of Botany, 60*, 2530–34.

Macnair, M.R., & Cumbes, Q.J. (1989). The genetic architecture of interspecific variation in Mimulus. *Genetics, 122*, 211–22.

Macnair, M.R., Macnair, V.E., & Martin, B.E. (1989). Adaptive speciation in Mimulus: An ecological comparison of *M. cupriphilus* with its presumed progenitor, *M. guttatus. New Phytologist, 112*, 269–79.

Macnair, M.R., & Cumbes, Q.J. (1990). The pattern of sexual resource allocation in the yellow monkey flower, *Mimulus guttatus*. Proceedings of the Royal Society of London B, 242, 101–07.

Montero, A.A., Gableman, W.H., & Williams, P.H. (1988). Use of sodium chloride solution to overcome self-incompatibility in *Brassic campestris* Hortiscience, 23, 876–77.

Mossop, M.R., Macnair, M.R., & Robertson, A.W. (1994). Within-population variation in sexual resource allocation in *Mimulus guttatus. Functional Ecology, 8*, 410–18.

Morell, V. (1996). Starting species with third parties and sex wars. *Science, 273*, 1499–1502.

Pennell, F.W. (1951). Mimulus. In L. Abrams (Ed.), *Illustrated flora of the pacc states* (Vol. 3, pp. 688–731). Stanford, CA: Stanford University Press.

Ritland, C., & Ritland, K. (1989). Variation in sex allocation among eight taxa of the *Mimulus guttatus* species complex (Scrophulariaceae). *American Journal of Botany, 76*, 1731–39.

Robertson, A.W., Diaz, A., & Macnair, M.R. (1994). The quantitative genetics of floral characters in *Mimulus guttatus. Heredity, 72*, 300–11.

Schoen, D. (1982). Male reproductive effort and breeding system in an hermaphroditic plant. *Oecologia, 53*, 255–57.

Vickery, R.L. (1964). Barriers to gene exchange between members of the *Mimulus guttatus* complex (Scrophulariaceae). *Evolution, 18*, 52–69.

Williams, P.H., & Hill, C.B. (1986). Rapid-cycling populations of *Brassica. Science, 232*, 1385–1389.

Yoon, C.K. (1995, September 5). For new species, a few genes are all that's needed. *The New York Times*, pp. Cl & Cll.

Modeling Modes of Evolution:
Comparing Phyletic Gradualism and Punctuated Equilibrium

 William F. McComas and Brian J. Alters

Overview

This activity provides students an opportunity to explore the tempo and mode of evolution by analyzing data and constructing two evolutionary trees, one gradual and one punctuated. The data included here are fictitious as are the creatures used as illustrations, but the simulation represents actual data.

Evolutionary Principles Illustrated

- Mode and tempo of evolution
- Punctuated and gradualist evolutionary patterns

Background Information

"Paleontologists have discovered two major patterns in life that make it difficult to support a totally uniformitarian view of life's' development" (Benton, 1993, p.100). These two views are known as phyletic gradualism and punctuated equilibrium.

Phyletic gradualism is the traditional Darwinian view that an interminable number of intermediate forms have existed, linking together all species in each group by gradations as fine as our existing varieties (Darwin, 1975).

Punctuated equilibrium, developed by Niles Eldredge and Steven Jay Gould (1972), offers a contrasting view that organic evolution is not steady and regular, but episodic and jerky with long periods of small changes interspersed with rapid bursts of large-scale transformation of species. The latter pattern explains that the "gaps" in the fossil record are not simply missing

---

This activity is based on "Modeling modes of evolution: Comparing phyletic gradualtion and punctuated equilibrium" by William F. McComas and Brian J. Alters (1994), in *The American Biology Teacher, 56*(6), 354–60. It has been adapted and reprinted with permission of the publisher.

data that will show up some day—as maintained by gradualists—but are real and must be interpreted as such.

Materials

Per group of students:

- Copies of the *Caminalcules* in Genera *Molluscaformis* (Figure 1a) and *Pedivarious* (Figure 2a). *Note:* Printing them on different colors of paper will be useful.
- Blank copies of geologic columns (strata sheets) for the two sites (Figures 1b and 2b) where each genus was found. Note that to perform the activity in the space provided, the blank strata sheets will have to be enlarged or the *Caminalcules* will have to be reduced so that the drawings ultimately fit in the space available.
- Scissors
- Graph paper (optional)
- Optional answer sheets for the stratigraphic columns are included as Figures 1c and 2c.
- Optional answer sheets for the graph are included as Figures 1d and 2d.

Procedures

Each student group should have photocopies of all the *Caminalcules* (Figures 1a and 2a) and the blank strata sheets (Figures 1b and 2b) located in the Support Materials section of this activity. The students should cut out all the *Caminalcules*, keeping the related data attached.

Each *Caminalcule* provided represents the morphological average of a number of *Caminalcules* found at a particular location. The "average of" number is located below each *Caminalcule* in parenthesis. For example, one *Caminalcule* might be represented by an average of four finds. This information, although fictitious, is provided to help the student understand that there is some morphological variation within the specimens of a given species found at a given site and that conclusions are based on a range of specimens rather than on a single individual.

The name listed with each *Caminalcule* is the name of the formation (geologic layer) in which it was found. If the specimen is listed as *Upper Wallacian*, it was found in the upper or more recent part of the layer called the Wallacian Formation. The amount of time (in thousands of years) that it took to form that particular layer is shown for each layer.

Following a discussion of the issues mentioned here, students should follow the specific instructions that follow:

Specific Instructions

1. Working with one genus at a time, each student group should arrange the *Caminalcules* from that genus (Figure 1a and 2a) on the appropriate stratrigraphic column (Figures 1b and 2b) by placing each individual in the stratum (layer) in which it was found on the appropriate blank worksheet.
2. Next, the species in the genus should be arranged into a logical morphology versus time tree (Figure 1). *Note: It is best if the students do not see these example trees prior to constructing their own.*
3. Draw the genus evolution tree on a chart showing morphology versus time. The time units are shown on the Y-axis. The extent of morphological change are estimated (no units) and shown on the X-axis. The answers are provided for teachers as Figures 1d and 2d.
4. Students should now repeat the steps above for the sample from the other genus.
5. To understand punctuated equilibrium, one must examine it point by point with the Darwinian view of phyletic gradualism. Therefore, have the students make a comparison list of the two trees. The two patterns of evolution along with implications for each are contrasted in Table 1.
6. Have students define the following terms with reference to their constructed trees:

   Transformation

   Speciation

   Lineage

   Strata

   Morphology

   Evolutionary Tree

   Evidence
7. Have students respond to the following questions with reference to their constructed trees:

   What is the geological meaning of "fast" and "slow"?

   What is the biological meaning of "fast" and "slow"?

   How do paleontologists decide if fossil organisms are of differing species?

Additional Considerations

After having students make the basic comparisons of phyletic gradualism and punctuated equilibrium, one could divide the class into two groups and study the range of professional opinion on the issue of punctuated equilibrium and then discuss the scientific merit of each evolutionary pattern. The following articles may prove to be useful. Many are available on the Internet along with websites devoted specifically to the debate regarding punctuated equilibrium generally. Those articles with an asterisk generally offer negative views about punctuated equilibrium while the others are either positive or provide an unbiased overview.

Alters, B.J., & McComas, W.F. (1994). Punctuated equilibrium: The missing link in evolution education. *The American Biology Teacher, 56*(6), 334–40.

Gould, S.J. (1977). Darwin's untimely burial. In *Ever since Darwin*. New York: Norton.

Gould, S.J., & Eldredge, N. (1977). Punctuated equilibria: The tempo and mode of evolution reconsidered. *Paleobiology, 3*, 115–51.

Eldredge, N., & Gould, S.J. (1972). Punctuated equilibria: An alternative to phyletic gradualism. In T.J. Schopf (Ed.), *Models in paleobiology* (pp. 82–115). San Francisco: Freeman, Cooper.

Eldredge, N. (1989). *Time frames: The evolution of punctuated equilibria*. Princeton: Princeton University Press.

Lewin, R. (1980). Evolutionary theory under fire. *Science, 210*(21), 883–87.

*Whitfield, P. (1993). *The natural history of evolution*. New York: Doubleday.

*Whitfield, P. (1993). *From so simple a beginning: The book of evolution*. New York: McMillan.

Students should be cautioned that the fossil record provides specific challenges to scientists because fossils may be broken and/or have missing parts, only 10% of geologic time is preserved in sedimentary layers (where fossils are likely to form and be preserved), and paleontologists generally decide if fossils are of differing species by comparing them to similar living organisms.

Debate and/or Discussion Topics

Some phyletic gradualists would state that the nine layers in the Pedivarious evolutionary sequence are not complete (Figure 3). Perhaps little or no rock is formed in a period between Gouldian and Eldredgean and consequently there are no fossils represented from this period. Therefore the actual evolution of the genus Pedivarious could be gradual!

The punctuationalists would counter by stating that the gradualists are arguing from lack of evidence (this is a great place to have a discussion about the nature of science, such as: what is scientific evidence?). Gould and Eldredge (1977) stated that "(p)hyletic gradualism was an a priori assertion from the start—it was never "seen" in the rocks . . . (w)e think that it has now become an empirical fallacy" (p. 115).

Acknowledgements

We acknowledge the contribution of the late J.R. Camin of the University of Kansas who developed the fictitious organisms called *Caminalcules*. He applied basic evolutionary principles and designed these creatures to be used in teaching various aspects of evolutionary biology. We have modified two of the *Caminalcules* for use in the activity presented here.

We thank Susan Lafferty, director of education at the Huntington Art Museum, Library and Botanical Gardens for lending her artistic talents by drawing the modified *Caminalcules*.

References

Benton, M. (1993). Four feet on the ground. In S.J. Gould (Ed.), *The book of life*. New York: W.W. Norton.

Darwin, C. (1975). *The origin of species. Introduced and abridged by Philip Appleman.* New York: W.W. Norton.

Eldredge, N., & Gould, S.J. (1972). Punctuated equilibria: An alternative to phyletic gradualism. In T.J. Schopf (Ed.), *Models in paleobiology* (pp. 82–115). San Francisco: Freeman, Cooper.

Futuyma, D.J. (1986). *Evolutionary biology*. Sunderland: Sinauer Associates.

Gould, S.J. (1977). Darwin's Untimely Burial. In *Ever Since Darwin*. New York: Norton.

Rhodes, F.H.T. (1984). Science correspondence: Darwin's gradualism and empiricism. *Nature, 309*, 116.

Van Andel, T. (1981). Consider the incompleteness of the fossil record. *Nature, 294*, 397–98.

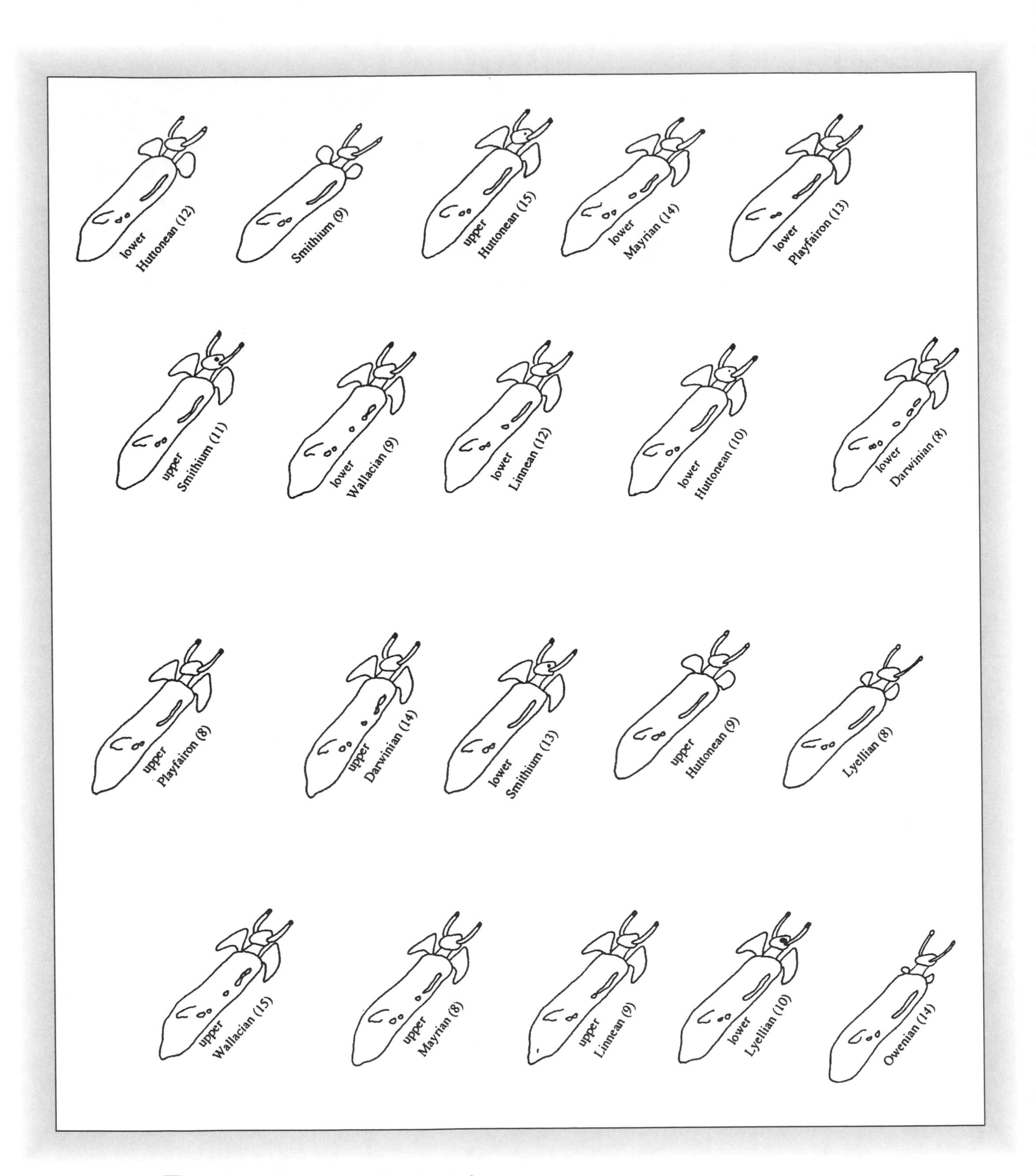

FIGURE 1A ■ Members of the Genus Molluscaformis from various strata.

FIGURE 1B Stratigraphic sequence for the genus Molluscaformis.

Formation	Duration (Years)	
Owenian	250,000	
Lyellian	300,000	
Smithium	150,000	
Huttonean	100,000	
Playfairon	80,000	
Linnean	175,000	
Mayrian	200,000	
Wallacian	50,000	
Darwinian	100,000	

FIGURE 1C ■ Answer key/members of the genus Molluscaformis shown in strategraphic sequence.

Formation	Duration (Years)	
Owenian	250,000	
Lyellian	300,000	
Smithium	150,000	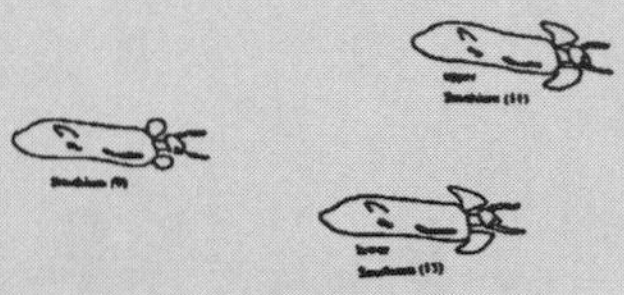
Huttonean	100,000	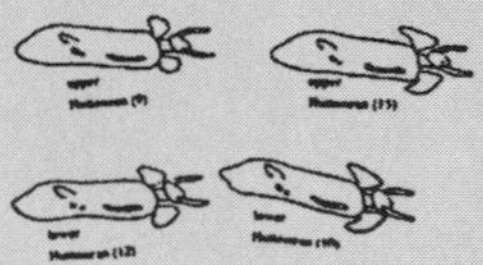
Playfairon	80,000	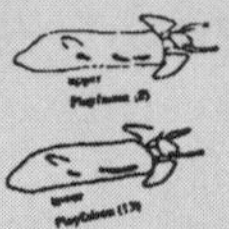
Linnean	175,000	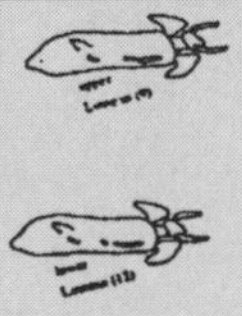
Mayrian	200,000	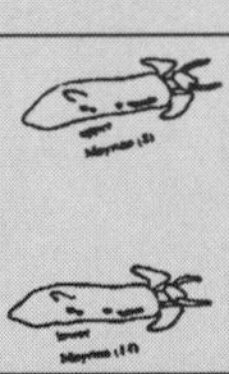
Wallacian	50,000	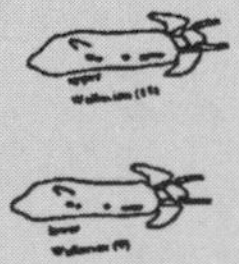
Darwinian	100,000	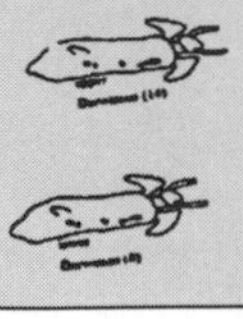

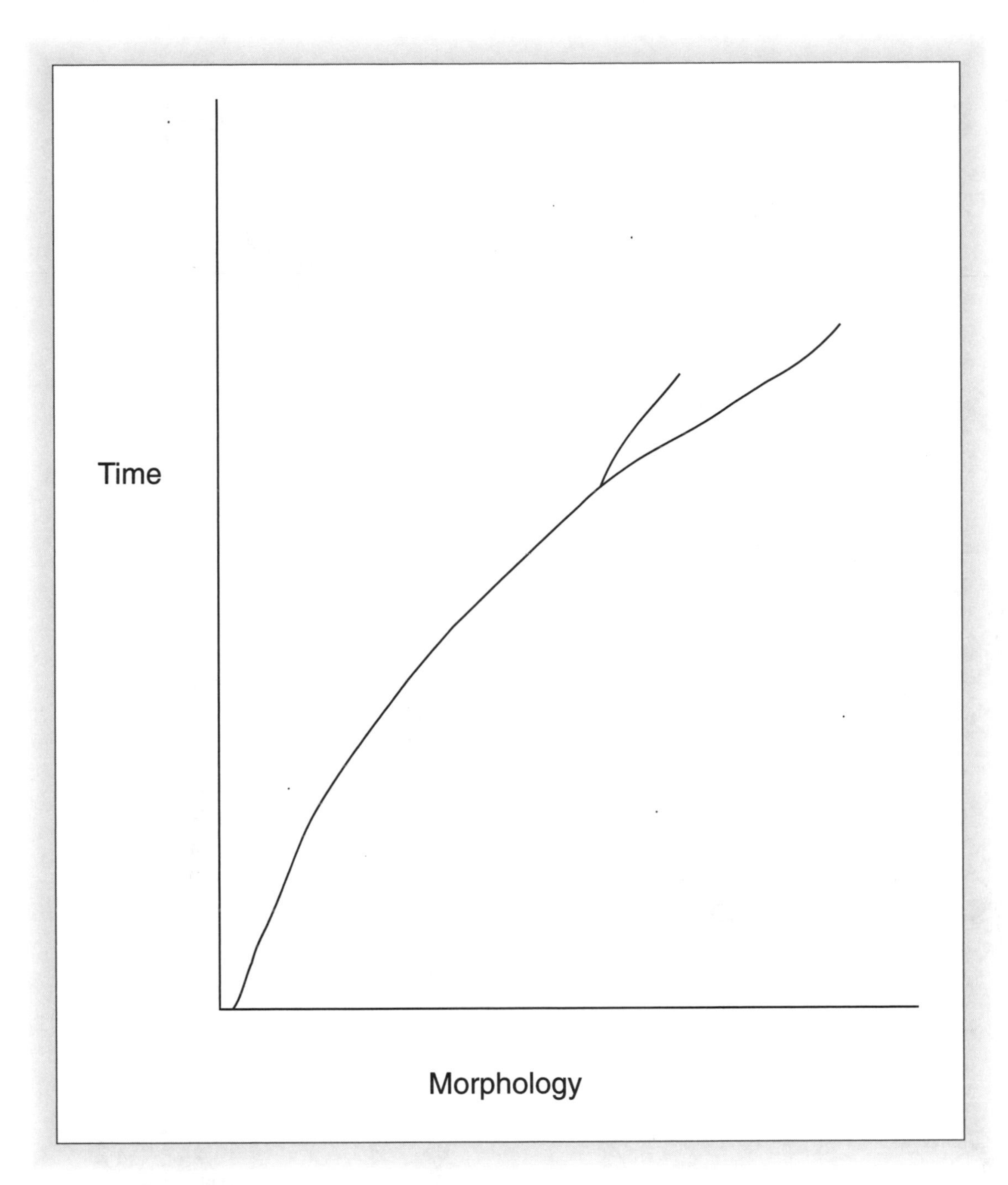

FIGURE 1D Answer key: The gradual pattern of speciation with Molluscaformis.

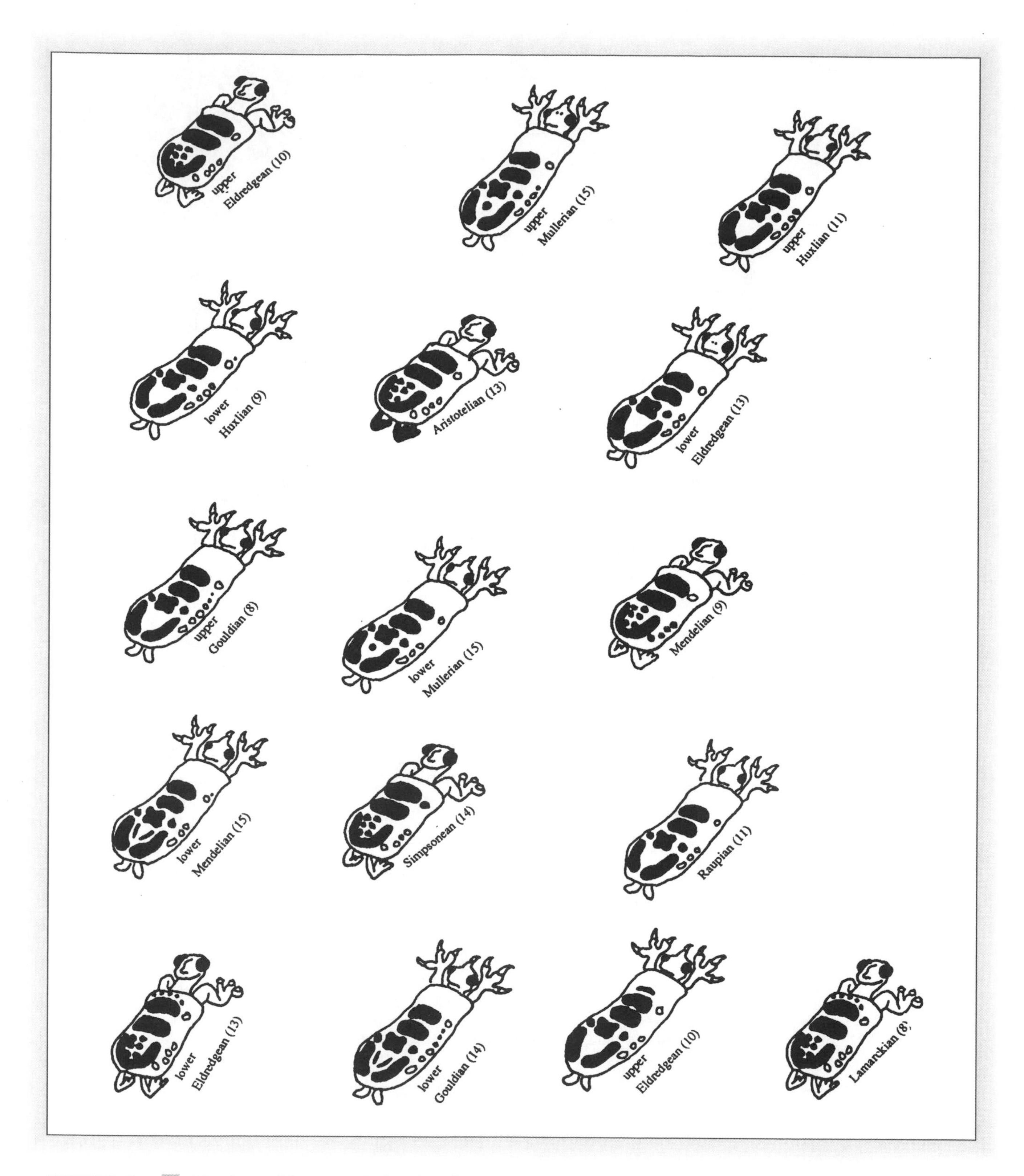

FIGURE 2A ▪ Members of the genus Pedivarious from various strata.

FIGURE 2B Stratigraphic sequence for the genus Pedivarious.

Formation	Duration (Years)	
Lamarckian	75,000	
Aristotelian	100,000	
Simpsonean	200,000	
Mendelian	100,000	
Eldredgean	35,000	
Gouldian	50,000	
Huxlian	250,000	
Raupian	100,000	
Mullerian	200,000	

FIGURE 2C Answer key.

Formation	Duration (Years)	
Lamarckian	75,000	
Aristotelian	100,000	
Simpsonean	200,000	
Mendelian	100,000	
Eldredgean	35,000	
Gouldian	50,000	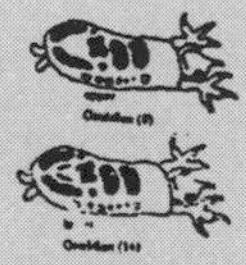
Huxlian	250,000	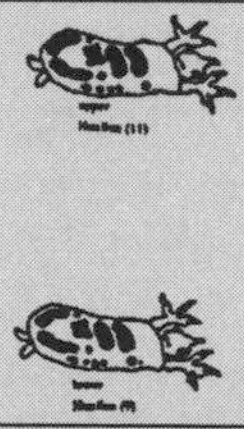
Raupian	100,000	
Mullerian	200,000	

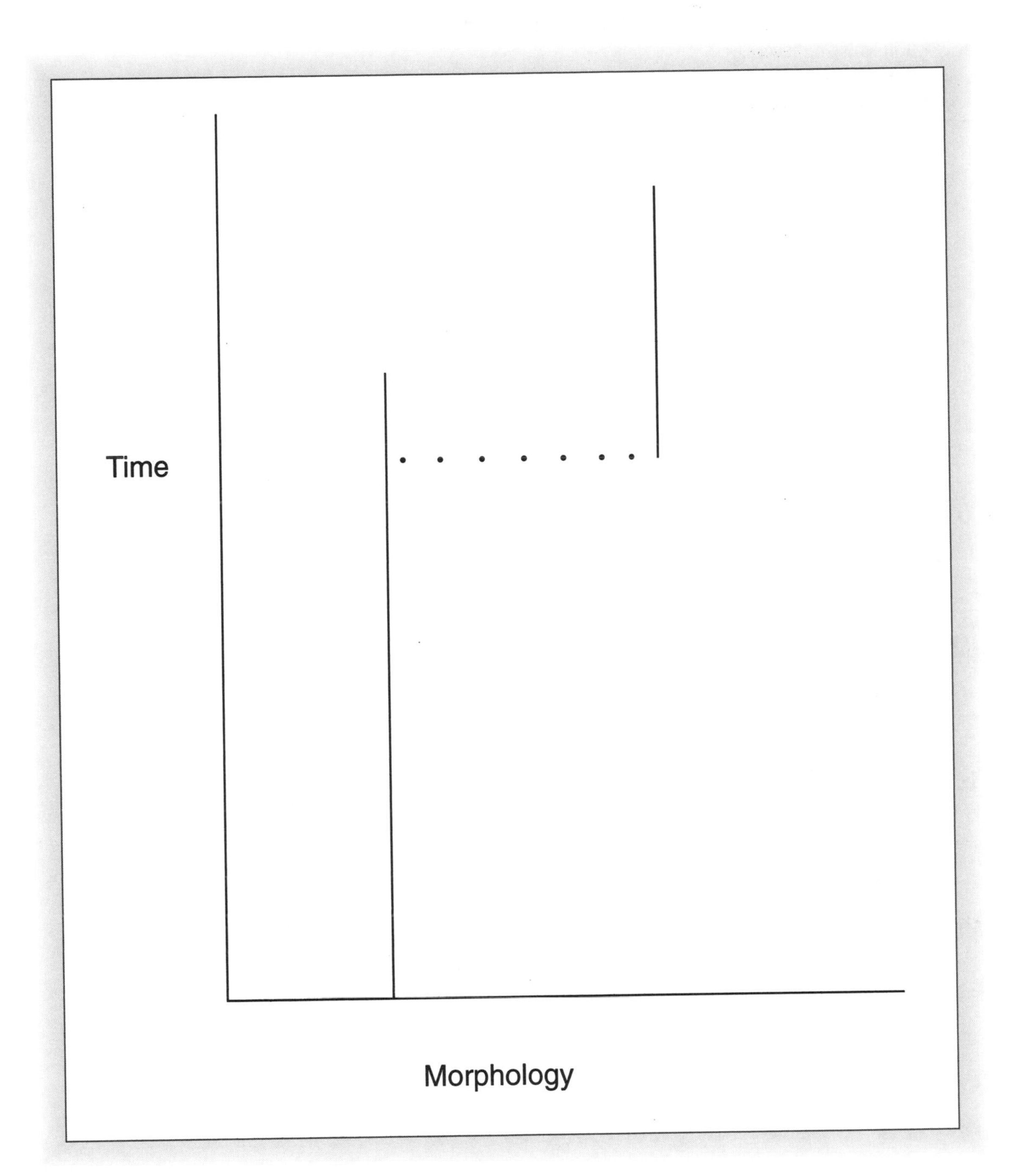

FIGURE 2D Answer key: The punctuated pattern of speciation with Pedivarious.

FIGURE 3 Missing strata: An explanation for the evolutionary development of Pedivarious based on unseen events within missing layers.

Formation	Duration (Years)	
Lamarckian	75,000	
Aristotelian	100,000	
Simpsonean	200,000	
Mendelian	100,000	
Eldredgean	35,000	
Gouldian	50,000	
Huxlian	250,000	
Raupian	100,000	
Mullerian	200,000	

Possible missing layers, representing up to 500,000 years

TABLE 1 Comparison of phyletic gradualism and punctuated equilibrium.

Caminalcules	
Fictional Genus: *Molluscaformis*	**Fictional Genus: *Pedivarious***
Name: Phyletic Gradualism	**Name: Punctuated Equilibrium**
Principal Proponent: Darwin	**Principal Proponents: Eldredge and Gould**
• New species develop gradually and slowly with little evidence of stasis	• New species develop rapidly and then experience long period of stasis
• The fossil record should contain numerous transitional forms within the lineage of any one type of organism	• The fossil record should contain few transitional forms with the maintenance of given forms for long periods of time
• New species arise via the transformation of an ancestral population	• New species arise as lineages are split
• The entire ancestral form usually transforms into the new species (sympatry)	• A small subpopulation of the ancestral form gives rise to the new species (allopatry)
• Speciation usually involves the entire geographic range of the species	• The subpopulation is in an isolated area at the periphery of the range

Adapted from Eldredge, 1989; Futuyma, 1986; Rhodes, 1984; and Gould & Eldredge, 1977.

Using DNA-DNA Hybridization Data to Build a Phylogenetic Tree of the Human and Ape Superfamily

 Caroline Alexandra Maier

Overview

In this 90-minute activity, students learn how the early technique of DNA-DNA hybridization reveals the genetic difference between species. Then they use actual genetic difference data to create a phylogenetic tree of the human and ape superfamily, Hominoidea. They calibrate their DNA clock and use it to estimate the divergence dates of the various branches on the tree. The activity expands theoretical studies of DNA-DNA hybridization, molecular phylogeny, and DNA clocks by allowing students to use real DNA difference data to understand species' evolutionary relationships. Since the generated tree shows the relationships among humans and our closest relatives, the activity can also serve as an introduction to a unit on human evolution.

Evolutionary Principles Illustrated

- DNA-DNA hybridization
- Phylogeny
- Divergence
- Molecular clock theory

Background Information

One of the important aspects of evolution is that it gives a historical context to biological diversity. In the eighteenth century, Carolus Linnaeus organized species into a hierarchy of increasingly inclusive groups based on physical similarity. However, because Linnaeus pre-dated Darwin, his taxonomy did not address familial relationships among species. For example,

---

This activity is based on the original work by Caroline Alexandra Mainer (2004), "Building a phylogenetic tree of the human and ape superfamily using DNA-DNA hybridization data," in *The American Biology Teacher*, *66*(8), 560–66. It has been adapted and reprinted with permission of the publisher.

Linnean classification could recognize the striking physical similarities between pygmy and common chimpanzees, but it could not address why these similarities exist. By recognizing that physical similarity can mirror familial relationships, Darwin's Law of Common Descent added a new historical dimension to Linnaean taxonomy and initiated the discipline of systematics (Campbell & Reece, 2002).

Systematics is a significant and dynamic discipline within the field of evolutionary biology whose products provide the foundation for other evolutionary and biological studies (Futuyma, 1998). Like many other biology textbooks, Campbell and Reece's *Biology* (6th ed.) has an informative section on phylogeny, with diagrams of several phylogenetic trees and a good general discussion of the principle that DNA sequence similarity provides exceptionally powerful insights into species' relationships. The goal of systematics is to understand the history, or phylogeny, of groups of related species. To do this, systematists compare physical similarities among several species, use the comparisons to infer the species' evolutionary backgrounds, and express the results in a phylogenetic tree (Diamond, 1992; Campbell & Reece, 2002). The earliest systematists compared large-scale morphological characteristics. Current researchers still use these valuable features, but advances in molecular biology now allow them to include DNA sequence comparisons in their studies (Diamond, 1992; Campbell & Reece, 2002). Since DNA is the fundamental unit of inheritance, sequence comparisons provide powerful insights into hereditary relationships. At the time two populations split from their common ancestor, they initially carry nearly identical pools of DNA sequences inherited from the ancestral species. Over time, independent mutations occur throughout the genomes of the two lineages, and this decreases their genetic similarity. The longer the time since two species diverged from their common ancestor, the greater the genetic difference. Since the average rate of DNA sequence evolution appears to be uniform and constant in related lineages, DNA divergence acts like a smoothly ticking clock (Sibley & Alquist, 1984). Therefore, difference in DNA sequence can be used to determine the pattern of relative divergence events among a group of related species. This can be illustrated as a branching pattern that shows the group's evolutionary relationships. Figure 1 on page 360 illustrates how DNA difference data are used to develop a phylogenetic tree for a hypothetical group of species.

Incidentally, if the actual divergence time of a pair of species in the group is known from the fossil record, the DNA clock can be calibrated to absolute values, so that DNA difference data estimate the date when pairs of species diverged from their common ancestor (Sibley & Alquist, 1984). Figure 1 explains how a hypothetical DNA clock is calibrated. Charles Sibley and Jon Alquist first applied DNA difference data to taxonomy in the 1970s. They used the newly developed technique of DNA-DNA hybridization to measure the amount of DNA sequence difference among bird species, and their work in avian taxonomy was pivotal. By the 1980s, Sibley and Alquist shifted their attention to the history of humans and our closest relatives: the two chimpanzee species, gorilla, orangutan, and the two gibbon species (Sibley & Alquist, 1984; Diamond, 1992). They constructed a phylogenetic tree of the human and ape superfamily, Hominoidea, using the Old World monkeys

(Cercopithecoidea) as an outgroup. The dates at which the Old World monkey and orangutan clades diverged from the main Hominoidea trunk are known from the fossil record, therefore, the DNA clock could be calibrated and used to date the divergence times of members of the superfamily (Sibley & Alquist, 1984).

However, specifically, how can the genetic difference among a group of related species be determined? How do DNA difference data reveal evolutionary relationships? Moreover, how are phylogenetic trees created? In order to understand the principles of phylogeny, students need to go beyond textbook reading assignments and use real data to develop phylogenetic trees of actual species. Unfortunately, activities for high school students and undergraduates that demonstrate principles of phylogeny are hard to come by and many of those that exist are simulation employing hypothetical species.

Materials Needed

Per group of two students:

- Envelope containing homologous 20-base pair DNA fragments from five hypothetical species
- Colored paper (at least five different colors)
- Scissors
- Copy of all figure sheets (Figures 1–7)

Procedures

Getting Started

In this activity, students learn how DNA-DNA hybridization measures genetic difference, then use Sibley and Alquist's genetic distance data to create their own phylogenetic tree of the hominoid superfamily. Furthermore, the students calibrate the DNA clock and use it to estimate the divergence dates of the various branches on the tree.

After a general overview of systematics, a simulation activity may be used to introduce the idea of genetic difference, the technique of DNA-DNA hybridization, and the principles of creating phylogenetic trees from genetic difference data. Pairs of students each receive an envelope containing homologous 20-base pair DNA fragments from five hypothetical species (Figure 2 on page 361).

The 5′-3′ and 3′-5′ strands of each fragment are on separate strips of paper; therefore, begin by reviewing DNA structure and base pairing rules as the students match complementary strands. The students count the number of hydrogen bonds holding each double-stranded fragment together and discover that the fragments from species B and C would denature at a higher temperature than the others since they are held by a greater number of H bonds (Figure 3 on page 362).

Next, the instructor explains that DNA-DNA hybridization was an early method for comparing the similarity between two DNA sequences before sequencing technology was developed. During the process of DNA-DNA hybridization, DNA from two species is denatured, brought together, and allowed to condense into a hybrid molecule composed of a single strand from each species. What students learn is that the homologous sequences from the two different species are similar, but not identical due to the independent mutations that have occurred since the two lineages split from their common ancestor. Furthermore, students will learn that hydrogen bonds do not form when mutations have resulted in the pairing of noncomplementary bases; thus, hybrid molecules denature at a lower temperature than parental fragments. Students will also learn from this exercise that there is a direct relationship between the genetic difference of two species' DNA and the amount by which the melting point of the hybrid is reduced. The term for this is the melting point depression. Incidentally, the students should know that a mathematical model converts actual depression values to percent genetic difference between two species' DNA. Therefore, even though DNA sequencing technology was not yet readily available in the 1970s, researchers were using melting point depression to accurately estimate genetic difference among groups of related species. Students see this direct relationship between the number of hydrogen bonds and genetic difference as they collect data on the hybrids formed by the five hypothetical species. Using this information, students fill in Figure 3, written on the board as a large table (can also be handed out as a worksheet for each group).

Creating a Phyogenetic Tree

Once students understand how DNA-DNA hybridization generates genetic difference data, they are ready to use the data to create a phylogenetic tree of the five hypothetical species. On the finished tree (Figure 4 on page 363), as on all phylogenetic trees, time is represented vertically. Modern species are listed along the top of the space that is flanked by both vertical axes, connected by branches that reach down through the space, and back into time, eventually splitting from the main trunk. Divergence points on the tree represent the common ancestor shared by the splitting lineages, and their vertical placement indicates the relative time the event occurred. Since the genetic difference among species is related to the time since lineages split, it is also represented as a vertical axis in Figure 4. Tracing any two species back to their common ancestor on the branching diagram reveals the percentage by which their DNA sequences differ. The genetic difference table for the five hypothetical species (Figure 3) contains all the information needed to create the branching pattern on a copy of the blank axes (Figure 5 on page 364).

First, students root the tree by identifying the outgroup, a species or group only distantly related to the study species. In the simulation, Species A is the outgroup since its DNA differs from the others by the greatest amount (50%). Students begin creating the diagram by drawing a deep "V" in the area delineated by the axes, with the divergence point positioned across from a 50% genetic difference point on the vertical axis, as shown in Figure 6 on page 365.

They label the top of the right arm "Species A." The empty left arm of the V is now ready to be expanded into a tree. Creating the tree is much like solving a jigsaw puzzle. When all the species are in the correct place on the tree, it is possible to trace any pair back to their common ancestor and read their genetic difference off the left axis.

Next, students build the tree by identifying the two most closely related species on the genetic difference table (D and E, Figure 3), drawing a branch from the main trunk of the tree at a point corresponding to the correct genetic distance between the taxa, and labeling the end of the branch with the name of the appropriate species. More distantly related lineages are added to the tree until it is complete (Figure 4).

Finally, as students finish the sample tree, point out that Species B has the same genetic difference to Species C as it does to Species D and E (30%). Since evolutionary rates are assumed to be uniform in related lineages, all groups branching from a single point should have an approximately equal genetic difference. Slight differences in evolutionary rates and chance events, among other things, can affect this pattern, but it is widespread enough that systematists use this "relative rate test" to double-check the trees they develop.

Working with Real Data

Now that students have learned to create phylogenetic trees from DNA difference data, they are ready to work with real data. Instructors introduce this part of the activity by showing students pictures of the common chimpanzee, pygmy chimpanzee, common gibbon, siamang gibbon, gorilla, human, and orangutan. Next, ask student groups to predict the evolutionary relationships among the species by organizing them into a possible tree. After recognizing the diversity in the students' ideas, explain that systematists traditionally argued over the relationships among these species. For example, in an attempt to clarify the phylogeny of this same group, Charles Sibley and Jon Alquist used DNA-DNA hybridization to collect genetic difference data on these species. Next, the instructor challenges the groups to use Sibley and Alquist's data to create a phylogenetic tree of the hominoid superfamily. Copies of the pair-based genetic difference data table (Figure 7 on page 366) and empty axes (Figure 5) provide the necessary information and structure. Incidentally, this tree is more difficult than the sample the students have just completed, so it is best to work in pencil with an eraser nearby. The split to the two species within the main gibbon lineage is perhaps the greatest challenge because divergence within a side branch, although common in nature, is initially unexpected by the students. This might confuse some groups, but with a couple of hints, these students will solve the problem and end up with the correct final tree (Figure 8 on page 367) which they can confirm with a relative rate test.

Calibrating DNA Clocks

As each group finishes its tree, students are given the information needed to calibrate the DNA clock. This is a simple matter of relating the two vertical axes of genetic difference and time to each other. Tell the students that the fossil record shows that the Old World monkey and ape lineages, which differ in 7.3% of their DNA, diverged approximately 30 million years ago. The fossil record also indicates that the orangutan lineage branched from the gorilla/chimp lineage approximately 16 million years ago. Orangutans differ genetically from the great apes by approximately 3.7% (Sibley & Alquist, 1984; Diamond, 1992). Challenge the students to calibrate the DNA clock so that it converts the genetic difference between pairs of species into their approximate divergence date. This is done by scaling the Years axis on the right side of the tree diagram. Students need only to place 30 on the Years axis across from the corresponding genetic difference of 7.3%, 16 across from the genetic difference of 3.7%, and divide the rest of the axis proportionally (Figure 8 on page 367).

Students then use their calibrated DNA clock to determine the approximate divergence time for the various lineages on the tree. They identify our closest and most distant relatives among the ape species and determine whether the two chimpanzee species are most closely related to gorillas or to humans. Finally, they identify which pair is most closely related: the two gibbon species or humans and chimpanzees.

As student groups finish their trees, they check their work by reading *The Third Chimpanzee* (Diamond, 1992, pp. 16–25). This delightful section describes the process of DNA-DNA hybridization and the history of its use by Sibley and Alquist in simple, straightforward, and interesting language that students easily understand. It describes Sibley and Alquist's data, shows a diagram of the tree generated by the data, and explains how a clock can be applied to the tree. In addition, it describes the tree's implications for human and chimpanzee classification. Having just finished using the actual data to create the tree described by Diamond, students become engrossed in the reading and understand the concepts more thoroughly than they otherwise would. Many students will likely continue reading the book outside of class. When this happens, the activity has fulfilled its purpose in making evolution relevant and interesting to students.

Additional Considerations

Although developed for advanced high school students and undergraduate in general biology courses, this activity can be adapted for younger students by leaving out the concept-laden section on DNA-DNA hybridization. Instead of generating their own genetic difference table, the students can use the data in completed tables to create phylogenetic trees, turning this into a simpler puzzle-solving activity.

References

Campbell, N.A., & Reece, J.B. (2002). *Biology* (6th ed.). San Francisco, CA Benjamin/Cummings.

Diamond, J. (1992). *The third chimpanzee.* New York: Harper Collins.

Futuyma, D.J. (1998). *Evolutionary biology* (3rd ed.). Sunderland, MA: Sinauer Associates.

Sibley C.G., & Alquist, J.E. (1984). The phylogeny of hominid primates, as indicated by DNA-DNA hybridization. *Journal of Molecular Evolution, 20*(1), 2–15.

Using DNA-DNA Hybridization Data to Build a Phylogenetic Tree of the Human and Ape Superfamily: Figures

When two populations initially diverge from their common ancestor, they carry nearly identical pools of DNA sequences inherited from the common ancestor. After divergence, independent mutations occur continuously throughout the genomes of the two lineages, and this gradually decreases their genetic similarity over time. The longer the time since two species diverged from their common ancestor, the greater the genetic difference (A). In this example, we can assume the lineage leading to modern species Y diverged more recently from those of species W and X than did Z, since species Y is more genetically similar to species W and X than is Z. Since the average rate of DNA sequence evolution appears to be uniform and constant in related lineages, genomic difference data can be used to determine relative divergence events among a group of related species (Sibley & Alquist, 1984).This information can then be used to develop a branching pattern that shows the group's evolutionary relationships. Notice that the principle of constant average rate of DNA sequence evolution means that all branches stemming from a divergence point on the tree (B) have identical numbers of genetic character states, as represented by horizontal slashes. In this example, the lineages of species W, X, and Y all reflect three genetic character states since the time they diverged from their common ancestor, represented on the tree by a solid circle. Dashed arrows trace the evolution of species W, X, and Y. Numbers on each arrow reflect the order of the three character states in each lineage. If the actual divergence times of a pair of species in the group are known from the fossil record, the DNA clock can be calibrated to absolute values. A calibrated clock uses DNA difference data to estimate the actual date when pairs of species diverged from their common ancestor. In the example (B), the hypothetical fossil record shows that species W and Z diverged 8,000 years ago. Since W and Z have experienced four genetic character states since they diverged from their common ancestor, genetic character states occur approximately every 2,000 years within this group. The lineage leading to modern species Y must have diverged from the main trunk of the tree approximately 6,000 years ago since three character states have occurred.

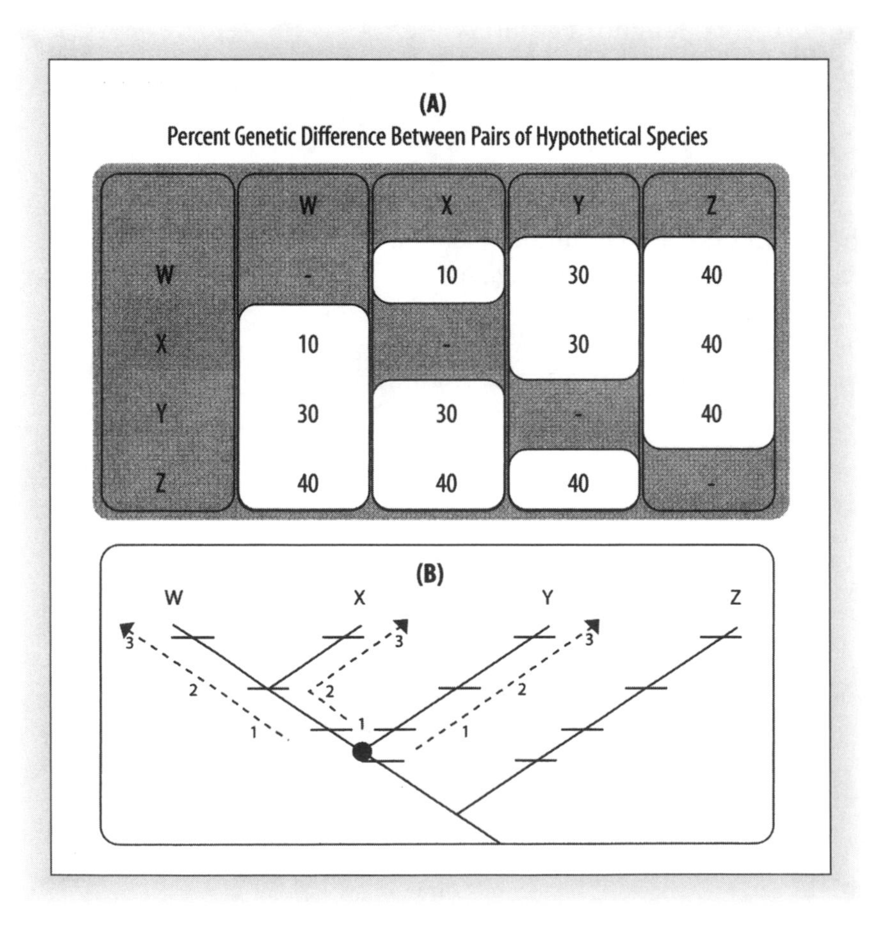
(A)
Percent Genetic Difference Between Pairs of Hypothetical Species

	W	X	Y	Z
W	-	10	30	40
X	10	-	30	40
Y	30	30	-	40
Z	40	40	40	-

FIGURE 1 ■ The use of genetic difference data in creating and calibrating a phylogenetic tree.

Species A		Species B		Species C		Species D		Species E	
5'	3'	5'	3'	5'	3'	5'	3'	5'	3'
G	C	A	T	T	A	T	A	T	A
C	G	G	C	A	T	G	C	G	C
G	C	G	C	G	C	G	C	G	C
A	T	G	C	G	C	C	G	C	G
C	G	C	G	C	G	C	G	C	G
C	G	C	G	C	G	C	G	C	G
C	G	T	A	A	T	A	T	A	T
T	A	T	A	T	A	T	A	T	A
T	A	T	A	T	A	T	A	T	A
T	A	A	T	C	G	A	T	A	T
T	A	T	A	T	A	T	A	T	A
C	G	C	G	A	T	A	T	A	T
A	T	C	G	C	G	C	G	T	A
A	T	C	G	C	G	T	A	C	G
A	T	G	C	G	C	G	C	G	C
G	C	G	C	G	C	G	C	G	C
G	C	T	A	G	C	G	C	G	C
C	G	C	G	C	G	C	G	C	G
C	G	A	T	A	T	A	T	A	T
A	T	A	T	A	T	A	T	A	T
3'	5'	3'	5'	3'	5'	3'	5'	3'	5'

FIGURE 2 Homologous 20-base pair DNA fragments from five hypothetical species.

To use these fragments in the DNA-DNA hybridization simulation, enlarge and copy each species' fragment on its own color of paper, then cut the 5′-3′ and the 3′-5′ strands apart so that students can form hybrid molecules.

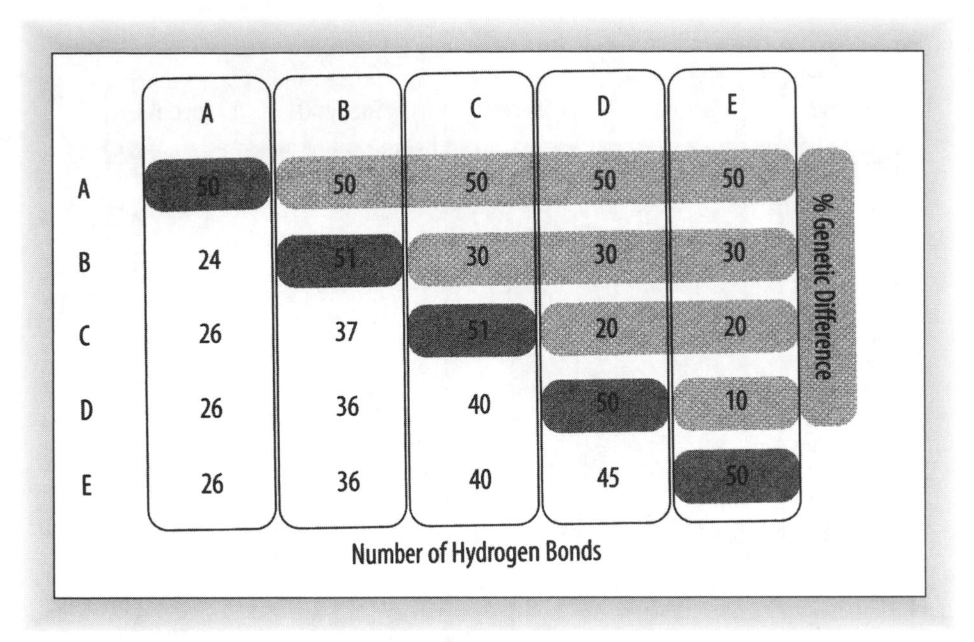

FIGURE 3 ■ The genetic difference and number of hydrogen bonds between homologous 20-based pair DNA fragments taken from the five hypothetical species used in the DNA-DNA hybridization simulation.

Complementary strands from two different species were aligned. To determine percent genetic difference, divide the number of mismatched bases in the hybrid molecule by the total number of bases in the fragment (20). Multiply the resulting product by 100. To determine the number of hydrogen bonds that would hold the hybrid molecule together, two bonds for each A-T pair and three bonds for each C-G pair were summed. The darkly shaded diagonal line shows the number of hydrogen bonds found in the native, nonhybrid molecules. White boxes below the diagonal show the number of hydrogen bonds holding together each hybrid molecule, while the lightly shaded boxes above the diagonal show the percent genetic difference between pairs of molecules. Since the bottom left and top right portions of the table are mirror images of each other, it is possible to compare the number of hydrogen bonds between hybrid molecules to their percent genetic difference by looking across the darkly shaded diagonal line.

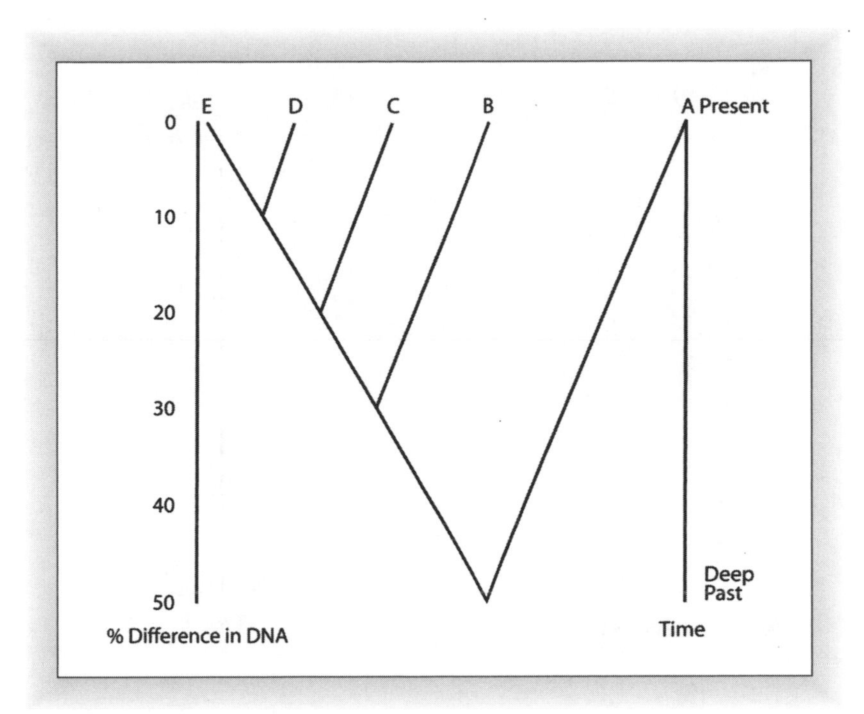

FIGURE 4 Phylogenic tree of five hypothetical species.

This diagram shows the branching pattern of the lineages leading to modern species A, B, C, D, and E. Tracing any two species back to their branch point allows their genetic difference to be read from the left vertical axis.

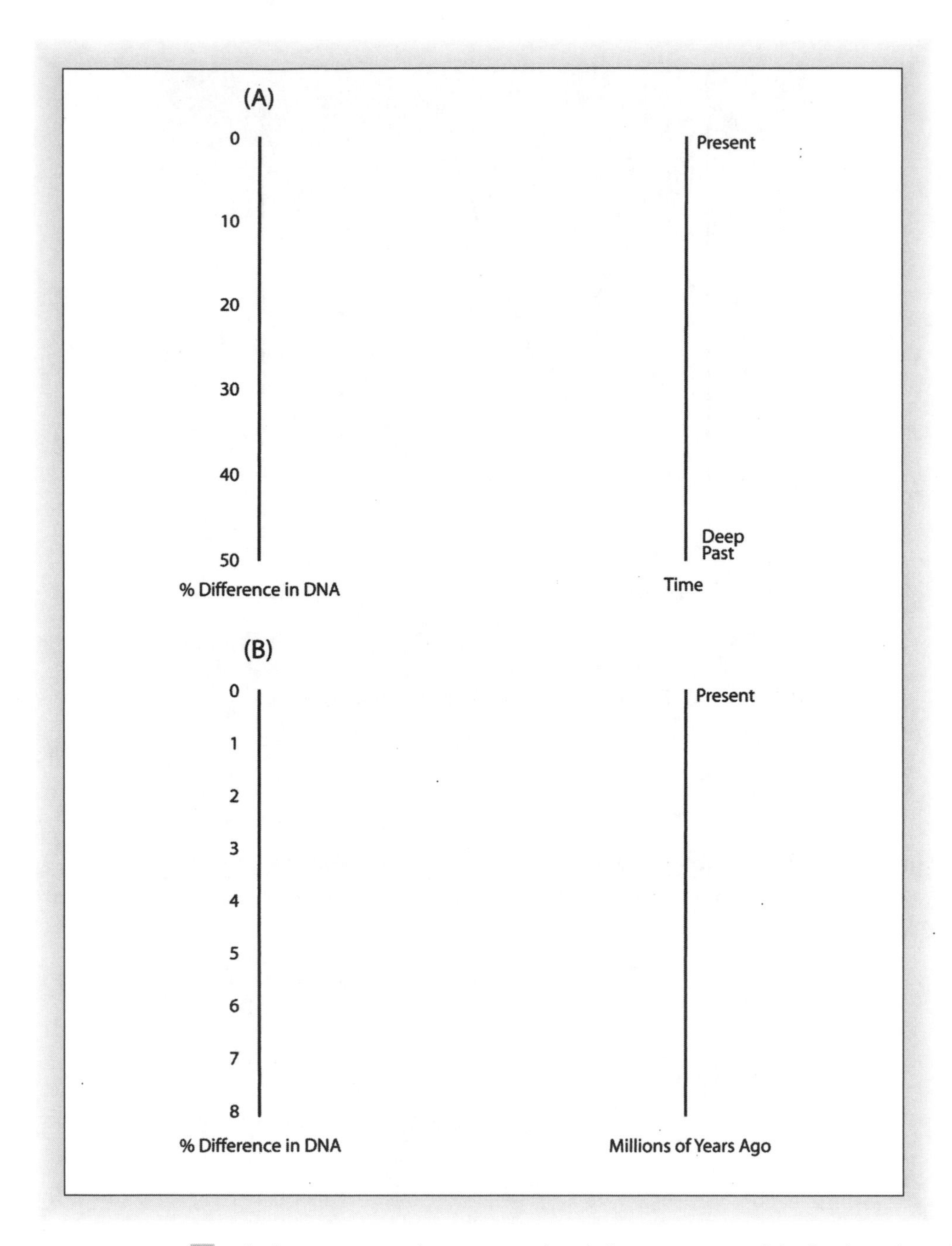

FIGURE 5 Blank axes to use when creating the phylogenetic trees of the five hypothetical species (A), and of the Hominoidea superfamily (B).

These axes are adapted from the diagram used by Sibley and Alquist (1984) and shown in *The Third Chimpanzee* (Diamond, 1992). The left axis corresponds to percentage of DNA difference, while the right axis depicts time and is used to calibrate a DNA clock to the tree. An enlarged copy of these axes guides students in creating their simulated phylogenetic tree.

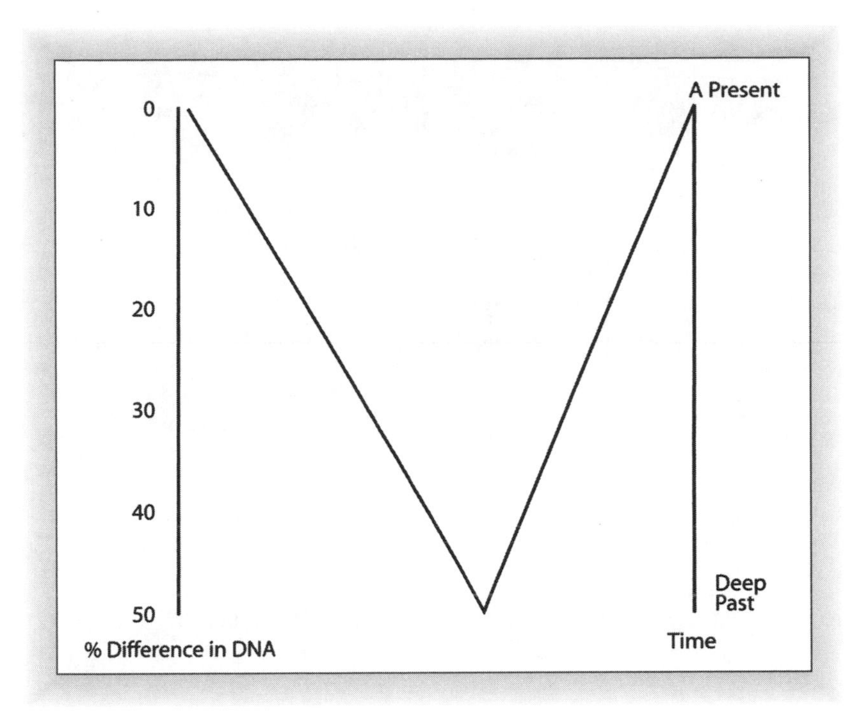

FIGURE 6 ■ Rooting the simulated phylogenetic tree of the five hypothetical species.

This diagram shows how the tree is started using Species A as the outgroup. The tree will be built along the left arm of the V. Notice that the branching point of the tree corresponds to a genetic difference of 50% since Species A differs from the other species by this amount.

	Human	Common Chimp	Pygmy Chimp	Common Gibbon	Siamang Gibbon	Gorilla	Old World Monkeys	Orangutan
Human	-	1.6	1.6	5.0	5.0	2.3	7.3	3.6
Common Chimp	1.6	-	0.7	5.0	5.0	2.3	7.3	3.6
Pygmy Chimp	1.6	0.7	-	5.0	5.0	2.3	7.3	3.6
Common Gibbon	5.0	5.0	5.0	-	2.2	5.0	7.3	5.0
Siamang Gibbon	5.0	5.0	5.0	2.2	-	5.0	7.3	5.0
Gorilla	2.3	2.3	2.3	5.0	5.0	-	7.3	3.6
Old World Monkeys	7.3	7.3	7.3	7.3	7.3	7.3	-	7.3
Orangutan	3.6	3.6	3.6	5.0	5.0	3.6	7.3	-

FIGURE 7 ■ Genetic difference matrix of species in the superfamily Hominoidea.

This matrix, developed frm Sibley and Alquist's DNA-DNA hybridization data (Sibley & Alquist, 1984) and used in *The Third Chimpanzee* (Diamond, 1992) shows the approximate genetic difference, in percent, between the genomes of all pairs of ape and human species.

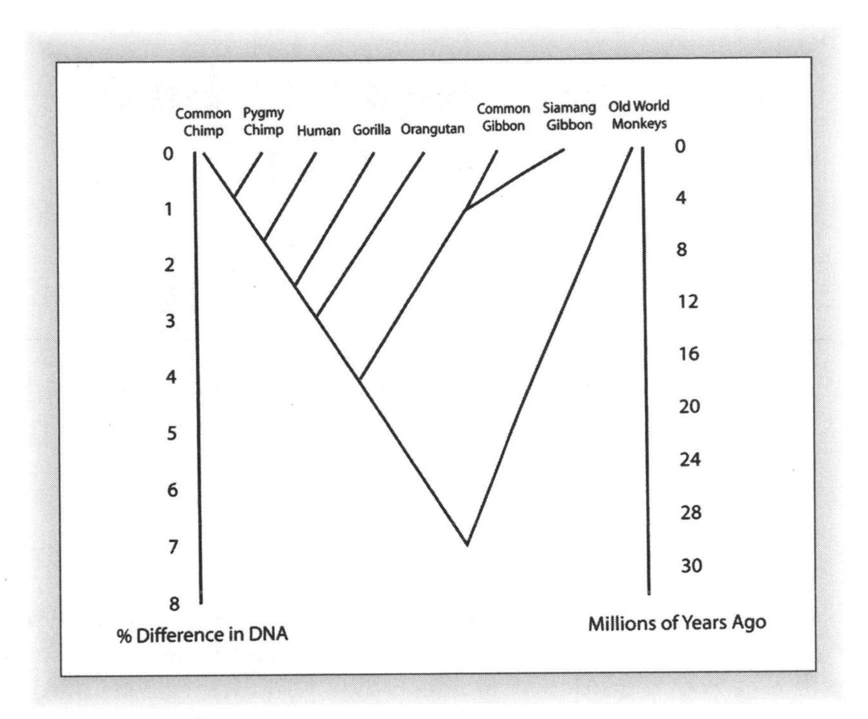

FIGURE 8 Phylogentic tree of the superfamily Hominoidae.

This diagram, based on Sibley and Alquist's (1984) DNA-DNA hybridization data and tree, and included in *The Third Chimpanzee* (Diamond,1992), shows the branching pattern of human and ape lineages. Tracing any two species back to their branch point allows their genetic difference to be read from the left axis. The right axis calibrates the molecular clock by relating actual divergence dates for the Old World monkey and orangutan clades known from the fossil record to their percentage of genetic difference. The date when any pair of species diverged from their common ancestor can be determined by tracing the two lineages back to their divergence point and reading the divergence date off the right axis.

Teaching Evolution through the Founder Effect

William H. Leonard and Elizabeth Edmondson

Overview

In this activity, students will learn how to use Hardy-Weinberg equations to calculate genotypic and phenotypic frequencies within a population. With the help of a guided worksheet, they will further consider how the founder effect can alter the genotypic (and thus phenotype) makeup of a population, resulting in evolution.

Evolutionary Principles Illustrated

- Founder effect
- Microevolution

Background Information

The specific biological concepts that are to be learned and/or reinforced from this activity are:

1. Most simple traits in humans have two gene loci, one on each homologous chromosome of the nucleus of each somatic cell. Only one of those loci is present in a gamete.
2. A simple trait can have contrasting alleles on each loci, one that is dominant and one that is recessive.
3. The human trait, widow's peak, is caused by a dominant allele. This phenotype is easily observed in a human individual.

This activity is based on "Teaching evolution through the founder effect: A standards based activity," by William H. Leonard and Elizabeth Edmondson (2003), in *The American Biology Teacher, 65*(7), 538-41. It has been adapted and reprinted with permission of the publisher.

4. Any given human will have one of three possible genotypes for the widow's peak trait: *WW*, *Ww*, or *ww*. The first two genotypes will code for widow's peak and the last for straight hairline.
5. Hardy and Weinberg have derived two equations that estimate the proportions in a population of genotypes and phenotypes for a simple trait such as widow's peak, as given in the following equation. Although there are several statistical assumptions in applying this equation to estimates of allele frequency change, the equation is nevertheless useful to estimate the changing allele proportions for a given trait in a population.

   $W + w = 1$ (for genotypes, where W = the frequency of the W allele and w = the frequency of the w allele) and

   $W^2 + 2\,Ww + w^2 = 1$ (for phenotypes, where W^2 = the frequency of individuals with a WW genotype, $2\,Ww$ = the frequency of individuals with a Ww genotype, and w^2 = the frequency of individuals with a ww genotype)

6. By observing the frequency of individuals expressing the recessive trait in a population, one can use the Hardy-Weinberg equations to estimate the frequency of the dominant and the recessive allele, the frequency of individuals that are homozygous dominant for the trait, and the frequency of individuals that are heterozygous for the trait.
7. Populations thrive or die depending on how well they can adapt to changing environmental conditions.
8. The founder effect, a type of genetic drift, is a phenomenon that changes the genetic composition of a population. This change occurs when a small population emigrates and becomes reproductively isolated from the parent population. This founding population may not be genetically representative of the parent population. As it grows, the smaller population may have a different gene pool with some alleles overrepresented or completely lost.
9. Natural selection results in the selection of traits based on how adaptive they are to the surrounding environment.
10. Evolution can be defined in both general and specific terms. Generally, and on a macro level, evolution means that life forms on Earth change over time. Specifically, and on a micro level, evolution is defined as a change in the allele frequency in a trait of a population over time.
11. A population is a group of organisms occupying a given area at the same time that are able to interbreed.

Materials

- One copy of the worksheet found in the Support Materials section for each student
- Calculators with square root function (per student pair)

Procedures

The procedures for this activity are contained within the student worksheet found in the Support Materials section. The first part of the activity is whole-class, while the second part of the activity will require the division of the class into four smaller groups.

Additional Considerations

Some organizational considerations when using this activity in your biology classroom are as follows:

Begin with a dramatic visual by showing the students a photo of the Munster family. Such a picture can be downloaded and printed from http://www.morticiasmorgue.com/munsters.html. If you have a color printer, you can make a beautiful, full-page overhead projection to share with your class. You can use another photo from http://www.ncrtec.org/tl/camp/gene/widow.htm that shows a more normal human with widow's peak. Finally, we found that it was crucial to help the students walk through the calculations for Table 1 from the Hardy-Weinberg equations. They could then complete Table 2 with their group.

Table 1 and Table 2 provide representative data for a typical biology class.

The Student Sheet, ready for double-sided photocopying and distribution to your students, follows on the next two pages.

TABLE 1 Frequencies of alleles, genotypes, and appearances of widow's peak for students in class.

Appearance and Genotype	W	w	W^2	$2\ Ww$	w^2
Frequencies	.155	.845	.024	.263	.714

TABLE 2 Frequencies of alleles/genotypes and appearances of widow's peak for four class groups.

Appearance and Genotype	W	w	W^2	$2\ Ww$	w^2
Group 1 Frequencies	.37	.63	.137	.4662	.397
Group 2 Frequencies	.29	.71	.084	.412	.504
Group 3 Frequencies	0	1	0	0	1
Group 4 Frequencies	.134	.866	.018	.232	.75

References

National Research Council (NRC). (1995). *National science education standards.* Washington, DC: National Academy Press.

Hardy, G.H. (1908). Mendelian proportions in a mixed population. *Science, 28,* 49–50.

Weinberg, W. (1909). Uber vererbungsgesetze beim menschen. Z. *Abst. u. Vererbl, 1,* 377–93, 440–60.

Hardy-Weinberg Equilibrium, Founder Effect, and Evolution: Student Materials

Overview

Do you have widow's peak? If you do, you may have a hairline like one of the "Munsters" instead of a straight hairline. (Widow's peak is rumored by folklore to foretell early widowhood.) It is caused by a dominant allele at the hairline gene site. We will call it *W*. But you have two hairline gene sites in each cell because you have a pair of homologous chromosomes, each with the same gene sites. Anyone who has a *W* on either of their chromosomes will have some form of peaked hairline such as the ones on the Munsters. Although the Munster hairline is a rather extreme form of widow's peak (that's Hollywood), it is easy to recognize in most humans as opposed to the straight-across hairline caused by genotype *ww*. How many of your classmates have widow's peak? How many are heterozygous for the trait (genotype *Ww* as opposed to the homozygous *WW*)? In this activity, you will use class data to find answers to these questions and be able to make predictions for future populations.

Materials

- Calculator with square-root function

Procedures

1. Observe each individual in the class and determine how many have a straight hairline *(ww)* and how many have widow's peak. Determine the percentage of those in the class with straight hairline (as opposed to those with widow's peak). Convert this percentage to a decimal. (For example 1% = .01 and the square root is 0.1.) The square-root of your class value of *ww* will be the frequency of *w* in the class population. What is this value?
2. The mathematicians Hardy and Weinberg proposed that, in the case of the hairline trait, all of the genes for hairline in a defined population (the total of all *W* and *w* genes) would be equal to 100% of the hairline alleles. This can be expressed mathematically:

   $$W + w = 1 \text{ (Equation 1)}$$

   They also proposed that all three possible genotype combinations of these alleles (homozygous dominants, heterozygotes, and homozygous recessives) are equal to 100%, represented by:

   $$W^2 + 2\,Ww + w^2 = 1 \text{ (Equation 2)}$$

   These two equations can be used to calculate for a given point in time both the frequencies of *W* and *w* alleles for a single trait in the population and also the frequencies of the three different genotype combinations. All one has to do to determine all genotype frequencies is to observe the percentage of homozygous recessives in a population (w^2) then use these two equations to calculate all other frequencies.

3. Substitute the value for *w* for your class data into Equation 1 and determine *W*.

4. Using Equation 2, calculate the percentages of all three phenotypes in your class.

5. Complete Table 1 for your class.

6. Describe the genotype percentages of the class with respect to hairline. How frequent are each the three genotypes?

7. Your teacher will randomly sort the class into four groups. Each group should determine its group data as was done in Table 1 and share these with the entire class, completing Table 2.

TABLE 1 Frequencies of alleles, genotypes, and appearances for students in class.

Appearance and Genotype	W	w	W^2	$2\ Ww$	w^2
Frequencies					

TABLE 2 Frequencies of alleles, genotypes, and appearances for four class groups.

Appearance and Genotype	W	w	W^2	$2\ Ww$	w^2
Group 1 Frequencies					
Group 2 Frequencies					
Group 3 Frequencies					
Group 4 Frequencies					

Interpretations

1. Describe how the frequency of a widow's peak differs in each group.

2. From examining Table 2, how would you describe the genetic differences in each group?

3. Identify the group that is most different genetically from the whole class.

4. Let's assume that each of the four groups migrates to a different place far away from each other, and only one group (the most different in #7 on page 373) survives the harsh new environment. This is an example of what is called founder effect. How would the observations for hairline trait in the surviving group be different in the future from that of your entire class?

5. Explain how this kind of allele shift and further selection could cause evolutionary change.

Applications

1. Your teacher will demonstrate the tongue-rolling trait in which you can either roll your tongue or not. Ability to roll your tongue is due to the gene *R*. Determine the frequencies of *R*, *r*, *RR*, *Rr*, and *rr* among your class or immediate family for the tongue-rolling trait. Use the same methods as you did for widow's peak.
2. Learn more about founder effect by reading or a class discussion. Summarize what you learned.

Demonstrating Natural Selection and Genetic Drift

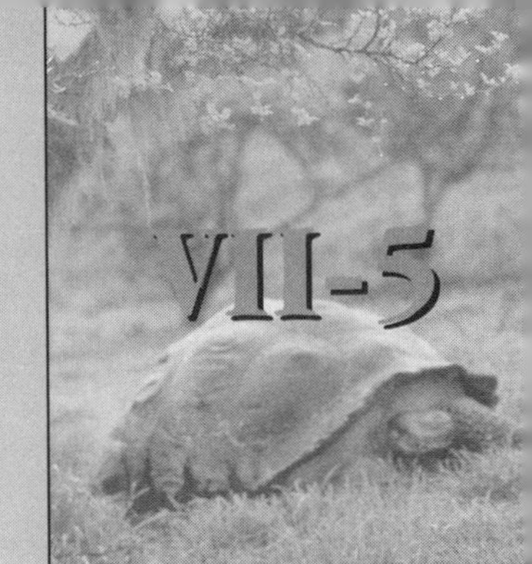

Helen J. Young and Truman P. Young

Overview

Part I of this activity introduces students to the mechanism of natural selection. Students are kept in suspense as to what the activity is demonstrating, during which they draw a series of fish. Eventually, students will come to see that evolution has occurred and that natural selection determines the direction (if any) of this change. Part 2, which can be done later on in the course, is similar to Part 1, but with a twist. Again the concepts—genetic drift, this time, along with Hardy-Weinberg equilibrium—are discovered by the students through the course of the activity.

Evolutionary Principles Illustrated

- Natural selection
- Genetic drift
- Hardy-Weinberg equilibrium

Background Information

Natural selection, the process by which individuals with favorable traits in a given environment pass on a greater proportion of their genes to the next generation than other individuals, is the mechanism for evolution that Darwin and Wallace proposed, thereby revolutionizing the discipline of biology. Yet, as the principle of Hardy-Weinberg equilibrium suggests, natural selection is but one cause of evolution. There are four others: genetic drift, nonrandom mating, migration, and mutation.

This activity is based on "A hands-on exercise to demonstrate evolution by natural selection and genetic drift," by Helen J. Young and Truman P. Young (2003), in *The American Biology Teacher, 65*(6), 444–48. It has been adapted and reprinted with permission of the publisher.

Procedures

Part 1: Evolution by Natural Selection

We perform this exercise in any class requiring an understanding of evolution by natural selection. With no introduction, the following exercise is carried out. (Students spend considerable time trying to figure out the purpose of the exercise while they are drawing the fish. We find that this searching for a purpose is helpful for the discussion that follows.)

- The instructor tapes to the wall/board a hand-drawn picture of a fish, with enough detail that variation will exist in the student copies of the fish (scales, gills, lateral line, etc.). Only put as much detail on the illustration as can be recreated by the students in two minutes—keep it relatively simple.
- Students receive five pieces of paper. They are instructed to draw one copy of the fish to the best of their ability in two minutes.
- These copies are collected. The instructor chooses one of the copies to be the model for the next generation. He/she can choose based on any apparent trait that occurs among the copies: the fattest fish, the longest fish, the fish with the skinniest fins, etc. The instructor may have a predetermined direction for selection, or may opportunistically choose interesting variants. It is also possible to select for major organizational change in the fish: Students may drop fins, add gill slits, and move body parts. The original fish is removed and is replaced with the chosen copy.
- Students are instructed to copy this new fish in two minutes.
- These copies are collected and the instructor chooses the one fish that best demonstrates a continuation of the trend chosen in the first generation (directional selection). If the fattest fish was chosen in Generation I, the fattest fish from Generation II should be selected. No oral clues should be given to the students as to what traits are used in the selection of the next fish.
- Continue this for about four to five generations, each time removing the fish just copied and taping up the chosen one (if you leave all the chosen fish on the board, the trend becomes apparent to the students and they tend to exaggerate their copies of the fish).
- Stop the exercise and tape the original fish, each of the chosen fish, and examples of variants produced in each generation next to their models (Figure 1).

In the subsequent discussion, ask the students to surmise what the exercise demonstrates. Some students will very quickly say "Evolution!" Agree with them and ask how the fish evolved through this process. Lead them in a discussion of the variation created when all the students copy the same fish. They were all instructed to copy the same fish; why didn't the copies look identical? State why you chose the fish you did among these variants (the longest, the fattest) using the terms "only this fish survived to reproduce."

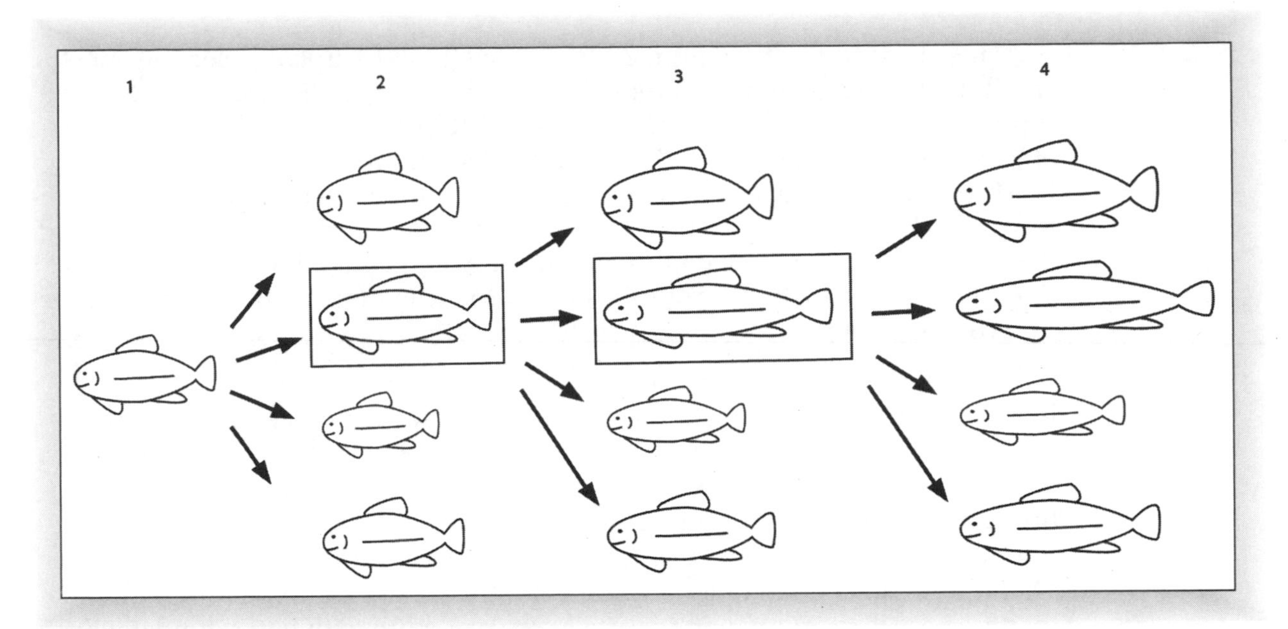

FIGURE 1 Sketch of the process of demonstrating evolution by natural selection. The original fish taped to the board is drawn under Generation 1. We have drawn only four possible renderings of the fish that the students might create. The fish "selected" by the instructor for each generation is indicated by the box around it.

Students then copied this survivor, creating new variation as they did. It usually becomes apparent at this point what you've done. Variation is created (through mutation and recombination) in the production of offspring; selection acts to determine which fish will reproduce. (Discuss that this is extremely strong selection: How would you repeat this demonstration with weaker selection?) Reproduction occurs again, variation is created again, and selection acts again. As you look at the original and final fish on the board, you can see that the fish did, indeed, evolve.

It is important to convey to the students that although mutation and recombination are essentially random, selection is not random. Organisms best adapted to their environments will have higher fitness (more likely to survive to reproduce, more offspring, more vigorous offspring) than organisms less well adapted to their environment. What happens when the environment changes? Different phenotypes are favored and evolution will follow a different phenotypic path. A nice example of the direction of evolution changing over time is finch beak shape documented by Peter and Rosemary Grant and their students. Selection favored birds with deeper bills during the drought of 1977 (Boag & Grant, 1981), but the El Niño event only several years later favored birds with smaller beaks (Gibbs & Grant, 1987). If you had sampled the birds only before the drought and after the El Niño, you would have noticed no net change in beak dimensions, even though researchers documented two episodes of directional selection (albeit opposite in direction) in this time period. So, evolution does not need to be directional over immense periods of time; it can happen quickly and it can reverse in its direction.

This exercise can be continued to demonstrate disruptive selection and stabilizing selection. For example, the instructor can choose the copy that best represents the original fish rather than the fattest fish, repeat this for five generations, and the students will see that the fish did not evolve in any particular direction. Does this mean that selection did not occur? No, in this case it means that stabilizing selection occurred: The biggest and smallest copies had the lowest fitness and the copies near the mean had the highest fitness. This demonstration clearly distinguishes evolution (the process) from natural selection (the mechanism).

An interesting question to explore with the students is why the copies look similar to the original or "selected" fish. Thus far, what has been discussed are the sources of variation among the "offspring" but not why there are fish that are similar. The answer is that many of the traits represented in the fish are heritable. In making "copies" of the fish, the students' close representation to the fish on the board is the thread we call heritability. Some traits are more variable than others because these traits are controlled for by more than one allele or more than one gene (or vary more with environmental differences). In our experience, each fish usually has one tail, three fins, gills, and a lateral line. For these traits, the heritability is 1.0 (there is no environmental variation among the copies). Other traits like body length and width, spacing of gills, and length of fins vary among the copies. This indicates that their heritability is something less than 1.0. This can lead to a discussion of whether nongenetic traits can evolve by natural selection. What if the source of variation is not genetic? Why might one fish be fatter for reasons other than its genes? This is a good time to talk about environmental influences on traits and Lamarck's misinterpretation that manifestations of traits affected by the environment are passed onto offspring. In this exercise (as in nature), genetic variation arises through random events (mistakes in copying the original, mutations); often variation is introduced via random recombination.

Students may also be asked to consider how the simulation differs from natural selection in the real world. First, evolution in the natural world is usually slower, mainly because variation among offspring is usually far less, especially for important traits (traits highly correlated with fitness). Second, although natural selection is *nonrandom* (even directional), it is *not* goal-directed. Instead, the most suitable offspring are favored in each generation based on their match with the environment *at that time*. In this demonstration, the instructor *was* goal-directed, intentionally choosing the fish to be copied based on its phenotype.

This exercise is even more precisely a demonstration of artificial selection, like breeders selecting for corn with high oil content. This is both faster than most natural selection, and it is explicitly goal directed. In fact, Darwin's knowledge of artificial selection, particularly in pigeons, was instrumental in his development of his theory of evolution by natural selection.

By the end of this demonstration, it should be clear that evolution by natural selection requires that the trait evolving shows variation in the population, is heritable, and is associated with an increase in fitness.

Part 2: Evolution by Genetic Drift

Before the concept of drift is introduced in the course, give each student three to four pieces of paper, and tape the same original fish to the board. Have the students copy this model in two minutes. Randomly take a fish out of the students' drawings, making it clear that you are not looking at phenotypic traits of the copies. Tape this fish to the board; have the students copy it; randomly choose one of their copies, etc. After three to four generations, stop and tape the models and their copies as you did before for natural selection. Have the students address the following questions:

1. *Did the fish evolve over the entire period?*

   It may not have changed noticeably, which demonstrates that drift alone does not necessarily result in evolution, but it can. The results depend on the phenotypes (and genotypes) that reproduce; by chance it may be that the smallest fish was "chosen"; then the fish will evolve to a smaller size. But if different phenotypes are chosen each generation, the traits may not evolve in a directional fashion over many generations.

2. *Was variation created each generation?*

   Yes, the variation among progeny in this model should be about the same as that in the model of natural selection. The same processes of mutation, segregation, and recombination are occurring in producing the variation.

3. *Were the traits that you observed changing heritable?*

   Yes, in the sense that the students' attempts to replicate the original drawing were simulating heritable traits.

4. *If the instructor wasn't being "selection," what process was determining which fish was chosen to copy each generation?*

   The random process is similar to a small number of individuals (or just one) colonizing an island: Only their genes (and traits) can be passed on to the next generation. If the smallest fish in its generation is the lucky one to colonize a new area, its "small genes" will be present among the descendents, not the "big genes" in the original population.

5. Or, you could modify this exercise to simulate multiple founder events. *What would happen if you took several different fish and started multiple lines?*

   This might be the case of an expanding species colonizing multiple archipelagos. Each island could receive a different phenotype of fish, and divergence would occur among islands, not because selection favored different phenotypes, but because drift occurred on each island.

6. *How can something evolve if natural selection has not taken place?*

   If the students don't already know this, now is the time to introduce the Hardy-Weinberg equilibrium, whose corollary is that five different processes can cause evolution of a trait: mutation, migration, genetic drift, nonrandom mating, and natural selection. These can act alone or in concert. So documenting that a trait has evolved is only the beginning; learning the causes of this evolution is the difficult and time-consuming part.

Additional Considerations

Both selection and drift may be happening at the same time. Imagine a group of snakes on a mainland, some of which are strong swimmers and can swim to adjacent islands. The representatives that arrive on the island are not a random subset of the mainland population; they are the strongest swimmers of the mainland population. But if only a few snakes swim to the island, you can see that "good swimming" will be well represented in the next generation (there are no "poor swimming" genes present to dilute the good swimming genes). When selection and drift act simultaneously, you expect rapid evolution of a trait.

References

Boag, P.T., & Grant, P.R. (1981). Intense natural selection in a population of Darwin's finches (Geospizinae) in the Galapagos. *Science, 214*, 82–85.

Gibbs, H.L., & Grant, P.R. (1987). Oscillating selection on Darwin's finches. *Nature, 327*, 511–13.

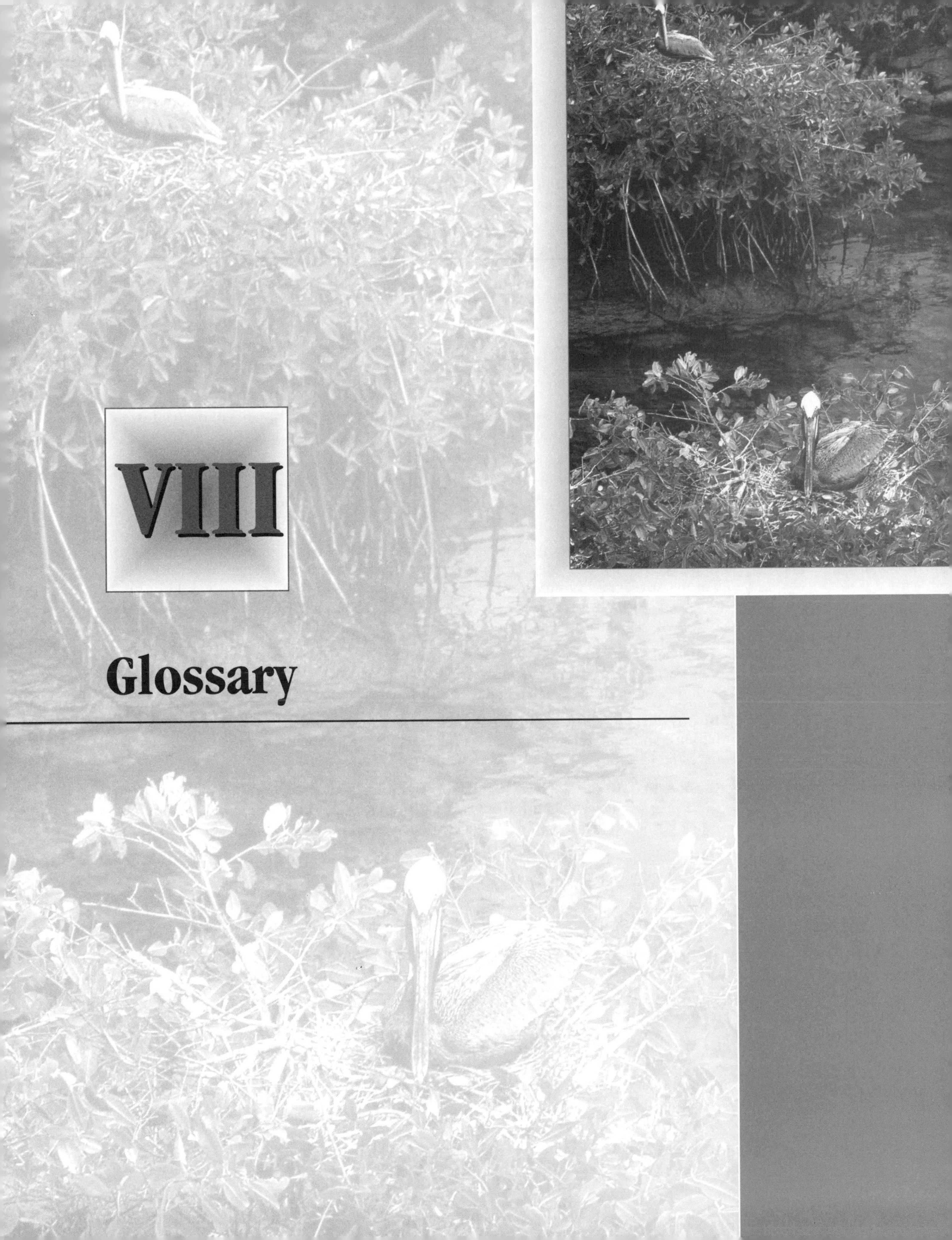

VIII

Glossary

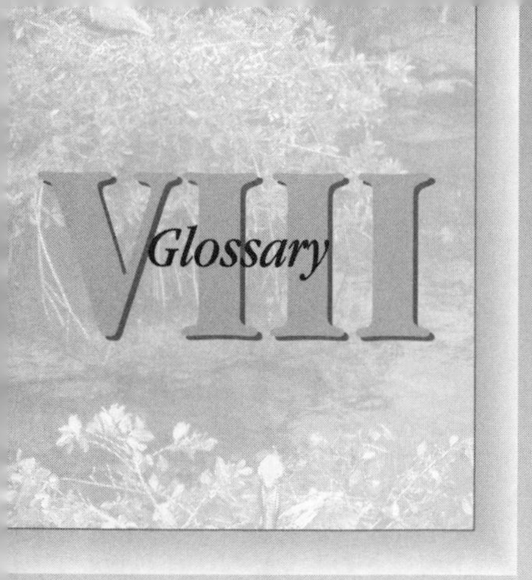

Absolute dating: Determination of the age of a rock layer or palenotological sample in real (rather than relative) terms. (See relative dating.)

Adaptation: Any characteristic (physical, behavioral or biochemical) that helps an organism to survive so that it can reproduce and likely transmit the adaptive character to the next generation. A characteristic that may be an adaptation in one environment is not necessarily an adaptation in all environments.

Allele: One of the various states of a gene for a particular trait. For instance, ear lobe attachment in humans is controlled by a pair of genes with two alleles for the trait, attached or free.

Allopatric: Species or subspecies together in different geographic areas. (See sympatric.)

Analogy: Two or more structures that have the same function, but different evolutionary origins. The classic example is the butterfly wing and the wing of a bird. (Contrast with homology.)

Analogous structures: Structures that have similar function but are not derived from a common ancestor; for example, butterfly wings and bird wings.

Apostatic selection: Selection by predators of the common forms of prey while rare ones are ignored. Presumably, the originally rarer ones will become more common since they have an advantage over the ones more easily found by predators and removed.

Artificial classification: A classification scheme that uses any traits (mostly physical) to place organism in categories with no concern for their evolutionary relationships. For instance, classifying organisms into groups by color, size, or shape would be an artificial system. This explains why students occasionally group whales and fish together. (See natural classification.)

Artificial selection: The process used by humans to increase the prevalence of particular varieties (usually economic or aesthetic) of organisms by choosing only those individuals with the desired characteristics for mating. (See natural selection.)

Biostratigraphy: Stratigraphy is the science examining the nature of rock layers (strata), and biostratigraphy is the science using the additional evidence of fossils to investigate strata.

Carbon 14 dating: Using the half-life of the radioactive isotope (C^{14}) of carbon to find the age of fossils. The half-life of C^{14} is 5720 years; therefore, any sample with half as much C^{14} as expected would be approximately 5700 years old. (See absolute dating.)

Cast: Original organism has decomposed and the resulting mold is filled in with another material, making a fossil copy of the original organism. (See mold.)

Comparative anatomy: The study of similarities and differences of structures in different organisms usually to make judgments about the degree of relatedness.

Comparative biochemistry: The study of the similarities and differences of the DNA base sequences of different organisms.

Comparative embryology: The study of the similarities and differences of the early phases of development of different organisms.

Convergent evolution: Organisms that may be distantly related but have evolved similar characteristics because of similar environmental conditions—for example, flippers in whales and fish. (See divergent evolution.)

Cladistic classification: A method of classification in which animals and plants are placed into taxonomic groups when they share characteristics that are thought to indicate common ancestry. It is based on the assumption that two new species are formed suddenly, by splitting from a common ancestor, and not by gradual evolutionary change.

Creationism: A nonscientific idea that has as it central premise the notion that species were created individually and independently of each other and, as such, have not evolved.

Cryptic coloration: Coloration that serves to conceal, especially in animals.

Darwin-Wallace model: The explanation of how evolution occurs—proposed independently by Charles Darwin and Russell Wallace in the mid-1800s. (See natural selection.)

Dating: One of several techniques used to determine the age of a particular layer or rock and/or the fossils within it. Such dating can be absolute or relative (see both).

Descent with modification: The term that Darwin used to describe what is now called evolution by "natural selection." (See natural selection.)

Divergent evolution: The process by which a group of organisms have changed through time into distinct species or varieties because of environmental pressure. The process may result in new species (such as the Galápagos finches) or new varieties (such as the Galápagos tortoises). (See convergent evolution.)

Evolution: The scientific principle that species alive today have descended (with changes) from related species that lived in the past.

Extinction: The complete disappearance of a species or variety.

Fitness: The degree to which a population of organisms responds to the pressures of natural selection based on the number of offspring produced. The more "fit" populations produce more offspring than less "fit" populations, presumably because they have more members with advantageous characteristics.

Fossil: Any preserved remains of a once living organism; examples include bones, casts, molds, imprints, petrified remains, and remains preserved in tar or amber; most often fossils are found in sedimentary rock. The remains of a long-dead organism that has not altered significantly are referred to as subfossils.

Gradualism: A principle inherent in the Darwin-Wallace Model of evolution by natural selection that there has been constant slow change in species through time. Contrast this with the idea of punctuated equilibrium.

Hardy-Weinberg equation (also known as the H-W Principle or the H-W Law): A mathematical relationship seen in large, randomly-mating populations. The law states that the gene frequency in the population stays the same as long as mutations, differential mating, and gene selection do not occur. The mutations causing new characteristics in organisms violate Hardy-Weinberg but provide the raw material of evolution.

Heterozygous: A condition in which the pair of genes that code for a particular trait contain the same alleles. In the case of eye color—controlled by a single pair of genes—a heterozygous condition exists when one gene codes for blue eye color, and the other gene codes for brown. (Compare with homozygous.)

Homology: Structures that now may look quite different and are descended from a common ancestral form. The arm of a human and the wings of birds and bats are homologous structures. (Contrast with analogy.)

Half-life: The average time it takes for one-half of the radioactive atoms present to undergo radioactive decay. Knowing the half-life of a substance and knowing how much radioactivity still exists in the remains of an organism enables one to determine when the organism died.

Homologous structures: Structures that are similar in origin but now have different uses. An example would be the ear bones of mammals and the jaw attachments in fish. The more changed the structures, the more distantly related the two organisms are.

Hypothesis: A testable statement about the natural world that can be used to build more complex inferences and explanations such as laws or theories. In other words, a hypothesis is a speculative idea that might actually be an immature theory or an immature law.

Lamarckism: The idea of "use and disuse" proposed by Jean Baptist de Lamarck suggesting that changes in an organism during its life will affect offspring of that individual. Changes in body cells do not have an effect on gametes and, thus, will not have an impact on nature of an organism's offspring, so evolution does not occur in this fashion.

Law: A descriptive generalization about how some aspect of the natural world behaves under stated circumstances: gravity is an example.

Macroevolution: Large-scale evolutionary change (see microevolution). The evolution of a branch of the reptile group into birds would be considered macroevolution.

Microevolution: Small-scale evolutionary change (see macroevolution). The acquisition of antibiotic resistance by bacteria would be considered microevolution.

Mold: A fossil that is a rock depression shaped like an organism. (See cast.)

Natural classification: A classification scheme that uses evolutionarily-derived traits to place related organisms together in categories only if they are actually related by descent not just appearance. For instance, although whales and dogs appear to be unrelated, they have enough evolutionarily derived characteristics that they are grouped together in the same class. (See artificial classification.)

Natural Selection: A theory used to explain how evolution occurs. In summary, natural selection states that there is natural variation within members of a species; species produce more offspring than can survive; and some characteristics are favored over others because of environmental conditions. Those individuals favored by the environment because of the characteristics they possess will survive, reproduce, and pass favored traits—and others—on to the next generation. (See artificial selection.)

New synthesis: A reference to research that has been done with respect to evolutionary biology since the time of the Darwin-Wallace model. The new evolutionary synthesis (sometimes called neo-Darwinism) has improved our knowledge of evolution but has neither negated the theory of evolution by natural selection nor the fact of evolution itself.

Paleontology: The study of fossils; founded by Georges Cuvier (1769–1832), an English vertebrate zoologist.

Parthenogenesis: Reproduction by development of an unfertilized gamete that occurs especially among lower plants and invertebrate animals.

Petrification: A fossil in which the hard parts of an organism are replaced by minerals such as occurs in petrified wood.

Phenetic classification: Classificatory systems or procedures that are based on overall similarity—usually of many characters—without regard to the evolutionary history of the organisms involved.

Phylogeny (line of evolutionary descent): Modern taxonomy is founded on the principle of phylogeny so that organisms that are thought to be descended from each other are classified together.

Phyletic gradualism: (See gradualism.)

Population: The members of a species living in one locale in which random mating occurs passing genes on to offspring

Punctuated equilibrium: An interpretation of the mode and tempo evolution proposed by Gould and Eldredge in which species remain unchanged (in equilibrium) for long periods of time, and then speciation suddenly (punctuated) occurs. (Contrast this with gradualism.)

Relative dating: Determination of the age of a rock layer or fossil sample with respect to the age of another layer or fossil. In other words, with relative dating one could know that sample is older or younger than another, but not know how old it is actually. (See absolute dating.)

Selective breeding: When humans choose organisms for breeding because of the traits that those organisms possess. (See artificial selection and contrast with natural selection.)

Species: A group of organisms that can potentially breed with each other to produce fertile offspring and cannot breed with the members of other such groups. One of the most hotly debated issues in modern biology.

Speciation: The divergence of one ancestral species into two different species. Speciation is thought to occur when a subpopulation of the ancestral group is separated for a prolonged period and exposed to different environmental conditions, thus making these organisms incapable to breeding successfully with those in the group from which they came.

Sympatric: Species or subspecies living together in the same geographic area. (See allopatric.)

Systematics: The study of classification systems and of the relationships among organisms.

Taxonomy: The study of the classification of organisms.

Theory: A well-substantiated explanation of some aspect of the natural world that may incorporate facts, laws, inferences, and tested hypotheses. An example would be the theory of evolution by natural selection. Note that evolution is not the theory, the mechanism proposed by Darwin and Wallace is.

Variation: Genetically determined differences in the characteristics of members of the same species such as the color of features or the shape of a leaf.

About the Editor

William F. McComas earned BS degrees in biology and secondary education from Lock Haven State University and MA degrees in biology and physical science from West Chester State University, both in Pennsylvania. He taught biology, life science, and physical science for thirteen years in middle and high schools in suburban Philadelphia before returning to graduate school at the University of Iowa, where he received a Ph.D. in science education. His dissertation research focused on exemplary laboratory teaching practices.

McComas founded the *Program to Advance Science Education* (PASE) in the Rossier School of Education at the University of Southern California (USC), Los Angeles, where he developed both masters and doctoral degree concentrations in science education. During his USC tenure more than 100 students received advanced degrees in science education; six PASE graduates are now professors of science education. In January 2006, McComas became the first holder of the *Parks Family Endowed Faculty Chair in Science Education* at the University of Arkansas, Fayetteville, where his work in educating the next generation of science educators continues.

He teaches courses in educational research, the philosophy of science, issues in science education, and advanced science teaching methods. His research and publications primarily target issues in biology education with particular focus on the teaching of evolution, the elements of effective laboratory and inquiry-based instruction, models of assessment, science learning in informal settings such as museums and field sites, and the education of gifted science learners. During his time in Los Angeles, he served as a science education advisor to the California Science Center, the Huntington Gardens, and the Los Angeles County Museum of Natural History.

McComas was named the 2004 winner of USC's highest teaching honor, the *Associates Award for Excellence in Teaching*. He was the 2001 winner of the *NSTA-Ohaus Award* for exemplary college curriculum design and was named *Outstanding Science Teacher Educator* in 1998 by the Association for Science Teacher Education (ASTE). He received the 1998 *Distinguished Achievement Award* from the Educational Press Association for his article, "The Discovery and Nature of Evolution by Natural Selection: Misconceptions and Lessons Learned from the History of Science," which originally appeared in the *American Biology Teacher.*

McComas has earned a private pilot's license to add to other interests, including photography, music composition, and piano and guitar performance. As a professional natural history photographer, he regularly conducts tours to ecologically important areas throughout the world, such as Indonesia, Malaysia, East Africa, Bolivia, Peru, Iceland, and the Galápagos Islands. His images have appeared in numerous magazines and academic journals and have formed the basis for various instructional units and a show titled *The Galapagos Islands: Evolution's Showcase*, which ran for over eighteen months at the Natural History Museum of Los Angeles County. He is married to Kim Krusen McComas, a geometry teacher and mathematics educator. Son Will and daughter Emily both, for some reason, are developing a keen interest in science, math, and travel!

Investigating Evolutionary Biology in the Laboratory joins *Investigating Ecology in the Laboratory* in a planned series of monographs featuring new ways to teach biology in the laboratory.